1990-1991
HOCKEY
Scouting Report

1990-1991

HOCKEY

Scouting Report

Michael A. Berger

Summerhill Press
Toronto

© 1990 Michael A. Berger

Published by Summerhill Press Ltd.
52 Shaftesbury Avenue
Toronto, Ontario M4T 1A2

Cover photography: Bruce Bennett
Cover design: Andrew Smith

Printed and bound in Canada

The National Library of Canada has catalogued this annual as follows:

Berger, Michael, 1960–

Hockey scouting report

Annual.
1986/1987-
ISSN 0836-5148
ISBN 0-9290991-24-8 (1990-1991)

1. Hockey - Scouting - Periodicals. 2. Hockey players—Periodicals. 3. National Hockey League—Periodicals. I. Davidson, John, 1953-.
II. McDonald, Jiggs. III. Title.

796.96'26

GV847.8.N3B4
C88-039002-6

DEDICATION

To hockey fans everywhere; after all, they're the true experts.

Acknowledgements

Every year we think this book will get easier. And every year it gets harder. But every year there are still people who help. Thanks go to:

As always to our sources: the coaches, general managers, chief scouts, scouts and players who help us compile these reports. And thanks to the NHL personnel who ask for copies — so they can see what the competition is saying.

Barry Watkins of the New York Rangers public relations office, and to Greg Bouris — Barry's counterpart for the New York Islanders. And thanks to the rest of the Ranger P.R. staff — Art Friedman, Ginger Killian and Kevin MacDonald — and those of the Islanders as well — Chris Botta, Steve Blinn, Cathy Schutte and Jim Johnson.

And finally to my publishers, Jim Williamson and Gordon Montador at Summerhill Press, for their continued belief in this project.

Thanks as always, boys and girls; Put this one on my tab.

Mike Berger NYC June 1990

Contents

Author Bio

Michael A. Berger

The editor of GOAL Magazine, the NHL's official program, Mike has frequently written about hockey in international publications like SPORT Magazine and The Hockey News, and for television on POWERSTICK HOCKEY WEEK. He has been heard as a featured commentator on the NHL Radio Network and for WFAN Radio in New York City, and has also served as a special color commentator for the Toronto Maple Leaf Radio Network.

Introduction

Welcome to year five of the most user-friendly reference book on NHL hockey players available to the public: The Hockey Scouting Report, the *only* hockey book that discusses players the way the hockey professionals do — by looking at what a player can and can't do, and why he can or can't do it.

What you're holding is the number one reference book on NHL player performance available today. Chances are, anything you see, hear or read about an NHL player's ability came from this book. Your team's radio and television broadcasters use it, the writers covering your team use it — and your team uses it.

Between these covers you get over 400 scouting reports presented in the same way hockey coaches, general managers, players and scouts all over the world present their views to their colleagues. And, in many instances, you're getting this info from those self-same coaches, general managers, players and scouts.

And you get all this with no-holds-barred — that's why our top-level sources have to stay anonymous. The truth, the whole truth and nothing but the truth has been our motto since starting this project five seasons ago.

And we can swear to that because of the thousands of hours we've spent researching during hundreds of games. We can swear to that because of the input we've gotten from NHL executives who share their expertise with us, and then read Hockey Scouting Report to see what the *other* big-wigs are saying.

And we can swear to that because we're the *only* hockey publication that analyzes players the way the pros do. Here's how the book works:

Each player's game is broken down into three parts, categories which consolidate the factors used by the pros to evaluate talent at all hockey levels. We discuss a player's skating, stickhandling, scoring, passing, play-making, checking and defensive abilities in The Finesse Game. How he uses his body, whether he takes advantage of his size and strength, his balance, his ability — and willingness — to play physically and to fight in The Physical Game. How he relates to his teammates, whether he's frequently injured, if he works hard to improve his game and if he's dedicated to his profession in The Intangibles.

Each player report is augmented by a graphic that instantly illustrates where a shooter is most dangerous from. For goaltenders that graphic shows areas of weakness.

Once again, the Hockey Scouting Report brings the game to you in an intelligent, articulate and concise discussion of the players behind the headlines.

We hope you enjoy reading it as much as we enjoyed creating it.

TEAM REPORTS

BOSTON BRUINS

RAY BOURQUE

Yrs. of NHL service: 11
Born: Montreal, Quebec, Canada; December 28, 1960
Position: Defenseman
Height: 5-11
Weight: 210
Uniform no.: 77
Shoots: left

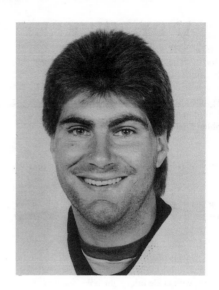

Career statistics:

GP	G	A	TP	PIM
794	230	610	840	628

1989-90 statistics:

GP	G	A	TP	+/-	PIM	PP	SH	GW	GT	S	PCT
76	19	65	84	31	50	8	0	3	0	310	6.1

LAST SEASON

All point totals were three-season highs. Finished second on club in scoring, first in assists and shots on goal. Finished third among NHL defenders in points, fifth overall in shots on goal. Missed four games with an abdominal injury.

THE FINESSE GAME

There is nothing Ray Bourque can't do. Class dismissed.

But seriously folks ...

Bourque is a world-class talent in any aspect of the game. His skating is superb, marked by agility, strength, explosive acceleration (for rink-length speed) and the balance and foot speed to change his pace and direction within a single stride.

His hand skills across the board are excellent. He controls the puck excellently at all speeds and in all situations, and he rushes the puck intelligently and with discretion. Bourque passes as well as he stickhandles, and he loves to make long passes up the middle of the ice to breaking wingers. His hand skill extends to his shot — or shots, we should say. His selection of shots is excellent, from a howitzer slap shot to a laser-like wrist shot, and any of his shots can beat any goaltender in the world. He switches to the right side on the power play and loves to sneak toward the net to fire an almost unstoppable wrist shot.

Firing all of this is Bourque's exceptional vision and play-reading ability — his hockey sense. He understands a play and its implications better than most any player in the world, in both the offensive (breakout, lead a teammate, create space) and defensive (gap control, transition play) modes.

THE PHYSICAL GAME

As with his finesse ability, Bourque's physical ability is truly superior. He's tremendously strong and can handle all of the League's bigger players; credit his upper body strength and balance here. Those two attributes also make him almost unbeatable in any confrontation in the corners.

His great strength also powers his great shot.

THE INTANGIBLES

It is hard to imagine a player more important to his team than Ray Bourque is to the Bruins (and no, this isn't a shot at Mark Messier's selection as the NHL's MVP last season). Bourque is one of the world's five best players, and his attitude, desire and character make him Boston's natural leader.

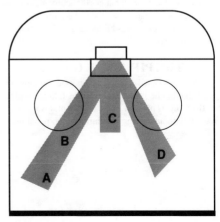

ANDY BRICKLEY

Yrs. of NHL service: 6
Born: Melrose, Mass., USA; August 9, 1961
Position: Left wing
Height: 5-11
Weight: 200
Uniform no.: 25
Shoots: left

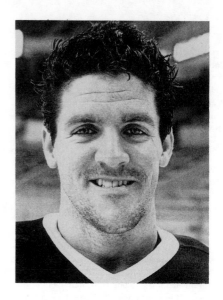

Career statistics:

GP	G	A	TP	PIM
308	70	112	182	69

1989-90 statistics:

GP	G	A	TP	+/-	PIM	PP	SH	GW	GT	S	PCT
43	12	28	40	11	8	6	0	1	0	69	17.4

LAST SEASON

Games played total was lowest of career, but assist and point totals were career bests. Missed nine games with ankle injury, three games with hip injury, eight games with groin injury, and rest of season with another hip injury. His plus/minus rating was fourth best among forwards.

THE FINESSE GAME

Brickley is a good skater and the Bruins put that skill to work on a checking line and the penalty killing unit. Andy has good lateral movement and quickness, and he reads the play well and knows how to angle the opposition to the boards; that accounts for his checking success. He is also a strong skater and has good endurance, making him almost tireless on his feet. He is not a speedster.

He is not a gifted puck handler, but his anticipation will carry him to the openings in the ice, where he can put a good wrist shot to work to the tune of 15-20 goals per season.

He sees the ice well but has difficulty moving the puck to an open teammate should he gain it through checking. Brickley brings his skating and anticipation to bear in his penalty killing role, and he does well there.

THE PHYSICAL GAME

Brickley is willing to use his body against the opposition, but he is not a thunderous hitter. He plays smartly and gets himself in his opponent's way, and is effective without hurting his club through penalties.

THE INTANGIBLES

This report is essentially unchanged, owing to Brickley's injuries last season. He's a role player and — through his night in, night out work ethic — a role model for the Bruins.

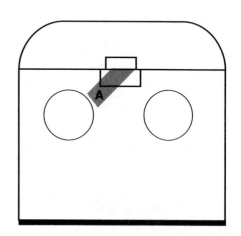

RANDY BURRIDGE

Yrs. of NHL service: 4
Born: Fort Erie, Ontario, Canada; January 7, 1966
Position: Left wing
Height: 5-9
Weight: 180
Uniform no.: 12
Shoots: left

Career statistics:

GP	G	A	TP	PIM
297	93	102	195	235

1989-90 statistics:

GP	G	A	TP	+/-	PIM	PP	SH	GW	GT	S	PCT
63	17	15	32	9	47	7	0	1	0	118	14.4

LAST SEASON

Games played and all point totals were three-season lows; missed 18 games with knee injury.

THE FINESSE GAME

Skating is primary among Burridge's skills, with speed and quickness primary among his skating abilities. He has a lot of power in his stride, and that power gives him good acceleration and a degree of rink-length speed. He also has good foot speed and balance, and those two ingredients combine to give him agility and lateral movement for his primary skill — his darting ability. His skating makes him a good checker, because he'll be strong in his pursuit of the puck.

Burridge has a dollop of hockey sense, and that sense combines with his one-step quickness to power his scoring game. His playreading ability and anticipation help him defensively by working in tandem with his quickness to close opposing openings. Those same abilities let him hit the openings himself, and his outstanding quickness makes him particularly dangerous when there are loose pucks around the net. He gets his shot away fairly quickly (as befits his style around the net), but he still hasn't demonstrated the ability to score from distances; that makes him fairly predictable. He has also taken to shooting the puck more; that makes him more dangerous.

He's not the best puckhandler in the world, but Burridge can handle the puck at his speed to beat defensemen. He looks to use his teammates when he can.

THE PHYSICAL GAME

He doesn't have great size. He probably doesn't even have good size. But none of that matters to Burridge. He'll go anywhere he has to against any oppponent he has to in order to make his plays, and his quickness can get him in and out of traffic areas unscathed.

But despite his willingness to use his good strength in any area of the ice, he's going to get out-muscled because of his size.

THE INTANGIBLES

Burridge is a tremendously enthusiastic player, one with great determination and heart. Though last season must be looked at as a disappointing campaign, Burridge's fine work ethic and attitude should allow him to regroup this season and post more Burridge-like numbers.

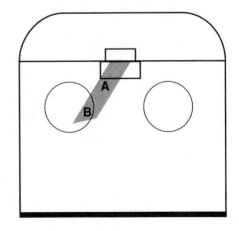

LYNDON BYERS

Yrs. of NHL service: 4
Born: Nipawin, Sask., Canada; February 29, 1964
Position: Right wing
Height: 6-1
Weight: 200
Uniform no.: 34
Shoots: right

Career statistics:

GP	G	A	TP	PIM
211	21	39	60	748

1989-90 statistics:

GP	G	A	TP	+/-	PIM	PP	SH	GW	GT	S	PCT
43	4	4	8	0	159	0	0	0		1	43	9.3

LAST SEASON

Games played and penalty minute totals were three season lows. Missed seven games with a knee injury, 14 games with a thumb injury, and 14 games with a foot injury.

THE FINESSE GAME

As befits his game, strength is the key to Byers' skating. He doesn't have a great deal of speed, but Lyndon's good balance and strength greatly aid him in his physical style.

His playreading isn't bad, but it is his desire more than his brains that can make him a serviceable checking forward. He needs time and space to make his plays when he has the puck, and the plays he makes will be simple ones at best.

His hands aren't good enough to fool NHL goaltending, so he'll have to score from near the net on rebounds and broken plays.

THE PHYSICAL GAME

Byers is not a card-carrying member of the kinder, gentler Bruins. In fact, he prefers forcing the opposition to see one thousand points of light.

Byers is a tough guy, a fighter — one of those guys who kind of loses it when he fights. He also tries to play a straightforward hitting and checking game, but he lacks the overall skating ability to be effective in that role. Byers can wipe a guy off the puck after trapping him in the corner, but he'll need a teammate to make the play of getting the puck out of the corner.

THE INTANGIBLES

Byers is a role player, and the role he plays requires him to put his body on the line every night. Now the role of tough guy in itself is a tenuous one, as you're always vulnerable for replacement by a guy a little bit tougher or more talented than yourself. But when you're a toughguy like Byers and your body can't withstand the punishment, well, maybe you shouldn't invest in any real estate.

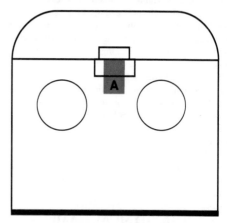

BOBBY CARPENTER

Yrs. of NHL service: 9
Born: Beverly, Mass., USA; July 13, 1963
Position: Center
Height: 6-0
Weight: 190
Uniform no.: 11
Shoots: left

Career statistics:

GP	G	A	TP	PIM
668	241	289	530	630

1989-90 statistics:

GP	G	A	TP	+/-	PIM	PP	SH	GW	GT	S	PCT
80	25	31	56	-3	97	5	0	5	0	220	11.4

LAST SEASON

Games played total was three-season high, and the sixth time in nine seasons Carpenter played 80 games. Goal total was four-season high.

THE FINESSE GAME

Though his best work is done in the physical areas of the game, Carpenter has a deep reserve of finesse skills at his disposal. He is first and foremost an excellent skater, equipped with acceleration and rink-length speed, quickness, balance and agility. He is not a fancy skater, but these skills (especially his balance) allow him to more than succeed in traffic areas.

He's not a fancy skater because his hand skills aren't at the same level of his foot skills, and it's taken Carpenter several seasons to realize that. His mistake was scoring 50 goals, because after that season he thought he was an artist with the puck and his play fell accordingly. Which is not to say that he is incapable of puck work. Rather, Carpenter carries the puck well and is good with it in traffic situations — but he is not Denis Savard, not even teammate Craig Janney.

He has good sense of the ice and anticipates well, and he uses that skill in tandem with his terrific slap shot and an accurate wrist shot to get into scoring position and then score.

THE PHYSICAL GAME

Balance and good strength are the keys to Carpenter's game, and when he applies both he can be an above average player. He has good strength and can hit people hard enough to hurt them, but the important aspect of his hitting is that he remains vertical after collisions so as to continue play. He has good upper body strength for one-on-one confrontations in tight quarters (balance helps here too), and he can wrestle the opposition off the puck.

The same upper body, arm and wrist strength that lets him pull the puck out of a tangle makes him a good faceoff man.

THE INTANGIBLES

Last season was a comeback year of sorts for Carpenter, for whom the last two seasons have been a disaster. If he keeps his head screwed on right, he can be a solid two-way performer capable of a 70 or 80 point season — when he wants to play the way he can.

The tag that followed him from Washington, through New York, out to Los Angeles and back to Boston is one that reads, "doesn't have great self-motivating qualities," but Carpenter said last year that he's finally playing for a coach who likes him. Perhaps that feeling will keep him on the right track.

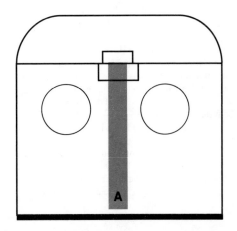

JOHN CARTER

Yrs. of NHL service: 2
Born: Winchester, Mass., USA: May 3, 1963
Position: Left wing
Height: 5-10
Weight: 175
Uniform no.: 31
Shoots: left

Career statistics:

GP	G	A	TP	PIM
135	29	34	63	52

1989-90 statistics:

GP	G	A	TP	+/-	PIM	PP	SH	GW	GT	S	PCT
76	17	22	39	17	26	2	1	1	0	142	12.0

LAST SEASON

First full NHL season after four previous tries; all point totals were career highs. Plus/minus rating was team's second best, best among forwards.

THE FINESSE GAME

Carter is a good skater with speed, agility and sound lateral movement. Balance is the key to any degree of agility or lateral movement and Carter has that balance. He's very sturdy on his skates, and that sturdiness serves him in his mucking role along the boards or when he works through the traffic in front of the opposing net.

He has good hands and handles the puck well when he carries it and when he operates in traffic, and Carter certainly has the ability to get the puck to his teammates.

Carter has a fairly highly developed sense of the ice and the play around him, and he combines that sense with his hand skills to be a player worth checking in the offensive zone. He also has a good shot from the traffic areas, and Carter will score many of his goals from near the net.

His sense extends to the defensive zone, where Carter plays a very strong positional game.

THE PHYSICAL GAME

Carter enjoys a bumping, hitting game and he plays that way at all times and in all situations: at home or on the road, one goal up or one goal down, early or late in the game. He has a good degree of strength in a body that — at least size-wise — isn't designed for such physical play, and Carter keeps himself in good condition.

He's afraid of no one and will go into a corner against any defenseman, but he can get out-muscled if he gets trapped. His balance serves him in good stead in his one-on-one battles for the puck and in his forays to the front of the opposing net.

THE INTANGIBLES

There are two. First (and we don't mean to cut on his play), Carter isn't cut out for the style he wants to play. He showed well during his first full season, but it would seem to be only a matter of time before he runs out of gas — through no fault of his own — after running himself into so many larger bodies.

And second, his age. To make the NHL on a full-time basis at age 27 is admirable, but there ain't a whole lot of time left for development. Carter has shown the ability to score at every level he's played, and he did fairly well last season, but we question how much better he can become.

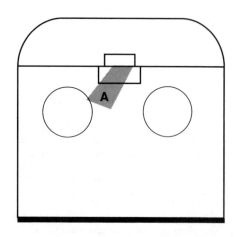

DAVE CHRISTIAN

Yrs. of NHL service: 10
Born: Warroad, Minn., USA; May 12, 1959
Position: Right wing/center
Height: 6-0
Weight: 180
Uniform no.: 27
Shoots: right

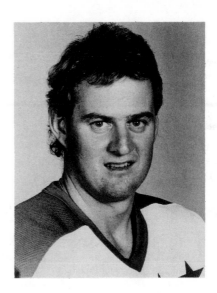

Career statistics:

GP	G	A	TP	PIM
784	284	371	655	190

1989-90 statistics:

GP	G	A	TP	+/-	PIM	PP	SH	GW	GT	S	PCT
78	15	25	40	-8	12	2	0	4	0	153	9.8

LAST SEASON

Acquired from Washington in exchange for Bob Joyce in December 1989. Goal and point totals were full-season career lows. Christian was plus-4 rated played during his Boston tenure.

THE FINESSE GAME

Goal scorers need two things: good hands and the ability to get into scoring position. Though lacking great speed or quickness, Christian knows how to get into position to score (he does kick up the juice a little when coming to the net from the outside on the backhand — down the left wing). He exploits defensive breakdowns regularly because of his excellent anticipation. He also possesses a scorer's patience and poise, and Dave waits as long as necessary for the defense or goaltender to commit before making his own play.

Christian's best asset is his shooting, and he is deadly accurate from around the net. He one-times shots with the NHL's best, and he likes to work between the crease and the lower edge of the right faceoff circle. On two-on-one breaks he wants the puck at the crease's edge for a shot upstairs.

His sensitive hands and excellent release — as well as his ability to get open — make him especially valuable on the power play. Dave moves well with the puck when he carries it and, when he does pass, gets the puck efficiently to open teammates. His defense, however, is often no better than perfunctory, and he needs to be teamed with a more defensively conscious teammate.

THE PHYSICAL GAME

Christian is a finesse player, and his physical game reflects that. Because of the balance he has on his skates, Christian avoids most hits, and he doesn't really go out of his way to instigate contact either. Most of the time he'll be on the outside of the scrum looking in.

He does, though, use his body well to protect the puck.

THE INTANGIBLES

Christian is not always intense in his approach to the game and his performances (both at even-strength and in individual games) can reflect that. Certainly his playoff series for Boston against Edmonton was a disappointment, and he needs to redeem himself for that performance this season.

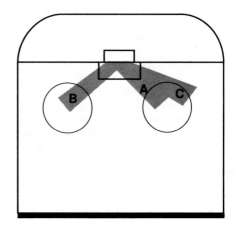

GARRY GALLEY

Yrs. of NHL service: 6
Born: Montreal, Quebec, Canada; April 16, 1963
Position: Defenseman
Height: 6-1
Weight: 190
Uniform no.: 28
Shoots: left

Career statistics:

GP	G	A	TP	PIM
382	46	135	181	394

1989-90 statistics:

GP	G	A	TP	+/-	PIM	PP	SH	GW	GT	S	PCT
71	8	27	35	2	75	1	0	0	0	142	5.6

LAST SEASON

Point and assist totals were second highest of career. Missed nine games with a sprained shoulder.

THE FINESSE GAME

Skating and puck movement are the keys to Galley's game, and the reasons why he can be a fairly successful offensive defenseman. He moves very well forward and back and demonstrates good lateral movement too. He can certainly control and contain the point in the offensive zone, and greater patience and poise has helped him use his skating to control the gap on the incoming puck carrier.

Galley uses his skating to both rush the puck and join the play as a late attacker without the puck. He carries the puck well while skating and he'll take a gamble by moving to the deep slot, but he's also learned that a good pass can beat a good rush in many instances.

To that end, Galley moves the puck well by finding open men and leading them to openings. His hockey sense, playreading and anticipation abilities serve him well here and that's why he'll see power play time. As for his own scoring, he'll notch 7-10 goals a season on shots from 40-60 feet; his shot is unremarkable.

THE PHYSICAL GAME

Let's make sure we phrase this the right way. Galley is a willing physical player, but not necessarily an able one. While willing to work along the boards and in the corners, Galley will nevertheless get knocked off the puck or plain out-muscled. His best bet is to contain the forward, and take the body and turn the play quickly if he can. Otherwise, Galley is apt to be outfought and trapped in the corner.

He works to be in good shape, and Galley will also sacrifice his body to block shots.

THE INTANGIBLES

Galley is an enthusiastic and coachable player, as well as being a determined competitor. He has matured fairly well in his NHL tenure, and his desire will go a long way toward deflecting any deficiencies he has.

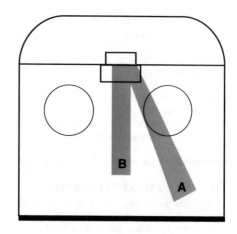

BOB GOULD

Yrs. of NHL service: 9
Born: Petrolia, Ontario, Canada; September 2, 1957
Position: Center/right wing
Height: 6-0
Weight: 195
Uniform no.: 18
Shoots: right

Career statistics:

GP	G	A	TP	PIM
697	145	159	304	572

1989-90 statistics:

GP	G	A	TP	+/-	PIM	PP	SH	GW	GT	S	PCT
77	8	17	25	-3	92	0	0	2	0	92	8.7

LAST SEASON

Games played total was three-season high, but point total was second-lowest full-season career mark. He missed three games with a knee injury.

THE FINESSE GAME

A good skater with a strong, steady pace, Gould uses that pace well in his role as a defensive forward, staying with his check up and down the ice. He has neither great speed nor outstanding agility.

His anticipation and vision — his superior hockey sense — help him excel in his defensive work. He counters the opposition's offense either by shadowing his check or by protecting a certain zone of the ice and cutting off passing lanes. He is a smart defensive player, so forget the plus/minus rating.

Though he doesn't show great offensive creativity, he can handle the puck fairly well, sometimes working a little give-and-go from the right corner. His goals will come from in close to the net, and he is a threat for the short-handed goal, using his anticipation to read the power play and find an opening.

THE PHYSICAL GAME

Intelligence rather than overt strength is the key to Gould's physical game. Though not unwilling to become involved, Bob is not the kind of player that throws his weight around. He uses his body intelligently, holding his man out of the play for the extra second necessary to make a good defensive play.

Gould does not run from contact and is not a thumper, but will certainly hit or be hit if the play dictates. He can't be intimidated.

THE INTANGIBLES

Gould is an excellent team man, working hard all the time for the team first and himself second. He is a role player and a fine defensive forward, so ignore the bad plus/minus. His durability, however, must be questioned, as he has played a complete NHL season just once in his career.

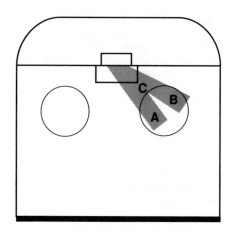

GREG HAWGOOD

Yrs. of NHL service: 1
Born: Edmonton, Alta., Canada; August 10, 1968
Position: Defenseman
Height: 5-8
Weight: 175
Uniform no.: 38
Shoots: left

Career statistics:

GP	G	A	TP	PIM
134	27	51	78	160

1989-90 statistics:

GP	G	A	TP	+/-	PIM	PP	SH	GW	GT	S	PCT
76	11	27	38	12	76	2	0	1	0	127	8.7

LAST SEASON

Alternated between defense and left wing.

THE FINESSE GAME

If it's true that good things come in little packages, then Hawgood bears that out — he is some package of finesse skills. He's an oustanding skater with great speed, agility and quickness, so he's going to get to those loose pucks, he's going to drive defensemen off the blue line, he's going to get breakaways. His ability in tight quarters is especially good, which means he'll work real well along the boards or in front of the net.

Hawgood amplifies his skating by virtue of his hand skills; he's a top-notch puckhandler and playmaker. He carries the puck very well when he rushes from his defense position, and he's just as good at wheeling and dealing in the offensive zone. He'll carry it into the offensive zone and become a fourth attacker; he isn't satisfied with gaining the blue line and dumpimg the puck. He's got good touch, so he distributes the puck well to his teammates regardless of their position on ice.

His hockey sense is also very high, and he'll succeed with high-risk/high-return offensive gambles. His skating is certainly strong enough for him to contain the point offensively and to challenge the puck carrier defensively.

Hawgood has a good shot from the point and he'll move in when given the room. He shoots off the pass very well, shoots frequently and his shot is good for tips and deflections.

THE PHYSICAL GAME

His size is a big problem for Hawgood, and always will be. If he gets trapped he's going to be outmuscled, so he has to stay away from being trapped — easier said than done. Not that he's afraid of contact — far from it. Hawgood is an aggressive player with the size he does have, and he'll fight anyone to earn the respect he needs to operate; he won't be intimidated.

But that doesn't alter physical fact — he's going to lose battles to stronger opponents of equal talent and better size.

Improved strength and a total off-season conditioning program would help, to a degree.

THE INTANGIBLES

Hawgood is an exceptionally dynamic player, and the Bruins aren't quite sure just what to do with him — forward or defense? They've already got a number of smaller players up front, and they have some good offensive players in back. Whatever the choice, Hawgood needs to settle into a stable and consistent role so he can best begin harnessing his considerable talents for NHL duty.

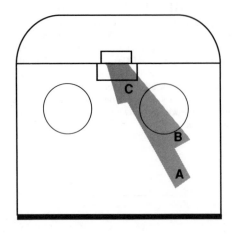

CRAIG JANNEY

Yrs. of NHL service: 3
Born: Hartford, Conn., USA; September 26, 1967
Position: Center
Height: 6-1
Weight: 190
Uniform no.: 23
Shoots: left

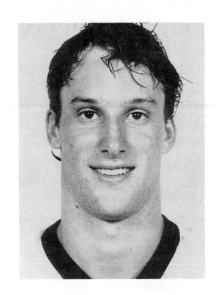

Career statistics:

GP	G	A	TP	PIM
132	47	93	140	16

1989-90 statistics:

GP	G	A	TP	+/-	PIM	PP	SH	GW	GT	S	PCT
55	24	38	62	3	4	11	0	5	2	105	22.9

LAST SEASON

Finished third on the club in points, second in assists (first among forwards) and power play goals. He led the club in game-tying goals and all regulars in shooting percentage. He missed 212 games with a groin injury, three games with a hip injury. Goal total was career best.

THE FINESSE GAME

Janney has many finesse skills, some of which show signs of being of the elite variety. He has good speed and quickness, and his balance and agility give him a very high ability to get to loose pucks. He has outstanding lateral ability that he sometimes minimizes by always moving to his forehand. He is more of a shifty skater than he is a speed demon, and he knows how to save his ice so as to make better use of the open space.

His hockey sense is very good, and his excellent anticipation keeps him a play or two ahead of the game. Janney not only recognizes openings and leads his teammates to them, but he can also manipulate play so as to create those openings. For obvious reason he is deadly on the power play.

That's when his hand skills come to the fore here, as Janney is a very good puckhandler. He passes equally well to both the forehand and backhand sides, and Janney has the touch to put the puck on a stick anywhere. His quick stick helps him snare loose pucks and also strip the puck from the opposition.

He retains his tendency to overhandle and overpass the puck, foregoing personal shooting and scoring opportunities that his sense and skating have created. He has the hands to score from in tight but he *must* shoot more.

His defense is not as unquestionable as his offense.

THE PHYSICAL GAME

He's not built like a physical player, and shouldn't play like one. But Janney's skills make him deadly in traffic and that's where he goes. The problem is — at least based on the evidence of the past two seasons — Janney's body can't take the pounding he receives; due to injury he's played only 117 of a possible 160 games over that span. There isn't a lot of bulk on his six-foot frame, and he'd better put some on if he intends to stay in one piece.

Until then, injuries will always be a concern.

THE INTANGIBLES

Don't get us wrong — our ankles aren't breaking from jumping off the Craig Janney bandwagon. But we would like to see him make the adjustments in his game (both physically and finesse-wise) that would propel him to the next NHL plateau. His position of pre-eminence is unchallenged on the Bruins — he's the number one center, playing with the number one winger — and maybe Janney needs that outside challenge to motivate him.

We await his answer.

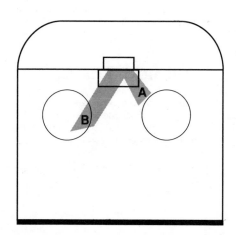

REGGIE LEMELIN

Yrs. of NHL service: 11
Born: Quebec City, Quebec, Canada; November 19, 1954
Position: Goaltender
Height: 5-11
Weight: 170
Uniform no.: 1
Catches: left

Career statistics:

GP	MINS	G	SO	AVG	A	PIM
456	25,232	1,448	11	3.44	15	93

1989-90 statistics:

GP	MINS	AVG	W	L	T	SO	GA	SA	SAPCT	PIM
43	2,310	2.81	22	15	2	2	108	1,002	.892	32

LAST SEASON

Teamed with Andy Moog to win Jennings Trophy for best team goals-against-average. Finished third in the NHL in goals-against-average, which was best of career.

THE PHYSICAL GAME

The strong stand-up style is Lemelin's style and he practices it almost to a fault. Though a reflex game has crept more and more into his style, Lemelin is still at his best when he squares himself to the puck so that all he has to do is let the shot hit him. In all, it is an unspectacular style.

He handles his rebounds fairly well by clearing them to safety, and the only other active thing he'll have to do with the puck is when he flags it down for his defense; Lemelin does not handle the puck.

Lemelin moves well laterally from post to post, and his angle-cutting game is powered by his good movement in and out of the net. He has good balance and that allows him to regain his stance quickly when he does go to the ice; he'll re-establish his position quickly for second shots. His hand speed is no better than good, and his feet remain his consistent weakness; he is vulnerable after his feet get moving and his stance has opened up.

THE MENTAL GAME

Lemelin anticipates and reads the play in front of him very well. His concentration is good, in terms of both individual shots from odd angles or scrambles around the net and throughout a game, and he helps himself here by getting good views of the puck. Bad goals don't generally affect him.

He also has the ability (because he plays with such coolness) to come into a game and immediately play his best. He certainly has big save capability and can get very hot.

THE INTANGIBLES

He's generally been a consistent player, but last season's playoffs suddenly made Lemelin look very old. His attitude and work ethic would indicate that he can play for another couple of seasons, but he has to answer some questions regarding last spring's performance.

ANDY MOOG

Yrs. of NHL service: 9
Born: Penticton, B.C., Canada; February 18, 1960
Position: Goaltender
Height: 5-8
Weight: 170
Uniform no.: 35
Catches: left

Career statistics:

GP	MINS	G	SO	AVG	A	PIM
328	18,283	1,049	3	3.44	15	70

1989-90 statistics:

GP	MINS	AVG	W	L	T	SO	GA	SA	SAPCT	PIM
46	2,536	2.89	24	10	7	3	122	1,145	.893	18

LAST SEASON

Teamed with Reggie Lemelin to win Jennings Trophy for lowest team goals-against-average. Finished fifth overall in that category among NHL goalies, fourth in wins and second in shutouts. Minutes played was three-season high.

THE PHYSICAL GAME

Where his goaltending partner relies on positioning and simplicity, Moog is more flamboyant. Unlike Reggie Lemelin, Moog primarily plays a reflex game — though Andy has toned down his scrambling and flopping.

Moog's learned that, quick as he is, he can't grow. In other words, if he doesn't cut his angles properly, smart shooters will just put the puck over his shoulders all night long. When playing well, Moog will be challenging the shooter from the top of the goal crease. You'll know he's in trouble when he's deep in his net (though his reflexes are good enough to bail him out even when he's struggling). He has very quick feet, but because he plays more of a butterfly style (weight on his inside edges) he's going to give up goals between his legs.

His quickness extends to his glove hand, though Moog is strong to both sides, and Moog sees the puck very well (making him effective on screen shots, despite the inequalities in height between him and the League's forwards).

Though he skates well and is proficient in using his stick to clear rebounds, Moog doesn't go that second step and handle the puck when he's out of the net. Instead, he prefers to leave it for his defense.

He regains his stance very quickly and is very balanced, always in position to make the second save.

THE MENTAL GAME

Moog is very tough mentally and recovers very well from mental lapses, tough losses or just plain bad goals. In fact, we may be doing him a disservice by saying he recovers well because that implies he suffers after these occasions. At any rate, his further play is untainted. He has excellent concentration and really knows how to play to the occasion (as demonstrated by his playoff performances in general and his play during Boston's triple-overtime contest against the Oilers in particular).

In short, he can make the big save and win the big game — sometimes all by himself. Moog can also come in cold and perform well.

THE INTANGIBLES

Moog is a goaltender to bank on, one of the NHL's finest. He should continue along that path for a number of seasons to come.

CAM NEELY

Yrs. of NHL service: 7
Born: Comox, B.C., Canada; June 6, 1965
Position: Right wing
Height: 6-1
Weight: 210
Uniform no.: 8
Shoots: right

Career statistics:

GP	G	A	TP	PIM
494	221	191	412	945

1989-90 statistics:

GP	G	A	TP	+/-	PIM	PP	SH	GW	GT	S	PCT
76	55	37	92	10	117	25	0	12	0	271	20.3

LAST SEASON

Led club in goals, power play goals, points and game winning goals. Goal and point totals were career highs. Finished 20th overall in NHL in points, third in goals, second in power play goals and first in both first goals and game winners.

THE FINESSE GAME

Neely is an amalgam of hockey skills, crossing both the finesse and physical borders. That means he skates, scores and hits. He is a corner and boards player with an excellent shot, and his entire game is powered by strength.

His strength and balance afoot are excellent, and he uses both to maximum in his work along the wood and in traffic. His strong stride makes him nearly impossible to stop as he charges the net and that same strength drives him through his checks (and almost drives his checks through the boards). His balance is crucial in one-on-one confrontations where he battles for the puck but retains body position (and thus the ability to shoot or make plays). His skating strength makes him an excellent forechecker because he'll punish the opposition.

In a slight paradox, Neely doesn't have good hands for passing or puckhandling but he has a great shot. His shot is heavy, quickly released and very accurate (as the numbers attest) and he is a terror in the slot on the power play. He likes the corners and the five-hole.

He has good hockey sense (as demonstrated by his scoring ability), but Neely's game is predicated more on bending a play to his will through his crash and burn style than it is on chess-like manipulation of open ice.

THE PHYSICAL GAME

Without question, Neely is the premier physical winger in the game and maybe second only to Mark Messier as the game's prototypical power forward. There is no one in the game who can match Neely for his ability pound the boards and gain the puck, and only the very strongest of the League's defensemen can even hope to control him.

His highlight film hits will relieve anyone of the puck when along the boards, and he is a formidable fighter when provoked — so don't.

THE INTANGIBLES

Neely returned to his successful style last season, concentrating on allowing more skilled puckhandlers to do just that while he crashed the net or mucked in the corners. That consistency of physical effort is the key to Neely's game, and he knows that. His scoring exploits last year are far from out of character (as we've said for years), and Neely's fine attitude and enthusiasm should guarantee that his success will continue.

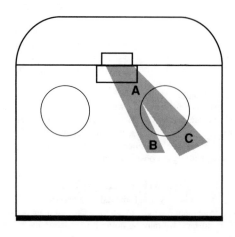

ALLEN PEDERSEN

Yrs. of NHL service: 4
Born: Edmonton, Alberta, Canada; January 13, 1965
Position: Defenseman
Height: 6-3
Weight: 210
Uniform no.: 41
Shoots: left

Career statistics:

GP	G	A	TP	PIM
276	2	25	27	301

1989-90 statistics:

GP	G	A	TP	+/-	PIM	PP	SH	GW	GT	S	PCT
68	1	2	3	-5	71	0	0	0	0	32	3.1

LAST SEASON

He was Boston's lowest scoring regular. Plus/minus was poorest among regular defensemen.

THE FINESSE GAME

Pedersen has a modicum of finesse skill, and he smartly stays within the limitations his skills proscribe. His skating is average at the NHL level, so that Pedersen must use discretion when he challenges the puck at either blue line. Because he lacks exceptional mobility Pedersen is slow in his turns. His ability to close the gap on the puck carrier isn't great, so Pedersen will have to be sure to angle the opposition to the boards.

He has the ability to get the puck to the open man and is a fair passer, but he won't be engineering any dynamic offensive plays from any zone; the simple play is his best way. He can make the correct pass from his own end quickly, and Pedersen generally makes correct decisions when moving the puck. Better ability to read and react at NHL speed would improve this apsect of his game.

He doesn't carry the puck and rarely joins the attack. He costs Boston some offensive pressure by not pinching in, and he doesn't add any offense from the point when he does station himself there.

THE PHYSICAL GAME

Pedersen can play a hitting game because he is a mobile enough player, and he uses size intelligently and often. He knows enough not to go charging around the defensive zone on search and destroy missions, and he applies his good size and strength to contain the opposition without taking penalties. He has the strength to win corner and crease battles and sacrifices his body as a good shot blocker but, though physical, is not a fighter.

THE INTANGIBLES

Pedersen is a strictly defensive defenseman, probably the only one among Boston's defensive corps. He is a steady and enthusiastic player, but is probably no better than fifth or sixth defenseman status.

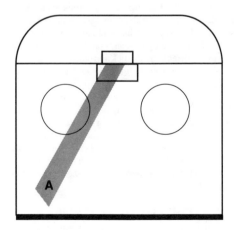

DAVE POULIN

Yrs. of NHL service: 7
Born: Timmins, Ontario, Canada; December 17, 1958
Position: Center
Height: 5-11
Weight: 190
Uniform no.: 19
Shoots: left

Career statistics:

GP	G	A	TP	PIM
499	167	252	419	315

1989-90 statistics:

GP	G	A	TP	+/-	PIM	PP	SH	GW	GT	S	PCT
60	15	27	42	16	24	0	1	1	1	88	17.0

LAST SEASON

Acquired by Boston from Philadelphia in exchange for Ken Linseman in January 1990. Games played and goal totals were full-season career lows. Missed 16 games with Philadelphia because of broken thumb. Plus/minus mark was team's third best, second among forwards.

THE FINESSE GAME

Poulin's best finesse asset is one that can't be measured, and that's his hockey sense and smarts. He reads plays excellently, both offensively and defensively. Poulin is an excellent checker and defensive player because of his speed and instincts, and those same attributes make him one of the NHL's premier penalty killers.

Physically, Poulin is a very strong skater with excellent speed and acceleration. Dave is smart enough to read the ice and give up his good shot for a teammate's better one. He's got good hands (soft enough to send a pass over a defenseman's stick and onto a teammate's), and they're strong enough to strip an opposing player of the puck.

He can score from a distance with a powerful wrist shot, but Poulin is more likely to score from within 15 feet or so (converting on opposing miscues). He should shoot more, in order to take advantage of the openings his speed and brains afford him. He prefers to go to his backhand when he is one-on-one with the goalie.

His skating and hockey sense make him a natural for penalty killing duty.

THE PHYSICAL GAME

Strength plays a large part in Poulin's skating game. His balance allows him to drive the net, but also keeps him vertical and positioned to make a play after a hit; he's very difficult to knock down. That's an important trait for a physical forward and Poulin can amplify his all-around physical play by playing mean at times.

Dave initiates contact in all three zones, taking men out of the play intelligently. His great arm, hand and wrist strength makes him an excellent faceoff man.

He willingly sacrifices his body to block shots, but the evidence suggests that Poulin's all-around physical play takes its toll in injuries.

THE INTANGIBLES

Poulin is a very intense and very intelligent player, the kind of player who needs to know why he's being asked to perform a certain way or use a certain tactic. A fine team man, Poulin characterizes everything a team leader should: intensity, determination, heart and willingness to sacrifice.

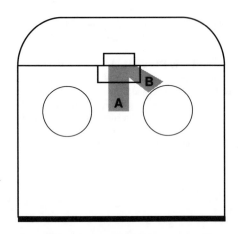

BRIAN PROPP

Yrs. of NHL service: 11
Born: Lanigan, Sask., Canada; February 15, 1959
Position: Left wing
Height: 5-11
Weight: 190
Uniform no.: 36
Shoots: left

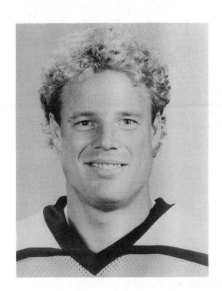

Career statistics:

GP	G	A	TP	PIM
804	372	489	861	679

1989-90 statistics:

GP	G	A	TP	+/-	PIM	PP	SH	GW	GT	S	PCT
54	16	24	40	5	41	5	1	0	0	153	10.5

LAST SEASON

Acquired by Boston in March 1990. Games played total was second lowest of career, all point totals were career lows. Missed 20 games with hand surgery, five games with a bruised shoulder.

THE FINESSE GAME

Propp has always succeeded as a finesse player by finding the openings and exploiting them with excellent anticipation and hockey sense complemented by fine skills. Once he sees the openings and gains them (because of his good speed and acceleration — his balance and lateral movement are excellent also) Propp can either make a play for a teammate or — more likely — himself. He knows how to get open.

He has outstanding stick skills, taking and giving passes smoothly at all speeds, but Brian is a scorer first and will take a bad shot even though a teammate is in better position. A negative commentator would call this trait "selfish."

Propp can score with an assortment of shots from all over the offensive zone (and his shot is very heavy), but his agility and one-step quickness make him a menace around the opposing goal, allowing him to easily convert loose pucks into points.

He remains a solid defensive player by playing his position well throughout all three zones. His anticipation and finesse skills also make him a regular in all specialty team situations.

THE PHYSICAL GAME

Brian is not big on physical contact, though he'll initiate some every once in a while (knowing his teammates will back him up). His balance, agility and hand skills allow him to control the puck in traffic, but Propp is not likely to be in the high-traffic areas.

THE INTANGIBLES

Consistency has always been Propp's hallmark, and we would expect it to be so again this season regardless of where he ends up. Though age and wear-and-tear are taking their tolls (he's no longer as fast as he once was, for example), Propp and his consistency remain an important part of any team he plays for.

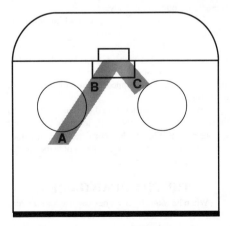

BOB SWEENEY

Yrs. of NHL service: 4
Born: Concord, Mass., USA; January 25, 1964
Position: Center
Height: 6-3
Weight: 200
Uniform no.: 42
Shoots: left

Career statistics:

GP	G	A	TP	PIM
239	60	65	125	291

1989-90 statistics:

GP	G	A	TP	+/-	PIM	PP	SH	GW	GT	S	PCT
70	22	24	46	2	93	5	2	6	0	147	15.0

LAST SEASON

Games played total was three-season low, but point total was career best. Led team in shorthanded goals and was second in game winners. Missed four games with a shoulder injury.

THE FINESSE GAME

Hand skills are the key to Sweeney's NHL success, from a finesse point of view. He handles the puck very well (his size and reach help here) in traffic though is less of a world-beater when carrying the puck up-ice on a rush; he can be a good one-on-one player in the offensive zone. He's got a good touch and can get the puck to open teammates, and he shoots fairly well from near the net but will not beat NHL goaltending from longer distances; he has a quick release and should shoot more. His hand skill does extend to the faceoff circle, where he is good on the draw.

Sweeney's skating is what slows him down and holds him back. Neither quick and agile nor outstandingly fast, Sweeney's skating actually gets in the way of his puck work. He won't always be able to get to the openings as he should because of his lack of foot speed, and he can get trapped defensively because of his skating.

Sweeney has demonstrated that he can read and understand the play at the NHL level, but he hasn't demonstrated that he can do it consistently. Sometimes he can be slow to react (although he's not helped in this department by his skating).

THE PHYSICAL GAME

When he wants to, Sweeney can use his size very effectively — in fact, he must in order to continue being successful at the NHL level. He's not outstandingly strong, but Sweeney's combination of balance and willingness to give and take hits can make up for any strength he may be lacking.

Sweeney can be a pretty tough player and he complements his size with his hand skills and the abil-ity to make plays coming out of the corner. His balance and reach also mean he can succeed in the traffic area near the net. And, college training aside, Sweeney will fight — and he ain't too bad at it.

THE INTANGIBLES

For Sweeney it all comes down to commitment and intensity. He needs to be pushed because he has a habit of playing comfortably and when he plays that way he fails to use all his tools. Sweeney must use everything he can muster to be successful at this level, and he's shown over three seasons that he can be at home in the NHL.

If he chooses to not put out, he becomes a marginal player.

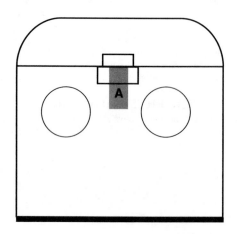

DON SWEENEY

Yrs. of NHL service: 1
Born: St. Stephen, N.B., Canada; August 17, 1966
Position: Defenseman
Height: 5-11
Weight: 170
Uniform no.: 32
Shoots: left

Career statistics:

GP	G	A	TP	PIM
94	6	10	16	78

1989-90 statistics:

GP	G	A	TP	+/-	PIM	PP	SH	GW	GT	S	PCT
58	3	5	8	11	58	0	0	0	0	49	6.1

LAST SEASON

First full NHL season; he missed five games with a separated shoulder.

THE FINESSE GAME

Sweeney is a player with offensive skills, skills that at his previous levels of play have been fairly strong. He skates well and his mobility should allow him to effectively and efficiently control and close the gap on the puck carrier, but Sweeney has a tendency to back in and look at the puck too much. He forces play wide well (and his plus/minus rating is a sound indication of his defensive ability), but he would do well to learn to be more active (versus reactive) at his own blue line.

His puckhandling skills allow him to carry the puck from the Bruins zone when necessary, and Sweeney demonstrates good intelligence in his rushing tendencies. He also moves the puck alertly to his forwards, and he will join the occasional rush up ice. He controls the point well, making prudent decisions as to when to pinch in and when to fall back.

Sweeney can come off the point to score, but he doesn't yet have a shot that will consistently fool NHL goaltending.

THE PHYSICAL GAME

Sweeney is a pretty tough kid, using the size he has in good fashion in front of the net and in the corners, but he is going to be out-muscled by bigger and stronger forwards — that's not a knock, simply a fact. He keeps himself in good muscular shape, so he clearly devotes time and energy to at least maintaining if not improving his strength, but bigger forwards are just going to reach around him for the puck.

He is helped in his willing physical game by the same balance that powers his skating game.

THE INTANGIBLES

Size is the big one (no pun intended). Outside of that, Sweeney is a hard working and dedicated kid who (if paired with the proper partner and allowed to exploit his strengths instead of having to concentrate on fixing an unfixable weakness) can develop into a pretty good NHL player.

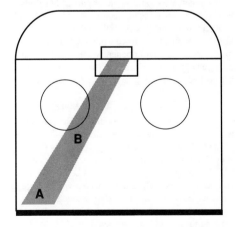

MICHAEL THELVEN

Yrs. of NHL service: 5
Born: Stockholm, Sweden; January 7, 1961
Position: Defenseman
Height: 5-11
Weight: 185
Uniform no.: 22
Shoots: left

Career statistics:

GP	G	A	TP	PIM
207	20	80	100	217

1989-90 statistics:

GP	G	A	TP	+/-	PIM	PP	SH	GW	GT	S	PCT
6	0	2	2	3	23	0	0	0	0	8	0.0

LAST SEASON

Games played total was career low (off-season knee surgery, followed by recurring knee problems and subsequent surgery).

THE FINESSE GAME

Skating and puck handling are the hallmarks of Thelven's game. Though not possessing great rink-length speed, Thelven can take advantage of the openings he sees and exploit them because he has a degree of foot quickness.

Michael handles the puck well in traffic, and Thelven likes to rush the puck and become a fourth attacker in the offensive zone. Once there, he's likely to run a give-and-go with the trailing forward and head for the slot. Most of his goals, however, will come not from the slot but from the point.

His defensive game is unexceptional, but Thelven will hold his own as the play comes down his side. He's more apt to use his skating skill to thwart the opposition (by stepping up to force a play) than he is to back in and try to take an opponent wide. That's because taking an opponent wide means Thelven would have to use his body, something he doesn't generally do.

THE PHYSICAL GAME

Michael will get his hits in when he can, on his terms. He is not an aggressive individual and won't really take the hits to make his plays, generally throwing snow instead of getting into the corner for the puck.

His front of the net coverage is going to be more tactical than physical, in that Thelven will attempt to block passes to the slot instead of bodying the opposing forward camped there. He can get out-muscled while working for the puck in cramped quarters.

THE INTANGIBLES

This report is virtually unchanged from last year in deference to Thelven's injury. That injury may or may not affect his skating. Here's what we said for intangibles last year: "As we've said, durability remains a major question mark for Thelven. Also of note is the fact that the Bruins have a host of defensemen who can play his kind of game, but will add greater degrees of physical involvement (Don Sweeney, Stephane Quintal, Greg Hawgood, Garry Galley).

All of this makes Thelven's continued presence with the Bruins a questionable circumstance."

We'll stand behind that.

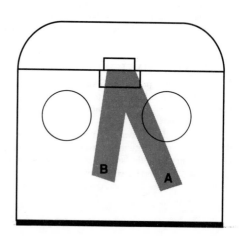

GLEN WESLEY

Yrs. of NHL service: 3
Born: Red Deer, Alta., Canada; October 2, 1968
Position: Defenseman
Height: 6-1
Weight: 195
Uniform no.: 26
Shoots: left

Career statistics:

GP	G	A	TP	PIM
234	35	92	127	178

1989-90 statistics:

GP	G	A	TP	+/-	PIM	PP	SH	GW	GT	S	PCT
78	9	27	36	6	48	5	0	4	0	166	5.4

LAST SEASON

Assist and point totals were lowest of career.

THE FINESSE GAME

Skating is the strongest of Wesley's considerable finesse skills, and his skating is marked by speed and mobility. His strong stride gives him very good speed in both directions, while his balance and foot speed give him strong one-step quickness and lateral ability. He is, however, just a little weak in his turns to the left, and he'll take penalties on forwards who beat him that way.

His fine hockey sense is marked by his poise, and the patience and confidence he demonstrates while handling the puck is remarkable for a player with lack of NHL experience. He shows good ability to find open men all over the ice, and Wesley anticipates well both offensively and defensively. He amplifies his sense with fairly good puckhandling ability and can move with the puck at any of his speeds. He passes well and with touch, and can not only find open men but can find openings and lead teammates to them.

Wesley uses both his skating and sense ability to be active at both blue lines. He contains the offensive zone very well, and he also controls the gap well on incoming puck carriers. He also has excellent shot selection, and he delivers both his slap and wrist shots quickly and accurately.

THE PHYSICAL GAME

He doesn't yet have a lot of bulk to offer, but that doesn't stop Wesley from playing an intelligently aggressive game. He's not a thumper, but he takes out his man very well, and Wesley's hand and foot skills guarantee that he can turn the play around quickly. He plays smartly in front of his own net (as in playing the oppositions' sticks when they are bigger than he), but he can be out-muscled by equally talented opposing forwards.

THE INTANGIBLES

We may have been a bit premature in predicting 25 goals a year for Wesley, who clearly faced more and better checking last season, but we maintain that he can approach that plateau. He is a character kid who will continue to improve because of his attitude and work ethic.

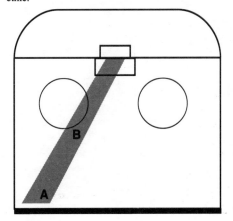

BUFFALO SABRES

DAVE ANDREYCHUK

Yrs. of NHL service: 7
Born: Hamilton, Ontario, Canada; September 29, 1963
Position: Left wing
Height: 6-3
Weight: 214
Uniform no.: 25
Shoots: right

Career statistics:

GP	G	A	TP	PIM
478	202	266	468	371

1989-90 statistics:

GP	G	A	TP	+/-	PIM	PP	SH	GW	GT	S	PCT
56	28	24	52	1	40	7	0	3	0	145	19.3

LAST SEASON

Games played total was full season low (knee injury). Andreychuk finished fifth in team scoring, third in goals. Goal total was second lowest of career, assist and point totals full season lows.

THE FINESSE GAME

Andreychuk's best finesse skills are concentrated in his head and his hands, not his feet. He's got a real good wrist shot that forces the goaltender to make saves, and Dave's hands are soft enough for him to release the puck quickly and while in traffic. He smartly makes use of his shot by shooting often, and Andreychuk makes his shooting in tight more effective by using his backhand when necessary (instead of circling to his forehand).

While primarily a finisher, Dave does look for his teammates. Because he handles the puck well and has excellent anticipation, Andreychuk is a good passer. He sees openings for his teammates and gets the puck to them well, but his anticipation is more likely to put him in scoring position (where he wants the puck).

As a skater, Andreychuk has little foot speed or quickness above the NHL average. While he has good balance which helps him maintain body position in front of the net), Andreychuk lacks the foot speed that — when working in tandem with balance — creates agility.

He is a good defensive player and pays attention to that aspect of the game, backchecking deeply in his own zone.

THE PHYSICAL GAME

His balance and strength on his skates are what makes Andreychuk a slot scorer. He drives the net and is almost impossible to move once he's planted himself there. Andreychuk also uses his great size to gain position either along the boards or in front of the net. Because he's practically impossible to move legally, he'll draw a lot of penalties.

He won't clobber people, but Dave will use his size while checking and will rub out the opposition along the boards. He uses his hand and arm strength to get the puck away while people are draped all over him; he'll also draw some faceoff duty because of that strength.

Andreychuk also puts his big wingspan to use around the net, first to gather in pucks (good hand and wrist strength helps here) and then to muscle a shot away despite checking.

THE INTANGIBLES

Andreychuk is one of the few Sabre youngsters who entered the League to big expectation who has actually come anywhere near fulfilling his notices. Though essentially a non-contributor in this season's playoffs (three assists in five games), Dave has shown that he can contribute in key situations. On a team as enigmatic as Buffalo, that's an important characteristic.

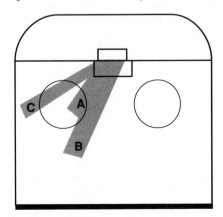

DOUG BODGER

Yrs. of NHL service: 6
Born: Chemainus, B.C., Canada; June 18, 1966
Position: Defenseman
Height: 6-2
Weight: 200
Uniform no.: 8
Shoots: left

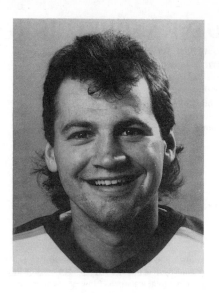

Career statistics:

GP	G	A	TP	PIM
431	54	208	262	408

1989-90 statistics:

GP	G	A	TP	+/-	PIM	PP	SH	GW	GT	S	PCT
71	12	36	48	0	64	8	0	1	0	167	7.2

LAST SEASON

Plus/minus rating was second lowest among defensemen. Missed eight games with a knee injury, one game with a shoulder injury.

THE FINESSE GAME

Skating and puck movement are the keys to Bodger's game. He has good to very good agility and mobility for a bigger man, and his lateral movement and one-step quickness will surprise opponents unaccustomed to such moves coming from a bulky guy. He uses his skating two ways to start Buffalo's transition game, either by stepping up to close the gap and force the play at his blue line, or by skating loose pucks from the zone himself. He is aggressive offensively, sometimes too much so in the attacking zone, and will always join a rush up-ice. Opponents must play the body on Bodger in order to slow him down.

He carries the puck confidently from the defensive zone, but Bodger is better at seeing and making a strong first pass. He gets good reads at both ends of the ice, and he'll find the open man ahead of him; he passes well to both sides, has pretty good touch and his vision is good enough to recognize openings and send his teammates into them. He is consistent defensively, if not the greatest defensive zone player ever, but he is susceptible to making blind passes around the boards that give the puck to the opposition.

Bodger's shot is probably the weakest of his finesse skills, in that it is only average in terms of speed and power. He does shoot well off the pass (a good power play skill), but there are still too many nights when his shot is absent without leave.

THE PHYSICAL GAME

Bodger is essentially a finesse player with size. He uses his body fairly effectively and efficiently around the net and on the boards, but he could use his size and develop his strength so that he becomes a punishing

hitter, making opposing forwards think twice before venturing near him. That would also give him some more room for his finesse plays.

THE INTANGIBLES

The general consensus with defensemen is that they take five years to mature; Bodger has just finished his sixth. He is a good player, not necessarily outstanding, and he certainly benefits from the fact that Phil Housley gets the lion's share of checking attention. How much further Bodger will develop is debatable, but for now he is a hard working, coachable — and fairly successful — NHL defenseman.

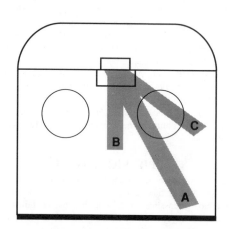

MIKE FOLIGNO

Yrs. of NHL service: 12
Born: Sudbury, Ontario, Canada; January 29, 1959
Position: Right wing
Height: 6-2
Weight: 195
Uniform no.: 17
Shoots: right

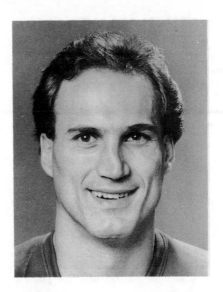

Career statistics:

GP	G	A	TP	PIM
819	320	342	662	1,755

1989-90 statistics:

GP	G	A	TP	+/-	PIM	PP	SH	GW	GT	S	PCT
61	15	25	40	13	99	3	0	1	1	107	14.0

LAST SEASON

Games played, goal and point totals were all career lows; Foligno missed four games with flu and 15 games with a broken thumb. His plus/minus rating was the club's third best, highest among forwards.

THE FINESSE GAME

As in his physical game, Foligno's strength is at the root of his physical game. He is not a pretty skater in the way teammate Pierre Turgeon is, but Foligno's powerful stride gives him power (and therefore a degree of speed) and driving strength. He's strong on his feet, making him effective in traffic situations, but he's not really an agile skater — despite his proclivity for the inside move near the net.

He's not a bad stickhandler (the root of that inside move in front), so Foligno can make a move coming off the boards; that same hand combines with his skate sturdiness to operate well in the crease. He is not, however, an outstanding passer. Foligno will shoot first — and he has a heavy, quick and *very* accurate shot that forces goalies to make saves — and ask questions later.

Foligno sees the play well both offensively and defensively, and he is then aided in his checking or playmaking by his skating. He uses those traits as an excellent checker, determined and successful.

THE PHYSICAL GAME

If his finesse attributes read more like physical ones, that's because Foligno was an NHL power forward before anyone knew what that was. His applications of his strength and physical gifts make him as a player. He initiates contact without fail, playing aggressively (sometimes too much so) and controlling play against the boards. He hits willingly and his sturdiness keeps him upright after collisions; his finesse ability makes his hitting all the more effective.

He backs down from nothing and is an excellent fighter. His upper body strength, especially in his hands, wrists and forearms, power his shot and it is that strength that makes him so effective along the boards.

THE INTANGIBLES

His outstanding conditioning betrays Foligno's attitude about the game and his work, and his work ethic simply underlines the point that he is always ready to play and give his best. That makes him a leader.

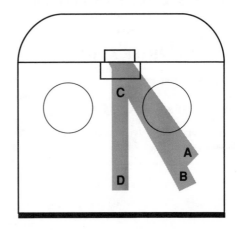

MIKE HARTMAN

Yrs. of NHL service: 3
Born: Detroit, Mich., USA; February 7, 1967
Position: Left wing
Height: 6-0
Weight: 183
Uniform no.: 20
Shoots: left

Career statistics:

GP	G	A	TP	PIM
165	25	23	48	686

1989-90 statistics:

GP	G	A	TP	+/-	PIM	PP	SH	GW	GT	S	PCT
60	11	10	21	-10	211	2	0	3	0	97	11.3

LAST SEASON

Point totals were all career bests, and his PIM total led the club. He finished next to last in plus/minus rating, worst among forwards. He missed nine games with ankle injuries.

THE FINESSE GAME

Finesse is not the strength of Hartman's game, so he's going to have to make his contributions in a checking and defensive sense. He has a fair degree of speed, and his skating strength and balance allow him to drive through checks. That balance doesn't necessarily translate into agility or lateral movement, and that's because Hartman has heavy feet.

His hand skills are no more exceptional than his foot skills. Hartman has no real ability to work with the puck when carrying or passing it, but he does have a degree of sensitivity when shooting. Still, because of his limited skills and because he doesn't demonstrate a real sense of the ice, he'll have to be opportunistic for his goals.

THE PHYSICAL GAME

Hartman is a strong player, and he uses that strength in his hitting. He'll hit when and wherever he can and is helped in his bodychecking by his strong stride and good upper body strength.

Also, Hartman beats people up. He likes to fight and is one of the League's top middleweights — maybe the best.

THE INTANGIBLES

Hartman is a gutsy, determined guy, a real competitor. He has excellent character and will continue to be valuable to the Sabres because of that mental outlook and attitude.

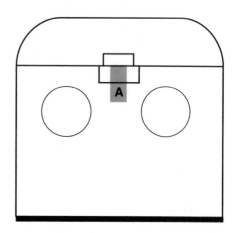

DALE HAWERCHUK

Yrs. of NHL service: 9
Born: Toronto, Ontario, Canada; April 4, 1963
Position: Center
Height: 5-11
Weight: 185
Uniform no.: 10
Shoots: left

Career statistics:

GP	G	A	TP	PIM
713	379	550	929	470

1989-90 statistics:

GP	G	A	TP	+/-	PIM	PP	SH	GW	GT	S	PCT
79	26	55	81	-11	60	8	0	2	0	211	12.3

LAST SEASON

Acquired June 1990 from Winnipeg in exchange for Phil Housley, Scott Arniel and Jeff Parker. Led the Jets in assists, points and shots on goal.

THE FINESSE GAME

There is nothing Dale cannot do finesse-wise. He is a deceptive skater in that he doesn't seem fast, but his long stride gives him power for acceleration and breakaway speed. Hawerchuk also has excellent one-step quickness which, when combined with his exceptional balance, give him exceptional agility and lateral movement. He can move in any direction within a step.

Hawerchuk's superior hockey sense complements his skating, pointing out the openings his quickness can gain. His sense and anticipation are the keys to his playmaking skills, but his excellent hands deserve equal credit. Dale can put the puck anywhere at any time (though he's historically used his right wingers better than his left wingers because the RW is on his forehand). He leads his teammates into the clear excellently, and likes to stop and turn in the offensive zone.

Hawerchuk can also tantalize the opposition with his stickhandling, but his ability can also be a curse. Dale tends to over-handle the puck and work himself into predicaments that lead to turnovers (one reason for his plus/minus), and his 1-on-1 work often leaves his teammates standing trapped deep in the zone.

He scores from most everywhere in the offensive zone. His great hands give him the ability to control the puck regardless of traffic, proximity to the goal or angle. He's deadly around the net, especially because his excellent eye/hand coordination makes him expert at deflecting the puck.

Simply, his defense stinks. He's a defensive liability, largely because he has a tough time playing within a structured system.

THE PHYSICAL GAME

Dale is not really a physical player, but he does play in the traffic areas. He will initiate some contact in the offensive zone, but just because he's giving and taking hits doesn't mean he likes them. Hawerchuk has a short fuse and he'll lose his temper over close checking, frequently taking stupid retaliatory penalties in the offensive zone.

THE INTANGIBLES

We've ridden Hawerchuk for his attitude in previous years. Now that he's gotten the trade he asked for, let's see if his attitude and outlook improve.

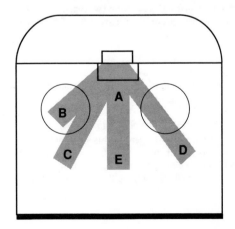

BENOIT HOGUE

Yrs. of NHL service: 2
Born: Repentigny, Quebec, Canada; October 28, 1966
Position: Center
Height: 5-10
Weight: 177
Uniform no.: 33
Shoots: left

Career statistics:

GP	G	A	TP	PIM
117	26	38	64	199

1989-90 statistics:

GP	G	A	TP	+/-	PIM	PP	SH	GW	GT	S	PCT
45	11	7	18	0	79	1	0	1	0	73	15.1

LAST SEASON

Point totals fell in second NHL season. He missed 20 games with a broken cheekbone, and another five games with a knee injury.

THE FINESSE GAME

Hogue is a finesse player, a good thing to be when you're a small guy. He demonstrates the requisite finesse abilities of skating, puckhandling and shooting, but only his skating is clearly at the NHL level. He has NHL speed and balance, but right now he operates best in a straight line.

One of the reasons for that is the fact that his playreading skills and understanding of the NHL game haven't reached the level of his skating. As such, his speed will create his opportunities but his brain hasn't caught up to his feet. Hogue particularly demonstrates this defensively, where he'll break too soon and leave his team out-manned in its own zone.

His hand skills are better than his foot skills at this point, in that Hogue can and will operate in traffic. He takes the puck off the boards well, and because he does know how to get into scoring position (positions near the net from which his hands will help him) he'll succeed down low. He's also got the eye/hand coordination to tip and deflect the puck. He shoots the puck with strength and accuracy, and he makes his shot better by getting it off quickly.

THE PHYSICAL GAME

Hogue plays bigger than his size, but that's not necessarily a benefit — his injuries are the kind one suffers from playing a physical game that can't be backed by bulk. In short, he'll take the pounding but

will pay a heavy price. His balance is a big key in his ability to gain position in front of the net and along the boards.

THE INTANGIBLES

Other clubs ask about Hogue in trades, so he's a fairly valuable commodity. Last season would not be a representative one of Hogue's NHL potential (because of injury), and Hogue's good attitude and great desire should power his continued NHL improvement.

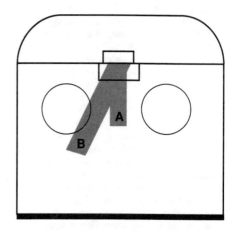

DEAN KENNEDY

Yrs. of NHL service: 7
Born: Redvers, Sask., Canada; January 18, 1963
Position: Defenseman
Height: 6-2
Weight: 203
Uniform no.: 26
Shoots: right

Career statistics:

GP	G	A	TP	PIM
441	15	75	90	684

1989-90 statistics:

GP	G	A	TP	+/-	PIM	PP	SH	GW	GT	S	PCT
80	2	12	14	-12	53	0	0	0	0	51	3.9

LAST SEASON

Acquired from Los Angeles as a waiver draft pick. Played 80 games for first time in career.

THE FINESSE GAME

Kennedy is not overly gifted in the finesse areas. He's no better than average as a skater, primarily because his agility (quickness plus balance) is very questionable. Because of his poor lateral movement, Dean is very prone to forwards faking one way and heading the other. When that happens he has no choice but to take penalties.

He could circumvent these negatives if gifted with above-average hokcey sense, vision or anticipation. But Dean is not so gifted, so his play *must* be the simple one. Fortunately for him, his play is most often characterized as such. As long as Dean sticks with the up-the-boards-and-out pass and doesn't look to make fancy glamourous passes, he'll function well.

He's essentially a throw-in on offense, though Kennedy will work to contain the puck at the point. He follows the play up-ice but his role is to be the safety valve — the one man back when necessary. The fact that he hardly shoots the puck indicates how little he is concerned with offense. When he does shoot, he fires a slap shot from the point that is no better than average in strength, speed or accuracy.

THE PHYSICAL GAME

Dean is a very physical player and this is the strength of his game. He'll try to thwart the play at the Sabre blue line by standing up the puck carrier, he ties up the opposition in front of the net, and Kennedy will outmuscle many players because of good upper body strength. He's a good body checker who makes the opposition pay for shots on goal or chances at the Sabres net, and Dean has to play that way to succeed.

Worth noting: Positive though it is that Kennedy hits frequently, he can also take himself out of the play by doing so because of his limited mobility.

THE INTANGIBLES

Kennedy is a very enthusiastic player with a great work ethic (as his physical condition demonstrates) and the smarts to play the way he must in order to be successful — alertly and aggressively while staying within his limitations; when he loses that focus, he is a very marginal NHLer.

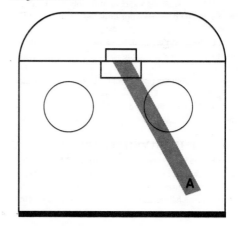

UWE KRUPP

Yrs. of NHL service: 4
Born: Cologne, West Germany; June 24, 1965
Position: Defenseman
Height: 6-6
Weight: 230
Uniform no.: 4
Shoots: right

Career statistics:

GP	G	A	TP	PIM
245	11	46	57	314

1989-90 statistics:

GP	G	A	TP	+/-	PIM	PP	SH	GW	GT	S	PCT
74	3	20	23	15	85	0	1	1	0	69	4.3

LAST SEASON

Assist and point totals were career highs. Missed two games with knee and ankle injuries. Plus/minus rating was team's second best.

THE FINESSE GAME

Steadiness is the key to Krupp's game, a game which highlights defensive play over offensive fireworks. He's improved his skills in all areas since his introduction to the NHL. He's a good skater and relatively agile laterally, but he'll use his size and defensive angles to protect his end; he'll step up when he can, but expect to see Krupp give the opposition an outside zone and then close it off.

Krupp can handle the puck, and he makes the most of his modicum of puckhandling skill by *not* handling the puck. In other words, Krupp makes sure to get the puck to his forwards as quickly and efficiently as possible. He gets a fairly good read of the play as it moves up-ice, and he can make not only the right play but a good play.

He has good sense of the game and always makes sure to get a good look at the ice before making a play. He is not a gifted offensive player (though he does have a good shot from the point), but he'll find the open man and get him the puck. That ability to keep his head up evidences itself at the offensive blue line, where Krupp knows to lift his shot over a sliding forward.

THE PHYSICAL GAME

Krupp can be very tough in front of his net, and he can fight, but he doesn't make consistent use of his size. He can get lazy and begin relying on pokechecking (a skill at which he is very good — as might be expected from a guy with a DC-10 wingspan) instead of using his body. Though his physical game is one of efficiency and not slam-bang bodychecks, he still must remember to apply himself at all times.

THE INTANGIBLES

As long as you don't look at Krupp and expect bombs to go off when he hits someone, you're okay. The Sabres know that, and that is one reason why Krupp's game has improved.

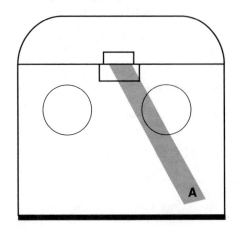

GRANT LEDYARD

Yrs. of NHL service: 6
Born: Winnipeg, Manitoba, Canada; November 19, 1961
Position: Defenseman
Height: 6-2
Weight: 190
Uniform no.: 3
Shoots: left

Career statistics:

GP	G	A	TP	PIM
373	42	101	143	398

1989-90 statistics:

GP	G	A	TP	+/-	PIM	PP	SH	GW	GT	S	PCT
67	2	13	15	2	37	0	0	1	0	91	2.2

LAST SEASON

Games played total tied third highest of career.

THE FINESSE GAME

Ledyard is a case of the sum not equalling the total of the parts. He has good to very good finesse skills beginning with his skating, which is very good. Ledyard is a very mobile player with good acceleration, quickness and balance. He moves just as well laterally as he does forward and back.

He can move well with the puck and can be a valuable player because of his puckhandling ability, but Ledyard mitigates that ability by hurrying his passes. He can make good passes when the play is clearly in front of him, but can be rushed into mistakes. His offensive play is better from the offensive blue line than elsewhere.

His modicum of ability in offensive playreading is not matched defensively. Ledyard doesn't use his skating as well as he could to close the gap on the opposition, and so he finds himself backing in way too much. Added to that, he has a tendency to be hypnotized by the puck. That hypnosis also means that he'll wander from his position.

His best talent is unquestionably his shot, which is one of the League's hardest — hard, accurate and fast from the blue line. But, again, Ledyard mitigates that talent by taking a lot of time getting the shot off.

THE PHYSICAL GAME

Despite his good size and strength, Ledyard is outfought in confrontational situations. We're not talking about fighting here, only those one-on-one battles that a defenseman has to win in the corners and the front of the net. He has the finesse skills to make his physical skills more effective, but he is undercut by his no-better-than-fair use of his physical gifts.

In short, he is a finesse player with size.

THE INTANGIBLES

Ledyard is a likeable guy, enthusiastic and hard working in his own right, but he needs help in the concentration department. As he's currently constituted (and we see no reason why he would change after a half-dozen NHL season), he's valuable to the Sabres in man-advantage situations and as a fourth-to-sixth (or even fifth-to-seventh) defenseman.

He's probably best described as a guy who's got all the tools but can't open the tool box. Don't be surprised if he finishes the season somewhere other than Buffalo.

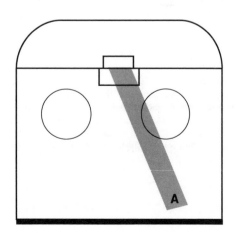

CLINT MALARCHUK

Yrs. of NHL service: 7
Born: Grande, Alta., Canada; May 1, 1961
Position: Goaltender
Height: 6-0
Weight: 190
Uniform no.: 30
Catches: left

Career statistics:

GP	MINS	G	SO	AVG	A	PIM
272	15,260	879	11	3.46	10	109

1989-90 statistics:

GP	MINS	AVG	W	L	T	SO	GA	SA	SAPCT	PIM
29	1,596	3.35	14	11	2	0	89	914	.903	14

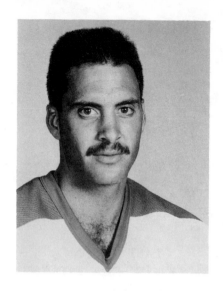

LAST SEASON

Games played total was five-season low.

THE PHYSICAL GAME

Strong standup angle play is the key to Malarchuk's goaltending success. When he is on his game, he may not have an equal to squaring himself to the puck and letting the puck do the work. He is a good skater with balance and quickness, and those assets allow him to move well in and out of the net and from post to post. They also serve to get him back into his stance quickly when Malarchuk goes to the ice.

His fast hands and feet make him very effective in scrambles near the net and those skills better help his effectiveness, because Malarchuk hangs in the net as play moves nearer the crease. His fast hands and feet will generally get him to most any puck.

That said, he tends to be weaker on his stick side. He could also do a better job of controlling his rebounds, both in terms of controlling the original shot (catching the puck instead of just batting at it) and the subsequent rebounds allowed.

He will leave the net to flag down loose pucks, but Malarchuk is not a great puckhandler.

THE MENTAL GAME

Mental toughness is a hallmark of Malarchuk's game, both in terms of preparation and concentration. Though he's had a tendency throughout his career to give up goals in bunches, Malarchuk will fight you for every goal you get. He also lets go of bad games and prepares well for his next assignment.

His ability to anticipate and concentrate also help his game physically by giving him his effectiveness during those scrambles near the net.

THE INTANGIBLES

Malarchuk has been the number one goalie throughout his NHL career, but he is now clearly the caddy to Daren Puppa. That move will test Malarchuk's ability to maintain his focus and concentration, as he can expect to play a like number of games this season as last.

ALEXANDER MOGILNY

Yrs. of NHL service: 1
Born: Khabarovsk, USSR; February 18, 1969
Position: Right wing
Height: 5-11
Weight: 186
Uniform no.: 89
Shoots: left

Career statistics:

GP	G	A	TP	+/-	PIM	PP	SH	GW	GT	S	PCT
65	15	28	43	8	16	4	0	2	1	130	11.5

LAST SEASON

First in the NHL. Missed two games with an ankle injury, five games with the flu.

THE FINESSE GAME

Mogilny has finesse ability across the board. He is an exceptional skater with speed and agility, so he can get anywhere at any time. He loves to dart through the middle, and he already makes his skating more effective by moderating his speed and throwing different changes of pace at the defense. He can also pull away from the defense.

Helping his foot skills are his hand skills. Mogilny handles the puck excellently, and can do just about anything he wants with it. He has excellent touch with his quick shot and works very well in traffic because of his soft hands (his balance helps here as well), but he also has the ability to drive the puck past any goaltender. He likes to cut to the forehand on an inside-outside-inside route.

His sense is very good, though Mogilny does need to be better acclimated to the speed and rhythm of the NHL game. Nevertheless, he has the ability to use his teammates (hands plus sense), even though he currently demonstrates one-on-one tendencies.

Mogilny is patient defensively, looking for the right time to leave his defensive zone and join or create an attack.

THE PHYSICAL GAME

Mogilny isn't big in terms of bulk, but he'll do the work along the wood. He won't slam anyone into the cheap seats, but his finesse skills make his bumping along the boards more effective — Mogilny can certainly make a play coming out of the corner.

Conversely, opponents must play the body against Mogilny if they harbor any hope of neutralizing him.

THE INTANGIBLES

Only the continuing huge one of adapting to the NHL and to North American life. Mogilny has shown signs that he has both made and not made some of the transitions necessary, and patience is necessary before he'll reach his considerable potential.

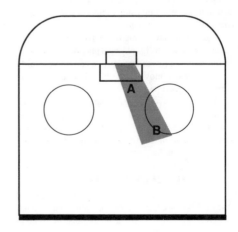

LARRY PLAYFAIR

Yrs. of NHL service: 12
Born: Fort St. James, B.C., Canada; June 23, 1958
Position: Defenseman
Height: 6-4
Weight: 225
Uniform no.: 27
Shoots: left

Career statistics:

GP	G	A	TP	PIM
688	26	94	120	1,812

1989-90 statistics:

GP	G	A	TP	+/-	PIM	PP	SH	GW	GT	S	PCT
4	0	1	1	-2	2	0	0	0	0	0	0.0

LAST SEASON

Games played total was career low; he was sidelined with a leg injury.

THE FINESSE GAME

Finesse has never been Playfair's game and most of his skills reflect that, but he does have a couple of finesse assets. He is not a good skater and has trouble with any kind of speed attack because of his lack of mobility. Playfair has a great deal of trouble stopping and starting, which means he won't be able to make the evasive maneuvers necessary to lose a forechecker when he goes back for the puck.

A defenseman without speed needs positional smarts, something Playfair does not have a great deal of. He is just average at playing his defensive angles, relying more on his imposing size to prevent the opposition from setting up camp in his zone than he does correct defensive positioning.

Larry does have some offensive ability that has been overshadowed by his physical play. While he won't join the rush as a fourth attacker, he can make a fairly positive offensive move at the blue line and he is an exceptionally good passer.

He can play a role on left wing as well as defense, functioning as the forward staying back to cover defensively or down low to plug the net. He'll get a goal or two a year from the front of the net, and another couple from the point.

THE PHYSICAL GAME

Playfair is a big tough guy, strong in his own end of the ice when he can catch the opposition. He is tough in the corners and in front of the net because of his good strength and he likes to hit — a lot. He is a punishing hitter and can also muscle the puck away from the opposition.

But he suffers from over-aggressiveness, charging at people, elbowing, obviously rubbing his gloves in their faces. Then the referee has no choice but to send him to the box.

He can contribute in a limited defensive role if he curbs his temper and he will sacrifice his body to block a shot or two. He is also an accomplished fighter.

THE INTANGIBLES

We've inlcuded Playfair's report unchanged from last season because of his injury. That said, his inclusion in the Sabres lineup (and perhaps in the NHL itself) is a highly questionable thing.

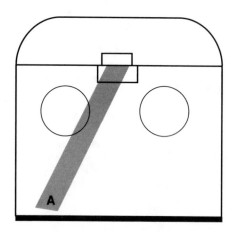

DAREN PUPPA

Yrs. of NHL service: 3
Born: Kirkland Lake, Ontario, Canada; March 23, 1965
Position: Goaltender
Height: 6-3
Weight: 191
Uniform no.: 31
Catches: right

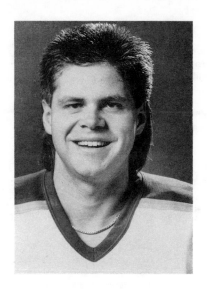

Career statistics:

GP	MINS	G	SO	AVG	A	PIM
120	6,609	358	3	3.25	9	22

1989-90 statistics:

GP	MINS	AVG	W	L	T	SO	GA	SA	SAPCT	PIM
56	3,241	2.89	31	16	6	1	156	1,610	.903	4

LAST SEASON

Finished second in wins among NHL goalies, third in save percentage and fourth in goals-against-average. Was third in minutes-played, with a career high mark.

THE PHYSICAL GAME

Puppa has outstanding size, and he uses that size to be a daunting — even intimidating — figure in the Sabres' goal. He has two styles, but is primarily a butterfly goalie, a bigger version of Tony Esposito. Puppa uses his size to advantage by standing up and challenging the shooter when the puck is above the faceoff circles, but as play moves nearer the net, Puppa will use his size and quickness to cover the bottom half of the goal.

He is very quick with his hands and feet, less so in regaining his stance after going to the ice. Puppa doesn't have great lateral ability, so he can be exploited on bang-bang plays — but just remember his size and reach.

Because he goes to the ice he leaves a lot of rebounds but, again, this is where his reflex ability comes through. Still, the corners of the net are going to be exploitable.

Puppa can handle the puck and will leave his net to pass loose pucks to his defense.

THE MENTAL GAME

As he's gained NHL experience and responsibility, Puppa has improved his concentration and mental ability. His outlook is the same good goal or bad goal, and he prepares himself to play each game; in short, he has improved his consistency while maintaining a high level of mental ability.

THE INTANGIBLES

As his performance in the All-Star Game and Skills Competition demonstrated, Puppa has moved from the back to the front of the NHL — he certainly was not out of place among the NHL's best and brightest. In fact, Puppa should be among the NHL's elite for a long time.

MIKE RAMSEY

Yrs. of NHL service: 10
Born: Minneapolis, Minn., USA; December 3, 1960
Position: Defenseman
Height: 6-3
Weight: 187
Uniform no.: 5
Shoots: left

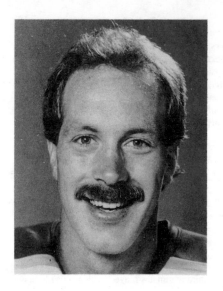

Career statistics:

GP	G	A	TP	PIM
741	62	220	282	791

1989-90 statistics:

GP	G	A	TP	+/-	PIM	PP	SH	GW	GT	S	PCT
73	4	21	25	21	47	1	0	2	0	91	4.4

LAST SEASON

Games played, assist and point totals were three-season highs. Plus/minus was club's best. He missed four games with a concussion, and other time with a hand injury.

THE FINESSE GAME

Ramsey's skills are understated, as often happens with an efficient yet unspectacular player. He is a very mobile player, and he combines his skating ability with his intelligence to play a positionally excellent defensive game. Ramsey will meet the opposition ahead of the blue line to close the gap when he can, but he is just as proficient at forcing the opposing winger to an outside lane. He plays his defensive angles very well.

Mike passes the puck from his zone very well, but he can carry the puck when necessary to take pressure off his forwards. He makes his puckhandling better by not overhandling the puck, getting it quickly and smartly out of his zone. Most of his assists will come that way, as his contributions from the offensive blue line are few and far between.

His smarts are what power his game. There are times when Mike will make defensive mistakes by gambling and trying to do too much but — as his plus/minus indicates — those times are few and far between.

THE PHYSICAL GAME

Ramsey is a quietly physical player. He's not likely to send someone flying into the cheap seats, but his takeouts and pins are strong and constant. He's very tough in front of his own net and takes the body very well along the boards, always positioning himself to make a play after a takeout; rare are the confrontations he won't win through some combination of strength and body positioning.

He steps up to hit very well in open ice, so forwards must keep their heads up. Ramsey is one of the few NHLers proficient at hip-checking, and he willingly sacrifices his body to block shots. The only downside to his shot-blocking is the fact he takes himself out of the play by going down to block the puck. That's what we meant by taking a defensive gamble.

THE INTANGIBLES

Ramsey is a terrific competitor, one who plays in pain and plays his best at all times. He works hard, he's smart and is a great team man. All these things add up to make him a leader and a player critical to any Sabres success.

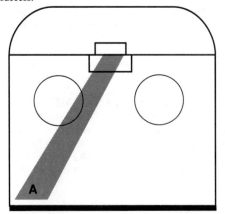

CHRISTIAN RUUTTU

Yrs. of NHL service: 4
Born: Lappeenranta, Finland; February 20, 1964
Position: Center
Height: 5-11
Weight: 194
Uniform no.: 21
Shoots: left

Career statistics:

GP	G	A	TP	PIM
291	81	175	256	311

1989-90 statistics:

GP	G	A	TP	+/-	PIM	PP	SH	GW	GT	S	PCT
75	19	41	60	9	66	4	1	2	1	160	11.9

LAST SEASON

Assist total set, and point total tied career, lows. Finished fourth on the club in scoring. Missed three games with flu. Plus/minus was third best among forwards.

THE FINESSE GAME

Creativity and smarts combine with above average offensive skills to make Ruuttu a fine finesse player. Ruuttu has outstanding hockey sense and anticipation ability, and those assets make him a very creative — and therefore very dangerous — player without the puck. He sees the ice well in both zones, playing conscientiously in the defensive zone and with ability to get into scoring position — or get a teammate there — in the offensive zone.

He's an excellent skater, and he can create openings with his speed and agility. He uses his excellent speed, quickness and acceleration (plus a great change of pace) to drive the defensemen off the blue line and create room for his teammates, and he likes to come back deeply into his own zone to start plays — opponents must play his body (especially in his defensive zone) in order to slow Ruuttu down. His balance and quickness combine to give him exceptional lateral movement, and Ruuttu uses those skills against the boards in the crease exceedingly well.

Ruuttu's got a quick stick, and his hand skills are not far below those of his feet. He carries the pucks very well and makes plays at top speed, one reason he succeeds in using his teammates. He drives a quick and accurate wrist/snap shot at the goalie and, because he rarely shoots from outside the slot area, his shots are usually high percentage plays. He also has soft hands, so Ruuttu can and will score from in tight while being checked.

All of his skills make him a specialty teams natural.

THE PHYSICAL GAME

Ruuttu is utterly fearless in his pursuit of the puck.

He belies his finesse image by mucking around in the corners and the crease, and he backs down from no one. He not only accepts contact but initiates it, and that physical willingness makes his finesse game better by opening up more ice for his use. He certainly has the skills to make plays after taking an opponent off the puck in the corner.

His one problem is his size. Because he puts himself in muscular situations, Ruuttu can be out-muscled by players bigger than he.

THE INTANGIBLES

We still think Ruuttu has more to offer in terms of scoring success than he's shown so far, and in that regard we consider him to be a bit of a paradox. But Ruuttu can never be accused of not pushing himself to reach his considerable potential. He's a very intense competitor, very smart, very coachable and very hard working. We just think he's better than 26 goals and 71 points — his NHL bests so far.

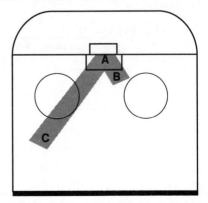

DAVE SNUGGERUD

Yrs. of NHL service: 1
Born: Minnetonka, Minn., USA; June 20, 1966
Position: Left wing
Height: 6-0
Weight: 170
Uniform no.: 18
Shoots: left

Career statistics:

GP	G	A	TP	+/-	PIM	PP	SH	GW	GT	S	PCT
80	14	16	30	8	41	1	2	2	0	120	11.7

LAST SEASON

First in the NHL. Led the club in shorthanded goals.

THE FINESSE GAME

Snuggerud is a fairly skilled player, one whose skills rest more in the invisible aspects of the game than anywhere else. That is, while he demonstrates NHL calibre skating skill and an average ability with the puck offensively, Snuggerud's strengths are in his vision and hockey sense.

He sees the ice very well and has strong anticipation ability; he also reads and reacts very well. Because of these abilities, Snuggerud is a good forechecker and an even better penalty killer.

He is an otherwise unremarkable player. He has a quick stick and is good at stripping opponents of the puck, and he looks to the net for open teammates before making plays. Snuggerud doesn't have great shooting ability so he'll have to be opportunistic with loose pucks.

THE PHYSICAL GAME

Snuggerud isn't big, but his sense makes him a bigger player by putting him where the puck is — or will be. He's not going to win a ton of battles along the boards, but his ability to be in the right place at the right time counters that. for that reason, the opposition has to play Snuggerud's body.

THE INTANGIBLES

As sometimes happens, circumstances combine to create success. The Sabres acquired Snuggerud in the 1987 Supplemental Draft and following his departure from the University of Minnesota Buffalo's new coaching staff found a way to use the youngster last season. They were greatly impressed by his intelligence and poise, and it is those qualities that will key Snuggerud's NHL progress.

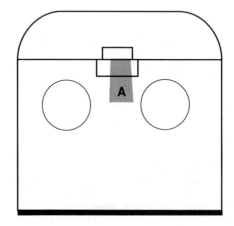

PIERRE TURGEON

Yrs. of NHL service: 3
Born: Rouyn, Quebec, Canada; August 29, 1969
Position: Center
Height: 6-1
Weight: 203
Uniform no.: 77
Shoots: left

Career statistics:

GP	G	A	TP	PIM
236	88	148	236	89

1989-90 statistics:

GP	G	A	TP	+/-	PIM	PP	SH	GW	GT	S	PCT
80	40	66	106	10	29	17	1	10	1	193	20.7

LAST SEASON

Led the club in scoring in all categories with career highs in all categories. Finished seventh in overall League scoring. Plus/minus was second best among forwards, and he led club in shooting percentage.

THE FINESSE GAME

Turgeon's finesse skills? Wow.

There is almost nothing he can't already do excellently at the NHL level in terms of finesse, and all his abilities will grow as he matures. He's not an excellent skater in the conventional sense in that he lacks overall rink speed (and we're certainly not saying he'll be caught from behind on a breakaway), but Turgeon is incredibly shifty for a man his size. He has exceptional — superior — balance and foot speed, and his change of direction and pace ability is very high. Those quick feet combine with his balance to make him almost unbeatable in one-step situations at any speed.

His hand skills are better than his overall foot skills. He can finesse a puck into any opening regardless of size. His hands are just as good in tight quarters in front of the net, and his quick release (combined with his balance and ability to shoot while checked) means he'll torture goalies to the tune of 50 goals a season. He carries the puck as well as he passes it — maybe better — and he'll make defenses look stupid unless they play his body.

His hockey sense, vision and anticipation are all excellent, nowhere more so than in specialty team situations. He sets up behind the net on the power play and distributes the puck from there, and is always a threat for a shorthanded goal while penalty killing. He always gets into scoring position, and more and more is putting his teammates there too.

THE PHYSICAL GAME

Turgeon will take hits to make plays (and clearly could get by just as he is), but he still prefers open ice to traffic areas. Now we're not saying he should pretend to be Cam Neely, but Turgeon has excellent size and balance (strength can be added) and those assets can amplify his finesse game. He could easily increase point

success by a third if he added a more robust physical element to his game.

He takes checks to make his plays and he uses his body very well to protect the puck; his balance is the key here. One can only imagine what would happen if he threw checks to make plays too (see Steve Yzerman and Pat LaFontaine — two players *smaller* than Turgeon).

THE INTANGIBLES

Turgeon responded very positively to the mantle of top gun for Buffalo, producing consistently throughout the season. He is already a dominant player in the Adams Division and will soon grow into a League-dominating player. He is the cornerstone of future Sabres success, and his presence almost automatically makes them a future Stanley Cup contender.

And his best is still ahead of him.

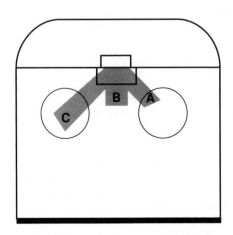

RICK VAIVE

Yrs. of NHL service: 11
Born: Ottawa, Ontario, Canada; May 14, 1959
Position: Right wing
Height: 6-09
Weight: 180
Uniform no.: 22
Shoots: right

Career statistics:

GP	G	A	TP	PIM
785	415	317	732	1,357

1989-90 statistics:

GP	G	A	TP	+/-	PIM	PP	SH	GW	GT	S	PCT
70	29	19	48	9	74	8	0	4	0	195	14.9

LAST SEASON

Goal and point totals were second lowest of career. Missed one game with flu, six games with groin injury, one game with concussion. Finished third on club in goals and shots on goal.

THE FINESSE GAME

Though 12 seasons of professional hockey have begun to take their toll on Vaive, he still retains some dynamic finesse skills. He is primarily a scorer and his skills reflect that. He delivers a big shot from down the wing that can still fool NHL goaltending, and his wrist shot is just as good. Vaive is a threat to score from anywhere inside the offensive zone because his strength drives the puck through the traffic and to the net, and because he is a goal scorer he'll look to the net before he looks to his teammates.

Vaive is an excellent skater, and that skill is marked by his strength and ability to drive through checks and to work in the traffic areas in the offensive zone. That strength also gives him good acceleration ability and rink-length speed. He'll pull away from checking within several strides.

While his skating is good enough to draw penalties on its own, Vaive helps things along by taking some of the NHL's best dives. His favorite diving tactic is to grab the opponent's stick — on the ref's blind side, naturally — to make it look like he's being hooked, and then fling himself to the ice and flop like a fish out of water.

As would be expected from a goal scorer, Vaive knows how to get into position to score. His skating gets him to that opening but so does his stickhandling, which helps him get tight to the net.

THE PHYSICAL GAME

Vaive is a tough hockey player, and he takes a beating in the offensive zone. He initiates a great deal of contact, and his skating strength will drive him through his checks and into possession of the puck. He'll also wrestle the puck away when mucking in the corners because of his good upper body strength.

He is very difficult to control in front of the net because of his strength, and he most always gets his shots away despite being checked. Vaive's entire game is based on playing in traffic and that's why he gets hammered every shift.

That style has betrayed him, in that he has never played a full NHL season.

THE INTANGIBLES

Vaive works hard in the offensive zone, less hard elsewhere on the ice, and he's not likely to play when injured. Nevertheless, he has been a consistent goal scoring force throughout his career. Of course, his goal scoring has also declined in each of the last three seasons. Has he taken too much abuse in his dozen pro campaigns?

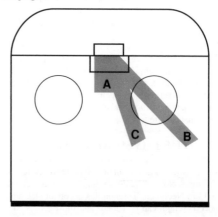

JAY WELLS

Yrs. of NHL service: 10
Born: Paris, Ontario, Canada; May 18, 1959
Position: Defenseman
Height: 6-1
Weight: 210
Uniform no.: 7
Shoots: left

Career statistics:

GP	G	A	TP	PIM
671	36	162	198	1,630

1989-90 statistics:

GP	G	A	TP	+/-	PIM	PP	SH	GW	GT	S	PCT
67	2	19	21	-3	184	0	0	0	0	67	3.0

LAST SEASON

Acquired by the Flyers from Los Angeles in exchange for Doug Crossman. Point total was four-season low. He was second in PIM among defensemen. He was sidelined by shoulder and finger injuries.

THE FINESSE GAME

Jay is one of those players for whom simple play is best. He grades out to average in all of his finesse abilities but Wells isn't a bad skater. He can contribute some speed and has some agility, and he can combine that agility with a degree of puckhandling talent so as to play more than just a defensive game.

But Wells runs into problems when he believes his skills to be better than they are. When he gets the puck it should be moved off his stick, preferably up the boards. Jay has a tendency — because he is a capable puckhandler — to force himself into situations where the puck gets pokechecked away while trying a 1-on-1 deke at his own blue line. More often than not the result of that poor play is a cheap goal against.

Wells reads the rush toward him well and is very difficult to beat one-on-one because of both his size and his positional play. He will follow the rush up-ice but doesn't jump into the play often, preferring to throw the puck around at the point to pinching into the zone. Once the puck is turned over, Wells is the first man back.

THE PHYSICAL GAME

Wells is very, very tough and very underrated in his toughness because he hasn't had to show it off for several seasons.

He is one of the best in the league at clearing the front of the net. And Wells doesn't care who's planted there, he'll take them on. He hits often and hard and is an excellent — and punishing — body checker. Wells will jar the puck loose with his hits and he's mean enough to add a little something extra if he can.

Wells will also sacrifice his body to block some shots and he can, by the way, throw 'em pretty good too.

THE INTANGIBLES

Jay's reputation has brought him that extra yard of room so he can function, but he's not always consistent in his output. Wells has to be constantly reminded to keep the play simple, to move the puck quickly and to take the body consistently.

When he does those things he's a force defensively. When he doesn't do them he's a very average defenseman.

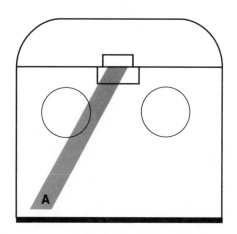

CALGARY FLAMES

THEOREN FLEURY

Yrs. of NHL service: 2
Born: Oxbow, Sask., Canada; June 29, 1968
Position: Center
Height: 5-6
Weight: 160
Uniform no.: 14
Shoots: right

Career statistics:

GP	G	A	TP	PIM
116	45	55	100	203

1989-90 statistics:

GP	G	A	TP	+/-	PIM	PP	SH	GW	GT	S	PCT
80	31	35	66	22	157	9	3	6	3	200	15.5

LAST SEASON

First full NHL season. Tied for club lead in shorthanded goals (Joe Mullen, Paul Ranheim), led club in game winners and game tying goals (led the League is last category). PIM total was club's third highest.

THE FINESSE GAME

Skating and stickhandling are Fleury's finesse claims to fame. He is a very agile and fast skater, blessed with speed and quickness up and down the scale. He complements that motoring ability with balance and lateral movement to become a very tricky, darting type of skater who can get in and out of holes easily.

His stickhandling ability works in tandem with this, allowing him to control the puck excellently as he dips and swoops around the opposing zone. He sometimes does too much of this and could be accused of doing too much one-on-one work, but he is too good a player to not correct this flaw as his NHL experience deepens.

Fleury does have good sense of the ice and he knows to open up to the ice so he can see the entire play. He's not ignorant of his teammates and can use them well, especially as he uses his quickness to open holes for them, and needs only to remember to more consistently look for them when he gets into trouble.

Because of his quickness he'll be very effective around the net, but he'll also score with wrist shots from 20-25 feet.

THE PHYSICAL GAME

Fleury is a very aggressive player in the use of his body and a very dirty player in the use of his stick. He rushes in where angels fear to tread, but of course Fleury is no angel. He exhibits absolutely no fear for his safety and will go barreling into anyone at any time — and he'll fight anybody who doesn't like that. His willingness and persistence will gain him more loose pucks than he'll lose, especially because Fleury has the skills and smarts to make plays after contact.

He will inevitably, however, be over-powered when matched against bigger and stronger opponents. The key for Fleury's success is not that he has to avoid traffic, but rather that he has to hit-and-run.

THE INTANGIBLES

Fleury is an enthusiastic, intense player and he brings that dedication to the rink every game and every shift. That mental set should guarantee that his NHL abilities will continue to grow.

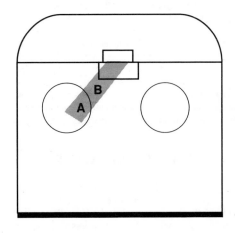

DOUG GILMOUR

Yrs. of NHL service: 7
Born: Kingston, Ontario, Canada; June 25, 1963
Position: Center
Height: 5-11
Weight: 185
Uniform no.: 39
Shoots: left

Career statistics:

GP	G	A	TP	PIM
534	199	331	530	362

1989-90 statistics:

GP	G	A	TP	+/-	PIM	PP	SH	GW	GT	S	PCT
78	24	67	91	20	54	12	1	3	1	152	15.8

LAST SEASON

Assist total was career best, point total second best. Finished second on the club in points, first in assists, third in power play goals.

THE FINESSE GAME

Hockey sense is the key to Gilmour's success as a finesse player, and that asset is certainly the best "tangible" quality he has. Gilmour sees, anticipates and reacts to the ice and his teammates as well as the best players in the game, and he does so at both ends of the ice.

He uses this mental ability to compensate for his less-than-dynamic skating. Don't get us wrong — Gilmour is far from being a poor skater. Rather, he uses his brain to make his excellent quickness and overall mobility (but not great speed) better. By knowing where the openings will be, Gilmour knows how to get to them for the Flames' use or to prevent their use by the opposition.

Or how to get his teammates to them — he is a very creative player with and without the puck. He backs up his smarts with his hands. Gilmour controls the puck very well when carrying it at all speeds (his balance allows him to work well with the puck in traffic), and he passes excellently. He can feather or fire a puck equally well to both his forehand and backhand sides.

Gilmour uses his one-step quickness to be extremely effective with loose pucks around the net and in open-ice (power play) situations. His skills make him a natural for all kinds of responsibilities, and he is a very strong defensive player.

THE PHYSICAL GAME

Someone forgot to tell Gilmour that he's a little guy — for the way he plays, he must think he sees Joel Otto looking at him when he stares into a mirror. Gilmour is a very aggressive player in all areas and aspects of the game, and his willingness to apply himself physically opens up his finesse game.

That style isn't always good for him because he'll get tired or fatigued, but it's not in Gilmour's nature to take a night off — and no one can complain about that.

His eye/hand coordination and arm and wrist strength make him a good faceoff man.

THE INTANGIBLES

If you can out-work Gilmour, you stand a chance of winning. Since your chances of out-working Gilmour are very slim, you're not going to win many games against him. He is a fanatically motivated player, one of the NHL's very best, and he just gets better as the games become more important.

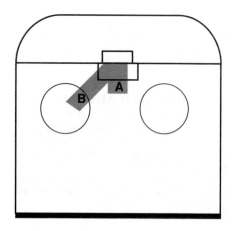

MARK HUNTER

Yrs. of NHL service: 9
Born: Petrolia, Ontario, Canada; November 12, 1962
Position: Right wing
Height: 6-0
Weight: 205
Uniform no.: 22
Shoots: right

Career statistics:

GP	G	A	TP	PIM
490	189	140	329	1,088

1989-90 statistics:

GP	G	A	TP	+/-	PIM	PP	SH	GW	GT	S	PCT
10	2	3	5	0	39	2	0	0	0	15	13.3

LAST SEASON

Missed 11 games originally with a knee injury, then was sidelined for the rest of the season with subsequent knee surgery. Games played and all point totals were career lows.

THE FINESSE GAME

Though he can make an impact in the finesse aspects of the game, Hunter is not a finesse player. He is a strong skater with good acceleration, but he's not very agile and could do better in the area of balance.

He has to have a center get him the puck because Mark isn't going to razzle-dazzle his way to the net from his own zone, nor is he going to make plays coming out of the corners. Because of his goal scoring success, Hunter doesn't use his teammates well, often shooting instead of passing to a more open teammate. Since he neither handles the puck well nor sees the ice well (which is why he needs that unselfish center in the first place), perhaps it's not a bad thing that Hunter shoots first and asks questions later.

His shot is the best of his finesse skills. Hunter gets great strength behind it and it will get to the net through traffic, but he'll need time to get it off. He'll chase his own rebounds and will get many goals on second effort. The best he'll do is 35 goals — maybe an honest 40, *maybe* — but no more than that. He works best from the faceoff circle for the original shot.

He's improved the level of his defensive game by backchecking more conscientiously, making better transitions from offense to defense, but he'll never be confused with Bob Gainey.

THE PHYSICAL GAME

The strength of Hunter's game is his strength. He's a hardnosed player and has to play that way to be successful. He has the strength and the size to play a dominant physical game, but could apply those assets more consistently. Mark can be very good in the corners at creating havoc because of his toughness, yet sometimes he does and sometimes he doesn't.

One area where he has improved his physical play is in the defensive zone, where he is taking the body better than ever.

THE INTANGIBLES

We wrote last season that Hunter's health was a big question; because of his absence last season we've left this report virtually alone. We continued, "Hunter has never played a full season. Secondly, he's not the hardest worker to ever put on skates. And considering the fact that he played less than half of last spring's Stanley Cup playoff games (so that essentially the Flames won without him), perhaps Mark shouldn't get too comfortable in Calgary."

Clearly they like him enough to have traded Joe Mullen, but Hunter must show he's recovered sufficiently from his knee surgery to contribute at his same level.

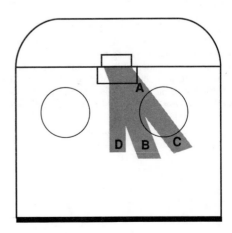

TIM HUNTER

Yrs. of NHL service: 8
Born: Calgary, Alta., Canada; September 10, 1960
Position: Right wing
Height: 6-2
Weight: 202
Uniform no.: 19
Shoots: right

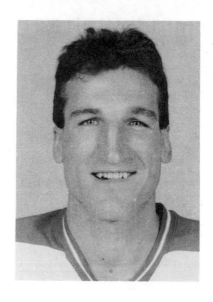

Career statistics:

GP	G	A	TP	PIM
481	43	54	97	2,095

1989-90 statistics:

GP	G	A	TP	+/-	PIM	PP	SH	GW	GT	S	PCT
67	2	3	5	-9	279	0	0	0	0	69	2.9

LAST SEASON

Games played total was four-season low, point totals full-season career lows. PIM total was five-season low, but still led club. Plus/minus rating was club's worst.

THE FINESSE GAME

Hunter is an average skater at best, with no real speed or agility in his stride. He does have good balance and strength on his skates and that serves him in his physical game. He has a slow driving stride that carries him from one end of the rink to the other.

Otherwise, Hunter is not gifted offensively. He does not have good hands with which to move or carry the puck, nor does he see the ice well. He is not a goal scorer, but maybe the pucks will bounce off him enough for 10 goals a year.

THE PHYSICAL GAME

Hunter is a one-man hammer-show, and his success is in his physical game. He is big, tough and strong, willing not only to mix it up but to provoke the battles. Hunter is also tough when he stations himself in front of the opposition net, where his strength and size make him a practically immovable object.

Because of his size and strength, Hunter is very difficult to out-muscle along the boards, but he will wander out of position because he's looking to belt someone. Hunter is also mean with his stick, and will use it with abandon. After all, something has to provoke his fights. He can, by the way, be forced (and it doesn't take much) into bad penalties.

He is always in great condition.

THE INTANGIBLES

Hunter knows what his role is, and he fills that role unquestioningly. He is an excellent team man but a limited player, and every limited player is subject to replacement.

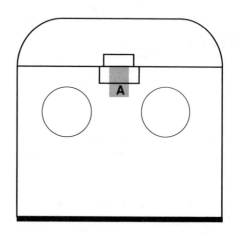

JIRI HRDINA

Yrs. of NHL service: 2
Born: Mlada Boleslav, Czechoslovakia; January 5, 1958
Position: Right wing/center
Height: 5-11
Weight: 183
Uniform no.: 17
Shoots: right

Career statistics:

GP	G	A	TP	PIM
143	36	55	91	59

1989-90 statistics:

GP	G	A	TP	+/-	PIM	PP	SH	GW	GT	S	PCT
64	12	18	30	10	31	0	0	3	0	96	12.5

LAST SEASON

Games played and all point totals fell in second NHL season.

THE FINESSE GAME

Hrdina is generally a skilled player across the board. He skates and handles the puck well, using his vision and hand skills in tandem to open ice and to create opportunities for his teammates. He can be a creative offensive player both with and without the puck.

He handles the puck well when he carries it and can pass well, but has also not shown the complete ability to understand and complete the play at the NHL level of speed. That flaw in understanding and reacting also affects his defensive play, where he is less than a sure thing. He does do well enough with open ice to merit some power play time, where his passing and vision work to good effect.

Like most Europeans he uses the wrist and snap shots almost exclusively and will sacrifice shots for passes to better positioned teammates. His goals will come from near the net.

THE PHYSICAL GAME

Hrdina is not a greatly physical player, but his skating skills of balance and strength afoot allow him to operate with a degree of success in the traffic areas. He can be successful coming off the boards because of his hand skills, but he's not going to do a lot of banging along the wood.

THE INTANGIBLES

Intensity from shift to shift and night after night are the questions here, especially considering how Hrdina has been worked in and out of the lineup. He needs to be able to maintain his intensity regardless of playing time or frequency, but on the other side of the scale is the fact that he hasn't shown himself to be anything other than a 32-year-old fourth liner.

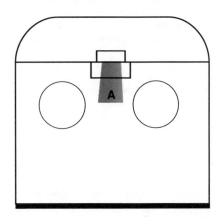

AL MACINNIS

Yrs. of NHL service: 7
Born: Inverness, N.S., Canada; July 11, 1963
Position: Defenseman
Height: 6-2
Weight: 195
Uniform no.: 2
Shoots: right

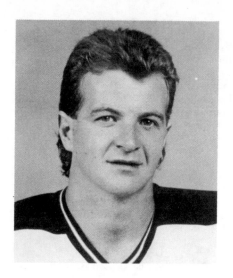

Career statistics:

GP	G	A	TP	PIM
528	126	380	506	621

1989-90 statistics:

GP	G	A	TP	+/-	PIM	PP	SH	GW	GT	S	PCT
79	28	62	90	20	82	14	1	3	0	304	9.2

LAST SEASON

All point totals were career bests. Finished third on the club in points, second in assists and power play goals, first in shots on goal total. Finished second in overall scoring among NHL defensemen (25th overall in NHL). Plus/minus rating was second best among Flames defensemen.

THE FINESSE GAME

May as well lead with your strength, and that's something MacInnis does quite well. While he is a good positional player and a fairly strong all-around defenseman, the whole world knows the best thing he does is shoot the puck — and MacInnis does that a lot. His slap shot from the point is the hardest in the NHL and it is intimidating in its strength: goalies fear being hit with it, defensemen won't go down to block it, some of MacInnis's own forwards won't go near the net to tip it. He shoots a lot (as his numbers indicate; figure three or four shots at goal for every official shot *on* goal), and many of his assists come off rebounds or other leftovers as his shots pinball around the crease. He fakes his shot and shoots off the pass extremely well.

That said, MacInnis is also a fairly alert passer, and he'll move the puck to teammates in better position. He joins the rush most always but is not generally inclined to start it by carrying the puck himself, and he'll move off the point and toward the net if the opening exists.

His skating has improved to the point that he can challenge and succeed against most any puckcarrier, but he is still a little weak in his turns to the middle of the ice (his left side). He forechecks and pinches in well, and MacInnis uses his hockey sense to tell him when it is and is not safe to do so.

THE PHYSICAL GAME

MacInnis has incorporated a more dynamic physical element to his game, as befitting his size and strength. Of course, that strength and leverage are the keys to his shot, but they also serve to power his work along the boards and in front of the net. He's not a big banger, but he'll throw his weight around. He uses his excellent reach to gather in loose pucks or to pokecheck the oppositions. Really, MacInnis is a finesse player who has added a solid physical element to his game.

THE INTANGIBLES

MacInnis has worked hard throughout the last several seasons to attain a high level playing plateau. He's become one of the NHL better all-around defensemen because of that intensity and dedication. He should continue in that vein for seasons to come.

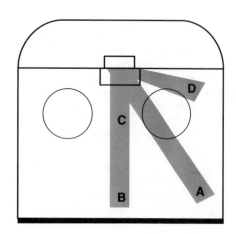

60

BRIAN MACLELLAN

Yrs. of NHL service: 6
Born: Guelph, Ontario, Canada; October 27, 1958
Position: Left wing
Height: 6-3
Weight: 215
Uniform no.: 27
Shoots: left

Career statistics:

GP	G	A	TP	PIM
526	158	222	380	458

1989-90 statistics:

GP	G	A	TP	+/-	PIM	PP	SH	GW	GT	S	PCT
65	20	18	38	-3	26	10	0	3	1	127	15.7

LAST SEASON

Games played total was four-season low; he suffered a late-season neck strain. Plus/minus rating was second worst aamong regulars. All point totals were career lows.

THE FINESSE GAME

His shot is the best of MacLellan's otherwise modest finesse skills. MacLellan releases his shot very quickly, and both his slap shot and wrist shot are heavy and accurate. His shots will carry into the net unless the goaltender is firmly in front of them.

He is an otherwise unremarkable finesse player. He doesn't handle the puck well enough or skate well enough to get into the open enough to put his shot to work (which is why he'll succeed at power play strength and fail at even strength). His skating lacks both speed and agility, but he does have good strength on his feet.

As with his limited puckhandling ability, MacLellan needs a lot of time and space to take advantage of his teammates via pass — and even then chances are he's not going to get a good enough read of the ice to make a strong offensive play because he lacks good anticipation or hockey sense.

His skating and sense — or lack thereof — make him a weak player defensively.

THE PHYSICAL GAME

MacLellan has a great body, perfectly designed for the power forward game of which he is capable but completely unwilling to play. He's big and strong and will succeed against the boards, but only if the puck happens to be where he is at the moment. He is otherwise a very passive player who may as well be a foot shorter and 50 pounds lighter, because that's the way he plays anyway.

He can score from in front of the net with defensemen draped all over him, and he'll fight and fight well when he feels compelled; all this is a testament to his strength and ability, but he gets almost nothing from his potential.

THE INTANGIBLES

Now this is the Brian MacLellan the Kings, Rangers and Stars knew and loved: 10 even-strength goals, terrible plus/minus, uninvolved physically (as indicated by the PIM total). You look at players like teammate Doug Gilmour and think, "What could he do if he had his desire in MacLellan's body?"

And all of that innate ability is just wasted because MacLellan is an unmotivated, un-intense, comfortable player. He has much better skills than his numbers indicate, but the bottom line with him is that if you expect anything above these numbers you're just fooling yourself.

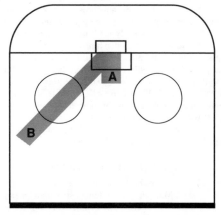

JAMIE MACOUN

Yrs. of NHL service: 7
Born: Newmarket, Ontario, Canada; August 17, 1961
Position: Defenseman
Height: 6-2
Weight: 197
Uniform no.: 34
Shoots: left

Career statistics:

GP	G	A	TP	PIM
470	53	157	210	527

1989-90 statistics:

GP	G	A	TP	+/-	PIM	PP	SH	GW	GT	S	PCT
78	8	27	35	34	70	1	0	1	0	120	6.7

LAST SEASON

Led club in plus/minus rating with third best mark in NHL.

THE FINESSE GAME

Macoun is like the Tasmanian Devil from those Bugs Bunny cartoons. He is just all over the ice, seemingly bordering on the edge of being out of control. But his helter-skelter style works, as the numbers over the course of his career indicate (plus-74 over the last two seasons).

He is an excellent skater with great, great speed, and he combines his speed with agility to be one of the NHL's most mobile players. He pinches in and forechecks as a matter of course, just as he steps up on the puckcarrier to close the gap at his own blue line. He uses his speed and one-step quickness (and the change-of-direction ability that accompanies that quickness) to join the rush as it moves up-ice, going all the way to the opposing net more often than not.

And he does all of this without the benefit of exceptional sense or anticipation — his skating skills just get him in and out of these situations with positive results. One thing though: Because he is so concerned with the puck, he can get deked by the puckcarrier.

Macoun passes fairly well, making the most of his ability to get into the open himself in order to gain the space to get the puck to a teammate. He's not an exceptional puckhandler, so he's more likely to join a rush than he is to start one by stickhandling from his own zone. In fact, his offense as a whole is not as exceptional as his skating might indicate; his goals and points will come primarily from the blue line.

His skating ability — especially his quickness — makes him a natural for penalty killing duty.

THE PHYSICAL GAME

His physical ability is almost as strong as his skating skill. Macoun is a big, tough, strong and mean player, one who exacts a price from every opposing player. His skating puts him in position to hit people and he does — and when he hits, he hurts. Macoun easily clears the front of the net (and he'll apply his stick liberally for help), and he's a dominating player in the corners. He'll out-muscle most any forward to gain the puck — all of this another reason why he'll kill penalties.

He uses his size to gain position and shield the puck along the boards, and he also uses his reach to pokecheck or deflect pucks. He has excellent eye/hand coordination and will occasionally be used for faceoffs. Macoun is also an excellent fighter.

THE INTANGIBLES

Macoun is a very intense player, a great athlete and dedicated player. He comes to play every night and his defensive ability makes him a very important player for the Flames.

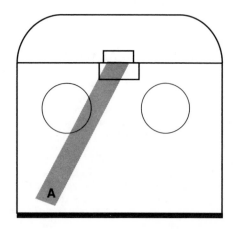

SERGEI MAKAROV

Yrs. of NHL service: 1
Born: Chelyabinsk, Soviet Union; June 19, 1958
Position: Right wing
Height: 5-8
Weight: 175
Uniform no.: 42
Shoots: left

Career statistics:

GP	G	A	TP	+/-	PIM	PP	SH	GW	GT	S	PCT
80	24	62	86	33	55	6	0	4	0	118	20.3

LAST SEASON

First NHL season. Finished second on the club in assists and plus/minus rating (fifth best overall in the NHL is the last category). Led all rookies in assists, points and plus/minus rating, was second in shooting percentage, fifth in both game winners and first goals.

THE FINESSE GAME

There may not be a faster pair of hands in the hockey world than those at the ends of Makarov's arms; no other explanation of his puckhandling and passing is necessary — or possible.

He makes his puck work even more effective with his skating ability. Makarov has great speed and mobility, and those skills out him in the open almost at will. Toss in his hand skills and he's able to *create* the open at will; that's hockey sense, and Makarov has a ton of it.

He sees the ice very well and is a creative player with the puck or near the opposition net — he can put the puck anywhere at any time for a teammate to take advantage of, and he makes the kind of plays that get you on your feet. He shoots the puck quickly and easily, using a wrist shot almost exclusively.

But when the puck is behind the red line Makarov might as well be in the locker room. As dynamic a player he is on offense, he is that sluggish in team defense situations.

THE PHYSICAL GAME

Makarov has tremendous physical gifts in the area of balance, and it is that balance that makes him the agile skater that he is. He doesn't play a strongly physical game in the barrel-into-the-opposition sense, but with Makarov a little shove is enough to knock you off balance so he can steal the puck — and he will.

THE INTANGIBLES

Among his comrades, Makarov made the best first-year impression. But his NHL road was not all sugar and spice. He needs to learn to apply himself in all situations and to get off the ice when he's supposed to — two areas that raised the hackles of his Flames teammates. He can be a world-class player when he wants to be, but he needs to motivate himself for 60 minutes a game, 80 times a season.

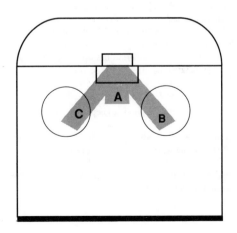

BRAD MCCRIMMON

Yrs. of NHL service: 11
Born: Dodsland, Sask., Canada; March 29, 1959
Position: Defenseman
Height: 5-11
Weight: 197
Uniform no.:
Shoots: left

Career statistics:

GP	G	A	TP	PIM
826	68	256	324	952

1989-90 statistics:

GP	G	A	TP	+/-	PIM	PP	SH	GW	GT	S	PCT
79	4	15	19	18	78	0	0	0	0	97	4.1

LAST SEASON

Acquired in June 1990 from the Calgary Flames in exchange for a draft choice.

THE FINESSE GAME

Powerful skating and defensive smarts make Brad one of the NHL's finest defensive defensemen. He's got a very strong stride and he uses it to close the gaps between himself and the opposition. He doesn't have a lot of rink-length speed, but in the confines of the defensive zone McCrimmon moves well. He's not a very agile skater, and his pivots and turns are not exceptional, but Brad counters that flaw with superior positioning.

He has excellent understanding of his defensive angles and almost always succeeds in forcing the play wide of the net. His positioning is also good in the offensive zone, where Brad knows when to challenge and when to fall back.

He's not much of a weapon in the offensive zone. He makes the simple play in his end and can rush the puck if necessary. He'll find the open forward when he's stationed at the offensive blue line.

THE PHYSICAL GAME

McCrimmon is good at keeping the front of the net clear and he does it physically and meanly. He's strong in the upper body and he'll muscle the opposition off the puck either in front of the net or along the boards.

His short reach betrays him when larger forwards are camped in the crease, but Brad makes them pay for every shot they get off.

THE INTANGIBLES

McCrimmon's begun to get some well-deserved recognition for his efforts. He may very well be the NHL's best defensive defenseman, but he fills another role for his club; when one defenseman is struggling, he's just teamed with McCrimmon — whose own stability and dependability straightens out the struggling player.

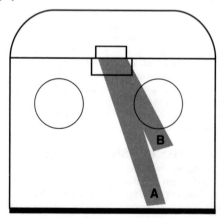

DANA MURZYN

Yrs. of NHL service: 5
Born: Calgary, Alberta, Canada; December 9, 1966
Position: Defenseman
Height: 6-2
Weight: 200
Uniform no.: 5
Shoots: left

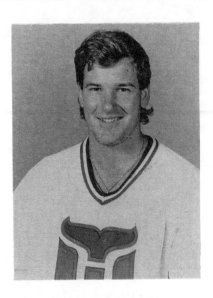

Career statistics:

GP	G	A	TP	PIM
367	29	85	114	641

1989-90 statistics:

GP	G	A	TP	+/-	PIM	PP	SH	GW	GT	S	PCT
78	7	13	20	19	140	1	0	0	0	97	7.2

LAST SEASON

Games played total tied career best.

THE FINESSE GAME

Skating is the beginning and ending of Murzyn's finesse game, and more like the ending than anything else. He is not a strong finesse player (let alone a strong offensive player) and this is because of his limited mobility. He has not become an agile player at the NHL level, so that while Murzyn is fine as he heads up and down the ice his ability to respond positively as the play moves laterally is average at best. He'll get deked by opposing players because he lacks the foot speed and agility to counter more mobile forwards.

His defensive style is reactive rather than active, so he needs to be paired with a more mobile partner. In short he concedes both blue lines without a fight, and because his skating doesn't gain him any time he gets forced into giveaways.

Paradoxically, Murzyn likes to handle and carry the puck despite his inability to move strongly with it. His best bets are to get the puck to the open man regardless of zone and let someone else do the offensive work. He does have good shots from the point (both his slap shots and wrist shots are accurate and low) but he's not going to get a lot of goals because his skating can't create many chances.

THE PHYSICAL GAME

Murzyn is a generally aggressive player, at least as much as his skating will allow. He takes the body and takes the man out fairly well against the boards, and he'll use his size and strength to advantage in front of the net. He sacrifices his body to block shots and uses his reach to pokecheck. He does not fight.

THE INTANGIBLES

There's not a whole lot in Murzyn's game, certainly not what you'd have expected from a number one draft choice (especially considering some of the players — Dave Manson, Sean Burke, Joe Nieuwendyk Mike Richter — chosen behind him). And there's no real indication that Murzyn will ever grow beyond what he is — a third or fourth defenseman who needs help gaining his intensity and work ethic and maintaining them from night to night.

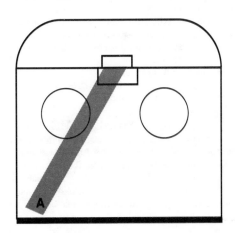

RIC NATTRESS

Yrs. of NHL service: 8
Born: Hamilton, Ontario, Canada; May 25, 1962
Position: Defenseman
Height: 6-2
Weight: 210
Uniform no.: 6
Shoots: right

Career statistics:

GP	G	A	TP	PIM
380	15	93	102	222

1989-90 statistics:

GP	G	A	TP	+/-	PIM	PP	SH	GW	GT	S	PCT
49	1	14	15	14	26	0	0	0	0	65	1.5

LAST SEASON

Missed six games with hand injury, 19 games with broken ankle.

THE FINESSE GAME

Nattress is not a gifted finesse player, probably no better than average in the application of his skills. His skating is certainly no better than average, as his limited mobility reveals. He is weak in his turn and overall agility, meaning that he must be a reactive player toward the puck — he can't take a chance of being beaten when challenging the puckcarrier, so Nattress's defensive play is going to have to be an attempt to force the play wide of the net.

His playreading ability isn't of much help here, because Nattress doesn't get real good looks at the ice. His play in both directions is going to have to be simple and immediate, and he can be pressured into giveaways by dynamic forechecking.

His hand skills are as limited as his foot skills and Nattress is not a good bet to rush the puck. He doesn't clear the zone well at all, either by skating the puck or moving it to a forward, so he's going to have to be paired with a more skilled partner.

He is not a goal scorer and any goals he gets will come on shots from the point.

THE PHYSICAL GAME

Nattress is a pretty tough customer in front of his net, getting most of his work done there by liberally applying his stick. He is unable to get the most from his size and strength because of his limited skating ability (he can't hit what he can't catch, but he also can't apply great force when he does catch someone because he lacks the leg strength and balance to do so).

Conversely, he can be bumped off the puck. He'll go up against anyone and is unintimidated, but he is not a good fighter.

THE INTANGIBLES

His lack of concentration and intensity can sometimes belie the fact that he's a coachable player, but Nattress generally succeeds with the Flames because the rest of the team's talent raises his own skill level. In other words they can afford him as a fifth or sixth defenseman, but that ranking leaves him eminently replaceable.

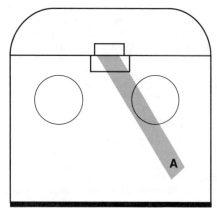

JOE NIEUWENDYK

Yrs. of NHL service: 3
Born: Oshawa, Ontario, Canada; September 10, 1966
Position: Center
Height: 6-1
Weight: 195
Uniform no.: 25
Shoots: left

Career statistics:

GP	G	A	TP	PIM
240	152	123	275	103

1989-90 statistics:

GP	G	A	TP	+/-	PIM	PP	SH	GW	GT	S	PCT
79	45	50	95	32	40	18	0	3	0	226	19.9

LAST SEASON

Led club in goals, points and power play goals, was third in plus/minus rating and shots on goal total. Finished 17th in overall League scoring. Goal total was career low, assist and point totals career highs.

THE FINESSE GAME

From top to bottom, Nieuwendyk is an exceptionally talented and exceptionally effective finesse player. Working from the bottom up, his skating is the least of his skills — but don't interpret that to mean anything other than above average. We mean only that he is not a spectacular or fancy skater, and so his forays up ice will not draw oohs and ahhs from the crowd. Rather, he has a very strong stride and deceptive speed, and he combines those assets with his balance to become a very agile, quick and balanced skater. His balance and sturdiness afoot key his work in front of the opposing goal.

His hand and sense skills are as much a function of one another as they are separate entities. His hands are made for goal scoring, and there may not be a better player in the League at deflecting and tipping pucks past goalies; that's how much hand speed and touch Nieuwendyk has. But to put that hand skill to use he has to get into position to use it — that's where his hockey sense comes in.

Nieuwendyk gets into scoring position superbly, as his sense and anticipation simply tell him where the puck and the opening will be next. And when he has to, Nieuwendyk uses his hand skills as a puckhandler, allowing himself to control seemingly unreachable pucks or to squeeze into seemingly unenterable spaces.

While he can use those skills to great advantage along the boards and out of the corners (where he gains the puck and moves it to an open teammate), Nieuwendyk is a scoring center who looks to the net before he looks to his teammates.

THE PHYSICAL GAME

Nieuwendyk's physical ability is very strong, and he uses every inch and pound of his lean but muscular body to drive the net and score. He sacrifices his body by taking tremendous abuse in front of the opposition goal, but he also doles out his own punishment when checking. He works the corners in both zones with the strength necessary to out-wrestle the opposition, is completely unintimidated can't be brutalized.

THE INTANGIBLES

Any critic would be hard pressed to find a flaw in Nieuwendyk's game. He plays strongly in both directions, has a tireless work ethic, fantastic determination, great heart and character. What else could you possibly ask for?

He is recovering, by the way, from a serious knee injury and may not play until after the New Year.

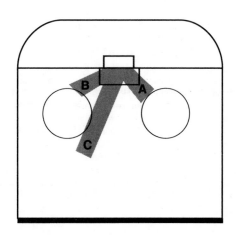

JOEL OTTO

Yrs. of NHL service: 5
Born: St. Cloud, Minn., USA; October 29, 1961
Position: Center
Height: 6-4
Weight: 220
Uniform no.: 29
Shoots: right

Career statistics:

GP	G	A	TP	PIM
373	97	162	259	926

1989-90 statistics:

GP	G	A	TP	+/-	PIM	PP	SH	GW	GT	S	PCT
75	13	20	33	4	116	7	0	0	0	96	13.5

LAST SEASON

Games played total was four-season high, assist and point totals full-season career lows. Missed three games with a hip injury. PIM total was career low.

THE FINESSE GAME

Since he is the immovable object applied to every irresistible force in the NHL, it is only natural that Otto's game be one based on strength. He is neither a fluid nor particularly agile skater, but Otto's long, strong stride lets him cover a lot of ice quickly en route to the puck. That strength also powers (pun intended) his checking game; he drives through his checks to take the opposition off the puck.

Otto combines a fairly strong understanding of the game and its implications — good hockey sense and vision — with his skating in his role as a premier checking center. He sees the ice well and can act instead of just react, but he'll succeed primarily by sticking with his check and working against him physically instead of mentally.

Many offensive opportunities will come Otto's way via his checking, and he'll pick up about 20 goals a season on opportunistic play around the net. Otto grabs a lot of loose pucks and should shoot more.

THE PHYSICAL GAME

Otto is a very physical player, as befits his role in stopping physical players. He's big and very strong, and he can also be very mean. He uses his body very well in checking and likes to hit, so he can take a lot of the starch out of the opposition (credit his skating strength here, as his ability in that regard lets him pound the opposition).

Conversely, he can be a titan in front of the opposition net — almost impossible to move because of his bulk and strength afoot. He'll also fight, but can't be pushed into it. His physical style takes its toll in fa-tigue and injury, and there are nights when (because there is no challenge lined up opposite him) he will coast.

THE INTANGIBLES

Otto's impact on the NHL over the last four or five seasons has been so great that every team is looking for a player that fits his profile. He is a quiet person off-ice, a player who lets his actions speak for him. Those actions include a tremendous work ethic and intensity level 12 months a year (he's on the ice all summer working out).

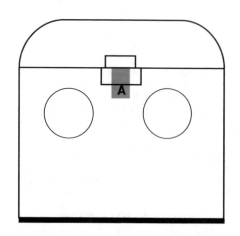

COLIN PATTERSON

Yrs. of NHL service: 6
Born: Rexdale, Ontario, Canada; May 11, 1960
Position: Left wing
Height: 6-2
Weight: 195
Uniform no.: 11
Shoots: left

Career statistics:

GP	G	A	TP	PIM
416	88	99	187	187

1989-90 statistics:

GP	G	A	TP	+/-	PIM	PP	SH	GW	GT	S	PCT
61	5	3	8	-4	20	0	0	0	0	56	8.9

LAST SEASON

All point totals were career low. Plus/minus was second lowest among regulars. Missed three games with groin injury, as well as suffering late season broken ankle.

THE FINESSE GAME

Patterson is an excellent skater in terms of speed. He can burn some rubber going up and down his wing and Patterson complements his overall speed with some good quickness, using both qualities to great effect as one of the NHL's top checking forwards.

Patterson gets to the puckcarrier and closes holes very well, and his skating is just one reason for that. A second reason is his excellent hockey sense and anticipation. Because of his understanding of the game's direction and a play's implication, Patterson can work at actively heading off that offensive thrust instead of just chasing the puck. Forget that plus/minus — it completely misrepresents Patterson's effectiveness.

His playreading abilities don't translate into offensive ability, and that's because Patterson's hands can't do the job offensively. His eyes let him see where the puck should go but he can't get the message to his hands fast enough. His shot release is no better than fair, and the strength of his shot may be less than that. So while he'll generate enough opportunities to score 25-30 goals, Patterson will convert on maybe half of those chances.

THE PHYSICAL GAME

Patterson is a strong player and he uses his speed and strength very well along the boards. He plays a take-no-prisoners style, which goes a long way toward explaining why he is always hurt.

THE INTANGIBLES

Health is always going to be *the* number one question when discussing Patterson — and again he must demonstrate recuperation from injury as this season opens. Otherwise he is a well-respected player, because of his character, work ethic and dedication.

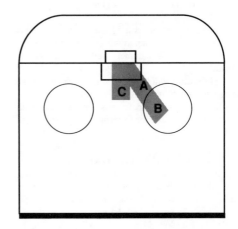

PAUL RANHEIM

Yrs. of NHL service: 1
Born: St. Louis, MO., USA: January 25, 1966
Position: Left wing/center
Height: 6-0
Weight: 195
Uniform no.: 28
Shoots: right

Career statistics:

GP	G	A	TP	PIM
85	26	28	54	23

1989-90 statistics:

GP	G	A	TP	+/-	PIM	PP	SH	GW	GT	S	PCT
80	26	28	54	27	23	1	3	4	2	197	13.2

LAST SEASON

First full NHL season. Tied for club lead (Joe Mullen, Theoren Fleury) in shorthanded goals. Finished second among NHL rookies in shorthanded goals, game tying goals and shots on goal, sixth in goals, game winners and first goals.

THE FINESSE GAME

Speed, speed and more speed are the keys to Ranheim's NHL game. His skating is marked by — you guessed it — speed, the kind that leaves the defense in cloud of dust.

The downside is that sometimes even Ranheim can't keep up with himself. His hands aren't as developed as his feet so he needs to moderate his speed to allow his hands to catch up to his feet. And by moderating his speed he'd lose some of the predictability that marks his play.

Nevertheless, his skating does open ice for his teammates and create opportunities for the Flames. He also uses his skating extremely well in penalty killing situations.

His scoring will be done from off the wing as he gains a step on the defense, and from near the net as he gets to loose pucks. His defense is pretty reliable, with Ranheim using his skating to get him into good position within his own zone.

THE PHYSICAL GAME

Ranheim is not an outstandingly physical player, in that he won't bash anyone into the boards— or get bashed into the boards himself in search of the puck. He succeeds in the open ice because of his skills and that's where he does most of his work. He'll drive the net for his goals, but he's not a power forward-type who will carry the opposition with him to the crease.

THE INTANGIBLES

A pretty good rookie season for a player generally overlooked because of the debut of Sergei Makarov. Ranheim has the smarts to succeed at the NHL level, and was demonstrating the changes in his game necessary for continued NHL development as last season progressed. He should continue to blossom this season.

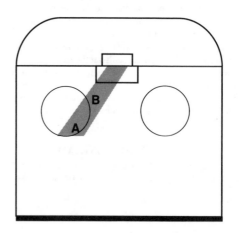

GARY ROBERTS

Yrs. of NHL service: 3
Born: North York, Ontario, Canada; May 23, 1966
Position: Left wing
Height: 6-1
Weight: 190
Uniform no.: 10
Shoots: left

Career statistics:

GP	G	A	TP	PIM
255	79	74	153	839

1989-90 statistics:

GP	G	A	TP	+/-	PIM	PP	SH	GW	GT	S	PCT
78	39	33	72	31	222	5	0	5	0	175	22.3

LAST SEASON

Games played and all point totals were career highs. He finished second on the club in goal and PIM totals, first in shooting percentage. His plus/minus rating was fourth best, third among forwards. Missed two games with a charley horse.

THE FINESSE GAME

Roberts has a finesse game overshadowed by his gruff physical style. He is a strong skater whose stride provides speed and acceleration ability. His agility is also good, so Roberts is a pretty mobile player. The result is Roberts is a very good forechecker, very strong on the puck.

His skating combines well with his hockey sense to give him a good view of the ice offensively. He's moving into holes more (although his style of going to the net is more responsible for his improved offense than anything else) and getting the puck to his teammates in better position.

Roberts can also use his degree of speed in tandem with his above average puckhandling ability to get around a defender or two, and since he generally keeps his head up he can find his teammates and the open space. He's shooting the puck with more confidence, releasing it more quickly so as to make it more effective. He also likes to fake his shot to gain some more room.

He uses his skills with equal enthusiasm in his defensive game, where he is a strong positional player.

THE PHYSICAL GAME

This is the immediately evident portion of Roberts' game, and he plays a dynamic physical game. Always aggressive, always hitting, Roberts uses his body 60 minutes a game, 80 games a season. His physical skill makes him an excellent corner and boards player, gaining either the puck or preferred position all over the ice. His insistent hitting can wear down the opposition, and Roberts will fight to back up his play.

THE INTANGIBLES

The temptation is to say that anyone playing with Joe Nieuwendyk and Sergei Makarov would score goals and collect points, and to a degree that analysis of Roberts' play is a correct one. But don't underestimate Roberts' own contributions to that line's success, gaining the puck and bulldozing paths for his linemates. So sure, he scored more goals because better players were getting him the puck — but Roberts' game is strong enough that he's going to earn points on his own.

He's a team leader and strong character man, so there's no fear that he will suddenly see himself as an artist and abandon his plumber way — he knows what to do to be successful and, much to the undoubted chagrin of the opposition, will keep doing the dirty work necessary for success.

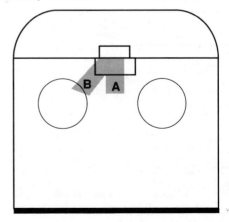

GARY SUTER

Yrs. of NHL service: 5
Born: Madison, Wisc., USA; June 24, 1964
Position: Defenseman
Height: 6-0
Weight: 190
Uniform no.: 20
Shoots: left

Career statistics:

GP	G	A	TP	PIM
362	77	269	346	512

1989-90 statistics:

GP	G	A	TP	+/-	PIM	PP	SH	GW	GT	S	PCT
76	16	60	76	4	97	5	0	1	0	211	7.6

LAST SEASON

Games played total was second highest of career; ditto assist and point totals. Finished fifth in scoring on club, fourth in shots on goal. Plus/minus rating was lowest among regular defensemen. Missed four games with knee injury.

THE FINESSE GAME

Suter is an exceptionally skilled finesse player with talent across the board — and all of it at a high level. He is an excellent skater in all facets of that skills, maybe one of the top five skaters in the NHL. He's mobile, fast, quick and balanced — Suter challenges and gains the puck all over the ice, and he does so better than most every other defenseman in the NHL. His lateral ability may be unmatched in the League.

His hockey sense is as developed as his skating ability, so he'll see openings and opportunities to be exploited and he'll exploit those opening because of his skating. He always joins the attack as it moves up-ice, and he'll go to the net on rushes.

Suter uses his hockey sense and skating in conjunction with his hand skills to become a very effective and dangerous puckhandler; his change of direction skills are particularly valuable here, and Suter uses all his skills to manipulate or even create the openings already mentioned. He passes the puck as well as he carries it and makes excellent use of his teammates with his soft passing touch.

His shooting skills are high (strong slap shot for deflections or tips, excellent wrist shot when closer to net) and he's smart enough to just put the puck in front on scrambles.

THE PHYSICAL GAME

Suter has excellent upper and lower body strength, and that strength demonstrates itself in his shooting and skating abilities. Suter can also battle along the boards, but his objective is going to be to get in and get out — get the puck, turn and make a play. He can cover the front of the net, but his job is going to be as the breakout and not takeout defenseman.

Which is not to say that Suter can't take men out along the boards; just that his skills are better in open ice. One example of that is his tendency toward injury; he has played 282 of 320 possible games over the last four seasons.

THE INTANGIBLES

Suter is a good character player, and certainly a superb hockey player (a good argument could be made for his being one of the best Americans to ever play the game), yet trade rumors continue to dog him. Of greater importance than those rumors, we think, is the fact that his long-time defense partner — Brad McCrimmon — has been dealt to Detroit. It was McCrimmon's steadiness that allowed Suter to reach the plateaus he has; we're curious how Suter will react to his partner.

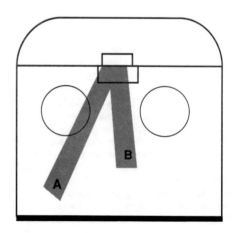

MIKE VERNON

Yrs. of NHL service: 5
Born: Calgary, Alta., Canada; February 24, 1963
Position: Goaltender
Height: 5-9
Weight: 170
Uniform no.: 30
Catches: left

Career statistics:

GP	MINS	G	SO	AVG	A	PIM
238	13,287	731	3	3.30	17	104

1989-90 statistics:

GP	MINS	AVG	W	L	T	SO	GA	SA	SAPCT	PIM
47	2,795	3.13	23	14	9	0	146	1,122	.870	21

LAST SEASON

Games played and win totals were four-season lows. Missed 17 games with back spasms.

THE PHYSICAL GAME

Vernon uses a standup, angle cutting style that maximizes his size. Because he's not exceptionally big he must occupy as much net as he can, and Vernon does that by coming out of his net to challenge shooters. His challenging style is powered by his excellent skating. Vernon has excellent balance and lateral movement, so not only is he tough to beat on crossing plays near the net but he's also going to quickly regain his stance if he's left his feet. He moves well in and out of the net, but Vernon doesn't usually leave the net to handle the puck. He holds his feet very well on breakaways and wraparounds, forcing the opposition to make the first move nine times out of ten.

He complements his standup work with exceptional reflexes, using the butterfly style on point and screen shots. If he's going to be beaten that's the time, because Mike won't make the mistakes that result in long shot goals, but because he regains his feet so quickly, those openings won't be open for long.

He has exceptionally quick hands and feet and he'll get a piece of most every puck that beats him — few of which will come on direct rush attacks. Corners are going to be a shooter's best bet.

THE MENTAL GAME

Vernon can certainly raise the caliber of his game to match the circumstance; he proved that during the Flames' Stanley Cup run. He has a tendency to go through hot and cold phases but he uses his anticipation to great effect every night, so he can pull out games where he is not playing well. He fights for every goal

and dismisses bad goals or games, and he has the capability of winning games singlehandedly.

THE INTANGIBLES

Health is a big one, and that's why the Flames have begun stockpiling goaltenders (Jason Muzzati, Trevor Kidd). Vernon is a competitor and he'll give whatever he's got to give; his talent makes him one of the NHL's best goalies. But he has to be able to play to demonstrate that ability.

RICK WAMSLEY

Yrs. of NHL service: 10
Born: Simcoe, Ontario, Canada; May 25, 1959
Position: Goaltender
Height: 5-11
Weight: 185
Uniform no.: 31
Catches: left

Career statistics:

GP	MINS	G	SO	AVG	A	PIM
358	20,408	1,126	12	3.31	8	50

1989-90 statistics:

GP	MINS	AVG	W	L	T	SO	GA	SA	SAPCT	PIM
36	1,969	3.26	18	8	6	2	107	855	.875	4

LAST SEASON

Minutes played total was three-season high, win total four season best.

THE PHYSICAL GAME

The stand-up, angle-cutting style is Wamsley's game. By playing that style (rarely leaving his feet), Rick maximizes his good size and minimizes his skating flaws.

He's no better than average as a skater; he'll move fairly well out of the net, less well back into it. His balance is no better than average, so when he does go to the ice he needs time recovering his feet. Rick keeps his feet in motion forward and back constantly, which inhibits his ability to move laterally. Because of that he's going to be vulnerable to shots on the ice toward the corners, and on bang-bang crossing plays in front. That's why Wamsley is smart to stand up and challenge as best he can.

For the most part, he handles rebounds well by directing them away from traffic. His hands are not especially fast so Rick benefits from cutting down the angles so the puck just hits him. He sees the puck fairly well and has good anticipation.

THE MENTAL GAME

Rick maintains a level-headed approach to the game mentally, neither getting too high after a win nor too low after a loss. He prepares well for each game and is ready to play, so he's largely unaffected by a bad performance the night before or a bad goal at any time.

His concentration is good, but it does tend to wander when he has nothing to do for stretches of time, and he looks unsteady on shots following that "empty" period.

THE INTANGIBLES

Wamsley is a strong team man, the kind of goalie a club likes to play for. He is a dependable player of fairly high ability, more suited for the role of backup than star because of his temperament and ability to play without excessive swings in performance — you may not get the jewelled performances, but you don't get the clinkers either.

CHICAGO BLACKHAWKS

KEITH BROWN

Yrs. of NHL service: 11
Born: Corner Brook, Nfld., Canada; May 6, 1960
Position: Defenseman
Height: 6-1
Weight: 192
Uniform no.: 4
Shoots: right

Career statistics:

GP	G	A	TP	PIM
677	55	240	295	691

1989-90 statistics:

GP	G	A	TP	+/-	PIM	PP	SH	GW	GT	S	PCT
67	5	20	25	26	87	2	0	0	0	111	4.5

LAST SEASON

Assist and point totals were three-season highs, goal total four-season high. Missed 10 games with bruised ribs. Plus/minus was club's third best, tops among defensemen.

THE FINESSE GAME

Skating has always been the strong point of Brown's finesse play, and it remains so even after 11 NHL seasons. He's a very mobile player with a ton of speed forward and back, as well as the quickness and agility necessary to step up and control the gap on the puck carrier. He can do those things but Brown plays a far more reactive than active game, thus minimizing rather than maximizing his skill in a defensive sense.

He has developed the patience to not just charge at the puck, so Brown is an effective defender in terms of using his angles. He remains a one-play player in this regard (in that he concentrates on his man and not necessarily on the other avenues of the play), but Brown secures his zone of the ice. He also is using his skating ability intelligently at the offensive blue line, making plays and pinching in with discretion.

He can rush the puck and handle it fairly well, and he's improved his use of his teammates by keeping his head up; when pressured, however, he is likely to just wrap the puck around the boards instead of looking for a play. Brown's rushes are much fewer in number than earlier in his career as he now concentrates primarily on defense.

He brings an above average shot from the blue line, and Keith will use his speed to cut to the right faceoff spot if the opening exists. Otherwise, his offensive contributions will be minimal.

THE PHYSICAL GAME

As skating has been Brown's top-shelf finesse asset, so too has been his strength. He's a very strong player in both his upper and lower body, with his leg strength powering his skating and his upper body strength keying his ability in front of the net and along the boards. He complements his strength with good balance (also the key to his agility) to out-wrestle many opposing forwards in one-on-one situations.

He plays a fairly aggressive but smart game.

THE INTANGIBLES

Brown's early career play was characterized by swings to each extreme — like the little girl with the curl, when he was good he was very good but when he was bad he was rotten. By and large he has tamed those excesses to become a fairly steady and dependable defensive player.

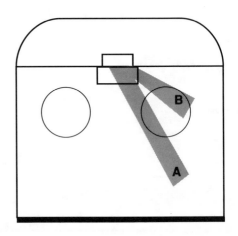

CHRIS CHELIOS

Yrs. of NHL service: 7
Born: Chicago, Ill, USA; January 25, 1962
Position: Defenseman
Height: 6-1
Weight: 187
Uniform no.:
Shoots: right

Career statistics:

GP	G	A	TP	PIM
402	72	237	309	783

1989-90 statistics:

GP	G	A	TP	+/-	PIM	PP	SH	GW	GT	S	PCT
53	9	22	31	20	136	1	2	1	0	123	7.3

LAST SEASON

Acquired from Montreal in June in exchange for Denis Savard. GAmes played total was four-season low; ditto goal total. Assist and point totals were full-season career lows. Missed six games with a groin injury, and also suffered a mid-season knee injury. Led defense in PIM total.

THE FINESSE GAME

Chelios is an excellent skater with speed, quickness and balance. Those three assets combine to give him great agility and lateral movement, and he teams his skating with his puckhandling to become an excellent rushing defenseman. He has the speed and the skills to go end-to-end to score.

He's an active — rather than re-active — defenseman, using his skills to quickly turn the play around. Chris handles the puck very well and can make plays at all speeds. He'll carry the puck to the opposing blue line, and then use his passing skills to hit the open man or lead a teammate into the clear. Chris draws on the combination of his vision/hockey sense and hand skills to become a superior playmaker.

Chelios has a strong slap shot from the point and he'll sneak to the top of the circle if he can. He also drifts into the slot for a good wrist shot. Chelios can take those chances because he is fast enough to recover if necessary.

His skating and sense allow him to challenge the puck at both blue lines. He forechecks and contains the point well offensively, and just as easily steps up to close the gap on the puck carrier (and then begin the transition game) defensively.

THE PHYSICAL GAME

Chelios is very strong, certainly strong enough to control the league's big forwards. He takes the body very well and crosses the border to mean; he's also liberal with his stick. His combination of strength and balance means he can take the puck away from anyone along the boards.

Chris can hold the opposition out of the play in the corner, and he can clear the front of his net too. He uses his body very well to shield the puck when he is rushing with it, and he will sacrifice his body by blocking shots.

He plays hurt and will fight.

THE INTANGIBLES

Chelios is a supremely talented player, the kind that can play any style of game and play it well. Attitude and desire fuel his game; when he has them, he plays a superior game. Without the desire, he's an ordinary player.

Now he must put those talents to work for a team on the way up, and in his hometown to boot. He's already won one Norris Trophy, and we think he's more than capable of winning another.

Need new diagram

JACQUES CLOUTIER

Yrs. of NHL service: 6
Born: Noranda, Quebec, Canada; January 3, 1960
Position: Goaltender
Height: 5-7
Weight: 167
Uniform no.: 31
Catches: left

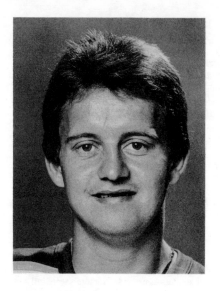

Career statistics:

GP	MINS	G	SO	AVG	A	PIM
187	9,620	571	3	3.56	7	37

1989-90 statistics:

GP	MINS	AVG	W	L	T	SO	GA	SA	SAPCT	PIM
43	2,178	3.09	18	15	2	2	112	931	.880	8

LAST SEASON

Games played total was career best, as was games won mark. He led Hawk goalies in minutes played, goals-against-average and wins. Missed six games with a groin injury.

THE PHYSICAL GAME

Cloutier is a little guy and as such must be able to play his angles very well or else the league's better shooters will put the puck over his shoulder before he can blink. He is at his best when he stays on his feet.

But that doesn't mean he does that often. He scrambles, he flops, he's very helter-skelter. To play angles and challenge the shooters requires confidence, something that is not always in long supply for Cloutier.

He handles the puck fairly well and will come out of his net to stop the puck from rolling around the boards. He is not a terrific skater, moving in and out of his net a little sluggishly, and that leaves him susceptible on rebound shots and two-on-ones where he must regain his position quickly. His balance problems are another reason why he's always flopping around.

He is very quick with his hands and feet, so he is successful in scrambles around the net, but Cloutier has difficulty with shots low to the glove and short sides, classic indications of failure to cut down the angle properly.

THE MENTAL GAME

Cloutier folds his tent if reached early and a bad goal destroys his confidence. He doesn't carry bad games with him, but can fall back into the same negative routine with the next bad goal.

THE INTANGIBLES

Cloutier is a tremendously hard worker in practice, always giving his best effort. But the Hawks have a plethora of goalies, so who knows what Cloutier's role will be next season?

ADAM CREIGHTON

Yrs. of NHL service: 5
Born: Burlington, Ontario, Canada; June 2, 1965
Position: Center
Height: 6-5
Weight: 210
Uniform no.: 22
Shoots: left

Career statistics:

GP	G	A	TP	PIM
295	89	110	199	512

1989-90 statistics:

GP	G	A	TP	+/-	PIM	PP	SH	GW	GT	S	PCT
80	34	36	70	4	224	12	0	3	0	156	21.8

LAST SEASON

Played 80 games for first time in career; all point and PIM totals were career bests. Finished third on club in PIM total, second in power play goals, and first in shooting percentage.

THE FINESSE GAME

Hand skills are the highlight of Creighton's finesse game, more so because of his build than because of any innate ability. He is able to handle the puck well while in traffic and that's important because Creighton plays a traffic game. He also does a good job of carrying the puck and his skating complements him here.

His balance and the agility that comes from balance are strong — especially given his size — but Creighton isn't the fastest guy around. He'll combine his size with his ability to lean and twist to create opportunities when he has the puck. Though lacking speed, Creighton has made his skating better by keeping his feet moving more than he ever has before. That allows him to drive the net, to get to loose pucks and to put his considerable bulk to work; he'll also draw penalties as the opposition is forced to foul him in order to stop him.

His anticipation and sense reveal the exploitable openings, and Creighton is now making better use of them than ever before. Still, he succeeds more as a scorer by virtue of his work and size — not because of Gretzky-like anticipation. Creighton remains an essentially straight-ahead player.

His lack of speed makes Creighton no better than average defensively.

THE PHYSICAL GAME

While he has certainly beefed up his willingness to play aggressively, Creighton is still selective in his use of his size. He must use his bulk to be successful and he needs to be reminded of that fact. When he gets himself moving he'll come up with pucks and win battles simply by virtue of inertia (an object in motion tends to stay in motion). But when he stops moving his feet he can be out-muscled. He does, by the way, have the habit of using his stick a lot.

He's a good faceoff man.

THE INTANGIBLES

Last season's performance is surely nearer what Buffalo had in mind when they drafted Creighton, and what Chicago had in mind when they traded for him. He can still improve his performances, as long as he picks up his intensity.

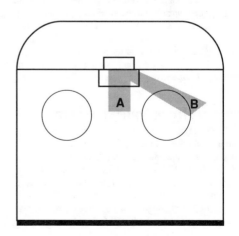

GREG GILBERT

Yrs of NHL service: 8
Born: Mississauga, Ontario, Canada; January 22, 1962
Position: Left wing
Height: 6-1
Weight: 191
Uniform no.: 14
Shoots: left

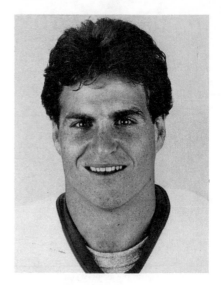

Career statistics:

GP	G	A	TP	PIM
499	105	163	268	378

1989-90 statistics:

GP	G	A	TP	+/-	PIM	PP	SH	GW	GT	S	PCT
70	12	25	37	27	54	0	0	3	1	108	11.1

LAST SEASON

Led club in plus/minus rating.

THE FINESSE GAME

Gilbert has found a niche as an above-average forechecker and defensive player, and one reason he can fill that role is because of his strong skating. He doesn't have a lot of speed or agility — the marquis items on a skating evaluation list — but he does have a good command of his balance and strength on his feet. He also has a strong steady pace that carries him to the puck and allows him to drive through puck carriers when hitting. His balance also serves him as he mucks around for the puck in the corners.

His sense of the game is limited offensively (as his numbers bear out), so he will have to make simple plays — and he'll need time to make even those. He doesn't handle the puck exceptionally well while carrying it and is more than likely to force himself into bad position. His hand skills are really no better for passing, but he can shoot fairly well. The problem is, he won't have gotten himself into good scoring position so he can't take advantage of his good release or power (except for his backhand shot, which is one of the League's best). He'll have to be near the net to score.

Gilbert plays a very strong defensive and positional game, thwarting numerous opposing scoring chances.

THE PHYSICAL GAME

Greg is a big, strong man and likes to hit, displaying a mean streak at times that allows him to cross-check opposing forwards into the boards after a play is whistled dead. His size best serves him in the corners where he digs the puck out well, and in front of the net where he can and will take the requisite pounding.

His game is the same in the defensive zone, where he will sacrifice his body to block shots or take out opposing forwards. Gilbert, though not a fighter per se, can more than handle his own because of his upper body strength.

THE INTANGIBLES

An enthusiatic, coachable and willing player, Gilbert is the kind of support player a team can build on. He has a fine work ethic and strong character — the kind of player who shows well in tough contests. In short, Gilbert is an honest hockey player who has begun to get some press for his defensive efforts.

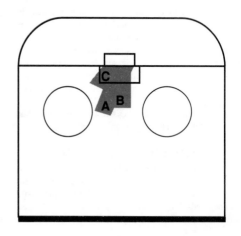

MICHEL GOULET

Yrs. of NHL service: 11
Born: Peribonqua, Quebec, Canada; April 21, 1960
Position: Left wing
Height: 6-1
Weight: 195
Uniform no.: 16
Shoots: left

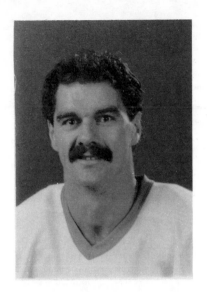

Career statistics:

GP	G	A	TP	PIM
821	460	490	950	622

1989-90 statistics:

GP	G	A	TP	+/-	PIM	PP	SH	GW	GT	S	PCT
65	20	30	50	-32	51	9	1	0	0	154	13.0

LAST SEASON

Acquired from Quebec in exchange for Dan Vincelette, Everett Sanipass and Mario Doyon in March 1990. Missed five games with Chicago with bruised ribs, as well as time out in Quebec with an ankle injury. Games played and all point totals were career lows, and his plus/minus rating was the club's worst.

THE FINESSE GAME

Michel has always used his skating to key the rest of his finesse game, but his skating is — only naturally, after a decade of pro hockey — losing some of its snap. Where once his foot speed and balance gave him exceptional agility and lateral movement, Goulet has lost some of that ability — making him eminently catchable. And, since he's really been more of a straight-ahead player than a shifty one, the loss of a step or two of speed is really telling.

Naturally then, because he doesn't get open as well as previously, his scoring totals diminish — his goal totals have fallen for eight seasons. When delivered, his shots are still good. His wrist shot is as dangerous as his slap shot and he will charge the net for second effort goals. He shoots often and accurately, forcing the goaltender to make saves and is especially devastating on the power play.

Michel has always demonstrated unselfishness despite his goal-scoring ability. His soft hands control the puck well, and he'll make the pass to a free teammate instead of gambling against a defender himself. The anticipation that gets him in position to score helps him make those passes.

His defense has always mirrored his offense, and now more than ever he needs a linemate with the speed and desire to play defense.

THE PHYSICAL GAME

Michel has never played a physical game — the occasional bump in the corner or charge through the traffic in the slot is the extent of his involvement with contact. His skating strength powers his drives to the net — and he'll accept the abuse while going there — but that's it.

He also has a temper and can sometimes be a little mean with his stick.

THE INTANGIBLES

How much new life can be breathed into this old warhorse? That is a question that only time can answer, and Goulet has competition in Chicago (a la Steve Thomas) he didn't have in Quebec. Can Goulet be successful with second-line duty? We'll have to wait and see.

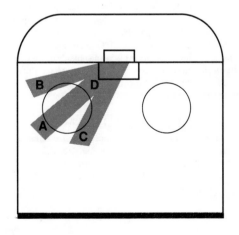

DIRK GRAHAM

Yrs. of NHL service: 6
Born: Regina, Sask., Canada; July 29, 1959
Position: Right wing
Height: 5-11
Weight: 198
Uniform no.: 33
Shoots: right

Career statistics:

GP	G	A	TP	PIM
421	139	175	314	509

1989-90 statistics:

GP	G	A	TP	+/-	PIM	PP	SH	GW	GT	S	PCT
73	22	32	54	1	102	2	3	1	0	180	12.2

LAST SEASON

PIM total was second highest of career, assist and point totals full-season career lows. Missed time with a bruised kneecap. Led team in shorthanded goals.

THE FINESSE GAME

Here's a case of the whole being greater than the sum of the parts. There isn't one particular skill that Graham performs better to the exclusion of others, but his determination makes all his skills better. He's an unexceptional skater, lacking great speed or quickness but countering with balance and good strength on his skates. He is also a fairly tireless skater, and that asset combines with his balance and sturdiness to make him a good checker.

Graham does have a degree of vision and anticipation ability (the ingredients of hockey sense) and those assets help him in his checking and penalty killing, but Graham's sense isn't so highly developed that he can wait for the puck to come to him — he's got to chase it. A lot of that chasing, by the way, will result in shorthanded goals.

As with his other skills, Graham has some ability to create and orchestrate some offense. He can find open teammates with his passes, just as he can recognize offensive openings for himself. Graham will try some shucking and jiving before hitting an outside move with the puck, and he can score 20-25 goals a season. But as with everything else, his offensive ability is keyed by his work ethic.

THE PHYSICAL GAME

Despite his less-than-impressive size, Graham plays a more-than-impressive game. He mucks and grinds in the corners against anyone, using his body well along the boards to take the opposition off the puck.

His balance works in his favor by keeping him upright, and his sturdiness means he's not likely to be knocked off the puck. He can take care of himself when the going gets rough and is a fairly good fighter.

THE INTANGIBLES

Graham is the exemplification of the cliche "where there's a will there's a way." Certainly he must work each shift each night to gain the most he can from his modest ability, and it is that character, that work ethic and determination that has made him a leader for Chicago.

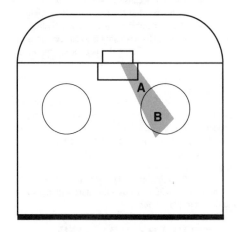

MIKE HUDSON

Yrs. of NHL service: 2
Born: Guelph, Ontario, Canada; February 6, 1967
Position: Left wing
Height: 6-1
Weight: 201
Uniform no.: 43
Shoots: left

Career statistics:

GP	G	A	TP	PIM
90	16	28	44	76

1989-90 statistics:

GP	G	A	TP	+/-	PIM	PP	SH	GW	GT	S	PCT
49	9	12	21	-3	56	0	0	3	0	51	17.6

LAST SEASON

Missed 12 games with a broken hand. Goal total improved from first season.

THE FINESSE GAME

Hudson is a good skater, a smooth skater with a fluid stride and a fair degree of mobility. He has good balance and foot speed, two elements which make up agility, and those ingredients combine to give Hudson a fairly good degree of lateral ability. He has good speed, but wouldn't really make a breakaway threat.

He has the finesse skills of passing and shooting, and that's because Hudson has fairly soft hands. He's got a good touch around the net and is a clever player, and Hudson can thread a needle or two for a pass or shot. He releases his shot quickly (important when working in the crowded areas around the net), and his hands also work well for passing to both the forehand and backhand sides.

His hand skills extend to his puckhandling, and Hudson can control the puck while carrying it and when in traffic (his balance and body control help here, keeping him in good position as he makes his plays). He is also a conscientious (if not necessarily) successful defensive player but, as is also the case in his offensive game, Hudson needs better understanding of the speed and ramifications of NHL play.

THE PHYSICAL GAME

Hudson is primarily a finesse player with size. His good size would allow him to impose himself on the opposition all over the ice, but Hudson doesn't really do that. His size and fairly good strength allow him to work in the traffic areas nearer the net, but he's not a big bump-and-grind player. He'll take a check to make a play, but won't initiate a lot of contact.

THE INTANGIBLES

Hudson needs a full NHL season, one without demotions or injuries in order to better indicate what kind of player he can be. He has a good attitude and strong desire (and is just 23 years old), so he can improve as an NHL player.

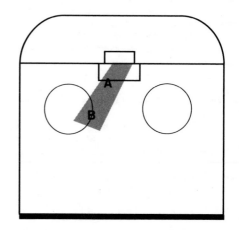

STEVE KONROYD

Yrs. of NHL service: 9
Born: Scarborough, Ontario, Canada; February 10, 1961
Position: Defenseman
Height: 6-1
Weight: 195
Uniform no.: 5
Shoots: left

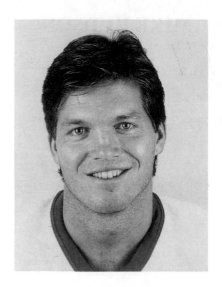

Career statistics:

GP	G	A	TP	PIM
650	34	145	179	647

1989-90 statistics:

GP	G	A	TP	+/-	PIM	PP	SH	GW	GT	S	PCT
75	3	14	17	6	34	1	0	0	0	93	3.2

LAST SEASON

Plus/minus rating was third best among defensemen.

THE FINESSE GAME

What may be Konroyd's best skill is one that has no tangible signs, no easy-to-point-to highlights. You have to be an intelligent hockey observer to understand Konroyd's best skill, and that is his ability to see the play defensively and understand its implications — to read and react, in the vernacular.

Konroyd is a super intelligent defensive player, and he uses his intelligence to recognize what is going on in front of him so as to thwart it. His skating is a big key here (no point seeing something if you can't do anything about it) and Konroyd uses his outstanding overall mobility to control the gap and step up on the puck carrier in excellent fashion. And he does this not only at his own blue line but in neutral ice as well, thus aiding the Hawks overall checking and transition games. This is a big reason he'll kill penalties.

He also uses his skating skill to elude forecheckers when he has the puck, but Konroyd won't have the puck for long because he knows it belongs to a breaking forward.

He moves the play from his own end with crisp passes, using the same vision to find the open man and get the puck quickly to him (which is why he'll see some occasional power play duty). He handles the puck when necessary, but Konroyd won't become part of the attack — the extent of his offense will be shots from the point.

THE PHYSICAL GAME

As with his finesse play, Konroyd is more efficient as a hitter than he is spectacular but make no mistake — he's big and strong and he can thump peo-ple. Konroyd is an intelligently aggressive player, using his size and strength against anyone without drawing penalties.

His aggressiveness and strength do not extend to fighting.

THE INTANGIBLES

Konroyd is probably Chicago's steadiest defensive defenseman, the kind of player who can free an offensively gifted partner to play that way, can clean up his partner's mistakes or back up a youngster (as in the playoffs, when he paired with Dave Manson, Trent Yawney and Bob McGill). Konroyd is a good team man who puts out solid effort night in and night out.

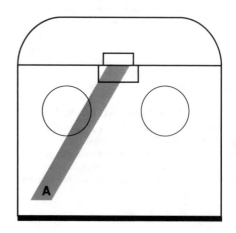

STEVE LARMER

Yrs. of NHL service: 8
Born: Peterborough, Ontario, Canada; June 16, 1961
Position: Right wing
Height: 5-11
Weight: 189
Uniform no.: 28
Shoots: left

Career statistics:

GP	G	A	TP	PIM
647	298	380	678	283

1989-90 statistics:

GP	G	A	TP	+/-	PIM	PP	SH	GW	GT	S	PCT
80	31	59	90	25	40	8	2	4	0	265	11.7

LAST SEASON

Led team in assists, points and shots on goal. Plus/minus total was third best on team, second best for forwards. Point total tied career best.

THE FINESSE GAME

How does Larmer do that voodoo that he do so well? He's not an exceptional skater in terms of glamorous assets (speed, agility), but he does possess great strength and balance on his skates critical to his success because of the amount of work he does in the traffic areas near the net.

He does have excellent hands for receiving the puck, and he shoots very well off the pass. His hand skills would extend to puckhandling (as would his balance — both would help him control the puck in traffic), but he shies away from handling the puck because his skating won't put him in the clear. When he does have the puck, Larmer passes extremely well, using his sense to find the openings.

Ah, his sense. What Larmer does better than all but the NHL's best goal scorers is get into scoring position and let the puck do the work — he's in position to shoot the puck before the puck gets to him. Then, his excellent shot does the rest.

His skating is good enough, combined with his brains, to make him a very solid defensive performer; that's why he'll kill penalties.

THE PHYSICAL GAME

Larmer isn't a big physical player; he's not a corner and boards winger. Sure, he goes to the traffic areas in the slot, but he doesn't impose himself on anyone.

He won't initiate a lot of contact and doesn't bang in the corners, but he'll take his punishment to score.

THE INTANGIBLES

Like Ole Man River, Larmer just keeps rolling along. His consistency is so great that you can actually forget he's playing and at what level he's performing. We have long held that Larmer is an essentially unknown commodity, but he is as dependable as he is unknown — which is all the Blackhawks care about.

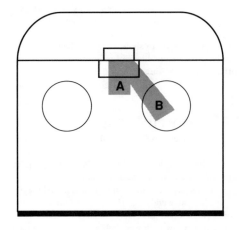

JOCELYN LEMIEUX

Yrs. of NHL service: 3
Born: Mont Laurier, Quebec, Canada; November 18, 1967
Position: Left wing
Height: 5-11
Weight: 215
Uniform no.: 26
Shoots: left

Career statistics:

GP	G	A	TP	PIM
150	25	22	47	244

1989-90 statistics:

GP	G	A	TP	+/-	PIM	PP	SH	GW	GT	S	PCT
73	14	13	27	-1	108	1	0	2	0	112	12.5

LAST SEASON

Acquired from Montreal at mid-season. Games played, all point and penalty minute totals were career highs. He was an even plus/minus player in Chicago.

THE FINESSE GAME

For a guy with a reputation as being a physical player, Lemieux demonstrated nice — and improveable — finesse skills. He skates forcefully and is well-balanced, and that helps him in his physical game, but Jocelyn also has some speed to go along with his strength. He uses his skating as an effective checker and penalty killer.

He does not yet handle the puck well at the NHL level and, because he is more of a physical than finesse player, that development may take some time. Even so, he will probably top out at the 25 goal level.

Jocelyn pays attention to his defensive responsibilities and has yet to show a creative bent in the offensive zone despite his hard offensive work. He gets off a strong wrist shot from within 20-feet of the net, but Lemieux hasn't demonstrated that he can create or force openings with his skating.

THE PHYSICAL GAME

This is the area of the game that is Lemieux's forte. He is big and strong and plays a very aggressive style in the offensive and neutral zones (he is too unsure of himself in his own zone to do the same).

Lemieux packs a lot of strength into his 5-11 body, and he hits often and hard. He is unafraid of either the corners or the opposition, and Lemieux isn't above using his elbows or his stick to help him gain an advantage while fighting for the puck.

His balance, as mentioned, helps him here by allowing him to remain vertical after he initiates collisions.

He does have a tendency to run around looking for hits, so sometimes he will get caught out of position.

THE INTANGIBLES

Maturity continues to be the big key for Lemieux, but the confidence shown in him by the Chicago coaching staff should go a ways in making him feel more comfortable and responsible. Lemieux does have a temper and can sometimes be guilty of being too aggressive, so he can be forced into foolish penalties.

Aside from that, his crash and bang style is perfect for Mike Keenan and Chicago Stadium.

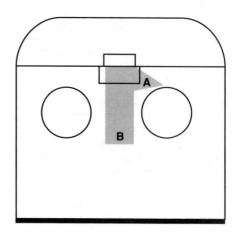

DAVE MANSON

Yrs. of NHL service: 4
Born: Prince Albert, Sask., Canada; January 27, 1967
Position: Defenseman
Height: 6-2
Weight: 202
Uniform no.: 3
Shoots: left

Career statistics:

GP	G	A	TP	PIM
255	25	73	98	984

1989-90 statistics:

GP	G	A	TP	+/-	PIM	PP	SH	GW	GT	S	PCT
59	5	23	28	4	301	1	0	1	0	126	4.0

LAST SEASON

Missed 16 games because of suspensions. Led defense in PIM total, second on club.

THE FINESSE GAME

Disguised and overshadowed by both the myth and reality of his physical play, Manson has tremendous finesse skills. He is a fine skater with speed, agility and quickness in surprising quantity for a bigger man, and he can use his mobility in both the offensive and defensive phases of the game. He certainly has the lateral ability to be an active versus reactive defenseman, stepping up and controlling the gap on the puck carrier near the Hawks blue line while containing and controlling the point at the opposing line.

But Manson is inconsistent his skating. He can carry the puck if need be, and Manson is also a good passer; when patient and poised he can make excellent use of his teammates. Manson generally gets good reads of the ice in both directions, and he can make not only the correct play but a smart play as well.

He shoots the puck very well, so much so that he can be a shooting as well as quarterbacking weapon for the Hawks on the power play. Manson has the ability to one-time the puck, and he's certainly a strong enough skater to charge the net (or at least come off the point) for shots.

THE PHYSICAL GAME

Manson is an outstanding bodychecker, one of the best hitters in the League. Leg strength has a lot to do with that, of course, as does upper body strength for holding the opposition out of the play. But the key to Manson's physical game (aside, that is, from meanness and willingness) is his balance. That balance allows him to smack people around at will, all the while remaining vertical and ready for the next play.

He uses his body and his strength to great advantage in gaining position in all areas of the ice, and is an especially dominating force in front of his own net; any opponent who scores from there has truly paid the price.

He is extremely tough and, though he can be goaded into penalties, will also absorb a few gloves to the face when he realizes the opposition is trying to get him off the ice. When he does want to fight, watch out — Manson is one of those guys who loses it when the gloves are dropped. He is an excellent team man and sticks up for his teammates as necessary.

He also sacrifices his body to block shots.

THE INTANGIBLES

If this guy ever gets 80-game confidence, watch out. The only thing standing in the way of Manson's permanent elevation to the League's elite level is Manson himself. His flaws are not flaws of omission, but errors of commission — he tries to do too much, fails at something, and then his confidence takes a beating.

He is a very intense and dedicated player, a hard worker who can be among the NHL's best players. So why does the Chicago Stadium crowd boo him?

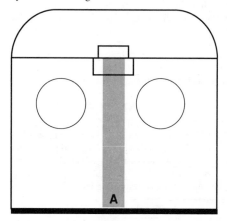

BOB MCGILL

Yrs. of NHL service: 9
Born: Edmonton, Alta., Canada; April 27, 1962
Position: Defenseman
Height: 6-1
Weight: 193
Uniform no.: 25
Shoots: right

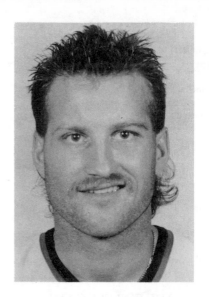

Career statistics:

GP	G	A	TP	PIM
500	9	46	55	1,447

1989-90 statistics:

GP	G	A	TP	+/-	PIM	PP	SH	GW	GT	S	PCT
69	2	10	12	-7	204	0	1	0		0	53	3.8

LAST SEASON

Games played total was second highest of career, assist and point totals career bests. PIM total was five-season high, fourth highest on club. Plus/minus was club's third worst, poorest among defensemen. Missed three games with broken cheekbone.

THE FINESSE GAME

McGill has modest skills at best to call on in the finesse game, and he must stay within the parameters of those skills in order to be successful in the NHL.

His skating is no better than average, maybe less so in the backward and lateral modes. He must play positional defense and concentrate on forcing the play wide of the net and toward the boards, and McGill must not put himself into situations from which his skating cannot recover; unless absolutely sure, he shouldn't pinch in or challenge at the blue lines.

His puckhandling and passing must be of the same simple-but-sure variety, but he can be forced into turnovers with forechecking. McGill is probably best off protecting the puck by tying up a forechecker and allowing a teammate to clear the zone.

His hand skill is not such that he should be rushing the puck, nor will he make great contributions from the offensive blue line. He'll collect a handful of goals a year on slap shots from the point.

Just as he must retain his poise and composure physically so too must McGill control himself mentally, for he can be forced into poor penalties.

THE PHYSICAL GAME

McGill is a physical hockey player, and he must be in order to play in the NHL. He has excellent size and strength, though those assets are mitigated by his skating: you can't hit what you can't catch. Nevertheless, McGill has made his physical play more effective by cutting down on his wandering and taking the hits as they come.

He benefits from playing in Chicago Stadium because of the smaller ice surface, which makes his skating better and his hitting more insistent.

THE INTANGIBLES

McGill can contribute in a limited way, but his toughness is mitigated by the fact that he cannot be played in every game situation. If he could, he would be a fine complement to Dave Manson, absorbing some of the toughness mantle that Manson must carry. But McGill can take on only a small part of those responsibilities, and because he has limited value he remains a replaceable player.

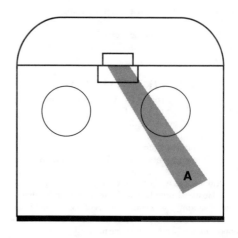

GREG MILLEN

Yrs. of NHL service: 12
Born: Toronto, Ontario, Canada; June 25, 1957
Position: Goaltender
Height: 5-9
Weight: 175
Uniform no.: 29
Catches: right

Career statistics:

GP	MINS	G	SO	AVG	A	PIM
591	34,832	2,225	17	3.83	19	72

1989-90 statistics:

GP	MINS	AVG	W	L	T	SO	GA	SA	SAPCT	PIM
49	2,900	3.38	19	25	5	1	158	1,471	.890	4

LAST SEASON

Traded twice, first from St. Louis to Quebec, and then from Quebec to Chicago.

THE PHYSICAL GAME

As he's matured, Millen has more and more utilized a standup style. That's not to say he isn't using his reflexes (he still works from deep in his net), but Greg is playing a more relaxed, energy-conservation game that allows the puck to just hit him than he ever has before. He's squaring himself to the puck excellently.

He's still a flamboyant, acrobatic goalie, popping up and down quickly and regaining his stance well (though he is likely to lose his angles after those acrobatics). He doesn't, however, have great balance (Millen keeps his weight on his inside edges excessively) and that means his movement across the crease is flawed. His lack of superior lateral movement — as well as his habit of hanging back in the net — are why he gives up goals inside the posts.

He skates out to snare loose pucks, but Millen prefers to leave them for his defense. His glove hand is good when he stands up, but since he goes to the ice on play around the net a lot of pucks elude him up high. He also hangs back on screens, another reason for pucks to fly over his hand and into the net.

Millen doesn't control rebounds off his chest protector well, leaving loose pucks floating around the front of the net.

THE MENTAL GAME

After a decade in the NHL, Greg knows how to prepare himself mentally. He has good concentration and above-average anticipation, and he's a tough competitor mentally. However, his concentration can wander from period to period and game to game. The fact that he can play excellent games merely underlines the fact that he can keep himself playing at a higher level, yet, after playing one game by standing on his head, his next game will be as if he has two left feet.

Still, he has a good attitude and approaches each game with confidence. That bolsters the team's confidence in him.

THE INTANGIBLES

Greg is the kind of goalie who makes the kind of saves that inspire a team — the dramatic, acrobatic kind of stops that a team draws strength from. Where he will fit into the Hawks plans for the future (they have an abundance of goalies) is anybody's guess.

BOB MURRAY

Yrs. of NHL service: 15
Born: Kingston, Ontario, Canada; November 26, 1954
Position: Defenseman
Height: 5-10
Weight: 185
Uniform no.: 6
Shoots: right

Career statistics:

GP	G	A	TP	PIM
1,008	132	382	514	869

1989-90 statistics:

GP	G	A	TP	+/-	PIM	PP	SH	GW	GT	S	PCT
49	5	19	24	3	45	3	0	1	0	84	6.0

LAST SEASON

Rotated in and out of lineup for third lowest games played total of career.

THE FINESSE GAME

Murray is almost a throwback to those days of strictly defensive defensemen — not that he's always been that way, but 15 NHL seasons will take some starch from your play.

He's still a good skater though slow, but Murray makes his skating work by playing his defensive angles smartly. He steps up when he can, but always forces the opposition wide and to the boards. He doesn't put himself into situations from which his skating cannot extricate him; he prudently pinches in at the blue line. As such he's unlikely to contribute much by way of offensive from the opposing blue line, but Murray can still turn the play around well from his end with a quick and intelligent pass.

He can still find the open man and retains his good instincts, so he'll see some power play time because of that (the extra open ice doesn't hurt, either). His slap shot from the point is his scoring weapon, and he'll pick up 5-8 goals a year with it.

THE PHYSICAL GAME

Murray's physical play is actually a credit to his brainwork. He learned early on that direct confrontation may not best serve his defensive purposes, so he forces the opposition to compete on his terms rather than vice versa. Murray plays the body and ties up his man's stick, but he also uses his hockey sense to amplify his physical play. He can't make the play in the corner on strength alone if he runs into a strong, hard-working forward.

Vision and ability to move the puck quickly to teammates once it's won are Murray's assets here.

THE INTANGIBLES

Murray is playing an off-the-bench role for the Hawks now, contributing when he can. His style is such that he could continue in this role for another season or two, but he remains vulnerable to replacement.

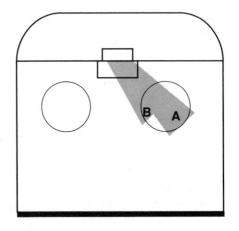

TROY MURRAY

Yrs. of NHL service: 8
Born: Winnipeg, Manitoba, Canada; July 31, 1962
Position: Center
Height: 6-1
Weight: 195
Uniform no.: 19
Shoots: right

Career statistics:

GP	G	A	TP	PIM
579	182	264	446	604

1989-90 statistics:

GP	G	A	TP	+/-	PIM	PP	SH	GW	GT	S	PCT
68	17	38	55	-2	86	3	1	4	0	111	15.3

LAST SEASON

Games played total was six-season low (elbow surgery, 11 games), but assist total was three-season high.

THE FINESSE GAME

Physically, skating key's Murray's finesse game — and his skating is keyed physically. That is, he is a very strong skater with a relentless pace. His skating allows him to pressure the puck well, and the strength allows Murray to close on the opposition and then drive through his checks; he'll stun people when he hits them. Toss in balance as an asset and Murray becomes almost impossible to impede or knock down — good qualities for traffic play.

Murray's anticipation and hockey sense are also strong, and he puts those qualities to work offensively and defensively. Defensively, he sees the openings the opposition will try to exploit, and thus thwarts the opposing center in his attempts to exploit them. Offensively, Troy's vision and anticipation allow him to use his teammates. In this way, he takes advantage of the loose pucks that his checking creates to be a well-rounded player (and not just a defensive role player).

His puckhandling and carrying abilities are not at the same level of his foot skills, thus keeping him from devloping offensive abilities to equal his defensive ones; Murray will dump the puck in rather than carry it over the blue line. His shooting ability is better than his dump-and-chase offense would infer. He's dangerous from the circles in with quick and accurate wrist and snap shots. Twenty goals a season is not an unreasonable number.

THE PHYSICAL GAME

Murray excels in physical play. His aformentioned ability to drive through his checks and punish the opposition separates him from many forecheckers; Murray's hitting really wears down the opposing defensemen and is a big key to his success as a forechecker (almost as important as his ability to get to the puck in the first place). He is, however, not always consistent in his use of his size and strength and needs to be reminded to apply himself.

His hand and arm strength also come to the fore in traffic, because that strength is such that Murray can either bull his way through crowds or gain the puck despite checking. And, because of that strength, Murray is a good faceoff man.

THE INTANGIBLES

Murray has a temper and can be goaded into foolish penalties, but paradoxically that intensity can sometimes be missing from his play. When it is not, Murray is one of the NHL's foremost defensive players. His ability to score some goals doesn't hurt either.

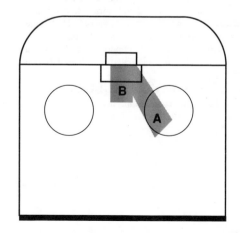

WAYNE PRESLEY

Yrs. of NHL service: 5
Born: Dearborn, Mich., USA; March 23, 1965
Position: Right wing
Height: 5-11
Weight: 180
Uniform no.: 17
Shoots: right

Career statistics:

GP	G	A	TP	PIM
284	78	74	152	371

1989-90 statistics:

GP	G	A	TP	+/-	PIM	PP	SH	GW	GT	S	PCT
49	6	7	13	-19	67	1	0	0	0	75	8.0

LAST SEASON

Point totals were all full-season career lows. Plus/minus rating was club's second worst.

THE FINESSE GAME

There are a lot of tools here, but Presley can't seem to take them all out of the toolbox when needed. He has good hockey sense and intelligence, but Presley has difficulty bringing those assets to bear consistently at the NHL level — certainly, his positional play wavers greatly from acceptable to unacceptable when he wanders all over the ice. So, while he's trying to create things offensively his defense — as previously in his NHL career — suffers.

He's developing the foot speed and quickness to exploit the openings he can find, and he can marshal those resources as a penalty killer. Otherwise, his offensive success has been inconsistent.

As such, his offense is limited to big slap shots from the faceoff circle.

THE PHYSICAL GAME

One reason Presley is all over the ice is because he wants to hit — an admirable trait but one that has undercut Presley's total game. And not that he has great size or strength to bring — Samson he ain't.

Still, willingness is important and Presley just needs to develop some discretion in his charging around.

THE INTANGIBLES

Presley is a conundrum. He has some outstanding finesse abilities and potential but has been unable to access them with any degree of consistency. We said last year, after Presley seemed to get a hold of himself, that this year would go a long way toward demonstrating what kind of NHL player Presley is. We don't think he's a six-goal scorer — and we also don't think he's going to get many more opportunities to prove otherwise.

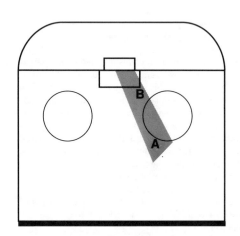

JEREMY ROENICK

Yrs. of NHL service: 2
Born: Boston, Mass., USA; January 17, 1970
Position: Center
Height: 6-1
Weight: 170
Uniform no.: 27
Shoots: right

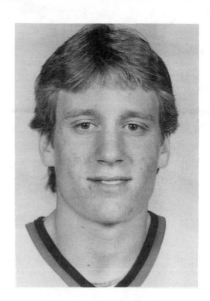

Career statistics:

GP	G	A	TP	PIM
98	35	49	84	58

1989-90 statistics:

GP	G	A	TP	+/-	PIM	PP	SH	GW	GT	S	PCT
78	26	40	66	2	54	6	0	4	0	173	15.0

LAST SEASON

Finished fifth among all rookie scorers, third among rookies in assists and shots on goal, fourth in goals and game winners.

THE FINESSE GAME

Speed and quickness of both foot and hand are what make Roenick the player he is, and what will power his growth into an NHL superstar. He's got remarkably fast feet and almost rocket-like acceleration abilities. Toss in balance and you've got a supremely agile and mobile skater: change of speed, change of direction, stop-start — it's all here.

His hand skills may not quite be a match for his feet, but they'll get awfully close with further NHL experience. He stickhandles very well at top speed and in crowded situations, and his touch extends to his passing: whatever is necessary to get the puck to either side — a touch of mustard or a little shave off the top — Roenick can do it.

His hockey sense is also very strong, and it too will improve as Roenick continues to adapt to the NHL's tempo. He reads the play very well, not just finding the open man but creating space to create open men; his hands and feet also allow him to exploit those openings himself, and he'll do a lot of damage near the net because he knows how to get into scoring position and can succeed in traffic.

His sense helps him in his defensive game, where Roenick is fairly conscientious positionally.

THE PHYSICAL GAME

Roenick's not a big kid, but he's a tough kid. He can't be intimidated and will not back down from a confrontation. He uses the size he does have very well in the corners, and he enjoys a hitting game. Of course, his finesse skills amplify his physical ability so as to make his hitting that much more effective (take the body, take the man off the puck, take the puck). Balance is the key here, keeping Roenick vertical and able to make plays after collisions.

He's not above bullying players smaller than himself.

THE INTANGIBLES

Roenick suffered through an horrific start to last season (one goal in his first 23 games), but through solid and steady work he achieved greater and greater success. We know he's an extremely talented young man with a bright future, but the question is how bright a future? Some observers say if his work ethic and desire remains high (and there's no reason to believe it won't) he can be the next Steve Yzerman.

We're inclined to agree.

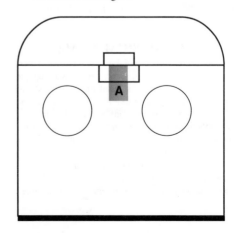

AL SECORD

Yrs. of NHL service: 12
Born: Sudbury, Ontario, Canada; March 3, 1958
Position: Left wing
Height: 6-1
Weight: 210
Uniform no.: 20
Shoots: left

Career statistics:

GP	G	A	TP	PIM
766	273	222	495	2,093

1989-90 statistics:

GP	G	A	TP	+/-	PIM	PP	SH	GW	GT	S	PCT
43	14	7	21	5	131	1	0	0	0	68	20.6

LAST SEASON

Signed as a free agent in summer 1989. Games played mark was six-season low; missed 17 games with a knee injury.

THE FINESSE GAME

Secord is a strong skater, but not a fancy one. He goes in and out of the corners and charges the net, all with a straight-ahead bull in a china shop style. There's not a lot of dipsy-doodling in his play, and Secord is generally smart enough to not play outside his limits.

He's a bull around the net, and it's from there that Secord will get his goals. He won't stickhandle past an entire team, and he won't blow the puck past a goaltender. He'll just knock in the rebounds and the garbage, and occasionally pot the odd 20-foot shot.

His assists will come from pucks he's knocked loose and his teammates have converted.

His problems have always come when he attempts to do too much, handling the puck when he should be passing it and so on. He lacks patience around the net, not taking that extra half-second to secure the puck and score.

THE PHYSICAL GAME

Secord remains one of the NHL's strongest men, courtesy of his fanatical approach toward working out. His upper body strength makes him difficult to dislodge from the puck, and it also adds to his power as a hitter.

Secord goes to the front of the net to take his beating there, knowing that in traffic his strength serves him best by allowing him to shrug off the opposition and shovel in the puck.

He has always been mean and tough, and he remains a vindictive player, determined to pay back every check. That tends to get him in trouble vis a vis penalties.

When he was scoring 40 and 50 goals a club could withstand Secord's penalties. But 15 goals makes his play a little excessive (less kind critics might call his play stupid).

THE INTANGIBLES

Last year Secord worked as hard as he ever has — and he is one tremendous worker on and off the ice in practice and in games. But age is a big question here, and Secord looks like he got old in a hurry.

DUANE SUTTER

Yrs of NHL service: 11
Born: Viking, Alberta, Canada; March 16, 1960
Position: Right wing
Height: 6-1
Weight: 188
Uniform no.: 12
Shoots: right

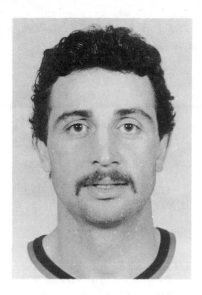

Career statistics:

GP	G	A	TP	PIM
731	139	203	342	1,333

1989-90 statistics:

GP	G	A	TP	+/-	PIM	PP	SH	GW	GT	S	PCT
72	4	14	18	-2	156	0	0	1	0	70	5.7

LAST SEASON

Goal total was career low.

THE FINESSE GAME

More than anything else, determination marks a Sutter game — and that's especially so in the finesse aspects. Duane gets where he is going on work, not fleet feet. He doesn't have great agility or lateral movement (we could even use the word slow), but his strong skating stride moves him up the ice and — more importantly — allows him to play his physical game.

Sutter can carry the puck, but his lack of hand skill combines with his lack of foot skill to make him below average in the puckhandling and puck movement categories. He's more effective on the right side, because his stick is open to the center of the ice and he's on his forehand.

His understanding of the creative game is limited too, as demonstrated by his tendency to go to his backhand when carrying the puck. Nor does he anticipate well; he won't lead teammates into openings — they're going to have to already be there.

His defense can suffer because of his lack of mobility, and he can be goaded into foolish penalties.

THE PHYSICAL GAME

Sutter's skating strength powers his physical game. It allows him to drive through his checks, thus helping him take the opposition off the puck. He's a persistent checker who works 100 percent of the time, and he's good in the corners because he works so hard and is fearless. He will throw his body to make plays, or take hits as well, and that corner work ties up

defensemen to allow openings for the pure goal scorers. For that reason, he just may be on the ice in a crucial situation.

He also uses his physical ability in his scoring, because he is tough in front of the net.

THE INTANGIBLES

What you get in Sutter is a leader by example. He stands up for the team, he's a character individual and plays his heart out. What more could you ask for?

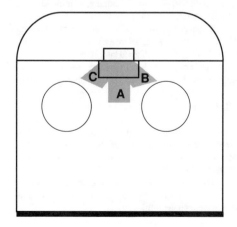

STEVE THOMAS

Yrs. of NHL service: 5
Born: Stockport, England; July 15, 1963
Position: Left wing
Height: 5-11
Weight: 185
Uniform no.: 32
Shoots: left

Career statistics:

GP	G	A	TP	PIM
312	130	128	258	352

1989-90 statistics:

GP	G	A	TP	+/-	PIM	PP	SH	GW	GT	S	PCT
76	40	30	70	-3	91	13	0	7	0	235	17.0

LAST SEASON

Goal and point totals were career bests. Led team in goals and game winners, and tied for lead in power play goals (Doug Wilson). Finished third in shots on goal. Missed three games with bruised ribs.

THE FINESSE GAME

Two S's characterize Thomas's game: shooting and skating. One thing's for sure: When Thomas shoots the puck, everyone in the rink knows it. Why? because he'll do one of three things: either score (big cheers and sirens), force the goalie to make a tough save (groans of disappointment), or miss the net entirely and hit the glass (loud smacking noise which wakes up sleeping fans). His big slap shot from the wing can beat any goaltender, but the slapper isn't his only weapon as he uses a good snap shot too. Accuracy, as implied, is not a big asset here.

Thomas's skating is as dynamic as his shooting. He has excellent speed, balance and strength, and those assets provide him with good lateral movement and the ability to make quick directional changes — like when he pulls his favorite move: gain the blue line, pull up short, and then shoot. He likes to come across on his off-wing in order to improve his shooting angle.

His sense of the offensive zone is fairly high, and Thomas uses that ability to get into scoring position. He also makes fairly good use of his teammates but make no mistakes: Thomas will shoot first and ask questions later.

His defense is less dynamic than his offense, so Thomas could benefit by paying more attention to his defensive responsibilities.

THE PHYSICAL GAME

He doesn't have great size, certainly not size that would match his finesse abilities, but Thomas is a pretty tough player. He gets in the corners and mucks around, and he can certainly make a play coming out of con-frontations (balance and skating strength help keep him vertical during those one-on-one battles).

He's fearless and will go into the corner with anyone, and when those confrontations turn fistic Thomas more than holds his own.

THE INTANGIBLES

Last season showed that Thomas can move into the elite level of left wings in the NHL. While his health will remain a concern (he's never played a full season) until proven otherwise, Thomas can remain at that elite level. He can even improve himself if his all-around game (read, *defense*) picks up.

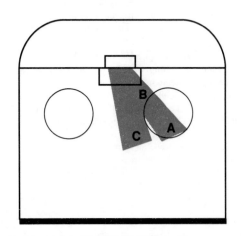

WAYNE VAN DORP

Yrs. of NHL service: 1
Born: Vancouver, B.C., Canada; May 19, 1961
Position: Left wing
Height: 6-4
Weight: 225
Uniform no.: 23
Shoots: left

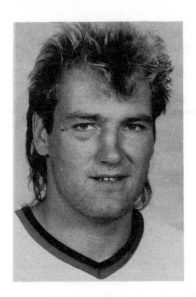

Career statistics:

GP	G	A	TP	PIM
96	8	7	15	431

1989-90 statistics:

GP	G	A	TP	+/-	PIM	PP	SH	GW	GT	S	PCT
61	7	4	11	-3	303	0	0	1	0	38	18.4

LAST SEASON

First full NHL season; games played, all point totals and PIM mark were career highs. Led team in PIM total and was club's lowest scoring regular.

THE FINESSE GAME

There really isn't one. Van Dorp's finesse skills would check in at no better than average in each category. He's neither a fast nor particularly agile skater, and his limited mobility limits his effectiveness as a checker. He does have a degree of balance, and that's critical for any player who functions as a fighter — you can't throw 'em if you can't stand up.

He demonstrates no creative sense for the offensive game, and his hand skills aren't good enough to support his thinking in any case. Van Dorp neither handles nor passes the puck with great skill, and his shooting ability is not much better. He'll need to be in front of almost-yawning nets to score, as he lacks the release or strength to beat NHL goaltenders with any kind of consistency.

THE PHYSICAL GAME

Take a guess — just look at those penalty minutes if you need a hint. Van Dorp is a fighter, plain and simple. He's not much of a hitter, because he can't catch anything to hit, and his limited finesse skills serve to limit his physical ability.

THE INTANGIBLES

If he were a more skilled player, Van Dorp would be a good complement to Dave Manson, able to pick up some of the tough guy responsibilities that prevent Manson from reaching his own potential. But Van Dorp is not the kind of player who can be played regardless of situation. And that means that he's replaceable as soon as a tough player with a higher degree of skill arrives.

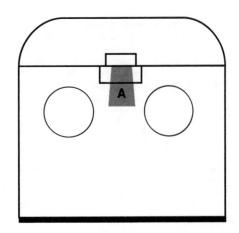

DOUG WILSON

Yrs. of NHL service: 13
Born: Ottawa, Ontario, Canada; July 5, 1957
Position: Defenseman
Height: 6-1
Weight: 187
Uniform no.: 24
Shoots: left

Career statistics:

GP	G	A	TP	PIM
887	214	525	739	734

1989-90 statistics:

GP	G	A	TP	+/-	PIM	PP	SH	GW	GT	S	PCT
70	23	50	73	13	40	13	1	2	0	242	9.5

LAST SEASON

Games played total was four-season high, goal total second best and point total third best of career (sixth overall among NHL defenders). Tied for team lead in power play goals (Steve Thomas) and led team's defense in scoring. Was fourth in plus/minus rating. Missed five games with knee injury.

THE FINESSE GAME

As a package, there's not much Wilson can't do. He has elite level finesse skills — truly world class talent — and his application of those talents begins with his skating. Despite the wear and tear, Wilson is among the NHL's best skaters — not best skating defensemen, best skaters period. He has speed, quickness, agility and balance — everything necessary to dominate play at the offensive and defensive blue lines.

He contains the point excellently at the offensive line, and closes the gap just as well at his own blue line. His skating also allows him to easily rush the puck from his zone (he's a superb stickhandler) or to join the play as an attacker — all without sacrificing his defense.

Wilson complements his skating with excellent hockey sense and playreading ability. That vision meshes with his excellent hand skills; Doug can put a pass anywhere, finessing or firing the puck when necessary — he likes to make the long breakaway pass, but Wilson hits singles as well as home runs.

His hand skill allows him to shoot off the pass very well, and he has an excellent slap shot: quick, strong, low and always on net. Wilson will also charge the slot for shots.

His skills make him a natural for all specialty team duty. In order to neutralize him, he must be checked closely and eliminated from the play — opponents must play his body.

THE PHYSICAL GAME

Though less likely to draw oohs and aahs, Wilson's physical game is as superb as his finesse game. He has good size and outstanding strength, and he takes the body to eliminate the man excellently. He covers the front of the net with intelligence and strength, stands up well at his blue line, and eliminates the opposition to prevent return passes. What more could you want?

His physical skill is amplified by his finesse ability, as Wilson can thwart the puck carrier and then turn the play up-ice himself. His strength and his balance are the outstanding attributes here.

THE INTANGIBLES

Wilson is a total player, almost without flaw in his game. He has long been (and continues to be) one of the top five defenders in the game, and the only thing that gets in Wilson's way is his health — the only intangible against him. He is otherwise an excellent and dedicated team man, and his attitude makes him a leader for Chicago

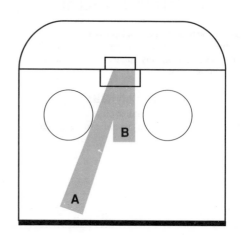

TRENT YAWNEY

Yrs. of NHL service: 3
Born: Hudson Bay, Sask., Canada; September 29, 1965
Position: Defenseman
Height: 6-3
Weight: 192
Uniform no.: 8
Shoots: left

Career statistics:

GP	G	A	TP	PIM
154	12	42	54	213

1989-90 statistics:

GP	G	A	TP	+/-	PIM	PP	SH	GW	GT	S	PCT
70	5	15	20	-6	82	1	0	1	0	58	8.6

LAST SEASON

Games played total was career high, but assist and point totals fell from first full season. Missed three games with a bruised kidney.

THE FINESSE GAME

Yawney is a strong skater, demonstrating balance and sturdiness on his feet but not yet at the NHL level in terms of foot speed or agility. He continues to improve in these areas, just as he continues to gain experience at playing at NHL speed.

He has good sense and instincts but is as yet unable to bring them to bear on a consistent NHL basis. When he does he'll be able to play an active rather than reactive game at both blue lines — a critical element for any player wishing to be among the League's better defenders.

Greater NHL experience will also flavor Yawney's puckhandling and puck moving ability. Again, though he's demonstrated good instincts (he's shown in isolated incidents that he can both jump into an opening or lead a teammate to it), he's not yet ready to make more sophisticated plays at the NHL level. To guarantee his success, Yawney must stick to simple plays and reads.

He's got a good shot from the blue line and will cheat into the zone for shots if he can.

THE PHYSICAL GAME

Efficiency rather than fireworks mark Yawney's physical play, and in this regard he is more like teammate Doug Wilson than he is Dave Manson. Yawney works to take the body well, and here too better NHL level skills would help him get to and hold his man out of the play. His physical play can be made more effective because of his ability to make a play coming away from the boards.

THE INTANGIBLES

Like most young defensemen, progress measurements for Yawney shouldn't really be made from season to season; that's because defensemen generally need five seasons to mature to the NHL level. Yawney has the skills and the potential to be an above-average NHL player, and his tremendous drive is more than likely to get him there.

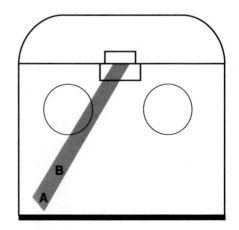

DETROIT RED WINGS

DAVE BARR

Yrs. of NHL service: 7
Born: Edmonton, Alta., Canada; November 30, 1960
Position: Right wing
Height: 6-1
Weight: 195
Uniform no.: 22
Shoots: right

Career statistics:

GP	G	A	TP	PIM
421	96	157	253	351

1989-90 statistics:

GP	G	A	TP	+/-	PIM	PP	SH	GW	GT	S	PCT
62	10	25	35	4	45	2	2	0	1	96	10.4

LAST SEASON

Goal total was full-season career low, point total second lowest. Played one month in Adirondack of the American Hockey League. Plus/minus was third-best among forwards.

THE FINESSE GAME

Primary among Barr's finesse ability is his hockey sense. He has a good understanding of both the offensive and defensive ends of the game, and he knows when to stretch his limits and when to play conservatively. His smarts make him a good forechecker (and not just in a puck pursuit sense), and they also key his solid defensive work. He makes good reads and good plays all over the ice.

His skating is unremarkable, with no appreciable speed or agility. He'll get from Point A to Point B fairly well, but Barr's footspeed won't blow anyone's doors off. Again, his ability to read and anticipate complement his skating to make that physical finesse skill more effective.

Because his scoring skill is not exceptional, Barr will not be a dynamic offensive force. Rather, his checking and heads-up play will create opportunities, and he will have to cash in those opportunities from near the net. He doesn't handle the puck particularly well, so don't expect any rink-length rushes or dynamic passing plays — but again, his sense will help him use his teammates.

THE PHYSICAL GAME

Barr is a corner and boards player, using his good size and strength willingly to take the opposition off the puck. He takes hits to make plays and consistently initiates contact throughout the rink's traffic areas.

He is also very tough in fights, though he does not fight often.

THE INTANGIBLES

His smarts and consistency are Barr's greatest strengths. He is an unglamourous player, but one with a fine work ethic and good team dedication. He is a solid, if unsung, player.

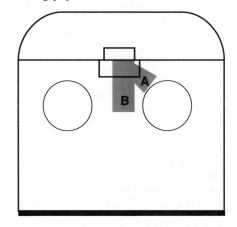

SHAWN BURR

Yrs. of NHL service: 4
Born: Sarnia, Ontario, Canada; July 1, 1966
Position: Left wing/center
Height: 6-1
Weight: 180
Uniform no.: 11
Shoots: left

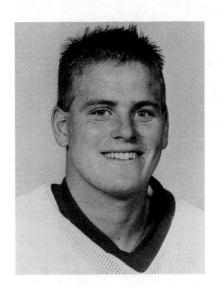

Career statistics:

GP	G	A	TP	PIM
313	83	107	190	370

1989-90 statistics:

GP	G	A	TP	+/-	PIM	PP	SH	GW	GT	S	PCT
76	24	32	56	14	82	4	3	2	0	173	13.9

LAST SEASON

Point totals were career highs. Finished third on club in plus/minus, best among forwards.

THE FINESSE GAME

Time is beginning to make Burr a more complete NHL player. While he has been a good skater since he entered the League (excellent balance and very good skating strength afford Burr rink-length speed and good acceleration; his balance also allows him a good degree of agility, and that balance keys his physical game too), his contributions in the offensive end of the rink have been outstripped by those in the defensive zone.

But last season, Burr showed that he can put his skating and fine hockey sense to work offensively. While he has been able to read the play well since entering the League (and has often created opportunities for himself) Burr hasn't consistently converted those opportunities. But his hands have begun to catch up to his feet. Burr has good hands for passing and shooting, but he could still improve the release of his shot.

His sense of the ice is good, showing him developing plays. Combined with his skating, Burr's hockey sense has made him one of the better defensive players in the League. He is a fine penalty killer (a strong shorthanded threat) and forechecker.

THE PHYSICAL GAME

Balance is the key to Burr's physical game, because it is balance that allows him to hit and yet remain vertical after collisions to make plays. He initiates contact all over the ice, and succeeds because of his ability to make plays out of the corner.

He is also a good faceoff man because of his hand and wrist strength.

THE INTANGIBLES

We said last year that Burr should be showing more to his game, that he was capable of 25 goals a season (so sue us for one goal), and that he should elevate himself out of the role player class.

He did raise his game last season; now we say he has to at least maintain that growth — and Burr is capable of better than that.

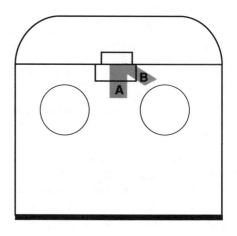

JIMMY CARSON

Yrs. of NHL service: 4
Born: Southfield, Michigan, USA; July 20, 1968
Position: Center
Height: 6-0
Weight: 185
Uniform no.: 10
Shoots: right

Career statistics:

GP	G	A	TP	PIM
288	162	163	325	111

1989-90 statistics:

GP	G	A	TP	+/-	PIM	PP	SH	GW	GT	S	PCT
48	21	18	39	-7	8	11	0	1	1	138	15.2

LAST SEASON

Acquired from the Oilers along with Kevin McClelland in exchange for Joe Murphy, Adam Graves, Petr Klima and Jeff Sharples. Was suspended by Oilers pending trade, and missed 21 games with a knee injury (and time with tonsillitis) after trade to Wings. Games played and all point toals were career lows.

THE FINESSE GAME

Carson's finesse skills are excellent — and still with potential to improve. He might look like a lumbering skater, but Carson has excellent quickness, the kind that allows him to stop and start in one direction or another within a step. He's not overly fast, but he has excellent acceleration, so he will pull away from the opposition. He has a smooth stride and is well balanced and agile in all three directions: forward, back and sideways.

Good as his skating is, Jimmy's hand skills are better — especially for scoring. His shot selection is excellent and is already among the League's best, both slap shot and wrist shot. He shoots often and accurately and makes the goalie stop him, rather than firing shots wide of the net.

Though a scorer, he uses his teammates fairly well. He regularly makes thread-the-needle passes and combines that skill with his ice vision and anticipation to be a very good playmaker. He anticipates very well offensively, particularly in making the transition from offense to defense.

THE PHYSICAL GAME

Though not primarily a physical player (Carson would never be called a power forward), Jimmy has good size and uses his body very well offensively. He protects the puck with his body very well and will certainly get stronger as he matures. He'd be helped by a tough winger who would open up ice for Carson to play in.

He's still a little too casual in his defensive aggressiveness, often getting out-fought and out-positioned because he's not as intense as he should be.

He also needs greater strength on faceoffs, particularly in the defensive zone — where he frequently loses more than he wins. When he loses those faceoffs he's beaten to the net by the opposing center.

THE INTANGIBLES

Carson is still a pup by NHL standards and, despite his holdout/suspension from Edmonton he wasn't a bad team guy. The Oilers didn't dislike him; Carson simply remained a loner while in Edmonton — he didn't socialize.

No matter. Now he's in Detroit — his hometown — where the pressure to perform (and to justify trading four good prospects) will be very heavy. If he succeeds, he and Steve Yzerman just may give Detroit the NHL's best one-two punch at center.

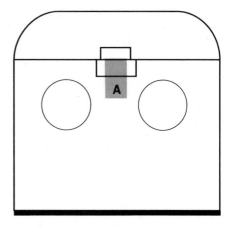

JOHN CHABOT

Yrs. of NHL service: 7
Born: Summerside, P.E.I., Canada; May 18, 1962
Position: Center
Height: 6-2
Weight: 200
Uniform no.: 16
Shoots: left

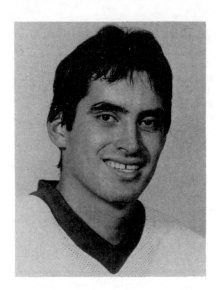

Career statistics:

GP	G	A	TP	PIM
481	79	223	302	81

1989-90 statistics:

GP	G	A	TP	+/-	PIM	PP	SH	GW	GT	S	PCT
69	9	40	49	5	24	0	2	0	0	91	9.9

LAST SEASON

Plus/minus was second best among forwards. Suffered a late season foot injury.

THE FINESSE GAME

Skating and puckhandling are the strengths of Chabot's game; his hand skills just may get the nod over his feet. He is an outstanding puckhandler with very quick hands and fine touch. He can rag the puck as a penalty killer better than most anyone in the NHL, and he also has the ability to win a faceoff and walk through to the net for a shot — his quick hands are the key. We'd also be remiss if we didn't credit his reach, a key factor in his puckhandling ability.

His skating is keyed by his balance and lateral movement. Though he lacks dynamic speed, Chabot is a quick player — fluid and snake-like; he is a very agile, mobile player, and can succeed in traffic because of that mobility. Chabot's skating and puckhandling combine with his good anticipation and hockey sense to make him a good checking forward and penalty killer. He can also use these skills offensively to create scoring chances for his teammates; his hands and sense will get the puck to them.

His checking also creates offensive opportunities for himself, but John is largely unable to take advantage of them because is he doesn't get his shot away quickly enough.

THE PHYSICAL GAME

Physical is not in Chabot's vocabulary. He does not hit or use his body to any degree, preferring to remain on the outside of the scrums, and he will not take hits to make plays. He does his defensive work by staying between the puck and his check, rather than by wearing his check down with hits.

In turn, he is difficult to hit because he is willowy on his skates, bending and swaying away from contact in order to keep working on the puck.

THE INTANGIBLES

What you see with Chabot is what you get — sometimes. He's never been accused of having an excess of character or work ethic, but Chabot does deserve credit for coming back from a poor 1988-89 effort with a solid effort in 1989-90. What the Wings will get from Chabot in 1990-91, however, remains to be seen.

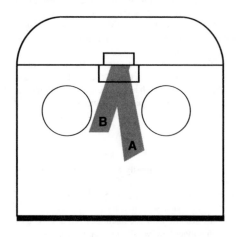

TIM CHEVELDAE

Yrs. of NHL service: 1
Born: Melville, Sask., Canada; February 15, 1968
Position: Goaltender
Height: 5-10 1/2
Weight: 176
Uniform no.: 32
Catches: left

Career statistics:

GP	MINS	G	SO	AVG	A	PIM
30	1,722	110	0	3.83	1	2

1989-90 statistics:

GP	MINS	AVG	W	L	T	SO	GA	SA	SAPCT	PIM
28	1,600	3.79	10	9	8	0	101	854	.882	2

LAST SEASON

First full NHL campaign. Second to Winnipeg's Bib Essensa in games played by rookie goaltenders. Joined Detroit for good in February, 1990.

THE PHYSICAL GAME

Cheveldae plays a challenging, angle-cutting game, a style that makes good use of his good — but not great — size. He complements his angle game with good positional awareness, moving well in and out of the net and from post to post across the crease.

His skating is good, so Cheveldae has the mobility to challenge shooters and then react for the second save. He has good balance and quick feet, so he can regain his position after going to the ice. Cheveldae works to limit offensive opportunities by covering his rebounds. His glove and stick hands are good.

THE MENTAL GAME

Cheveldae has good concentration, and he uses that ability to insure he gets sight of the puck. He is very alert to play in front of him and around the net, and that helps make his physical play better.

THE INTANGIBLES

In all, not a bad debut for a goalie whose team allowed 35 more goals than it scored — and allowed fourth-most shots in the NHL. Cheveldae showed well enough last season that he'll be given ample opportunity to claim the number one spot this year, which might spell the end of Glen Hanlon's or Greg Stefan's tenure in Detroit.

STEVE CHIASSON

Yrs. of NHL service: 4
Born: Barrie, Ontario, Canada; April 14, 1967
Position: Defenseman
Height: 6-0
Weight: 202
Uniform no.: 3
Shoots: left

Career statistics:

GP	G	A	TP	PIM
206	29	76	105	393

1988-1989 statistics:

GP	G	A	TP	+/-	PIM	PP	SH	GW	GT	S	PCT
67	14	28	42	-16	114	4	0	2	0	190	7.4

LAST SEASON

Led Detroit blueliners in scoring; games played and goal totals were career highs. Plus/minus was club's worst, SOG total third highest. Missed seven games with groin injury, three games with knee injury, two games with heel injury.

THE FINESSE GAME

Chiasson is currently the Wings' best offensive threat from the blue line, courtesy of his still-developing skating and puckhandling skills. He is a good skater in all directions (though he can be caught flat-footed going to his left when he back-skates), and he has developed a good degree of agility and quickness. He uses his skating to join the offensive play (and not just support it) as it heads up-ice, and he'll go to the net for that play. He'll also come off his point position to challenge in the slot.

He's a fairly solid puckhandler and he likes to carry the puck up-ice (probably Detroit's only sure thing as far as rushing goes), but he's also smart enough to move the puck to players in better position in both his defensive and offensive zones. Though his judgement has improved, he could be more consistent in his puck movement — sometimes he tries to be too fancy.

He reads the rushes well in both directions, and can step up to strip the puckcarrier and then turn the play around. Steve has a very good slap shot, heavy, low and on net, and he'll slide to the openings to deliver it.

THE PHYSICAL GAME

Chiasson mixes his physical and finesse abilities to play a balanced, all-around game. He is a big man and plays aggressively; his improved skating and balance greatly help his physical game (by getting him to guys to hit and by keeping him vertical), and he has the upper body strength to control most anyone in the corners and in front of his net.

He uses his body smartly to protect the puck when he carries it.

THE INTANGIBLES

Chiasson is a character kid at the rink, a hard-nosed, mentally tough individual with tremendous desire. He brings a fine attitude to the Wings, and is a team leader.

We continue to say that, at age 23, his best days are ahead of him.

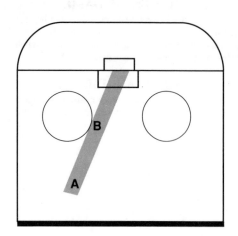

BERNIE FEDERKO

Yrs. of NHL service: 14
Born: Foam Lake, Sask., Canada; May 12, 1956
Position: Center
Height: 6-1
Weight: 190
Uniform no.: 42
Shoots: left

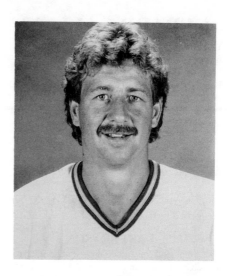

Career statistics:

GP	G	A	TP	PIM
1,000	369	761	1,130	487

1989-90 statistics:

GP	G	A	TP	+/-	PIM	PP	SH	GW	GT	S	PCT
73	17	40	57	-8	24	3	0	0	0	108	15.7

LAST SEASON

Point totals were second-lowest full-season marks of Federko's career. Finished third on Wings in scoring. Missed three games with a groin injury.

THE FINESSE GAME

Federko is a slowing down superstar, and his skills reflect that — or, rather the results of his skills reflect that. He's never been a speed merchant, so to say that Federko has lost a step may be a bit rhetorical. But the point is, the game has gotten faster (and more talented) around him; his skating gives him less and less time to make plays. His balance is exceptional and allows him to work well in the traffic areas — where his hand skills work to their best advantage. He can make plays almost regardless of body position.

His hockey sense still powers his finesse game, but his hands are more and more showing themselves to be slowing down in translating what his eyes are seeing. For a playmaker who makes his living with his hands and brain, that's not a good sign. Still Federko retains outstanding sense and anticipation. He sees the ice excellently and immediately looks to make plays once he gains the offensive blue line.

Bernie's 35-goal days are past, especially since — if given a choice — Bernie's going to pass. He'll pick up loose pucks around the net for his goals, and his sensitive hands are ideal for slot scoring.

THE PHYSICAL GAME

Federko takes his hits to make his plays and, as mentioned, works willingly in traffic and protects the puck well — but he has never been a physical player. His excellent balance allows him to bump along the boards and gain control of the puck there, but he's never going to knock anyone into the cheap seats.

THE INTANGIBLES

In his defense, Federko's disappointing season is not solely his fault. Accustomed to being the number one center (and playing with first-line teammates), he was not last season. Already concerned about his ice time, Federko will be pushed further into the background because of Steve Yzerman and Jimmy Carson. We wouldn't be surprised to see Federko finish this season in a different uniform.

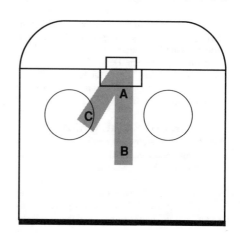

GERARD GALLANT

Yrs. of NHL service: 6
Born: Summerside, P.E.I., Canada; September 2, 1963
Position: Left wing
Height: 5-10
Weight: 185
Uniform no.: 17
Shoots: left

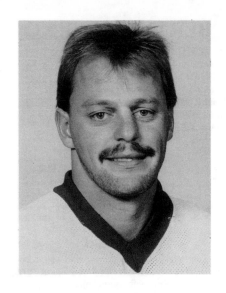

Career statistics:

GP	G	A	TP	PIM
382	173	202	375	1,114

1989-90 statistics:

GP	G	A	TP	+/-	PIM	PP	SH	GW	GT	S	PCT
69	36	44	80	-6	254	12	3	5	1	219	16.4

LAST SEASON

Point total was second highest of career. Second on club in all offensive categories. PIM total was career high and club's second highest.

THE FINESSE GAME

Power is reflected throughout Gallant's game, as befitting a power forward. He is a strong skater and that makes him a strong forechecker, despite the fact that he is not exceptionally talented in the agility, quickness and speed areas. His balance, however, is exceptional and it is that skill that makes him so effective physically — he remains vertical after collisions.

Strength, again, powers Gallant's goal scoring ability. His shooting skill is very good, with a wrist shot that is very heavy (Gallant's shots will power their way through traffic), and his skating strength will put him in position near the net. He is otherwise not remarkably gifted in the hand skills department, even though Gerard has the ability to use his teammates.

That skill comes from his vision and ability to make a play after knocking an opponent off the puck in the corner. Gallant looks up and finds the open man, and he can get the puck to him. He's successful when he remembers not to overhandle the puck.

His defensive play is fairly solid and Gallant will see ice time in crucial situations.

THE PHYSICAL GAME

Gallant is a very physical player, whose strength is the key to his entire game. He uses that strength to great effect in the corners and along the boards, where he can be a dominating player. His strength carries him to the net for shots, and also allows him to overpower defensemen in the crease. He drives through his checks to take the opposition off the puck, and that is why he can be an important player in defensive situations (getting the puck out of the zone when it is against the boards).

He is also more than willing to mix it up, as his PIM total suggests.

THE INTANGIBLES

Gallant is a very competitive person, a player driven to succeed. He is a good team man and a character player. His offense can go in streaks, but his work ethic will never be in doubt. Like his center, Steve Yzerman, Gallant is a leader for the Wings.

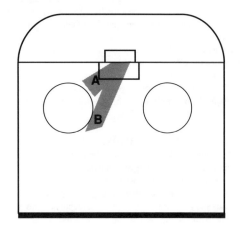

MARC HABSCHEID

Yrs. of NHL service: 5
Born: Swift Current, Sask., Canada; March 1, 1963
Position: Center
Height: 6-0
Weight: 185
Uniform no.: 25
Shoots: right

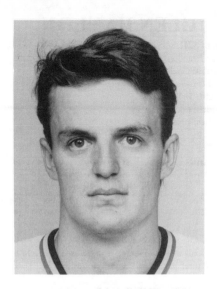

Career statistics:

GP	G	A	TP	PIM
253	56	72	128	107

1989-90 statistics:

GP	G	A	TP	+/-	PIM	PP	SH	GW	GT	S	PCT
66	15	11	26	1	33	0	0	0	0	114	13.2

LAST SEASON

Games played and all point totals were second highest of career.

THE FINESSE GAME

Habscheid is an excellent skater, with agility and lateral movement his best assets. Marc has extremely quick feet, and they combine with his exceptional balance to make him very shifty. He likes to combine that agility with his good quickness to drive the defense off the blue line, then pull up short and wheel 360-degrees to open ice. His acceleration ability is also outstanding, and he'll beat opponents to the outside.

His hand skills well complement his skating skill, because Marc handles the puck well at top speed. He likes to carry the puck over the blue line (and can be guilty of overhandling it), but he'll also look for the trailer and head to the net after gaining the offensive zone. Otherwise, he's not real creative without the puck. He's got a good shot, not a great one, but he makes the most of his opportunities because of his ability to dart to loose pucks around the net. He should shoot more when he finds an opening.

His anticipation and smarts are such that he can play in all situations, and Habscheid is also a conscientious and attentive defensive player — an acquired trait. He is a particularly effective penalty killer.

THE PHYSICAL GAME

Habscheid plays an involved physical game — he's willing to get his nose dirty — and that willingness amplifies his finesse game. But he doesn't have a lot of strength, and doesn't have great size, so his best work is going to be done in the open ice.

His eye/hand coordination is very good, making him an excellent faceoff man.

THE INTANGIBLES

Habscheid has a tendency to worry too much about his performance, but better than not worrying at all. He's popular with his teammates and is a fairly skilled player; the Wings need that kind of player — they have plenty of muckers.

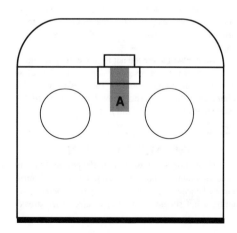

GLEN HANLON

Yrs. of NHL service: 12
Born: Brandon, Man., Canada; February 20, 1957
Position: Goaltender
Height: 6-0
Weight: 185
Uniform no.: 1
Catches: right

Career statistics:

GP	MINS	G	SO	AVG	A	PIM
458	25,175	1,515	13	3.61	11	233

1989-90 statistics:

GP	MINS	AVG	W	L	T	SO	GA	SA	SAPCT	PIM
45	2,290	4.03	15	18	5	1	154	1,159	.867	24

LAST SEASON

Goals-against-average was five-season high. He missed three games with a groin injury.

THE PHYSICAL GAME

Hanlon plays a hybrid game of angles and reflexes. When he is standing up and squaring himself to the puck, challenging the shooter and letting his body stop the shot, then he is successful. He does have a tendency, however, of squaring himself to the puck while remaining deep in the net. Because he is likely to leave rebounds, opposing shooters have good angles to the goal.

Which brings us to the second part of Hanlon's game. His innate quickness is very good, and he's a .500 shot to get a piece of (or completely thwart) that follow-up opportunity. But this helter-skelter play reveals a flaw.

Hanlon's balance is not exceptional, and he'll lose it once he moves his feet — that means he's going to be on the ice where, as stated, he can be down and out of the play.

Hanlon will leave the net to move the puck up to his defense, is weak on his glove side on any shot below the waist, but is good above it. He goes to his knees immediately on screen shots (but doesn't butterfly his pads) so when shots miss him he has to lunge with his upper body.

THE MENTAL GAME

Hanlon responds well to challenges, and he can come up with big games. He maintains his concentration well during games, and can keep his concentration during a hot streak, but will also have other streaks where his concentration falters. He is no longer, however, adversely affected by bad games or goals.

THE INTANGIBLES

The emergence of rookie Tim Cheveldae will cut into Hanlon's time. Hanlon's a good team man, valued in the dressing room because of his attitude. He'll need that positive attitude as he slips into a backup role for the Wings.

DOUG HOUDA

Yrs. of NHL service: 2
Born: Blairmore, Alta., Canada; June 3, 1966
Position: Defenseman
Height: 6-2
Weight: 190
Uniform no.: 27
Shoots: right

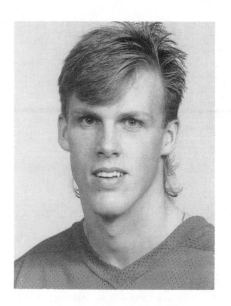

Career statistics:

GP	G	A	TP	PIM
147	5	21	26	208

1989-90 statistics:

GP	G	A	TP	+/-	PIM	PP	SH	GW	GT	S	PCT
73	2	9	11	-6	127	0	0	0	0	59	3.4

LAST SEASON

Games played total was career high. Led defense in PIM total Missed five games with knee injury.

THE FINESSE GAME

Houda continues to develop his already fairly solid defensive skills. His skating continues to improve and he does more than his share of challenging at the defensive blue line; he is a solid positional player. His agility and lateral movement have improved (he does move well in all directions), but he still succeeds positionally at least as much because of his size as he does because of his mobility.

He gets fairly good reads of the ice, and he is difficult to beat one-on-one. Still, he needs to continue his acclimation to NHL speed, particularly on plays across the front of the net.

Houda is not spectacular in his puck work, but he will make the right play more often than the wrong one. He doesn't overhandle the puck or try to do things he's not capable of. He contributes rarely from the blue line, acting more as the fall-back defender than as the fourth attacker.

THE PHYSICAL GAME

He's a big boy and Houda plays that way. He hits often, putting his good size and strength to use in front of the net and in the corners. He cleans the crease well and will play aggressively, as his growing PIM total indicates. Doug will win the battles in the high traffic areas, and because he makes simple and effective plays his physical play is that much more effective.

THE INTANGIBLES

Increased confidence is the cause of Houda's improved play; that just makes sense. He'll continue to improve as his ice-time and responsibilities increase (he currently does not play in specialty team situations). The Wings have smartly paired him with experienced players (Lee Norwood and Borje Salming last season), and Houda has rewarded them.

He is already fairly tough defensively, and he'll do nothing but improve.

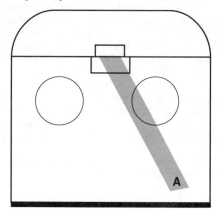

JOE KOCUR

Yrs. of NHL service: 5
Born: Calgary, Alta., Canada; December 21, 1964
Position: Right wing
Height: 6-0
Weight: 195
Uniform no.: 26
Shoots: right

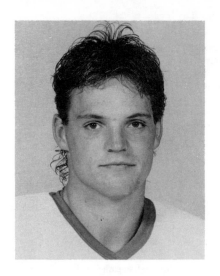

Career statistics:

GP	G	A	TP	PIM
347	51	51	102	1,461

1989-90 statistics:

GP	G	A	TP	+/-	PIM	PP	SH	GW	GT	S	PCT
71	16	20	36	-5	268	1	0	5	0	128	12.5

LAST SEASON

Goal, assist and point totals were career highs; games played total second highest of career. Led team in PIM total. Missed two games with a hand injury, one with a groin injury and was also sidelined with late season knee injury.

THE FINESSE GAME

Kocur has more finesse skill than he is generally given credit for. He demonstrates balance and a degree of speed in his skating, so much so that he can pull an inside move or two on a defender. He is also a very strong skater, so that he drives through his checks. Limiting his skating ability are his lack of quickness, and turning ability that is below his straightaway skill; his agility is no better than average.

He also has better hands than he is given credit for, and his goal-scoring last season was no fluke. He shoots the puck very well, and his improved goal total can be attributed to the fact that he shot more last season (1.8 shots per game) than he did in 1988-89 (1.27 shots per game).

Kocur has some puckhandling ability, so he's not afraid to carry the puck and challenge the defense. He sees passing openings and he can get the puck there (he also takes a pass fairly well), but he generally succeeds in these skills because of the room he gets from the opposition.

His defense is unreliable, mostly because of his agility problems.

THE PHYSICAL GAME

Kocur is one of the NHL's most feared players, and that fear is generated because of his fighting ability. He is an exceptional fighter, a true NHL heavyweight who can literally knockout opponents with one punch. He fights more at home than he does on the road, but a player with his record couldn't be called a homer.

His hitting is just as fearsome, although it is less feared(because of his limited agility, Kocur has difficulty nailing the opposition). All and all, when Kocur hits people they stay hit.

His physical game betrays him physically — despite his conditioning — in that his hands are always hurt, and that he has never played a full NHL season.

THE INTANGIBLES

Highly prized around the League, Kocur is a good team man. He could work harder, and — as his point totals last season showed — he has other things to offer besides his fists. He can score 20 goals a year, and that would make him a threat in more ways than one.

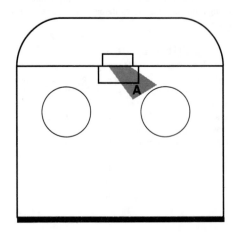

KEVIN MCCLELLAND

Yrs. of NHL service: 8
Born: Oshawa, Ontario, Canada; July 4, 1962
Position: Right wing/center
Height: 6-2
Weight: 205
Uniform no.: 18
Shoots: right

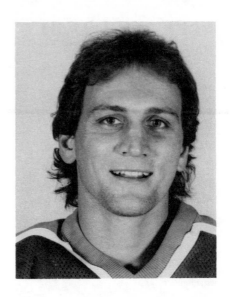

Career statistics:

GP	G	A	TP	PIM
561	68	111	179	1,613

1989-90 statistics:

GP	G	A	TP	+/-	PIM	PP	SH	GW	GT	S	PCT
71	5	6	11	-6	196	0	0	0	0	31	16.1

LAST SEASON

Acquired from Edmonton along with Jimmy Carson in exchange for Adam Graves, Jeff Sharples, Petr Klima and Joe Murphy. Games played total was five season low (missed three games with a shoulder injury). Finished third on club in PIM total.

THE FINESSE GAME

McClelland isn't much of a finesse player; whatever he accomplishes comes from work and desire. He's a strong skater, a good skater with a burst of speed keyed by his powerful stride, but he won't out-race anyone over the length of the ice. He's basically a straight-ahead player, and uses his skating strength to pursue the puck relentlessly.

Because he may not have the agility to stick with the fancier forwards, Kevin must succeed in his checking by playing positionally and remaining with his check up and down the ice. He's decent defensively.

He can combine his anticipation with his skating to shut down the opposition, but he doesn't translate those skills into offensive contributions. McClelland needs time and space to get the puck to the open man, and he rarely takes advantage of an opportunity by shooting the puck himself. Kevin doesn't have a great shot, so he'll have to do his scoring from within close proximity of the net.

THE PHYSICAL GAME

The physical game is McClelland's game, and he plays it with gusto. His excellent upper body strength and leg power make him very effective along the boards and his balance enters into play here, keeping him upright and driving after collisions.

He loves to hit and play it rough all over the ice, and he fears nothing and no one; Kevin is only too willing to back up his play with his fists.

He sacrifices his body to block shots, a rare trait among forwards, and stands up for his teammates in any situation.

THE INTANGIBLES

When there's enemy ground to be gained, McClelland is going to get the call. He's an agitator, the type of player who will do anything to win, and Kevin's yeoman effort in the trenches is the type that's crucial to any team's success. McClelland works hard and has tons of heart and enthusiasm making him a leader and an important part of the Wings.

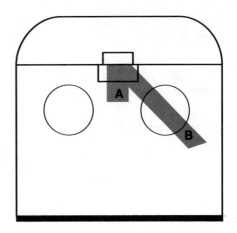

LEE NORWOOD

Yrs. of NHL service: 7
Born: Oakland, Calif, USA; February 2, 1960
Position: Defenseman
Height: 6-1
Weight: 198
Uniform no.: 23
Shoots: left

Career statistics:

GP	G	A	TP	PIM
356	46	125	171	773

1989-90 statistics:

GP	G	A	TP	+/-	PIM	PP	SH	GW	GT	S	PCT
64	8	14	22	15	95	1	0	1	0	60	13.3

LAST SEASON

Point total was full-season career low. Plus/minus was team's second best. Was sidelined with with hip and wrist injuries.

THE FINESSE GAME

Positional and relatively intelligent play are the keys to Norwood's continued success; he must play that way because he is otherwise no better than average in his finesse skills.

He doesn't have a lot of speed or agility, so Norwood wouldn't be among the more mobile rearguards in the League. But he uses his skills to play positionally, to force the opposition wide of the net by using his defensive angles, and in that way he's a triumph of function over form.

Norwood doesn't have great hand skills, but he does like to move into the slot for shots; he'll also pinch in when he can. Otherwise, he smartly concentrates on moving the puck to the more talented players in all three zones.

He'll see power play time as the defensive safety valve, and he'll also see fairly regular penalty killing duty.

THE PHYSICAL GAME

Norwood is very aggressive, but he is generally smart in his play (as his PIM totals indicate). He plays a very tough style of game (he's very good at his take-outs, the second step of playing defensive angles) and is a fearless player without regard for his body. He blocks shots, he mixes it up in front of the net, he muscles with forwards against the boards. He enjoys the physical game and makes the most of his size.

THE INTANGIBLES

When he stays within his limits, Norwood thrives. There are times when he makes mistakes because he tries to do too much, but he'll come through when needed. Now, as one of the elder statesmen for the Wings' defensive corps, he'll be counted on to rotate in and out of the lineup (with no change in effectiveness) and to impart his smarts to the youngsters.

He's a hard worker, a coachable athlete, and a tremendously intense competitor. That makes him a leader.

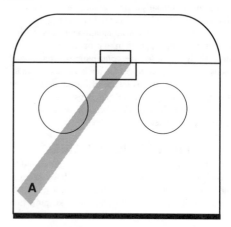

MIKE O'CONNELL

Yrs. of NHL service: 12
Born: Chicago, Ill., USA; November 25, 1955
Position: Defenseman
Height: 5-9
Weight: 180
Uniform no.: 2
Shoots: right

Career statistics:

GP	G	A	TP	PIM
860	105	334	439	605

1989-90 statistics:

GP	G	A	TP	+/-	PIM	PP	SH	GW	GT	S	PCT
66	4	14	18	-11	22	0	0	0		57	7.0

LAST SEASON

Plus/minus was team's second worst. PIM total was full-seasoncareer low. Missed four games with back spasms.

THE FINESSE GAME

Smarts are the key to O'Connell's current and future NHL success, although the ravages of time haven't scarred him too badly. Though still a good skater (O'Connell retains a degree of the agility that marked his skating game throughout his career, and he has enough quickness left to intercept a pass and start a rush up-ice), he succeeds more now by thwarting the opposition with his anticipation and play reading. Where previously O'Connell was adept at meeting and forcing the play at his blue line, he now uses his defensive angles to deflect the attack.

He won't carry the puck as much as he did earlier in his career, and O'Connell will no longer pinch in at the opposing blue line as successfully as he has, but he still makes good first passes from his zone and lead passes in the other zones. His smarts and reading ability put him on-ice in all situations.

He no longer shoots the puck as he once did, so O'Connell's goals will be few and far between.

THE PHYSICAL GAME

The physical game has never really been O'Connell's hallmark — it couldn't be because of his size. He's always played a smart physical game, tying up wingers along the boards or in front of the net, but the League's crops of bigger and stronger players will continue to out-muscle O'Connell. That's where his smarts (tying up a stick, intercepting a pass) come in.

He's always been willing to use the size he has, but his hitting won't punish anyone.

THE INTANGIBLES

Knowledge and steadiness (despite the poor plus/minus numbers) are the qualities O'Connell is now most valued for. He's a good team man, and his upbeat attitude is one that will help the Wings tutor their young defenders. Of course, it is the presence of those youngsters that just might spell the end of O'Connell's days in Detroit.

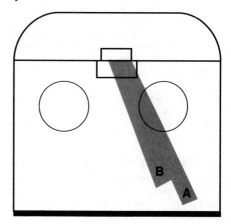

ROBERT PICARD

Yrs. of NHL service: 13
Born: Montreal, Quebec, Canada; May 25, 1957
Position: Defenseman
Height: 6-2
Weight: 207
Uniform no.: 7
Shoots: left

Career statistics:

GP	G	A	TP	PIM
899	104	319	423	1,025

1989-90 statistics:

GP	G	A	TP	+/-	PIM	PP	SH	GW	GT	S	PCT
44	0	8	8	-4	48	0	0	0		0	39	0.0

LAST SEASON

Acquired from Quebec in exchange for Tony McKegney. Games played and all point totals were career lows. He missed time while with Detroit because of a foot injury.

THE FINESSE GAME

Picard is a good skater, both forward and backward, though he needs work on his pivots. Picard has good acceleration up-ice and will carry the puck if the opportunity presents itself. Because of his weakness in turning, however, Picard is a good target for forecheckers. When forced, he throws blind passes around the boards.

Offensively, Picard is a good passer and can spot the open man, though he has no better than average anticipation skills. Still, he sees the ice and can make use of it by jumping into the openings himself or by leading a teammate with a pass.

Picard has a fairly good shot from the point and will see time on the power play because of his passing and shooting skills. He also likes to charge the net when he can.

Defensively, Picard still shows a tendency to gamble too frequently, pinching into the offensive zone too often and too deeply. Though he has the speed to recover, Picard doesn't hustle back and will also wander from his position in the defensive zone, making things difficult for his partners.

THE PHYSICAL GAME

Picard can be a pretty good hitter. He has a mean streak and that makes a good defenseman, but he doesn't hit consistently. He can hurt you when he hits, but sometimes is left checking air because he is so unsubtle.

He has good, not great, strength and can be muscled off the puck by the opposition. Though he hits hard,

Picard also does a lot of pushing and shoving and he would be better served by increased upper body strength.

THE INTANGIBLES

We told you last year that Picard's tenure with Quebec was coming to an end. He played well enough in Detroit to earn another chance this season, but what you see with Picard is probably more than you're going to consistently get. Because he plays comfortable and isn't driven to succeed, Picard's consistency is questionable at best.

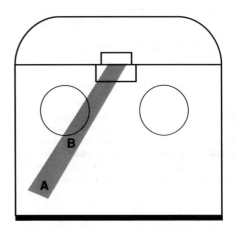

BOB PROBERT

Yrs. of NHL service: 4
Born: Windsor, Ontario, Canada; June 5, 1965
Position: Right wing
Height: 6-3
Weight: 215
Uniform no.: 24
Shoots: left

Career statistics:

GP	G	A	TP	PIM
210	57	59	116	932

1989-90 statistics:

GP	G	A	TP	+/-	PIM	PP	SH	GW	GT	S	PCT
4	3	0	3	0	21	0	0	1	0	12	25.0

LAST SEASON

Returned late in season after serving League-mandated expulsion for cocaine smuggling.

THE FINESSE GAME

While he may produce offensively like a fine finesse player, Probert is not necessarily a well-rounded finesse player. His skating is average at best, lacking agility and foot speed. He does have great balance, and that balance is the key to Probert's physical game, as it allows him to remain upright after hitting an opposing player. Bob is facilitated in his skating by the fact that no one comes near him, and by his long stride which pulls him away from the opposition. Just don't confuse that with speed.

His great finesse strength is in his hand skill, which is very good. Probert carries the puck well while skating and has the talent to handle the puck in traffic and tight to the net. He can certainly make a play coming out of the corner with the puck, and he has enough talent to get the puck over sticks or through traffic to his teammates. He's dangerous enough with the puck to draw penalties.

He doesn't have a lot of anticipation or hockey sense in the offensive zone, and if in doubt he'll just throw the puck behind the net.

He doesn't have an outstanding shot (his slap shot is easily blocked because it takes him so long to release it) in terms of blazing speed or power, but Probert gets his wrist shot off very quickly from in front of the net: He's a power play regular there, and his hand skills are good enough for him to finesse the puck into a small opening.

Because of desire rather than anticipation or skating talent, Probert is good defensively. He stays with his check up and down the ice, and is fairly disciplined in terms of positional play, not wandering from his lane.

THE PHYSICAL GAME

Next to his hand skills, power is the greatest component in his game. He hits people hard and he hurts them when he checks them. He has tremendous strength, and he couples that with great reach to be more effective in traffic.

He is one of the League's toughest players — maybe the toughest — and he is the NHL's best fighter. Unlike teammate Joe Kocur, who remains relatively calm during a fight, Probert loses control.

That threat of physical punishment is why he's avoided on the ice, and why players from all teams allow him to camp in front of the net. Better, they think, to leave the big guy alone than to wake him up.

They're right.

THE INTANGIBLES

This report is reprinted from edition three of the *Hockey Scouting Report*. We said then, "Time is on his side. After all, he's still only 23 years old. We hope he can take control of his life." He is attempting to do just that now. If he does, he will become a force to be reckoned with.

Time will tell.

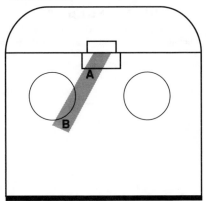

DANIEL SHANK

Yrs. of NHL service: 1
Born: Montreal, Quebec, Canada; May 12, 1967
Position: Right wing
Height: 5-10
Weight: 190
Uniform no.: 34
Shoots: right

Career statistics:

GP	G	A	TP	+/-	PIM	PP	SH	GW	GT	S	PCT
57	11	13	24	1	143	0	0	1	0	61	18.0

LAST SEASON

Shank's first in the NHL. He joined the wings from Adirondack of the American Hockey League in November 1989, and later missed two games with an abdominal injury. He finished fourth on the club in PIM total.

THE FINESSE GAME

Shank doesn't have a real good idea of where he's going when he's on the ice, but he's in a hurry to get there and nail somebody. He works with what he sees in front of him, so that means he's going to be going right at the puck and the puck carrier. His skating isn't bad in terms of speed or mobility, and Shank is a very strong skater — so he'll drive through his checks.

He doesn't get a good read of the ice, and his hand skills aren't at the level of his Tasmanian devil skating, but Shank can put the puck in the net — and he'll get the chance by bowling over someone in the crease to get at the puck. He's smart enough to go to the front of the net.

THE PHYSICAL GAME

As we've already implied, Shank is a physical player. He hits as often as he can, and he isn't shy about fighting either. He hits with good strength and can take the opposition off the puck, but he has yet to demonstrate the ability to make a play after checking.

THE INTANGIBLES

He's a peppery player, is Dan Shank. Aggressive and agitating, he's the kind of guy who drives the opposition nuts (kissing his stick after he scores doesn't calm them down either). Anyway, he's got developable finesse skills, and his physical play will buy him the time necessary to improve.

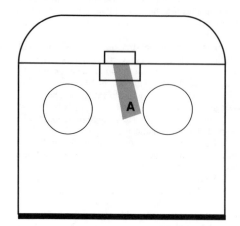

GREG STEFAN

Yrs. of NHL service: 8
Born: Brantford, Ontario, Canada; February 11, 1961
Position: Goaltender
Height: 5-11
Weight: 180
Uniform no.: 30
Catches: left

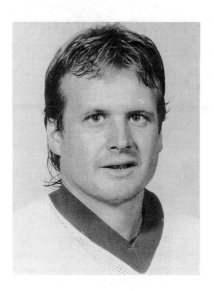

Career statistics:

GP	MINS	G	SO	AVG	A	PIM
299	16,333	1,068	5	3.92	15	210

1989-90 statistics:

GP	MINS	AVG	W	L	T	SO	GA	SA	SAPCT	PIM
7	359	4.01	1	5	0	0	24	147	.837	4

LAST SEASON

Games played total was full season career low (back and knee injuries). Posted third consecutive winning season, but GAA was three-seasons high.

THE PHYSICAL GAME

Stefan's skating, particularly his exceptional balance, are the keys to his reflex style of goaltending. His balance allows him to regain his stance very quickly after making a save or flopping to the ice, and that balance also allows him to lunge in one direction to get a piece of the puck, even after leaning the other way.

Greg frequently goes to the ice because he doesn't cut his angles as well as he should. Since he isn't squared with the puck, Greg will make phantom saves and has to regain his stance quickly after flashing out a skate toward the puck. Greg's quickness means he'll usually get a piece of any puck, even the ones that get past him for goals. He uses his quickness to its best advantage in goal-mouth scrambles and on deflections, whipping an arm or leg into the path of a seemingly inevitable goal.

Stefan sees the puck well and tracks the play alertly. He will not generally leave his net to handle the puck, and is content to allow it to skitter behind the goal instead of stopping it for his defense. His hands are fast (like his feet), but Stefan is not particularly adept at handling the puck.

THE MENTAL GAME

Greg is one of those hot-and-cold goalies. When he's on he's super, but Stefan is erratic in his performances because he plays so emotionally. One aspect of that emotional game has been his temper and his PIM totals (and, we might add, League-mandated suspensions), but the positive side of that is mental toughness.

He has the ability to come back from bad goals or games, and he can lift his game to fit the circumstances.

THE INTANGIBLES

Because of his abbreviated 1989-90 season, we've left Stefan's report essentially untouched. He has the ability to reach high heights when his concentration is on, but he also has the ability to plummet when his emotions get the better of him. A pressure situation such as the playoffs makes Greg work harder, but he has gone as far as he can as an NHL goaltender. Despite the fact that he can carry the team when hot, Stefan isn't good enough often enough to be placed with the NHL's best goalies.

Add the emergence of Tim Cheveldae, and we may be seeing the last of Stefan in a Detroit uniform.

STEVE YZERMAN

Yrs. of NHL service: 7
Born: Cranbrook, B.C., Canada; May 9, 1965
Position: Center
Height: 5-11
Weight: 185
Uniform no.: 19
Shoots: right

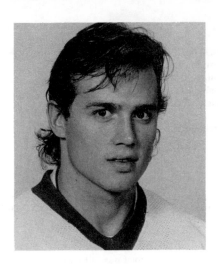

Career statistics:

GP	G	A	TP	PIM
514	291	401	692	334

1989-90 statistics:

GP	G	A	TP	+/-	PIM	PP	SH	GW	GT	S	PCT
79	62	65	127	-5	79	16	7	8	2	332	18.7

LAST SEASON

Yzerman finished third in NHL scoring, second in goals. He led the NHL in shorthanded goals and was second in shots on goal. He led the Wings in every point category, and in shooting percentage. He missed one game with a bruised ankle. Point totals were second highest of career.

THE FINESSE GAME

Easier to say what he can't do: He can't leap tall buildings in a single bound. Otherwise, Yzerman is a superior hockey player in every phase of the game.

His skating combines explosive acceleration and breakaway speed (though his speed is marginally behind the rest of his skating skills), exceptional balance and quickness — across the mobility range, Yzerman is one of the top skaters in the League. He loves to stop and turn, and he's back at top speed in stride.

Ditto his hand skills, which are just as effective when he is standing still as when he's flying down the wing or twisting away from a defender in the crease. The puck goes where he wants it when he wants it there — whether that means passing it or carrying it. He excels at using his teammates.

His scoring ability is frightening from all ranges. He's got a heavy slap shot from outside, and his wrist shot is a blur. He has the hands to work in traffic and needs only the slightest opening to score. He shoots the puck a lot (though his SOG total did fall by about 14 percent from last season — 388 in 1988-89 to 332 last season — and assists from those rebounds may account for his assist total falling from 90 in 1988-89 to 65 last season).

His hockey sense and positional play in all situations are outstanding.

THE PHYSICAL GAME

Yzerman plays big, certainly much bigger than his size, and his willingness to absorb punishment combines with his skills to make him one of the toughest players in the League. He is fearless in all areas of the ice and will hit anyone, and he has deceptive strength. He'll fight to protect himself, and he retaliates with his stick when necessary.

He uses his body well in all three zones in all situations.

THE INTANGIBLES

Considering that his nearest teammate was 47 points behind him (the largest gap in the League), considering that he lacks the offensive defenseman to give him the puck (a la Paul Coffey for Mario Lemieux and Steve Duchesne for Wayne Gretzky) and considering the fact that he was involved in almost 50 percent of his club's goals, there's a good basis for argument that Yzerman is the NHL's best player. We wouldn't argue too hard against that thesis.

Yzerman is an exemplary leader. His character, work ethic and dedication are second to none, and the Wings are lucky to have him to hang their collective hats on.

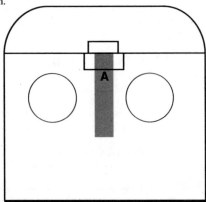

RICK ZOMBO

Yrs. of NHL service: 4
Born: Des Plaines, Illinois, USA; May 8, 1963
Position: Defenseman
Height: 6-1
Weight: 195
Uniform no.: 4
Shoots: right

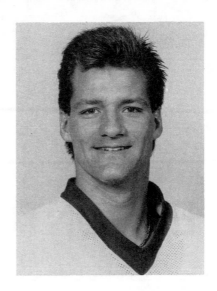

Career statistics:

GP	G	A	TP	PIM
273	10	59	69	372

1989-90 statistics:

GP	G	A	TP	+/-	PIM	PP	SH	GW	GT	S	PCT
77	5	20	25	13	95	0	0	0	0	62	8.1

LAST SEASON

Games played, goal and point totals were career highs. Plus/minus was fourth best.

THE FINESSE GAME

Zombo is your prototypical throwback, the kind of defensive defenseman hardly seen nowadays — and greatly, vastly, underrated as a player. He's a pretty good skater for a big man, certainly mobile enough to step up and challenge at both blue lines (though he does so more at his own line than at thee opposition's), but also smart enough to know which forwards to *not* challenge.

He is a solid positional player, he makes good first passes from his own end to the players ahead of him (thus gaining zones for the Wings), and he demonstrates the patience necessary to handle the puck when he has to.

Zombo reads the ice well in all three zones and can both find the open man and close the defensive hole. Because he concentrates on defense, he's not likely to contribute to the offense; entire games will elapse without his shooting the puck. As such, his points will come on breakout assists and rare blue line shots.

THE PHYSICAL GAME

Zombo is a fairly big man, and he plays a big man's game. He takes the body very well in his own zone and is solid in his crease coverage, but there are times when he is too concerned with hitting (he a l - ways wants to belt someone) and will lose his position — not that you could prove it by his plus/minus rating.

He is also very intelligent in his physical play, keeping himself on the ice and out of the penalty box.

THE INTANGIBLES

By knowing his limitations and staying within them — and while working hard at the same time — Zombo has developed himself into a fine NHL defenseman. He is a player's player, in that his NHL brothers on all teams know and respect his ability — even if the outside world has no idea who he is. For that reason, he just may be the NHL's most underrated player.

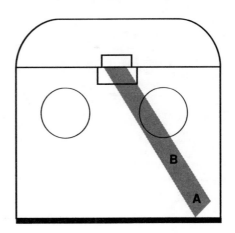

EDMONTON OILERS

GLENN ANDERSON

Yrs. of NHL service: 10
Born: Vancouver, B.C., Canada; October 2, 1960
Position: Right wing
Height: 6-1
Weight: 190
Uniform no.: 9
Shoots: left

Career statistics:

GP	G	A	TP	PIM
754	389	452	841	712

1989-90 statistics:

GP	G	A	TP	+/-	PIM	PP	SH	GW	GT	S	PCT
73	34	38	72	-1	107	17	1	7	1	204	16.7

LAST SEASON

All point totals were second lowest of career. Led club in power play goals and game winners, was second in shots on goal total. Missed six games with a hand injury.

THE FINESSE GAME

Anderson's ability to do things faster than almost anyone in the League (with the possible exception of teammate Mark Messier) makes him a remarkable finesse player. Glenn is an excellent skater with tremendous speed; no one can catch him. His speed is made better because of his balance, so Glenn adds fantastic agility and quickness to his repertoire. His balance makes the opposition suffer the brunt of the physical punishment when Anderson gets hit, rather than the other way around.

Anderson's feet and hand skills are made better by each other, in that Glenn needn't slow down to make his plays. He works excellently at full throttle. His shot gains most from this ability. Because of his lightening-quick release and soft hands, Anderson can score anytime from anywhere — and into any part of the net. He's most usually on net with his shot, and he excels in the traffic around the net for tough goals too.

He's a creative player in the offensive zone without the puck (except that he likes to go to the net from the right side), and his good vision and anticipation allow him to make good use of his teammates.

THE PHYSICAL GAME

Glenn plays like a kamikaze, flinging his body into people with abandon. As mentioned, his exceptional balance makes him successful here. He initiates a good deal of contact and is unafraid of the hitting that accompanies his work in the corners, and he'll also get his stick into people.

THE INTANGIBLES

Those who came to bury Anderson and not to praise him were a bit premature last season. He rebounded — to a degree — during the regular season, but he once again demonstrated that it is in Stanley Cup play that he shows best — he was one of Edmonton's five best players, especially in the Cup Final.

Which is not to say that he doesn't have to play during the regular season, only that his career — both as an Oiler and as an NHLer — isn't quite in the downturn certain people thought it might be.

Mea culpa.

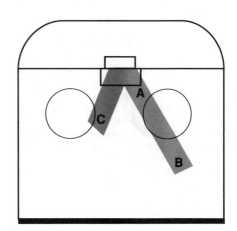

JEFF BEUKEBOOM

Yrs. of NHL service: 4
Born: Ajax, Ontario, Canada; March 28, 1965
Position: Defenseman
Height: 6-4
Weight: 215
Uniform no.: 6
Shoots: right

Career statistics:

GP	G	A	TP	PIM
199	9	45	54	505

1989-90 statistics:

GP	G	A	TP	+/-	PIM	PP	SH	GW	GT	S	PCT
46	1	12	13	5	86	0	0	0	0	34	2.8

LAST SEASON

Assist total was second highest of career.

THE FINESSE GAME

Beukeboom has made improvements in his NHL game, most notably in his skating and playreading ability. He is a smoother skater with improved speed, quickness and agility both forward and back, but he is a little weak in his turns to his left.

Jeff has also improved his understanding of the NHL play, including reading the play and reacting to it more quickly. He is recognizing the rush toward him earlier and combines that better read with his better skating to more consistently force the play wide and to more consistently close the gap on the puck carrier.

He can make the plays to the forwards and has improved in this aspect of his game (better skating equals more time to look and make a play), but right now is content to be the takeout defenseman, rather than the breakout defender. That role befits his modest finesse ability.

THE PHYSICAL GAME

Jeff is big and likes to hit, so he can certainly be said to get the most from his size. He is an aggressive player in front of the net and in the corners and he punishes people when he hits them, but he does need to be reminded to use his physical gifts at all times.

Again, his improved finesse skills — notably his skating — help him to be a better physical player. Since he moves his feet better, Jeff is better able to get to the opposition and use his strength.

THE INTANGIBLES

Beukeboom is a sincere and mature young man, one who works hard at improving his skills. He needs to develop the intensity necessary to play at his best level — and with his best skills working for him — every night. More than anything, that will gain him ice time.

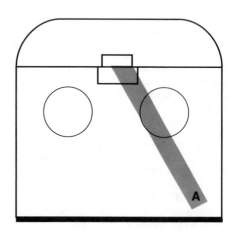

DAVE BROWN

Yrs. of NHL service: 7
Born: Saskatoon, Sask., Canada; October 12, 1962
Position: Right wing
Height: 6-5
Weight: 205
Uniform no.: 32
Shoots: right

Career statistics:

GP	G	A	TP	PIM
395	33	37	70	1,234

1989-90 statistics:

GP	G	A	TP	+/-	PIM	PP	SH	GW	GT	S	PCT
60	0	6	6	-3	145	0	0	0	0	32	0.0

LAST SEASON

Finished fifth on club in PIM total.

THE FINESSE GAME

Brown remains a below-average finesse player, though he has improved his skills. He still lumbers up and down the ice, though smoother and with better balance than previously. He has little speed and less agility.

He can handle the puck when going straight forward in his wing position, but is not really an accomplished puck handler. If given time and space, he can get the puck to his teammates, but he lacks the vision and anticipation (the hockey sense, really) to be a consistent offensive player.

His scoring will have to be done from directly in front of the net. He can play well defensively if matched against an equally-talented opponent.

THE PHYSICAL GAME

A physical style of game would seem to benefit Brown, but that's not so. Because he's unable to catch most everyone, and thus can't hit them, a mucking role is currently out of Brown's grasp; opponents just step out of his way and let him thunder by. Additionally, when he is able to connect he's probably going to get the worst of the bargain because his balance is bad.

He is a fighter, and that's what keeps him in the NHL. Brown's fighting clears the way for players like Esa Tikkanen to be pests on the ice, for Brown will take care of anyone who disapproves of Tikkanen's tactics. While he has a big reputation, Brown is not one of the NHL's best fighters, as he has had trouble with smaller opponents who won't be intimidated.

THE INTANGIBLES

What's to say — the guy knows his role and plays it. As with any other limited player, he is on the edge of replacement — all that's necessary is a guy to show up who's anywhere near as tough and more talented.

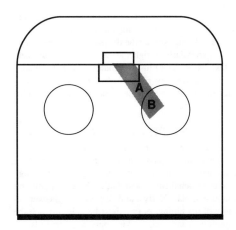

KELLY BUCHBERGER

Yrs. of NHL service: 2
Born: Langenburg, Sask., Canada; December 2, 1966
Position: Left wing
Height: 6-2
Weight: 205
Uniform no.: 16
Shoots: left

Career statistics:

GP	G	A	TP	PIM
140	8	15	23	483

1989-90 statistics:

GP	G	A	TP	+/-	PIM	PP	SH	GW	GT	S	PCT
55	2	6	8	-8	168	0	0	2	0	35	5.7

LAST SEASON

Plus/minus rating was third worst among regulars, PIM total third highest. Suffered a late season shoulder injury.

THE FINESSE GAME

Strength more than finesse is the hallmark of Buchberger's game. He's a strong skater with some speed, but not yet consistent agility or quickness at the NHL level. He lacks an understanding of the NHL game in terms of speed, so Kelly is going to have trouble making a play or reading a rush.

That means he has to succeed as a puck pursuing type of forward, rather than one who actively reads the ice and makes decisions that affect the opposition. But since he has to do that, he frequently finds himself out of position — thus, the poor plus/minus. He needs to develop judgement (read and react) skills.

He doesn't yet handle the puck well when carrying it, particularly at higher speeds, so he's as unlikely to take advantage of his teammates as he is to create a scoring opportunity for himself. He uses his skating strength to drive to the crease, and he'll have to get his goals from there.

THE PHYSICAL GAME

This is where Buchberger can shine. His strength gives a relentless quality to his skating, so his checking is insistent and physical. He can rap guys pretty good, *if* he can catch them — and that's where the agility bit comes into play. Kelly can be a good forechecker because of his hitting, but he must be able to reach the defensemen and backchecking opposing forwards.

Obviously too, he has no problem throwing his fists.

THE INTANGIBLES

Buchberger can make his mark as one of the ground soldiers who opens up space for the better players — the infantry clearing the way for the cavalry, so to speak. Improved mental skill would greatly improve his overall game, and his growing NHL experience may speak to that issue.

For a physical player, one who must succeed by using his body and strength, Buchberger has suffered some fairly substantial injuries (broken ankle two seasons ago, shoulder injury last season).

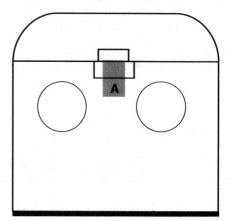

GRANT FUHR

Yrs. of NHL service: 9
Born: Spruce Grove, Alta., Canada; September 28, 1962
Position: Goaltender
Height: 5-10
Weight: 185
Uniform no.: 31
Catches: right

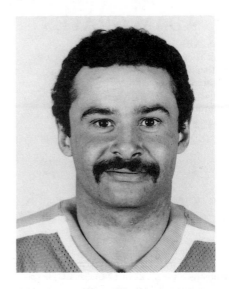

Career statistics:

GP	MINS	G	SO	AVG	A	PIM
410	23,132	1,431	8	3.71	36	54

1989-90 statistics:

GP	MINS	AVG	W	L	T	SO	GA	SA	SAPCT	PIM
21	1,081	3.89	9	7	3	1	70	532	.868	2

LAST SEASON

Games played total was career low; missed six games with appendectomy, missed 32 games with shoulder injury and surgery, and then was sidelined again with recurring shoulder injury.

THE PHYSICAL GAME

Fuhr combines his outstanding reflexes with a modified stand-up style to great succes as the NHL's best goaltender. He has the NHL's best hand and foot speed, and he maximizes those skills by squaring himself to the puck and cutting down the shooter's angle excellently.

When forced to move, Grant does so with great ease because of his excellent skating skill. Fuhr has tremendous balance, so his lateral movement is exceptional. He regains his feet (after going to the ice) or his stance (after movement) almost instantaneously. He moves in and out of the net and around the defensive zone excellently.

His one weakness is between the pads, and that's because Grant keeps his weight on his inside edges — because he likes to butterfly. That weight distribution sometimes makes it difficult for Fuhr to snap his legs closed but — really — his foot and leg speed usually closes that hole very quickly.

He handles the puck better than almost any other goaltender and often starts plays up ice by sending the puck to the forwards. Grant handles his stick well and has the fastest glove hand — just pure radar — in the world.

THE MENTAL GAME

His attitude and mental outlook are at least as large a reason for Fuhr's success as is his physical skill. He is unaffected by the circumstances of the game and is essentially nerveless. Pressure means nothing to him. Stanley Cup games, Canada Cup games, mid-December Norris Division games — they're all the same to Fuhr.

Neither bad goals nor bad performances bother him; Fuhr just shrugs them all off. His concentration is excellent and he maintains it throughout any type of game, but Fuhr also pulls his game to the level of the game being played.

Right now, he's still the NHL's best money goaltender.

THE INTANGIBLES

Our choice as the world's best goaltender needs to demonstrate complete recuperation from his shoulder problems (which have plagued him throughout his career). Until then, everything else is on hold — including discussion about his being replaced by Bill Ranford as the club's number one goalie (a move which would be premature, in our opinion).

ADAM GRAVES

Yrs. of NHL service: 2
Born: Toronto, Ontario, Canada; April 12, 1968
Position: Left wing/center
Height: 5-11
Weight: 200
Uniform no.: 12
Shoots: left

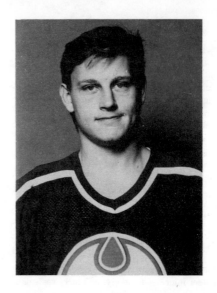

Career statistics:

GP	G	A	TP	PIM
141	16	19	35	204

1989-90 statistics:

GP	G	A	TP	+/-	PIM	PP	SH	GW	GT	S	PCT
76	9	13	22	0	136	1	0	1	0	94	9.6

LAST SEASON

Acquired along with Petr Klima, Joe Murphy and Jeff Sharples from Detroit in November in exchange for Jimmy Carson and Kevin McClelland. Games played and all point totals were career highs.

THE FINESSE GAME

Graves is a very talented finesse player. He's an excllent skater with balance, strength and agility. He has good-to-very-good quickness, and that trait combines with his balance to give him good change of direction and lateral movements skills.

Adam's stick skills match his foot skills. He controls the puck very well (especially when he plays in traffic), and he also shoots the puck well. His shot is hard and accurate, forcing the goaltender to make saves.

His physical finesse skills are amplified by his hockey sense. Graves has a great sense of where the puck will be and what is the best way for him to get there. He also plays an aware and disciplined defensive game, and his skills make him a good transitional player — he'll skillfully get the play started from the defensive zone.

THE PHYSICAL GAME

Though he doesn't have great size, Graves has great strength and he plays a very physical game. He works very well against the boards and in traffic because of his strength and balance, and he likes to play a hitting game.

He's an aggressive player but a smart one, so he won't hurt his team with penalties. His strength powers his shot and also makes him a good faceoff man.

THE INTANGIBLES

Here's a guy with the talent and determination to control a game — particularly in the mucking aspects, the dirty-nose areas of the offensive zone. He is a dedicated player with great intensity; already he is being talked of as a junior Mark Messier. That kind of description might be a bit premature, but there's no questioning the innate talent and inner drive Graves brings to the Oilers. He will be a leader for Edmonton in a very short time.

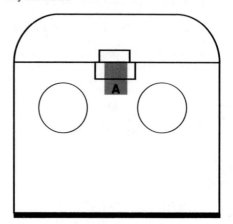

MARTIN GELINAS

Yrs. of NHL service: 1
Born: Shawinigan, Quebec, Canada; June 5, 1970
Position: Left wing
Height: 5-11
Weight: 195
Uniform no.: 20
Shoots: left

Career statistics:

GP	G	A	TP	PIM
52	18	10	28	30

1989-90 statistics:

GP	G	A	TP	+/-	PIM	PP	SH	GW	GT	S	PCT
46	17	8	25	0	30	5	0	2	2	71	23.9

LAST SEASON

First full NHL season. Led club in shooting percentage.

THE FINESSE GAME

Gelinas is a tremendously talented finesse player, one with talent across the board. He has rink-length speed, the kind that can blow the doors off the defense, and he also has the balance and agility to race past the defense and then cut inside to the net. His balance also serves him in the traffic areas near the net where he maintains excellent body position and control.

In turn, his hand skills feed off that balance. He controls the puck excellently and is very dangerous in traffic because of his ability to make plays and shoot the puck while being leaned on or otherwise checked. He has the hand skills to finesse the puck from in tight, and his shooting skill is very high: quick, accurate shots that force goalies to make saves.

Gelinas is a primarily a scorer, so he's going to look to the net before he looks to his teammates. He does have the ability to float passes to them, but his sense is primarily a goal scorer's: get into scoring position and the puck will follow.

He works at his defensive game, and is playing fairly well positionally.

THE PHYSICAL GAME

Gelinas is not a physical player per se, but he'll take his share of knocks as he works around the opposing goal. He leans in on the opposition well enough that his hand skills can go to work taking the puck away, and Gelinas will plant himself in front of the net on the power play and take his punishment.

THE INTANGIBLES

Gelinas' play during the Stanley Cup playoffs was the most eye-opening of the three kids (Adam Graves and Joe Murphy) Edmonton put together as a line, but that's only because his skills are the most obviously spectacular. Nevertheless, Gelinas showed all the weapons in his arsenal during the NHL's most difficult time to shine, and that just bodes well for Gelinas' future NHL success — which can be considerable.

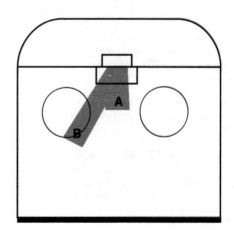

RANDY GREGG

Yrs. of NHL service: 8
Born: Edmonton, Alta., Canada; February 19, 1956
Position: Defenseman
Height: 6-4
Weight: 215
Uniform no.: 21
Shoots: left

Career statistics:

GP	G	A	TP	PIM
453	40	148	188	299

1989-90 statistics:

GP	G	A	TP	+/-	PIM	PP	SH	GW	GT	S	PCT
48	4	20	24	24	42	0	0	0	0	41	9.8

LAST SEASON

Games played total was second lowest of career (missed significant time with preseason groin injury, and three games with leg injury). Plus/minus was club's overall best.

THE FINESSE GAME

Gregg is a good skater both forward and backward, with an efficient more than spectacular style. He's fairly fluid though not exceptionally agile, and he lacks real speed or quickness, but his hockey sense more than compensates for any skating deficiencies he might have.

He is a defensive style defenseman, moving the puck quickly for the forwards to carry up-ice. Though he will make a foray or two, rushing the puck is not Gregg's strong point. Rather, he quickly turns the puck up-ice.

Randy reads the rush very well and channels it wide of the net effectively. He rarely makes a defensive mistake and that's important for as it allows the Oilers to rev up their speed game for offense knowing someone can not just hold the fort but successfully defend it.

Gregg will join the play up-ice and he will control the point well, but rarely pinches in. He has an average shot from the point but will find the open man for a pass.

THE PHYSICAL GAME

As with his finesse play, steady and unspectacular describes Gregg's physical game. He takes the body very well, is strong and clears the front of the net or holds the opposition out of the play well.

He puts his reach to work deflecting passes and pokechecking the puck, and he will also sacrifice his body to block shots.

THE INTANGIBLES

Gregg is an excellent defensive defenseman, one of the League's best in that regard. The steadiness and stability he provides to the Oilers is probably the biggest (though unmeasureable) intangible of all.

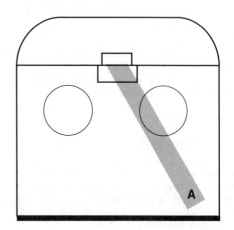

CHARLIE HUDDY

Yrs. of NHL service: 9
Born: Oshawa, Ontario, Canada; June 2, 1959
Position: Defenseman
Height: 6-0
Weight: 210
Uniform no.: 22
Shoots: left

Career statistics:

GP	G	A	TP	PIM
641	76	265	341	468

1989-90 statistics:

GP	G	A	TP	+/-	PIM	PP	SH	GW	GT	S	PCT
70	1	23	24	-13	56	1	0	1	0	119	.8

LAST SEASON

Games played total was three-season low and second-lowest full-season mark of career. Goal total was career low, assist and point totals second lowest full-season marks of career. Plus/minus mark was poorest among regulars.

THE FINESSE GAME

Charlie's hockey sense is his outstanding finesse skill. He reads plays very well, breaks up rushes excellently by forcing the opposition wide of the net and he can step into an offensive rush up-ice if need be, moving the puck quickly and smoothly. That playreading ability makes him one of the best pinching defensemen in the League.

Huddy combines his ice vision with his hand skills to move the puck to the open man well in both zones. He controls the point well because he is a good stickhandler, much better than he is given credit for. When shooting, Charlie delivers a hard slap shot from the point, one that is accurate and low, good for tip-ins and deflections. He'll move to the deep slot if he can.

Huddy is a good skater, probably above average but without any exceptional skill in this asset. Neither tremendously agile nor exceptionally fast, Charlie skates well both forward and backward and is smooth in his pivots.

THE PHYSICAL GAME

Huddy doesn't have great size or strength, but he'll hold his own against most players in the corner and crease battles. He'll make a play quickly because of his balance and hand skills, but Charlie will find himself out-matched against the League's bigger and stronger forwards; he'll be paired with a stronger partner because of that.

He will sacrifice his body by blocking shots.

THE INTANGIBLES

Huddy is a dependable NHL defenseman, the kind who can contribute at both ends of the ice. Still, the Oilers have a backlog of defensive prospects and it wouldn't be surprising to see Huddy playing elsewhere within a season.

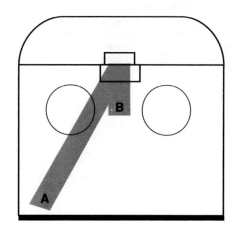

PETR KLIMA

Yrs. of NHL service: 5
Born: Chaomutov, Czechoslovakia; December 23, 1964
Position: Left wing
Height: 6-0
Weight: 190
Uniform no.: 85
Shoots: left

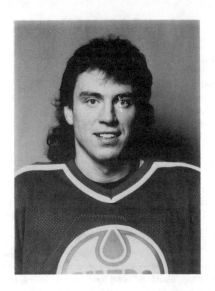

Career statistics:

GP	G	A	TP	PIM
356	154	121	275	220

1989-90 statistics:

GP	G	A	TP	+/-	PIM	PP	SH	GW	GT	S	PCT
76	30	33	63	-9	72	9	0	3	0	186	16.1

LAST SEASON

Acquired along with Joe Murphy, Jeff Sharples and Adam Graves in November in exchange for Jimmy Carson and Kevin McClelland. Point total was second highest of career, assist total career high. Plus/minus was second poorest among regulars, worst among forwards.

THE FINESSE GAME

Klima is an excellent skater in all skating areas: quickness, speed, balance, power and agility. He will out-race most any checker, or cut inside most any defenseman. He stops on a dime, has tremendous one-step quickness, and his explosive acceleration puts him in the clear within two strides.

Petr's hand skills are as superior as his foot skills. He plays with the defense when he carries the puck, and he's got the hands to work with the puck in tight situations. That skill extends to his shot. His shot selection is excellent, and his slap shot from the wing will beat any goaltender in the League — if it gets on net; Klima will shoot 10-15 times a game and have just 2-3 shots on goal. He must make goaltenders work to stop his shot.

His abilities to anticipate and get into position to score are very high. He has excellent hockey sense in the offensive zone, and he uses his finesse skills to drive for the openings. All of his skills make him a natural for specialty teams duty.

His defense has improved from peremptory to something-better-than-casual, but he remains inconsistent in his defensive play from shift to shift and game to game.

THE PHYSICAL GAME

While primarily an open ice player, Klima has gradually edged closer and closer to the boards and corners. He's getting his body in the way of the opposition. There is still room for improvement in this area, as Klima still prefers the outside of the scrum. But Klima even tosses the occasional check here and there.

THE INTANGIBLES

The Oilers have done wonders over the years for players who were characters who needed to become character players. We're not saying they can do that for Klima; he has to want to do that himself. But surely the best thing possible for a pointer to the right road is a Stanley Cup win, and perhaps that experience will help Klima in his attempts to mature.

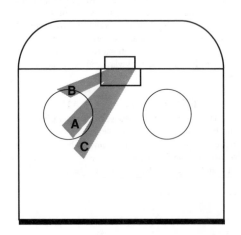

JARI KURRI

Yrs. of NHL service: 10
Born: Helsinki, Finland; May 18, 1960
Position: Right wing
Height: 6-1
Weight: 195
Uniform no.: 17
Shoots: right

Career statistics:

GP	G	A	TP	PIM
754	474	569	1,043	348

1989-90 statistics:

GP	G	A	TP	+/-	PIM	PP	SH	GW	GT	S	PCT
78	33	60	93	18	48	10	2	2	1	201	16.4

LAST SEASON

Assist total was four-season high, but point total was third lowest of career. Finished second on club in assists and points, tied for third in plus/minus rating among regulars (Kevin Lowe, and third in shots on goal totals. Missed one game with groin injury.

THE FINESSE GAME

Kurri is an outstanding finesse player. He's an outstanding skater with exceptional balance, quickness and speed, and he uses those abilities to dip and duck around and behind the defense to snare passes and loose pucks. His outstanding one-step quickness translates into excellent lateral movement and direction changing ability, and Kurri uses those to hit the openings in the offensive zone.

Jari complements that ability — in fact, makes that ability what it is — by using his great instincts and anticipation to get into scoring position. Kurri may be the NHL's most creative player without the puck, using the ice well to create openings by moving from lane to lane.

His shot is probably the best of his physical finesse skills. Jari needs just the slightest opening (and gets it with his quickness) and his quickly released, hard and accurate wrist shot is goal-bound. He excels at one-timing the puck. He is dangerous around the net because his balance and superior hand skills allow him to control the puck in traffic.

His puckhandling is excellent, he takes a pass in stride better than most NHLers, and his sense and hands combine to make him a good passer. When he chooses to carry the puck into the offensive zone, he likes to skate parallel to the blue line from the left wing to the right wing boards, and then jet around the defense.

Kurri's skills make him an exceptional specialty teams player. His scoring ability is evident on the power play, and he uses his breakaway speed and anticipation to score short-handed. He is also a fine positional player defensively.

THE PHYSICAL GAME

Kurri isn't a physical player per se, in that he doesn't smash the opposition into the boards, but Jari excels at taking the body efficiently along the boards — thus allowing his balance and hand skills to come into play.

He is un-intimidatable, going into the corners and taking any abuse aimed his way.

THE INTANGIBLES

Kurri is a fantastic two-way player, and he is also a player with great mental toughness, intensity and dedication. He's one of the finest NHLers of this or any other decade, and he most certainly can and has been successful without Wayne Gretzky at his side. We're sorry some people are more interested in headlines than thay are at truth, and we're sorry they savage Kurri for headlines' sake — this future Hall of Famer deserves better.

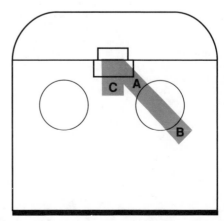

MARK LAMB

Yrs. of NHL service: 2
Born: Ponteix, Sask., Canada; August 3, 1964
Position: Center
Height: 5-9
Weight: 180
Uniform no.: 7
Shoots: left

Career statistics:

GP	G	A	TP	PIM
103	16	25	41	64

1989-90 statistics:

GP	G	A	TP	+/-	PIM	PP	SH	GW	GT	S	PCT
58	12	16	28	10	42	2	0	2	0	81	14.8

LAST SEASON

First full NHL season; point totals were all career highs.

THE FINESSE GAME

Lamb is a small, tricky forward with the kind of finesse skills that befit that image. He's a good skater wih quickness and fine mobility, and he uses those skills to great effect as a checker and forechecker. He's gifted with a good degree of hockey sense, and he uses that ability to be an active force in the offensive zone instead of just reacting to the puck.

He handles the puck very well and can get it to his wingers, but he still hasn't quite got the feel for NHL speed. As well, because he's not overly fast, he's not going to see or create a lot of openings. In that sense, his offense has to come reactively as he pounces on mistakes or loose pucks.

Despite his puck skills he'll have to be near the net to score, using his skills opportunistically. He's a strong defensive and positional player.

THE PHYSICAL GAME

Lamb doesn't have good size, but he uses what he does have aggressively. He uses his good balance and strength afoot to make good takeouts in his checking, suprisingly strong for his size. That said, Lamb will be overwhelmed in traffic situations when playing against players anywhere near his equal skill-wise.

He has to be used wisely, so as to minimize his physical limits and maximize his finesse strengths.

THE INTANGIBLES

Lamb's a worker, the kind of guy who can succeed by filling a role on a stronger club. He can continue to do that for Edmonton, and his as yet untapped offensive potential (he was a dominant player in the American Hockey League) may be able to surface enough keep him just above that role player (and therefore easily replaceable) line.

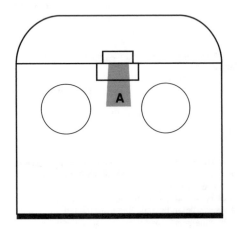

KEVIN LOWE

Yrs. of NHL service: 11
Born: Lachute, Quebec, Canada; April 15, 1959
Position: Defenseman
Height: 6-2
Weight: 195
Uniform no.: 4
Shoots: left

Career statistics:

GP	G	A	TP	PIM
838	68	275	343	908

1989-90 statistics:

GP	G	A	TP	+/-	PIM	PP	SH	GW	GT	S	PCT
78	7	26	33	18	140	2	1	0	0	74	9.5

LAST SEASON

Games played total was five-season high, point total three-season high. Plus/minus rating tied for fourth best (Jari Kurri).

THE FINESSE GAME

Smarts are what make Lowe the defensive force he is. His oustanding hockey sense and vision give him superior understanding of the defensive play, and he uses that skill to make both the correct plays and the good ones.

Kevin easily forces the play wide of the net, and his sense makes his skating better — it allows him to step up and challenge the play at his blue line, but he won't force a play where one doesn't exist. He's a good skater in all directions, and he maintains good agility and lateral movement. Lowe isn't very fast, but his strength and balance help him work in traffic.

And even as he makes his move, Lowe knows what he's going to do after he gains the puck. Kevin's anticipation and vision work on the second half of the defensive play, when he relieves the enemy of the puck and starts the play up ice.

He sees the best play presented, Lowe will make that best play eight-to-nine times out of 10. He moves the puck quickly and crisply to the forwards, using his good hand skills on breakouts and at the opposing blue line (when he follows the play up ice).

Lowe can skate the puck if necessary, but he isn't a puck carrying defender. Nor is he an offensive threat at the NHL level, so the handful of goals he scores each year will come from the point.

THE PHYSICAL GAME

Lowe plays a very efficient physical game, one marked — like his finesse game — by smarts. Instead of immediately pounding the opposition into tomorrow (which Lowe despite his good size and strength isn't really suited for), Kevin waits for the correct moment to start pounding. By doing so he stays physical and avoids penalties.

His crease coverage is excellent, and he takes people off the puck with authority in the corners. His good balance leaves him in position to make plays after hits, making his hitting more valuable. He uses his good reach to pokecheck or deflect pucks efficiently.

He's an excellent open-ice hitter, and Lowe is absolutely fearless in sacrificing his body to block shots.

THE INTANGIBLES

You couldn't find a more determined, intense player anywhere in the NHL — and we're including Lowe's teammate Mark Messier. Lowe plays in pain and regardless of personal concern. He is a tremendous team man and a tremendous leader, just as he is a tremendous player.

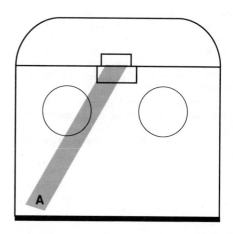

CRAIG MACTAVISH

Yrs. of NHL service: 9
Born: London, Ontario, Canada; August 15, 1958
Position: Center
Height: 6-1
Weight: 195
Uniform no.: 14
Shoots: left

Career statistics:

GP	G	A	TP	PIM
610	144	179	323	390

1989-90 statistics:

GP	G	A	TP	+/-	PIM	PP	SH	GW	GT	S	PCT
80	21	22	43	13	89	1	6	5	0	109	19.3

LAST SEASON

Third straight 80-game season. Point total was second highest of career. Tied for team lead in shorthanded goals (Mark Messier).

THE FINESSE GAME

MacTavish has become a good skater with a lot of strength in his stride. He is neither exceptionally fast nor outstandingly quick, but he pursues the puck well at a steady pace. He has good balance — which helps his physical game — and he uses his skating skills to be a good two-way player who's able to contribute at both ends of the ice. Craig can move the puck fairly well within his class of player, and he can get it to his teammates effectively. He also demonstrated a scoring touch around the net.

Craig's anticipation, hockey sense and ice vision are his primary tools as a defensive center. He recognizes where the openings will be and uses his strong skating to thwart the opposition's intentions.

THE PHYSICAL GAME

MacTavish complements his checking by bodychecking. He initiates contact along the boards and in open ice, and he also absorbs his share of abuse when camped out in front of the opposition's net. He applies himself along the boards and can muscle the opposition off the puck. He's still not a belter, more of a pusher and shover, but he's become increasingly effective in the traffic areas.

One reason for that is his improved balance, for it is that skill that adds to his leg strength and helps keep him vertical in contact situations.

He is strong on faceoffs because of his eye/hand coordination.

THE INTANGIBLES

By contributing so strongly at both ends of the ice, MacTavish has raised himself from the mere role-player class. His dedication and work ethic are the underpinnings of his success, just as his performance is one of the underpinnings for Edmonton's success.

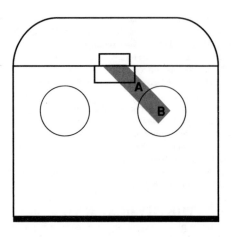

MARK MESSIER

Yrs. of NHL service: 11
Born: Edmonton, Alta., Canada; January 18, 1961
Position: Center
Height: 6-1
Weight: 210
Uniform no.: 11
Shoots: left

Career statistics:

GP	G	A	TP	PIM
798	380	590	970	1,088

1989-90 statistics:

GP	G	A	TP	+/-	PIM	PP	SH	GW	GT	S	PCT
79	45	84	129	19	79	13	6	3		2	211	21.3

LAST SEASON

Finished second overall in NHL in points and assists, third in shorthanded goals, second in first goals. Led club in all point and shots on goal categories, was second in power play goals, shooting percentage and plus/minus rating among regulars (first among forwards). Assist and point totals were career highs.

THE FINESSE GAME

Messier is the League's best combination of finesse and physical skills — the prototypical power forward. He's an excellent skater with blazing speed and superior agility and lateral movement; he literally changes direction and speed within a stride. Messier consistently does more things faster than anyone else in the League.

Mark's hand skills are the equal of his foot skills. He's an excellent puckhandler who can do anything with the puck at any speed. He can get the puck to a teammate anywhere, or he can work around an opposing defenseman just as easily.

He has superior anticipation and hockey sense, making him dangerous at both ends of the rink. Defensively he is unparalleled, simply skating over the opposing center almost without exception. He backchecks excellently and is aided by his playreading ability and hockey sense.

His best scoring weapon is his wrist shot, made especially effective by his ability to deliver it in stride. He uses that shot almost exclusively and, though Mark is another player who can score from anywhere, the majority of his goals will come from the high traffic area near the net.

All his skills combine to make him a specialty team natural. His quickness and sense make him a shorthanded scoring threat, and his ability to either work the corners or the front of the net, or keeping the passing lanes open with his one-step quickness, gives him power play success.

THE PHYSICAL GAME

Though tremendously strong, it is Messier's balance that keys his physical game. It allows him to crash into the opposition yet remain vertical, and thus able to continue the play.

Mark has excellent size and strength, and he will out-muscle anyone anywhere, hit often and punishingly (thanks to leg and upper body strength) and hurt the people he hits. Mark will fight and he has a nasty temper — which helps make him mean with his stick.

His hand and wrist strength, combined with his quickness and eye/hand coordination, make him one of the best faceoff men in hockey.

THE INTANGIBLES

We told you last year that Messier's combination of awesome playing ability and incredible drive, desire and intensity made him the best all-around player in the world. This season — after a career year, after a fifth Stanley Cup — he was voted the League's Most Valuable Player. Nothing else need be said.

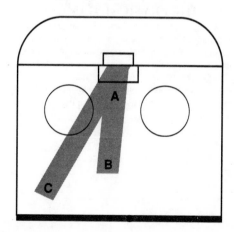

CRAIG MUNI

Yrs. of NHL service: 4
Born: Toronto, Ontario, Canada; July 19, 1962
Position: Defenseman
Height: 6-3
Weight: 200
Uniform no.: 28
Shoots: left

Career statistics:

GP	G	A	TP	PIM
310	21	64	85	320

1989-90 statistics:

GP	G	A	TP	+/-	PIM	PP	SH	GW	GT	S	PCT
71	5	12	17	22	81	0	2	0	0	42	11.9

LAST SEASON

All point totals were career lows (missed eight games with a broken finger). Led all regulars in plus/minus rating.

THE FINESSE GAME

Muni is a deceptive skater, in that he doesn't seem to possess either great speed or quickness, balance or agility. But somehow, he gets to where he has to be when he has to be there. He uses his modest speed and quickness to challenge the opposing forward, and Craig makes those plays work by not over-extending himself or challenging foolishly.

He remains essentially a conservative player, and Muni succeeds by identifying the best play and making it. He doesn't get fancy with the puck, he just gets the job done. He knows to move the puck with his head up, so he sees his options and his best opportunities.

Because he'll fall back to defend, Muni isn't an offensive threat. But when given the time, Muni can find the open man in the offensive zone. His shot is no better than average, and he'll do his scoring from the point.

THE PHYSICAL GAME

Craig has good size and strength, and he uses them smartly and efficiently. He takes men out of the play in front of the net and along the boards with little flair but great success, and the use of his strength is made better by the fact that he stays out of the penalty box.

He takes the body well along the boards, and Muni makes sure to complete his takeouts so the opposition can't sneak behind him — and back into the play. He sacrifices his body to block shots.

THE INTANGIBLES

No one's exactly sure how he does it, but that mystery can't detract from the fact that Muni has become one of the NHL's best defensive players over the last several seasons.

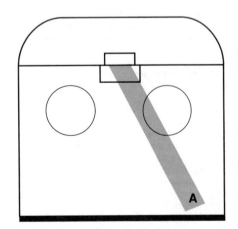

JOE MURPHY

Yrs. of NHL service: 3
Born: London, Ontario, Canada; October 16, 1967
Position: Left wing/center
Height: 6-1
Weight: 190
Uniform no.: 8
Shoots: left

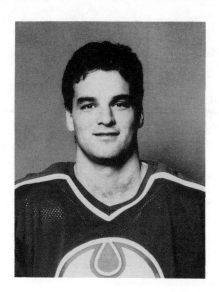

Career statistics:

GP	G	A	TP	PIM
152	21	36	57	127

1989-90 statistics:

GP	G	A	TP	+/-	PIM	PP	SH	GW	GT	S	PCT
71	10	19	29	5	60	2	0	1	0	117	8.5

LAST SEASON

Acquired from Detroit in November 1989 along with Petr Klima, Jeff Sharples and Adam Graves in exchange for Jimmy Carson and Kevin McClelland. Games played, assist and point totals were career highs.

THE FINESSE GAME

Murphy is a good skater with foot speed, acceleration ability and balance. The three combine to make him fairly agile, but he could improve on all three at the NHL level (right now, only his acceleration stands out).

He handles the puck with average skill at the NHL level, more because the play is still a little too quick for him than because he doesn't have the hand skills. He can stickhandle and control the puck in traffic, and that's because Murphy has sensitive hands for puck work.

His hockey sense and passing skills can combine to make him a good playmaker, but again he's not yet reacting with NHL speed, so his passes will hit skates and the opposition instead of finding their intended targets. Still, he can pass well to both sides.

His sense and vision also help him get into position to score, but he has yet to show that he reads the ice fully or that his anticipation is above the ordinary. He plays with his head up, and that always helps all phases of the game.

Murphy has a good slapshot, heavy and quick, and he can deliver it from a distance. Right now, because of his checking/mucking role, most of his goals will come from loose pucks forced free near the net. That's okay, because Murphy's wrist shot is also good (well released and accurate) and he can shoot off the stickhandle too.

He's playing fairly sound defense, but he needs to concentrate on staying with his man all the way back to the Oiler net.

THE PHYSICAL GAME

Murphy has good size and strength, and he's putting it to use by going into the corners and by banging along the boards. He bodychecks well and his balance helps him stay involved in the play by keeping him vertical after collisions.

THE INTANGIBLES

There's nothing more questionable — and questioned — than a first round draft choice. Unless it's a first round draft choice with a bad reputation.

That's why the cliched change of scenery will probably be the best thing that could ever happen to Murphy. His play throughout the end of last season and through the playoffs gave a strong indication that this young man is ready to fully accept the rigors of the NHL, and is ready to work and apply the intensity necessary for NHL success.

BILL RANFORD

Yrs. of NHL service: 4
Born: Brandon, Man., Canada; December 14, 1966
Position: Goaltender
Height: 5-10
Weight: 170
Uniform no.: 30
Catches: left

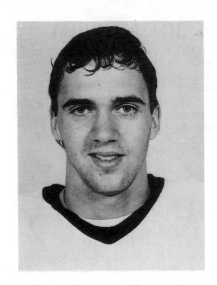

Career statistics:

GP	MINS	G	SO	AVG	A	PIM
136	7,415	403	5	3.26	5	28

1989-90 statistics:

GP	MINS	AVG	W	L	T	SO	GA	SA	SAPCT	PIM
56	3,107	3.19	24	16	9	1	165	1,463	.887	18

LAST SEASON

Games played total was career high, fourth-highest total in NHL. Finished fifth overall in wins. Missed six games with ankle injury.

THE PHYSICAL GAME

Ranford is a standup goaltender, coming out of his net to challenge the shooters because he is a strong skater. When he is on Ranford plays his angles very well, but he does have the tendency of losing his net at times. He stands up well and maintains that stance — instead of going to the ice — on screen shots and shots from the point with crowds around the net.

He has very quick reflexes and moves well in and out of the net (Ranford leaves the net to handle the puck), but his movement across the crease — his lateral movement — could improve. He has not yet learned to control a rebound after a save, so the second save is a problem for him. Of particular concern would be his tendency to leave fat rebounds off pad saves.

Because Bill frequently gets by on the speed of his hands and feet, he has a tendency to not get back into his stance — surviving, as it were, on reflex. Because of that, he is often too deep into his net when the puck is in the slot. The results are goals allowed to the corners, especially low.

THE MENTAL GAME

He's got good confidence in his ability, and Ranford showed beyond question during last season's playoffs that he can raise the level of his intensity and concentration — and therefore the level of his game — to match the importance of the contest. He demonstrated big-save, game-stealing ability.

THE INTANGIBLES

We said last year that playing along-side Grant Fuhr actually meant playing behind Grant Fuhr. We're not quite ready to say that Ranford could replace Fuhr, simply because Ranford lacks the depth of competitive and championship experience that Fuhr has. On the other hand, and especially considering his history of injury and his age, Fuhr may never be more marketable than he is now.

At any rate, Ranford has matured tremendously in his game and mental outlook, remaining confident in his innate — and preferred — ability to stop pucks by reflex but maximizing that talent by using it when necessary (by playing a challenging style) instead of always.

CRAIG SIMPSON

Yrs. of NHL service: 5
Born: London, Ontario, Canada; February 15, 1967
Position: Right wing/left wing
Height: 6-2
Weight: 195
Uniform no.: 18
Shoots: right

Career statistics:

GP	G	A	TP	PIM
374	157	149	306	443

1989-90 statistics:

GP	G	A	TP	+/-	PIM	PP	SH	GW	GT	S	PCT
80	29	32	61	-2	180	7	0	2	1	129	22.5

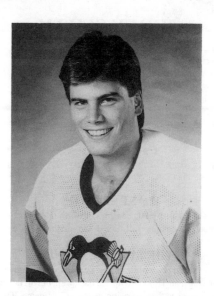

LAST SEASON

Played 80 games for second time in career; all point totals were three-season lows. Led club in PIM total and shooting percentage (among regulars).

THE FINESSE GAME

Simpson has great hands, so it's natural that stick skills and smarts would be the keys to his finesse game. He's an excellent passer and puckhandler, putting his reach to work for him in the rink's congested areas to pull the puck from traffic. But he also uses his hand skills to control the puck in those tight areas, and his quick release makes his shot (both forehand and backhand) an exceptional one; that's one big reason for his power play success. He also excels on tip-ins and deflections.

Craig's anticipation and vision are very good, getting him into position to score. His vision is excellent and he tries to make the most of his teammates by finding the openings and getting the puck there.

He's not a bad skater, but his foot skills remain behind his hand skills — even after five NHL seasons. He lacks outstanding foot speed, quickness and agility (the absences of which might actually make his scoring success more remarkable). He does have a lot of strength, so he can drive the net, and that also allows him to put his balance —the one exceptional component of his skating — to work. That balance keys his ability to work in traffic by allowing him to maintain body position and control of the puck. He's almost impossible to knock down, but he could use another step.

Simpson's defensive play remains weak, largely because he works so deep to the opposing net that his lack of foot speed prevents him from getting back into the play in time. When he can get into position, Craig plays a conscientious defensive game.

THE PHYSICAL GAME

Craig is very strong, and that's the ability that lets him drive the net. He is unafraid of traffic or the fear-

some areas in front of the net and in the corners. Most important is the fact that Craig not only takes hits to make plays, but he takes hits and makes successful plays. He could benefit by initiating more of that contact, rather than just accepting it when it occurs.

He uses his reach very well in keeping the puck from the opposition, or to snare loose pucks, and he uses his body well to protect the puck when he carries it.

THE INTANGIBLES

This guy has such good hands, he could get 70 goals. He's a pretty conscientious player in terms of work ethic and intensity, although he does have a little bit of the hot dog in him. His performances are largely based on his teammates, so if they're successful in getting him the puck — if the team itself succeeds — then Simpson succeeds too.

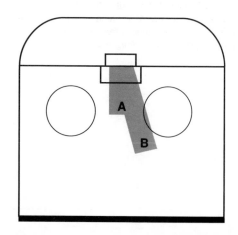

GEOFF SMITH

Yrs. of NHL service: 1
Born: Edmonton, Alta., Canada; March 7, 1969
Position: Defenseman
Height: 6-2
Weight: 190
Uniform no.: 25
Shoots: left

Career statistics:

GP	G	A	TP	+/-	PIM	PP	SH	GW	GT	S	PCT
74	4	11	15	13	52	1	0	0	0	66	6.1

LAST SEASON

First full NHL season. Plus/minus rating was second best among full-time defensemen.

THE FINESSE GAME

Smith is a mobile skater, perhaps surprisingly so for a big man. He moves up and back well, but his lateral movement is the surprising aspect of his game. That total mobility combines with his strong hockey sense to allow him to play an active and challenging game at both blue lines. He gets good reads on containing the point offensively, and he also steps up to control the gap on the puck carrier defensively.

Smith has some developable offensive skills. He moves the puck well and smartly to the open man to get play moving from the Edmonton end and Smith can carry it if need be (but don't look for too much of that).

He'll get his points on work from the blue line (although he will challenge the net if given the chance — and he does so in strongly intelligent fashion), and his skating and sense combine to make him a penalty killing regular.

THE PHYSICAL GAME

Smith has good size and uses it efficiently, if quietly. Though unlikely to hammer anyone through the boards, Smith's skating skill allows him to take the opposition to the boards and hold them there. He also gains good body position in front of his net; again, his physical play reflects intelligence.

THE INTANGIBLES

All in all a pretty auspicious rookie season. Smith is a player to build on, which means that certain of the older Oiler defenders may see their ice time further curtailed.

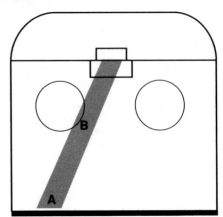

STEVE SMITH

Yrs. of NHL service: 5
Born: Glasgow, Scotland; April 30, 1963
Position: Defenseman
Height: 6-4
Weight: 215
Uniform no.: 5
Shoots: right

Career statistics:

GP	G	A	TP	PIM
308	33	131	164	887

1989-90 statistics:

GP	G	A	TP	+/-	PIM	PP	SH	GW	GT	S	PCT
75	7	34	41	6	171	3	0	1	0	125	5.6

LAST SEASON

Assist and point totals were second highest of career. Smith led Oiler defensemen in all point categories and shots on goal total, and was second on club in PIM total. He missed four games with a foot injury.

THE FINESSE GAME

Smith has become — considering his size and bulk — a very good skater at the NHL level. He moves well both forward and backward, and his improved quickness has given deceptive agility and lateral movement. He uses his skating skill well in an active — rather than re-active — role at both blue lines.

He reads the rush and anticipates well, and Smith makes that talent work thrice: closing the gap on the puck carrier, taking him off the puck and starting the play up-ice.

Steve can carry the puck from the zone, but is more likely to move it to the forwards and then join the play as it heads up ice. His playreading ability extends to the offensive zone (and has been improved by his improved skating) and Steve will not only find the open forward but will find an opening and lead a forward to it with a good pass.

His hand skills have developed along with his foot skills and Smith contains the play very well at the offensive blue line, so much so that he will get good power play time. He has a good slap shot, nothing exceptional, and Smith wil shoot from the point or the middle of the blue line.

THE PHYSICAL GAME

Steve is an excellent and aggressive physical player, especially now that his skating allows him to completely track down the opposition and consistently put his excellent size and strength to work against them.

He's very strong in front of his net and will succeed against most all NHL forwards, including those of the power variety. He's just as sure to win the battles in the corners, and his ability to make plays coming out of the corner magnifies his already superb physical play. He uses his body excellently to gain position against the opposition.

His size makes him very difficult to get around at the blue line and Smith will sacrifice his body to block shots.

THE INTANGIBLES

Smith is the kind of player every team hopes for, a defenseman with skill in all areas and the intensity and dedication to put all his skills to work. He would be no worse than a number two defender on any team in the NHL, and since that's what he is with the Stanley Cup champions chances are he'd be front-line on 20 other clubs.

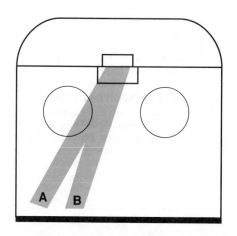

ESA TIKKANEN

Yrs. of NHL service: 5
Born: Helsinki, Finland; January 25, 1965
Position: Left wing
Height: 6-1
Weight: 200
Uniform no.: 10
Shoots: left

Career statistics:

GP	G	A	TP	PIM
337	125	181	306	554

1989-90 statistics:

GP	G	A	TP	+/-	PIM	PP	SH	GW	GT	S	PCT
79	30	33	63	17	161	6	4	6	0	199	15.1

LAST SEASON

Point total was full-season career low, goal total second lowest full-season mark of career. Finished fourth on club in PIM total, second in game winners.

THE FINESSE GAME

Tikkanen is an excellent skater with great speed, acceleration, quickness, balance and agility. His balance allows him to retain his body position (and thus control of the puck) as he's being fouled. Esa also moderates his speed to make it more effective, but he does perform well at high speed.

He's a smart player and uses his playreading ability both offensively and defensively. He's very good at turning the play around by intercepting a pass or closing a hole, and his smarts combine with his skating to make him an excellent forechecker and penalty killer.

Esa's hand skills are just as advanced as his foot skills, and he makes particularly good use of his hands in traffic and around the net. His smarts amplify the ability of his hand skills by putting him in places where his hands can go to work.

Tikkanen has an excellent wrist shot, and he can put it anywhere courtesy of his soft hands. It's quickly released and accurate, and Esa would benefit by using it more often. He's most dangerous from the top of the circle and in.

He excels defensively, playing his position and checking well in all three zones.

THE PHYSICAL GAME

Tikkanen is a very tough player and loves hitting and working in the trenches. He plays bigger than his size and is fearless in the corners, a style that belies the European stereotypes. Esa's excellent balance aids him in his physical play by allowing him to remain vertical after he initiates a hit, and he more than has the skills to make the play coming out of the corner.

He's also fairly liberal in the use of his stick.

THE INTANGIBLES

Tikkanen makes a lot of players crazy, including some on his own team, through his yapping. He shows respect to no one on ice, which is why the opposition can't stand him — but he is still a tremendously talented player (albeit flamboyant one).

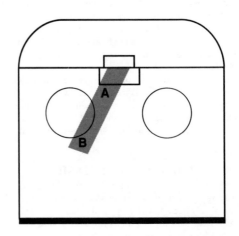

HARTFORD WHALERS

MIKAEL ANDERSSON

Yrs. of NHL service: 4
Born: Malom, Sweden; May10, 1966
Position: Center
Height: 5-11
Weight: 185
Uniform no.: 34
Shoots: left

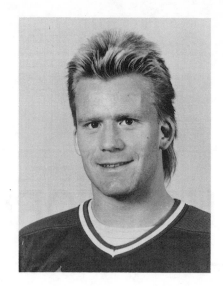

Career statistics:

GP	G	A	TP	PIM
149	17	57	74	24

1989-90 statistics:

GP	G	A	TP	+/-	PIM	PP	SH	GW	GT	S	PCT
50	13	24	37	0	6	1	2	2	0	86	15.1

LAST SEASON

Games played and all point totals were career bests. Missed six games with a knee injury, two games with a bruised leg, 11 games with a second knee injury, and further time with a late-season hamstring injury.

THE FINESSE GAME

Speed, speed and more speed. Are you getting the picture? Andersson can skate like he was shot from a cannon, and his skating and speed will open things up for his teammates. He's a very agile player, but his hand skills can't catch up to his foot skills so he doesn't have the ability to cash in on the opportunities he creates.

So what do you do with him? Why, make him a checker of course. And Andersson filled that role well for Hartford last year. He has a good sense of the offensive zone and is already a defensively responsible player, so it's easy to go that one extra step and just make him a checker. He forces loose pucks because of his speed and functions very well on the penalty killing unit, where his speed and hockey sense make him a threat for shorthanded goals.

As mentioned, he doesn't really have a scoring touch so he's going to have to be opportunistic around the net to get goals.

THE PHYSICAL GAME

As long as Andersson can stay in the open field, so to speak, he's okay. But once he gets trapped near the boards he's easily out-muscled. There's almost no point in his going to the corner to attack the puck because he's not going to succeed, so don't interpret his staying in open ice as fear or timidity. Instead, Andersson is doing the things that will insure his NHL success.

THE INTANGIBLES

Andersson is a role player, and successful though he was last season all role players are eminently replaceable players.

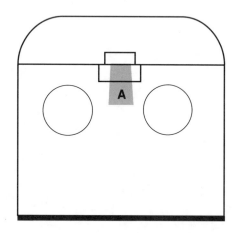

DAVE BABYCH

Yrs. of NHL service: 10
Born: Edmonton, Alta., Canada; May 23, 1961
Position: Defenseman
Height: 6-2
Weight: 215
Uniform no.: 44
Shoots: left

Career statistics:

GP	G	A	TP	PIM
731	117	438	555	642

1989-90 statistics:

GP	G	A	TP	+/-	PIM	PP	SH	GW	GT	S	PCT
72	6	37	43	-16	62	4	0	1	0	164	3.7

LAST SEASON

Games played total was five-season high, but point total was second lowest of career. Missed two games with a sore neck, and missed time with a late-season foot injury. Led Hartford defensemen in points, but plus/minus rating was the defensive corps' worst (second poorest on club).

THE FINESSE GAME

Long known as a smooth and talented skater, Babych is slowing up in the agility and one-step quickness areas, making him more vulnerable to opposition attempts to cut inside him or to gain loose pucks. He retains a good degree of his forward and back mobility and can join rushes but seldom does so. He has never been strong at gap control, and his decreasing agility hasn't helped. He plays defense reactively, rather than actively.

He still uses his speed as a weapon in the offensive area of the game, where he can create and execute plays based on skating, puck movement and space; he is still Hartford's power play general. He combines his skating with good puckhandling skills and is especially effective in traffic.

His vision and hockey sense allow Dave to use his teammates well, but again, his decreasing quickness means loose pucks once snared may now be lost — or an opening once recognized may be closed before the puck gets through it. He passes well, but Babych likes to shoot the puck when he can.

THE PHYSICAL GAME

He's never been a big hitter, and he's never going to be a big hitter. Babych is inconsistent is his use of his size for clearing the net or taking men off the puck, two aspects of defensive play he's not real interested in. In short, he's a finesse player with size.

THE INTANGIBLES

He's a one-dimensional, aging hockey player saved from dismissal by the fact that no other Hartford defenseman has come to the offensive fore. He doesn't really want to be cast in a leadership role of any type, and the fact that he doesn't play with intensity in every game demonstrates that.

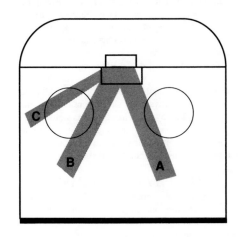

147

ADAM BURT

Yrs. of NHL service: 1
Born: Detroit, Mich., USA; January 15, 1969
Position: Defenseman
Height: 6-0
Weight: 195
Uniform no.: 6
Shoots: left

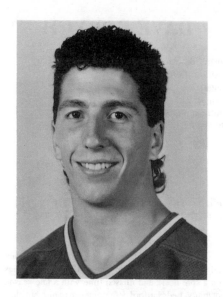

Career statistics:

GP	G	A	TP	PIM
68	4	8	12	111

1989-90 statistics:

GP	G	A	TP	+/-	PIM	PP	SH	GW	GT	S	PCT
63	4	8	12	3	105	1	0	0	1	83	4.8

LAST SEASON

First full NHL season. Missed five games with hip injury, eight games with separated shoulder.

THE FINESSE GAME

Burt has a fairly good complement of NHL-level finesse skills, the best of which is probably his skating. Though not possessed of outstanding speed, Burt is an agile skater with good lateral ability. That mobility is important for his defensive game, as Burt is certainly a strong enough skater to challenge the puck carrier and control the gap; he has the skating ability to force plays at his own blue line, and greater NHL experience will help him solidify this skill.

He likes to handle and carry the puck and Burt does a good job of both when in motion; again, his mobility allows him to orchestrate an attack by carrying the puck himself, or to join the attack as a late man. He plays a fairly intelligent game at the offensive blue line, containing the point and pinching in prudently. This aspect of his game should also become stronger with greater NHL experience.

Burt gets fairly good reads of the ice when carrying or passing the puck (or when playing defense, for that matter) and one reason why is because he keeps his head up when making plays. That shows confidence in his ability. He uses his eyes and hands to pass well on both the forehand and backhand sides, and he has a strong shot from the point. He'll see occasional power play time because of his combination of skills.

THE PHYSICAL GAME

Burt has good — not great — NHL size, and good strength and he uses both in an intelligently aggressive style. His mobility allows him to take the opposition to the boards and pin his man out of the play, while his finesse skills complement his physical ability by allowing him to make plays coming out of the corners.

His balance is a big part of Burt's success and he helps his physical game by being smart; Burt knows how to use his body to establish position, a critical skill for front of the net coverage. He takes hits to make his plays.

THE INTANGIBLES

Like a number of other young Hartford players, Burt made a solid NHL debut last season. He has the skills and intelligence to be an above average NHL player, and his work ethic and strong competitive attitude should help him along that road.

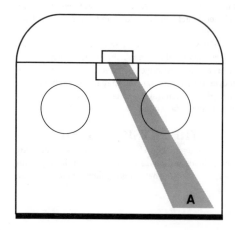

YVON CORRIVEAU

Yrs. of NHL service: 3
Born: Welland, Ontario, Canada; February 8, 1967
Position: Left wing
Height: 6-2
Weight: 205
Uniform no.: 20
Shoots: left

Career statistics:

GP	G	A	TP	PIM
159	27	19	46	242

1989-90 statistics:

GP	G	A	TP	+/-	PIM	PP	SH	GW	GT	S	PCT
63	13	7	20	2	72	1	0	1	0	90	14.4

LAST SEASON

Acquired from Washington in exchange for Mike Liut in March 1990. Games played, goal and point totals were all career highs. Missed four games with a broken nose while with Washington.

THE FINESSE GAME

Though the physical game is where Corriveau will excel (if he is to succeed at the NHL level), he does have finesse skills that can be brought to bear.

He is a strong skater, not particularly agile or fluid, but with good balance and a strong stride. That portends some speed in his future, and the balance means he can become more agile (greater foot speed is necessary there). He pursues the puck very well as a forechecker because of his strong skating ability.

Corriveau has good hands for a big man, but as yet he's not shown tha ability to consistently contribute offensively at the NHL level. He'll move the puck to the open man and lead a teammate into an opening, and he also has the ability to handle the puck in traffic (balance helps here), but right now the NHL game moves too quickly for him.

He has a good wrist shot, heavy and generally accurate, and Corriveau will score from the faceoff circle and in.

He intends to be a conscientious defensive player and will contain his check well, but he also has a tendency to get hypnotized by the puck and wander from his position.

THE PHYSICAL GAME

Corriveau has good size and strength, thick in the upper body and willing to put that strength to use at all times. He can be a punishing hitter because of his size and strength, and he uses his body well along the boards.

He'll overpower people along the boards because of his strength and balance. He enjoys a physical contest.

THE INTANGIBLES

Yvon has great desire and a very good attitude. He works extremely hard and wants to succeed, and he is very coachable. Time is needed to see whether that desire can be translated into NHL-level ability commensurate with first-round selection.

SYLVAIN COTE

Yrs. of NHL service: 5
Born: Quebec City, Quebec, Canada; January 19, 1966
Position: Defenseman
Height: 5-11
Weight: 185
Uniform no.: 21
Shoots: right

Career statistics:

GP	G	A	TP	PIM
309	24	49	73	130

1989-90 statistics:

GP	G	A	TP	+/-	PIM	PP	SH	GW	GT	S	PCT
28	4	2	6	2	14	1	0	1	1	50	8.0

LAST SEASON

Games played total was full-season career low (missed time with a broken toe, 21 games with a knee injury, and several months with ankle injuries). Point total was correspondingly low.

THE FINESSE GAME

Skating is Cote's best skill both offensively and defensively. He uses his speed and quickness very effectively as the play moves up ice and those same assets counter any positional mistakes he makes. Cote uses his skating prowess instead of solid positional play to play defense (and he can get burned because of that). Still, his speed, quickness and agility insure that he won't often be beaten 1-on-1.

He has sort of stagnated in his ability to handle the puck at NHL speed, whether that means skating it from the zone (which he does frequently) or making the breakout pass. He's got the ability to make correct decisions and just needs to exercise some patience to do so.

Sylvain does anticipate plays in both directions fairly well, and he's shown confidence in his own abilities by taking chances — things like charging the net, knowing that his skating can help him recover.

THE PHYSICAL GAME

Cote rides the fence in this area. While not necessarily averse to a physical game, Cote doesn't really have the size or strength to play an effective physical game. So what you get instead is a lot of pushing and shoving, and some out-muscling by the opposition when Cote gets caught in front of the net.

He'll try to tie up the opposition along the boards, and if Cote can get both himself and the puck free he can make a play.

THE INTANGIBLES

We've left this report alone, due to Cote's abbreviated 1989-90 season. Our report continued, "While still an NHL youngster (in terms of both age and experience), Cote needs to learn better positional play and should develop some strength." No changes here.

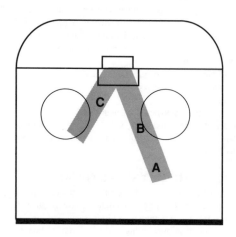

RANDY CUNNEYWORTH

Yrs. of NHL service: 6
Born: Etobicoke, Ontario, Canada; May 10, 1961
Position: Center/left wing
Height: 6-0
Weight: 190
Uniform no.: 7
Shoots: left

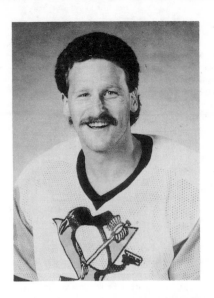

Career statistics:

GP	G	A	TP	PIM
387	117	134	251	637

1989-90 statistics:

GP	G	A	TP	+/-	PIM	PP	SH	GW	GT	S	PCT
71	14	15	29	-11	75	4	0	2	0	121	11.6

LAST SEASON

Acquired from Winnipeg in exchange for Paul MacDermid in December 1989. Point totals were full-season career lows, plus/minus rating was team's fourth worst (third poorest among forwards).

THE FINESSE GAME

Balance and strength are the keys to Cunneyworth's game, both physically and finesse-wise. His balance keeps Randy upright through collisions and that's important, given his play-the-body style. His skating strength allows him to both drive through his own checks and to drive to the net against opposing checking. He also uses that balance to key a fairly agile skating style, one that provides him with some speed and quickness.

His hockey sense is at a fairly high level, though Cunneyworth does tend to out-think himself in search of goals. Still, he acts and reacts well at NHL speed, looking over the ice before making a play.

His hand skills are good, but Cunneyworth will not usually try to stickhandle through a team to score. He'll give the puck to an open teammate and charge the net.

His balance and strength render him impervious to the traffic close to the net, and it is those assets that let him deliver a good wrist shot while being checked, or while off-balance.

THE PHYSICAL GAME

Cunneyworth is a very tough, aggressive player — despite the fact that he has less than intimidating size — and he uses his body in all three zones. He likes to hit (sometimes he's too aggressive), and his style is powered by the balance and strength mentioned earlier.

His physical play is more valuable because of his ability to make plays out of traffic.

He also sacrifices his body to block shots.

THE INTANGIBLES

Cunneyworth is a support player, the kind of guy whose strong work ethic allows him to work the boards and grind it out shift after shift and night after night. He brings good intensity to the rink every day, and as long as he remembers that it is the unglamorous aspects of NHL play that have gotten him here, and not artistic playmaking, he'll perform just fine. And when you can get 20-25 goals from a player like Cunneyworth, your team is ahead of the game.

KEVIN DINEEN

Yrs. of NHL service: 6
Born: Quebec City, Quebec, Canada; October 28, 1963
Position: Right wing
Height: 5-11
Weight: 195
Uniform no.: 11
Shoots: right

Career statistics:

GP	G	A	TP	PIM
412	193	200	393	902

1989-90 statistics:

GP	G	A	TP	+/-	PIM	PP	SH	GW	GT	S	PCT
67	25	41	66	7	164	8	2	2	2	214	11.7

LAST SEASON

Games played total was four-season low, with point total five-season low. Finished third on the club in goals, assists, points and shots on goal, first in game-tying goals. Missed five games with a back injury, one game with a groin injury, and time late in the season with a back injury.

THE FINESSE GAME

Dineen is a crash-and-bash player, and the finesse root of his success is his strong skating skill. Balance and skating strength are what Dineen uses to power his power forward style of game, putting both to work as he muscles along in the corners and the crease. His balance keeps him upright as he wrestles for the puck and also allows him to get away his shot while being checked, while his strong stride provides him with speed and the ability to drive through his checks and punish the opposition. He also has a degree of lateral ability that belies his straight-line style.

He passes and carries the puck well at full speed, but his shooting ability highlights his hand skills. Dineen has a very hard wrist shot that he uses to great success from the faceoff circle and in, and he has the hand strength to bull the puck home from close quarters.

Dineen can pass well, but he generally looks to shoot first and thus leaves his teammates standing around when he has the puck. He has the anticipation to be a playmaker (just as he has the sense to get into scoring position). A more negative commentator would say Dineen is a selfish player.

THE PHYSICAL GAME

Dineen has outstanding physical ability, when he wants to use it. He has absolutely no fear when it comes to banging bodies in the corner or the slot, and Dineen is built for success courtesy of his strength and balance.

He is at his best when he plays to his strengths, but he sometimes lacks the intensity to do so every night and every shift.

THE INTANGIBLES

The aforementioned intensity and lack thereof, as well as what may or may not be a strained relationship with coach Rick Ley. There's no denying that Dineen is a hustler and worker but he is sometimes his own worst enemy, as his undisciplined play and tendency toward poor penalties attests.

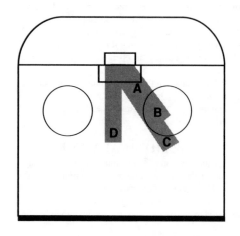

DEAN EVASON

Yrs. of NHL service: 5
Born: Flin Flon, Man., Canada; August 22, 1964
Position: Center
Height: 5-10
Weight: 180
Uniform no.: 12
Shoots: left

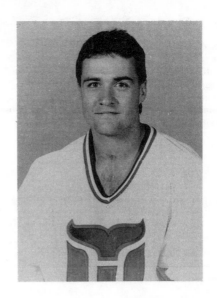

Career statistics:

GP	G	A	TP	PIM
376	84	129	213	449

1989-90 statistics:

GP	G	A	TP	+/-	PIM	PP	SH	GW	GT	S	PCT
78	18	25	43	7	138	2	2	2	0	150	12.0

LAST SEASON

Games played total was three-season high and second highest of career; ditto all point totals.

THE FINESSE GAME

Evason has good offensive skills, notably in the skating and shooting departments. He is a fine skater with acceleration and power for rink-length speed, as well as quickness and balance for agility and darting ability.

His shooting skills are best maximized from the area near the net, where Evason can convert loose pucks into goals because of his quick and fairly accurate shot. His skating contributes here by getting him to those loose pucks in the first place, and he can be especially dangerous on the power play because of the added open ice.

He has a fair degree of anticipation skill and view of the ice, and Evason can put that hockey sense to work as a checker and a penalty killer; again, his skating is the physical key to Evason's success. Evason also uses his sense and hand skills to a fair degree in finding open teammates for his passes.

THE PHYSICAL GAME

Size is going to be a problem for Evason, because he'll be out-muscled by bigger opponents. He won't be intimidated but that doesn't help when he's overwhelmed in the traffic areas.

THE INTANGIBLES

He's got the heart and the character and it seems as if Evason has found a niche as a checker, but as the League gets bigger and stronger he will have more and more trouble remaining competitive.

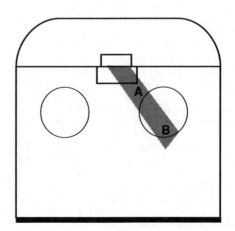

RAY FERRARO

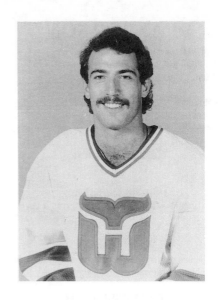

Yrs. of NHL service: 6
Born: Trail, B.C., Canada; August 23, 1964
Position: Center
Height: 5-10
Weight: 185
Uniform no.: 26
Shoots: left

Career statistics:

GP	G	A	TP	PIM
427	155	189	344	415

1989-90 statistics:

GP	G	A	TP	+/-	PIM	PP	SH	GW	GT	S	PCT
79	25	29	54	-15	109	7	0	4	1	138	18.1

LAST SEASON

Goal and point totals were second lowest full-season marks of career. Plus/minus rating was club's third worst, second poorest among forwards.

THE FINESSE GAME

Ferraro is a dynamic package of finesse skills and his skating is the most dynamic of all his finesse ingredients. He has two speeds, fast and faster, and Ferraro uses them to his utmost. He is a breakaway threat because of his rink-length speed, but he also has outstanding quickness afoot that allows him to dart and scurry in any direction within a step. He's very dangerous near loose pucks, and he'll bury rebounds near the net.

His excellent agility and lateral movement (credit his balance) work in tandem with his above average stick skills to make him a tricky and deceptive puckhandler. He loves to carry the puck and throw fake after fake at the opposing defenseman, and he can exploit the openings he earns because of his quickness. His hand skills do not always mesh well with his skating, in that his feet can out-race his hands' ability.

His scoring ability is a direct reflection of his ability to get to loose pucks and get his shot off, and he makes the most of his opportunities by shooting often and quickly.

His defensive play reflects none of his offensive ability, because Ferraro is very weak in completing his defensive assignments in all three zones.

THE PHYSICAL GAME

Ferraro doesn't have great size, but that doesn't mean he won't play a physical game. He'll do the work along boards, taking his hits to make his plays, and his balance really helps him absorb the punishment; he certainly is not intimidated. Nevertheless, Ferraro will be physically overwhelmed by bigger players — that's just a fact. While working along the boards he must remain opportunistic and get to those loose pucks before bigger, stronger opponents he'll be unable to out-muscle.

THE INTANGIBLES

We're tempted to say that Ferraro is following in the Hartford tradition of offensively prolific and defensively sluggish forwards like Blaine Stoughton and Mike Rogers, but those guys at least scored 100 points a season while being poor defensively. Because of his plus/minus and the fact that he scored just 19 goals at even-strength, Ferraro was essentially a four-goal scorer last season.

He works diligently at his offensive game, but he needs to incorporate that same effort into his defensive responsibilities. Should he not, the end of his Hartford career may be nearer than farther.

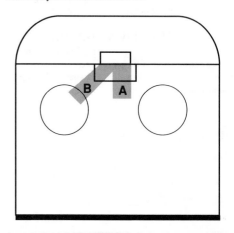

RON FRANCIS

Yrs. of NHL service: 9
Born: Sault Ste. Marie, Ontario, Canada; March 1, 1963
Position: Center
Height: 6-2
Weight: 200
Uniform no.: 10
Shoots: left

Career statistics:

GP	G	A	TP	PIM
647	243	502	745	487

1989-90 statistics:

GP	G	A	TP	+/-	PIM	PP	SH	GW	GT	S	PCT
80	32	69	101	13	73	15	1	5	1	170	18.8

LAST SEASON

All point totals were career highs, as Francis led club in assists, points and power play goals. Finished thirteenth in overall League scoring. Plus/minus rating was club's second best, tops among forwards.

THE FINESSE GAME

As demonstrated by his career-best numbers last season, Francis is an excellent playmaking center. There are two keys to his success here: passing and hockey sense. He has great vision of the ice, as well as the patience and poise to wait that split-second more to reach the opposition's panic zone; Francis simply forces the opposition into committing itself, and then exploits the opening he has essentially created. He reads the ice very well, and not only finds the open man but also sees the openings into which he can lead teammates.

The physical side of this is his passing, which is excellent. Francis has great touch with the puck and can deliver anywhere in any way necessary, be it feathered or fired.

Francis's skating is good to very good, equipped with speed and agility that is a little surprising to find in a man with his size and bulk. He can dipsy-doodle, and his balance gives him both superior lateral ability and the skill to lean away from checks. He also functions well in traffic because of his balance.

Because he is unselfish, Francis is a better playmaker than scorer. He's most effective from the slot, because his balance allows him to maintain body position and get his shot off in traffic. Francis can also blast a slap shot past the goaltender from farther away.

Francis is also a reliable defensive player, playing a responsible game in all three zones.

THE PHYSICAL GAME

Francis has better than good size, but he doesn't initiate a lot of contact. That's not to say he's afraid of playing physically or that he won't take a hit. What we're saying is that he doesn't take advantage of his size by imposing himself on the opposition.

He has good upper body strength and can combine that strength with his superior balance to muscle the opposition off the puck, but Francis rarely puts his size to work for him in congested areas. Instead he waits outside the scrums to snare loose pucks with his good reach. He is a good faceoff man, and he loves to go forward with the puck off the draw.

THE INTANGIBLES

Let's start with this: Francis is a character player and a good team man, though he might be miscast in the captain's role because of his less-than-intense attitude off the ice. No complaint here from us.

He's clearly an upper level player in the NHL and a strong two-way center, and if he were to include a more robust physical game (doubtful at this stage of his career) Francis could be an elite level player. As is, he is on a plateau below players like Steve Yzerman and Pat LaFontaine.

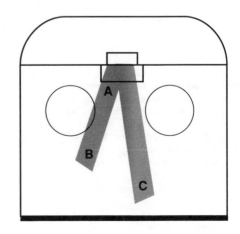

JODY HULL

Yrs. of NHL service: 2
Born: Cambridge, Ontario, Canada; February 2, 1969
Position: Right wing
Height: 6-2
Weight: 200
Uniform no.: 8
Shoots: right

Career statistics:

GP	G	A	TP	PIM
98	23	28	51	31

1989-90 statistics:

GP	G	A	TP	+/-	PIM	PP	SH	GW	GT	S	PCT
38	7	10	17	-6	21	2	0	0	0	46	15.2

LAST SEASON

Missed two games with a charley horse, but bounced back and forth between Hartford and Binghamton of the American Hockey League.

THE FINESSE GAME

Hull has excellent finesse skills across the board. He is a fine skater with gifts in each of the requisite skating departments: speed, balance, quickness, agility. He accelerates well with a strong stride and his foot speed combines with his balance to give him a good degree of lateral movement. His balance and skating strength pave the way for him to drive the net and work the corners, as well as giving him outside speed.

He has good puckhandling skills (working well in the traffic areas — his balance needs crediting here too), and Hull demonstrates his good hands by giving and taking passes in stride. His shot is accurate, quickly released, and hard, forcing the goaltender to make saves, and he would benefit by shooting the puck more.

His smarts are very good and Hull has a fine understanding of the play as it develops both offensively and defensively. He uses his sense to get into scoring position and to lead teammates into openings with his passes, and he uses that same sense as a solid defensive player.

THE PHYSICAL GAME

In the physical realm Hull has the tools but can't open the tool box. He has outstanding size and must learn to use his size consistently and aggressively. He's not unaware of his body, as he works hard to stay in good shape, but he must realize that his size and strength are weapons to be used like anything else.

He goes to the net well, but he must demonstrate more willingness to work in the corners.

THE INTANGIBLES

His sophomore season must be considered a disappointment, and one reason for that is Hull's inability to fire up his game. He seems to play unemotionally and one symptom of that is his inconsistent use of his body. He'll have a long road to NHL stability if he doesn't work on those drawbacks.

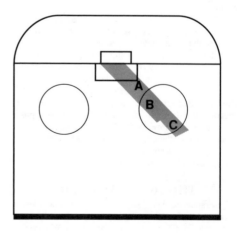

GRANT JENNINGS

Yrs. of NHL service: 2
Born: Hudson Bay, Sask., Canada; May 5, 1965
Position: Defenseman
Height: 6-4
Weight: 220
Uniform no.: 25
Shoots: left

Career statistics:

GP	G	A	TP	PIM
119	6	16	22	313

1989-90 statistics:

GP	G	A	TP	+/-	PIM	PP	SH	GW	GT	S	PCT
64	3	6	9	-4	154	0	0	0	0	45	6.7

LAST SEASON

Games played total rose, point total fell in second full season. Missed eight games with a shoulder injury, eight games with a knee injury. PIM total was second highest among defensemen.

THE FINESSE GAME

Nice and easy does it every time should be the Grant Jennings credo, and Jennings's play shows that he already subscribes to that philosophy. He's not lacking in finesse ability but the strength of his game is clearly in the physical department. As such, Jennings is pretty smart about playing within the parameters of his modest skills.

His skating remains a little slow by NHL standards, and last season's knee trouble surely did nothing to improve that skill. He doesn't bring a lot of speed or agility to the table but Jennings plays a fairly composed angle and zone game, at least forcing the opposing winger into a narrower and narrower zone along the boards. A forward with speed and good lateral ability, however, can get Jennings turned. He is usually prudent about pinching in at the offensive blue line.

Jennings will not handle the puck or skate with it, as he knows that his best play is the quick pass to an open forward. He can be forced by aggressive forechecking. He doesn't have great hand skills, so his assists are going to come on plays he's started from the Hartford zone, and his goals are going to come from the blue line — few and far between.

THE PHYSICAL GAME

Jennings is big and tough, and he's willing to use his size and strength to punish the opposition. His physical game is mitigated though by his limited mobility — in other words, he can't hit what he can't catch.

He is very effective in clearing the crease and when using his size in the traffic areas.

THE INTANGIBLES

Jennings can be a very important part of Hartford's future because of his ability to clean up his own end. He can fall into lazy funks and needs to be reminded to do the things that guarantee his NHL success. Just as important, he's shown a tendency toward injury during his first two NHL seasons.

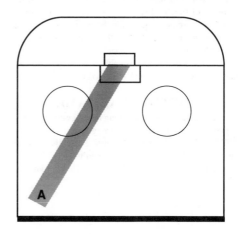

ED KASTELIC

Yrs. of NHL service: 3
Born: Toronto, Ont., Canada; January 29, 1964
Position: Right wing
Height: 6-4
Weight: 215
Uniform no.: 22
Shoots: right

Career statistics:

GP	G	A	TP	PIM
150	8	5	13	447

1989-90 statistics:

GP	G	A	TP	+/-	PIM	PP	SH	GW	GT	S	PCT
67	6	2	8	-3	198	0	0	0	0	35	17.1

LAST SEASON

Games played, all point totals and PIM marks were career highs. He finished second on the club in PIM total.

THE FINESSE GAME

Underneath the gruff bluster of Kastelic's physical game are some finesse skills that might be underrated at the NHL level — which is not to say that his exterior hides a Denis Savard just waiting to burst forth, but that there are some skills Kastelic can bring to bear.

He's not a bad straight-ahead skater but he lacks good foot speed and balance, so he's going to have trouble keeping pace with quicker and shiftier NHL opponents.

Kastelic doesn't handle the puck particularly well, nor does he have a great sense of the ice and a play's implications in either the offensive or defensive modes. If he's going to make plays he needs Einstein-like amounts of time and space — lots of both. He does, however, have pretty good hands for shooting and he can score some goals if given the chance, maybe 15 a year at his optimum NHL capacity.

His lack of real speed or ability to see the ice mean that he is going to be weak defensively.

THE PHYSICAL GAME

Kastelic can be a punishing hitter, courtesy of his aggressiveness and size and strength, but his lack of agility will mitigate against his hitting effectiveness. In other words, he can't hit what he can't catch.

His aggressiveness will cross the line to fighting.

THE INTANGIBLES

Kastelic walks a fine line. While he has certain finesse skills he's not skilled enough to play in the NHL on skill alone, and while he has toughness he may not be tough enough to play in the NHL on toughness alone. He must work hard to bring everything in his modest arsenal to bear every night he plays.

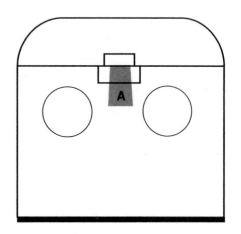

TODD KRYGIER

Yrs. of NHL service: 1
Born: Northville, Michigan, USA; October 12, 1965
Position: Center
Height: 5-11
Weight: 180
Uniform no.: 17
Shoots: left

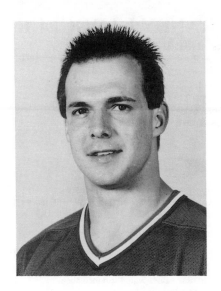

Career statistics:

GP	G	A	TP	+/-	PIM	PP	SH	GW	GT	S	PCT
58	18	12	30	4	52	5	1	3	1	103	17.5

LAST SEASON

Krygier's first full NHL campaign. Spent two weeks in Binghamton of the American Hockey League, and then missed time later in the season with a heel injury.

THE FINESSE GAME

Krygier is a fairly talented finesse player, gifted with speed and agility in his skating. That allows him to drive the defensemen off the blue line with outside speed and Krygier also has the ability to cut inside off that outside move.

He's shown fairly good ability to read and react at the NHL level in both his offensive and defensive games, as evidenced by all his numbers. He has a certain degree of patience and poise in his play, which is not to say that Krygier will delay forever before making his plays; rather, he gets a good read of the ice to spot both his teammates and the openings and then he makes a play to exploit those factors. He handles the puck well in traffic, and he's demonstrated a previous ability to get the puck to his teammates.

He shoots the puck fairly well, and Krygier knows how to work himself into fairly good scoring position. While his skating will allow him to take advantage of loose pucks around the net, Krygier can also lay claim to a fairly good shot (accurate and well-released, if not necessarily powerful).

THE PHYSICAL GAME

Krygier is built like a college finesse player, and he tends to play that way. He doesn't have a lot of strength or size to muster against the opposition, so Krygier will have to exploit his finesse abilities.

Not that he's afraid of physical play, but Krygier will be out-muscled in close quarters. Willing is one thing and able is another, and to that end Krygier should work to develop his strength (he already has the balance) in order to improve his physical game.

THE INTANGIBLES

In all, a pretty auspicious NHL debut for a very determined young man, one who seems likely to do the things necessary for continued NHL success. Added strength and bulk would help protect Krygier from the rigors of the NHL, especially considering he is playing in the rough-and-tumble Adams Division.

He'll see greater checking pressure this year because he's no longer a secret. How he reacts to that pressure will go a long way toward determining his future NHL course.

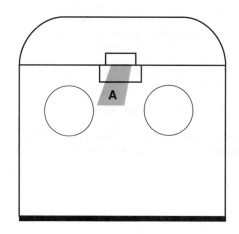

RANDY LADOCEUR

Yrs. of NHL service: 8
Born: Brockville, Ontario, Canada; June 30, 1960
Position: Defenseman
Height: 6-2
Weight: 220
Uniform no.: 29
Shoots: left

Career statistics:

GP	G	A	TP	PIM
539	22	94	116	828

1989-90 statistics:

GP	G	A	TP	+/-	PIM	PP	SH	GW	GT	S	PCT
71	3	12	15	-6	143	0	0	0	0	45	6.7

LAST SEASON

Assist and point totals were four-season highs. Plus/minus was second worst among defensemen. Missed nine games with a sprained knee.

THE FINESSE GAME

There isn't much Ladoceur has to offer at the NHL level, and in order to be successful he *must* play within his limitations. He's a no better than average skater, without exceptional speed or agility. His defense will have to be played positionally, for he lacks the foot speed or smarts to effectively or consistently step up and close the gap on the puck carrier. So too must he play offensively, making sure he challenges and forechecks prudently.

He doesn't get great reads of the ice, so he needs time and space to make his plays at both ends of the ice; that's why he can be forced into giveaways when pressured. He does very little handling of the puck, leaving that for the backchecking forward or his defensive partner. He will not carry the puck from the defensive zone and rarely joins the rush as an attacker. He is susceptible to fakes because of his lackluster foot speed and reading ability.

His few goals a season will come on shots from the point.

THE PHYSICAL GAME

Ladoceur has fairly good size and strength, and he will use those assets in his hitting game. His limited skating ability serves to limit his hitting ability, and his lack of balance means he can be knocked off the puck. He'll take the rough going but isn't a fighter.

THE INTANGIBLES

Ladoceur is a competent but no better than average NHL player. He helps give Hartford depth on the blue line but he'll never be more than a fifth defensemen.

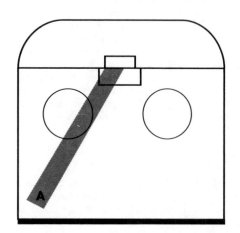

JOEL QUENNEVILLE

Yrs. of NHL service: 12
Born: Windsor, Ontario, Canada; September 15, 1958
Position: Defenseman
Height: 6-1
Weight: 200
Uniform no.: 3
Shoots: left

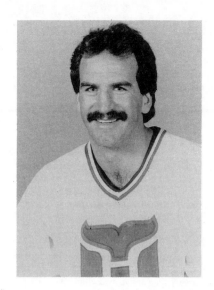

Career statistics:

GP	G	A	TP	PIM
794	53	136	189	705

1989-90 statistics:

GP	G	A	TP	+/-	PIM	PP	SH	GW	GT	S	PCT
44	1	4	5	9	34	0	0	0	0	17	5.9

LAST SEASON

Games played total was second lowest of career, goal total tied and assist and point totals set career lows. Plus/minus was defense's second best.

THE FINESSE GAME

After a dozen years of the NHL wars and the requisite wear and tear, Quenneville succeeds now more on smarts than he does strong finesse play. He uses his ability to see the play and its implications to force the incoming forward to a lane wide of the net, and he contains the play well that way even though his ability to close the gap has waned.

Once he gains the puck Quenneville wastes no time in moving it to the forwards so it gets out of the defensive zone. Rare are the times he'll take more than three strides while holding the puck, and Quenneville will make almost no offensive contributions from the opposing blue line.

Which is not to say he can't contain the blue line or find an open man. Rather, as with his defensive play, Quenneville makes the most of his play at the offensive end by staying within his limitations and making simple but effective plays.

THE PHYSICAL GAME

Quenneville is less a physical player in terms of thumping than he is an effective player by virtue of smart body positioning. He takes the body well along the boards and establishes inside position near the crease. And when that fails, Quenneville isn't above hooking or holding to get the job done. He uses his body well to protect the puck along the boards to kill time or get a faceoff, but he doesn't otherwise sacrifice his body (he doesn't block shots).

THE INTANGIBLES

Quenneville can contribute because of the smarts he's gained over the course of his career, but the growing depth of the Whaler defense corps may keep Quenneville more out of the lineup than in it.

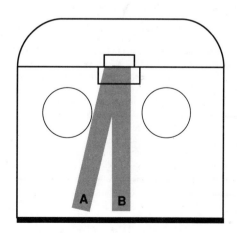

ULF SAMUELSSON

Yrs. of NHL service: 6
Born: Fagersta, Sweden; March 26, 1964
Position: Defenseman
Height: 6-1
Weight: 195
Uniform no.: 5
Shoots: left

Career statistics:

GP	G	A	TP	PIM
401	28	126	154	926

1989-90 statistics:

GP	G	A	TP	+/-	PIM	PP	SH	GW	GT	S	PCT
55	2	11	13	15	167	0	0	0		0	57	3.5

LAST SEASON

Games played and all point totals were full-season career lows. Missed 25 games because of off-season knee surgery. Plus/minus was club's best and he led defense in PIM total.

THE FINESSE GAME

Samuelsson has outstanding finesse abilities, and his skating is at the heart of all of them. He is an excellent skater in all aspects of that skill, with strength for speed, acceleration and driving ability, and balance and foot speed for one-step quickness and excellent lateral movement. He practices outstanding gap control and closes on the puck carrier excellently, and his skating also allows him to control the point, forecheck and pinch in his offensive play.

He easily takes the opposition off the puck and just as easily turns the play around. He finds open men very well at both ends of the ice, and Samuelsson will make not only a correct play in the transition game but a good play.

His ability to read and react in both his offensive and defensive games is very high, and he can convert high risk plays to high return. He uses his hockey sense and vision in his passing and puckhandling, and uses it more strongly in his defensive zone play to break up passes and turn the play around.

His offensive contributions are made better by virtue of the fact that Samuelsson sacrifices nothing defensively to make those plays. He is not an offensive dynamo, but will score 40 points a season — and is capable of much more.

THE PHYSICAL GAME

Samuelsson's physical game is at least as strong as his finesse game — in fact, it's probably stronger. He's big, strong, tough and mean in all areas of the defensive zone and he likes to hit and punish the opposition. He is absolutely fearless in his confrontations and his high calibre finesse skills blend excellently with his physical gifts of size and strength.

If he didn't have the mobility and balance that he has, Samuelsson wouldn't be able to play the robust elite-level physical game he does. He's an outstanding bodychecker and will beat almost any player in a one-on-one battle. He makes the opposition pay the price in front of the net, blocks shots with impunity (he's one of the very best in the NHL at this skill) and will generally sarifice his body in any way necessary.

Except fighting, which Samuelsson does not do.

THE INTANGIBLES

You get the idea we like Samuelsson? We sure do. He is an elite level player if unlimited potential and ability, a world-class player with tremendous character and work ethic. He may very well be Hartford's best and most important player.

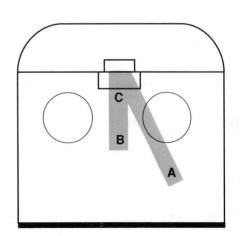

BRAD SHAW

Yrs. of NHL service: 1
Born: Cambridge, Ont., Canada; April 28, 1964
Position: Defenseman
Height: 5-11
Weight: 170
Uniform no.: 32
Shoots: right

Career statistics:

GP	G	A	TP	PIM
78	4	34	38	44

1989-90 statistics:

GP	G	A	TP	+/-	PIM	PP	SH	GW	GT	S	PCT
64	3	32	35	2	40	3	0	0	0	65	4.6

LAST SEASON

First full NHL season after four previous attempts. Games played and all point totals were career highs. Missed nine games with recurring back spasms, seven games with a foot injury.

THE FINESSE GAME

Though he's played just one NHL season, Shaw has demonstrated that he is Hartford's best puckhandling defensemen — so much so that he can control the game. Though not an outstanding skater (and skating is usually necessary to fully implement puckhandling ability) in terms of speed, Shaw can make the puck dance. He'll rush from his end to create offense, though he likes to pass off the rush, and he can distribute the puck excellently at the offensive blue line. He also uses his puckhandling skill to create ice for his teammates, and then he leads them into that ice with fine passes. As might be expected, he's a killer on the power play.

As mentioned, his skating lacks great speed but Shaw is a fairly mobile player. He demonstrates good instincts in his play around his own blue line (if only so as to force turnovers so he can go on offense), and his defensive zone coverage is aided by his hockey smarts. He may never be mistaken for Rod Langway, but Shaw is better than okay in his own end. Just as he does at the offensive blue line Shaw finds the open man well in his own zone, but he'll rush the puck as necessary — even if not to create a rush.

His stick skills do not necessarily translate to his goal scoring ability, and that may be because he lacks superior upper body strength.

THE PHYSICAL GAME

Shaw has to be smart with the puck because he's certainly not going to run anyone over with his skating strength. As mentioned, he would benefit from improved upper body strength; that added strength would allow him to compete more evenly in traffic situations, or even in simple one-on-one battles for the puck. Right now, he's going to be out-muscled. Because of that, he must be paired with a stronger partner who can act as the takeout man while Shaw is the breakout man.

THE INTANGIBLES

Shaw has been a star at every level at which he's played, and last year's performance shows that he has star potential in the NHL as well. He must stay away from injury (another reason why added strength and bulk is important), and he will have to demonstrate the ability to work through the added checking he will see this season — after all, he's not a secret any more.

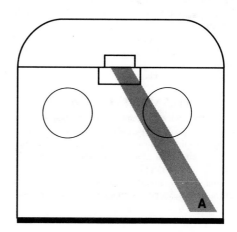

PETER SIDORKIEWICZ

Yrs. of NHL service: 2
Born: Dabrown Bialostocka, Poland; June 29, 1963
Position: Goaltender
Height: 5-9
Weight: 180
Uniform no.: 30
Catches: left

Career statistics:

GP	MINS	G	SO	AVG	A	PIM
91	5,398	300	5	3.33	4	4

1989-90 statistics:

GP	MINS	AVG	W	L	T	SO	GA	SA	SAPCT	PIM
46	2,703	3.57	19	19	7	1	161	1,203	.866	4

LAST SEASON

Games and minutes played totals rose in second full NHL season. He led Whaler goalies in those categories.

THE PHYSICAL GAME

Contrary to stereotype Sidorkiewicz is a smaller goaltender who plays a bigger man's standup style. That's a smart choice, because that angle-cutting and challenging game maximizes his size. His skating is good and Sidorkiewicz moves smoothly in and out of his net as he challenges shooters. He also uses his skating to flag down loose pucks in an attempt to help his defense, but he doesn't otherwise handle the puck.

He abandons his standup style on short-game play around the net, preferring to use a butterfly style to cover the lower portion of the goal, but his balance allows him to rapidly regain his stance. He succeeds more by his angle play than he does his reflex play, so plays that alter the direction of the puck (tip-ins, deflections) will succeed.

Like many goaltenders, he tends to cheat to his stick side. That, and his tendency to not completely square himself to the puck, make him more vulnerable to his left side than his right.

THE MENTAL GAME

Sidorkiewicz can maintain his calm and poise after horrendous goals or periods and come right back strongly — that's because he generally plays a controlled, unemotional game. When he does have trouble maintaining his confidence, the symptoms reveal themselves in his failing to cut the angle properly, as well as in the tendency to struggle throughout a game.

He otherwise has fairly good concentration and anticipation.

THE INTANGIBLES

What with Mike Liut's departure, Sidorkiewicz has been installed as the incumbent for the number one goalie slot. He'll still have to contend with Kay Whitmore, but Sidorkiewicz would seem to be the more securely entrenched of the two so the job should be Sidorkiewicz's to lose.

DAVE TIPPETT

Yrs. of NHL service: 6
Born: Moosomin, Sask., Canada; August 25, 1961
Position: Left wing/center
Height: 5-10
Weight: 180
Uniform no.: 15
Shoots: left

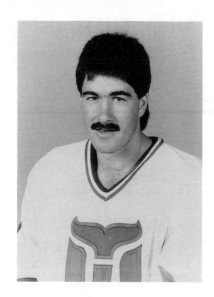

Career statistics:

GP	G	A	TP	PIM
483	75	120	195	183

1989-90 statistics:

GP	G	A	TP	+/-	PIM	PP	SH	GW	GT	S	PCT
66	8	19	27	0	32	0	1	3	0	91	8.8

LAST SEASON

Thumb surgery (13 games) prevented Tippett from recording his sixth consecutive 80-game season. All point totals were five-season lows.

THE FINESSE GAME

If you judged him just by his surface skills, Tippett wouldn't seem to be anything out of the ordinary. His skating is average in terms of speed and quickness, maybe a little better than that in the area of lateral movement and a degree higher in terms of strength and sturdiness.

His hand and stick skills certainly don't stand out. Tippett is not better than average at carrying the puck, maybe less than average when handling it in traffic. He doesn't have a goal scorer's ability to get into scoring position, nor does he demonstrate anything but average passing, playmaking and shooting skills. He's going to have to make relatively simple offensive plays, and the goals he scores are going to have to be opportunistic ones.

But look below the surface and you'll find the strength of Tippett's game: his understanding of the play and its implications, his ability to anticipate — his hockey sense, in short.

Tippett sees the ice very well and he uses his vision and anticipation to stay with his check excellently. That sense also makes him an excellent penalty killer, his anticipation makes his average skating better — he can be relentless in puck pursuit, and his skating strength gives him an almost tireless pace.

THE PHYSICAL GAME

Tippett is not an exceptionally physical player, so here too it is the subtle play that is his hallmark. While he won't bounce anyone into the bleachers, Tippett is certainly strong enough to hold up any of his opposing checks. His balance and his sturdiness on his skates are big helps here, especially when he is battling his check for control of the puck.

He excels at establishing position along the boards or in front of his goal, using his smarts to angle his body correctly and smartly so as not to hurt the club via penalties.

THE INTANGIBLES

We've said it before: it seems Tippett doesn't do anything exceptionally well — except succeed. He's one of the League's best checkers and defensive players, and his work ethic and determination are big reasons why he's found the success he has.

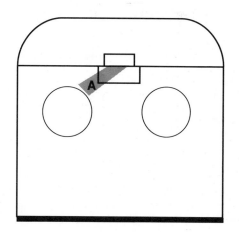

MIKE TOMLAK

Yrs. of NHL service: 1
Born: Thunder Bay, Ontario, Canada; October 17, 1964
Position: Left wing
Height: 6-3
Weight: 205
Uniform no.: 28
Shoots: left

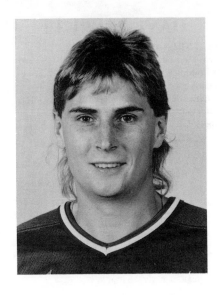

Career statistics:

GP	G	A	TP	PIM

1989-90 statistics:

GP	G	A	TP	+/-	PIM	PP	SH	GW	GT	S	PCT
70	7	14	21	5	48	1	1	2	0	64	10.9

LAST SEASON

First full NHL campaign. Missed one game with the flu, seven games with a broken wrist.

THE FINESSE GAME

Intelligence and hockey sense are the values Tomlak brings to his NHL game. He gets good reads of the ice and he uses that playreading ability as a strong checker and penalty killer. He forces play well during forechecking in the offensive zone more through smarts and strong angle play than he does through his skating, for Tomlak doesn't have a lot of speed to bring to his game. He is, however, a strong player and that strength is reflected in his skating stride, pace and endurance.

His hockey sense could carry into the offensive parts of the game, but Tomlak has not yet demonstrated the ability to recognize or create scoring opportunities. He doesn't handle the puck particularly well, and his shot is no better than average at this time. When he scores it's going to have to be opportunistically off pucks turned over due to his checking.

THE PHYSICAL GAME

Tomlak has size and he's willing to use it in his checking. Though mitigated to a degree because of his lack of NHL speed, Tomlak's smart angle play gets him near his opponent and from there he can rub him out along the boards. He is more of an efficient hitter than he is a spectacular one, but his strong skating stride and balance give him the ability to drive through his checks and take his man off the puck.

THE INTANGIBLES

Like teammates Todd Krygier and Brad Shaw, Hartford's new regime gave Tomlak a chance to show what he could do and Tomlak showed fairly well. He certainly held his own in his checking role and gave indication that he can contribute and grow in the NHL.

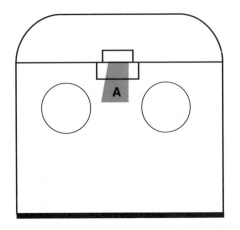

PAT VERBEEK

Yrs. of NHL service: 7
Born: Sarnia, Ontario, Canada; May 24, 1964
Position: Right wing
Height: 5-9
Weight: 195
Uniform no.: 16
Shoots: right

Career statistics:

GP	G	A	TP	PIM
543	214	196	410	1,171

1989-90 statistics:

GP	G	A	TP	+/-	PIM	PP	SH	GW	GT	S	PCT
80	44	45	89	1	228	14	0	5	1	219	20.1

LAST SEASON

Played 80 games for the first time in his career. Assist and point totals were career highs, goal total second highest of career. Led club in goals, PIM total and shooting percentage, finished second in assists, points, power play goals and shots on goal.

THE FINESSE GAME

Life is timing. All you have to do is be in the right place at the right time. Just ask Pat Verbeek.

The winger's best finesse asset is his timing, or anticipation if you will (though less charitable observers might call it conditioned response and nothing else). Whatever, Verbeek has learned to be a goal scorer by going to where the puck is going to be. He scores off scrambles in front and is opportunistic, picking up rebounds and other garbage. That skill makes him a premier power play player, and you'll find him posted in front of the net in the man-advantage situation. But he's more than just a power play specialist, as his 30 even-strength goals demonstrate.

He's a strong skater and can plant himself in the crease, but his balance remains a little high because of his barrel-like upper body. He doesn't have great foot speed (so there's not a lot of quickness), but Pat does have some rink length speed he can apply, and he can move pretty quickly once he gets his fireplug body moving.

He handles the puck no better than averagely when he carries it, and don't expect him to make Savard-like moves with it because he can't. Despite what his improved goal totals might indicate, Verbeek's straight ahead style reflects itself in his playmaking ability. He doesn't have great playreading creativity.

THE PHYSICAL GAME

The physical game is Verbeek's game, and he must play that way to be successful. He packs a lot of strength into a small package and is very aggressive, so he can hurt people when he hits them. Certainly he's willing to take hits, and he does so in the slot in order to score.

One disadvantage he suffers is in reach. If he's tied up with a bigger opponent who matches him in strength, Verbeek's lack of reach mitigates against him. But this is a not a major disadvantage, as most of Verbeek's opponents will be knocked on their behinds.

THE INTANGIBLES

As long as he remembers how he scores — which is as an offshoot of his physical play — Verbeek will be all right. His style is perfect for the crash-and-bang Adams Division, and there's no reason why he can't continue to be among the NHL's offensively potent right wings.

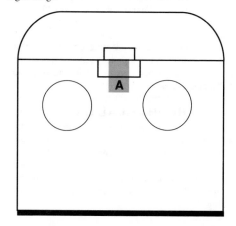

SCOTT YOUNG

Yrs. of NHL service: 2
Born: Clinton, Mass., USA; October 1, 1967
Position: Right wing
Height: 6-0
Weight: 190
Uniform no.: 27
Shoots: right

Career statistics:

GP	G	A	TP	PIM
163	43	80	123	76

1989-90 statistics:

GP	G	A	TP	+/-	PIM	PP	SH	GW	GT	S	PCT
80	24	40	64	-24	47	10	2	5	0	239	10.0

LAST SEASON

Games played and goal totals rose from rookie NHL season. Led team in shots on goal, but plus/minus rating was team's worst. Finished fourth on club in points.

THE FINESSE GAME

Skating is what key's Young's finesse abilities. He brings a good degree of speed to the Hartford lineup and he complements that speed with agility and sound lateral movement. His mobility is especially valuable for those times he falls back to defense, even if only while playing the point on the power play.

Young is a smart player with good anticipation, playreading and hockey sense abilities. He uses his sense in two ways that are really the same way, and that is either getting into scoring position himself or maneuvering a teammate to scoring position via his passing. Young is a good passer with fine touch on his passes, so he can feather or fire a pass as the situation dictates.

His hand skills extend to his ability to both carry the puck and shoot it, and he uses his balance to get his shot off while being checked; he releases his shot quickly and accurately.

He needs to continue adapting to the tempo of an NHL game so as to better understand how quickly he needs to make his decisions regarding passing and challenging as a skater.

THE PHYSICAL GAME

Young plays an efficient and unspectacular physical game, using his smarts and good size to win body position along the boards or in front of the net — in short, to command one-on-one confrontations. He's not a big banger, but Young uses the size and strength he has (and which could be improved) more than willingly.

He drives the net on offense and hits when he can, and his balance and leg strength help him maintain control in physical situations. He will also sacrifice his body to block shots.

THE INTANGIBLES

Young has a lot of potential, glimpses of which have been visible over the past two seasons. He has a strong attitude and works hard to improve, so that bodes well for his future. We are, by the way, at a loss to explain his plus/minus figure — which has been bad for two seasons now.

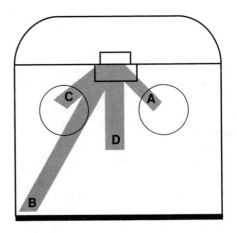

LOS ANGELES KINGS

MIKE ALLISON

Yrs. of NHL service: 10
Born: Ft. Francis, Ontario, Canada; March 28, 1961
Position: Right wing/center
Height: 6-1
Weight: 195
Uniform no.: 10
Shoots: right

Career statistics:

GP	G	A	TP	PIM
499	102	166	268	630

1989-90 statistics:

GP	G	A	TP	+/-	PIM	PP	SH	GW	GT	S	PCT
55	2	11	13	-6	78	0	0	1	0	25	8.0

LAST SEASON

Point totals were all full-season lows.

THE FINESSE GAME

Smarts and not skills are the keys to Allison's game, and the reason why he has played — and played well — in the NHL for a decade. Mike sees and reads the ice very well, especially in defensive or pursuit situations. That reading ability makes him a good forechecker, despite his limited skating ability. He gets good angles on the puck carrier, forcing the man into smaller and smaller space and then ultimately into bad plays. He is also a very good penalty killer for the same angle reasons.

Allison's play-reading ability and ice vision don't necessarily translate into offensive success — more a reflection of his physical finesse skills than anything else. He is a below average skater (too wide a stride means not much speed and even less agility), and the knee and leg injuries that have hobbled him throughout his career are directly attributable to his stride.

Because it so wide and his feet are so far apart, his weight is really planted when his feet are on the ice. When he gets hit, he is unable to shift his weight or dance away from the check, and so all the force is absorbed by one knee or the other.

He is smart defensively, so his plus/minus mark is a misleading indication of defensive ability.

THE PHYSICAL GAME

Allison has always played the best physical game he can muster, succeeding as a grinder and a mucker. That helps him in his boards work (his wide stance makes him hard to move off the puck), and he can knock people off the puck.

He is also a good faceoff man, one who can be used in crucial situations.

THE INTANGIBLES

Like fellow former Ranger Tom Laidlaw, Allison's physical condition (bad knees) will keep him out of games. But like Laidlaw, Allison is a strong team man and a very positive player. What he lacks in skill he makes up for in desire and heart, so Mike brings an excellent attitude and work ethic to the Kings.

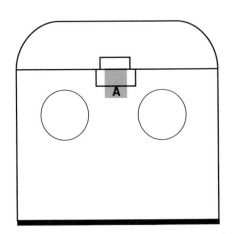

BRIAN BENNING

Yrs. of NHL service: 4
Born: Edmonton, Alta., Canada; June 10, 1966
Position: Defenseman
Height: 6-1
Weight: 185
Uniform no.: 2
Shoots: left

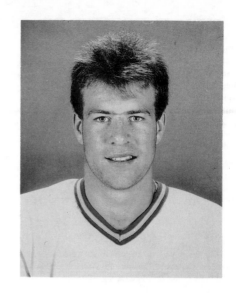

Career statistics:

GP	G	A	TP	PIM
280	35	112	147	425

1989-90 statistics:

GP	G	A	TP	+/-	PIM	PP	SH	GW	GT	S	PCT
55	6	19	25	-2	106	3	0	0	0	122	4.9

LAST SEASON

Acquired from St. Louis in November 1989. Games played and all point totals were full-season career lows (missed nine games with appendectomy).

THE FINESSE GAME

Brian has a whole package of finesse skills, and his skating is primary among them. His excellent balance and foot speed make him a very agile skater and give him excellent lateral ability. That allows him to force the opposition at the blue line, to be active instead of re-active. He also has good speed and acceleration, enough to back the defense off the opposing blue line.

Benning carries the puck very well and likes to rush from his own zone. He stickhandles well and his hockey sense shows him the openings; Brian looks to use his teammates and he jumps into the offense himself as a fourth attacker. He's an excellent one-on-one player.

While he can be a good scorer, he doesn't have exceptional goal scoring ability. Most of his goals will come from the point, but he'll cheat to the faceoff circle if there's an opening.

His skating allows him to cheat defensively, and he takes a lot of chances (many of which demonstrate poor judgement). While he can turn the play around quickly, Benning needs to play better positionally in his own zone and not try to run down every loose puck.

THE PHYSICAL GAME

Brian has good size and strength and he's not afraid to combine a physical game with his finesse one. He gets into the corner and mucks around, but his taking the body is more like pushing and shoving than it is hitting. He has difficulty pinning his man defensively.

Importantly, he'll initiate contact. His balance and hand skills make that contact more effective because they allow him to make plays away from the boards after hitting. The best part of his physical game is that he not only takes his hits to make plays, but he makes the plays after taking hits.

THE INTANGIBLES

He's a coachable player and, at 24 years old, Benning has plenty of time remaining in his NHL career. He's begun to strengthen some of his weaknesses, but he's still going to have to be paired with a tougher, more defensively oriented partner.

KEITH CROWDER

Yrs. of NHL service: 10
Born: Windsor, Ontario, Canada; January 6, 1959
Position: Right wing
Height: 6-0
Weight: 190
Uniform no.: 23
Shoots: right

Career statistics:

GP	G	A	TP	PIM
662	223	271	494	1,354

1989-90 statistics:

GP	G	A	TP	+/-	PIM	PP	SH	GW	GT	S	PCT
55	4	13	17	2	93	0	0	1	0	48	8.3

LAST SEASON

Games played and all point totals were full-season career lows. Missed 10 games with a neck injury, as well as time late in the season with a knee injury.

THE FINESSE GAME

Not a greatly skilled finesse player to begin with, Crowder's game is showing the signs of age and NHL wear and tear. While he has great strength on his skates (making him relentless in his pursuit of the puck), Keith has little speed or agility — and he's losing a step or two of what he does have. He does have great balance, and that trait is what makes his physical game work, keeping upright and in the play after collisions, but generally he slows his linemates down.

Keith can make use of his teammates because he keeps his head up, looking for that play from the corner instead of blindly flinging the puck goal-ward.

Using his physical style to open ice for his teammates is a great strength of Crowder's game, and he complements that style by effectively moving the puck to his now-open teammates. However, when he gets near the net he just barges through.

Most of Keith's goals are of the second effort variety, with Crowder shooting from the bottom of the faceoff circle and chasing the puck. But he also likes to work his way around the back of the net and tuck the puck in.

THE PHYSICAL GAME

Crowder is fearless in the corners and works them excellently. He sacrifices his body shift after shift. His strength and willingness to take physical abuse makes Crowder successful when he charges the net and, because of his strength, his shot is a powerful one.

Keith plays the same way at both ends of the ice and will rub out the opposition in the defensive zone as well as the offensive zone. Physical though he is, Crowder isn't a real fighter. He won't back down, but he won't fight unless heavily provoked.

THE INTANGIBLES

We told you last year that Crowder was expendable as a Bruin, not through lack of effort but through lack of result and lack of health. We say the same thing this season, especially considering the presence of Tomas Sandstrom and Tony Granato.

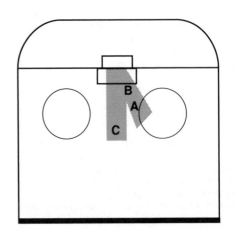

STEVE DUCHESNE

Yrs. of NHL service: 4
Born: Sept-Iles, Quebec, Canada; June 30, 1965
Position: Defenseman
Height: 5-11
Weight: 195
Uniform no.: 28
Shoots: left

Career statistics:

GP	G	A	TP	PIM
304	74	156	230	331

1989-90 statistics:

GP	G	A	TP	+/-	PIM	PP	SH	GW	GT	S	PCT
79	20	42	62	-3	36	6	0	1	1	224	8.9

LAST SEASON

Point totals were second highest of career. Led defensemen in scoring (ninth overall in NHL). Finished third on club in shots on goal. Plus/minus was worst among full-time defensemen.

THE FINESSE GAME

Duchesne is a exceptionally gifted in the finesse departments, making him a dangerous offensive player. He's a very mobile skater, with speed, quickness and agility, and those skills allow him to join rushes as a fourth attacker, to cheat into the slot for shots, to rush the puck himself, and to challenge at the points.

He doesn't use his skating as well defensively as he does offensively, though he certainly possesses the ability to step up and force the puck carrier at the Kings' blue line. This is more a play reading flaw than a physical one and, as such, can be corrected. He can turn the play around quickly, but because of that reading problem Duchesne can also make some bad giveaways.

He handles the puck well at top speed, making and accepting passes very well (he excels at controlling bouncing pucks), and he makes his offensive puckhandling better by doing it with his head up. He sees the open man, and he also sees challenging opponents at the offensive blue line — he'll skate around sliding shot-blockers.

He has an excellent shot from the point (strong and low), and shoots off the pass very well. He likes to go high glove with his wrist shot, but he's also smart enough to just put the puck on net when he has no other play.

His skills are best demonstrated on the power play, and he may very well be a better man-up player than he is an even-strength one.

THE PHYSICAL GAME

The physical game isn't really Duchesne's game, despite his fairly good size, so he can be less effective in a more physical contest. His corner and crease game is no better than average, and he'll have to be paired with a stronger partner ... but, because he is the breakout and not takeout defenseman, Duchesne is okay if holds his own.

THE INTANGIBLES

Duchesne is an above average player, and an above average offensive defenseman. His package isn't so good that he can compete with the likes of Paul Coffey (but then, who can?), but Duchesne needs to understand that he can still make his own game better.

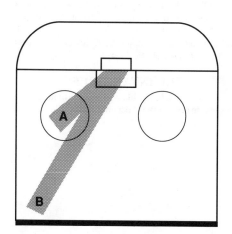

TODD ELIK

Yrs. of NHL service: 1
Born: Brampton, Ont., Canada; April 15, 1966
Position: Center
Height: 6-2
Weight: 190
Uniform no.: 6
Shoots: left

Career statistics:

GP	G	A	TP	+/-	PIM	PP	SH	GW	GT	S	PCT
48	10	23	33	4	41	1	0	0	0	86	11.6

LAST SEASON

First NHL season; joined the Kings in December 1989.

THE FINESSE GAME

Elik is an offensive player, one who likes to handle the puck and make plays. He's not a great skater in terms of speed or agility, but he has a certain degree of quickness that gets him to loose pucks or allows him to turn a defenseman.

His greatest finesse ability is concentrated in his hands. He handles the puck and shoots it very well (bordering on excellent as a shooter because of his quick release), but he doesn't shoot the puck anywhere near often enough (his slow skating speed also thwarts him in his attempts to get open). He has a tendency to overhandle the puck, but that's because he has a high degree of success in making good plays. He likes to carry the puck over the blue line.

His defensive play is adequate at best, and he could pay a lot more attention to his defensive responsibilities.

THE PHYSICAL GAME

Elik is a big guy, but there's not a lot of muscle on him; he can be out-muscled for the puck. Still, he's willing to tough it out along the boards or in traffic in pursuit of the puck — the question is just one of success. He's not afraid of physical play.

THE INTANGIBLES

Time will tell for Elik, who will see more ice time this season because of the departure of Bernie Nicholls.

He's a confident kid, bordering on cocky, which may or may not be a good thing for a player just finishing his first NHL season. Improved skating and attention to defense will go a long way toward insuring Elik's future NHL success.

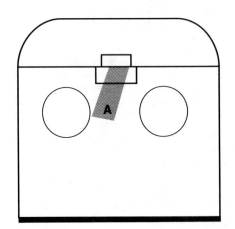

MARIO GOSSELIN

Yrs. of NHL service: 6
Born: Thetford Mines, Quebec, Canada; June 15, 1963
Position: Goaltender
Height: 5-8
Weight: 165
Uniform no.: 31
Catches: left

Career statistics:

GP	MINS	G	SO	AVG	A	PIM
218	11,751	723	6	3.69	8	40

1989-90 statistics:

GP	MINS	AVG	W	L	T	SO	GA	SA	SAPCT	PIM
26	1,226	3.87	7	11	1	0	79	587	.865	0

LAST SEASON

Games played total was full-season career low (he spent time inNew Haven of the American Hockey League).

THE PHYSICAL GAME

Gosselin lives and dies with his reflexes. Because of his fast hands and faster feet (his left foot in particular) he'll get to almost every puck he can see.

He uses his speed to great effect on scrambles in close to the net, and though he flops to the ice constantly his balance helps him regain his footing — so he can fling himself at the next shot. The problem, however, is that his butterfly style leaves the top of the net open for rebounds — of which there are plenty.

Mario is a good skater and he moves well in and out of the net to counter screens. He tracks down loose pucks, but doesn't help himself with puck movement; he just leaves the puck for his defense.

Because he doesn't conserve energy by cutting down the angle and just letting the puck hit him, Gosselin suffers fatigue both within games and throughout the season.

THE MENTAL GAME

Gosselin has good concentration skills, and he can certainly raise the level of his game to make big saves (he loves pressure situations), but he's been largely unable to do that with any consistency.

His concentration within a game is good, especially as he tracks the puck near the net, and he's easygoing in that bad goals or games don't stay with him.

THE INTANGIBLES

We told you last year that Mario would be out of Quebec and that he may in fact be running out of NHL time. We again say that his time in the NHL could be coming to an end, what with LA's development of Robb Stauber. Gosselin may be able to hang around through expansion, but minor league duty is almost certainly in his future.

TONY GRANATO

Yrs. of NHL service: 2
Born: Downers Grove, Illinois, USA; July 25, 1964
Position: Right wing
Height: 5-10
Weight: 175
Uniform no.: 14
Shoots: right

Career statistics:

GP	G	A	TP	PIM
134	48	51	99	262

1989-90 statistics:

GP	G	A	TP	+/-	PIM	PP	SH	GW	GT	S	PCT
56	12	24	36	-1	122	2	0	0		0	120	10.0

LAST SEASON

Acquired along with Tomas Sandstrom in exchange for Bernie Nicholls. Games played and all point totals were career lows. Missed 12 games with a groin injury.

THE FINESSE GAME

Clearly, Granato's best finesse skill is his skating. His speed makes him a breakaway threat and his quickness combines with his balance to make him a very agile skater. Currently, he uses his skating in a north/south way, in that he's very much a charge up-and-down the ice player. His agility will give him good lateral movement (east/west, as it were) once he begins to think in that dimension.

His skating is made better by the fact that he can handle the puck at his top speed; that may change should he integrate more of a lateral game into his own. Right now, he's going to go right at the defenseman — and then right around him.

Granato's shot is fairly dynamic, in that he gets it away quickly, strongly and accurately. He's got the hands to score on breakaways and to finesse the puck while in traffic, but most of his goals will come from being opportunistic near the net — using his quickness to snare loose pucks.

THE PHYSICAL GAME

Granato plays a very physical game, perhaps even too physical. He certainly doesn't have great size (though Tony is in excellent shape and has good strength for his size), but that doesn't stop Granato from flinging himself at anything he can in true kamikaze fashion.

And because his style (and his mouth, and his stick) drives the opposition to distraction, Granato also absorbs a lot of punishment from players anxious to make him pay for his misdeeds.

THE INTANGIBLES

Granato's a good team man, a good man in general. He's a character individual because of his work ethic and intensity, but he is not (as we mentioned last year) a big goal scorer. Rather, he gives the Kings speed, good forechecking and penalty killing, and outstanding effort and coachability.

His size will continue to be a concern in the current NHL, though that may change after expansion.

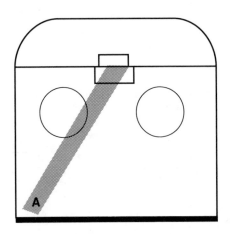

WAYNE GRETZKY

Yrs. of NHL service: 12
Born: Brantford, Ontario, Canada; January 26, 1961
Position: Center
Height: 6-0
Weight: 170
Uniform no.: 99
Shoots: left

Career statistics:

GP	G	A	TP	PIM
847	677	1,302	1,979	406

1989-90 statistics:

GP	G	A	TP	+/-	PIM	PP	SH	GW	GT	S	PCT
73	40	102	142	8	42	10	4	4	1	236	16.9

LAST SEASON

Games played, assist and point totals were second lowest of career. Goal total tied career low. Led NHL in scoring and assists, led club in shorthanded goals. Second on club in goals and shots on goal, third in power play goals. Second among forwards in plus/minus. Sidelined late in season with back injury.

THE FINESSE GAME

Physically, it is Gretzky's balance that keys his exceptional finesse game. That balance makes him agile and mobile, letting him lean forward, backward and sideways in order to weave his puckhandling magic. That balance makes him an outstanding skater, even though he doesn't have breakaway speed. His lateral movement, though, is almost unparalleled.

He sees plays with computer-quickness, evaluating potential developments and choosing the play that best suits the moment. What makes all this better is his phenomenal patience. Though predictable in his rushes (up the right wing he's going to cut to center along the offensive blue line, and up the left wing he heads to the faceoff circle and then loops back to the blue line) Gretzky just stalls the opposition while waiting for the late man. This is no secret — he just has the game's furthest panic point and uses that patience to his advantage.

His stick skills match his foot and brain skills. He uses his entire team better than anyone in the world, his touch as a passer is unmatched and he steals the puck from behind better than anyone. His shooting is just as exceptional as his passing. He'll put the puck anywhere at anytime, regardless of circumstance, making the puck rise or sink depending upon how he releases it.

THE PHYSICAL GAME

Gretzky is not afraid of physical contests, but he doesn't embrace them either. He can become frustrated when he's hit or at all impeded (he'll go to the ice looking for a call), but his balance is such that he spins off most every check aimed at him — if his anticipation hasn't gotten him away from the hit in the first place. He plays in the high traffic areas all the time.

THE INTANGIBLES

The level of play in the NHL has grown to the point that, on any given night in any given game, any one of several players — Gretzky, Steve Yzerman, Denis Savard, Pat LaFontaine, Brett Hull, Mario Lemieux, Mark Messier, Ray Bourque — can be the League's best player. That evolution is only natural, even if the observation is heretical (*"Someone other than Gretzky the best player? Come On!"*).

We've documented our thoughts about the Great One through four previous editions, and to win one game we'd still choose Wayne over anyone. Which is not to say that he is the best, bar none. Rather, because of a variety of factors (not the least of which are the toll 13 NHL seasons take on a body, and the aforementioned evolution of talent), the who's better debate has grown to include a new cast of characters.

We mean no disrespect to Gretzky and his accomplishments; we're just trying to say that his margin of greatness is less vast than it was 10, five or even two years ago.

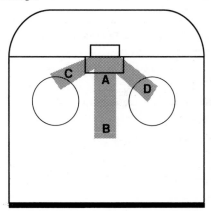

KELLY HRUDEY

Yrs. of NHL service: 7
Born: Edmonton, Alberta, Canada; January 13, 1961
Position: Goaltender
Height: 5-10
Weight: 180
Uniform no.: 32
Catches: left

Career statistics:

GP	MINS	G	SO	AVG	A	PIM
309	17,453	1,028	9	3.53	10	125

1989-90 statistics:

GP	MINS	AVG	W	L	T	SO	GA	SA	SAPCT	PIM
52	2,860	4.07	22	21	6	2	194	1,532	.873	18

LAST SEASON

Games and minutes played totals were second highest of career. Finished eighth in NHL in minutes played, second in goals allowed, fifth in shots faced. He missed five games with a virus.

THE PHYSICAL GAME

Hrudey is an excellent standup goaltender who complements that style with outstanding reflexes. He positions himself very well in the net, squaring himself to the shooter and letting the puck do the work. By cutting the angle, he also makes certain to get a good look at the puck, and Hrudey's vision is better than most; rare is the shot that gets by that he hasn't seen and made an attempt at.

That vision combines with his reflexes (he has outstandingly quick hands and feet) to make Hrudey outstanding in scrambles near the front of the net. His quick feet and excellent balance mean that he moves across the crease very well; those assets also get him to the ice and back on his feet just as well. As with his vision, his exceptionally fast hands and feet insure that he'll get a piece of every puck that comes his way.

His speed and vision also mean he's almost impervious to first shots, so tips and other redirections are the key to beating him.

Hrudey handles the puck well and will move it to his defensemen, but he is generally restrained in his wandering.

THE MENTAL GAME

Hrudey is exceptionally tough mentally, the kind of goaltender who is unaffected by a bad goal or game and will bounce back to fight for the next save or win. He also has superb concentration (which greatly aids his vision), and these assets combine with his physical play to give him big save capability — the ability to win games by himself.

He is always prepared for that night's game.

THE INTANGIBLES

Like another former Islander-turned-King (Roland Melanson), Hrudey is discovering that his style and that of the Kings may be incompatible. He can't count on open wingers being covered on cross-ice passes, so more and more Hrudey looks like he's off-balance. Rather, he's just throwing himself across the crease to cover for another's mistake.

Despite the looks, Hrudey remains one of the NHL's best goalies.

STEVE KASPER

Yrs. of NHL service: 9
Born: Montreal, Quebec, Canada; September 29, 1961
Position: Center
Height: 5-8
Weight: 170
Uniform no.: 11
Shoots: left

Career statistics:

GP	G	A	TP	PIM
670	161	263	424	491

1989-90 statistics:

GP	G	A	TP	+/-	PIM	PP	SH	GW	GT	S	PCT
77	17	28	45	4	27	1	1	4	0	72	23.6

LAST SEASON

Games played total was five-season low, goal, assist and point totals were four-season lows.

THE FINESSE GAME

Mental finesse skills are the keys to Kasper's game, and they are the things that continue to power his game after a decade of NHL service. His ice vision and anticipation — his hockey sense — are excellent, and he uses those abilities in an active rather than reactive way. That is, he doesn't have to chase the puck — he'll go to where it's going to be, not follow where it's been. He always knows where he is on the ice in relation to his man, the puck and the net, and these skills make him an obvious choice for penalty killing duty.

He can use his smarts to get the puck to his teammates (and his checking will create loose pucks), but he is not often cast in an offensive role.

His skating stamina and endurance are the highlights of his physical finesse skills, making his good (but not great) speed and quickness more effective.

He's a good puckhandler and can move it smoothly to his wingers. His hand skills continue to his hard wrist shot from the slot and NHL-caliber slap shot, and those skills are best shown off in Kasper's faceoff ability. He's the guy most likely to take those crucial draws in the Kings' zone late in the game.

THE PHYSICAL GAME

Conditioning is obviously the key to Kasper's game, re his skating. Don't bother trying to stop him by double-shifting against him—it won't work. He doesn't have great size, but Kasper makes the most of what he has by playing smartly. He can hit but is not punishing when he does so, and rare are the times that he hits anyway. He does, however, have the strength necessary to hold his man out of the play, and he can do it as effectively at the end of his shift as at the beginning.

THE INTANGIBLES

On a team that charges ahead as much as the Kings and neglects the defensive zone almost as frequently, a player who takes pride in playing defensively — and plays well — is an important character. Steve Kasper is that character.

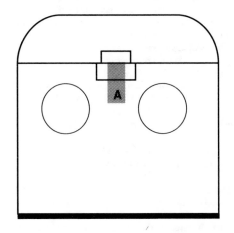

MIKE KRUSHELNYSKI

Yrs. of NHL service: 9
Born: Montreal, Quebec, Canada; April 27, 1960
Position: Left wing/center
Height: 6-2
Weight: 200
Uniform no.: 26
Shoots: left

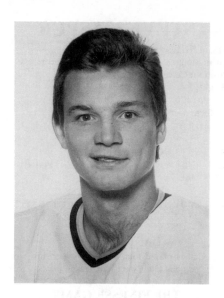

Career statistics:

GP	G	A	TP	PIM
593	188	257	445	473

1989-90 statistics:

GP	G	A	TP	+/-	PIM	PP	SH	GW	GT	S	PCT
63	16	25	41	7	50	2	2	2	1	101	15.8

LAST SEASON

Games played total was second lowest of career; ditto point total. He missed 17 games with a wrist injury. Plus/minus was third best among forwards.

THE FINESSE GAME

Krushelnyski is a superior skater, one of the NHL's best (even if he's not recognized as such). His long stride and acceleration pull him away from the opposition and put him in the clear, and his high degree of balance gives him great agility in closer quarters. That balance also keeps him vertical after collisions, ready and able to make plays.

His reach and soft hands make him a fine puckhandler and, added to his balance (the ability to work while being checked), make him exceedingly dangerous in tight. He'll tease a defender with the puck to force an opening, and then take advantage of that opening with either a pass or a shot. He combines his physical finesse skills with vision and anticipation to find the open man and take advantage of him. Those same hand skills make Krushelnyski an outstanding faceoff man.

He shoots well, using his quickly released, hard and accurate wrist shot to force the goaltender to make saves. He is an opportunist and will swoop to the net to pick up a loose puck in an attempt to shovel it home.

THE PHYSICAL GAME

Paradoxically, Krushelnyski is a tough player who doesn't always play tough. Rather, he stays to the outside of crowds and works — for lack of a better word — as an artist and not a plumber. Though his skills make him an ideal traffic player, he prefers to stay out of the high traffic areas in the corners and in front of the net.

He will make his plays while being hit, uses his reach very well in snaring pucks and powers his shot with good arm and wrist strength (that's where his faceoff ability comes from).

THE INTANGIBLES

Krushelnyski is essentially an underachiever, a player who could accomplish more than he does because he has the package to be better. He needs to bring more intensity and effort to his game — he doesn't push himself as often as he could.

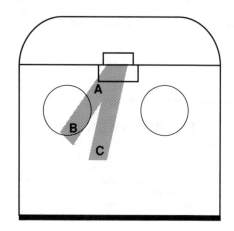

ROBERT KUDELSKI

Yrs. of NHL service: 2
Born: Springfield, Mass., USA; March 3, 1964
Position: Right wing
Height: 6-1
Weight: 200
Uniform no.: 37
Shoots: right

Career statistics:

GP	G	A	TP	PIM
102	24	17	41	74

1989-90 statistics:

GP	G	A	TP	+/-	PIM	PP	SH	GW	GT	S	PCT
62	23	13	36	-7	49	2	2	3	0	135	17.0

LAST SEASON

First full NHL season after two previous tries. He missed 15 games with a hand injury.

THE FINESSE GAME

Kudelski is paradoxical as a player, in that he has an excellent shot but isn't a great scorer. Lack of skating skill is the problem here, specifically a lack of speed. While Kudelski can get going once he gets revved up, he needs a long runway for takeoff. Because of that, he rarely gets open for scoring chances — which makes his 23 goals all the more remarkable.

He has an excellent wrist shot and his good ice vision and anticipation show him the openings (he's also intelligent enough to go to the net), but he's otherwise hampered by his skating.

He's a decent defensive player, aided as he is by his intelligence and vision.

THE PHYSICAL GAME

Kudelski is not an outstandingly physical player, and he could be more aggressive on the puck, but he is one of Los Angeles' better boards players because of his size and strength. He won't drive anyone through the boards with his hitting but he will take them off the puck, and his hands are certainly good enough to make plays after those hits.

His size and strength also help him as he drives the net, as well as serving to make him a fairly good faceoff man.

THE INTANGIBLES

Kudelski is an intelligent player (not surprising for a Yale man), and as his ice time and NHL experience grow, so too will his ability. Improved skating ability would further that improvement.

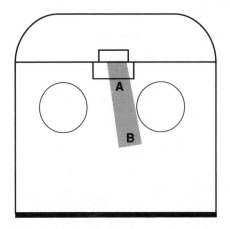

TOM LAIDLAW

Yrs. of NHL service: 10
Born: Brampton, Ontario, Canada; April 15, 1958
Position: Defenseman
Height: 6-1
Weight: 205
Uniform no.: 3
Shoots: left

Career statistics:

GP	G	A	TP	PIM
705	25	139	164	717

1989-90 statistics:

GP	G	A	TP	+/-	PIM	PP	SH	GW	GT	S	PCT
57	1	8	9	4	42	0	0	0	0	27	3.7

LAST SEASON

Games played tied, and assist and point totals set, career marks. Missed four games with an eye injury, nine games with knee injuries, and time with a back injury. He was LA's lowest scoring regular player.

THE FINESSE GAME

Every year we say the same things about Laidlaw — and we don't mean that as an insult, we mean it as a compliment to his consistency and determination. He succeeds because of his smarts, and it is those smarts that keep him within the boundaries of his game. He's a dependable defensive defenseman — maybe the club's best (Tim Watters might give him a run for that title), and he uses his knowledge of positional play and good play reading ability to earn that ranking.

Laidlaw has to play that way, because his finesse skills are unexceptional. His skating is slow and lacks anything above average mobility; he's slow turning and won't challenge at either blue line. But Laidlaw knows his limits, so he applies his smarts as compensation.

His hand skills mirror his foot skills (as his numbers would indicate), and he'll move the puck so he doesn't have to handle it. Laidlaw makes simple plays, and he makes them well. He almost never shoots the puck, but he has developed the tendency of sneaking two or three strides off the line for wrist shots.

THE PHYSICAL GAME

The physical game is Laidlaw's game, and he plays it in as smart a way as he plays his finesse game. Nothing fancy or earth-shattering — just solid takeouts along the boards and cleared creases in front of the Kings' goalies. Laidlaw is consistently physical and aggressive, even if he won't bounce anyone into next week. He sacrifices his body by blocking shots.

THE INTANGIBLES

Health will always be a question with Tom, especially now because of his age and his proclivity for playing physically. He's going to be hurt at least once during a season (for the above reasons, although better conditioning might help), and his ability to play strong back-to-back games is fading.

That said, he's a super team man, popular and always positive, always up.

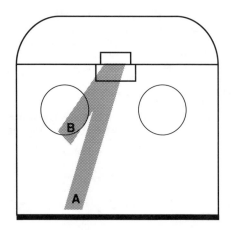

MIKKO MAKELA

Yrs. of NHL service: 5
Born: Tampere, Finland; February 28, 1965
Position: Right wing
Height: 6-2
Weight: 193
Uniform no.: 24
Shoots: left

Career statistics:

GP	G	A	TP	PIM
352	102	138	240	114

1989-90 statistics:

GP	G	A	TP	+/-	PIM	PP	SH	GW	GT	S	PCT
65	9	17	26	-14	18	1	0	0	1	82	11.0

LAST SEASON

Acquired by the Kings in exchange for Hubie McDonough and Ken Baumgartner. Games played and all point totals were full-season career lows. Plus/minus was club's worst. He missed time with a bruised shoulder.

THE FINESSE GAME

Makela has everything needed finesse-wise to be an NHL star. He's an exceptional skater in all aspects of that skill: speed, quickness, agility, balance. He can change speed and direction within a stride, providing him with superior mobility and lateral movement.

Mikko complements his skating skill with brains; his sense tells him where to be, his feet put him there. Makela knows how to get into scoring position, but also knows how to find and exploit the openings for his teammates. His peripheral vision is excellent and reveals the position of everyone on-ice.

His hand skills are just as good as his other attributes. Makela can carry the puck and make plays with it at any speed. He has great passing touch, and can deliver or accept a pass in full stride.

Makela's shot is the best of his hand skills. While he has the ability to hit the top of the net off a one-time from 10-feet (*that's* touch), he also has the strength to blow the puck past any goaltender from the distances. He's a very dangerous scorer, very creative with the puck.

THE PHYSICAL GAME

Makela's size and strength are just as major-league as his finesse skills — and even if they weren't, he's almost talented enough to make the physical part irrelevant. But nevertheless, Mikko is strong enough to hold off the biggest defensemen in order to make his plays.

He uses his balance and reach excellently in his puckhandling, teasing the defense with the puck. He is willing to take his knocks to make his plays, and his balance and low center of gravity aid him in working for the puck along the boards and in traffic.

THE INTANGIBLES

Makela has continued his backward slide; he must be the most enigmatic (and frustrating to coach) player in the NHL. None of what we've written above means a thing, because Makela simply refuses to put his talent to work. Some other team might get fooled, but — because of his attitude — we can't imagine Makela remaining in the NHL much longer.

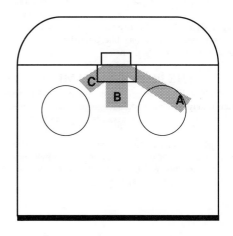

MARTY MCSORLEY

Yrs. of NHL service: 7
Born: Hamilton, Ontario, Canada; May 18, 1963
Position: Defenseman/right wing
Height: 6-1
Weight: 230
Uniform no.: 33
Shoots: right

Career statistics:

GP	G	A	TP	PIM
388	49	78	127	1,558

1989-90 statistics:

GP	G	A	TP	+/-	PIM	PP	SH	GW	GT	S	PCT
75	15	21	36	2	322	2	1	0	1	127	11.8

LAST SEASON

Games played and all point totals were career highs. PIM total was second highest of career, third highest in NHL and highest on team. He missed one game with a bruised thigh.

THE FINESSE GAME

McSorley is an average skater at the NHL level, making do more with his power and strength than with any speed, quickness or agility. McSorley's skating greatly improved through his association: By playing and practicing with and against the world's best players (when he was with the Oilers), Marty naturally became a better skater. That said, his agility is still no better than average and he can be deked by opposing forwards. He will, however, join rushes up-ice.

Marty doesn't handle the puck all that well, and he counters that weakness by not handling the puck except when necessary. When playing defense and moving the puck from the defensive end, rare is the time that he'll take more than three strides with it.

He plays a fairly well disciplined game positionally (and he plays almost exclusively at defense now), but needs to be paired with a more mobile partner. He shoots mainly from the blue line, but will take chances heading to the slot and the net.

THE PHYSICAL GAME

McSorley hits at every opportunity and does so punishingly. He has good strength and will win the battles in the corners and the boards, as well as the front of both nets.

McSorley is a fighter and sees more than his share of action. He is one of those players with a Jekyll-and-Hyde personality, and he can 'click out' (as the vernacular goes) on the ice and go crazy.

THE INTANGIBLES

McSorley is an irritating player to play against, and he can draw penalties that help the Kings. But, because he plays so emotionally, he can also take penalties that hurt the Kings. He needs to hold that balance.

He knows his role as a tough guy and plays that role willingly. He defends the team's smaller and better players, and McSorley also works constantly at improving his modest finesse skills.

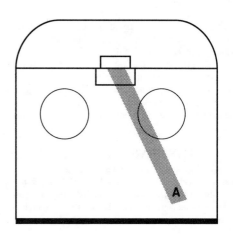

JAY MILLER

Yrs. of NHL service: 5
Born: Wellesley, Mass., USA; July 16, 1960
Position: Left wing
Height: 6-2
Weight: 210
Uniform no.: 29
Shoots: right

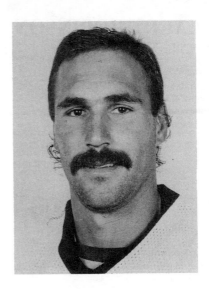

Career statistics:

GP	G	A	TP	PIM
313	28	25	53	1,215

1989-90 statistics:

GP	G	A	TP	+/-	PIM	PP	SH	GW	GT	S	PCT
68	10	2	12	-6	224	0	0	1	0	44	22.7

LAST SEASON

Games played and goal totals were career highs. PIM total was club's second highest, tops among forwards.

THE FINESSE GAME

Mobility is a problem for Miller, especially on larger ice surfaces and against better skating teams. He is an average skater at best, lacking real speed or quickness. His balance is the best of his skating assets, and that balance aids him in his physical game by keeping him vertical after collisions and upright and rooted when fighting.

He demonstrates no real ability in handling the puck, whether by carrying it or passing it to teammates, and rarely — if ever — shoots when he is in position to do so. If he's going to make a play, Miller needs plenty of time and space. As such, his scoring must be of the opportunistic kind from in front of the net.

His checking duty will be rare, both because of his skating and because his understanding of the NHL game and his ability to read the ice — though improved — remain weak.

THE PHYSICAL GAME

Miller is a fighter, ready and willing. His size and strength combine with his balance to make him one of the NHL's better fighters, and his willingness creates room for his more talented teammates.

He can be a punishing hitter when he catches someone, but his skating works against him in the bodychecking department. Still, his excellent strength and size means he can hurt the opposition.

THE INTANGIBLES

Miller is essentially a one-dimensional player, and because he can't play in a skating game his ice time will continue to be limited to tough games and enforcer situations. Not that he doesn't work to improve (he's a tenacious practice player), but that effort hasn't been translated into effect.

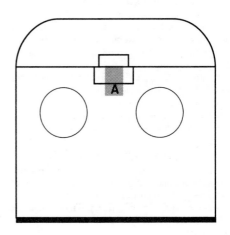

LARRY ROBINSON

Yrs. of NHL service: 17
Born: Winchester, Ontario, Canada; June 2, 1951
Position: Defenseman
Height: 6-4
Weight: 225
Uniform no.: 19
Shoots: left

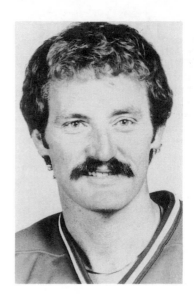

Career statistics:

GP	G	A	TP	PIM
1,266	204	718	922	740

1989-90 statistics:

GP	G	A	TP	+/-	PIM	PP	SH	GW	GT	S	PCT
64	7	32	39	7	34	1	0	1	1	80	8.8

LAST SEASON

Games played total was second lowest of career, point total third lowest. Plus/minus was second best among defensemen.

THE FINESSE GAME

Despite age and the requisite wear and tear, Robinson still skates well. While his rushes up-ice have generally fallen by the wayside the odd rush to relieve pressure on his forwards isn't out of the question. He is slower afoot than ever before, so he can be beaten to the corners or left a step behind by a successful fake.

Larry still moves the puck for the breakout pass extremely well, and he'll still see power play time because of his ability to find the open man. Larry does a little cheating into the zone, and he still does well in containing the play.

Smarts and almost two decades of NHL experience are the keys to Robinson's success now. He knows when to challenge and when to stay within his diminishing range of skills.

His positional play is almost textbook-like, courtesy of his anticipation and play-reading capabilities. Robinson sees the ice defensively as well as any superstar forward sees it offensively. The question as time goes by, though, is what can he do about it?

THE PHYSICAL GAME

Though less aggressive than earlier in his career, Robinson still plays a physical game. He does whatever is necessary to contain the play and gain the puck; if that means just taking the body, fine. If it means thumping a little harder to clear the crease, fine.

Larry is still a strong player, and he'll often shoulder the responsibility of handling the League's bigger and tougher forwards. Perhaps the most startling thing is that his physical game has remained effective without Robinson growing into larger PIM totals. In other words, his physical play doesn't hurt the team.

THE INTANGIBLES

The Big Bird is more and more less and less a factor on the ice. But he remains a titan in the locker room. He is a team leader of the highest order, one who can still lift a team when necessary. We mean no disrespect when we say Robinson's skills have diminished. In fact, his ability to contribute in the NHL despite 18 years of combat shows just how extraordinary Robinson is.

His will to win remains unsurpassed, and is an invaluable example to the team's younger players.

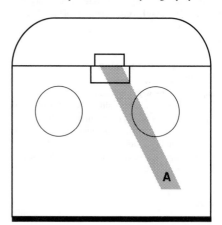

LUC ROBITAILLE

Yrs. of NHL service: 4
Born: Montreal, Quebec, Canada; February 17, 1966
Position: Left wing
Height: 6-1
Weight: 190
Uniform no.: 20
Shoots: left

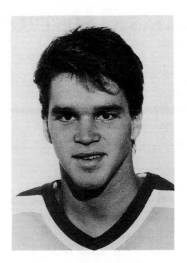

Career statistics:

GP	G	A	TP	PIM
317	196	198	394	213

1989-90 statistics:

GP	G	A	TP	+/-	PIM	PP	SH	GW	GT	S	PCT
80	52	49	101	8	38	20	0	7	0	210	24.8

LAST SEASON

Played 80 games for second time. Goal and point totals second highest of career. Finished second on club in points, first in goals, power play goals, game winners and shooting percentage. Led NHL in shooting percentage, was fifth in power play goals. Finished 12th overall in League scoring. Plus/minus tied for club's third best (Wayne Gretzky), second best among forwards.

THE FINESSE GAME

Robitaille's hands are the hallmark of his game, the hands of a premier NHL scorer. Overwhelmingly, his shot is his finest finesse skill. He has great hands in front of the net and a very quick stick, and his touch is demonstrated by his ability to score to the most difficult areas of the net while being checked — up high, and between the goalie's legs by re-direction as the goaltender moves. His hand skill extends to his puckhandling; he can make plays at most speeds, but Robitaille is far better at getting into scoring position without the puck than he is at deking an entire team.

The second half of his superior scoring ability is his sense, the skill that puts him in position to score. As reflected in his shot itself (Robitaille knows intuitively where he's shooting before he even gets the puck), Luc reads the ice very well and he uses that anticipation to create openings or slip into holes.

His skating is nowhere near his hand skills, but nor is it as poor as has been made out. Rather, he succeeds by using his best assets to his best result. Nevertheless, he's a strong and well-balanced skater (he'll makes plays and release his shot while being checked), but he lacks the dynamic skating ability evidenced by the League's flashier skaters.

Robitaille's defense is average, but he can still be mesmerized by the puck and he will make absent-minded plays.

THE PHYSICAL GAME

The physical game is not Robitaille's forte, in that he doesn't initiate a lot of contact. He's not afraid of physical play, and he'll work in the traffic areas along the boards and in front of the net, but he's not necessarily equipped with the size and strength to dominate those areas. On the other hand, if you're not Cam Neely, why play like Cam Neely?

His balance and skating strength give him an advantage in this area.

THE INTANGIBLES

Robitaille is a quality kid, one with strong desire and determination. His work ethic is good, but he does need occasional reminding to bear down. His scoring consistency remains questionable; in 1988-89, he tallied only 12 times in his last 28 games. Last season, he scored just 11 goals in his last 19 games, of which just six were at even-strength. Could his conditioning need work?

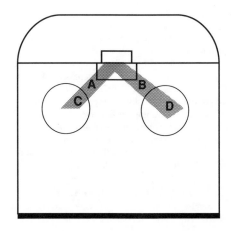

TOMAS SANDSTROM

Yrs. of NHL service: 6
Born: Jakobstad, Finland; September 4, 1964
Position: Right wing
Height: 6-2
Weight: 204
Uniform no.: 7
Shoots: left

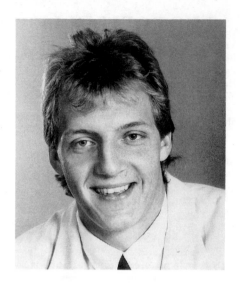

Career statistics:

GP	G	A	TP	PIM
435	186	227	413	591

1989-90 statistics:

GP	G	A	TP	+/-	PIM	PP	SH	GW	GT	S	PCT
76	32	39	71	-11	128	7	1	3	1	249	12.9

LAST SEASON

Acquired along with Tony Granato in exchange for Bernie Nicholls. Games played total was second highest of career, point total third highest. Finished third on Kings in goals and points, second among forwards in PIM total, and first in shots on goal. He missed five games with a facial fracture.

THE FINESSE GAME

Where previously skating and shooting were the hallmarks of Sandstrom's game, he's now added play-making to the list. He's an excellent skater with speed and agility, and Tomas has learned to bull defensemen off the blue line with his skating and to then use the extra space created to make a pass and lead a teammate. Previously, if he got a step he was making the play himself.

His very good hands combine with his balance to make him an ideal traffic player. He maintains body position despite being checked, and he makes plays from all of those contortions.

His great hockey sense shows him the openings, his speed puts him in the holes and his hands power his exceptional shot. His slap shot is among the League's best, and it can beat *any* goalie. He likes the long side of the net, low on the ice, and he gets his shot away in one touch. Lately, he's added the top of the net to his repertoire.

Though he still doesn't shoot anywhere near enough, Sandstrom has allowed his passing skills (he passes and takes a pass extremely well, and he can execute with all of his skills at top speed) to work.

Sandstrom has improved to average defensively. He still plays a far more interested game in the neutral and offensive zones, but Sandstrom can be a strong defensive player; his penalty killing stints showcase his sense and skating to illustrate the point.

THE PHYSICAL GAME

Sandstrom is a very aggressive player, in all manners of the game. He takes the body and checks very well, and he is also among the League's chippiest players with his stick and elbows. The word is out on him now, but despite that he still draws penalties by getting under the skin of the opposition; he thrives on their retaliation.

He is not a fighter, but Sandstrom will bump with anyone.

THE INTANGIBLES

When he wants to, Tomas can dominate a game; all he needs is intensity. But the Rangers were displeased with his performance early in the season when his center — Carey Wilson — was injured, and Sandstrom picked up none of the slack. That made him expendable when Bernie Nicholls became available.

Still, Tomas is one of the NHL's better players, and we still maintain that — when he wants to be — he's among the League's best.

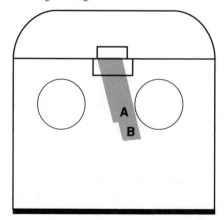

DAVE TAYLOR

Yrs. of NHL service: 12
Born: Levack, Ontario, Canada; December 4, 1955
Position: Right wing
Height: 6-0
Weight: 190
Uniform no.: 18
Shoots: right

Career statistics:

GP	G	A	TP	PIM
880	388	577	965	1,301

1989-90 statistics:

GP	G	A	TP	+/-	PIM	PP	SH	GW	GT	S	PCT
58	15	26	41	17	96	2	0	1	0	100	15.0

LAST SEASON

Games played and assist totals were second lowest of career, goal and point totals career lows. Second on club in plus/minus, first among forwards. Missed 16 games with a groin injury.

THE FINESSE GAME

A dozen years of the NHL wars have taken their toll on Taylor, but he is still an effective player. He has never had blazing speed, so in that regard Taylor's skating seems unchanged. He is, however, less quick than he used to be, so that the openings he gained by quickly changing direction — and the angling he did during his exceptional forechecking — are less likely to be exploited. The best of his skating skills have always been his strength and balance, and he retains those characteristics. He's very difficult to knock off his feet, and his skating strength serves him in traffic situations and while driving the net.

His hockey sense, anticipation and smarts compensate for his waning skating ability. He has always been a strong positional player both offensively and defensively (credit the smarts), and in the offensive zone can still make plays coming out of the corner. His hand skills mirrors his foot skill in traffic, and he can make plays in congested areas, further solidifying his ability as a corners and crease player. Like his feet, his hands have seen their best days, but he can still shoot the puck. In a healthy season, 25 goals is a reasonable expectation.

Those goals are made more valuable by Taylor's ability to play offense without sacrificing defense.

THE PHYSICAL GAME

As a prototypical corners-and-boards guy (or, in the parlance, "along the wood"), Taylor has beaten the hell out of his body. Here especially, a dozen years of pounding show their effects — and, in fact, he's never played a full NHL season.

But we're not saying that Taylor can't take the punishment (there's no 'chute pulling going on here, and Taylor plays hurt). Instead, because he so assiduously plays a physical game, he gets hurt. Nevertheless, Taylor is a very strong physical presence. His balance and skating strength are the keys to this game, allowing him to remain vertical after hitting and to drag the opposition to the net if necessary. Taylor hits hard and often, and is not intimidated by anyone, regardless of size or reputation.

THE INTANGIBLES

Taylor is a top character player, a worthy captain who demonstrates his leadership by example.

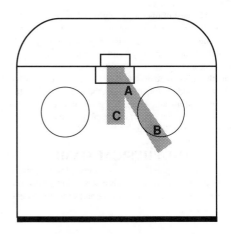

JOHN TONELLI

Yrs. of NHL service: 12
Born: Milton, Ontario, Canada; March 23, 1957
Position: Left wing
Height: 6-1
Weight: 200
Uniform no.: 27
Shoots: left

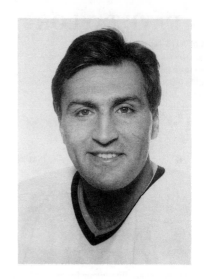

Career statistics:

GP	G	A	TP	PIM
905	308	484	792	811

1989-90 statistics:

GP	G	A	TP	+/-	PIM	PP	SH	GW	GT	S	PCT
73	31	37	68	-8	62	15	0	4	0	163	19.0

LAST SEASON

Games played total was six-season low (missed time with the flu), point total four-season high. Plus/minus was club's fourth worst. Was second on club in power play goals.

THE FINESSE GAME

Tonelli has always been a player who could be labelled, "if wishing could make it so," by which we mean that he has accomplished more than his tools would allow on their own.

His skating has always been marked not by agility but by strength and balance; that remains the case today. His speed down the wing has largely disappeared but again, he succeeds more on determination than skill. He doesn't get great reads of the offensive zone while forechecking, but he can succeed by being a good puck chaser (again, age and decreasing foot speed take their tolls here). His determination has never spilled into his defensive game, nor does it now. Tonelli coasts back to his zone, hoping to conserve energy for another rush up-ice.

The best of his finesse abilities has been his slap shot off the wing, but more and more it accomplishes less and less. He now holds the puck too long while looking to make his plays, and he helps the defense by running himself out of room both vertically (heading into the corner) and horizontally (curling to the boards). He goes wide a lot, but lacks the speed to beat the defense. More and more, his goals will come from nearer the net on opportunistic play — as his power play goal total illustrates.

THE PHYSICAL GAME

Tonelli's proclivity for physical play frequently leaves him in an awkward body position, but it's in those situations that his skating balance and strength come to the fore. He's always had a reputation for physical play, charging the corners with reckless abandon, but he does less of that now, and a lot more leg grinding to look busy.

Tonelli can be cavalier with his stick, but he does not fight.

THE INTANGIBLES

Tonelli posted his second strong year in Los Angeles numbers-wise, but those numbers bear inspection. He scored just 16 even-strength goals, just three of those in his last 12 games.

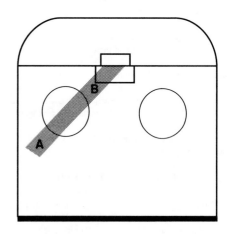

TIM WATTERS

Yrs. of NHL service: 9
Born: Kamloops, B.C., Canada; July 25, 1959
Position: Defenseman
Height: 5-11
Weight: 180
Uniform no.: 5
Shoots: left

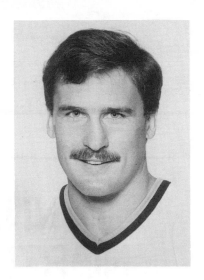

Career statistics:

GP	G	A	TP	PIM
576	25	129	154	1,020

1989-90 statistics:

GP	G	A	TP	+/-	PIM	PP	SH	GW	GT	S	PCT
62	1	10	11	23	92	0	0	0	0	50	2.0

LAST SEASON

Plus/minus rating was team's best. He missed nine games with a bruised ankle.

THE FINESSE GAME

Watters is a triumph of function over form, substance over style. He is not an outstandingly gifted player in any one physical area, and his conservative — and tremendously effective — defensive style reflects that. He is a good skater in all three directions (forward, backward and laterally) and he uses that ability in tandem with his play-reading skill to close the gap on the puckcarrier and to force him out of harm's way.

He handles the puck well and is poised with it, though he is unlikely to be the rushing defenseman. Watters' play is to the breaking forward and he knows that, so the puck will be off his stick as soon as possible — but not so soon that it creates giveaways. His puckhandling ends at his blue line, and he is almost completely uninvolved in the offensive zone; he'll be the safety valve on offense.

Any scoring opportunities he gets will come on infrequent shots from the point.

THE PHYSICAL GAME

Watters plays much bigger than his size, sometimes too big. He is fearless in his use of his body and has good strength for his size, but he'll be overmatched against the League's bigger forwards. Because of that, he has a tendency to take penalties when trying to be too tough. Still, because of his smarts (and the strength he does have), Watters can be effective against the boards and in the crease in most any situation.

Watters is also fearless in his shotblocking, and he remains one of the few NHL practitioners of the hip check. Like two of his stylistic peers — Detroit's Mike O'Connell and Chicago's Bob Murray — Tim is not a big guy and must play a smart physical game.

THE INTANGIBLES

Watters is a great team man, and any coach would suffer the sins of his errors of commission. His greatest strength lies in his character and dedication and those qualities are at least as important to the Kings as are his defensive abilities.

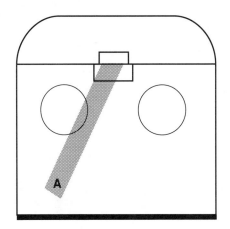

MINNESOTA
NORTH STARS

DON BARBER

Yrs. of NHL service: 2
Born: Victoria, B.C., Canada; December 2, 1964
Position: Left wing
Height: 6-2
Weight: 205
Uniform no.: 37
Shoots: left

Career statistics:

GP	G	A	TP	PIM
67	23	24	47	40

1989-90 statistics:

GP	G	A	TP	+/-	PIM	PP	SH	GW	GT	S	PCT
44	15	19	34	4	32	4	0	2	0	100	15.0

LAST SEASON

Began season with Kalamazoo of the International Hockey League. Games played and all point totals rose in second season. Plus/minus rating was third best overall among all North Stars, regardless of games played.

THE FINESSE GAME

Barber's best assets as a potential NHLer are in the physical game, but there are certain finesse skills that key that physical game. He succeeds by going to the net and taking his punishment, and Don has the balance and skate strength necessary to succeed in confrontation situations. He remains vertical after getting hit, and his skating strength allows him to drive through checks to the goal.

Don has fairly good hands, as one must for scoring work in close quarters. He gets his shot off quickly and on net (hard to miss from gimme-putt distance), and he's going to score most of his goals in opportunistic fashion (on the power play particularly): In other words, don't expect him to whip slappers past anyone from the blue line.

He handles the puck fairly well when carrying it, though he is still not completely acclimated to NHL speed, but his ability will show best by his gaining the puck and controlling it in traffic — not in rink-length rushes.

Barber is a fairly conscientious defensive player, with a good understanding of — and attentive to — his positional play.

THE PHYSICAL GAME

Unlike some players who succeed in traffic, Barber isn't going to plow anyone over. What he will do is drive ceaselessly for the net and take the punishment once he gets there. He makes his physical play better by having good hand skills, and he'd be even more valuable if he initiated some of that contact instead of solely accepting it.

THE INTANGIBLES

He came to camp last season believing he'd already won a roster spot, and he had — in Kalamazoo. Barber has a strong enough work ethic (and he can become a strong NHLer) but he must realize that he has a new coach and new general manager to impress, and to do that he must apply himself from the first practice.

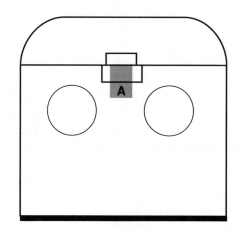

BRIAN BELLOWS

Yrs. of NHL service: 8
Born: St. Catherines, Ontario, Canada; September 1, 1964
Position: Right wing
Height: 5-11
Weight: 195
Uniform no.: 23
Shoots: right

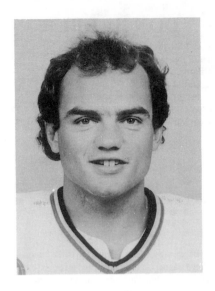

Career statistics:

GP	G	A	TP	PIM
593	277	295	572	453

1989-90 statistics:

GP	G	A	TP	+/-	PIM	PP	SH	GW	GT	S	PCT
80	55	44	99	-3	72	21	1	9	0	300	18.3

LAST SEASON

Games played and all point totals were career highs. Led Stars in goals (fourth in NHL), points (14th in NHL), power play goals (fourth overall), game winners (fifth overall), shots on goal and shooting percentage.

THE FINESSE GAME

Bellows is a very strong skater with balance and sturdiness the primary assets of his skating. His balance and skating strength work in tandem to power his physical game, allowing him to drive through checks and remain vertical and in position to make plays after collisions. He uses that skill well in driving the net or when working in traffic, maintaining body position and thus puck control. He is not, however, a particularly fast or agile player.

As he has great strength in his feet, so too does he have it in his hands. Bellows uses his hands to free pucks trapped between bodies, and he just as easily sends a pass to an open teammate (though he is more likely to drive the net with the puck himself). He carries the puck fairly well when skating, but because his agility is below his hand ability he's more likely to just charge straight ahead than he is to dipsy-doodle past a defender.

Bellows has excellent touch as a scorer, able to shoot the puck very quickly to take advantage of the small openings he gains near the net. He can get the puck to the top of the net from in tight, but he can also beat any NHL goalie from a distance. He shoots a lot (as his numbers indicate) and a good number of his goals will come as he drives for rebounds.

His sense and strength on the puck will make him a regular in all situations, and he is usually a conscientious defensive player.

THE PHYSICAL GAME

Bellows' physical game powers his finesse game, and it is his ability to work the corners and boards that make him the player he is. His aforementioned skating ability is the key, as is Bellows' desire — when he wants to be, he's pretty close to unstoppable; he can initiate a lot of intelligent and effective hitting. He is also very strong in the upper body, so he gets his shot off while being checked or out-wrestles a defenseman for a loose puck.

THE INTANGIBLES

Players like Bellows, the NHL's power forwards, are the League's most valued commodities. Bellows can maintain his position of preeminence with Minnesota, but he — like the rest of his team — will have to get accustomed to yet another new coach. Bellows has been out-spoken in the past about Minnesota's volatile management circumstances, and the new coach may have his hands full in trying to get Bellows with his program.

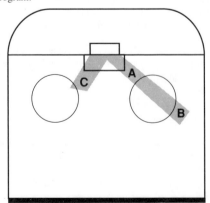

PERRY BEREZAN

Yrs. of NHL service: 5
Born: Edmonton, Alta., Canada; December 5, 1964
Position: Center
Height: 6-2
Weight: 190
Uniform no.: 21
Shoots: right

Career statistics:

GP	G	A	TP	PIM
232	35	58	93	191

1989-90 statistics:

GP	G	A	TP	+/-	PIM	PP	SH	GW	GT	S	PCT
64	3	12	15	-4	31	0	0	0	0	75	4.0

LAST SEASON

Games played total was career high. Missed eight games with sprained ankle, and suffered late season broken nose.

THE FINESSE GAME

Skating is the heart and soul of Berezan's game, the skill that allows him to work as a checker, forechecker and penalty killer. He has speed and balance, quickness and strength in his stride, so he's going to be very strong in his puck pursuit and very strong on the puck when he has it.

He puts his skating to work in tandem with his smarts to play a fairly intelligent game away from the puck, seeing the ice and reading its possibilities so as to thwart the opposition.

Those skills would naturally extend to the offensive game, but Berezan's hand skills aren't at the level of his skating skills. He can control the puck and maintain possession in traffic and other tough situations, but he doesn't have the ability to make the consistent passes or puckhandling moves that would exploit open ice or open teammates. He has touch around the net and the strength to score from a little farther away, but Berezan's goals will usually be few and far between.

THE PHYSICAL GAME

Berezan plays a physical game best characterized as efficient. He uses his skating ability to impose himself on the opposition and to gain good body position along the boards, but he's not going to smack anyone into the middle of next week. Berezan will initiate contact in the traffic areas and use his balance and sturdiness afoot to bump the opposition off the puck.

THE INTANGIBLES

Due to injury, Berezan always has trouble keeping himself in the lineup. His next problem will be one of style; he needs the new general manager and coach to understand what he brings to the game and to accept that. In other words, Berezan (because of the limited nature of his contributions) could be on the bubble in Minnesota.

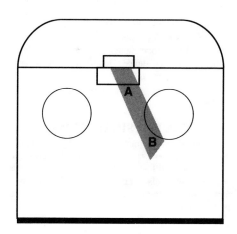

AARON BROTEN

Yrs. of NHL service: 9
Born: Roseau, Minn., USA; November 14, 1960
Position: Left wing
Height: 5-10
Weight: 180
Uniform no.: 14
Shoots: left

Career statistics:

GP	G	A	TP	PIM
676	171	316	487	389

1989-90 statistics:

GP	G	A	TP	+/-	PIM	PP	SH	GW	GT	S	PCT
77	19	17	36	-23	58	1	2	2	0	148	12.8

LAST SEASON

Acquired in January 1990 from New Jersey in exchange for Bob Brooke. Games played total was four-season low, point total six-season low and assist total lowest full-season mark of career. His plus/minus rating was the club's worst.

THE FINESSE GAME

Broten's finesse skills are of the subtle variety (so subtle they sort of disappeared last season). Skating and smarts are the keys to his game, a game made better by open ice created by physical linemates.

He doesn't have outstanding speed, but his balance makes him agile enough to change direction in a step or hit the holes to get to open ice. That balance also allows Broten to handle the puck well in traffic, and his anticipation helps him find the openings for his teammates. Broten can pass well to both sides, and his puck skills make him indispensable on the power play.

Broten's a playmaker before he's a goal scorer, and his shot isn't good enough to overpower any NHL goaltender from a distance. That's why his teammates have to open up ice for him, so he can get closer to the net. He likes to go to the upper right corner with his shot.

THE PHYSICAL GAME

Broten's size mitigates against his physical play, so his strength game is a minimal one. He can — but not necessarily will — gain the puck along the boards because of his hands and balance, and he'll bump bigger forwards, but he certainly won't knock anyone into the sixth row.

He is a durable player.

THE INTANGIBLES

Broten's is the kind of game that improves as his team improves. He needs help to make his finesse game successful, teammates who can cash in on the opportunities he can create. His last two seasons have been anything but strong ones, and he needs a better effort in order to show he is anything above average as an NHL player.

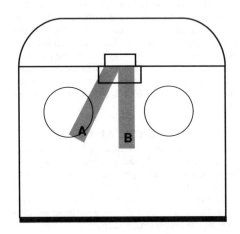

NEAL BROTEN

Yrs. of NHL service: 9
Born: Roseau, Min., USA; November 29, 1959
Position: Center
Height: 5-9
Weight: 170
Uniform no.: 7
Shoots: left

Career statistics:

GP	G	A	TP	PIM
632	216	444	660	393

1989-90 statistics:

GP	G	A	TP	+/-	PIM	PP	SH	GW	GT	S	PCT
80	23	62	85	-16	45	9	1	4	0	212	10.8

LAST SEASON

Games played total was four-season high, assist total second highest of career. Point total was four-season high and fourth highest of career. Finished tops on club in assists and second in points, but plus/minus rating was team's second worst.

THE FINESSE GAME

Skating, sense and hand skills: Broten's got them all, and they combine to make him Minnesota's top offensive center. He is an excellent skater in a darting, quick way — very dangerous around loose pucks and well able to create those pucks by forcing the opposition into mistakes. His agility level is very high and he can change directions and speeds within a stride. Add acceleration and you've got a top-level skating threat.

Broten's hockey sense, his ability to see the openings and his teammates in relation to those openings (as well as his ability to anticipate and to even manipulate those openings), is very high. He'll use his skating to create space for his teammates to skate into, or he'll throw a pass that a teammate will suddenly snare. He knows how to get people into scoring position. He is a very creative player.

His hand skills are the third leg of this offensively dangerous triangle. Broten is a superb playmaker, able to take advantage of a teammate any time, anywhere. He either fires or feathers his passes, and he uses both his forehand and backhand sides equally well. He also puckhandles extremely well, so defenses must pay attention to him and can't just play him to pass. Strangely, his shot lags behind his other hand abilities in terms of delivery; he'll get most of his goals from close proximity to the net.

His skills make him a regular in all situations. He makes the transition from offense to defense, but his size and strength work against him defensively.

THE PHYSICAL GAME

Broten is not a physically inclined player, and he operates better in the non-traffic areas. He'll take his hits to make plays, but he's unlikely to barge into a crowd in search of the puck. His exceptional finesse skills can allow him to make a play away from the boards, but if he gets trapped one-on-one he's going to get out-muscled.

THE INTANGIBLES

When he's at his best, Broten is still Minnesota's best offensive pivot. But his health has been questionable the last several seasons, and his injuries make him an old 31. Two other factors out of his control may also affect his performance: the continued development of Mike Modano (relatively minor for the short-term, as in this season) and the introduction of yet another new coach.

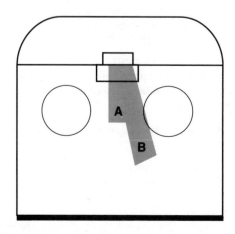

JON CASEY

Yrs. of NHL service: 4
Born: Grand Rapids, Minn., USA; March 29, 1962
Position: Goaltender
Height: 5-10
Weight: 155
Uniform no.: 30
Catches: left

Career statistics:

GP	MINS	G	SO	AVG	A	PIM
158	8,517	472	4	3.33	4	36

1989-90 statistics:

GP	MINS	AVG	W	L	T	SO	GA	SA	SAPCT	PIM
61	3,407	3.22	31	22	4	3	183	1,757	896	18

LAST SEASON

Games and minutes played totals were career highs, second highest among all NHL goalies; ditto shots faced. Finished third overall in wins, fifth in shutouts (career best in shutouts).

THE PHYSICAL GAME

Casey has succeeded over the last two seasons by refining his somewhat unorthodox game into a more normal one. He's at his best when he stands up well and cuts the shooter's angle, challenging by moving out from his net. He doesn't have great size so he must maximize what he has by limiting the amount of net a shooter sees.

When he's at his best he takes position to insure he sees the puck well, and then he lets his good reflexes work for him; he's fast enough to reach out or behind him to grab a puck if he's cut an angle poorly, speed he needs when his glove hand is the short side (Casey doesn't 'hinge' off the post as well as he could to cut the angle on that side).

By staying on his feet he's able to move well across the net for slot play, but he's weak moving completely from post to post; he can be beaten on re-directed pucks. He also lets a lot of rebounds go and needs help in controlling those pucks. He does use his stick very well for pokechecking, but he is less sure of himself when called upon to handle the puck.

THE MENTAL GAME

Casey has good concentration abilities, both within games and from game to game, and he also has fairly strong anticipation abilities (which makes him a faster goaltender than he might otherwise be). He has confidence in his play, as evidenced by his increased ability to play a stand-up style. He's a self-motivated player and doesn't respond well to outside criticism; he knows when he's turned in a poor performance, and he just wants to get back in the net.

He's got big save capability.

THE INTANGIBLES

Sometimes he's scary to watch (from Minnesota's point of view) because every shot looks like it could go in. But somehow they stay out, and Casey wins games. He has grown well into his position as the Stars' first-string goalie, and he enjoys the responsibility that goes along with that ranking. He'll have some additional competition for time this season what with the presence of Daniel Berthiaume, but Casey should prevail again.

SHAWN CHAMBERS

Yrs. of NHL service: 2
Born: Royal Oaks, Mich., USA; October 11, 1966
Position: Defenseman
Height: 6-2
Weight: 200
Uniform no.: 26
Shoots: left

Career statistics:

GP	G	A	TP	PIM
169	14	44	58	182

1989-90 statistics:

GP	G	A	TP	+/-	PIM	PP	SH	GW	GT	S	PCT
78	8	18	26	-2	81	0	1	2	0	116	6.9

LAST SEASON

Games played, goal and point totals rose in second season. Led defense in shorthanded goals and game winners.

THE FINESSE GAME

Chambers is a mobile skater, suprisingly so for a player with his size and bulk, and he likes to use his mobility in an offensive fashion. He gets up and down the ice well, using his foot speed to forecheck and pinch in in the offensive zone in hopes of containing the point and continuing the North Stars play there. He gambles there and needs to develop a better sense of opportunity, because he can get trapped as the play passes him back down ice.

He likes to handle the puck and will do so whenever possible, whether that means rushing it from his zone or carrying it into the opposition end. He uses his skating to join the rush, though generally stays behind at the opposing blue line instead of going all the way to the net. His ability to relieve some of the logjam in the Stars' zone by skating with the puck is an important one, and one that improved judgement will make more valuable.

He has the skating ability to play an active defensive style, stepping up and challenging the puck carrier at the goal line so as to force play. Again, improved judgement and ability to read the ice will help him develop this skill. He does have fairly good vision when the play is moving away from him, and he can move the puck to open teammates. He looks for the winger at the net for a pass or a deflection, and smartly takes something off his shot so that teammate can get to the puck. Chambers has a good shot from the point in terms of accuracy, but he could improve his release.

His skills (particularly skating) make him a regular in specialty team situations.

THE PHYSICAL GAME

Chambers has good size and he's not afraid to use it. He bodychecks fairly well and covers the front of the net effectively, though he'd be a better physical player if he replaced some of his bulk with muscle so as to more successfully wrestle with the opposing forwards. His physical game is helped by his ability to make plays coming away from the boards, and his reach will get him to a lot of loose pucks.

THE INTANGIBLES

Chambers is a fairly talented kid who is already pretty close to being a steady NHL player; a more consistent work ethic in practice will get him to that plateau. As the Stars enter another transitional period, Chambers has youth and talent on his side.

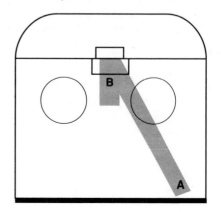

SHANE CHURLA

Yrs. of NHL service: 2
Born: Fernie, B.C., Canada; June 24, 1965
Position: Right wing
Height: 6-1
Weight: 200
Uniform no.: 27
Shoots: right

Career statistics:

GP	G	A	TP	PIM
122	4	9	13	595

1989-90 statistics:

GP	G	A	TP	+/-	PIM	PP	SH	GW	GT	S	PCT
53	2	3	5	-4	292	0	0	1	0	40	5.0

LAST SEASON

First full NHL season. Finished second on club in PIM total.

THE FINESSE GAME

Churla's finesse skills are limited, to say the least. He has no real mobility or speed as a skater at the NHL level, lacking the foot speed or exceptional balance that would provide him with any real degree of quickness or agility.

He doesn't see the ice very well and so will have to make straight-ahead, first-play-seen plays — assuming he can get to and hold on to the puck that long.

His goal scoring will have to be from in front of the net, with the goalie down and out. Churla's defense isn't much better than his offense, though not from lack of effort. Rather, he's handicapped by his skating and slow reads of the ice.

THE PHYSICAL GAME

For every NHL goal he's scored, Churla has accumulated 148.75 minutes in penalties; what do you think his physical game is all about? He is a fighter and a very tough player, but he also tries to hit and play a standard physical game. The problem is Churla's skating isn't good enough for him to do that — he can't hit what he can't catch.

THE INTANGIBLES

Churla does his job by protecting his smaller teammates (Mike Modano in particular last season), but like any one-dimensional player he is out the door the minute someone tougher — or someone near as tough with better skills — comes along.

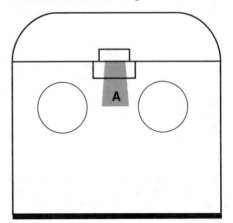

ULF DAHLEN

Yrs. of NHL service: 3
Born: Ostersund, Sweden; January 12, 1967
Position: Right wing
Height: 6-2
Weight: 195
Uniform no.: 22
Shoots: left

Career statistics:

GP	G	A	TP	PIM
202	73	64	137	106

1989-90 statistics:

GP	G	A	TP	+/-	PIM	PP	SH	GW	GT	S	PCT
76	20	22	42	-3	30	13	0	4	0	135	14.8

LAST SEASON

Acquired from New York in March 1990 in exchange for Mike Gartner. Games played total was career high, point total career low. All PPG were scored with New York, and Dahlen was a plus-1 with Minnesota.

THE FINESSE GAME

Dahlen is an excellent skater, and it is his exceptional balance that makes him so. While not possessing great speed or quickness (and therefore not having exceptional agility or lateral ability), Dahlen's balance is equal that of the NHL's best players. That balance excellently complements his willingness to play a physical game and go into traffic, where he is almost impossible to knock down.

He amplifies his ability to maintain body position with the hands, the eyes and the brain to create opportunities. He controls the puck very well when carrying it, and Ulf passes well because he sees the open man and has the hands to get the puck to his teammates. He could improve in his reaction time, because Dahlen has a tendency to hold onto the puck longer than necessary — simply because he can.

Though he's got good hands and controls the puck well at all speeds, Dahlen won't make end-to-end rushes because of his skating; he'll use his hands to make plays away from the boards. He'll get into scoring position, where he'll use his good, quickly released shot — and that makes him a natural for power play duty.

THE PHYSICAL GAME

Ulf takes a beating because of his complete physical willingness. His balance makes him a extraordinary player against the boards or in the slot, where he has the strength to hold onto the puck despite tough checking and fouling.

He has good size, but he needs greater muscle strength and bulk so as to avoid the injuries he's bound to accumulate as a physical player. He initiates contact in all situations, and certainly accepts hits to make his plays, and Ulf isn't above a scrap or two a season.

Another thing that makes him successful in confrontations is his reach. When that reach is combined with his hand skills, Dahlen is able to not only gain the puck in the corner and then move out to make a play, but he's often able to create an excellent scoring chance for himself.

THE INTANGIBLES

A matter of philosophy: The Rangers felt that Dahlen's skating wouldn't improve enough for him to make strong contributions at even-strength. The North Stars felt they were getting a young player whose potential is still ahead of him.

At any rate, Dahlen is a well-liked and likable young man, an enthusiastic and coachable player with a fine work ethic and strong intensity. It remains to be seen which judgement — that of the Rangers or that of the North Stars — will prove correct.

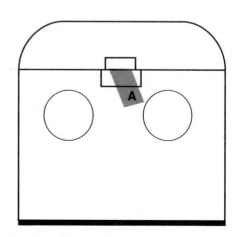

GAETAN DUCHESNE

Yrs. of NHL service: 9
Born: Les Saulles, Quebec, Canada; July 11, 1962
Position: Left wing
Height: 5-11
Weight: 200
Uniform no.: 10
Shoots: left

Career statistics:

GP	G	A	TP	PIM
673	131	190	321	416

1989-90 statistics:

GP	G	A	TP	+/-	PIM	PP	SH	GW	GT	S	PCT
72	12	8	20	5	33	0	1	1	0	93	12.9

LAST SEASON

Assist and point totals were career lows. He missed eight games with a knee injury. Plus/minus was club's second highest.

THE FINESSE GAME

Duchesne is one of the NHL's top checkers, and he's able to perform in that role because of two above average skills: he skates exceptionally well and he sees the ice with good vision.

Duchesne is an almost tireless skater, not possessing great speed or quickness but able to run down most every puck; he just seems to be able to go and go, and his skating strength is the secret here — it makes him very strong in his puck pursuit. He is a very mobile skater.

Duchesne uses his vision to direct his skating, finding the openings that need to be closed and then getting to them. He enjoys his role as a defensive specialist, and is particularly effective as a penalty killer because of his talents.

He'll gain some opportunities because he'll force pucks loose, but Duchesne lacks the hand skill necessary to completely exploit the chances he creates. He'll need to be opportunistic to score (and one reason is because he has a very slow release on his shot). His ability to use his teammates is similarly handicapped by his hand skills.

THE PHYSICAL GAME

Duchesne uses his body willingly in his checking but he's not the strongest guy ever, so his chances of out-wrestling an opposing player are not high. But he does succeed in physical battles by establishing good position and letting his strength and balance do their jobs for him. He initiates and accepts contact, but he does not fight.

THE INTANGIBLES

Duchesne is a dedicated athlete, a tireless worker and a character player. His actions make him a leader, but as with many of the Stars his future is in the hands of the new general manager and new coach — who may or may not want a 28 year old role player.

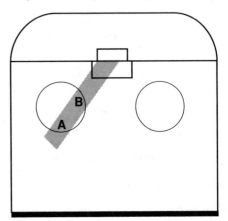

DAVE GAGNER

Yrs. of NHL service: 4
Born: Chatham, Ontario, Canada; December 11, 1964
Position: Center
Height: 5-10
Weight: 180
Uniform no.: 15
Shoots: left

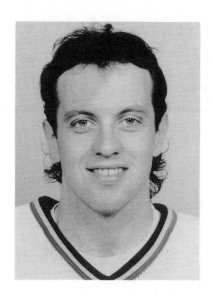

Career statistics:

GP	G	A	TP	PIM
285	94	108	202	260

1989-90 statistics:

GP	G	A	TP	+/-	PIM	PP	SH	GW	GT	S	PCT
79	40	38	78	-1	54	10	0	3	0	238	16.8

LAST SEASON

Games played and goal totals were career highs. Finished third on club in scoring, second in goals and shots on goal. Plus/minus was third best among fulltime forwards.

THE FINESSE GAME

Intelligence and dedication are the keys to Gagner's NHL success, in particular the application of those qualities to his finesse skills. He is an above average (but not exceptional) skater, with balance and quickness the primary attributes of his skating. Gagner has a degree of speed because of his strong stride, but his skating keys his game by allowing him to play the body and remain vertical and to be a mobile player because of his lateral movement.

He uses his skating in conjunction with his intelligence to get good reads of the offensive zone, reads that he uses as a forechecker and scorer. His quickness allows him to close on the puck carrier or to get to loose pucks, and his mobility allows him to stay with his checks.

Gagner uses his hockey sense more as a scorer than as a playmaker, smartly getting into position to receive the puck or pounce on rebounds. That ability will take him to traffic areas, where his balance allows him to maintain body position, but it also takes him to open space where he doesn't have to fight off bigger players. His scoring shows patience even though he scores from high-speed areas where quick release of his shot is critical to success. But patience just means making sure of the target and of the puck, and that poise equals more goals. That patience also allows his teammates time to get open.

Gagner's skills insure that he sees ice in all situations.

THE PHYSICAL GAME

He's a little guy, but Gagner plays as if he were twice his size. He's afraid of no one and no situation, and there isn't a puck he won't chase. He uses his balance to keep him upright after hitting, and Gagner's skating strength and sturdiness helps him drive his checks off the puck. He's an aggressive player who initiates contact at every opportunity, and certainly accepts hits to make plays.

In fact, there are times when he'd be better served by getting out of the traffic areas so he could take better advantage of his finesse skills.

THE INTANGIBLES

Gagner is one of — if not the — hardest working players in the NHL, and that's what we mean by dedication. He's got great enthusiasm and plays with the same high level of intensity at home or on the road, ahead or behind. He was having disagreements with former coach Pierre Page on his role with the club (as to how much offense and defense should be in his game), and Gagner will need to settle that question with his new coach.

But regardless of the decision, Gagner's work ethic will be a good example to the rest of the club.

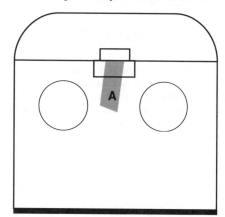

STEWART GAVIN

Yrs. of NHL service: 9
Born: Ottawa, Ontario, Canada; March 15, 1960
Position: Left wing
Height: 6-0
Weight: 190
Uniform no.: 12
Shoots: left

Career statistics:

GP	G	A	TP	PIM
632	111	139	250	462

1989-90 statistics:

GP	G	A	TP	+/-	PIM	PP	SH	GW	GT	S	PCT
80	12	13	25	9	76	0	3	1	0	146	8.2

LAST SEASON

Played 80 games for second time in career. Goal total was three-season high. He led club in plus/minus rating and shorthanded goals.

THE FINESSE GAME

Speed and acceleration ability are the keys to Gavin's excellent skating game, and he uses that skill to its fullest as a checking winger and fine penalty killer. He forechecks very well because of his skating ability and he's helped in that aspect of the game by his very strong hockey sense and vision of the ice. Gavin combines his skating and sense to be an active checker and penalty killer, one who can dictate a style rather than just chasing the puck. He can also create some chances for the Stars because of his skating.

Gavin handles the puck fairly well as he rushes up-ice and he uses good vision to help him make good passes to his teammates. He'll score by driving for the openings (remember his speed) and does his best work from near the net by pouncing on loose pucks. He also has a big slap shot off the wing and will use it often.

He uses his smarts and skating in his own end of the ice (as his plus/minus rating indicates) as a very sound positional player.

THE PHYSICAL GAME

Gavin is a tenacious player, the kind who gives and takes checks along the boards without a second's thought. His balance and skating strength help him here by driving him through his checks or carrying him to the net, and then keeping him vertical for playmaking after collisions. He uses his underrated physical ability to separate the opposition from the puck in all three zones.

THE INTANGIBLES

Gavin's a very strong team man, well respected by his teammates because of his intensity and work ethic. He is a good character player for Minnesota, an unfortunately overlooked and little known NHL player.

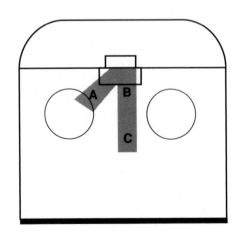

CURT GILES

Yrs. of NHL service: 11
Born: The Pas, Manitoba, Canada; Nov. 30, 1958
Position: Defense
Height: 5-8
Weight: 180
Uniform no.: 2
Shoots: left

Career statistics:

GP	G	A	TP	PIM
764	38	184	222	637

1989-90 statistics:

GP	G	A	TP	+/-	PIM	PP	SH	GW	GT	S	PCT
74	1	12	13	3	48	0	0	0	0	55	1.8

LAST SEASON

Led defense in plus/minus rating. Suffered a groin injury, missed four games with back spasms.

THE FINESSE GAME

Skating has always been the bedrock of Giles' rock-solid defensive game, a game that he plays actively at both ends of the ice. Giles steps up well at both blue lines, getting good reads of the ice to challenge the puck at both ends. He has good speed and better lateral movement, making him a very mobile player. Giles reads and reacts well to come across the ice for hits, and he also steps up to close the gap on the puck carrier and force the play at his own blue line; he's very good at breaking up odd-man rushes because of his positioning.

He uses his skating offensively to rush the puck when necessary, but mostly he will support the attack by containing the point to keep play concentrated in the offensive zone.

He uses his good view of the ice to get the puck to open men smartly regardless of situation, but he won't create a lot of offense from the point. He'll see some infrequent power play time because of his passing (and a lot more penalty killing time because of his smarts) but he's not a tremendous offensive force. He has an average slap shot from the point and could shoot more.

THE PHYSICAL GAME

Giles has very strong physical ability. He may be the only practitioner of the hip check left in the NHL, and he is a very strong all-around bodychecker. His skating and low center of gravity are a big help to him here, and he'll hit anyone. He also uses his body smartly along the boards in terms of gaining position, so that he doesn't always have to out-wrestle the opposition.

He sacrifices his body to block shots, but it is his willingness to put himself on the line that has kept him from ever playing a complete NHL season.

THE INTANGIBLES

In a quiet way Giles is the kind of player a team like Minnesota needs. His work ethic and off-ice demeanor can serve as examples to the club's younger players (he's a great person in the locker room, with an enthusiastic and positive attitude), while his on-ice play can be a lesson to the younger defensemen.

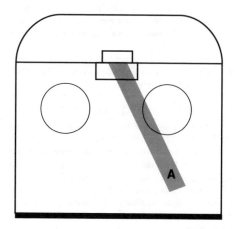

BASIL MCRAE

Yrs. of NHL service: 6
Born: Beaverton, Ontario, Canada; January 5, 1961
Position: Left wing
Height: 6-2
Weight: 205
Uniform no.: 17
Shoots: left

Career statistics:

GP	G	A	TP	PIM
343	42	58	100	1,592

1989-90 statistics:

GP	G	A	TP	+/-	PIM	PP	SH	GW	GT	S	PCT
66	9	17	26	-5	351	2	0	2	0	95	9.5

LAST SEASON

Games played total was three-season low, point total second highest of career. Missed nine games with knee injury. Led NHL in PIM total (three-season personal low).

THE FINESSE GAME

McRae is a limited finesse player, but there are some weapons he can bring to bear that aren't necessarily fistic in origin. He's a fairly strong skater in terms of stride or power, and he can use that strength in his hitting game. He lacks, however, the balance that would render him a better bump and grind player; right now, he's as good a bet to go to the ice as is the guy he hits. McRae can't lay claim to any real degree of agility or quickness; he's a straight-ahead player.

McRae can and will handle the puck, and he gets some room to operate because of his reputation. He's developed some confidence in his puckhandling and no longer panics when he has the puck, so he can make some plays. He doesn't have a great shot, so he'll have to be close to net (as when plugging it on the power play) to score.

He works hard at being a strong defensive player, but his modest skating and below average vision mitigate against his efforts.

THE PHYSICAL GAME

McRae plays a willing physical game, and he's made that game stronger and of greater importance by learning to accept being hit. He doesn't necessarily play like an idiot. If the other team is keeping its nose clean regarding McRae's teammates, Basil will behave too.

That allows him to use his good strength in confrontations along the boards. He can hurt people when he hits them, as his leg strength allows him to drive through checks.

As for fighting — well, Basil is more than willing to go with anyone. Not a heavyweight in himself (in terms of punching power or casting fear into anyone), McRae nevertheless goes willingly with the League's heavyweights. But just because people know they're going to fight him doesn't mean they're afraid of him, and the League's heavyweights aren't.

THE INTANGIBLES

Yes, he's an enforcer (we wouldn't say goon — though maybe someone else would — because of McRae's willingness to play when fighting is unnecessary), but he is also a very strong team man, someone with heart and intensity. As they go through another period of acclimation and change the North Stars need as many dedicated and team-oriented players as they can get.

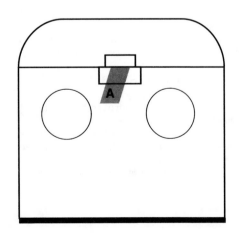

MIKE MODANO

Yrs. of NHL service: 1
Born: Livonia, MI, USA; June 7, 1970
Position: Center
Height: 6-3
Weight: 188
Uniform no.: 9
Shoots: left

Career statistics:

GP	G	A	TP	+/-	PIM	PP	SH	GW	GT	S	PCT
80	29	46	75	-7	63	12	0	2	0	172	16.9

LAST SEASON

First NHL season (appeared in two 1989 playoff games). Finished third on club in assists, fourth in points, third in power play goals. Finished second in overall rookie scoring, first in power play goals, second in assists, third in goals, fourth in shots, fifth in shooting percentage.

THE FINESSE GAME

Modano is a complete package of finesse skills, but perhaps first among equals for his talents are his hand skills. Modano controls the puck excellently in traffic, and not only controls the puck but dominates play. His hands are as soft and sensitive as you could want, so he'll stickhandle through players, maintain control while being checked, pass with equal touch to both the forehand and backhand sides — in short, do just about anything he wants to.

Other skills are necessary for hand skills to be effective, skills like skating and hockey sense; Modano has both in abundance. Though not yet a speed demon at the NHL level, Modano is already a very agile player whose balance and foot speed power his ability in traffic. That balance and agility allows him to stop, start and change direction in very confined spaces.

He has outstanding sense of the ice, his teammates and the permutations of the play. Modano is a very creative player who can exploit opportunities — can *create* opportunities — by either getting the puck to his teammates or doing the damage himself.

Modano can score in any number of ways, both from near and far. He'll finesse the puck through the smallest opening allowed, shoots off both the pass and the stickhandle, gets into scoring position.

He needs some help in his transition game, but he works at playing a two-way style.

THE PHYSICAL GAME

Modano is like a Mario Lemieux, in that his great natural size will automatically work for him in terms of strength, leverage and balance. He uses his size excellently to protect the puck from the opposition and, like Lemieux, is very difficult to take the puck from because of his wing span and balance.

He doesn't initiate a lot of slam-bang play, but Modano takes the body well in a quiet way by forcing the opposition to the boards and then relieving them of the puck.

THE INTANGIBLES

The North Stars did the smart thing last season, putting Modano in situations where he wasn't expected to be a superstar so that he could just get the feel of the NHL. As it was, often playing with offensively-limited teammates like Shane Churla, Basil McRae and Gaetan Duchesne (the first two for protection, the last for defensive coverage) Modano posted some great numbers.

His potential is a sky-high one, and he has thus far shown the enthusiasm and coachability necessary to become an elite NHL player. It's the responsibility of the new Stars management to help him along that road

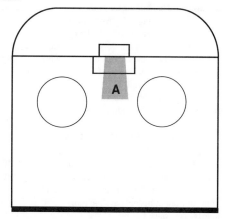

FRANTISEK MUSIL

Yrs. of NHL service: 4
Born: Pardubice, Czechoslovakia; December 17, 1964
Position: Defenseman
Height: 6-3
Weight: 205
Uniform no.: 6
Shoots: left

Career statistics:

GP	G	A	TP	PIM
263	14	44	58	524

1989-90 statistics:

GP	G	A	TP	+/-	PIM	PP	SH	GW	GT	S	PCT
56	2	8	10	0	109	0	0	1	0	78	2.6

LAST SEASON

Goal and point totals set, and assist total tied, career lows. Suffered from back spasms; games played total was second lowest of career. PIM total was second highest among defensemen.

THE FINESSE GAME

Musil is kind of a give with one hand and take with the other type of player. He has outstanding finesse potential, and despite four NHL seasons those skills remain more in the potential realm than in the realm of reality. He's a strong skater with speed, balance and good mobility, so he can certainly challenge the puck at both blue lines — at least physically.

He has also shown good puckhandling and rushing abilities, as well as the ability to make passes to teammates. The problem is not physical, but mental. For example, Musil can still be hypnotized by the puck.

Musil is still not reading plays well at the NHL level, despite the signs of his intelligence. Since he's not getting those reads his skating becomes one-dimensional: force the play wide, instead of stepping up and controlling the gap on the puck carrier. Falling back instead of containing the point. Carry the puck until checked, or just dump it after skating. In short, he is still a reactive instead of active player.

Musil can make not only correct plays but good ones offensively — every once in a great while, a strong play falls out of his tool box. But right now he is a limited player who covers his own zone well but contributes almost nothing in the offensive area of the game — in effect leaving Minnesota to play 4-on-5.

THE PHYSICAL GAME

Luckily, Musil contributes well in the physical game. He is big and strong, mean and unafraid. His skating ability has certainly helped him become a better hitter, and Musil also makes sure that anyone who camps in front of his net pays the rent — and he does it smartly, generally keeping himself on the ice and out of the box. There are times, however (as in the first game of the playoffs last spring), when he got too aggressive and took four minors in a period and a half.

THE INTANGIBLES

All the tools and can't get into the toolbox — not yet anyway. Musil has every ingredient necessary to be not just an above average NHL defender but a great one. Patience is important, but he's not getting any younger — he'll be 26 in December, with four NHL seasons already under his belt and no real sign that he's moved toward his potential.

He's got the work ethic and intelligence necessary, and it will be the job of Minnesota's new coach to tap Musil's ability.

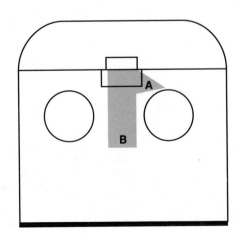

LARRY MURPHY

Yrs. of NHL service: 10
Born: Scarborough, Ontario, Canada; March 8, 1961
Position: Defenseman
Height: 6-2
Weight: 208
Uniform no.: 8
Shoots: right

Career statistics:

GP	G	A	TP	PIM
785	151	478	629	643

1989-90 statistics:

GP	G	A	TP	+/-	PIM	PP	SH	GW	GT	S	PCT
77	10	58	68	-13	44	4	0	1	1	173	5.8

LAST SEASON

Assist and point totals were three-season highs. Led Stars defense in points, second on club in assists. Plus/minus rating was team's third worst, poorest among defenders. Missed two games with groin injury.

THE FINESSE GAME

Skating is at the heart of Murphy's success, almost all of which comes in the offensive zone (and much of which comes at the expense of his defense). He has a good range of speed up and down the scale, and he uses those changes of pace to rush the puck from the Stars' zone. He also uses his skating to contain the point and control the Minnesota offense, but he's not as effective using his skating defensively. He gets hypnotized by the puck as he skates back and can be beaten because of that.

While intelligent at the point when on the offensive, Murphy takes chances that often result in turnovers and his getting caught out of the play. In other words, his plus/minus rating is not unwarranted.

His puckhandling and playmaking abilities are critical in Minnesota's transition game, and are nowhere more valuable than on the power play (Murphy was on ice for over 60 of Minnesota's 80-plus power play goals). He finds open men in the offensive zone and can skate the puck from his own end. He uses his teammates well.

Murphy will primarily score from the point, though he will slide to the faceoff circle or the slot for shots. His shot is low and accurate to the net, allowing for deflections, rebounds and tip-ins. That shot does create a lot of offense.

THE PHYSICAL GAME

Murphy's got size and strength, but he's not a hitter and really doesn't come close to playing an all-around game. He pushes and shoves along the boards and goes to the wood only if he feels he'll have a high degree of success in gaining the puck. He's no better than adequate in front of his net and will really have to be paired with a more consistently physical partner.

THE INTANGIBLES

Freed from the defensive constraint he played under in Washington, Murphy has fallen back into his sloppy defensive ways — so that his 68 points are reduced to 53 points by his minus-13 rating (and we haven't begun deducting his power-play points). The point is, he's made himself into a one-dimensional player, and one dimensional players are always replaceable — especially when the club has a new general manager and coach.

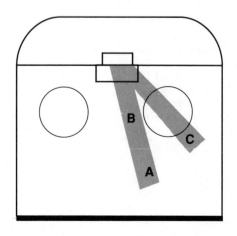

VILLE SIREN

Yrs of NHL service: 5
Born: Tampere, Finland; February 11, 1964
Position: Defenseman
Height: 6-2
Weight: 190
Uniform no.: 5
Shoots: right

Career statistics:

GP	G	A	TP	PIM
290	14	68	82	276

1989-90 statistics:

GP	G	A	TP	+/-	PIM	PP	SH	GW	GT	S	PCT
53	1	13	14	1	60	0	0	0	0	53	1.9

LAST SEASON

Games played and point totals were second-lowest of career, goal total tied career low. Plus/minus was second highest among defensemen.

THE FINESSE GAME

Siren's skills have topped out at average at the NHL level. His skating is consistently at the NHL level now, and he skates well backward and with greater agility and lateral movement, so he's consistently able to angle the opposition to the boards.

His skating has gained him the time to read the play better, and Siren now sees the rush both ways fairly well. He is able to react to the play at the NHL level, and his improved defensive play is attributable to that. He understands the play better and moves better when necessary. He also moves the puck better now than ever before, courtesy of his improved playreading ability. Ville generally makes correct passing decisions — he's a pretty intelligent player at both ends of the ice. He'll carry the puck to center if he can, but Siren doesn't charge into the offensive zone.

Siren reads the offensive play better than before, pinching in and containing the point, but still concentrates on defense. He shoots nowhere near frequently enough, and his shot could use improvement in strength and quickness of release.

THE PHYSICAL GAME

Siren is not an overtly physical player in terms of hitting and banging, but his physical game reflects the same smarts that his finesse game shows. He's not afraid of a tough game and he uses his body to gain position well along the boards and in front of the net. His takeouts are strong but unspectacular, and Siren is helped in his physical play by his ability to make plays off the boards.

THE INTANGIBLES

He can get the job done in an understated way, but Siren's been caught in a position where younger players with at least the same set of skills are being worked into the lineup. And with a new coach and general manager in Minnesota, who knows what will become of Siren?

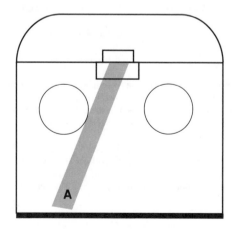

KARI TAKKO

Yrs. of NHL service: 4
Born: Uusikaupunki, Finland; June 23, 1962
Position: Goaltender
Height: 6-2
Weight: 182
Uniform no.: 1
Catches: left

Career statistics:

GP	MINS	G	SO	AVG	A	PIM
129	6,669	426	1	3.83	1	30

1989-90 statistics:

GP	MINS	AVG	W	L	T	SO	GA	SA	SAPCT	PIM
21	1,012	4.03	4	12	0	0	68	482	.859	2

LAST SEASON

Games and minutes played fell for fourth straight season. Win total was career low.

THE PHYSICAL GAME

Takko is a hybrid as a goalie, using his good size to its best advantage by playing a challenging stand-up style when the puck is at the distances but reverting to a reflex-butterfly style as the puck gets closer to his net. He's not the best angle-cutting goaltender ever, and that's why he's invariably moving from one side or the other to make what should be routine saves.

He has very quick feet and he uses them well in that butterfly style when play is near the net, and he is an agile player overall. He gets to the ice and off the ice relatively quickly, but because he's got so many parts to put back into place (it takes time to gather those long legs) it can't be said that he regains his stance well.

His quick feet help him move well across the front of the net and he'll try to take up as much net as he can with his legs, but he's vulnerable on slot shots because he gives away the top of the net. As a corollary to being on the ice, he cannot handle his rebounds well. His agility and quickness will generally get him in the way of those second shots, but he shouldn't have to make those saves.

He uses his stick well around the goal to deflect passes and pokecheck pucks off the opposition's stick.

THE MENTAL GAME

Takko has fairly good concentration and anticipation abilities, and he maintains his intensity from game to game. Now he needs to concentrate on maintaining his intensity after not playing for long periods of time, as Jon Casey takes more and more of the bulk of games for Minnesota.

THE INTANGIBLES

Takko is a solid NHL goaltender, a little better than middle-of-the-road, but he's going to be facing a lot of competition from Daniel Berthiaume in search of that second spot behind Casey. Takko's got a good attitude (he's also popular among his teammates) and he's going need all his positive enthusiasm.

MARK TINORDI

Yrs. of NHL service: 2
Born: Red Deer, Alta., Canada; May 9, 1966
Position: Defenseman
Height: 6-4
Weight: 206
Uniform no.: 24
Shoots: left

Career statistics:

GP	G	A	TP	PIM
137	6	12	18	397

1989-90 statistics:

GP	G	A	TP	+/-	PIM	PP	SH	GW	GT	S	PCT
66	3	7	10	0	240	1	0	0	0	50	6.0

LAST SEASON

First full NHL campaign. All point totals were career highs, as was PIM total; he led defense in last category (third on club). Suffered a concussion, missed six games with the flu.

THE FINESSE GAME

Tinordi's finesse abilities have grown through his abbreviated NHL tenure, and his play has improved correspondingly. He's not the greatest skater in the League but he is a fairly mobile player, and he makes his defense more effective by consciously and consistently staying within his limitations. You won't find Tinordi galloping all over the ice in search of either loose pucks or bodies to hit. He stays in his lane and keeps the puck ahead of him, forcing the play wide of the net when he can.

He is limited in his hand skills so he'll have to make simple up-the-boards plays in order to be successful — and Tindordi does just that; the puck's gone as soon as he can get rid of it. He finds the open man ahead of him and moves the puck quickly and efficiently.

Any scoring he does will have to come from the blue line, although Tinordi will make a rare appearance at the faceoff circle for shots. His shot is no better than average, and he'll get a handful of goals per season.

His poise and positional play make him an important part of the Stars' penalty killing unit.

THE PHYSICAL GAME

Tinordi is a very physical player, consistently and intelligently (despite what the PIM total indicates) using his size and strength to bang away at the opposition. He takes men out of the play very effectively, and he punishes the opposition in front of the Stars' net.

He is a patient and very effective fighter and will drop the gloves against anyone.

THE INTANGIBLES

Tinordi is a poised and hard working player, one who has worked his way from marginal to important player and can improve still more. He is a fine team man and can be a strong part of the Stars' foundation as they prepare for the Nineties.

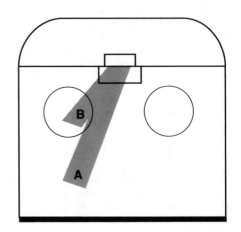

MONTREAL
CANADIEANS

GUY CARBONNEAU

Yrs. of NHL service: 8
Born: Sept-Iles, Quebec, Canada; March 18, 1960
Position: Center
Height: 5-11
Weight: 180
Uniform no.: 21
Shoots: right

Career statistics:

GP	G	A	TP	PIM
622	165	244	409	453

1989-90 statistics:

GP	G	A	TP	+/-	PIM	PP	SH	GW	GT	S	PCT
68	19	36	55	21	37	1	1	3	0	125	15.2

LAST SEASON

Games played total was career low, assist total tied career high. Finished fourth on club in scoring, third in assists. Missed nine games with knee injury, two games with arm injury.

THE FINESSE GAME

As good as Wayne Gretzky and Mario Lemieux are at anticipating the offensive play, that's how good Carbonneau is defensively. He reads plays and situations almost perfectly and thus knows where the puck is headed or how the opposition intends to operate. He blocks shots just by being in position, because Guy always knows where he is in relation to the puck, the net, the opposition and his teammates.

Factor in his exceptional skating (superior in all categories) and you've got the NHL's best forechecker, penalty killer and defensive forward — tireless in his pursuit of the puck.

And as if this isn't contribution enough, Carbonneau can also put the puck in the net. He doesn't have the 50-goal ability that many people think he has, but 25-30 goals a season is definitely in character for him.

His skating and sense get him to the loose pucks his checking creates, and Carbonneau's excellent hands can thread the puck through a crowd onto a teammate's stick or handle the puck well at full speed and in traffic.

Carbonneau has a fast wrist shot and is particularly effective from the edges of the faceoff circles, though he has the touch to score from in tight as well.

THE PHYSICAL GAME

Carbonneau uses his body excellently, despite the fact that he lacks great size. What he does, firstly, is use his skating to take the body — then his hand skills take over. But Guy also uses his body to gain good position along the boards when contesting the puck in traffic; his balance helps him remain vertical

He willingly sacrifices his body as the NHL's best

shot-blocking forward, and Carbonneau excels at faceoffs because of his hand speed, strength and balance (the latter skill gives him an excellent base of support).

THE INTANGIBLES

Carbonneau's a very intelligent player and he has to be treated as such; he needs to know the whys and wherefores of why a team philosophy is the way it is. Much of his success comes from thinking about the game, and the evidence of that thought is his superior play. He is a worker and leader, and his all-around game has too long been hidden by his defensive prowess. Nevertheless, he's the prototypical defensive forward.

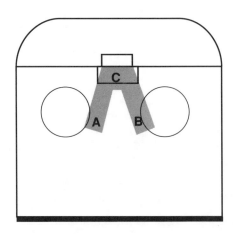

SHAYNE CORSON

Yrs. of NHL service: 4
Born: Barrie, Ontario, Canada; August 13, 1966
Position: Center
Height: 6-0
Weight: 175
Uniform no.: 27
Shoots: left

Career statistics:

GP	G	A	TP	PIM
287	81	106	187	635

1989-90 statistics:

GP	G	A	TP	+/-	PIM	PP	SH	GW	GT	S	PCT
76	31	44	75	33	144	7	0	6	1	192	16.1

LAST SEASON

All point totals were career highs. Finished second on club in points, goals, plus/minus rating and PIM totals, first in assists. Was third in shots on goal total. Missed two games with a separated shoulder.

THE FINESSE GAME

Consistent with his overall style, strength is the hallmark of Corson's game. His above average skating strength gives him some speed and acceleration ability. He has good foot speed and balance, but not sufficient to be labelled an agile forward. Rather, his balance and skating strength key his physical game, driving him through checks and keeping him vertical (and able to make plays) after hits.

He is a smart player in terms of ice vision and playreading, and he combines that intelligence with his skating to become a good forechecker and penalty killer.

He's not a fancy puckhandler, but since he's more inclined to skate over the defense instead of around it that's okay; Shayne can carry the puck at his top speed, but he's not likely to finesse the puck though traffic to a teammate. He is smart enough, though, to open up to the center of the rink and to keep his head up. He likes to carry the puck over the blue line — rather than dump it in — whenever possible.

Shayne will succeed as a scorer by being around the net to force turnovers, and then by pouncing on the loose pucks he forced. He's especially effective plugging the net on the power play.

THE PHYSICAL GAME

Corson is a very aggressive player, sometimes too aggressive for his own good. His temper often gets the better of him, and he's not mature enough to take a check and keep playing — he's going to go right back at the guy that hit him. That's bad, because it distracts Corson from the game.

His skating strength makes him a hard hitter, and he plays that style consistently. He is also a willing fighter, but not one who is feared by other fighters.

THE INTANGIBLES

Corson is a pretty intense young man, but he does need to be reminded to do the things that will allow him to succeed, to keep his intensity at consistent levels at all times and to always use his physical ability. When he doesn't do those things, he's a pretty ordinary player. When he does do those things he can be an exceptional NHLer.

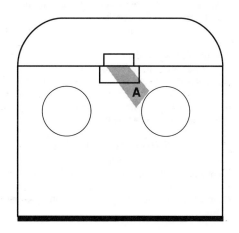

RUSS COURTNALL

Yrs. of NHL service: 6
Born: Duncan, B.C., Canada; June 2, 1965
Position: Center
Height: 5-11
Weight: 180
Uniform no.: 9
Shoots: right

Career statistics:

GP	G	A	TP	PIM
453	139	177	316	285

1989-90 statistics:

GP	G	A	TP	+/-	PIM	PP	SH	GW	GT	S	PCT
80	27	32	59	14	27	3	0	2	2	294	9.2

LAST SEASON

Games played total was career high, goal total second highest of career, point total three-season high. Finished third on club in points and goals, first in shots on goal total.

THE FINESSE GAME

Skating and shooting are the hallmarks of Russ Courtnall's finesse game. He's an excellent skater, possessing breakaway speed, superior balance, excellent quickness and agility. Russ puts that speed to use by driving the defensemen off the blue line, forcing them to backpedal and open up ice for his teammates. He doesn't need to coast to make his plays, and can handle and move the puck at almost full speed. He changes direction and speeds within a step. He's a great forechecker and penalty killer.

Courtnall has good hands and vision, and he combines those abilities with anticipation to become an effective playmaker. However, he undercuts his playmaking ability by overhandling the puck (too much 1-on-1 play versus the opposition). He tries to make a play from a crowd, leading to turnovers. If he'd move the puck a little quicker and then jump into the holes he'd be twice as effective.

Russ has an excellent wrist shot, just packed with power. It is a dangerous offensive weapon, and Courtnall uses it to great effect from right in front of the net. He'll often be at a wing position on offensive zone faceoffs in order to take advantage of his shot.

THE PHYSICAL GAME

For a little guy, Courtnall plays awfully tough. He is not a physically imposing player and he isn't going to knock anyone out with his physical game, but Courtnall hits willingly, frequently and with a good bit of strength.

He plays the body well in open ice (his balance on his skates is the key to that ability), but he won't win many battles along the boards because of his stature. Courtnall is unafraid and — though much more suited to a finesse game — will fight when he has to.

THE INTANGIBLES

Courtnall has a good attitude. He wants to win and he works hard, and can be a super player for the Habs because of that combination of attitude and talent.

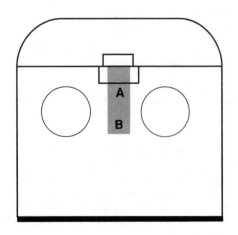

TODD EWEN

Yrs. of NHL service: 3
Born: Saskatoon, Sask., Canada; March 26, 1966
Position: Right wing
Height: 6-2
Weight: 215
Uniform no.: 36
Shoots: right

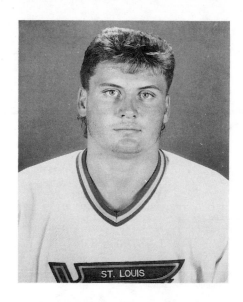

Career statistics:

GP	G	A	TP	PIM
165	14	13	27	651

1989-90 statistics:

GP	G	A	TP	+/-	PIM	PP	SH	GW	GT	S	PCT
44	4	6	10	-1	169	0	0	2	0	29	13.8

LAST SEASON

Acquired from St. Louis in December 1989. Assist and point totals were career highs, and he led the club in PIM total.

THE FINESSE GAME

Not a whole lot here. Ewen doesn't have a lot of skating skill, though he is fast and strong on his feet. He's tough to move off the puck should he have it, which makes him effective in front of the net, but he's only effective in front of the net if the goaltender's having coffee and the defensemen are discussing the weather.

Like an Einstein equation, Ewen needs plenty of both time and space to make any kind of play; he certainly won't finesse the puck into a small opening. Anything he gets will have to be because of brute strength.

He wanders from his position, but that's not surprising because he needs the whole rink to make a turn. His speed, however, indicates that he might — *might* — have some NHL success as a checker.

THE PHYSICAL GAME

When he catches anybody, Ewen's pretty tough player. He's got great strength and uses it well when checking and along the boards, but he can't make the strength pay off in points because he has no hands — at least not at the NHL level.

He's also a pretty good fighter, and that's why he's in the NHL.

THE INTANGIBLES

He's a willing guy, very intelligent off-ice. But he is a limited player on-ice, and as such is subject to eminent replacement by the next tough guy on the block.

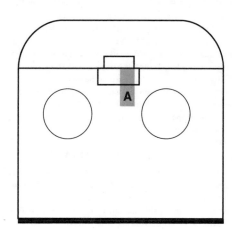

BRENT GILCHRIST

Yrs. of NHL service: 2
Born: Moose Jaw, Sask., Canada; Aril 3, 1967
Position: Center
Height: 6-1
Weight: 190
Uniform no.: 41
Shoots: left

Career statistics:

GP	G	A	TP	PIM
106	17	31	48	44

1989-90 statistics:

GP	G	A	TP	+/-	PIM	PP	SH	GW	GT	S	PCT
57	9	15	24	3	28	1	0	0	0	80	11.3

LAST SEASON

Second NHL appearance; scored one more goal, one fewer assist than in 1988-89. Missed three games with cheek laceration.

THE FINESSE GAME

Though he exhibited a scorer's profile while in junior and the American Hockey League, Gilchrist has yet to demonstrate any significant finesse ability at the NHL level. He's no better than average as a skater, showing neither exceptional speed nor superior quickness or agility. Strength would have to be listed as the principle quality in Gilchrist's skating, and he uses that ability to get where he's going as a checker.

He doesn't yet show great flair in understanding the offensive zone at the NHL level, so his use of his teammates and his own ability to get into scoring position is limited. Better experience will show him the NHL's speed, an aspect to which he has yet to become completely acclimated. For now, his offense is going to have to be generated down low.

Gilchrist plays a fairly strong and determined defensive game.

THE PHYSICAL GAME

Gilchrist has good size and he's not loathe to use it; again, greater NHL experience will show him his hitting opportunities better. He's shown an ability to establish good position against the opposition, and to use his body while working both ends of the ice.

THE INTANGIBLES

Gilchrist is currently showing himself to be in the workhorse mold, a la Mike McPhee or Ryan Walter — though he currently lacks their skating ability. He's a motivated kid, and he'll have to be to improve his skills for the NHL level.

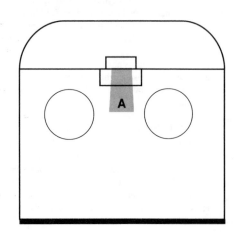

BRIAN HAYWARD

Yrs. of NHL service: 8
Born: Georgetown, Ontario, Canada; June 25, 1960
Position: Goaltender
Height: 5-10
Weight: 175
Uniform no.: 1
Catches: left

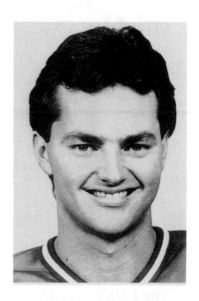

Career statistics:

GP	MINS	G	SO	AVG	A	PIM
306	17,297	1,054	6	3.66	12	77

1989-90 statistics:

GP	MINS	AVG	W	L	T	SO	GA	SA	SAPCT	PIM
29	1,674	3.37	10	12	6	1	94	770	.878	4

LAST SEASON

Games played total was six-season low; ditto win total. Missed five games with knee injury.

THE PHYSICAL GAME

Hayward is a cool, consistent and stand-up goaltender, adept at squaring himself to the puck and cutting down the shooters' angles. He challenges the shooters in almost all situations and lets the puck do the work by just hitting him; you won't often see Hayward flinging himself flying around the ice.

His style is based on smarts and self-knowledge, because Brian is not a great skater. While he has good foot speed and moves around the net well, he has below average balance and does not recover his stance quickly. His lateral movement reflects that, making him vulnerable in scramble situations because he is unable to get into position to stop second and third attempts.

He also fails to use his challenging style sufficiently on screen shots, where he hangs back in the net instead of coming to the top of the screen. That's when you'll see him beaten to the extreme ends of the net — beyond his feet and inside the posts on both sides.

Hayward is average at controlling the puck after a save, usually able to direct it out of danger. He does not frequently leave his net to retrieve loose pucks and that's smart because he does not handle it well.

THE MENTAL GAME

Brian's concentration and mental toughness have grown steadily since his time in Montreal, to the point now that he applies himself mentally throughout a game. He's less affected by bad goals or games, knowing that a good outing isn't far away. He's competitive and wants to play more often than he gets a chance to, so he does his best to make the most of his opportunities.

THE INTANGIBLES

Hayward is a steady goaltender, and that consistency makes him a more dependable goaler than Patrick Roy. Hayward gives the Canadiens a solid performance most every night out, but he lacks Roy's potential (albeit Patrick's only shown it once — but it won Montreal a Stanley Cup) to raise his game to the situation, to become a hot and thus unbeatable goaltender.

MIKE KEANE

Yrs. of NHL service: 2
Born: Winnipeg, Man., Canada; May 28, 1967
Position: Right wing
Height: 5-11
Weight: 175
Uniform no.: 12
Shoots: right

Career statistics:

GP	G	A	TP	PIM
143	25	34	59	141

1989-90 statistics:

GP	G	A	TP	+/-	PIM	PP	SH	GW	GT	S	PCT
74	9	15	24	0	78	1	0	1	0	92	9.8

LAST SEASON

Games played total rose, but all point totals fell in second NHL season. Missed one game with sore neck.

THE FINESSE GAME

Keane is a player whose physical style both disguises and powers his finesse game. He's a good skater who uses his skating strength and balance to charge the net, but he also has good vision and hockey sense — so he can make a play en route to the goal.

Mike generally keeps his head up to look over the ice, but he doesn't yet move the puck at NHL speed. He has the hands to make good backhand passes, and he accepts passes well too. His hands are good enough for him to one-time the puck, and he delivers his to the net with a good release and some power. Right now, though, he's going to have to be more opportunistic than artistic in order to score.

THE PHYSICAL GAME

He doesn't have great size, but Keane is a tough physical forward. His skating and balance help him greatly in the traffic areas. He takes the body and rubs out his man well in all three zones, and Mike has the strength to be good hitter.

He's not primarily a fighter, but he can go pretty well. He fights lefty, making him a more difficult opponent. He'll sacrifice his body by blocking shots.

THE INTANGIBLES

There's some solid potential here, 25 goals worth (maybe more) with sufficient NHL experience though there's always going to be concern that he's too small for the fiesty style he plays. Keane's a good worker and the kind of dependable player who can be on the ice in any situation. As a type, he comparable to Mike McPhee or Ryan Walter.

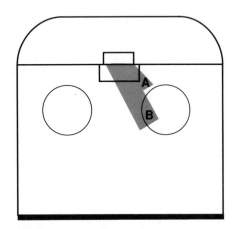

STEPHAN LEBEAU

Yrs. of NHL service: 1
Born: St.-Jerome, Quebec, Canada; February 28, 1968
Position: Center
Height: 5-10
Weight: 180
Uniform no.: 47
Shoots: right

Career statistics:

GP	G	A	TP	PIM
58	15	21	36	11

1989-90 statistics:

GP	G	A	TP	+/-	PIM	PP	SH	GW	GT	S	PCT
57	15	20	135	13	11	5	0	3	0	79	19.0

LAST SEASON

First full NHL season. Finished fourth among rookies in first goals.

THE FINESSE GAME

Lebeau is a very talented finesse player, a skater and stickhandler as befits his nifty-sort of size. He has some rink-length speed he can throw at the opposition, but his quickness and one-step ability makes him more of an agile/lateral/darting type player than anything else.

He handles the puck well at his top speeds and while in traffic, and he uses his balance and hand skills to great effect in front of the opposing goal. He's got great hands for shooting and scoring, so he can get off those quick shots from a crowd that result in goals.

Lebeau looks to use his teammates, but he's going to shoot when he can. Right now shooting is a good option because he doesn't yet have a great sense of the NHL game's speed, so his playmaking is more apt to go awry while a shot is at least a guaranteed offensive opportunity.

He plays a very aware defensive game, working his way back deeply into the Habs' zone.

THE PHYSICAL GAME

Lebeau is a little guy, but he'll go to the net and take his beatings. And then he'll go back for more. He's not going to impose himself to any great degree on the opposition (as in a corners and boards game), but he does have the talent to play hit-and-run, bumping the opposition off the puck and then scooting away.

THE INTANGIBLES

Size is always going to be the question with Lebeau (especially as the NHL gets bigger and stronger), as his coach will have to determine how many small players he wants on the ice at one time. He has some talent, but whether that is translatable to the NHL on a consistent basis remains to be seen.

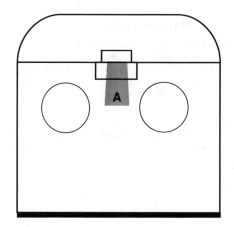

SYLVAIN LEFEBVRE

Yrs. of NHL service: 1
Born: Richmond, Quebec, Canada; October 14, 1967
Position: Defenseman
Height: 6-2
Weight: 187
Uniform no.: 3
Shoots: left

Career statistics:

GP	G	A	TP	+/-	PIM	PP	SH	GW	GT	S	PCT
68	3	10	13	18	61	0	0	0	0	89	3.4

LAST SEASON

First full NHL season.

THE FINESSE GAME

Lefebvre is a strong skater with good agility, speed and strength in his feet. All these qualities combine to allow him to play intelligently and aggressively, challenging the puck and the puck carrier at both blue lines.

He plays a more defensive style, so Lefebvre is less apt to forecheck or pinch in to contain the point than he is to fall back and protect his zone (a role he plays occasionally on the power play). Whatever scoring he's going to do is going to come from the blue line.

When he gets the puck he moves it quickly and efficiently, using his good vision to find the open man and get him the puck. Because he is still getting acclimated to NHL speed, determined and immediate forechecking can pressure him into giveaways.

THE PHYSICAL GAME

Lefebvre has good size and rangy strength, and he combines both with his mobility to take men out of the play very well. His takeouts are very sound, and his defensive zone coverages are marked by efficient and intelligent use of his body.

THE INTANGIBLES

Lefebvre is an understated player, but a steady and dependable one nonetheless. He makes his job easy by making the easy play, and he can grow into an above average NHL defenseman.

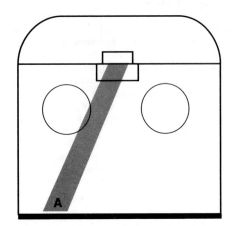

CLAUDE LEMIEUX

Yrs. of NHL service: 5
Born: Buckingham, Quebec, Canada; July 16, 1965
Position: Right wing
Height: 6-1
Weight: 206
Uniform no.: 32
Shoots: right

Career statistics:

GP	G	A	TP	PIM
281	97	92	189	576

1989-90 statistics:

GP	G	A	TP	+/-	PIM	PP	SH	GW	GT	S	PCT
39	8	10	18	-8	106	3	0	1	0	104	7.7

LAST SEASON

Games played and all point totals were full-season career lows. Missed 41 games with abdominal surgery. Plus/minus rating was club's worst.

THE FINESSE GAME

Claude is a power forward, a combination of strength aqnd finesse. His skating is represented by strength, as his stride gives him acceleration, speed and driving ability. His balance is good enough to keep him upright after checking, but Lemieux lacks the fine edge that would make him an agile player. He's just charges straight ahead with the puck.

Lemieux has good hockey sense and a solid read of the ice, and he combines those mental attributes with his skating to be a good forechecker. He does not, however, make good use of those skills when he has gained the puck.

While he does carry it well at top speed, Claude undercuts his chances by keeping his head down — he's focussed on the puck and the defenseman in front of him. If he looked up, he'd make better use of his teammates. Additionally, Lemieux is a goal-scorer — so he shoots first and asks questions later.

His shot is excellent, strong and accurate, quickly released, and he certainly has the hands to nail the far corner. His release (as well as his ability to work in traffic) benefit the Habs on the power play, when Claude camps in front of the net for garbage goals. He has enough power to blow the puck past the goaltender from the top of the circle.

Lemieux's improved his defensive play, but he'll never be mistaken for teammate Guy Carbonneau.

THE PHYSICAL GAME

Lemieux has superior strength, and that asset works in tandem with his balance to make him a good traffic player. He uses his skating strength to drive the net, and Lemieux has the upper body and arm strength to get his shot off despite the checking he encounters in the slot.

Because he's so strong in his upper body — and because he has excellent balance on his feet to remain vertical after collisions — Lemieux can be a terror up and down the boards. He bangs around with reckless abandon in the corners and continues around the opposition net.

There is, however, a big but.

THE INTANGIBLES

Lemieux is an enigma. He's a big strong winger, an agitator and a chippy/dirty player who can handle most anything his play stirs up — but therein lies the contradiction: He won't always do so.

Lemieux is hugely inconsistent in his use of his physical ability; there are games that he floats through without touching a soul. He needs to consistently apply himself in his very strong physical game; he'd rather dive for penalties than muscle his way into position.

Thus far in his NHL career Lemieux has but scratched the surface of what he is capable of.

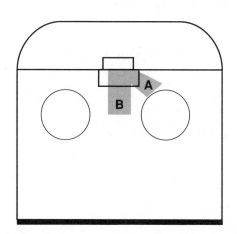

223

CRAIG LUDWIG

Yrs. of NHL service: 8
Born: Rhinelander, Wisconsin, USA; March 15, 1961
Position: Defenseman
Height: 6-3
Weight: 217
Uniform no.: 17
Shoots: left

Career statistics:

GP	G	A	TP	PIM
597	26	111	137	619

1989-90 statistics:

GP	G	A	TP	+/-	PIM	PP	SH	GW	GT	S	PCT
73	1	15	16	24	108	0	0	0	0	49	2.0

LAST SEASON

Games played total was three-season low, assist total six-season high. Led defense in plus/minus rating. Suffered a late-season shoulder injury.

THE FINESSE GAME

Finesse is not really the name of Ludwig's game, so he succeeds by smartly staying within his limitations. He's not a bad skater, though no one element in his skating leaps to the fore. Craig doesn't have exceptional speed, quickness or agility, but he can step up and close the gap on the puckcarrier.

Because he sees the defensive zone fairly well, Ludwig can get away with the occasional fancy pass, the pass up the middle to the breaking forward. But he'll most often make the pass necessary to get the puck out of danger. His good vision also powers his transition game; he can make the takeout and get the play up ice quickly.

Ludwig generally serves as the defensive safety valve — the last man back. As such, he doesn't usually become a fourth attacker in the offensive zone. He does, however, have a good enough read of the offensive zone that he can successfully drop the puck and charge the net.

His offense is otherwise minimal.

THE PHYSICAL GAME

Ludwig is a tough guy and a mean sonofagun, as his suspension-earning elbow to Trent Yawney proved. Craig is aggressive in the corners and the front of the net, but he will take shots as well as give them. He frequently uses his stick, so forwards won't make too many plays with their heads down.

He also sacrifices his body by blocking shots.

THE INTANGIBLES

Teams love mean defensemen, especially those who don't usually accrue many penalties. Ludwig fits into this mold, and he's pretty good defensively too. Craig's non-fancy style of just clearing the man and moving the puck perfectly complements that of any offensively oriented partner, and that's part of Ludwig's great value.

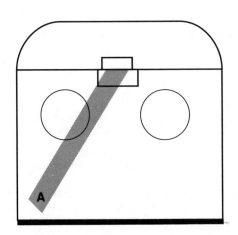

MIKE MCPHEE

Yrs. of NHL service: 7
Born: Sydney, N.S., Canada; July 14, 1960
Position: Left wing
Height: 6-1
Weight: 200
Uniform no.: 35
Shoots: left

Career statistics:

GP	G	A	TP	PIM
439	124	126	250	462

1989-90 statistics:

GP	G	A	TP	+/-	PIM	PP	SH	GW	GT	S	PCT
56	23	18	41	28	47	0	1	1	2	118	19.5

LAST SEASON

Games played total was full-season career low, but goal total tied career high. Suffered early-season abdominal injury. Plus/minus rating was team's third best.

THE FINESSE GAME

Strength is the basis of McPhee's game, so it's only fitting that strength marks his skating. That power gives him speed and acceleration, as well as making him an almost tireless skater. Mike has a good helping of balance, which combines with his skating strength to allow him to drive through checks. He has a modicum of foot speed, but not so much that he could be labelled an exceptionally agile skater.

McPhee combines speed with anticipation to become a very good forechecker and penalty killer. His checking creates many loose pucks and McPhee is talented enough to convert on those opportunities around the net.

Though he lacks the sensitive hands needed to be considered a true goal scorer (McPhee isn't going to finesse three inches of puck into two inches of net), his anticipation will get him to scoring position and loose pucks.

And, because he gets a good read of the ice, McPhee can make plays because his hands are sensitive enough to give and take soft passes.

McPhee is a determined back checker and plays good, positional defense, rarely wandering from where he is supposed to be when in his defensive zone.

THE PHYSICAL GAME

McPhee is a very strong player, and he uses his strength to play a very aggressive game. He gets into the corners and bulls around, and his balance helps keep him vertical and ready to make plays after banging into the opposition. Mike can be a punishing hitter and he hits relentlessly.

He will win more than his share of battles along the boards.

THE INTANGIBLES

His all-around skills serve to take McPhee out of the role-playing category, and he's a much-sought after commodity. He is a very driven individual, the kind of hard-working player who would be referred to as "honest."

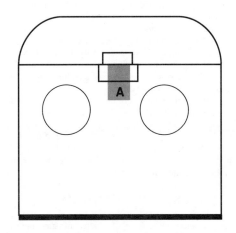

STEPHANE RICHER

Yrs. of NHL service: 5
Born: Ripon, Quebec, Canada; June 7, 1966
Position: Right wing/center
Height: 6-2
Weight: 200
Uniform no.: 44
Shoots: right

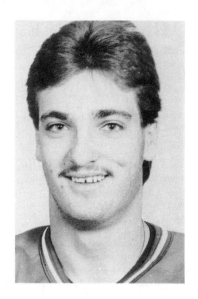

Career statistics:

GP	G	A	TP	PIM
338	167	138	305	309

1989-90 statistics:

GP	G	A	TP	+/-	PIM	PP	SH	GW	GT	S	PCT
75	51	40	91	35	46	9	0	8	0	269	19.0

LAST SEASON

Games played and all point totals were career highs. Led club in goals (seventh in NHL), points (22nd in NHL), power play goals, plus/minus rating (second in NHL), game winners and shooting percentage, second in shots on goal. Suffered a late season hip pointer.

THE FINESSE GAME

Richer has exceptional finesse skills, primary of which is his slap shot, one of the two or three best in the League. That shot is pretty much unstoppable from the edge of the faceoff circle and in, but Stephane is more than just a one-hit wonder. His soft hands make him extremely dangerous around the net, as he can finesse the puck through the smallest opening regardless of checking.

He's an excellent skater whose powerful stride gives him explosive acceleration and rink-length speed. His speed will not only get him to the openings but will create them as well. His exceptional foot speed and balance give him one-step quickness, and they also combine to make Richer a very agile player — he has excellent lateral movement.

His excellent hockey sense works in tandem with his skating to put Richer into position where he can unleash his shot; he gets into scoring position excellently. He uses his anticipation to lead his teammates into openings with his passes.

Primarily a goal-scoring center, Richer's hand skills extend to his puckhandling and passing. He carries the puck excellently at all speeds, but he can also take and give passes at full speed because of his soft hands. He likes to work 1-on-1 against the defense, and is that rare player who could stickhandle through an entire team and score.

THE PHYSICAL GAME

Richer has excellent physical tools. He's got size, strength and balance — all of which could guarantee a successful physical game. His use of his physical skills is limited, however, to occasional forays into the corners. Still, he's bumping the opposition for the puck.

His strength can also help him in the high traffic area around the net, allowing him to hold the puck longer and withstand checks. He uses his body well to protect the puck, and Richer's reach and arm strength help him pull loose pucks from traffic.

And like Mario Lemieux, Richer's bulk is such that once he gets moving he's very difficult to slow down.

THE INTANGIBLES

He seems to have finally hit the stride for which he was destined (two out of the last three seasons would say so, anyway). He is the kind of player who can control and dominate each game in which he plays, as long as his intensity and dedication level is where it belongs — which, if he chooses to be that dominant player — is at a high level. Richer must continue to keep his attitude strong if he wants to keep his on-ice performances as sensational as they were last season.

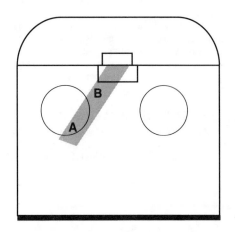

PATRICK ROY

Yrs. of NHL service: 5
Born: Quebec City, Quebec, Canada; October 5, 1965
Position: Goaltender
Height: 6-0
Weight: 175
Uniform no.: 33
Catches: left

Career statistics:

GP	MINS	G	SO	AVG	A	PIM
241	13,860	651	12	2.82	17	28

1989-90 statistics:

GP	MINS	AVG	W	L	T	SO	GA	SA	SAPCT	PIM
54	3,173	2.53	31	16	5	3	134	1,524	.912	0

LAST SEASON

Finished first in the NHL in goals-against-average, save percentage and in wins, fourth in shutouts. Games and minutes played totals were career highs. Missed four games with the flu.

THE PHYSICAL GAME

While he's added a certain degree of stand-up play to his game. Roy lives and dies with his reflexes. He flops a lot (sometimes too early and too frequently) but that works for him because of his size; his long legs cover almost the entire bottom of the net. His fast feet cover the low corners, and serve as his version of lateral ability.

His balance is good, and Roy quickly springs from the ice to regain his stance. However, it's while he's on the ice that he's often left scrambling for loose pucks around the net. He does not generally roam from his net to handle the puck and that's good, because he's not a particularly gifted stickhandler and doesn't show great puck movement judgement any way.

Because he doesn't cut his angles or square himself to the puck as best as he can, Patrick is weak on his short stick side. and that indicates failure to properly cut down the angle. He's also stiff on his glove side with shots that are close to his body and don't allow him to extend his arm.

He also does not handle rebounds off his chest protector well, leaving the puck to bounce loose in front of him.

THE MENTAL GAME

Patrick has big save capability. He can be tough mentally and return from bad goals or games, and his confidence helps him in that.

His concentration and vision are excellent, especially on scrambles around the net. He sees the puck very well and tunnels in on it, and he keeps his concentration intact within games.

THE INTANGIBLES

A second Vezina Trophy would certainly seem to demonstrate Roy's goaltending brilliance. But he is still an inconsistent player, one who is just as likely to be out of synch with his teammates' performances on one night as he is to win a game by himself on the next night.

DENIS SAVARD

Yrs. of NHL service: 10
Born: Pointe Gatineau, Quebec, Canada; February 4, 1961
Position: Center
Height: 5-10
Weight: 175
Uniform no.: 18
Shoots: right

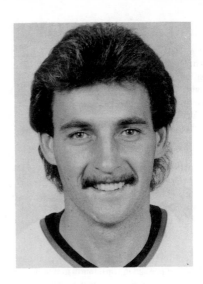

Career statistics:

GP	G	A	TP	PIM
736	351	662	1,013	828

1989-90 statistics:

GP	G	A	TP	+/-	PIM	PP	SH	GW	GT	S	PCT
60	27	53	80	8	56	10	2	4		1	181	14.9

LAST SEASON

Missed 17 games with a broken finger, as well as time with an ankle injury. All point totals were second lowest of career. Finished second on club in scoring.

THE FINESSE GAME

Skating is surely the best of Savard's formidable finesse skills, and balance and foot speed are sure the best aspects of that asset. In tandem they serve to make him the NHL's best one-on-one skater. Savard can literally stop and start, as well as change direction inside of a stride — and he can get to top speed almost as fast. That makes him extremely dangerous near any opening or loose puck, and almost impossible to take the body on. He also has great breakaway speed, and he'll lurk near the red line looking for a breakaway pass.

A close second to his skating skill is his puckhandling ability. There are many great ones in the NHL, but in a one-on-one situation no one is a better puckhandler than Savard. His hands are as agile as his feet, and he needs only the thinnest of openings to make his moves — whether that means beating a defender himself or threading the puck to a teammate.

His combination of soft hands and amazing ice vision and anticipation make Savard not only an excellent playmaker but an excellent scorer as well. He can put the puck in the net anywhere in any way. He has an excellent wrist shot (accurate, quickly released, heavy), and works very well in the traffic areas in front of the net because of his sense, balance and quick release.

He has a tendency to be a bit too much of a one-on-one player (and that leaves his teammates standing around), but at this stage of his career that won't change. About the only thing he's not exceptional at are faceoffs.

THE PHYSICAL GAME

Savard doesn't really have one. He works best in open ice and keeps himself there, and his finesse skills make him really difficult to hit or even bump. He stays away from crowds and uses his skill to dart in and out of crowded areas.

THE INTANGIBLES

Until his retirement (or Mike Keenan's departure from Chicago — whichever comes first) Savard will perpetually be mentioned as trade bait. He's a sensitive player and trade talk (and the lack of confidence implicit) can affect his game. Savard does need a kick start every once in a while, but he's shown that he can still be a dominating player even after a decade of NHL service.

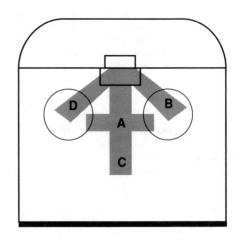

MATT SCHNEIDER

Yrs. of NHL service: 1
Born: Woonsocket, R.I., USA: June 12, 1969
Position: Defenseman
Height: 5-11
Weight: 180
Uniform no.: 18
Shoots: left

Career statistics:

GP	G	A	TP	PIM
48	7	14	21	27

1989-90 statistics:

GP	G	A	TP	+/-	PIM	PP	SH	GW	GT	S	PCT
44	7	14	21	2	25	5	0	1	0	84	8.3

LAST SEASON

First full NHL season. Led defense in power play goals. Joined Montreal from Sherbrooke of the American Hockey League in December 1989. Suffered from late-season flu.

THE FINESSE GAME

Schneider is a fairly mobile defenseman and he plays an aggressively intelligent style at both blue lines despite the fact that he is not overly fast. He uses his good ice vision and hockey sense to show him the openings offensively and to read the rush defensively, and he moves to aid or counter those plays.

He can get the puck to open teammates because of his vision and hand skills, and he shoots the puck well from his point position; he will, occasionally, cheat from the blue line for a shot.

He moves up with the attack well but doesn't really jump into the offense, preferring to play a more conservative all-around game. His skill at reading the ice and finding the open man combines with his skating to make him a specialty teams asset.

THE PHYSICAL GAME

Schneider is not big, and though he'll play an efficient physical style regarding his takeouts he can be out-muscled in one-on-one confrontations. He does use his body well to establish position and his hand skills will certainly help him make a play coming out of the corner, but he would benefit from additional upper body strength.

THE INTANGIBLES

All sorts of possibilities exist now, what with Chris Chelios gone to Chicago. Not that we're saying Schneider is another Chelios, but he can fill some of the hole left on the backline — with more NHL experience and greater physical strength, that is.

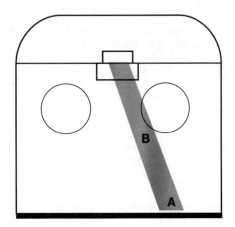

BRIAN SKRUDLAND

Yrs. of NHL service: 5
Born: Peace River, Alta., Canada; July 31, 1963
Position: Center
Height: 6-0
Weight: 188
Uniform no.: 39
Shoots: left

Career statistics:

GP	G	A	TP	PIM
353	55	114	169	416

1989-90 statistics:

GP	G	A	TP	+/-	PIM	PP	SH	GW	GT	S	PCT
59	11	31	42	21	56	4	0	1	0	70	15.7

LAST SEASON

Games played total was career low, assist and point totals career highs. Suffered early season ankle injury.

THE FINESSE GAME

Quickness and strength make Skrudland a good skater and very effective defensive forward. His skating is strong and almost tireless and, while Skrudland is not a tremendously agile player, his foot speed and quickness help him stay on his man all the time. That extra step helps him close the passing lanes and thus deny puck movement.

Good — and improving — anticipation and sense of the NHL game help Brian in his checking role. That means he can use his skating more efficiently when necessary by closing off areas of the ice through smarts. His offensive skills are growing apace as Skrudland takes greater and greater advantage of the loose pucks his checking creates, but he's never going to be a great scorer.

His good vision serves him in those offensive moments as he looks for plays around the net instead of just slamming the puck into the goaltender. Like others on the Canadiens checking staff, his growing ability to contribute offensively makes him more valuable and moves him out of the role player category.

THE PHYSICAL GAME

Skrudland plays an aggressive and consistently physical game, with his quickness allowing him to close the gaps between himself and the puck carrier. His good strength makes him a hard checker and he bumps his man at every opportunity, though sometimes to his disadvantage. Penalties and missed checks are the result, but this aspect of Skrudland's game is also improving.

He plays that physical style home and away and at both ends of the ice. He uses his size well against the boards and can take the puck away from the opposition fairly frequently, and his improving offensive ability makes his physical play more effective. He does not fight.

THE INTANGIBLES

Skrudland is a character player, the kind who gives 100 percent every night. He is also a good road player, and that's an indication of his consistent intensity and work ethic.

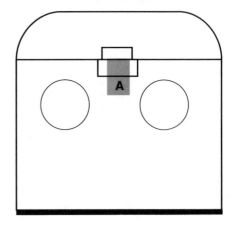

BOBBY SMITH

Yrs. of NHL service: 12
Born: North Sydney, N.S., Canada; February 12, 1958
Position: Center
Height: 6-4
Weight: 210
Uniform no.: 15
Shoots: left

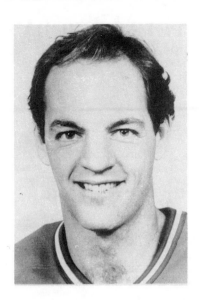

Career statistics:

GP	G	A	TP	PIM
891	328	604	932	738

1989-90 statistics:

GP	G	A	TP	+/-	PIM	PP	SH	GW	GT	S	PCT
53	12	14	26	-4	35	4	0	2		1	102	11.8

LAST SEASON

Games played and all point totals were career lows; missed three games with a charley horse, seven games with a separated shoulder, 18 games with a broken jaw. Plus/minus rating was club's second worst.

THE FINESSE GAME

Smith is a very smooth and fluid skater, with a long stride that belies his speed: that stride gets him away from the opposition quickly. He also has excellent balance and lateral movement, and he adds his skating to that agility to make plays beyond the capabilities of many NHLers.

Smith's vision and anticipation skills are also very high, and he uses those traits to recognize and exploit openings with either his own exceptional puck control, or by leading a teammate into the openings with soft and accurate passes.

Bobby's outstanding hand skills and hockey sense combine to make him a very dangerous scorer who can score in many ways, from almost anywhere in the offensive zone. Smith has an excellent selection of shots (hard and accurate wrist shot, very good slap shot), but his sneakiest weapon is the League's best backhand — it the upper right corner almost every time. The Canadiens set Smith up for that shot on the power play, otherwise he's more likely to score from deeper in the slot.

His transitional game down-ice is good, and he's a solid and consistent defensive player.

THE PHYSICAL GAME

Though he plays exceptionally well in traffic, Smith is not primarily a physical player. Rather, his excellent balance and reach allow him to dislodge opponents from the puck or to take it from them while he maintains body position.

He does not shy away from contact and he takes more physical punishment now than ever before. Bobby also initiates a great deal of contact, though not of the body-bashing kind.

His reach is exceptional and allows him access to the puck while on the outside of the crowd, and he certainly has the ability to make a play coming away from the boards. Hand and wrist strength help him snare those pucks, and they also make him a good faceoff man.

THE INTANGIBLES

Many called for his head last season, pointing at his woeful offensive totals. But history has shown Smith to be a consistent player, and we wouldn't yet give up on this disciplined player with upper-level finesse skill, and a solid team attitude and work ethic.

Because, geez, isn't a guy allowed to get hurt?

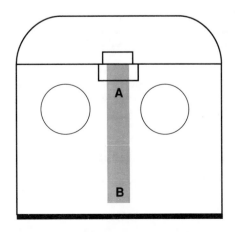

PETR SVOBODA

Yrs. of NHL service: 6
Born: Most, Czechoslovakia; February 14, 1966
Position: Defenseman
Height: 6-1
Weight: 170
Uniform no.: 25
Shoots: left

Career statistics:

GP	G	A	TP	PIM
416	30	152	182	615

1989-90 statistics:

GP	G	A	TP	+/-	PIM	PP	SH	GW	GT	S	PCT
60	5	31	36	20	98	2	0	2	0	90	5.6

LAST SEASON

Games played total was career low, assist and point totals second highest of career. Led defensemen in scoring. Missed 15 games with groin injury.

THE FINESSE GAME

Skating is the key to Svoboda's total game, and he demonstrates speed, quickness, agility and balance. Petr moves forward and back with equal ease and agility, as his balance and foot speed give him outstanding mobility and lateral movement. He uses that skill to challenge the puck at both blue lines.

He complements his skating ability with good hand skills, and Petr will rush the puck to take pressure off the Canadiens' forwards. Petr handles the puck well and has soft hands that make him a good passer. He also takes the puck off the boards extremely well in the defensive zone and starts the play away almost in one motion.

Svoboda uses his hand skills to get the puck to his teammates and to contain the point well, but his ice vision still does not completely jibe with NHL speed. He doesn't always find the open man as easily as possible, and Svoboda also has a tendency (because his head is dropped) to drive a shot into a charging opposing player. His shot is accurate but lacking in strength. He'll cruise to the top of the faceoff circle if he can.

THE PHYSICAL GAME

Petr is an aggressive player, especially in the use of his stick. He'll get nailed for his cross-checks and slashes, but one reason Svoboda has to resort to stickwork is because his strength isn't sufficient to clear the front of the net or take the opposition off the puck.

He needs more muscle on his frame, or else he'll continue to be bounced off the puck and out-muscled in front of the net.

THE INTANGIBLES

Svoboda's matured into a fairly dependable and consistent two-way defenseman. His aggressive style of play doesn't always work against him, as that style often takes the opposition out of the game — they're too busy trying to clobber him, instead of paying attention to the play.

And with Chris Chelios gone, Svoboda is going to be in the game more than ever; he'll undoubtedly pick up the brunt of Chelios's responsibilities.

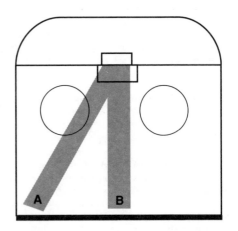

RYAN WALTER

Yrs. of NHL service: 11
Born: New Westminster, B.C., Canada; April 23, 1958
Position: Center/left wing/right wing
Height: 6-0
Weight: 195
Uniform no.: 11
Shoots: left

Career statistics:

GP	G	A	TP	PIM
886	255	370	625	875

1989-90 statistics:

GP	G	A	TP	+/-	PIM	PP	SH	GW	GT	S	PCT
70	8	16	24	4	59	1	0	1	0	109	7.3

LAST SEASON

All point totals were career lows. Missed four games with broken toe, four games with leg injury.

THE FINESSE GAME

Like many of his teammates, Walter's finesse game springs from his physical one. His skating is particularly marked by his strength, especially in his ability to pursue the puck as a checking forward. He has good balance and power, and those assets help him in his physical game by driving him through his checks and by making him a tenacious checker.

Walter has learned to read the ice and anticipate the play fairly well, so he's able to break up a pass or find an opening by positioning himself well.

Because of his vision, Ryan can capitalize on the opportunities his checking creates by getting the puck to his teammates. He'll need to be opportunistic for his own scoring, picking up junk near the net, because his shot lacks the quick release that will fool NHL goaltending. He'll also be used to plug the front of the goal on the power play.

THE PHYSICAL GAME

Ryan gets the most from his physical ability by playing a controlled but aggressive game. He's got a mean streak, and Walter plays aggressively in all three zones — at home or on the road, winning or losing — without taking penalties. Because of his balance, Walter comes out of most collisions vertical and ready to make a play.

He backs down from nothing and he uses his body well, showing good strength along the boards where he out-muscles the opposition.

THE INTANGIBLES

He gives 100 percent of himself at all times, but there was an increasing chorus of voices last season who wondered whether Walter had much of anything left to give. His work ethic alone makes him a valuable player, but with the excess of bodies the Canadiens have up front Walter may find himself on the way out.

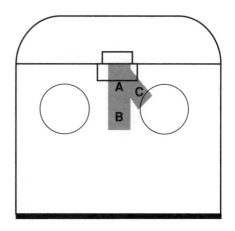

NEW JERSEY DEVILS

TOMMY ALBELIN

Yrs. of NHL service: 3
Born: Stockholm. Sweden; May 21, 1964
Position: Defenseman
Height: 6-1
Weight: 198
Uniform no.: 26
Shoots: left

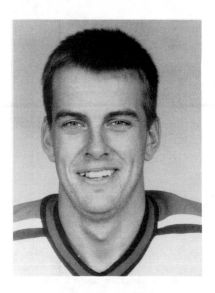

Career statistics:

GP	G	A	TP	PIM
188	18	74	92	177

1989-90 statistics:

GP	G	A	TP	+/-	PIM	PP	SH	GW	GT	S	PCT
68	6	23	29	-1	63	4	0	0	0	125	4.8

LAST SEASON

Games played total was career high. Missed four games with a knee injury.

THE FINESSE GAME

Albelin is a talented finesse player with good potential but with improvement yet to be done. He skates well in both directions and is smooth in his pivots, but he needs to improve the general speed and quickness of his movement. His defense is solid and Albelin showed that he understands how to force a play wide of the net by angling off the forward.

The improvement can come in his ability to read and understand the play and its ramifications so that he can use his fine skating to be more than a one-play (as in simply react and force the play wide instead of stepping up) defenseman. In the vernacular, this is his read and react game, and it could be stronger.

He handles the puck well and is unafraid to do so at this level. He plays with poise and confidence at the point, smoothly pinching in to contain and control the offensive play. Tommy also handles the puck very well, taking it off the boards and shooting it with ease. He'll cheat to the faceoff circle for shots if he can.

THE PHYSICAL GAME

Albelin has good size but could use greater strength in his upper body for confrontations in the defensive zone. Right now he can be overpowered in the traffic areas, and even though he's going to be more of an offensive contributor he'll need strength for the times his defensive partner can't cover the front of the net.

THE INTANGIBLES

Albelin showed pretty well for a guy shuttled in and out of the lineup. He gets a lot of responsibility in terms of power play and penalty killing assignments, and he has become (in three abbreviated seasons) a pretty reliable defenseman. Greater experience can only make him better.

BOB BROOKE

Yrs. of NHL service: 6
Born: Melrose, Mass., USA; December 18, 1960
Position: Center/right wing
Height: 6-1
Weight: 205
Uniform no.: 10
Shoots: right

Career statistics:

GP	G	A	TP	PIM
447	69	97	166	520

1989-90 statistics:

GP	G	A	TP	+/-	PIM	PP	SH	GW	GT	S	PCT
73	12	14	26	-2	63	0	3	1	0	109	11.0

LAST SEASON

Acquired from Minnesota in exchange for Aaron Broten in January 1990. Goal and point totals were three-season highs. Suffered late season foot injury. Was a plus-3 with New Jersey.

THE FINESSE GAME

Brooke is an excellent skater with strength, speed, and balance, and he uses those assets best as a checking forward. He plays the game at very high speed, and he can do that because his strong stride gives him the power necessary for acceleration. He doesn't have the quickness that creates one-step agility.

His hockey sense and vision are excellent and they serve him in both the offensive and defensive game. His smarts and skating ability will create many offensive opportunities for him, almost none of which he will cash in on. As good as Bob's foot skills are, that's how bad his hands are. They betray him when giving or accepting passes, and when he is carrying the puck. He'll be able to get into scoring position because of his speed and sense, but he'll never be able to get the puck away fast enough. He'll have to get his goals, therefore, by being opportunistic around the net.

And forget that plus/minus; his defensive play is excellent. Brooke is always aware of his check and plays his position deep into the defensive zone.

THE PHYSICAL GAME

Brooke is in excellent condition, and his conditioning allows him to take full advantage of his size and strength (as well as to maximize his skating skill). He uses his strength and balance to work the corners and boards ceaselessly, and he can come away with the puck (what he does with it after gaining it — see 'hand skills' — is another matter). His balance keeps him upright after collisions, and ready to make plays.

He is an aggressive player who backs down from no one (don't interpret this to mean he's a fighter, however) and he hits well at both ends of the ice.

He has excellent eye/hand coordination, so he'll get loose pucks and win faceoffs.

THE INTANGIBLES

He's an honest, hard working player, and Bob also has the ability to play both forward and defense. That versatility is important for a role player.

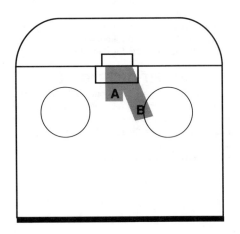

DOUG BROWN

Yrs. of NHL service: 3
Born: Southborough, Mass., USA; June 12, 1964
Position: Right wing
Height: 5-11
Weight: 180
Uniform no.: 24
Shoots: right

Career statistics:

GP	G	A	TP	PIM
206	43	42	85	51

1989-90 statistics:

GP	G	A	TP	+/-	PIM	PP	SH	GW	GT	S	PCT
69	14	20	34	7	16	1	3	3	0	135	10.4

LAST SEASON

Assist and point totals were career highs. Missed one game with back injury.

THE FINESSE GAME

Brown is an excellent — really outstanding — checker, and it is his skating that makes him so. He has tremendous quickness in his skating (more so than speed), and that makes his ability to excel in cramped quarters very high. He darts in and out of spaces, stopping, starting and changing direction within a stride excellently.

His quick feet will let him get a jump on a loose puck or on a puck carrier, and then he uses his quick hands to gain that loose puck or to knock the puck off that puck carrier's stick — and then it's off to the races. This combination of hand and foot quickness make him a very important member of the penalty killing squad, and he is a good bet for a shorthanded attempt.

Notice we didn't say shorthanded goal; that's because Brown's scoring ability is less pronounced than his pokechecking ability. He doesn't handle the puck well near the opposition *or* at top speed, so he's really going to have to be opportunistic in his goal scoring — cashing in on loose pucks his checking can create.

THE PHYSICAL GAME

Unfortunately for Brown, willing doesn't always translate into able. So though he deserves all the credit in the world for throwing his body around recklessly, Brown lacks the strength necessary to tie up the NHL's stronger forwards — doesn't, in fact, even have the strength to at least slow down most NHL wingers.

Improved upper body strength would help Brown hold his own when simply playing the body, and that alone would amplify his checking ability.

THE INTANGIBLES

Given his lack of physical effectiveness, Brown's checking success is even more remarkable since it's all based on brains and skating. He is an enthusiastic and hard working player who responds well in any situation, but his physical shortcomings may mean he'll be shuttled in and out of the lineup depending on the size of the opposition.

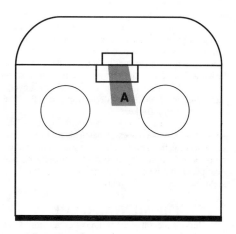

SEAN BURKE

Yrs. of NHL service: 3
Born: Windsor, Ontario, Canada; January 29, 1967
Position: Goaltender
Height: 6-3
Weight: 205
Uniform no.: 1
Catches: left

Career statistics:

GP	MINS	G	SO	AVG	A	PIM
127	7,203	440	4	3.67	4	98

1989-90 statistics

GP	MINS	AVG	W	L	T	SO	GA	SA	SAPCT	PIM
52	2,914	3.60	22	22	6	0	175	1,453	.880	38

LAST SEASON

Games and minutes played totals fell in second full season, but still finished sixth in the NHL in games played.

THE PHYSICAL GAME

Burke has all the tools for NHL greatness with — astoundingly — almost none of the weaknesses to prevent him from attaining that success. He has outstanding and intimidating size coupled with the quickness and reflexes of a much smaller goaltender, and those natural assets cover just about all the goaltending bases.

He uses his size in a stand-up style (especially on breakaways, where he almost always forces the opposition to make the first move), but his extremely fast feet and legs belie the general wisdom about shooting to the feet of big men.

He is a fine skater with excellent balance, so he moves in and out of the net and from post to post in a compact, almost seamless, package. He puts his size to work by moving to the top of screens to take up as much space as possible and to minimize deflections, yet his outstanding balance and quickness get him back to his stance and ready for the next save if he does choose to butterfly to the ice. He does have the tendency to hold the ice with his inner edges, so he is vulnerable to five-hole goals. Because of his ability to reach most every puck, re-directed pucks (tips, deflections) have the best chance of beating Burke.

Sean has a good glove hand and a quick stick, though his hand speed doesn't match his foot speed. He really benefits from his size on high shots. He handles the puck well in moving it to his teammates and has great puckhandling strength; if he were so inclined, he could shoot the puck for goals.

THE MENTAL GAME

Burke's mental game is almost as accomplished as his physical one. He has excellent anticipation and vision and is very tough mentally. His concentration is unfazed by bad goals or games. He is always prepared to play and not only has the capability of making the big save, but of winning games by himself.

His confidence and concentration are strong enough that he couldn't be called a front-runner (better when he's winning a game than when he's losing it), but he certainly feeds off early game success stronger as games go on.

THE INTANGIBLES

Burke needs the confidence of his team in order to be successful. But he received mixed signals from the club last season, so much so that he fully expected to be traded before this season started.

Something is wrong when one of your (and maybe your only) world class players feels vulnerable. That must be addressed if he is to fulfill his notices. He is a very hard worker and solid team man, very popular with his teammates, and he keeps himself in great shape at all times (his body looks more like a defenseman's in its trim muscularity than it does a goalie's).

KEN DANEYKO

Yrs. of NHL service: 6
Born: Windsor, Ontario, Canada; April 17, 1964
Position: Defenseman
Height: 6-0
Weight: 210
Uniform no.: 3
Shoots: left

Career statistics:

GP	G	A	TP	PIM
369	19	53	72	1,048

1989-90 statistics:

GP	G	A	TP	+/-	PIM	PP	SH	GW	GT	S	PCT
74	6	15	21	15	216	0	1	1	0	64	9.4

LAST SEASON

Games played was full-season career low, but all point totals were career highs. Tied with Alexei Kasatonov for best plus/minus rating among defensemen. Led team in PIM total, despite three-season low in that category. Missed three games with wrist and thumb injury.

THE FINESSE GAME

You wouldn't think it to look at him (considering the Superman-like body), but Daneyko has strong finesse skills that — when applied — make him one of the better defenders in the NHL. He has good (maybe very good) quickness, if not necessarily rink-length speed, and Daneyko should be able to apply that quickness to meet the opposing puck carrier outside his blue line. He doesn't always do this, and Daneyko needs to have greater confidence in his mobility. Yes, he'll get beaten, but his feet will allow him to get back into the play. Strangely, he challenges at the offensive blue line (where he doesn't always make good decisions) but often refuses to do so at his own blue line.

He doesn't have an exceptional degree of hockey sense or read and react skills, so Daneyko will need to make the simple play when he handles the puck. He is not apt to carry the puck from his zone, leaving that breakout task to his partner while Daneyko acts as the takeout defenseman.

Even with the career-best numbers, Daneyko would not be characterized as an offensive threat. He doesn't shoot the puck with any exceptional skill, and his passing skills aren't much better than his shooting skills.

THE PHYSICAL GAME

Daneyko is big, strong and tough. He thrives on a physical contest and he really punishes the opposition when he hits them along the boards or in front of the net; he is one of the toughest defenders in front of the net in the League. His balance and strength combine to keep him vertical after his many collisions, and his skating strength powerfully drives him through his checks.

His is a good fighter, a lefty with very fast hands, and he'll go with anyone.

THE INTANGIBLES

We've said for several years that Daneyko has potential but needs molding and direction; he showed last year just how powerful a player he can be. And don't get us wrong when we speak of his deficiencies; Daneyko knows what he can and can't do and generally stays smartly within his limitations. But he must also be taught to play up to his ability and not just back away from what he cannot do well.

He is a worker, enthusiastic and a pretty good team man.

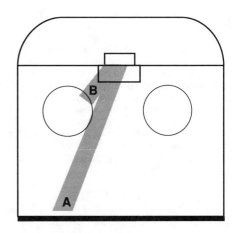

BRUCE DRIVER

Yrs. of NHL service: 6
Born: Toronto, Ontario, Canada; April 29, 1962
Position: Defenseman
Height: 6-0
Weight: 185
Uniform no.: 23
Shoots: left

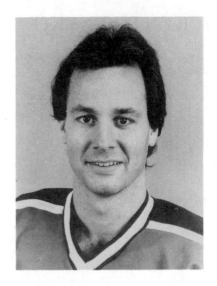

Career statisitics:

GP	G	A	TP	PIM
361	41	169	210	253

1989-90 statistics:

GP	G	A	TP	+/-	PIM	PP	SH	GW	GT	S	PCT
75	7	46	53	6	63	1	0	0	1	185	3.8

LAST SEASON

Games played, assist and point totals were career highs. Led Devils' defense in scoring and shots on goal, and finished third on club in assists. Missed one game with a groin injury, and was sidelined again late in the season with a second groin injury.

THE FINESSE GAME

The most important thing a defenseman can do is control the gap on the puck carrier, which means allowing a certain space between the defense and the puck and then closing the gap. If a defenseman can do that, he's going to win more than his share of one-on-one battles at all levels of hockey. That's an active versus reactive defensive play, and a player who can perform that skill consistently is a valued and valuable commodity.

Ladies and gentlemen, may we present Bruce Driver? Skating and smarts — particularly mobility and read and react ability — are the keys to playing a strong gap-control game, and Driver has both of those skills at his command. He is a very mobile skater with outstanding lateral movment, and he sees the ice defensively as well as he does offensively (and his numbers tell you how well he does *that*). He is an excellent one-on-one player.

He is also a fine offensive, aided by the combination of his skating ability, puckhandling skill and hockey sense. He carries the puck smoothly and can easily find the open man for a breakout pass or shot on goal. He contains the point well because of his skating and reading ability, and his hand skills help him take the puck off the boards and move to the center of the zone for shots.

He is a good shooter, smart enough to wrist the puck at the net when he has no other play and adept at one-timing his shot. His skills make him a natural for specialty teams work.

THE PHYSICAL GAME

Driver plays a willing physical game, but willing doesn't necessarily mean able. He'll take on any player (and his smarts and finesse ability make his physical play more effective) and he'll sacrifice his body by blocking shots, but Driver will get out-muscled in close quarter one-on-one confrontations — in areas like the front of the net, for instance. He will play along the boards but doesn't match up well strength-wise against the opposition, so he's forced to push and shove.

One aspect of his game that is way above average is his pokechecking ability. Driver will break up many rushes via pokecheck, and he'll use his exceptional finesse abilities to turn the puck up ice.

THE INTANGIBLES

Bruce Driver is an underrated player, one who is made better by having a better cast of characters around him. He proved that last year via a relatively injury-free year (though his durability is still questionable), and showed himself to be a very important piece of the Devils' puzzle.

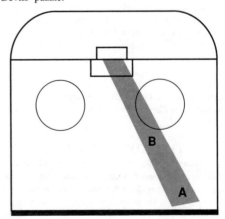

VIACHESLAV FETISOV

Yrs. of NHL service: 1
Born: Moscow, Soviet Union; May 20, 1958
Position: Defenseman
Height: 6-1
Weight: 205
Uniform no.: 2
Shoots: left

Career statistics:

GP	G	A	TP	+/-	PIM	PP	SH	GW	GT	S	PCT
72	8	34	42	9	52	2	0	0	0	108	7.4

LAST SEASON

First NHL season. Plus/minus rating was second among Devil defensemen. Led Devil defense in goals. Missed six games with knee injury.

THE FINESSE GAME

Though clearly possessed of ultra-high physical finesse abilities, hockey sense is the best of Fetisov's overall finesse abilities. He has shown in the past what could best be described as Gretzky-like anticipation and play manipulation skill, but at the NHL level only glimmers of this asset were visible. He certainly has strong read and react skills and he thinks very creatively — perhaps too creatively for his teammates. He contains and challenges at both ends of the ice very well and is an active rather than reactive defenseman.

His skating and puckhandling abilities mirror his mental facilities. Despite age and injury (and Fetisov is an old 32) he retains great balance for lateral mobility, if not necessarily rink-length speed or outstanding quickness. But his ability to stop, start and turn in confined spaces will make up for some of the quickness he has lost.

He handles the puck very well when carrying it and can certainly rush it from his zone, and he is a very good passer with excellent touch. But Fetisov overhandles the puck at the NHL level, and he tries too many high risk/high return passes (to mix our metaphors, he loves the long bomb-home run pass) that result in too many mistakes.

Fetisov is an excellent shooter, and there may not be a better wrist shot from an NHL defenseman. As was Denis Potvin, Fetisov is extremely dangerous with that shot when he moves off the point. Fetisov also shoots very well off the pass, and he has a fine slap shot.

THE PHYSICAL GAME

Fetisov isn't afraid of NHL traffic or hitting, but that doesn't mean he's always effective in that mode. He uses his body very well to establish position along the boards and in front of the net, but he can be bumped off the puck by strong forwards (one reason why his overhandling of the puck is dangerous). He can also be a dominating hitter because of his skating strength.

He'll sacrifice his body to block shots and will certainly take hits to make plays.

THE INTANGIBLES

All things considered, a pretty remarkable debut for Fetisov. He still has a lot to learn regarding the NHL and how to pace himself for the 100 games he'll play a year, but Fetisov's strong desire to prove himself in this hemisphere should guarantee he'll make the necessary improvements to his game. There is also a feeling that the full-season presence of former Soviet National team teammate Alexei Kasatonov (a former friend of Fetisov's who is now a rival, and who made an immediate and positive impact on the Devils upon his arrival) will pressure Fetisov into better play.

By the way — how could the Professional Hockey Writers' Association not have voted him to the NHL's All-Rookie team?

MARK JOHNSON

Yrs. of NHL service: 11
Born: Madison, Wisconsin, USA; September 22, 1957
Position: Center/left wing
Height: 5-9
Weight: 170
Uniform no.: 12
Shoots: left

Career statistics:

GP	G	A	TP	PIM
669	203	305	508	260

1989-90 statistics:

GP	G	A	TP	+/-	PIM	PP	SH	GW	GT	S	PCT
63	16	29	45	-8	12	4	0	1	0	82	19.5

LAST SEASON

Games played and point totals were three-season highs.

THE FINESSE GAME

Johnson is a smart player, particularly in the offensive end of the ice. He has great smarts and vision, and his excellent patience with the puck forces opposing defenses to panic and commit themselves.

He complements his vision and anticipation with strong stick skills. Johnson handles the puck very well, both in motion and when still, and he passes with equal ease to both his forehand and backhand sides. He has great touch and can feather or fire passes, and his puckhandling in traffic is an indication of that — he can retain the puck while being checked because of his soft hands. His anticipation and vision combine with his hand skills to make him a good playmaker, above average at leading teammates into the clear. He'll see power play duty (sometimes at the point) because of his ability to exploit the open man.

His skating skills enter the picture here, and his skating assets are of the subtler variety. He's not very fast and after a decade of NHL hockey Johnson doesn't have a lot of one-step springiness left in his stride either, but he does have great balance and that allows him to lean every which way while maintaining control of the puck.

Johnson concentrates on playmaking and will often sacrifice better shooting positions. He'll convert on loose pucks around the crease, and he also excels at tips and deflections.

THE PHYSICAL GAME

Johnson doesn't have one. He assiduously avoids the traffic areas of the ice, preferring to work from the outside of scrums in hopes of a puck popping loose. He's not likely to initiate contact either.

He does have excellent eye/hand coordination, allowing him to succeed at the tip-ins and deflections we mentioned earlier.

THE INTANGIBLES

At this point Johnson is a useful player off the bench, someone who can give a foreseeable result. He's never played a full season and won't play in pain, but his versatility in many situations (he can center or wing, kills penalties and plays the power play) will probably insure his continued NHL employment.

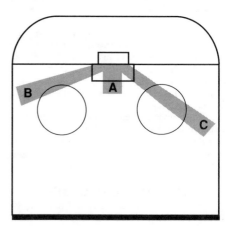

ALEXEI KASATONOV

Yrs. of NHL service: 1
Born: Leningrad, Soviet Union; October 14, 1959
Position: Defenseman
Height: 6-1
Weight: 210
Uniform no.: 7
Shoots: left

Career statistics:

GP	G	A	TP	+/-	PIM	PP	SH	GW	GT	S	PCT
39	6	15	21	15	16	1	0	0	0	60	10.0

LAST SEASON

First NHL season. Joined New Jersey in January 1990.

THE FINESSE GAME

Unlike fellow Soviet Viacheslav Fetisov, Kasatonov's skills are far more subtle and far less dramatic. All he does is get excellent reads of the ice at both ends, contain and control both blue lines, force turnover and speed the transition game. He just doesn't do it with the flair Fetisov does — when Fetisov does it.

Kasatonov is an excellent skater across all aspects of that skill, possessing speed, agility, quickness and balance. He uses that skating to its best degree in all aspects of his game and his excellent hockey sense and read and react abilities play off his skating very well.

He makes solid and sure passes from his end, willing to accept low risk options. Kasatonov finds the open man excellently, but he is not such an offensive dynamo that he will create open ice for his teammates. Kasatonov handles the puck very well and can rush with it, but he knows not to hang onto it for long spans of time — one very important reason he had the immediate NHL success he did.

He'll score his goal from 40-feet out and back, and his points will come from intelligent play if not necessarily creative play.

THE PHYSICAL GAME

As with his finesse game, Kasatonov's physical game is a subtle one but highly defined nevertheless. His excellent skating ability puts him in good position for takeouts, and his strength and balance allow him to pin his man to the boards. He excellently uses his body to gain position, plays a willing physical game in all areas and cannot be intimidated.

THE INTANGIBLES

A very strong NHL debut for Kasatonov, who just may have sneaked past all the hoopla and pressure by joining the Devils in mid-season. Like fellow Soviet Fetisov, Kasatonov is the rare kind of player who can make his teammates better just by his presence — which is to be expected from a world class player. He has fine desire and a strong attitude and can only improve with greater NHL experience — though it's hard to imagine his being any more effective.

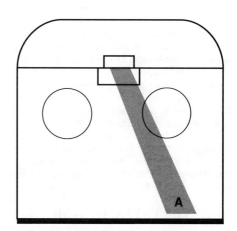

JOHN MACLEAN

Yrs. of NHL service: 7
Born: Oshawa, Ontario, Canada; November 20, 1964
Position: Right wing
Height: 6-0
Weight: 200
Uniform no.: 15
Shoots: right

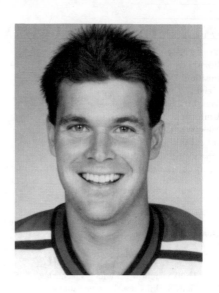

Career statistics:

GP	G	A	TP	PIM
468	172	191	363	640

1989-90 statistics:

GP	G	A	TP	+/-	PIM	PP	SH	GW	GT	S	PCT
80	41	38	79	17	80	10	3	11	0	322	12.7

LAST SEASON

Led Devils in goals, plus/minus, game-winners (third in NHL) and shots on goal (fourth in NHL). Played 80 games for second time in career, and all point totals were second best of career. PIM total was five season low.

THE FINESSE GAME

MacLean is a goal scorer, and what are the two things goal scorers do best? Shoot and get into scoring position. MacLean's shot is definitely the best of his finesse tools — heavy, fast, accurate and *quickly* released. He shoots from anywhere (as his SOG total might suggest) but the flip side is he can score from anywhere. Both his slap shot off the wing and his wrist shot from in tight are exceptional, and his shot is made better by its accuracy, forcing the goaltender to make saves. He is especially dangerous in the slot, and is a power play natural.

His ability to put himself in position to use his shot is his second best attribute, an ability best described as hockey sense because he really doesn't have great skating ability. But MacLean knows where to be to receive a pass, and he gets there somehow.

The rest of his finesse skills are rather plebeian. His skating style and general offensive thought processes are of a more straight line variety, as opposed to being creative. He's neither an exceptionally agile nor mobile skater, lacking the requisite foot speed, and his playmaking ability is nothing to write home about either. He is the line's designated shooter, and he'll look to the net before he looks to pass.

THE PHYSICAL GAME

MacLean doesn't have great size, but he does use what he has effectively. He initiates play in the trenches, and he's well aided by his balance (which keeps him vertical and ready to make a play after collisions). Still, he can get out-muscled if matched against larger forwards or defensemen.

Obviously, it is his strength that powers his shot, and that same strength allows him to deliver the puck goal-ward even while in traffic.

THE INTANGIBLES

As long as MacLean maintains his intensity, he's okay. He does have a tendency to be goaded into foolish penalties, but he cut down on that last season — that's an indication of his working to keep himself in the game. He's the Devils' best offensive threat, as well as their most consistent, and he must perform well in order for New Jersey to have a good chance at success.

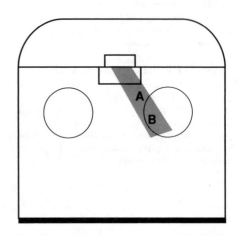

DAVID MALEY

Yrs. of NHL service: 4
Born: Beaver Dam, Wisconsin, USA; April 24, 1963
Position: Center/left wing
Height: 6-2
Weight: 205
Uniform no.: 8
Shoots: left

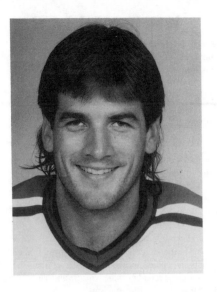

Career statistics:

GP	G	A	TP	PIM
230	23	37	60	529

1989-90 statistics:

GP	G	A	TP	+/-	PIM	PP	SH	GW	GT	S	PCT
67	8	17	25	-2	160	0	0	2	0	82	9.8

LAST SEASON

Games played and all point totals were career highs. Finished second on the club in PIM total, first among forwards. Missed eight games with knee surgery, five games with a subsequent knee injury.

THE FINESSE GAME

Not a lot here. Maley's skating is probably the best of his finesse skills, and he's not blessed with a great deal of speed, quickness or agility. He'll get up and down the ice on effort, and his willing physical game is mitigated by the fact that he may not catch anyone to hit. Because of his skating, he's probably better played at wing than at center.

His hand skills are at about the same level of his foot skills, so he will need time and space to make his plays. Any goals he gets will have to be of the opportunistic variety.

THE PHYSICAL GAME

This is where Maley can succeed in the NHL and he must play this way to succeed. He has good size and strength and is willing to use both of those assets, and he can hit hard when he tags somebody. He's a fighter and can fight lefty, so he'll win some decisions because opponents will be confused when he switches to a southpaw style.

THE INTANGIBLES

Maley's a pretty hard worker in game situations, and a good team man. He is a limited player who must consistently use all of the tools at his disposal in order to play in the NHL.

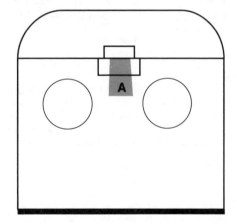

KIRK MULLER

Yrs. of NHL service: 6
Born: Kingston, Ontario, Canada; February 8, 1966
Position: Center/left wing
Height: 6-0
Weight: 205
Uniform no.: 9
Shoots: left

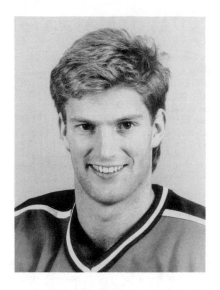

Career statistics:

GP	G	A	TP	PIM
476	166	284	450	496

1989-90 statistics:

GP	G	A	TP	+/-	PIM	PP	SH	GW	GT	S	PCT
80	30	56	86	-1	74	9	0	6	1	200	15.0

LAST SEASON

Third consecutive 80-games season. Led club in assists and points (second highest career totals in those categories), second in game winners and shots on goal. PIM total was four-season low.

THE FINESSE GAME

Muller's style is a hybrid one, one that indicates he's probably better off as a winger than a center. His skating (for instance) is far more suited for work along the wood and in the corners than it is for work in the middle of the ice, and that's because strength, sturdiness and balance are the upside of his skating skill rather than speed, agility and lateral movement. He's very strong on his feet and has a strong pace to his skating, so he can drive through his checks and remain vertical and in the play.

Which is not to say that Muller can't turn or lean or do anything fancy — far from it. But his skating also meshes well with his playmaking abilities, which are of the straight-ahead, one-play-in-advance kind. He's smart enough to know where to look when he gains the puck, but Muller lacks the dynamic hockey sense and anticipation that marks true playmaking centers.

He handles the puck well enough when he carries it and has a strong shot while in stride, certainly above average. He puts his balance and sturdiness afoot to work when he jams the net (especially on the power play) and he's adept at tipping and deflecting pucks. The same eye/hand coordination that allows him to tip pucks also makes him a good faceoff man.

He continues to be weak defensively, but as a winger can at least battle for the puck along the boards.

THE PHYSICAL GAME

Muller has a high degree of physical ability and, while he is slightly inconsistent in his use of his size and strength from night to night, his overall physical play is high. He drives the net very strongly (balance and strength are the keys here) and goes to the crease almost all the time. He certainly has the upper body strength to out-wrestle many defenders for loose pucks and will score many goals from within ten feet of the net.

His strength and balance serve him well in one-on-one battles along the boards, and he'll win more of those battles than he loses. He has the ability to make a play coming out of the corner, and that makes his physical play more effective.

THE INTANGIBLES

Though he still has the occasional intensity lapse, Muller is a pretty hard worker. But both Muller and the Devils still possess Jekyll-and-Hyde ability to be comfortable and then intense. It is the captain's job to prevent this — hard to do if he can't prevent it in his own play first.

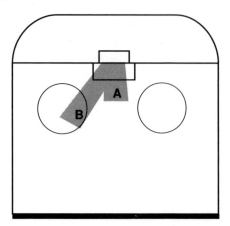

JANNE OJANEN

Yrs. of NHL service: 1
Born: Tampere, Finland; April 6, 1966
Position: Center
Height: 6-2
Weight: 185
Uniform no.: 22
Shoots: left

Career statistics:

GP	G	A	TP	PIM
67	17	14	31	14

1989-90 statistics:

GP	G	A	TP	+/-	PIM	PP	SH	GW	GT	S	PCT
64	17	13	30	-5	12	1	0	1	1	76	22.4

LAST SEASON

First full NHL season. Shooting percentage was best among team's regulars.

THE FINESSE GAME

Ojanen doesn't fit the NHL stereotype of European players, the one that says they're all the greatest skaters on Earth. Ojanen is not a fleet skater and not tremendously agile either, but he is a strong skater with a high degree of balance and strength on his feet. Those skills allow him to battle for the puck all over the ice, and may determine that he is better on the wing than he is at center.

What might keep him as a center ice-man is his puckhandling ability. Ojanen works well with the puck, especially in crowded traffic situations where his balance and skating strength allow him to maintain body position and thus playmaking ability. He sees the ice fairly well but needs more experience of the NHL's tempo before he moves into anything above the see-one-play-and-make-it plateau.

He has pretty good hands for shooting, and because he's going to be shooting and scoring from within 20 feet of the net, Ojanen's balance is a factor here too.

His defense needs work, and it is here that he is betrayed by his lack of skating speed.

THE PHYSICAL GAME

Ojanen can play a fairly accomplished physical game (again going against and admittedly diminishing European stereotype) courtesy of — here are those words again — balance and skating strength. He won't bang anyone into oblivion but he can effectively use his body in close contact situations, and he can certainly make a play coming off the boards.

THE INTANGIBLES

A big guy with skills is always going to be a valued and valuable commodity and may especially be so to New Jersey, a team which needs to swing its pendulum back toward players willing to get their noses dirty. Ojanen can be one such player. He is young and enthusiastic and should continue to improve.

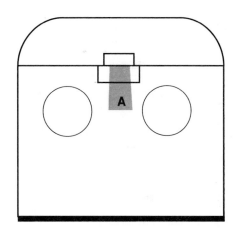

WALT PODDUBNY

Yrs. of NHL service: 8
Born: Thunder Bay, Ontario, Canada; February 14, 1960
Position: Center
Height: 6-1
Weight: 205
Uniform no.: 21
Shoots: left

Career statistics:

GP	G	A	TP	PIM
447	179	230	409	438

1989-90 statistics:

GP	G	A	TP	+/-	PIM	PP	SH	GW	GT	S	PCT
33	4	10	14	-4	28	1	0	0	1	50	8.0

LAST SEASON

All point totals were career lows. Rotated in and out of the lineup, but also missed at least six games with a recurring back problem as well as time with torn ligaments.

THE FINESSE GAME

Balance and the attendant agility make Poddubny a good skater, and his skating and scoring skills make him a good player.

He has rink-length speed to out-race the opposition, and his balance and lateral movement make him agile and allow him to absorb checks and still make plays.

Walt combines his foot speed and puckhandling ability with his anticipation skills to get into the open, or to get the puck to his open teammates. Those passing and anticipation skills — along with an excellent wrist/snap shot — make Poddubny a power play stalwart.

Poddubny shoots the puck well and often, using a fast (but not exceptionally hard) wrist shot to beat goaltenders from 30-feet or so. Because he has good hands, Poddubny can also operate well in the traffic around the net, and is very dangerous around the crease.

THE PHYSICAL GAME

Poddubny's balance keys his physical game and allows him to operate with the puck in traffic. He's willing to get involved along the boards, but he's not really a mucker. He'll go into traffic for a loose puck but won't muscle anyone out of the way for it; Walt will let his hand skills pull the puck out for him.

His balance also makes him difficult to dislodge from the puck. Though not an extraordinarily physical player, Poddubny will take his licks and can dish some out as well.

THE INTANGIBLES

Because of his injury-plagued season (and he's never played more than 77 games in a season) we've left Poddubny's report unchanged from last year. He had a great deal of difficulty carving out a role for himself after joining New Jersey last season, and he will likely have the same trouble this season. Not good news for a player who needs to be constantly praised in order to maintain his performance level.

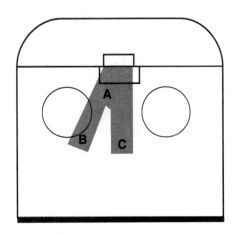

BRENDAN SHANAHAN

Yrs. of NHL service: 3
Born: Mimico, Ontario, Canada; January 23, 1969
Position: Center/right wing
Height: 6-3
Weight: 205
Uniform no.: 11
Shoots: right

Career statistics:

GP	G	A	TP	PIM
206	59	89	148	383

1989-90 statistics:

GP	G	A	TP	+/-	PIM	PP	SH	GW	GT	S	PCT
73	30	42	72	15	137	8	0	5	0	196	15.3

LAST SEASON

Games played, all point totals and PIM mark were career highs. Finished tied for second on club in goals and plus/minus rating, second among forwards in PIM total and fourth overall in shots on goal total.

THE FINESSE GAME

Don't let Shanahan's physical play fool you: There's a pretty good finesse player underneath that steamroller exterior. He's not a great skater and may never be by NHL standards in terms of speed or beauty, but he has a strong stride and good sturdiness and balance. Those skills certainly key his physical game by allowing him to work the corners and drive through checks, but his stride also happens to get him where he's going.

In a way he should be glad that he doesn't have rocket-like speed, because his hands might not be able to keep up with his feet if that were the case. But it is not and Shanahan's hand skills dovetail well with his level of skating, allowing him to make his plays at what is his best speed. Those hands combine with his improving ability to see the ice at the NHL level (by which we mean getting the message from his brain to his hands faster), as his improved scoring statistics attest. He's not a fancy playmaker, but Shanahan knows to move the puck to a teammate in better position (and he's lucky to be playing with Patrik Sundstrom, who knows how to get into that better position). He will not, however, succeed in stickhandling around an entire team.

Shanahan also knows to head to the net after he makes that pass, and he gets his goals from being in the right place to pick up rebounds and other leftovers. He shoots the puck fairly well, certainly well enough to be effective in the traffic areas where quick release and touch to find the holes are necessary. He also has the strength to score from longer distances.

THE PHYSICAL GAME

Shanahan is a tough player and likes a tough game — most of the time. By that we mean he has a tendency to coast and to forget to play to his size, but that can be ascribed to growing pains; after all, he's still just 21 years old.

But make no mistake, he's a very physical player and it is his physical play that frees his finesse game. His balance and strength serve him well in the traffic areas, and he can hurt people when he drives through his checks. Shanahan will go into a corner against anyone. He'll fight if need be, and he's a good scrapper.

THE INTANGIBLES

Shanahan's play over the last season and a half has been very strong, so strong that if he continues in this vein he'd deserve selection to the NHL's mid-season All-Star Game. And after that? Based on the last year and a half, a post-season All-Star berth isn't out of the question.

But first things first. Shanahan must maintain his concentration (the word intensity may be substituted), so that he continues to improve — especially physically, where his body and strength still have room to mature.

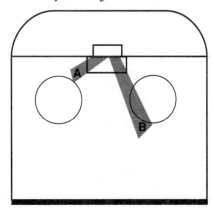

PETER STASTNY

Yrs. of NHL service: 9
Born: Bratislava, Czechoslovakia; September 18, 1956
Position: Center
Height: 6-1
Weight: 200
Uniform no.: 29
Shoots: left

Career statistics:

GP	G	A	TP	PIM
749	385	674	1,059	703

1989-90 statistics:

GP	G	A	TP	+/-	PIM	PP	SH	GW	GT	S	PCT
74	29	44	73	-46	40	12	0	1	1	156	18.6

LAST SEASON

Acquired at the trading deadline from Quebec in exchange for Craig Wolanin. Assist and point totals were career worsts, goal total second poorest of career. His plus/minus rating was the NHL's second worst, worst among all NHL forwards; he was minus-1 while with New Jersey.

THE FINESSE GAME

Even factoring in age and NHL wear and tear, Peter remains an elite level player. His hockey sense and anticipation are the keys to his game. His vision reveals the entire ice surface, and his anticipation and sense show him the soon-to-be-openings. He is excellent at using his teammates because of these skills.

He complements his sense with his skating, even though time has eroded some of his ability. Never a rink-length speed demon, Stastny's skating is still marked by balance and agility; he has great lateral movement and one-step quickness. Allowing him to swoop into openings and snare loose pucks. Peter's balance allows him to make plays while being checked.

Stastny combines his head and foot skills with his hand skills to become a superior playmaker. He skims passes through the openings to his teammates, but Peter can also stickhandle his way into the opening for a shot himself; he is one of the NHL's best puckhandlers on the backhand.

Like most Europeans, Peter uses an accurate wrist shot almost exclusively, and he's going to get as near to the net as he can before shooting.

He's never been keenly interested in defense, so his plus/minus rating is nowhere near unjustified.

THE PHYSICAL GAME

Stastny can play in tough games (and he makes room for himself with his stick; he's very liberal in his lumber-work, certainly fulfilling the European stereotype in this regard), but he's not really a physical player. He's more likely to be found in mid-ice than he is near the congested board areas, and he doesn't initiate a lot of contact.

THE INTANGIBLES

Stastny responds to a lot of responsibility — he loves ice time and wants to be counted on when the game is on the line. Which is nice, except he also has a tendency to take more than the odd night off — so if the Devils were looking for veteran leadership out of him they're going to have to look awfully hard. But if all they are counting on is a talented player who can put points on the board, they're looking in the right place. Of course, he is 34 years old and his point totals have fallen for three straight seasons ...

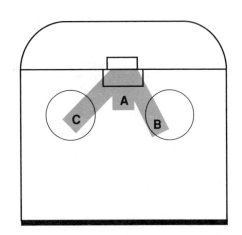

PATRIK SUNDSTROM

Yrs. of NHL service: 8
Born: Skelleftea, Sweden; December 14, 1961
Position: Center/left wing
Height: 6-0
Weight: 200
Uniform no.: 17
Shoots: left

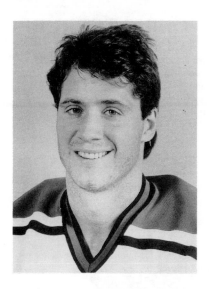

Career statistics:

GP	G	A	TP	PIM
591	203	335	538	293

1989-90 statistics:

GP	G	A	TP	+/-	PIM	PP	SH	GW	GT	S	PCT
74	27	49	76	15	34	8	1	0	2	142	19.0

LAST SEASON

Assist and point totals were second highest of career. Finished third on the club in points, second in assists and tied for second with three other Devils for second best plus/minus rating. Missed two games with a leg injury, as well as time late in the season with a recurring back injury.

THE FINESSE GAME

Sundstrom is one of the most complete players in the NHL and his finesse skills reflect that. He is an excellent skater across the boards; he has balance and strength, foot speed and agility. He has great mobility (Sundstrom can stop and start and change direction within a stride) and excellent speed (he'll beat all but the very fastest skaters to an opening or a loose puck).

His hockey sense (the ability to anticipate plays and see undeveloped openings) is keen, and he combines his skating with his sense to use the entire ice. He saves his ice to keep opportunities in front of him, and he uses his brains and his exceptional hand skills to lead teammates into the openings he has created.

His puckhandling and playmaking abilities are superb. Sundstrom can not only carry the puck well at top speed but he can also make any play he sees at that speed, controlling the puck as if it were nailed to his stick. His passing reveals excellent touch for any give situation; he can either fire or feather a pass and he uses both his forehand and backhand sides equally well.

Sundstrom possesses shooting skills that equal his other hand skills, but he doesn't exploit them as well as he could. Instead, he prefers to set up his teammates.

He plays the game as well defensively as he does offensively, and his smarts and skills make him a specialty teams necessity.

THE PHYSICAL GAME

If John Cameron Swayze were to describe Sundstrom he'd say, "Takes a licking and keeps on ticking." Sundstrom is absolutely oblivious to personal safety on the ice, using his body to take and give hits with impunity. His outstanding balance allows him to lean away from hits and still maintain sufficient body position to make plays, and that same balance serves to keep him upright and ready to make plays after giving or taking hits.

Sundstrom gains body position excellently, and he will sacrifice his body to make whatever play is necessary — including blocking shots (he's not only one of the best shot-blocking forwards in the NHL, but one of the best shot-blocking players period).

His hand and wrist strength make him a fine faceoff man, the man most likely to take those critical draws (when penalty killing, by the way, he most always tries to go forward to clear the puck).

THE INTANGIBLES

Sundstrom is the kind of player who makes other players better. He is a durable and, considering how he plays with pain from his back injuries, we would say a courageous player. He has a fine character and is a top person, and is also New Jersey's best player.

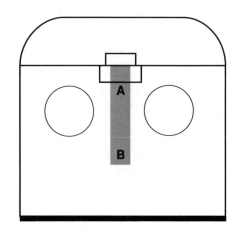

CHRIS TERRERI

Yrs. of NHL service: 1
Born: Providence, R.I., USA: November 15, 1964
Position: Goaltender
Height: 5-9
Weight: 160
Uniform no.: 31
Catches: left

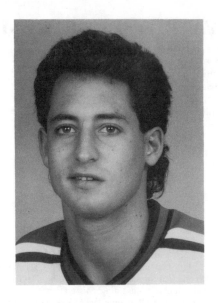

Career statistics:

GP	MINS	G	SO	AVG	A	PIM
50	2,619	149	4	3.41	0	0

1989-90 statistics

GP	MINS	AVG	W	L	T	SO	GA	SA	SAPCT	PIM
35	1,931	3.42	15	12	3	0	110	1,004	.890	0

LAST SEASON

Terreri's first full NHL season after two previous tries.

THE PHYSICAL GAME

Though a degree of control and poise has entered his game Terreri still plays goal like a jack-in-the-box, popping up and down and flinging himself from pillar to post. If he were a kid, his mother would cut back on his sugar cereal — that's how hyperactive his style can be.

He is a small goalie with tremendous athletic and acrobatic ability and he relies primarily on that ability to succeed. The results are exciting saves and many stopped pucks, but Terreri can also stop some hearts (mainly those of his teammates) with all those spectacular saves. He has tremendously fast hands and feet and there may not be any goalie in the NHL quicker in getting to the ice and then getting back on his feet.

He leaves a lot of rebounds as a result of his scrambling style, and then he leaves more rebounds after making saves on the first set of rebounds — which he got to only because of his speed, and which existed only because of his style.

He has begun to incorporate a more controlled style of play into his own personal style, and we must credit him with working hard to succeed in this attempt to improve. Nevertheless, he remains a player who lives and dies by his reflexes.

THE MENTAL GAME

The general belief is that butterfly goaltenders play the way they do because they don't have confidence enough in themselves to just stand still and stop the puck — they have to make some move or the puck is going in the net. Terreri is very confident in his style, and he can make the big saves that inspire a club, but he can also allow goals that deflate the club. He comes back strong after poor performances, determined to fight for every goal. His willingness to add a more stand-up phase to his game also says that he has a degree of maturity in his play.

THE INTANGIBLES

Because spectacular sometimes looks better than efficiency, there are those who believe Terreri should supplant Sean Burke as the Devils' number one goalie. We don't agree. In fact, we wonder for just how long Terreri can go on playing off emotion and adrenalin — two factors that are large reasons for the inconsistent performances he suffers. He needs to add consistency and flatten the emotional roller-coaster if he is to have a long-term NHL career.

SYLVAIN TURGEON

Yrs. of NHL service: 7
Born: Noranda, Quebec, Canada; January 17, 1965
Position: Left wing
Height: 6-0
Weight: 195
Uniform no.: 16
Shoots: left

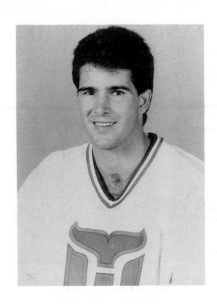

Career statistics:

GP	G	A	TP	PIM
442	208	167	375	447

1989-90 statistics:

GP	G	A	TP	+/-	PIM	PP	SH	GW	GT	S	PCT
72	30	17	47	-8	81	7	0	3	0	218	13.8

LAST SEASON

Games played and goal totals were four-season highs. Suffered a late season groin injury. Finished third on club in shots on goal.

THE FINESSE GAME

Skating and shooting are Turgeon's primary skills, and he uses them well in tandem but one-dimensionally in his total game. He has excellent outside speed and just as strong lateral ability, and he will use his skating to drive the defenseman off the blue line and to get closer to the net to score. He is not an exceptionally creative skater, doesn't save his ice and does very little other than shoot with the open ice his skating creates.

He carries the puck well at top speed but looks to do nothing other than shoot. Turgeon has the power to blast the puck past a goaltender from the distances but also likes to dip behind the defense and go one-on-one with the goalie, fake him to the ice, and deposit the puck in the far corner. He releases his shot quickly and with excellent touch, but he lacks the ability to truly get into scoring position. For Turgeon, scoring position is wherever he happens to be at the time.

In fact, he doesn't read the ice well at all and that shows up in his playmaking — or lack thereof. Because he thinks shoot before pass he doesn't use his teammates well at all, making his skating and hand skills less effective than they might be.

His defense is highly unreliable.

THE PHYSICAL GAME

There isn't one. Turgeon doesn't get involved in the physical part of the game and he doesn't want to get involved either. While he can take the puck off the boards very quickly and make a play with it, Sylvain won't do even the most elementary body work along the boards — thus rendering his finesse ability ineffective.

THE INTANGIBLES

How many other ways can we say what we've said before: Turgeon is the kind of player that gets coaches fired and gives general managers ulcers: tremendous talent matched only by his lack of intensity. He is one of the NHL's biggest enigmas.

He's not a bad kid, and he's not a problem discipline-wise off-ice; he's not a bad liver. Turgeon is just unmotivated. There was thought that a change of scenery might help and he did post better goal numbers last season than he had in three previous campaigns, but consider that he scored just eight goals and seven assists in his final 33 games.

We're afraid New Jersey is in for more of what Hartford got when Turgeon was there: disappointment.

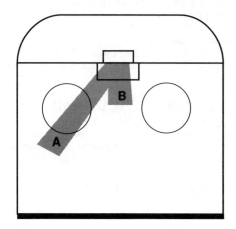

RANDY VELISCHEK

Yrs. of NHL service: 7
Born: Montreal, Quebec, Canada; February 10, 1962
Position: Defenseman
Height: 6-0
Weight: 200
Uniform no.: 27
Shoots: left

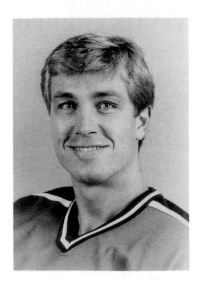

Career statistics:

GP	G	A	TP	PIM
392	17	63	80	337

1989-90 statistics:

GP	G	A	TP	+/-	PIM	PP	SH	GW	GT	S	PCT
62	0	6	6	4	72	0	0	0	0	34	0.0

LAST SEASON

All point totals were full-season career lows.

THE FINESSE GAME

There is no one particular skill that Velischek performs at an especially high level, but he uses his intelligence to stay within his limitations and make his game better as a whole than it would be piece-meal. He is not an exceptional skater in any phase of that skill, but he is a mobile enough player to either do some stepping up on the puck carrier or some hitting along the wood.

He uses his skating primarily to force the puck carrier into a narrower and narrower zone along the boards before finally running him out of room. Velischek is not a gifted offensive player, and he takes pains to stay out of situations (forechecking, pinching in, joining the attack) where his skating won't back him up.

He doesn't usually handle the puck, preferring to leave that task to his partner, but when Velischek does handle the puck he moves it quickly from his end of the ice. He can, however, be forced into giveaways via strong forechecking.

His shot — which he almost never uses because he is the safety valve (falling back to defense) — is no better than average.

THE PHYSICAL GAME

Velischek plays physically the same way he does finesse-wise — intelligently. He doesn't have great size or strength, but by using his body to gain position he can succeed in physical situations. Velischek likes to hit and he'll take the body when he can; he effectively bangs in the corners and clears the front of the net.

He does not fight.

THE INTANGIBLES

The Devils have a plethora of defensemen trying to get into the lineup and, despite his relative reliability, Velischek may find himself on the outside looking in — much like he did through the early part of last season.

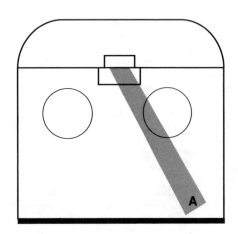

NEW YORK ISLANDERS

KEN BAUMGARTNER

Yrs. of NHL service: 3
Born: Flin Flon, Manitoba, Canada; March 11, 1966
Position: Defenseman
Height: 6-1
Weight: 200
Uniform no.: 24
Shoots: left

Career statistics:

GP	G	A	TP	PIM
144	4	11	15	699

1989-90 statistics:

GP	G	A	TP	+/-	PIM	PP	SH	GW	GT	S	PCT
65	1	5	6	-4	222	0	0	0	0	48	2.1

LAST SEASON

Acquired from Los Angeles in November 1989 along with Hubie McDonough in exchange for Mikko Makela. Games played, assist and point totals were career highs. Was second on club in PIM total, first among defensemen. Missed one game with a groin injury.

THE FINESSE GAME

Baumgartner is generally at average or below average in his finesse skills. He's a decent enough skater but he lacks the agility and mobility that would allow him to become an active versus reactive player. He'll have a lot of difficulty with lateral movements or fakes from the opposition, and a direct speed attack will exploit him as well.

He does not anticipate or read the rush well. On a 3-on-1 or 4-on-2 with a late man, Baumgartner almost always commits totally to the puck carrier. His reading and containing ability up ice are also weak, but Baumgartner is an intelligent guy and he is improving in this regard.

His passing and shooting skills are as marginal as his skating and vision, so his offensive contributions are going to be minimal. Defensively, he *must* make the simple up-the-boards play to be successful.

THE PHYSICAL GAME

This is a horse of another color. Baumgartner is a very tough player who likes to fight and will beat people up. He creates aggressive play and will fight all the League's heavyweights, but he can sometimes be too aggressive and hurt his team through penalties. He brooks no abuse of his smaller teammates and settles scores immediately.

He also tries to hit as often as possible, but he lacks the skating ability to play a consistent hitting game. He uses his good strength and meanness to clear the front of the net, but must remember to always play the man and not the puck.

THE INTANGIBLES

A lot of the credit for the Islanders resurgence last season was laid at Pat LaFontaine's doorstep — and deservedly so. But it wasn't until Baumgartner (and Hubie McDonough) arrived from Los Angeles that the Isles turned their season around, and one very large reason was because Baumgartner's presence allowed LaFontaine to run wild without fear of retribution.

Unless he upgrades his skills Baumgartner will still be a borderline player subject to replacement when a tougher guy comes along (difficult though that is to imagine), but a full season under Al Arbour's tutelage may work wonders for Baumgartner.

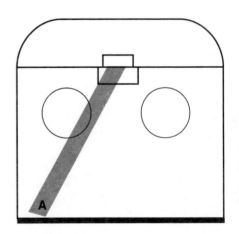

DOUG CROSSMAN

Yrs. of NHL service: 9
Born: Peterborough, Ontario, Canada; June 30, 1960
Position: Defenseman
Height: 6-2
Weight: 190
Uniform no.: 3
Shoots: left

Career statistics:

GP	G	A	TP	PIM
705	85	287	372	434

1989-90 statistics:

GP	G	A	TP	+/-	PIM	PP	SH	GW	GT	S	PCT
80	15	44	59	3	54	8	0	1	2	159	9.4

LAST SEASON

All point totals were career highs. Finished third on club in scoring (first among defensemen) and assists. Plus/minus rating was second best among defenders. Was one of only two Islanders (David Volek) to play all 80 games.

THE FINESSE GAME

Vision and hand skills are the hallmarks of Crossman's game, and they were certainly demonstrated last season. He finds the open man very well in all three zones because of his vision and sense, and then he gets the puck to that teammate with good touch. Crossman can also lead teammates to open space with his passes; again, sense and anticipation are the keys here.

He handles the puck well and is the Islanders best bet to rush it from the zone, and he'll dish it to a teammate to start a give-and-go. Crossman joins most every rush and he'll come off the offensive point to pinch in and force the play; he's successful much of the time.

He is not overwhelmingly fast or quick as a skater, but his smarts will make up for that. He plays an active game at his own blue line, looking to step up and turn the play around. His transition game is strong and he'll see time in all situations because of his skills.

He doesn't have a great shot from the point in terms of power, but Crossman lets it go pretty well. He fakes his shot a lot, and then will move in for a closer opportunity.

THE PHYSICAL GAME

Crossman is a very un-physical player, both in intent and effect. He can be overpowered by most any opposing player with strength, so Crossman needs backup in both the corners and in front of the net. He does have a good reach and can pokecheck effectively, but he's of questionable value in tough situations.

THE INTANGIBLES

Certainly Crossman came through in spades for the Islanders, and he can continue to do that if: 1) he's paired with a tougher partner 2) he's not expected to perform in a demonstrative leadership role 3) no one asks that he change from his low-key personality to a more emotional one. In the meantime he can continue to act as a bridge between the past of Denis Potvin and the future of Jeff Norton/Wayne McBean/Jeff Finley.

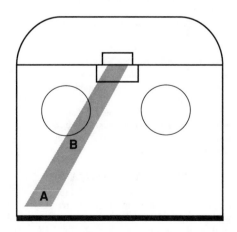

GERALD DIDUCK

Yrs. of NHL service: 5
Born: Edmonton, Alta., Canada; April 6, 1965
Position: Defenseman
Height: 6-2
Weight: 207
Uniform no.: 4
Shoots: right

Career statistics:

GP	G	A	TP	PIM
314	29	63	92	580

1989-90 statistics:

GP	G	A	TP	+/-	PIM	PP	SH	GW	GT	S	PCT
76	3	17	20	2	163	1	0	0	0	102	2.9

LAST SEASON

Games played and PIM totals were career bests. PIM total was club's third highest, second among defensemen. Missed two games with a shoulder injury.

THE FINESSE GAME

Unspectacular finesse skills are what allow Diduck to be an above average NHL defender. When we say unspectacular we don't mean poor; rather, we just don't mean headline-making. He is a strong skater in the most direct meaning of that word — he has great strength in his lower body, strength he puts to work in his checking. Diduck also has a fair degree of agility (though he lacks rink-length speed or dipsy-doodle agility), so he moves well laterally.

The result, when combined with his maturing patience and ability to read and react, is an active defensive game. Diduck acts upon the opposition now, no longer content to let the puck carrier come to him. He also has the ability to contain the point by pinching in and forechecking. Correct decisions are Diduck's key here, as he must remember his key to NHL success is defense and not offense.

He doesn't usually rush the puck, preferring to make smart passes to open wingers. Diduck gets the Islanders from there zone fairly well, at least making correct plays (and often making good ones too). He'll find the open man from the offensive blue line and can see some power play time because of that. His own goals will come on a very strong slap shot from the point; Diduck would score more often if his shot were more accurate.

THE PHYSICAL GAME

Diduck is a very strong physical player, and by that we mean both his innate body strength and his willingness to use it. He's big, tough and strong, and he'll go after anyone anywhere any time. He drives through his checks excellently and is very good at pinning men to the boards so they can't rejoin the play. Diduck is also mean in front of his own net, so anyone who scores from there will have really paid the price.

He is also a fairly good fighter.

THE INTANGIBLES

Diduck's game has matured strongly over the course of his five-year NHL career, and it can get better still. He's doing the things necessary for not just his own success but for the team's, and he's developing into a leader because of that.

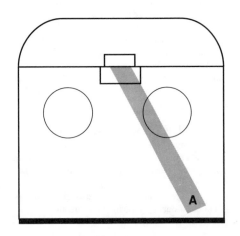

MARK FITZPATRICK

Yrs. of NHL service: 2
Born: Toronto, Ontario, Canada; November 13, 1968
Position: Goaltender
Height: 6-1
Weight: 190
Uniform no.: 29
Catches: left

Career statistics:

GP	MINS	G	SO	AVG	A	PIM
75	4,236	255	3	3.61	4	22

1989-90 statistics:

GP	MINS	AVG	W	L	T	SO	GA	SA	SAPCT	PIM
47	2,653	3.39	19	19	5	3	150	1,472	.898	18

LAST SEASON

Games and minutes played totals were career highs. Finished third in NHL in shutouts. Missed two games with a groin injury.

THE PHYSICAL GAME

Fitzpatrick is a standup goaltender, and that style maximizes his good size. He challenges the shooters by moving out on point shots, and Mark also stands up well on plays in close so as to force the opposition into the first move.

He is a good skater with good balance, and he moves well in and out of the net, and from post to post. He does have good reflexes and will close the gap between his legs (the five-hole) fairly quickly, but he falls prey to the problem many tall goalies have and that is low shots to the corners. His glove hand is very strong.

Mark clears his rebounds fairly well, but he could improve in his use of the stick for pokechecking. He also needs to improve his puckhandling; he loses time and accuracy by changing hands to shoot the puck.

THE MENTAL GAME

Fitzpatrick plays a positional game, and he uses his good vision to see the puck and anticipate the play; he's a thinking goaltender. He's also got the ability to maintain his concentration, as his shutout string during the season showed. He also maintains his intensity throughout games, whether ahead or behind. He has big save capability.

THE INTANGIBLES

Fitzpatrick is a confident player with a good attitude, a player with intensity and dedication. He wants the responsibility of being the Islanders' number one goaltender.

PAT FLATLEY

Yrs of NHL service: 7
Born: Toronto, Ontario, Canada; October 3, 1963
Position: Right wing
Height: 6-2
Weight: 197
Uniform no.: 26
Shoots: right

Career statistics:

GP	G	A	TP	PIM
373	92	169	261	419

1989-90 statistics:

GP	G	A	TP	+/-	PIM	PP	SH	GW	GT	S	PCT
62	17	32	49	10	101	4	0	2	0	136	12.5

LAST SEASON

Goal total was four-season high, games played total three-season best. Plus/minus was tired (Mick Vukota) for second best among forwards. Missed two games with a toe injury, six games with a groin injury.

THE FINESSE GAME

Flatley is not a glamorous player by any stretch of the imagination, but his determination keys the success he has found in the finesse areas. He is a strong skater but not a mobile one, so he needs to be in close quarters to succeed — that's why he's so good along the boards or in traffic, because he can put his strength to work. He also pursues the puck well, if without speed.

He is a fairly smart player, certainly smarter than his corner and boards game might imply, but he mitigates his smarts by overhandling the puck once he gains it. Flatley sees the ice well and can find his open teammates, but he holds the puck too long in hopes of beating defenders with quickness or dekes — and neither his hands nor feet can back up that play. He needs to learn that if he moved the puck, he might get it back in better scoring position.

He uses his skating strength to go to the net and he does shoot the puck well, using his strength to shoot or dig rebounds even when checked. He gets his shots away quickly, and can surprise some defensemen this way.

THE PHYSICAL GAME

Flatley is a hellbent for leather player, a crash and bang type of guy who is absolutely fearless in his puck work — and, we might add, always successful in the corners because of his strength and sturdiness. He doesn't care if he hits someone or gets hits himself but (as we said in Book 3) those hits are going to turn into injuries — he's never played a full season, and played just 206 of a possible 320 games over the last four seasons.

He protects the puck well with his body, one reason he can come out of the corner with it, and he uses his size and strength to good effect by jamming the net on the net on the power play.

THE INTANGIBLES

Health will always be a question mark, but Flatley's commitment and dedication will not. He is an honest player who earns all his success.

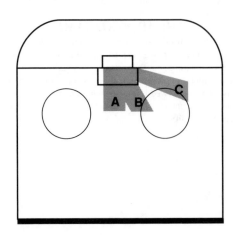

JARI GRONSTAND

Yrs. of NHL service: 4
Born: Tampere, Finland; November 14, 1962
Position: Defenseman
Height: 6-3
Weight: 197
Uniform no.: 44
Shoots: left

Career statistics:

GP	G	A	TP	PIM
182	8	25	33	133

1989-90 statistics:

GP	G	A	TP	+/-	PIM	PP	SH	GW	GT	S	PCT
48	3	5	8	-1	29	0	0	2	0	26	11.5

LAST SEASON

Acquired from Quebec in November 1989. Missed two games with a lacerated forehead.

THE FINESSE GAME

Gronstand's finesse skills are good and improving, but are still not at a consistent NHL level. He skates well forward and has fairly good agility moving toward the offensive zone, but his backskating and turns are weak and need improvement.

Jari moves the puck well from the defensive zone because he has good hands and good vision, but he's not a real threat to rush the puck himself. He can handle the puck well enough when he skates, but Gronstand is going to get the puck to the open man and then fall back defensively. He won't force an offensive play, and he can be forced into giveaways by pressured forechecking.

He does, however, follow the play up-ice and will contribute to a small degree at the offensive blue line but — as his shot and point totals indicate — Gronstand is not a big offensive player.

He understands defensive angles well and usually uses them to his advantage in angling off the opposition. He forces the play wide and can start the play up-ice after gaining a loose puck.

THE PHYSICAL GAME

Gronstand has height and reach, but he's not a very strong defender. He uses his reach well in pokechecking and in tying up an opponent's stick, but he will be outmuscled in front of the net and along the boards.

That said, Gronstand isn't afraid to suffer physical abuse. He'll take whatever hits are necessary to make his plays, and he'll certainly initiate contact regardless of the opponent. He also sacrifices his body by blocking shots.

THE INTANGIBLES

Gronstand's persistence has fooled a lot of people, especially his willingness to play physically and to not back down in a confrontation. He can continue to progress in the NHL but age mitigates against him, so he'll probably continue to shuttle in and out of the lineup.

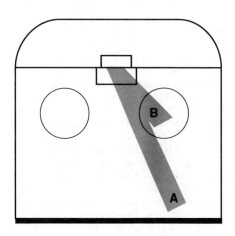

GLENN HEALY

Yrs. of NHL service: 3
Born: Pickering, Ontario, Canada; August 23, 1962
Position: Goaltender
Height: 5-10
Weight: 175
Uniform no.: 35
Catches: left

Career statistics:

GP	MINS	G	SO	AVG	A	PIM
122	6,816	461	3	4.06	4	41

1989-90 statistics:

GP	MINS	AVG	W	L	T	SO	GA	SA	SAPCT	PIM
39	2,197	3.50	12	19	6	2	128	1,210	.894	7

LAST SEASON

Shutout number was career best.

THE PHYSICAL GAME

Healy is the opposite of stable-mate Mark Fitzpatrick. Where Fitzpatrick plays a controlled angle game, Healy is a reflex goalie and a guesser. When he's hot, he's hot — but when he's not, he's not.

Healy skates well, and he uses his skating to come out of the net to gain loose pucks, but he doesn't have great balance — so he'll have trouble regaining his stance after flopping to the ice. He moves well laterally, and his quick feet help him cover bang-bang plays across the crease and from post-to-post.

He is very quick and acrobatic, and he needs to be because he loses his position in the net (which wasn't a strong position to begin with, hence all his flailing around. That flailing also leaves a lot of rebounds.

While his fast hands and feet will get him to most any gettable puck, Glenn's big problem is his failure to sufficiently and correctly cut down the shooter's angle. Because of that, he is weak on direct rush attacks — forwards breaking down the wing. He'll allow soft goals to the corners to very average shooters because of this weakness. And, because he hasn't set his angles properly to begin with, Healy has great difficulty finding the net again after one of his flopping forays.

THE MENTAL GAME

Healy's a tough customer mentally, in that he drops the bad games from his memory and begins the next game prepared to play. He could use help in maintaining his concentration within games, but he does have the ability to get very hot. However, one downside of streaky goalies is that they also get very cold. When he's hot he'll win the game regardless of how many shots he faces; when he's cold he'll lose the game reagrdless of how few shots he faces. And when he's cold he's got to get the hook.

THE INTANGIBLES

Healy showed well in his role of number 1A with the Islanders last season, and he'll be confined to that role as Fitzpatrick and later Jeff Hackett continue their development. Don't be surprised if the Isles find themselves with three goalies this season, and don't be surprised if Healy finds himself on the outside looking in.

ALAN KERR

Yrs. of NHL service: 4
Born: Hazelton, B.C., Canada; March 28, 1964
Position: Right wing
Height: 5-11
Weight: 195
Uniform no.: 10
Shoots: right

Career statistics:

GP	G	A	TP	PIM
324	69	84	153	686

1989-90 statistics:

GP	G	A	TP	+/-	PIM	PP	SH	GW	GT	S	PCT
75	15	20	35	-1	129	3	0	1	0	127	11.8

LAST SEASON

Games played total was second highest of career, goal and point totals three-season lows. PIM total was second highest among forwards. Missed two games with elbow injury.

THE FINESSE GAME

Kerr is a good skater at the NHL level in terms of speed and its offshoots. He accelerates well down the wing and can leave a trail of dust and he's also fairly quick in confined situations, so he'll have some success at getting to loose pucks. He likes to forecheck and his speed makes him good at it, but he lacks a strong degree of balance in his skating. He can be knocked off the puck in one-on-one battles, and his lack of balance also slows him in getting back into position — after all, it takes time to get up off the ice.

He has neither great hands nor exceptional anticipation sense, so Kerr will need some time and space to make his plays. He does see the ice fairly well, but his hands don't react as quickly as necessary to make sure plays. He has improved his ability to handle the puck while skating, and that will allow him to drive defensemen off the blue line.

He'll need to be an opportunistic player in order to make up for his modest finesse skills, but Kerr adds a degree of value to his offense by being fairly consistent defensively.

THE PHYSICAL GAME

Kerr uses his body very aggressively in his checking. He likes a hitting game and succeeds at it, powered by his strong skating to drive through checks. Those checks will take the opposition off the puck, but they may also take Kerr off his feet.

He is generally tough, and crosses the line to mean because of his stickwork. He's also a pretty good fighter, but usually remains outside the pileup he's caused.

THE INTANGIBLES

Kerr can be a positive player when he remembers to stay within his game. He is an enthusiastic worker whose success will always be determined by his physical play, and he demonstrates that enthusiasm both home and away (there aren't a lot of players who play tough both at home and on the road).

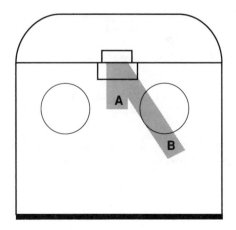

DEREK KING

Yrs. of NHL service: 3
Born: Hamilton, Ontario, Canada; February 11, 1967
Position: Left wing
Height: 6-1
Weight: 203
Uniform no.: 27
Shoots: left

Career statistics:

GP	G	A	TP	PIM
163	39	80	119	64

1989-90 statistics:

GP	G	A	TP	+/-	PIM	PP	SH	GW	GT	S	PCT
46	13	27	40	2	20	5	0	1	0	91	14.3

LAST SEASON

Games played total was three-season low (began season with Springfield of the American Hockey League, missed nine games with knee injuries).

THE FINESSE GAME

Hand skills are the heart and soul of King's game, particularly in terms of shooting the puck. He has a very quick release on his shot, making him dangerous from near the net, but he also has the shooting ability to convert from further away.

King is also a clever puckhandler but he's undercut in that area by his skating, which lacks the NHL level of speed or quickness that would drive him past the defense — or give him the ability to dance past them; King is not very agile. Often, then, Derek is easily driven to the boards or the corners and forced to make 40- and 50-foot plays, when shorter passes are always more effective.

He has great hockey sense and smarts, and he's shown throughout his pre-NHL career that he knows how to get into scoring position and how to exploit openings, but King has been unable to demonstrate that skill at the NHL level.

THE PHYSICAL GAME

Careful might be a good way to describe King's less-than-imposing physical game. He has good size but uses it poorly, staying generally uninvolved in traffic situations and throwing a lot of snow. When he does get involved it's more to push and shove than hit.

THE INTANGIBLES

King has played at a particular level during his short NHL career, and has given no sign that he will mature beyond said level. His profile currently is that of a one-dimensional player, and any one-dimensional player is a tenuous NHLer at best.

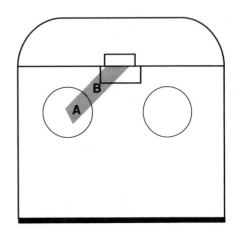

PAT LaFONTAINE

Yrs of NHL service: 7
Born: St. Louis, Missouri, USA; February 22, 1965
Position: Center
Height: 5-10
Weight: 177
Uniform no.: 16
Shoots: right

Career statistics:

GP	G	A	TP	PIM
455	246	235	481	267

1989-90 statistics:

GP	G	A	TP	+/-	PIM	PP	SH	GW	GT	S	PCT
74	54	51	105	-13	38	13	2	8	1	286	18.9

LAST SEASON

All point totals were career highs. Led club in goals, assists, points, game winners and shots on goal, finishing eighth in overall League scoring (fifth in goals). Finished second on club in power play goals and shooting percentage, last in plus/minus rating. Missed six games with hand injury.

THE FINESSE GAME

There's a scoreboard graphic the Islanders use when LaFontaine scores, making reference to the cartoon character Roadrunner — nothing could be truer. He has excellent speed and his game radiates from that skill. He has afterburner speed and just as good quickness, and those abilities dovetail with his excellent balance and agility to make him a very dangerous player in both open ice and contained spaces. Few are the pucks he can't get to, so few are the pucks he can't exploit.

His hands are as gifted as his feet for all kinds of puck work. While he is a scoring center first he also uses his teammates very well, looking to them if they are in better scoring positions. Of course, because of LaFontaine's shooting abilities, few players will ever be in better scoring positions. LaFontaine can beat a goaltender in many ways; he's not picky. He can deke in tight because of his balance and hands, and he's deadly when left alone in front because of his quick release and his ability to make the puck dance on his stick. He can score from anywhere with any shot.

He also carries the puck well at his top speed, which means he can burst in off the wing and succeed one-on-one. He uses his skills well in all situations and, despite the woeful plus/minus rating LaFontaine is a conscientious and responsible defensive player.

THE PHYSICAL GAME

LaFontaine and Steve Yzerman are our two favorite examples of finesse players who have gained their successes by incorporating physical elements into their games. LaFontaine is not a big guy, but he plays that way. He's built up his body so as to better absorb the punishment he's going to face, and he also uses his increased strength and bulk in an active way by hitting and getting his nose dirty. LaFontaine aggressively works in the traffic areas of the corner and the front of the net, and his finesse skills kick in to make him more effective there.

His size is one reason, by the way, that he suffers defensively.

THE INTANGIBLES

Hard as it might be to believe — and many people believe it to be a put-on to some degree — Pat LaFontaine is really the person he projects: determined, a leader, full of heart, dedicated, sincere, great team man. He combines that off-ice demeanor with his play to become one of the NHL's very best players, and he deserves every bit of recognition he earns.

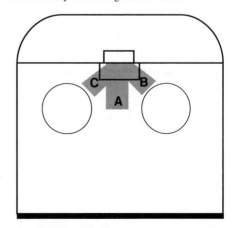

BRAD LAUER

Yrs. of NHL service: 4
Born: Humboldt, Sask., Canada; October 27, 1966
Position: Left wing
Height: 6-0
Weight: 195
Uniform no.: 32
Shoots: left

Career statistics:

GP	G	A	TP	PIM
207	33	52	85	153

1989-90 statistics:

GP	G	A	TP	+/-	PIM	PP	SH	GW	GT	S	PCT
63	6	18	24	5	19	0	0	2	0	86	7.0

LAST SEASON

Assist total tied career high, point total was second highest of career. Missed four games with knee injury, suffered last season thigh injury. Began season with Springfield of the American Hockey League.

THE FINESSE GAME

Lauer's finesse game is a limited one. He is not an exceptional skater in terms of speed and quickness or agility, and he can be left behind in fast games. What he does offer in his skating is excellent sturdiness afoot; that strength on his feet keys his very effective boards game.

As with his foot skills, his hand skills are unexceptional — and he lacks the exceptional hockey sense that would maximize his minimal hand ability. Lauer isn't strong in handling or passing the puck, and he lacks solid understanding of the speed and dimension of play at the NHL level. The result is poor use of his teammates and some giveaways.

Lauer also does not position himself to score and that certainly undercuts his best finesse skill, which is his shot. His slap shot off the wing is a strong one and it can beat NHL goaltending, but he doesn't get it off fast enough and his feet don't often get him in the open to get it off; despite his ability, he will actually have to be at relatively short range to score.

THE PHYSICAL GAME

Lauer has excellent strength that he can put to use, but he hasn't learned how to use his body. Despite his strength and sturdiness afoot, he often gets knocked off (or otherwise relieved) of the puck because he doesn't keep his feet moving — and in hockey, most planted objects get uprooted when hit by moving objects.

He must make greater and more consistent use of his size, strength and ability along the wall.

THE INTANGIBLES

Lauer must make the conscious effort to be more aggressive in all aspects of his game, and by that we don't mean fighting — we just mean not passive. Without that keyed up mental approach, he cannot play at levels high enough to sustain an NHL career.

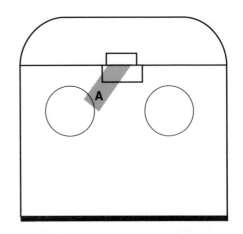

DON MALONEY

Yrs. of NHL service: 12
Born: Lindsay, Ontario, Canada; September 5, 1958
Position: Left wing
Height: 6-1
Weight: 190
Uniform no.: 28
Shoots: left

Career statistics:

GP	G	A	TP	PIM
753	214	345	559	809

1989-90 statistics:

GP	G	A	TP	+/-	PIM	PP	SH	GW	GT	S	PCT
79	16	27	43	6	47	0	1	2	0	113	14.2

LAST SEASON

Signed by the Islanders as a free agent in September 1989. Games played total was six-season high, point totals three-season high.

THE FINESSE GAME

Balance and a low center of gravity are the keys to Maloney's skating and to his game. Because of them, he can gain the puck in the corners and that makes him valuable as a forechecker. Otherwise, he has no real speed and is not particularly adept at carrying the puck while moving.

The extent of Maloney's playmaking prowess is throwing the puck in front after gaining it in the corners. His shot is fair and any goals he gets are going to have to come from in tight. He's sound defensively, despite his lack of speed in making the transition from offense to defense.

THE PHYSICAL GAME

Though no longer the dominating corner-man of his youth, Maloney remains a strong, physical hockey player. It is difficult to knock him down and he has a knack of pushing opponents in the direction he wants to go.

Clearly, injuries play a key part in Maloney's career at this point and he'd have to be judged as somewhat brittle. That is the consequence of his physical style.

THE INTANGIBLES

Don is finishing his career as a role player and checker, a role in which he performs extremely well. He has a fine work ethic and dedication, and he was a quiet leader in that regard for the Islanders, a team rediscovering its personality.

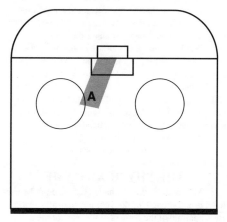

HUBIE MCDONOUGH

Yrs. of NHL service: 1
Born: Manchester, NH, USA; July 8, 1963
Position: Center
Height: 5-9
Weight: 180
Uniform no.: 39
Shoots: left

Career statistics:

GP	G	A	TP	PIM
80	21	16	37	38

1989-90 statistics:

GP	G	A	TP	+/-	PIM	PP	SH	GW	GT	S	PCT
76	21	15	36	14	36	0	3	4	0	105	20.0

LAST SEASON

First full NHL season. Acquired in November 1989 from Los Angeles along with Ken Baumgartner in exchange for Mikko Makela. Led team in plus/minus rating and shooting percentage.

THE FINESSE GAME

As his size might indicate, McDonough is a darty, tricky skater and player. He's got rink-length speed, but his quickness is more acute, getting him to loose pucks or allowing him to force those pucks. He is a strong checker because of his skating skill, and he also uses his skating as a fine penalty killer.

He has good sense and gets good reads of the ice (McDonough is a fairly strong read and react player), so he can do more than just chase the puck. His sense also gives him good reads after he gains the puck, and his skating gets him to the openings he sees. He can also create openings because of his darting ability.

McDonough's hand skills support his skating skills by allowing him to work in tight circles and close quarters. He has good balance and that allows him to stay vertical in traffic, and his hands are soft enough to retain the puck and shoot it quickly.

He is a very strong player positionally.

THE PHYSICAL GAME

McDonough doesn't have great size but he uses the size and strength he does command in all situations. He's unafraid of the corners or the front of the net, and his skating strength will help him knock the opposition off the puck or drive him free of checking.

THE INTANGIBLES

McDonough is a player of great heart and enthusiasm, a player who last season proved many critics ("too small") wrong, and who will look to prove them wrong again. We think he will.

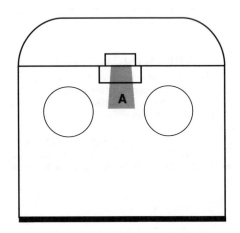

JEFF NORTON

Yrs. of NHL service: 3
Born: Cambridge, Mass., USA; November 25, 1965
Position: Defenseman
Height: 6-2
Weight: 195
Uniform no.: 8
Shoots: left

Career statistics:

GP	G	A	TP	PIM
144	6	85	91	153

1989-90 statistics:

GP	G	A	TP	+/-	PIM	PP	SH	GW	GT	S	PCT
60	4	49	53	-9	65	4	0	0	0	104	3.8

LAST SEASON

All point totals were career highs. Finished second on club in assists, fourth in points. His plus/minus rating was the defense's worst. Missed four games with a bruised hand, one game with the flu, five games with a groin injury and eight games with a bruised ankle.

THE FINESSE GAME

Last year we said Norton had all the tools but couldn't open the tool box. This year we say he's got the box open but sometimes takes too much out. He is an excellent skater and that skill is the basis for any and all of his NHL success. Norton must learn to use his mobility in an active defensive style, and not just in an offensive mode. Judgement defensively is what he needs, as Norton already has the ability to force play at his blue line by closing the gap on the puck carrier.

He can take advantage of his skills offensively, and his assist numbers back him up. Norton has excellent hockey sense offensively, and he has the hand skills to back up his brains. He finds the open man and gets the puck to him in both zones, but he also sees open ice and can maneuver his teammates to those openings too. Added sense of the NHL game in terms of speed and style will insure Norton's improvement, because right now he forces plays that lead to turnovers.

Norton carries the puck well and uses his hand and foot skills to good effect. Though still making some questionable decisions at the opposing blue line re pinching and forechecking, he is now taking an active role — making mistakes of effort and not of indecision. Norton also has a dynamic shot (low, hard and quickly released) and he must use it more.

THE PHYSICAL GAME

Norton has great size and strength for a finesse player, and an attitude toward physical play that is just as strong. He works the corners and the boards aggressively and well, especially when he concentrates on one task at a time.

His finesse abilities (balance, ability to make a play out of the corner) all make his physical game better, as does his ability to take his hits to make plays. He also demonstrates a mean streak (and some fighting ability) that bodes well for an NHL defenseman.

THE INTANGIBLES

Norton played more within his limits last season, and can do an even better job of that this season. He knows that, just as he knew he had to show up in better shape last season than he did for his rookie year — so he did. He has a tremendous amount of potential but not a tremendous amount of time to bring it to bear; he is already 25 years old. Follow the five-year defensemen rule and he'll be at least 28 before reaching his prime — and 28 is old to first be reaching your best NHL level, far different, say, from Kevin Hatcher who has achieved that level at age 24 and has more time ahead of him than behind him.

He is a highly skilled player who can be a dominating NHL player, and he must re-double his efforts to gain that plateau.

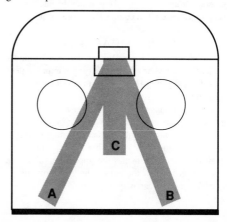

GARY NYLUND

Yrs. of NHL service: 8
Born: Surrey, B.C., Canada; October 23, 1963
Position: Defenseman
Height: 6-4
Weight: 210
Uniform no.: 36
Shoots: left

Career statistics:

GP	G	A	TP	PIM
507	29	119	148	1,077

1989-90 statistics:

GP	G	A	TP	+/-	PIM	PP	SH	GW	GT	S	PCT
64	4	21	25	8	144	2	0	0	2	65	6.2

LAST SEASON

Games played total was six-season low, assist total was career high. Led full-time defensemen in plus/minus. Suffered a late-season knee injury.

THE FINESSE GAME

Nylund's game is one where the style matches the substance. He is a fairly mobile skater — better than fairly when his size is factored into the judgement — and he is now using his mobility in conjunction with his improved smarts to play a strong defensive game.

His play shows him concentrating on a single aspect of a play at a time, so that his overall play is more controlled. Nylund now meets the play well at his own blue line and forces it wide of the net, and he uses his mobility to make smart decisions regarding closing the gap on the puck carrier.

In keeping with that one-play-at-a-time philosophy, Nylund makes simple plays from the defensive end that become effective because of their simplicity — find the open man, get him the puck. He generally makes those plays simple by not overhandling the puck.

He'll get his points the same way, by finding open men in the offensive zone and moving the puck to them. He shoots from the point and one-times the puck on net exceptionally well, but could shoot more frequently.

THE PHYSICAL GAME

With poise and control his watchwords, Nylund's physical game has shown the same type of improvement as his finesse game. He's taking men out of the play with authority, and anyone who's ever seen him up close knows Nylund has the size and strength to pin men against the boards forever. He works at improving his already excellent strength (he's always in the weight room), and Nylund enjoys using that strength in a physical game; he punishes the opposition along the boards or in front of the net — the guy looks like a linebacker, and he can play like one.

Nylund is not a fighter per se, so his penalties will usually be ones of over-aggression. He will sacrifice his body to block shots.

THE INTANGIBLES

Nylund's coachability and strong attitude are to be credited for his development into a steady and dependable defensive defenseman. As long as he stays within his limits (and there's no reason to believe he won't), Nylund will be a defensive force.

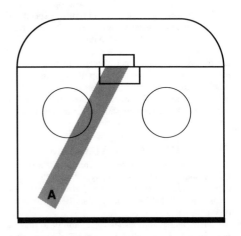

RICHARD PILON

Yrs. of NHL service: 2
Born: Saskatoon, Sask., Canada; April 30, 1968
Position: Defenseman
Height: 6-0
Weight: 202
Uniform no.: 47
Shoots: left

Career statistics:

GP	G	A	TP	PIM
76	0	16	16	273

1989-90 statistics:

GP	G	A	TP	+/-	PIM	PP	SH	GW	GT	S	PCT
14	0	2	2	2	31	0	0	0	0	5	0.0

LAST SEASON

Suffered eye injury November 4, 1989; sidelined rest of season.

THE FINESSE GAME

Pilon is an under-rated finesse player, particularly in the area of his skating. But Pilon could not play the dominating physical game he does play if not for his skating. That skating is marked by a strong stride and some good foot speed, both of which allow Rich to close the gap on the puck carrier. After all, you can't hit what you can't catch.

His finesse game is otherwise limited. Pilon will make the simple play up the boards to get the puck to the forwards, and he will be the last one up ice and the first one to head back to defense. A greater degree of offensive involvement would help the Islanders, because otherwise the team is essentially operating 4-on-5.

He does read the rush toward him very well, and that vision is a big part of his ability to step up and separate the puck carrier from the puck.

Any scoring he does, of which there will not be much, will be done on an average shot from the point.

THE PHYSICAL GAME

There are not many defensemen in the NHL who can hit like Pilon can, and few who attempt it — and fewer still the number who do it as consistently. He's tremendously strong and he can really punish the opposition as they head his way. Pilon uses his good strength in the board and crease battles, and he won't often lose. He is fearless about hitting, and will line up any player.

The one disadvantage to his play is that he is not yet able to consistently make a play after taking the opposition off the puck; that should change with greater NHL experience.

THE INTANGIBLES

We've left Pilon's report unchanged from last season in response to his injury, but include it here in the hopes that he returns. We concluded last season, "Pilon is a throwback to the era of the pure defensive defenseman. His play fell off at the end of the year because of a sore back, and that ailment raises the question of Pilon's continued banging. But such was his impact (pun intended) that the opposition made great attempts to stay away from him. Pilon, in turn, must become more intelligent in his hitting and picked his spots.

He's a very enthusiastic player who just loves to play, and he can be a very important part of the Islanders' next phase. His hitting has made him a marked man, but an indication of his intensity is that he plays better when he knows he's a target."

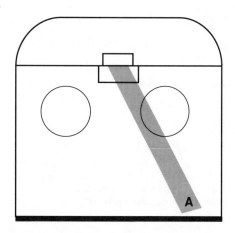

271

BRENT SUTTER

Yrs of NHL service: 9
Born: Viking, Alberta, Canada; June 10, 1962
Position: Center
Height: 5-11
Weight: 180
Uniform no.: 21
Shoots: left

Career statistics:

GP	G	A	TP	PIM
611	262	285	547	706

1989-90 statistics:

GP	G	A	TP	+/-	PIM	PP	SH	GW	GT	S	PCT
67	33	35	68	9	65	17	3	3	0	198	16.7

LAST SEASON

Games played total was four-season low, but goal and point totals were five-season highs. Finished second on the club in goals, assists and points, first in power play and shorthanded goals. His plus/minus was fourth best among forwards. Missed three games with a groin injury, three games with a back injury, five games with a leg injury.

THE FINESSE GAME

As might be expected when talking about a Sutter, strength and determination will be the operative words — but those words shouldn't be read to mean "inept finesse-wise." His strong stride and sturdiness afoot drives him to and through his checks, as well as to loose pucks. While neither exceptionally fast nor outstandingly agile, Sutter is a very strong forechecker in his pressuring of the puck. He also uses his strength when scoring, driving to loose pucks around the net, and Sutter's hands are good enough to do some finessing of the puck in those tight quarters.

He has strong hockey sense and read and react skills, and he uses those skills fairly well in his offensive game. He carries the puck (sometimes too much so) or finds the open man, but Sutter is not an especially strong offensive player in even-strength situations. He succeeds on the power play because of his work when coming to the front of the net.

He is a defensively complete player, using his sense and reading abilities very well as he heads back down the ice, and those abilities also make him one of the Islanders' best penalty killers — despite his relatively weak agility.

THE PHYSICAL GAME

His is a game based on the physical, and Sutter uses his body very well in gaining position on the puck. He is not a thunderous hitter but he uses his body aggressively, and the combination of balance and finesse that he does possess does the job. He drives through his checks because of his skating strength, and that same strength afoot serves him in the crease.

He is also a very good faceoff man.

THE INTANGIBLES

Has anyone noticed that Sutter has scored at least 20 goals in each of his NHL seasons — nine years in a row? Talk about consistency, and it's the work ethic and dedication behind that result that has made him a leader for the Islanders. And it's hard to find a more complete player.

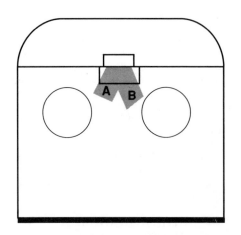

BRYAN TROTTIER

Yrs. of NHL service: 15
Born: Val Marie, Sask., Canada, July 17, 1956
Position: Center
Height: 5-11
Weight: 195
Uniform no.: 19
Shoots: left

Career statistics:

GP	G	A	TP	PIM
1,123	500	853	1,353	798

1989-90 statistics:

GP	G	A	TP	+/-	PIM	PP	SH	GW	GT	S	PCT
59	13	11	24	-11	29	4	0	0	0	84	15.5

LAST SEASON

Games played and all point totals were career lows. Missed 12 games with rib injury, two games with back spasms. Plus/minus was second poorest on club.

THE FINESSE GAME

The strength factors of Trottier's finesse game are the factors that remain in his game today; the speed or finesse factors are the factors that have waned. He has always been a more powerful than artistic player and he retains the balance and sturdiness that have marked his skating, so much so that he may now be more effective along than wing than at center. His speed and quickness, however, are not as demonstrative as they have been in the past. In other words, he's slowing down.

Trottier's second primary finesse asset has always been his sense of the game, and this sense continues to make his skills better. He sees and understands the game's patterns very well, but he's not able to make the moves his brain is telling him about as he once did. He sees the openings but needs more time to complete his passes or to get himself to the openings.

He's always been a traffic scorer, and will continue to be the grind-it-out type. He'll make all his plays by being in the right place, and he will more and more have to rely on his knowledge of the game in order to succeed.

THE PHYSICAL GAME

Trottier has always been a strong player, and he retains a good degree of that strength today. He has excellent upper body strength and that combines with his sturdiness afoot to make him a very successful player in traffic; he'll win many one-on-one battles because of his leverage and hand and arm strength.

He doesn't hit as hard as he used to but he can still be a mean player, and Trottier gives or takes checks with impunity. He is a good — down from excellent — faceoff man, with his hand speed decreasing.

THE INTANGIBLES

As his career winds down Trottier can still make contributions, not the least of which is the example of working night in and night out after winning four Stanley Cups and a wheelbarrow full of individual awards. He's no longer going to be as effective as he was (and his even strength scoring is an example of that: 15-12-9 goals over the last three seasons) but he's still a good player. There's nothing wrong with him mentally or physically, and he can still go when he wants to.

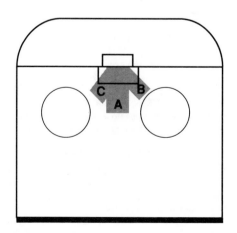

RANDY WOOD

Yrs. of NHL service: 3
Born: Princeton, New Jersey, USA; October 12, 1963
Position: Left wing
Height: 6-0
Weight: 195
Uniform no.: 11
Shoots: left

Career statistics:

GP	G	A	TP	PIM
182	62	53	115	167

1989-90 statistics:

GP	G	A	TP	+/-	PIM	PP	SH	GW	GT	S	PCT
74	24	24	48	-10	39	6	1	3	0	185	13.0

LAST SEASON

Games played total was career low, but all point totals were career highs. Finished third on club in goals, and third worst in plus/minus rating. Missed two games with shoulder injury.

THE FINESSE GAME

Speed and plenty of it is what Wood brings to his NHL game, and it is that speed that is at the root all his ability. He is actually an excellent skater in all phases of that skill, using his strength to create acceleration ability and breakaway speed while his balance and foot speed add a hefty degree (though not matching his speed) of lateral mobility. He's more of a straight ahead player than he is a dipsy-doodler.

Wood's speed creates openings, openings that he primarily exploits himself. He's pretty singleminded as he charges the net with the puck, looking to blow the doors off some defenseman with an outside-in move. He carries the puck fairly well at his top speed but hasn't yet demonstrated exceptional ability to use his teammates at the same speed, regardless of his career-best assist number. His anticipation ability is not high, so Wood must work with his head up in order to amplify his own game.

Because Wood shoots the puck fairly well, and because his balance lets him work well in traffic, most of his goals will come from fairly close to the net. He needs great help defensively, both in using his skating to make better transitions from offense to defense and in not turning the puck over through poor passing.

THE PHYSICAL GAME

Wood has excellent upper body strength, and that strength combines with his skating power to make him a very effective checker and corner and boards player. He can out-wrestle many players along the wood, but he does have to make sure that he maintains his balance — that upper-body strength can sometimes make him top-heavy.

He is a willing physical player and can be a punishing hitter because of the force he generates. He is not a fighter.

THE INTANGIBLES

Wood is a smart and coachable player, and his performance last season is more akin to what he is capable of. But in order to maximize his contributions he *must* energize his defensive play. Otherwise, his 24 goals become 14 goals because of his minus-10 rating. Then compensate for his specialty team goals and he's a whopping 9-goal man at even-strength — less than earthshattering numbers.

He is the kind of player who worries about his performances, sometimes to adverse effect.

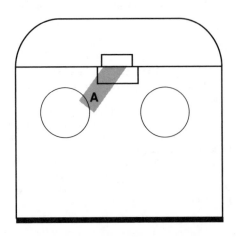

DAVID VOLEK

Yrs. of NHL service: 2
Born: Czechoslovakia; June 18, 1966
Position: Left wing
Height: 6-0
Weight: 185
Uniform no.: 25
Shoots: left

Career statistics:

GP	G	A	TP	PIM
157	42	56	98	65

1989-90 statistics:

GP	G	A	TP	+/-	PIM	PP	SH	GW	GT	S	PCT
80	17	22	39	-2	41	6	0	0	0	181	9.4

LAST SEASON

One of only two Islanders (Doug Crossman) to play all 80 games. Point totals fell in second NHL season.

THE FINESSE GAME

Volek is a very dynamic finesse player, possessing above average hand and foot skills. His skating is exceptional, marked by outstanding quickness and agility (although he also possesses good speed). He'll get to and force many loose pucks because of his darting capability, and he'll change speed and direction within a stride to get to an opening.

His hand skills complement his foot skills very well, in that he can operate with the puck at high speed and in contained space. At this point he may be developing a tendency to overhandling the puck, but that's a relatively common second-year mistake ("This play worked last year and it's not working now, so maybe if I just add *this* move ...," while the defense continues to close in). As he opens up his playmaking game to take greater advantage of his teammates, so too will his puckhandling game improve — in no small part by being less predictable one-on-one.

His hand skills certainly extend to his passing (he releases the puck very quickly) and to his shot in general. He'll get a lot of goals on tips and deflections because of his hand speed, and his hand sensitivity will net him goals in tight, but he can score from the distances; he can be devastating on the power play.

Volek's mental set is very strong, in that he has great understanding of the offensive zone and its possibilities. He is very creative away from the puck and knows how to get into scoring position, and he's showing better understanding of his defensive responsibilities.

THE PHYSICAL GAME

Volek is a very physical player, despite his less than imposing physique. We're not saying he can't go to the beach for fear someone will kick sand in his face, but Volek is built as his game would imply — he's lean, almost greyhound-thin. But Volek isn't at all shy about using his body in any and all situations against any opponent. He gives and takes hits with impunity and his finesse skills perfectly amplify his physical ones — allowing him to check the opposition and take the body, and then make plays coming away from the boards.

THE INTANGIBLES

As might be expected, Volek had a tougher time — at least point-wise — in his second season than he did in his first. That's normal; after all, he's not a surprise any more and teams know they have to pay special attention to him. He is too dedicated and too determined to succeed to not rebound strongly. He demands a lot from himself, is a worker and a coachable young man whose attitude bodes well for his future.

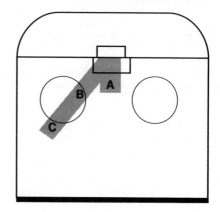

MICK VUKOTA

Yrs. of NHL service: 3
Born: Saskatoon, Sask., Canada; September 14, 1966
Position: Right wing
Height: 6-2
Weight: 195
Uniform no.: 12
Shoots: right

Career statistics:

GP	G	A	TP	PIM
141	7	10	17	609

1989-90 statistics:

GP	G	A	TP	+/-	PIM	PP	SH	GW	GT	S	PCT
76	4	8	12	10	290	0	0	0	0	55	7.3

LAST SEASON

Games played, all point and PIM totals were career highs. Led team in PIM total, and plus/minus rating was second best on club. Missed two games with an elbow injury, one game with a sore back.

THE FINESSE GAME

The finesse game is not Vukota's game, so in order to play regularly in the NHL he must play intelligently and well within the limits of his — at best — average finesse skills.

He is a strong skater but lacking in speed, quickness or agility. He's not especially mobile, and so his attempts at hitting will often go awry. His hand skills are not much better than his skating skill, so Vukota will not do much carrying of the puck. When he does have it he needs to move it quickly to a teammate in better position. His shot is unexceptional, and he'll have to be near the net to score.

Here's the other shoe: We said last year that he needs to shore up his defensive play in order to play regularly in the NHL (he was minus-17 during 1988-89). We also said that Vukota is an intelligent player in the application of his physical skill. Well, he also showed he's intelligent enough to know how to get a regular shift — his plus-10 rating last season was a swing of plus-27 from two seasons back, in large part because he cured himself of his wandering tendencies and played his position.

He won't ever be confused with Bob Gainey, but Vukota's value increases every time he takes a regular shift.

THE PHYSICAL GAME

Vukota can't be said to be an effective physical player because his checking game is thwarted by his limited mobility. But as a policeman/tough guy/enforcer, however, he is very effective; he knows what to do and when to do it (and this doesn't necessarily mean fighting) to slow down the opposition's momentum or to light a fire under his club.

He drives the opposition's good players crazy, is a hell of a fighter (and throws lefty, by the way) and he certainly won't let anyone take advantage of his teammates.

THE INTANGIBLES

For one, he'll be serving the remainder of his League-mandated suspension for his part in a post-game brawl during last season's playoffs. Apart from that, Vukota can continue to be an important player for the Islanders if he maintains his defensive vigilance.

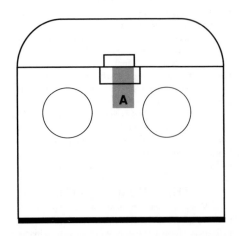

NEW YORK RANGERS

JAN ERIXON

Yrs. of NHL service: 7
Born: Skelleftea, Sweden; July 8, 1962
Position: Right wing
Height: 6-0
Weight: 196
Uniform no.: 20
Shoots: left

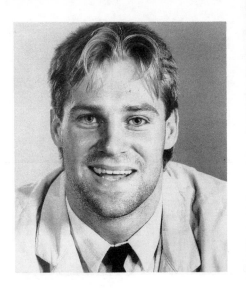

Career statistics:

GP	G	A	TP	PIM
412	37	121	158	145

1989-90 statistics:

GP	G	A	TP	+/-	PIM	PP	SH	GW	GT	S	PCT
58	4	9	13	-17	8	0	0	1	0	61	6.6

LAST SEASON

Assist and point totals were career lows; missed 21 games with recurring back injury. Plus/minus rating was club's third worst, second worst among forwards.

THE FINESSE GAME

Hockey sense and skating skills are the finesse keys to Erixon's exceptional checking ability. He is an almost tireless skater, and a very strong one as well. He has the ability to go stride for stride with the players he's checking, and that's because of both his endurance and his overall mobility. He is extremely strong on his skates, and his great balance and quickness combine to give him exceptional lateral ability. He does not have rink-length speed.

Erixon uses the anticipation and vision aspects of his hockey sense to their best degrees when he forechecks. His brains and skating combine to make him an active forechecker, a player who angles extremely well while forechecking so as to force a play instead of just chasing the puck. His sense works to show him the holes, and he plugs those holes or intercepts the puck during his individual checking assignments.

His hand skills are a paradox. He makes and takes passes exceptionally well and, because the puck is almost impossible to get off his stick, once it's there he's very strong in traffic and puck control situations. In fact, he is almost impossible to separate from the puck by legal means because of his hand skill and balance.

Unfortunately, Erixon has no more success getting the puck off his own stick than the opposition does at trying to get it away from him. His hands are as poor for scoring as his feet are good for checking. He hits posts, misses the net, forces goalies into great saves — all because he lacks even average scoring ability.

That's a shame because he's great at getting the puck into scoring position.

THE PHYSICAL GAME

The components of skating strength are balance and, obviously, strength or power. Erixon puts both to use in his checking, and he can be a physically over-whelming player because of those assets. Not physi-

cally overwhelming as in a stick of dynamite, but his insistent and persistent hitting wears down the opposition like the ocean wears down a beach. He also uses his body very smartly to gain good position on the puck.

He is a finely conditioned athlete and he needs every ounce of his strength and conditioning to both absorb the tremendous punishment he receives (his checks abuse him unmercifully in attempts to get away from him) and to avoid injury — somnething he has been unable to do.

THE INTANGIBLES

Question number one is his health; he averages just 59 games per season. Secondly, as good a player as he is, we find it curious that on a team that was plus-12 Erixon should minus-17 — that means he was on ice for 29 more goals against than he was goals-for. We know that he's a fine defensive player and strong from night to night in individual contests, so where did that number come from?

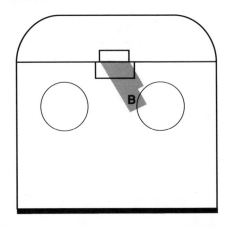

BOB FROESE

Yrs. of NHL service: 8
Born: St. Catharines, Ontario, Canada; June 30, 1958
Position: Goaltender
Height: 5-11
Weight: 178
Uniform no.: 33
Catches: left

Career statistics:

GP	MINS	G	SO	AVG	A	PIM
242	13,451	694	13	3.10	10	90

1989-90 statistics:

GP	MINS	AVG	W	L	T	SO	GA	SA	SAPCT	PIM
15	812	3.33	5	7	1	0	45	355	.873	0

LAST SEASON

Games played total was career low, missing only one game because of injury.

THE PHYSICAL GAME

Bob is an excellent standup goaltender who plays a superior angle game strengthened by strong reflex play. He has good balance and quick feet, and regains his position fairly speedily, but is much better on his feet than off them. Froese will come out of his net to handle the puck, but will only wrap it around the boards, rather than passing it to a teammate.

He generally prevents rebounds by directing shots to the corners, and Bob moves well in and out of his net, but his lateral movement is not as strong as his movement forward and backward, so he is vulnerable on criss-cross plays across the slot. He's also vulnerable to dekes (particularly to his right) on breakaways.

He sees the puck and anticipates well, and Froese will move out to the top of the screen before butterflying his pads on the ice to cover the lower part of the net.

THE MENTAL GAME

Though his concentration will wander at times, Froese is most always in the game. He prepares well for each contest and has just a small swing in his range of performance. He has the ability to sit for several consecutive games and then play well when he finally appears.

He is apt to lose his temper if he gets fouled too frequently around the crease, but opponents find it pretty tough to knock Froese off his game.

THE INTANGIBLES

He didn't appear in a game after January 25, 1990 — didn't start one after January 8 (and his report here remains unchanged because of that fact). What do you think that says about Froese's ability to get into the lineup if both John Vanbiesbrouck and Mike Richter remain in front of him?

Froese is a very popular team guy and the team enjoys playing for him; it just may be a team other than the Rangers that gets to enjoy that privilege this season.

MIKE GARTNER

Yrs. of NHL service: 11
Born: Ottawa, Ontario, Canada; October 29, 1959
Position: Right wing
Height: 6-0
Weight: 190
Uniform no.: 22
Shoots: right

Career statistics:

GP	G	A	TP	PIM
850	449	440	889	810

1989-90 statistics:

GP	G	A	TP	+/-	PIM	PP	SH	GW	GT	S	PCT
79	45	41	86	-4	38	21	4	5	0	288	15.6

LAST SEASON

Acquired from Minnesota in March 1990 in exchange for Ulf Dahlen. Goal total was fourth highest of career, best on club. Led club in power play goals (third in NHL), shorthanded goals and shots on goal. Was a plus-4 player in New York.

THE FINESSE GAME

As a successful finesse player, Gartner has two main skills he brings to bear against the opposition: his skating and his shot. He has explosive skating speed coming down the wing, speed that he puts to use by blowing past his check and breaking wide on a defender before cutting behind him for a swoop in on goal.

Mike's acceleration is outstanding and he commands an almost instantaneous burst of speed from a stationary position. He is tremendously agile, has terrific lateral movement for his inside cuts and an outstanding change of pace to turn his speed up another notch.

Gartner's slap shot is just as lethal. It is a rocket from the edge of the right faceoff circle that drives goaltenders backward because of its speed and heaviness. If a goaltender isn't fully in front of that shot, it's going in the net, and obviously, the NHL's goaltenders see a lot of shots from Gartner. He gets into position to score and is a shooter first and a playmaker second.

Mike handles the puck well at top speed and his vision shows him the entire ice surface. He'll look for a play (and is a good passer), but Gartner expects the puck.

Gartner is also a good defensive player, making a concerted effort to play a solid defensive game.

THE PHYSICAL GAME

Gartner has long known the value of adding a physical element to a finesse game. Though not a thunderous hitter, he willingly hits and takes the body well along the boards and in all three zones. He excel-

lently protects the puck with his body, shielding it from the opposition when he swoops around the defenseman and leans away from checks.

He's also very strong on his skates and almost impossible to dislodge from the puck.

THE INTANGIBLES

Gartner is an excellent character player, a hard worker who aims to contribute at all times — a leader by example who, remarkably, has shown no signs of slowing down despite a dozen years of professional hockey.

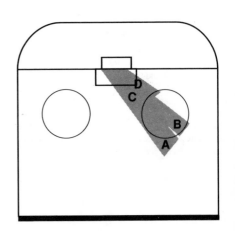

RON GRESCHNER

Yrs. of NHL service: 16
Born: Goodsoil, Sask., Canada; December 22, 1954
Position: Defenseman
Height: 6-2
Weight: 208
Uniform no.: 4
Shoots: left

Career statistics:

GP	G	A	TP	PIM
982	179	431	610	1,226

1989-90 statistics:

GP	G	A	TP	+/-	PIM	PP	SH	GW	GT	S	PCT
55	1	9	10	-7	53	0	0	0	0	26	3.8

LAST SEASON

Played fewer than 60 games for third consecutive season. Goal total tied career low, assist and point totals third lowest of career. Missed one game each with neck and shoulder injuries, four games with a subsequent shoulder injury, three games with a knee injury and 10 games with a broken toe. Plus/minus rating was lowest among full-time defenders.

THE FINESSE GAME

There aren't a whole lot of rabbits left in the hat for Greschner to keep pulling out. Never known as a speed demon (in football we'd call him a possession receiver), Greschner has slowed tremendously in his skating. He has to give large spaces to the opposition in order to keep the puck in front of him, and those spaces simply give the opposition more room to develop their own speed or offensive play.

Greschner is an intelligent player and will use his smarts to head the opposition off at the pass, but he needs more time than ever to get the message from his brain to his hands and feet.

He handles the puck fairly well but has less time than ever to make a play with it because of his slowed skating. He must move the puck quickly in order to remain a valuable commodity in the transition game.

THE PHYSICAL GAME

To his credit, Greschner has increased the tenor of his physical game even as his finesse game has stilled. He has good size and strength and his balance afoot is particularly effective as he takes men out of the play along the boards or wrestles for the puck in the crease.

He is not, however, Hercules and he will lose many battles against younger and stronger opponents — especially if they gain the Rangers zone or Greschner's area with a full head of steam.

He will fight if provoked, and uses his reach to stay away from the opposition in those fights.

THE INTANGIBLES

If he were willing to accept sometime status, Greschner could probably extend his NHL career. But he wants to play often, and he no longer has the capacity for regular-shift, 80-games-a-season contributions. If he remains in New York it will be as a part-time player, and should he leave New York his fate won't be much different.

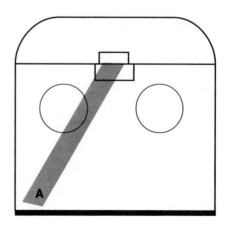

MARK HARDY

Yrs. of NHL service: 10
Born: Semaden, Switzerland; February 1, 1959
Position: Defenseman
Height: 5-11
Weight: 195
Uniform no.: 14
Shoots: left

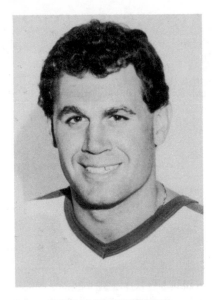

Career statistics:

GP	G	A	TP	PIM
722	59	277	336	1,023

1989-90 statistics:

GP	G	A	TP	+/-	PIM	PP	SH	GW	GT	S	PCT
54	0	15	15	4	94	0	0	0	0	55	0.0

LAST SEASON

Games played was three-season low, all point totals full-season career lows. Missed two games with bruised ribs, two games with foot injuries, nine games with knee injuries and 13 games with an ankle injury. Plus/minus rating tied for best (James Patrick) among regular defensemen.

THE FINESSE GAME

Hardy is a strong skater, well balanced on his skates and equipped with a good burst of speed up ice. He is fairly agile while carrying the puck and is able to rush the puck from the defensive zone to relieve forechecking pressure.

Hardy sees the ice well and makes good use of his teammates. He makes for a good point man on the power play because of his puckhandling ability, anticipation and shot. He contains the point well and knows when to pinch in and when to fall back. His shot is low and hard from the blue line and is excellent for tip-ins or deflections. Smartly, Hardy shoots often.

Except for the occasional rush he's a fairly conservative defenseman and takes few chances with the puck. He forces the play wide of the net by using his defensive angles, and he is adept at moving the puck quickly from his own end. He is poised with the puck and will generally make the right play.

THE PHYSICAL GAME

Hardy plays a physical game when he can and will dish out checks whenever possible. He has good strength along the boards, but on occasion is guilty of not completely taking the opposing winger out of the play.

He's effective in front of the net, tying up the opposition, but his game is more in hitting and gaining the puck and then starting a play.

THE INTANGIBLES

Hardy can contribute to the Rangers in a variety of ways and his steadiness is primary among them. Given the cast of characters he has to share time with (James Patrick, Brian Leetch, David Shaw, Randy Moller and Norm Rochefort), it's hard to see him in anything but a supporting role — and we haven't begun to talk about any of the younger defensemen the Rangers may want to integrate into their lineup.

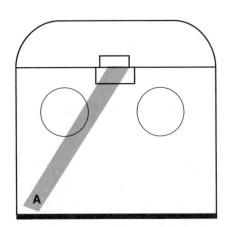

MARK JANSSENS

Yrs. of NHL service: 1
Born: Surrey, B.C., Canada; May 19, 1968
Position: Center
Height: 6-3
Weight: 195
Uniform no.: 15
Shoots: left

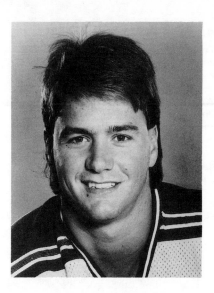

Career statistics:

GP	G	A	TP	PIM
86	5	8	13	161

1989-90 statistics:

GP	G	A	TP	+/-	PIM	PP	SH	GW	GT	S	PCT
80	5	8	13	-26	161	0	0	0		61	8.2

LAST SEASON

First full NHL season. Plus/minus rating was club's worst, PIM total third highest on club.

THE FINESSE GAME

Janssens is not yet a gifted finesse player at the NHL level. The highlights of his limited finesse ability include his skating and — to a degree — his hockey sense. He is not an artistic skater by any stretch if the imagination, showing neither particular quickness nor speed in his stride, but he does have a steady pace that he uses in his forechecking and defensive work.

His sense comes into play here, showing him the offensive zone and allowing him to slow down the opposition. Janssens is a good forechecker and not just a puck chaser, and he uses his vision and sense to angle the opposition into narrower and narrower zones as they attempt to rush up-ice.

As for offensive ability, it lags way behind his defensive skill. Janssens can handle the puck when skating, but is hesitant to make any play that will take him from his defensive role. His checking will produce loose pucks, but right now he hasn't demonstrated the NHL ability to cash in via scoring; he releases his shot too ponderously for that.

THE PHYSICAL GAME

Janssens has some fine physical tools, tools which — with proper development — can become exceptional. He has great size but less strength than his size would indicate, and he needs to improve his upper body strength so as to neutralize the big centers he checks when in front of his own net.

In the meantime he uses his body for takeouts fairly well (better strength helps here too) and he puts his body to work on a consistent basis. He will also fight when need be.

THE INTANGIBLES

If it sounds as if we're down on Janssens, we're not. Actually, it's not much of a stretch to say that he has begun to resemble the silhouette of the prototype big defensive center, Joel Otto. And Janssens himself knows what he needs to improve in order for his entire game to improve. Not originally a self-confident young man, Janssens is another of the young Rangers to have been positively affected by the new management's acceptance of mistakes en route to learning philosophy, and that is a mindset that will combine with Janssen's desire to create a better player.

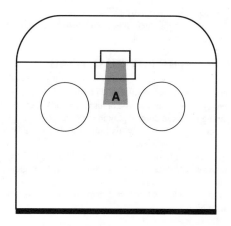

KRIS KING

Yrs. of NHL service: 2
Born: Bracebridge, Ontario, Canada; February 18, 1966
Position: Left wing
Height: 5-11
Weight: 210
Uniform no.: 12
Shoots: left

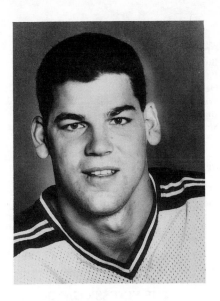

Career statistics:

GP	G	A	TP	PIM
126	9	10	19	456

1989-90 statistics:

GP	G	A	TP	+/-	PIM	PP	SH	GW	GT	S	PCT
68	6	7	13	2	286	0	0	0	0	49	12.2

LAST SEASON

First full NHL season. Finished second on club in PIM total (second highest in team history). Did not dress for 11 games, missed one game with League-mandated suspension.

THE FINESSE GAME

King is not an especially gifted finesse player, but he does have certain skills that can be brought to bear constructively. He is a very strong skater and he uses his skating skill to pursue the puck relentlessly during his forechecking. He also uses his strong stride and balance to drive to the net in offensive situations.

He carries the puck fairly well for his speed though he demonstrates no particular flair for scoring or playmaking. He will work himself into positive situations but his hand skills aren't sophisticated enough to take advantage of them: he'll overhandle the puck when he should pass, or fail to get just the right touch on his shots. That's a shame, because his net-driving style does provide him with opportunities.

His scoring, therefore, will have to be done on an opportunistic basis near the net.

THE PHYSICAL GAME

King is a very physical player. He takes the body and hits in every situation, and he succeeds in one-on-one confrontations because of his upper and lower body strength; he can control play in the corners, but is undercut in that ability by his limited ability to make a play coming out of that corner.

He is a fighter — more of a middleweight than a heavyweight because of his size — and will go against any opponent. His penalty minutes are generally good ones, in that he tends to take a member of the opposition with him.

THE INTANGIBLES

King's acquisition by Neil Smith is one of those small deals that means a lot. He gave the Rangers an immediate physical presence on the ice, and off the ice his tremendous attitude, desire and work ethic serve to make him a leader.

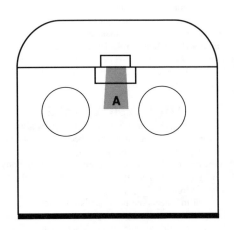

KELLY KISIO

Yrs. of NHL service: 8
Born: Peace River, Alberta, Canada; September 18, 1959
Position: Center
Height: 5-9
Weight: 180
Uniform no.: 11
Shoots: right

Career statistics:

GP	G	A	TP	PIM
521	163	304	467	532

1989-90 statistics:

GP	G	A	TP	+/-	PIM	PP	SH	GW	GT	S	PCT
68	22	44	66	11	105	7	2	1	0	128	17.2

LAST SEASON

Point total was third highest of career, but goal total was four-season low. Games played total was full-season low (missed five games with back injuries, six games with leg bruise). Tied for team's best plus/minus rating with John Ogrodnick.

THE FINESSE GAME

Kisio's finesse skills are rooted more in his physical ability than they are grounded in any outstanding finesse quality. His skating, for best example, is marked more by its power and strength than it is any fanciness. He has a strong stride with good balance and Kisio uses that power and sturdiness to battle for the puck in traffic or along the boards. He pursues the puck and fights through checks very well.

Kisio has a good understanding of the game and its implications, and he uses that degree of sense in his checking and in his offensive game. He has good hands and gets the puck to his teammmates well, and he also carries the puck well at all speeds.

He releases his shot quickly and accurately, important skills because he is usually in traffic when he shoots, but he could shoot the puck still more.

His skills and sense make him a natural for specialty teams duty.

THE PHYSICAL GAME

Kisio plays bigger than his size. He takes the body aggressively and relentlessly against all members of the opposition, and his good strength combines with his skating balance and sturdiness to enable him to win more battles than he loses. He plays that way all game every game and at both ends of the rink, one very big reason he has never played a full NHL season.

He also has a propensity for using his stick as an equalizer, and can be a chippy — even dirty — player in this regard.

THE INTANGIBLES

His heart and determination serve to make him a leader for the Rangers, speaking loudly where his otherwise quiet demeanor does not.

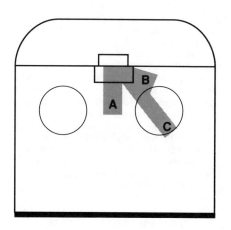

BRIAN LEETCH

Yrs. of NHL service: 3
Born: Corpus Christi, Texas, USA; March 3, 1968
Position: Defenseman
Height: 5-11
Weight: 185
Uniform no.: 2
Shoots: left

Career statistics:

GP	G	A	TP	PIM
157	36	105	141	76

1989-90 statistics:

GP	G	A	TP	+/-	PIM	PP	SH	GW	GT	S	PCT
72	11	45	56	-18	26	5	0	2	1	222	5.0

LAST SEASON

Plus/minus was club's second worst, poorest among defensemen. Finished second on club in assists, third in shots on goal total. Missed eight-games with a late-season broken ankle.

THE FINESSE GAME

Leetch is an excellent skater in every skating category. He has breakaway speed, exceptional one-step quickness, superior balance and tremendous agility and lateral movement. Leetch challenges the opposition at both blue lines — and usually succeeds — knowing his skating will allow him to recover if he makes a mistake.

His skating is made even more impressive by the fact that his hand skills and his hockey sense operate not only at the same high level as his foot skills, but at the same high speeds. Leetch handles the puck exceptionally well and easily goes end-to-end; he handles the puck as if it were nailed to his stick.

But he also passes excellently. He has excellent hands and can put the puck anywhere, and his superior hockey sense tells him when to move the puck to a teammate and when to hold it — and that stands for play at both ends of the ice. Like the NHL's best players, he sees the play earlier than anyone else on the ice. Defensively, however, he made mistakes that shouldn't be made in pick-up hockey — watching the puck too much and letting men slide behind him. That kind of mental mistake is especially surprising given Leetch's otherwise strong hockey intelligence.

Maybe the weakest of his skills is his shot, but that's quibbling. His shot is very good, strong, low to the net from the point, and accurate from anywhere. He takes good advantage of it by shooting often. He releases the puck quickly on his wrist shot, coming off the point well to put that loose puck on goal.

THE PHYSICAL GAME

The physical game is never going to be Leetch's strong point (no pun intended) but he can play a smart and aggressive physical game nonetheless. He already knows to play the sticks of the League's bigger forwards when he opposes them in front of his own net, realizing that he cannot bulldoze them out of the slot. He can also succeed by executing hit-and-run plays, using his balance to knock the opposition off the puck for just the second it takes Leetch's hands to gain control of the puck.

He already takes hits to make plays, and he does use his body very well to gain position.

THE INTANGIBLES

He can and will dominate games for years to come, but last season was a big learning experience for Leetch. He saw increased checking and defensive pressure and made mistakes (as mentioned) he should never have made as his confidence plummeted. But the key thing is he cares about his performances in all areas, and is determined to improve. He must show that improvement physically and mentally this season, as he recovers both from an injured ankle and an injured psyche.

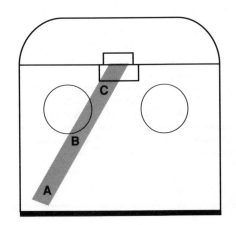

TROY MALLETTE

Yrs. of NHL service: 1
Born: Sudbury, Ontario, Canada; February 25, 1970
Position: Left wing/center
Height: 6-2
Weight: 190
Uniform no.: 26
Shoots: left

Career statistics:

GP	G	A	TP	+/-	PIM	PP	SH	GW	GT	S	PCT
79	13	16	29	-8	305	4	0	1	0	107	12.1

LAST SEASON

Mallette's first in the NHL. Led club in PIM total, setting a club record.

THE FINESSE GAME

A legitimate question based on the above numbers would be, "Is there one?" The answer is yes, and it is a function of Mallette's physical ability. He is a strong skater and his stride gives him some speed. He has a degree of sturdiness and balance in skating, but he is not what you'd call an agile skater.

He handles the puck with average ability at the NHL level, improving as the season progressed. He carries the puck fairly well, but in order to insure no turnovers Mallette will dump the puck at the blue line and then chase it down.

Mallette's playmaking and goal-scoring will be of the same order: make a safe play, work in the traffic, find an open teammate. He has demonstrated no real offensive flair as yet, no real ability to get into scoring position. He shoots the puck with strength, but needs some time and space to do so.

He needs work in the defensive aspect of the game, holding his position down the ice, being aware of the puck and so on.

THE PHYSICAL GAME

Well, what can we learn from 305 penalty minutes? This is one tough kid, afraid of nothing and no one. He wants to play the game physically and enjoys that style, so he initiates contact all over the ice (sometimes taking himself out of position while looking for hits). He is very strong and will hurt people when he hits them, and he backs up his play with his fists — and he's a pretty good fighter, though not necessarily among the League's heavyweights.

THE INTANGIBLES

Mallette is a heart-and-soul, emotions on his sleeve player. Like the other rookies on the squad he benefitted from management's willingness to accept the mistakes while looking for the good. And Mallette will continue to improve; just because he hasn't demonstrated Gretzky-like scoring ability doesn't mean he won't develop finesse-wise — parallels are already being made to Rick Tocchet and Cam Neely.

Those comparisons are a bit premature, but if Mallette continues to apply his intensity and work ethic those comparisons may shortly prove accurate.

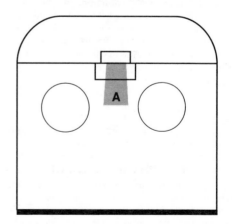

287

RANDY MOLLER

Yrs. of NHL service: 8
Born: Red Deer, Alta., Canada; August 23, 1963
Position: Defenseman
Height: 6-2
Weight: 207
Uniform no.: 24
Shoots: right

Career statistics:

GP	G	A	TP	PIM
568	34	131	165	1,141

1989-90 statistics:

GP	G	A	TP	+/-	PIM	PP	SH	GW	GT	S	PCT
60	1	12	13	-1	139	0	0	0	0	47	2.1

LAST SEASON

Acquired from Quebec in October 1989 in exchange for Michel Petit. Games played total was career low; ditto goal and point totals. Missed 14 games with shoulder injuries, five games with back spasms but led defense in PIM total (fourth on club).

THE FINESSE GAME

Skating and play-reading ability are the traits that make Moller a dependable defenseman. He has good speed, quickness and balance, and those traits combine to make Randy an extremely mobile defender. His acceleration and lateral movement serve him at both blue lines, where he will successfully challenge the puck more often than not. He forechecks and contains the point smartly and well, and Moller also steps up to force the puck carrier at his own blue line.

He is not generally a rushing defenseman, but — when necessary — he can avail himself of good puck carrying skills to relieve pressure on the forwards. His sense and vision allow him to find the open man in both zones but Moller's passes are safe ones more than they are designed to create offense. He has a very effective transitional game.

Randy has a strong slap shot and will score his goals from the point, but he should shoot more frequently.

He is a penalty killing natural because of his skills, and he can also contribute on the power play.

THE PHYSICAL GAME

Moller plays a quiet but effective physical game. He covers the front of the net well and makes the opposition pay for its shots (thus the majority of his penalty minutes). His strength allows him to rub out and keep out the opposition along the boards, and his balance and finesse skills make his physical play more effective by keeping him vertical and ready to continue the play after hits.

THE INTANGIBLES

Night in and night out, Moller plays a strong and consistent game. He's a leader through his discipline and hard work, and he's a strong team player.

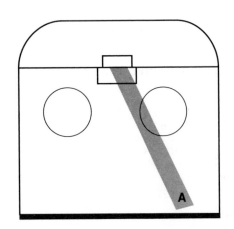

BRIAN MULLEN

Yrs. of NHL service: 8
Born: New York City, NY, USA; March 16, 1962
Position: Left wing
Height: 5-10
Weight: 180
Uniform no.: 19
Shoots: left

Career statistics:

GP	G	A	TP	PIM
600	205	277	482	276

1989-90 statistics:

GP	G	A	TP	+/-	PIM	PP	SH	GW	GT	S	PCT
76	27	41	68	7	42	7	3	3	1	186	14.5

LAST SEASON

Assist total tied career high and point total was second highest of career, best in five seasons. Plus/minus was club's fourth best, third among forwards. Missed two games with a foot infection.

THE FINESSE GAME

Quickness and agility are the qualities that mark Mullen as a player, and they mark his skating especially well. Mullen is lightening-fast within a single step, and he also has the ability to stop and turn — in any direction — within a stride; he has excellent lateral movement ability. That makes him exceedingly dangerous around the front of the opposition net and near loose pucks. That skill also allows him to create space near a defense. While he can burn some rubber up the rink, he is more quick than fast.

His shot reflects the same principles that his feet demonstrate. Mullen lets his shot go very quickly so as to best exploit that opening he has just gained. He forces goalies to make saves with a very accurate shot, and he manufactures scoring opportunities by shooting from bad angles.

He handles the puck very well when he carries it, so he loses none of his agility. He is a very creative player both with and without the puck and his sense will get him into scoring position. He has hands soft enough to succeed in playmaking but Mullen exposes himself as a goal scorer by thinking shot before he thinks pass.

Mullen uses his skills to his benefit defensively, where he plays a fairly conscientious game.

THE PHYSICAL GAME

He neither looks like nor really plays like a physical hockey player, but Mullen has added a physical segment to his game over the last two seasons and has become a more complete player. He will never bounce anyone into the blue seats but he doesn't have to, because his balance, quickness and hand skills are such that he can accomplish a lot by just leaning into or bumping an opponent.

Once the opposition is off-balance, Mullen just puts his quickness to work to grab the puck and run. And he will get his nose dirtier than that, using his skills to good success in the traffic areas in front of the net.

THE INTANGIBLES

Mullen has continued to play the more-rounded game that he has developed over the past several seasons. He is still a streak player, but he has succeeded in lessening the times when he doesn't succeed at all. In short, he's pulled his bottom closer to his top. If he continues to maintain his intensity he'll continue to contribute evenly across a season and in all situations.

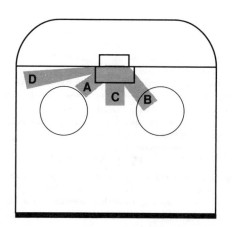

BERNIE NICHOLLS

Yrs. of NHL service: 9
Born: Haliburton, Ontario, Canada; June 24, 1961
Position: Center
Height: 6-0
Weight: 185
Uniform no.: 9
Shoots: right

Career statistics:

GP	G	A	TP	PIM
634	339	456	795	785

1989-90 statistics:

GP	G	A	TP	+/-	PIM	PP	SH	GW	GT	S	PCT
79	39	73	112	-9	86	15	8	1	0	287	13.6

LAST SEASON

Acquired from Los Angeles in January in exchange for Tomas Sandstrom and Tony Granato. Led club in assists and points (finishing sixth in NHL in both categories), finishing second in shots on goal. Assist and point totals were second highest of career.

THE FINESSE GAME

For all his finesse skill, Nicholl's is not an exceptional skater. If he was judged just on his touch of quickness and good balance, he wouldn't be expected to score 50 points let alone 150. But because he has such high levels of anticipation and hockey sense — and the other physical finesse skills necessary to utilize that anticipation and sense — Nicholls leaps from ordinary to extraordinary.

Despite the fact that he doesn't pursue the puck well, Nicholls reads the offensive zone fantastically. He picks off passes, takes the puck off the boards and gets into scoring position exceptionally well.

Now add his superior hand skills, and you begin to see how Nicholls succeeds. He's very patient with the puck along the boards, getting the puck under control before making a play, and Bernie can slip the puck through the smallest opening to a teammate.

His puckhandling is excellent. His favorite play is to fake his slap shot (a shot the defense *must* respect) and then deke to his forehand. That slap shot is an excellent one, among the League's best, and Bernie makes it better by being an excellent one-touch shooter. When he shoots more he scores more: 385 SOG in 1988-89 and 70 goals, versus last season's numbers.

All his talents make him not just a specialty teams regular, but a specialty teams star.

THE PHYSICAL GAME

Nicholls is extremely strong on the puck, so don't try the ol' stick-lifting trick; it won't work. That strength and balance combine to make him an exceptional traffic player, and he not only accepts checks and the physical game, but initiates contact as well. That hitting helps get him into the game.

His big, strong hands power his wrist shot and help him win faceoffs, and his wiry strength complements his size.

THE INTANGIBLES

Nicholls is among the NHL's very best players, not necessarily a 150-point scorer, but 50-60 goals and a like number of assists is never out of the question. He's a great competitor who loves the pressure to perform, and that's no small reason why we think he can approach last season's success.

But can we do something about that plus/minus ... please?

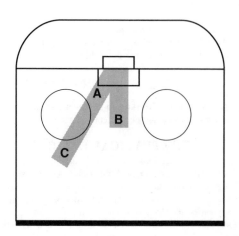

CHRIS NILAN

Yrs. of NHL service: 10
Born: Boston, Mass., USA; February 9, 1958
Position: Right wing
Height: 6-0
Weight: 205
Uniform no.: 30
Shoots: right

Career statistics:

GP	G	A	TP	PIM
591	98	99	196	2,506

1989-90 statistics:

GP	G	A	TP	+/-	PIM	PP	SH	GW	GT	S	PCT
25	1	2	3	-8	59	0	0	0	0	24	4.2

LAST SEASON

Games played was full-season career low; missed 35 games with a broken forearm, 20 games with a knee injury.

THE FINESSE GAME

Though physical performance is why Chris Nilan is in the lineup, he keeps himself there because of often-obscured finesse skills. Though he's no better than average as a skater, Nilan is a good forechecker because of persistence and determination. He also has a small dose of speed that he can use effectively, mostly because it surprises he opposition.

He is disciplined in playing his wing, and he has a pretty good view of the ice and ability to anticipate. He stays with his check fairly deeply into the defensive zone, and his presence in an area often forces the opposition to surrender the puck or pursue it with less vigor.

For a fighter, Chris has good hands, and he can make plays to his teammates and even operate in a little bit of traffic. He'll score by lurking around the net and putting home defensive mistakes.

THE PHYSICAL GAME

If it moves in an opposition uniform, Nilan will hit it. He is an exceptionally hard hitter (made so because he has great strength and fairly good balance, so he remains vertical after collisions) and most difficult to dislodge from his skates.

He's one of the NHL's better fighters (certainly unafraid of any opponent) and he uses his stick liberally.

Chris has good upper body strength and can out-muscle many opponents along the boards, but he can often be guilty of being overaggressive and cancelling his good work out with an extra elbow that loses him the puck he could gain.

THE INTANGIBLES

Injury has taken its toll on Nilan, not surprising consoidering the tenor of his physical game. They will love him in his hometown of Bostonbut he has to stay in the lineup to be effective. Yes, he's one of the League's great leaders, a heart-and-soul guy whose own attitude and desire improves that of his club. But over the last three easons he's shown himself to be a 30-plus years old player who can't stay healthy.

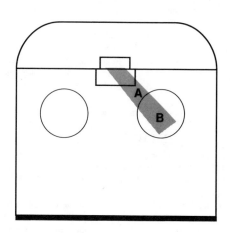

JOHN OGRODNICK

Yrs. of NHL service: 11
Born: Ottawa, Ontario, Canada; June 20, 1959
Position: Left wing
Height: 6-0
Weight: 206
Uniform no.: 25
Shoots: left

Career statistics:

GP	G	A	TP	PIM
775	348	383	731	226

1989-90 statistics:

GP	G	A	TP	+/-	PIM	PP	SH	GW	GT	S	PCT
80	43	31	74	11	44	19	0	8	0	215	20.0

LAST SEASON

Games played total was seven-season high, goal total second best and point total fourth best of career. Tied with Kelly Kisio for team's best plus/minus rating, finished second on club in power play goals. Led club in game winners and shooting percentage, was fourth in shots on goal total.

THE FINESSE GAME

Ogrodnick is an above average skater, equipped with good acceleration ability and he puts it to use well, jetting into the clear on his wing and unloading on the goaltender. He drives the defense backward with his skating and that opens space for his teammates.

His shot is exceptional, quickly released in all its forms and all its forms can beat goaltenders from most anywhere in the offensive zone. He shoots accurately, as his numbers demonstrate, and he gets to loose pucks quickly so as to be doubly dangerous (and one very big reason why he succeeds on the power play). He also uses the defense as a screen very well.

He has a scorer's mentality, so he'll look to shoot before he looks to his teammates. He reads the play well and certainly knows how to get into position to score, but his style is more of a straight ahead, get-a-step-on-the-defenseman-and-blast-at-the-net mode than a dipsy-doodle one.

He also stepped up the pace of his defensive game.

THE PHYSICAL GAME

Ogrodnick is playing a more nose-dirtying style than he'd played for several seasons, and that willingness to go to the traffic areas pays off in goals. He's taking hits to make his plays, and he's also rubbing out the opposition in the offensive zone. He won't ever be mistaken for Cam Neely, but Ogrodnick's physical performances are now positives where they were previously negatives.

THE INTANGIBLES

A confident player can do almost anything and the Rangers' new regime gave Ogrodnick his confidence back. They didn't give up on him as the previous regime did, and he responded by having a great season. He's certainly capable of repeating a good deal of that success, which is something the Rangers are expecting, and Ogrodnick's positive attitude and work ethic can lay the base that results in that success.

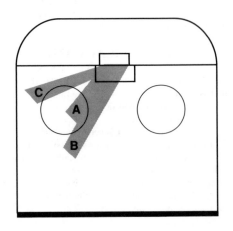

JAMES PATRICK

Yrs. of NHL service: 6
Born: Winnipeg, Man., Canada; June 14, 1963
Position: Defenseman
Height: 6-2
Weight: 192
Uniform no.: 3
Shoots: right

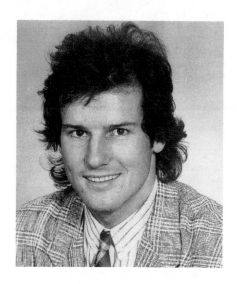

Career statistics:

GP	G	A	TP	PIM
451	75	233	308	366

1989-90 statistics:

GP	G	A	TP	+/-	PIM	PP	SH	GW	GT	S	PCT
73	14	43	57	4	50	9	0	0	0	136	10.3

LAST SEASON

Games played total was three-season high, as was point total. Missed three games with separated shoulder, three games with broken finger, one game with back spasms. Led defense in goals and points.

THE FINESSE GAME

Patrick is an exceptionally gifted finesse player, and his skating is unquestionably his most exceptional skill. He is one of the NHL's very best skaters in terms of total mobility; he has speed, quickness, balance — all the factors that create truly world-class skating skill. He can out-race the opposition up-ice, beat them to the loose pucks and openings — he skates better backwards than many players do forwards. He uses his skating skill to excellently control and close the gap on the puck carrier, and he plays a very dynamic active game at both blue lines (credit his excellent lateral ability here).

His hand skills make his skating better, and vice versa. He controls the puck excellently when rushing it, and his ability to turn the play around by taking the puck off the boards and then starting up-ice is outstanding. He could stickhandle in a shoebox and can certainly handle the puck in traffic, and he'll become an integral part of his team's offense. Patrick passes the puck with intelligence and touch and he's helped here by that third element of great play: hockey sense. That sense makes itself evident not just in his playmaking but also in his defense, his forechecking — in all aspects of Patrick's game.

He has several shooting weapons, all of them good to very good. His slap shot is ideal for tips and deflections because it is low and accurate to the net, but he'll also cut to the slot to use a wrist shot that can beat any NHL goaltender.

His one weakness comes in front of his net, where he'll play off his man in order to be active against the puck. This calculated gamble somtimes backfires when the puck gets through to the unguarded forward.

THE PHYSICAL GAME

Patrick's physical game is marked by an understated quality. He doesn't bang anyone into the bleachers, but his excellent skating ability and balance combine with his good strength to make him good at takeouts. He will get out-muscled in confrontations against stronger forwards whether that means along the boards or in front of the net, and there are times when they can drive through his checks. He succeeds in physical situations more by intelligent application of skills then he does by sheer muscular ability.

THE INTANGIBLES

One sign of maturity is the ability to judge people for what they are, not what they can be or what you want them to be. With that in mind (and it's taken us five years to get to this point), we offer this about James Patrick: He is a dedicated team man, one whose smoothness of effort can sometimes belie his desire or intensity. He is one of the NHL's most consistent and dependable players, and his efforts and success night in and night out only serves to underline that point.

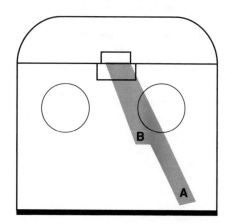

MIKE RICHTER

Yrs. of NHL service: 1
Born: Abington, PA, USA; September 22, 1962
Position: Goaltender
Height: 5-10
Weight: 185
Uniform no.: 35
Catches: left

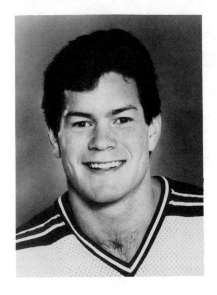

Career statistics:

GP	MINS	AVG	W	L	T	SO	GA	SA	SAPCT	PIM
23	1,320	3.00	12	5	5	0	66	686	.904	0

LAST SEASON

First full NHL season; played one playoff game during 1989.

THE PHYSICAL GAME

Richter's is a very strong hybrid style of goaltending based primarily on challenging the shooter and cutting down the angles but seasoned with aggressive reflex ability.

He comes out of the net courtesy of his balance and skating skill, and lets the puck do the work of hitting him. That allows Richter to stay in a compact stance and move well to face a pass or second shot. When playing well he is a model of efficiency: move out, stop the puck, clear the rebound, prepare for the next save — all with little spectacular motion.

But Richter also has exceptional reflexes. His hands and feet are very fast, so he'll fare well in those scrambles around the front of his net when he has to leave his feet; his balance and foot speed get him to and from the ice with speed.

Because of his angle ability, the extremes of the net are going to be the only available shooting spaces.

THE MENTAL GAME

Richter is a very tough competitor, one who can raise the level of his game to match the level of the game being played. He has big save capability, and just may be on the verge of showing the ability to win games himself. He maintains his intensity well both within games and from game to game.

THE INTANGIBLES

About the only sure thing in the Ranger goal this season will be Richter, by which we mean his presence (based on his performance last season) could easily allow the Rangers to move any of their other goaltenders. Richter's debut was a strong one, as befits a player of strong character and work ethic, and as he improves he could become one of the game's best goaltenders.

NORMAND ROCHEFORT

Yrs. of NHL service: 10
Born: Trois-Rivieres, Quebec, Canada; January 28, 1961
Position: Defenseman
Height: 6-1
Weight: 200
Uniform no.: 5
Shoots: left

Career statistics:

GP	G	A	TP	PIM
522	36	110	146	494

1989-90 statistics:

GP	G	A	TP	+/-	PIM	PP	SH	GW	GT	S	PCT
31	3	1	4	2	24	0	0	1	0	30	10.0

LAST SEASON

Games played total was second lowest of career; he missed 42 games with knee surgery, two games with a broken finger.

THE FINESSE GAME

Rochefort is an excellent defensive defenseman and his mobility is the reason. He's a good skater, both forward and backward and he is agile on his skates, so he moves well laterally too. His skating and excellent positional play means that Rochefort is rarely beaten one-on-one.

He steers the play wide excellently and once he takes the opposition off the puck (his good foot speed helps him close the gap on the puckcarrier), Normand has ability to make a quick breakout pass.

Normand sees the ice well, and he plays two-on-ones and three-on-twos well because of his vision and his ability to anticipate the cross-ice pass. He passes well because of that vision and his good hands. Though he doesn't usually rush the puck from his own zone, Rochefort's skills are such that he could do so safely if necessary.

Normand is not a goal scorer, so anything he gets will have to be on shots from the point.

THE PHYSICAL GAME

Rochefort is a good and aggressive player. He hits frequently and well and can rub out a forward along the boards, although he does tend to look for the hit instead of letting the hit come to him. Rochefort is very strong and very tough in front of his net.

He can out-muscle forwards for the puck along the boards or in the corners, or he can hold them out of the play when necessary. Rochefort is good at shielding the puck with his body in the corners and he will sacrifice his body to block shots.

THE INTANGIBLES

Health is a big question now, as Rochefort has played just 184 of a possible 400 games over the last five seasons. A healthy Rochefort is an important player, especially when his work ethic and desire are added to the mix.

LINDY RUFF

Yrs. of NHL service: 11
Born: Warburg, Alta., Canada; February 17, 1960
Position: Left wing/defense
Height: 6-2
Weight: 200
Uniform no.: 44
Shoots: left

Career statistics:

GP	G	A	TP	PIM
677	105	194	299	1,234

1989-90 statistics:

GP	G	A	TP	+/-	PIM	PP	SH	GW	GT	S	PCT
56	3	6	9	-10	77	0	0	2	0	59	5.1

LAST SEASON

Games played total was three-season low; missed six games with a fractured rib, one game with a charley horse. Plus/minus total was second worst among defensemen.

THE FINESSE GAME

As a finesse player, Ruff isn't. He's never been better than average as a skater, and a decade-plus of NHL service (combined with the injuries acquired) have slowed Ruff down. He just cruises up and down the ice.

Ruff isn't a good puckhandler but that's all right, because he doesn't know what to do with the puck anyway. He has little vision of the ice or his teammates, and less anticipation for possible plays. If he wins the puck during a foray into the corner, the best Ruff will do with it is the blind pass to the slot.

His shot is consistent with his other finesse skills, and he's unlikely to score from any place other than the edge of the goal crease by shovelling home rebounds and other garbage.

Lindy is a conscientious back checker, very concerned with his defensive play and disciplined enough to stay on his wing and not create any openings by leaving the zone too soon. He is aided in his defensive play by his experience as a defenseman and understands what angles are all about so as to keep his man from the puck.

But when forced to play defense, his lack of skating skill betrays him.

THE PHYSICAL GAME

Ruff is.

He's big and strong and uses that strenth to bang around in the corners and jar the puck loose from opposing defensemen. He doesn't have the skills to make a play out of the corner, so his physical game is one-dimensional in that regard.

Ruff also uses his strength to wreak havoc in front of the opposition goal, daring a defenseman to move him from the crease. He is aggressive and will take pokes at people when he has to stand up for the team. Lindy also applies himself physically in the defensive zone, where he will rub out an opposing winger along the boards.

His injury record is a direct result of his play, rather than an indication of any fragility on his part. Ruff counters the injury problem by staying in great condition.

THE INTANGIBLES

Ruff can contribute to the Rangers on a part-time, fill-in basis at either wing or defense, and any chance he has to be a more active participant will come up front. He has always been a fine team man and knows when to assume leadership in the locker room or on the ice so as to produce the best effect for the club. Hard work is all he knows and he has the ability to play well after sitting for long stretches, but he can no longer be a front-liner.

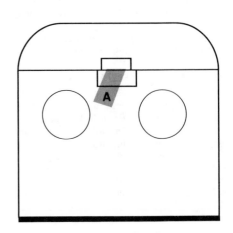

DAVID SHAW

Yrs. of NHL service: 6
Born: St. Thomas, Ontario, Canada; May 25, 1964
Position: Defenseman
Height: 6-2
Weight: 204
Uniform no.: 21
Shoots: right

Career statistics:

GP	G	A	TP	PIM
320	22	84	106	368

1989-90 statistics:

GP	G	A	TP	+/-	PIM	PP	SH	GW	GT	S	PCT
22	2	10	12	-3	22	1	1	0	0	24	8.3

LAST SEASON

Games played total was five-season low; missed 54 games with shoulder injury and subsequent season-ending surgery.

THE FINESSE GAME

Shaw combines his skating ability with his smarts to become a strong player at both ends of the ice. His skating is quietly effective (which is another way of saying he doesn't have any particularly spectacular skating skill) and Shaw is a fairly mobile defender. He uses his hockey sense to command his skating, reading the ice and challenging the puck by pinching in at the offensive blue line or stepping up to close the gap on the puckcarrier at his own blue line.

The same could be said of Shaw's hand skills. He moves the puck quickly and correctly from his own zone and, though he wouldn't be considered an offensive weapon, Dave also contributes well from the opposing blue line. He moves the puck to his teammates well because of his vision and good hands, and he augments his passing with a howitzer shot from blue line; the shot is his best physical finesse skill.

Shaw would be even more effective from the blue line if he could lose the bad habit of putting his head down once he decides to shoot. Many times he tucks his head in for a slapper, only to drive the puck into a shot-blocking forward who made the challenging move after Shaw looked down. The results are far too many odd-man advantages for breaking opponents, an ironic twist for a conservative defender.

THE PHYSICAL GAME

In his quiet and dependable way, Shaw uses his size and strength very well. Dave isn't a thundering hitter or great fighter — he just forces the opposition from the crease, or ties up the incoming forward along the boards 99 percent of the time. And, he does it smartly — without drawing penalties that harm the team.

He takes the body well and can hit hard (skating balance and strength afoot are the keys here). He also puts his reach to work excellently in poking the puck or deflecting shots on goal.

THE INTANGIBLES

Shaw remains an underrated defensive commodity, the kind of player a coach can rotate the rest of his defense around because of his steadiness and dependability. He is an enthusiastic, hard working and coachable player who must work through his rehabilitation to regain his defensive standing.

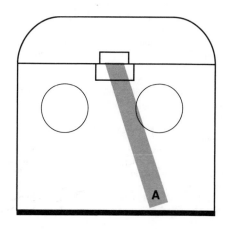

DARREN TURCOTTE

Yrs. of NHL service: 1
Born: Boston, Mass., USA; March 2, 1968
Position: Center
Height: 6-0
Weight: 185
Uniform no.: 8
Shoots: left

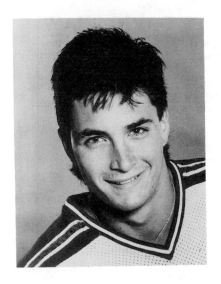

Career statistics:

GP	G	A	TP	PIM
96	39	37	76	36

1989-90 statistics:

GP	G	A	TP	+/-	PIM	PP	SH	GW	GT	S	PCT
76	32	34	66	3	32	10	1	4	0	205	15.6

LAST SEASON

First full NHL season. Finished fourth in overall rookie scoring, first in goals and shots on goal, second in power play goals and first goals, third in game winners. Missed one game with a bruised foot, three games with the flu.

THE FINESSE GAME

Turcotte has speed galore, and it is the basis — but not sole fine point — of his game. He has breakaway speed and tremendous quickness — one stride and he's gone. His agility and lateral ability are just as high as his foot speed. In short, he's a very dangerous skater who both creates and exploits openings.

His hands are almost as talented as his feet, and sometimes it's a toss-up between the two for top honors. His hands are soft and remarkably sensitive, so he releases his excellent shot quickly and acuurately — and Turcotte can score from literally any place in any position because of his balance and hand skill.

He gets open very well, and while his skating is one function of that his hockey sense is the other. He is, however, a scorer first so he looks to the net before he looks to his teammates. Which is not to say that he won't pass or can't pass well; Turcotte is smart enough and talented enough to move the puck to a teammate in better position. It's just that with all things being equal, he's going to shoot the puck.

He plays a fairly consistent defensive game, and his skills combine to make him a natural for specialty teams duty.

THE PHYSICAL GAME

Turcotte is a tough and willing kid who'll take his knocks to make his plays. He's unafraid of working in the traffic areas near the net, and actually succeeds there because of his finesse abilities.

That said, he's not an overwhelming physical player in terms of size or strength and though he may impose himself on the opposition by initiating contact he's going to get more accomplished with hit-and-run missions than he is bumping and grinding.

THE INTANGIBLES

Turcotte is a very dynamic player, and his scoring achievements of last season are not out of character for him. He must, however, work to eliminate the inconsistencies that plague him; he admits to being a streak player, and strings of eight and seven (twice) games without goals indicate that. He'll see better checking in his second full-season, and his response to that will go a long way toward determining how he will develop as an NHLer.

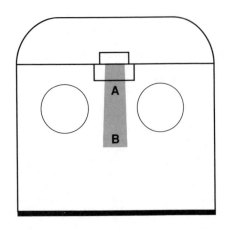

JOHN VANBIESBROUCK

Yrs. of NHL service: 6
Born: Detroit, Mich., USA; September 4, 1963
Position: Goaltender
Height: 5-8
Weight: 179
Uniform no.: 34
Catches: left

Career statistics:

GP	MINS	G	SO	AVG	A	PIM
316	17,840	1,060	7	3.57	18	153

1989-90 statistics:

GP	MINS	AVG	W	L	T	SO	GA	SA	SAPCT	PIM
47	2,734	3.38	19	19	7	1	154	1,362	.887	24

LAST SEASON

Games played was five-season low, second lowest full-season total of career. Goals-against total was full-season low.

THE PHYSICAL GAME

When he's on his game, Vanbiesbrouck may be the best goaltender in the League at squaring himself to the puck and letting the puck do the work of staying out of the net. He is generally a very strong angle goaltender at any rate, and he makes the most of his ability and size by challenging most every shooter.

He is an excellent skater and has a high degree of balance, the result being that Vanbiesbrouck moves in and out of the net well to challenge, to flag down loose pucks, and to move with good (not great) authority from post to post. His balance and foot speed also mean that he goes to the ice and gets back into a stance very quickly; he's generally in a good position for follow-ups to the initial save.

His hand and foot speed are above average, and Vanbiesbrouck will usually come to the top of a screen or deflection before going to the ice for a save; tight traffic near his net, however, tends to pin him into his net. One sign that he is struggling is when Vanbiesbrouck plants himself so solidly on his inside edges (in order to butterfly his pads and then get up from that maneuver) that he cannot take advantage of his feet.

His glove hand is one of the NHL's very best, and he uses his stick well to corral and move pucks (his judgement on passing seems to have improved); he generally handles and clears rebounds well.

He is faster moving from right to left, so the right side of the net is where he is more vulnerable.

THE MENTAL GAME

Vanbiesbrouck's whole style is keyed by confidence — as is the style of any goaltender who challenges the puck. When he feels confident he will play that strong style and not over-extend himself, not out-think himself and try to do everyone's job (as in, stay back in the net because the defense isn't covering the front, so what happens when the shot goes wide and so on).

He prepares himself to play every game and has very high intensity, and he certainly has big save capability. He is one of the few goalies who can win games by himself but needs to play a stretch of games to bring his concentration and confidence to their best levels. He is strong when a game is within a goal either way, but can become disinterested if he falls behind by a couple.

THE INTANGIBLES

Vanbiesbrouck needs to know he is the team's number one goalie; that's what we mean by saying the team has to show confidence in him. He is an exceptionally driven athlete and one who believes his ability dictates he should be the top gun. Which, because of the emergence of Mike Richter, has become a topic open to debate.

CAREY WILSON

Yrs. of NHL service: 6
Born: Winnipeg, Man., Canada; May 19, 1962
Position: Center
Height: 6-2
Weight: 205
Uniform no.: 17
Shoots: right

Career statistics:

GP	G	A	TP	PIM
431	143	221	364	251

1989-90 statistics:

GP	G	A	TP	+/-	PIM	PP	SH	GW	GT	S	PCT
41	9	17	26	4	57	4	0	1	0	64	14.1

LAST SEASON

Games played total was full-season career low (missed 34 games with knee injuries, three games with a charley horse, two games with injured shoulder).

THE FINESSE GAME

Wilson is loaded with upper level finesse skills. To begin with, he is an excellent skater with speed, quickness and agility. He can move laterally or change directions at will.

He has exceptional hands and hockey sense and he can be an excellent playmaker because of those skills. He has the ability to give the soft pass and knows where to send that pass, leading his teammates to the opening if he doesn't take advantage of them himself. Wilson also likes to carry the puck (especially across the opposing blue line) and beat people 1-on-1 (he is an excellent 1-on-1 player), so he won't always make those passes.

Wilson has good sense around the net and is dangerous if left unguarded. He has an accurate and quick wrist shot that is effective both in close and from a distance.

He combines all his skills to be an excellent defensive player as well and he's also a very smart one doing the job without taking penalties that hurt the club.

THE PHYSICAL GAME

Wilson has outstanding physical skills that should not be confused with board-bashing ability. His balance makes him a superior player in traffic — both along the boards and when checked in front of the net. He'll maintain his puck control through most all physical situations, is very strong and will out-muscle many opponents along the boards, staying vertical and ready to make plays after those collisions.

He has terrific eye/hand coordination (which makes him an excellent faceoff man) and is a remarkably conditioned athlete and works very hard at staying in shape year round.

THE INTANGIBLES

Assuming health, Wilson can be a strong two-way hockey player of above average demeanor. Of course, he has to want to be that player. His reputation (unfairly, we would say) speaks of his lack of concentration and intensity, questioning his desire to always play at his best level. He's answered that question since coming to New York.

He has been the Rangers number one center offensively since joining New York, but that is no longer the case with Bernie Nicholls in the lineup — and Wilson has already expressed displeasure at the shifting of responsibilities. It is up to Wilson to prove he deserves those responsibilities once again.

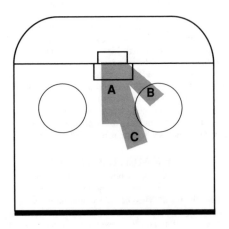

PHILADELPHIA
FLYERS

KEITH ACTON

Yrs. of NHL service: 11
Born: Stouffville, Ontario, Canada; April 15, 1958
Position: Center
Height: 5-8
Weight: 170
Uniform no.: 25
Shoots: left

Career statistics:

GP	G	A	TP	PIM
737	195	303	498	821

1989-90 statistics:

GP	G	A	TP	+/-	PIM	PP	SH	GW	GT	S	PCT
69	13	14	27	-2	80	0	2	0	0	94	13.8

LAST SEASON

Games played total was second lowest of career, assist and point totals lowest of career.

THE FINESSE GAME

Skating and smarts key what remains of Acton's finesse game. His foot speed and balance give him good lateral movement and one-step quickness on his skates, and those assets combine particularly well with his hockey sense to make him a good forechecker and penalty killer. The opposition has to respect his speed, and Acton uses that speed to draw penalties (not that he's above a good dive).

His checking work is good at both ends of the ice, so his plus/minus mark is a deceiving measure of his defensive ability.

Never truly exceptional with the puck (Acton's offensive success has always come more from the opportunities his skating created and from his read of the ice), Acton now is not a bet to stickhandle through the opposition. What offense he does generate will come from pouncing on loose pucks and getting the puck to open teammates.

THE PHYSICAL GAME

Listed at 5-foot-8, Acton plays bigger than his size. He is aggressive and is an agitator (another reason he draws penalties), and is unafraid to work against bigger competition. He uses his stick freely, but he does not fight.

THE INTANGIBLES

A character player and a smart veteran, Acton is a worker and a dedicated team player. His example can be valuable to a team trying to make the transition from older to younger players.

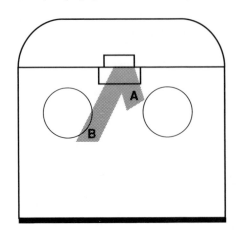

CRAIG BERUBE

Yrs. of NHL service: 2
Born: Calahoo, Alberta, Canada; December 17, 1965
Position: Left wing
Height: 6-1
Weight: 205
Uniform no.: 17
Shoots: left

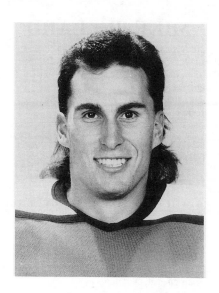

Career statistics:

GP	G	A	TP	PIM
161	8	17	25	655

1989-90 statistics:

GP	G	A	TP	+/-	PIM	PP	SH	GW	GT	S	PCT
74	4	14	18	-7	291	0	0	0	0	52	7.7

LAST SEASON

Games played, all point totals and PIM mark were career highs. Led club in PIM total (ninth overall in NHL).

THE FINESSE GAME

Berube is a limited finesse player, and his overall play reflects that. His best finesse skill would be his skating, but even that asset is no better than average at the NHL level. He is a straight-ahead skater without a great deal of agility or quickness, which means that better skaters can easily avoid him.

He patrols his wing with little imagination or understanding of the game's flow, and must keep the play ahead of him in order to be successful. His positional play needs to improve so that he doesn't remain a defensive liability when the play turns past him into the Flyer zone.

Berube doesn't handle or carry the puck well, and he doesn't shoot it well either. Any goals he does get will have to come from directly in front of the net.

THE PHYSICAL GAME

This is the heart of Berube's game, and if he can catch somebody he'll hit him. He has good strength along the boards and in the corners, but will not be able to make a play after taking the man off the puck.

He backs down from no one and is a willing fighter, one of the NHL's more punishing pugilists. He can, however, be goaded into stupid "extra tough" penalties.

THE INTANGIBLES

Berube is a good team guy, understanding and willingly filling his role. As with other one-dimensional players, Berube must develop his other skills so as to keep pace with the competition. That improvement is something he works very hard at after practice, but the degree to which he can develop remains debatable.

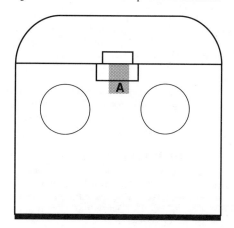

MIKE BULLARD

Yrs. of NHL service: 10
Born: Ottawa, Ontario, Canada; March 10, 1961
Position: Center
Height: 6-0
Weight: 195
Uniform no.: 10
Shoots: left

Career statistics:

GP	G	A	TP	PIM
662	315	331	646	663

1989-90 statistics:

GP	G	A	TP	+/-	PIM	PP	SH	GW	GT	S	PCT
70	27	37	64	0	67	6	0	4	0	181	14.9

LAST SEASON

Games played total was five-season low (late season groin injury). Finished second on club in goals and shots on goal, third in points.

THE FINESSE GAME

Bullard is a skilled offensive player, as his almost a point-per-game NHL average testifies. With a decade of NHL hockey taking its toll on his body, Bullard's hands are now his best finesse weapon. He's a gifted puckhandler and shooter, shooting well off the pass. He has a good selection of shots (especially from his off wing), and he has a goal scorer's ability to find the scoring position.

Speed had been his primary skating asset, and it was that skill that brought Bullard to those scoring positions. He has a good degree of balance and agility, resulting in good lateral movement. Because of his ability in open space, Bullard is a natural for power play duty.

Bullard can use his skills to work well with his teammates, but he is more apt to look to the net than he is to his wings. His defense is no better than average, not a strong sign for an aging offensive player.

THE PHYSICAL GAME

Bullard is not really a physical player, which is just as well because his strengths are not in the physical game. He operates best in the low traffic areas, despite the fact that he has the hand skill to succeed in the congested areas near the net.

He'll take his hits if he's in proximity to the boards, but don't expect Bullard to come charging out of the corner with loose pucks.

THE INTANGIBLES

An aging goal scorer, one who scored just nine goals in his last 30 games last season (after a 1988-89 season that saw him tally just 13 times in his last 36 games) — and only six of those were at full strength. That says something about Bullard's ability, whether it be a conditioning question or a determination question.

What we think it says is that Bullard's skills are declining, not a good sign for a player on a rebuilding team.

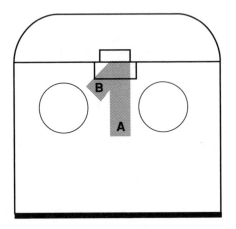

TERRY CARKNER

Yrs. of NHL service: 4
Born: Smith Falls, Ontario, Canada; March 7, 1966
Position: Defenseman
Height: 6-3
Weight: 212
Uniform no.: 29
Shoots: left

Career statistics:

GP	G	A	TP	PIM
256	20	87	107	593

1989-90 statistics:

GP	G	A	TP	+/-	PIM	PP	SH	GW	GT	S	PCT
63	4	18	22	-8	167	1	0	1	0	60	6.7

LAST SEASON

Assist and point totals were three-season lows. Plus/minus was club's third worst, second poorest among defensemen. Missed 15 games with knee injury.

THE FINESSE GAME

Passing would be primary among Carkner's finesse skills, skills that might otherwise best be termed "modest." Carkner can read the offensive blue line fairly well — which is one reason why he'll see power play time — and he can also make a good, quick pass from the defensive zone. If he can continue to develop his first-pass ability from the Flyers' end, his play for Philadelphia will be that much more valuable.

Carkner's puckhandling and skating continue to improve, but neither so much that it can compensate for the other; Terry is best moving the puck and leaving the rushing to others.

Carkner's skating is only slightly better than average at the NHL level, and improved quickness and foot speed would aid him in this category. He compensates for skating flaws by holding his position and not challenging, but Carkner would be a better defenseman if he could better close the gap on the puck carrier.

Last on the finesse list would be Carkner's scoring ability. Terry doesn't drive the puck as well as his size and strength would indicate, and — if he plays a full season and continues with power play time — he'll net 10-13 goals.

THE PHYSICAL GAME

Physically strong and very tough, Carkner's only flaw here is that he needs to be reminded to play to his size. Not that he isn't willing — he may be one of the most willing players in the NHL. Rather, his concentration lapses and Carkner forgets to do what he does best.

He clears the front of the net well and can be mean while doing so, and Carkner makes his physical play more effective by being able to make a play after a hit. He will take the puck away from most players along the boards.

He will fight, and can hold his own against the NHL's heavyweights.

THE INTANGIBLES

Though occasionally prone to making a big error (note the lapsed concentration again), Carkner is nevertheless a tremendously dedicated player with a great team attitude and work ethic. He sacrifices to win, and is capable of scaling greater NHL heights.

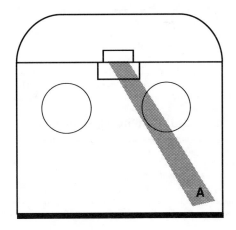

JEFF CHYCHRUN

Yrs. of NHL service: 2
Born: LaSalle, Quebec, Canada; May 3, 1966
Position: Defenseman
Height: 6-4
Weight: 212
Uniform no.: 6
Shoots: right

Career statistics:

GP	G	A	TP	PIM
163	3	11	14	503

1989-90 statistics:

GP	G	A	TP	+/-	PIM	PP	SH	GW	GT	S	PCT
79	2	7	9	-12	250	0	0	1	0	52	3.8

LAST SEASON

Second on the club in PIM total (first among defensemen, fifth among defensemen in NHL). Plus/minus rating was team's second worst, worst among defensemen.

THE FINESSE GAME

Chychrun's finesse game is a limited one, limited both by his skills and by his imagination. He's a no better than average skater in both directions, lacking the foot speed and agility that would move his skating to a higher level. He'll have trouble with the League's faster, shiftier forwards because of his trouble turning, and he can be deked because of that.

His hand skills don't do much to offset his foot skills, and his reads of the ice — particularly in an offensive scheme — add little to his physical finesse abilities. When he succeeds finesse-wise — which is to say, when he rids himself of the puck successfully — it is because he has not overstepped his personal limits. As long as Jeff sticks to forcing the play wide and making the first safe pass he can, he's not a defensive liability. But he'll make mistakes if he's rushed (and must be paired with a more talented partner), and he can be driven off the blue line because of his limited mobility.

His offensive ability is almost non-existent, mostly because Chychrun doesn't attempt any offense. He's the safety valve at the point, and rarely shoots the puck.

THE PHYSICAL GAME

Chychrun is a very tough player, one who has taken on all of the NHL's heavyweights and has become one of the NHL's top fighters himself. But his physical play is not limited to fighting. He moves players from the front of the net extremely well, but he is apt (both in the crease and in the corners) to take dumb penalties by being too tough.

Improved finesse skills would make his physical play that much more impressive.

THE INTANGIBLES

Don't get us wrong — we're certainly not saying Chychrun has nothing but toughness to contribute at the NHL level; in fact, he's already improved during the time he's been in the League. However, in order to remain a full-time player (and thus retain his effectiveness), Jeff must be able to consistently keep up with the play around him — and to improve as the League improves.

MURRAY CRAVEN

Yrs. of NHL service: 7
Born: Medicine Hat, Alta., Canada; July 20, 1964
Position: Left wing
Height: 6-2
Weight: 185
Uniform no.: 32
Shoots: left

Career statistics:

GP	G	A	TP	PIM
480	134	233	367	266

1989-90 statistics:

GP	G	A	TP	+/-	PIM	PP	SH	GW	GT	S	PCT
76	25	50	75	2	42	7	2	3	0	175	14.3

LAST SEASON

Games played total was three-season high, assist mark career best. Finished second on team in scoring.

THE FINESSE GAME

Craven is a good finesse player, the kind who can be a constant (if not necessarily explosive) offensive threat. His above-average skating keys that game, and his balance and agility key his skating. Despite his relative height, Craven is a shifty skater. Balance is important here, and Craven's quickness and foot speed also give him a fair degree of overall speed as well.

Complementing his skating skill is his puckhandling ability. He handles the puck well at top speed, and combines these two physical skills with his on-ice smarts to find and exploit the holes; he reads the ice well and, for that reason, may be better at center.

That said, Craven reduces his playmaking potential by too frequently going one-on-one against the defense, and by shooting more than passing — which is not necessarily bad, because Craven has goal-scorer's hands. He shoots well off the pass, especially on the power play.

His defense does not suffer because of his offense.

THE PHYSICAL GAME

The temptation is to say that the word "physical" comes after the word "pass" in Craven's dictionary — and that he's missing that page. While not a physical player, Craven is imposing himself somewhat upon the opposition while against the boards — as a winger, he must. But he still won't initiate much contact, and he prefers to work outside the congested areas.

Rick Tocchet, he ain't.

THE INTANGIBLES

Craven is very bright, and his play-reading ability reflects that. The departure of Brian Propp, combined with the thus far disappointing development of Scott Mellanby, helps cement Craven in his top line position. His ability as one of the Flyers' few tested offensive talents further makes him a valuable player.

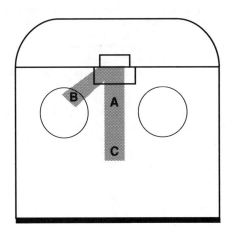

PER-ERIK EKLUND

Yrs. of NHL service: 5
Born: Stockholm, Sweden; March 22, 1963
Position: Center
Height: 5-10
Weight: 175
Uniform no.: 9
Shoots: left

Career statistics:

GP	G	A	TP	PIM
362	80	214	294	65

1989-90 statistics:

GP	G	A	TP	+/-	PIM	PP	SH	GW	GT	S	PCT
70	23	39	62	7	16	5	3	2	0	126	18.3

LAST SEASON

Games played total tied career low (missed three games with groin injury, five with knee injury). Goal total was career high. Plus/minus was club's third-best, best among forwards. Tied for club lead (Ilkka Sinisalo) for shorthanded goals.

THE FINESSE GAME

Eklund is a very skilled player, gifted in all finesse areas. His skating is of the shifty style because of his agility and lateral ability. Balance is obviously the key here, as Eklund's style is more one of darting than breakaway speed.

He handles the puck exceptionally well while in motion, and can exploit the smallest openings because of that ability. Additionally, his excellent ice vision (particularly peripherally) and superb anticipation combine to show him those openings. In the parlance, he has great hockey sense — and that is best demonstrated by his work during man-advantage situations.

We said last year that Eklund should shoot more, and he did increase his SOG total marginally (1.8 SOG per game, up from 1.53 during the 1988-89 season). He could still do better.

THE PHYSICAL GAME

Eklund is a small player and plays that way; he can be intimidated in physical situations. Because of that, he needs to be used properly by the coaching staff — and, to date in the NHL, has been.

THE INTANGIBLES

Because of his physical limitations (and especially in an ever-growing NHL) Eklund may never grow into more than a talented-but-confined-to-a-role player. His tendency to take some nights off doesn't help either. Nevertheless, he remains Philadelphia's most innately talented forward, and maybe the Flyers' most talented player overall.

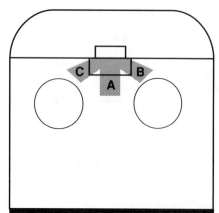

RON HEXTALL

Yrs. of NHL service: 4
Born: Brandon, Manitoba, Canada; May 3, 1964
Position: Goaltender
Height: 6-3
Weight: 192
Uniform no.: 27
Catches: left

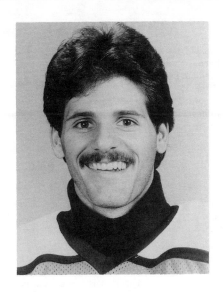

Career statistics:

GP	MINS	G	S0	AVG	A	PIM
200	11,534	629	1	3.27	20	335

1989-90 statistics:

GP	MINS	AVG	W	L	T	SO	GA	SA	SAPCT	PIM
8	419	4.15	4	4	1	0	29	219	.868	14

LAST SEASON

Games and minutes played totals were career lows (League suspension, pulled hamstring, recurring groin injury).

THE PHYSICAL GAME

If — other than stopping the puck — there can be trends in goaltending, then Hextall is the prototypical 1990s NHL goalie (as also exmplified by goalers like Patrick Roy and Sean Burke): great size combined with outstanding athletic skills.

By mixing a solid, standup angle game with his outstanding reflex ability, Hextall forms a perfect package to thwart today's stronger, faster and harder NHL shooters. He maximizes his size by moving from the net to cut the shooter's angles, but he also uses his superior skating ability and foot speed (all keyed by his excellent balance) to make the reaction saves necessary on deflections and tips. He moves around his crease very well, and easily regains his stance after going to the ice.

His puckhandling is only the most obvious of his hand skills. He's good-to-very-good with both hands, though his main weakness is high to the stickside. He handles the puck better than any other goalie in the game, but can also be guilty of overhandling it. Still, he is a scripted part of the Flyers' play — especially on the penalty killing unit where he kills time by stickhandling.

THE MENTAL GAME

Ron is outstandingly tough mentally, capable of winning games singlehandedly. Anticipation and vision — what in skaters is called hockey sense — are also keys to his game, and allow Hextall to stop most every stoppable shot and many unstoppable ones as well. He comes back tougher after bad outings and bad goals.

While he has improved control of his temper, he can still be rattled by physical contact. His tantrums, however, have grown fewer and fewer in number as his NHL tenure has lengthened.

THE INTANGIBLES

Last year was obviously a wash, one that — for Hextall — began badly (NHL suspensions followed by his contract holdout) and ended worse. While a subject of trade rumors for several seasons, Hextall is a committed strong leader for the Flyers and it is fair to say that Philadelphia's entire game revolves around his extraordinary ability.

MARK HOWE

Yrs. of NHL service: 11
Born: Detroit, Mich., USA; May 28, 1955
Position: Defenseman
Height: 5-11
Weight: 185
Uniform no.: 2
Shoots: left

Career statistics:

GP	G	A	TP	PIM
746	182	461	643	391

1989-90 statistics:

GP	G	A	TP	+/-	PIM	PP	SH	GW	GT	S	PCT
40	7	21	28	22	24	3	1	1	0	63	11.1

LAST SEASON

Games played total was lowest of career (Howe's third consecutive year of declining attendance; recurring back injury); all point totals were correspondingly low. He led the club in plus/minus.

THE FINESSE GAME

Though gradually succumbing to age, Howe remains an excellent skater, certainly still among the best of the NHL's defensemen. He combines agility with excellent hand skills to become very dangerous with the puck, and — as such — remains the key man for developing Philly's offense.

Mark rushes the puck excellently, and he'll stay as a fourth attacker even after he's forced to dish it off because his speed gets him back into the defensive play.

He combines his hand skills with excellent vision and anticipation to become an excellent passer, especially (and this is his greatest value) in getting the puck from the Flyers' defensive zone. He's Philadelphia's most consistent player in that area.

Offensively, he has a low and accurate shot from the left point (perfect for deflections), and he'll sneak into the slot if he can. Mark also likes to tail away to the right wing boards for a shot, because he'll get a better angle at the net.

His finesse skills make him a specialty teams natural.

THE PHYSICAL GAME

Not known as a physical player, Howe nevertheless applies himself physically. He won't crush anyone with a hit, but Mark takes the body along the boards (and he's aided here by his ability to remain balanced and in position to make a play from the boards). Because he's just average at clearing the front of the net, Mark can be overpowered by stronger forwards. He can also be worn down by constant physical abuse.

By pairing him with a stronger, more physical defense partner (first Brad McCrimmon and now Kjell Samuelsson), Howe is free to play the game he knows best — that of starting plays, rather than stopping them.

THE INTANGIBLES

This report — in light of Howe's abbreviated 1989-90 season — has been left virtually untouched. His health remains a factor (though last season he was on pace to maintain his 58 points-per-season average), and a healthy Howe is critical to Philadelphia success. At 35 years old, however, he may find himself working for another organization this season.

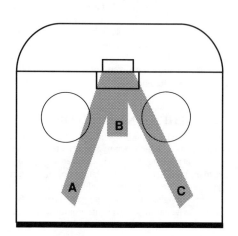

TIM KERR

Yrs. of NHL service: 10
Born: Windsor, Ontario, Canada; January 5, 1960
Position: Right wing/center
Height: 6-3
Weight: 230
Uniform no.: 12
Shoots: right

Career statistics:

GP	G	A	TP	PIM
574	353	273	626	569

1989-90 statistics:

GP	G	A	TP	+/-	PIM	PP	SH	GW	GT	S	PCT
40	24	24	48	-3	34	9	0	2	2	162	14.8

LAST SEASON

Games played total was third lowest of career (missed at least 37 games with recurring shoulder injury), but he still finished second on the club in power play goals and fourth in shots on goal.

THE FINESSE GAME

Kerr's career — or what's left of it — is based on his shot, and that's why his shoulder problems are so devastating. He may not have an equal in the NHL in terms of quickness of release, and it is that skill alone that makes him a threat when he has the puck. He'll cash in on any loose puck around the net, and he certainly gets his chances — as his SOG totals have always indicated.

His skating skill is nowhere near his shooting skill, particularly in the areas of agility and lateral movement. Kerr is a straight-ahead skater, without exceptional speed, whose greatest skating asset is his sheer bulk; when he gets driving to the net he's unstoppable. Otherwise, he's no better than average as an NHL skater.

He can be a selfish player, although his reach and size let him work the corners fairly well. He protects the puck well, but cannot stickhandle exceptionally well.

Kerr is not a reliable defensive player.

THE PHYSICAL GAME

Despite his overwhelming physical size and strength (only the NHL's biggest and strongest defensemen can even attempt to control him), Kerr is not a dominating physical player in the way teammate Rick Tocchet is. Not only doesn't Kerr impose himself physically, he is far more likely to retaliate with his stick than he is with his body or fists.

His strong hands and arms also allow the Flyers to use him on offensive zone faceoffs, especially on the power play.

THE INTANGIBLES

His comebacks speak about his dedication and work ethic, but his sometimes selfish and sulky play can be less than team-oriented — not good traits in a 29-year-old, wounded, one-dimensional player. He'll play in pain, but his health will always be in question — as might be his continued service with the Flyers.

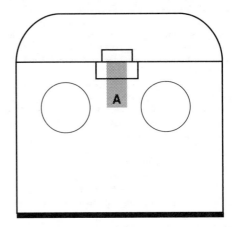

KEN LINSEMAN

Yrs. of NHL service: 12
Born: Kingston, Ontario, Canada; August 11, 1958
Position: Center
Height: 5-11
Weight: 180
Uniform no.: 18
Shoots: left

Career statistics:

GP	G	A	TP	PIM
802	249	522	771	1,629

1989-90 statistics:

GP	G	A	TP	+/-	PIM	PP	SH	GW	GT	S	PCT
61	11	25	36	5	96	2	0	0	0	79	13.9

LAST SEASON

Acquired from Boston in exchange for Dave Poulin (Jan. 1990). Games played total was second lowest full-season total of career (missed 14 games with arm injury). Was minus-7 in 29 games with Flyers.

THE FINESSE GAME

Despite a dozen NHL seasons, Linseman remains a superlative skater. He has very good speed, and his one-step skills (lateral movement, agility and quickness) make him one of the League's shiftiest and most difficult to contain skaters. He can turn, change direction, stop and start within a single stride.

His superior puckhandling ability makes his skating better. Linseman performs excellently with the puck at any speed, and he combines those skills with ice vision and anticipation to exploit openings for himself or teammates. His vision and one-step quickness keep the passing lanes open in all situations.

His goal scoring comes from anticipation and quickness, not from great shot selection; he is not good scorer. Linseman gets his goals from in close — deflections and the like (eye/hand coordination help here). He should shoot more.

His checking and defensive game are as solid as his offensive output, and Linseman's play without the puck is strong in all three zones. He is one of the NHL's best faceoff men and will take many of the important defensive zone faceoffs.

THE PHYSICAL GAME

Ken is a very physical player — certainly playing bigger than his size — and is unafraid to hit in the corners. He is also mean with his stick and elbows, doing whatever necessary to stop an opponent — like pitchforking the defenseman after he gets rid of the puck. He is also one of the NHL's best holders, making him a frustrating player to play against. Linseman is not, however, a fighter.

His physical game is made better by the fact that Linseman certainly has the hand skills to make plays from the corners.

THE INTANGIBLES

Injuries have become a concern for Linseman, and he must remain healthy to be of value to Philadelphia.

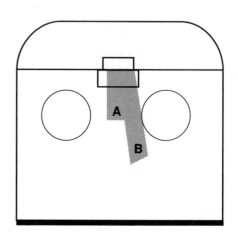

SCOTT MELLANBY

Yrs. of NHL service: 4
Born: Montreal, Quebec, Canada; June 11, 1966
Position: Right wing
Height: 6-1
Weight: 205
Uniform no.: 19
Shoots: right

Career statistics:

GP	G	A	TP	PIM
281	63	93	156	539

1989-90 statistics:

GP	G	A	TP	+/-	PIM	PP	SH	GW	GT	S	PCT
57	6	17	23	-4	77	0	0	1	0	104	5.8

LAST SEASON

Games played total was full-season career low; ditto point totals (recovery from off-season arm injury).

THE FINESSE GAME

Mellanby brings a number of weapons to bear in his finesse game, although all must still be described as nearer potential than fulfilled. He reads the ice well and can get into position to score, and Mellanby has the hands to do 25-30 goals worth of damage a year. He gets his shot off quickly and strongly (or did, pre-injury), and Mellanby has the hand skills to score from in tight as well.

He is not a graceful skater by NHL standards; rather he is a driving skater, and that power generates speed for him down the wing. He would improve as a skater (and, therefore, as a player) if he could improve his balance and foot speed. The result would be greater agility and quickness to complement his current straight-ahead style.

Mellanby's defensive game — as with his overall game — has a tendency to waver. Though he can be defensively reliable, Mellanby can also make mistakes in his positional play in all three zones.

THE PHYSICAL GAME

Scott is a hitter, which is a good thing in a player his size. His upper body strength and strength on his skates serve him both along the wood and in his drives to the net, and he can out-muscle many of his opponents in both areas.

He will fight, but isn't a particularly pugnacious player.

THE INTANGIBLES

We said last season that Mellanby has all the tools to be an exceptional NHLer, and that the 1989-90 season was a critical one for him. His off-season arm injury (suffered in a bar fight) essentially short-circuited last season. This year, we say the same thing.

One important ingredient for Mellanby's success (and one reason why his performances can be erratic) will be his willingness to motivate himself — he needs to be pumped up on some nights. Self-motivation is the sign of a mature professional, and that maturity must precede Mellanby's improvement as a player.

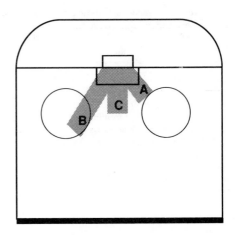

GORD MURPHY

Yrs. of NHL service: 2
Born: Willowdale, Ontario, Canada; March 23, 1967
Position: Defenseman
Height: 6-2
Weight: 190
Uniform no.: 3
Shoots: right

Career statistics:

GP	G	A	TP	PIM
150	18	58	76	163

1989-90 statistics:

GP	G	A	TP	+/-	PIM	PP	SH	GW	GT	S	PCT
75	14	27	41	-7	95	4	0	1	0	160	8.8

LAST SEASON

Goal, point and PIM totals were career bests. Led defensemen in scoring and shots on goal. Missed one game with flu.

THE FINESSE GAME

Increased confidence that comes from understanding of the NHL is the reason Murphy contributed the way he did to the Flyers' offense last season. He has good offensive skills, if not outstanding ones, but judgement and intelligence make his assets better.

Gord's not a flashy skater, but his foot speed has improved and allows him to get to the puck for a first pass, to step up and close the gap on the puck carrier, to contain the point and to rush the puck from the zone. Poise and patience help Murphy here, and will continue to guide his improvement.

His intelligence is evident in his passing choices, and he gets a good read of the ice both from the offensive blue line and as he moves back through the neutral zone.

His experience and adaptation to the NHL has also improved his scoring ability. By reading faster he sees he has to release his shot quicker, and by releasing his shot quicker he's scoring more.

THE PHYSICAL GAME

Despite his lean build — there's not a lot of muscle on his frame — Murphy is pretty tough in front of his own net. He could afford to improve his upper body strength for his battles in the traffic areas (especially as the NHL's forwards get bigger), but that's not to say Gord can't handle himself in the crease (his balance helps here).

He is unafraid of the opposition and will go into the corners with anyone.

THE INTANGIBLES

Murphy is a quality kid, really coachable with a solid work ethic. He's improved dramatically during his short NHL tenure, and everything about him indicates he will continue to do so.

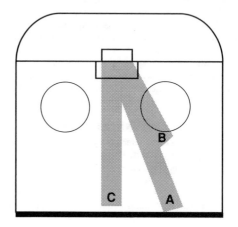

PETE PEETERS

Yrs. of NHL service: 11
Born: Edmonton, Alta., Canada; August 17, 1957
Position: Goaltender
Height: 6-1
Weight: 195
Uniform no.: 33
Catchs: left

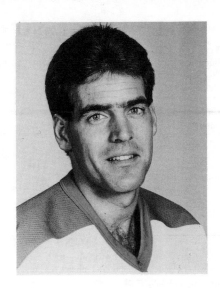

Career statistics:

GP	MINS	G	SO	AVG	A	PIM
463	26,429	1,362	20	3.09	13	190

1989-90 statistics:

GP	MINS	AVG	W	L	T	SO	GA	SA	SAPCT	PIM
24	1,140	3.74	1	13	5	1	71	606	.883	2

LAST SEASON

Signed by Flyers as free agent, summer 1989. Games played total was full-season career low, goals against average second highest of career. Had club's only shutout.

THE PHYSICAL GAME

Like stablemate Ron Hextall, Peeters has envious size for an NHL goaltender. But, unlike Hextall, Peeters is a standup goaltender who rarely leaves his feet. He plays an angle game almost to a fault and has a very strong first-save game, containing rebounds or leaving loose pucks for the defense.

Peeters has good hand quickness and he handles the puck well when he leaves the net, making good passes and helping his defense.

Strangely, because he is a good skater, Peeters' foot work is suspect; he's very vulnerable once his feet are moving. Peeters doesn't handle the puck well at all when it is shot at his feet, and he allows rebounds by failing to clear the puck to the corner. His lack of foot speed and lateral movement across his crease make low shots to the net's corners — and scrambles in front — almost sure scoring plays.

In the game's parlance, he has trouble with his "short game", — passouts from behind the net, wraparounds and scrambles. All these are plays around the net where footwork is key.

THE MENTAL GAME

When he maintains his concentration, Peeters can be very sharp. When his concentration wavers, so too does his game. He's demonstrated that he can maintain that mental toughness through long stretches (as in the 1979-80 season during which he went 27 games without a loss, and the 1982-83 season when he won 40 games and went 31 contests without a defeat).

But he has also had difficulty gaining extended playoff success and, in fact, his playoff goals against average is higher than his regular season average. That calls into question his big save capability.

THE INTANGIBLES

As a player, Peeters is an enigma. After all, which performances are the true barometer of his ability? He's got a good work ethic and is a good team man, but could easily be the odd man out for the Flyers because of the presence of Ron Hextall and Ken Wregget.

KJELL SAMUELSSON

Yrs. of NHL service: 5
Born: Tyngsryd, Sweden; October 18, 1958
Position: Defenseman
Height: 6-6
Weight: 235
Uniform no.: 28
Shoots: right

Career statistics:

GP	G	A	TP	PIM
294	17	67	84	561

1989-90 statistics:

GP	G	A	TP	+/-	PIM	PP	SH	GW	GT	S	PCT
66	5	17	22	20	91	0	0	1	0	88	5.7

LAST SEASON

Games played total was full-season career low (missed 13 games with shoulder injury), but point totals were second highest of career. Plus/minus rating was club's second best.

THE FINESSE GAME

Smart is the best way to describe Samuelsson's vastly underrated game, because those smarts make his skills better. He is a much better skater than generally given credit for, and it is his skating that makes him so difficult to get around. Though far from overwhelmingly fast or quick, Samuelsson still closes the gap on the opposition in order to force plays.

Though his skill with the puck is as modest as his skill on his skates, Samuelsson makes the most of that puck skill by making the quick and easy plays. Kjell won't carry the puck, but will make the correct pass to an open winger. He'll get power play time because of that, but more to act as the safety valve than as an offensive force.

He will score a handful of goals on an average slap shot.

THE PHYSICAL GAME

In his own way, Samuelsson is a pretty tough player. He plays hurt and is unafraid in physical contests, although he doesn't fight and is more of a pusher and holder than is a hitter. His fantastic reach makes him a great pokechecker, and combines with his skating to make him almost impossible to beat one-one-one; he is omnipresent.

THE INTANGIBLES

Samuelsson succeeds by sticking to the basics and by doing the things that will make him successful. He's a very effective player, certainly Philadelphia's most dependable defenseman inside the team's blue line, and he complements his abilities with a good work ethic and willingness to sacrifice.

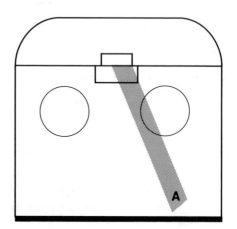

ILKKA SINISALO

Yrs. of NHL service: 9
Born: Valeakoski, Finland; July 10, 1958
Position: Right wing
Height: 6-0
Weight: 200
Uniform no.: 23
Shoots: left

Career statistics:

GP	G	A	TP	PIM
526	199	210	409	180

1989-90 statistics:

GP	G	A	TP	+/-	PIM	PP	SH	GW	GT	S	PCT
59	23	23	46	6	26	4	3	4	0	102	22.5

LAST SEASON

Shooting percentage was best among club's regulars. He tied for team lead (Pelle Eklund) in shorthanded goals. Missed 10 games with a knee injury, three games with collarbone injury.

THE FINESSE GAME

Skating skill — particularly speed — is the key to Sinisalo's game. He's fast from the get-go, and Sinisalo can use his speed in either an offensive or defensive game plan. Sinisalo also has the agility and lateral movement to complement his straight-ahead ability; he cuts well to the net.

Second to his skating ability is his shot, quickly released and accurate, as his shooting percentage attests; he loves the upper right hand corner of the net, and his hand speed is an advantage in the close quarters around the enemy net.

His hand and stick skills combine with his intelligence (which itself is a combination of experience, vision and anticipation) to make him valuable in both power play and penalty killing situations.

THE PHYSICAL GAME

The downside of Sinisalo's game, especially as he gets older and even more prone to injury. Though strong on his skates, Sinisalo does little work in the trenches or along the wood; he is essentially a perimeter player.

THE INTANGIBLES

He's never played a full season during his NHL career, and it's been four seasons since he played at least 70 games. Though he can contribute when healthy, his health remains a question mark and combines with his age to spell the coming end of his "full-time" career.

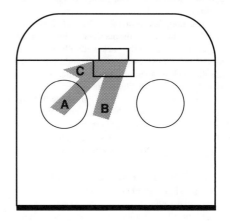

DERRICK SMITH

Yrs. of NHL service: 6
Born: Scarborough, Ontario, Canada; January 22, 1965
Position: Left wing
Height: 6-2
Weight: 215
Uniform no.: 24
Shoots: left

Career statistics:

GP	G	A	TP	PIM
422	69	77	146	301

1989-90 statistics:

GP	G	A	TP	+/-	PIM	PP	SH	GW	GT	S	PCT
55	3	6	9	-15	32	0	0	0	0	72	4.2

LAST SEASON

Games played, all point totals and PIM mark were career lows. Missed 15 games with ankle injury, six games with rib injury. Minus-15 was club's worst.

THE FINESSE GAME

Let us begin by saying that Smith is one of the NHL's top defensive wingers — plus/minus rating aside. He is a tireless skater and very strong on his skates, making him an exceptional checker away from the puck. His insistent skating ability keeps him in the opposition's face. His puck pursuit is strong, making him a fine forechecker.

That said, Smith is a fine example of "Look Ma, no hands." His ability with the puck is very limited, neither shooting nor handling the puck well; if he had to make the NHL on his puck work, Smith wouldn't. He can run with the puck in a straight line, but that is about the extent of Derrick's stickhandling ability.

His shot isn't much better, and he will have to pounce on the loose pucks his checking creates in order to score. He lacks the confidence that would breed the patience necessary for scoring success, and is — in fact — perfectly happy to be a defensive player.

THE PHYSICAL GAME

Smith is a very physical player, and his insistent hitting will wear down the opposition. He is very strong along the boards, and credit must be given not only to his physical strength but also to his balance on his skates. That balance allows Smith to apply his hitting ability yet remain vertical and in the play after collisions.

He shines in physical contests and regularly out-muscles the opposition, but Smith is not a fighter.

THE INTANGIBLES

Smith is a tireless worker, a role player who is above average in his role—limited though it is. A player of his ability will always have a place to play in the NHL, despite his essentially silent contributions.

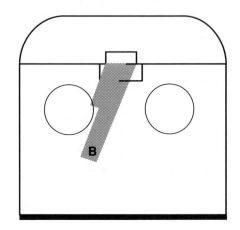

RON SUTTER

Yrs. of NHL service: 7
Born: Viking, Alta., Canada; December 2, 1963
Position: Center
Height: 6-0
Weight: 180
Uniform no.: 14
Shoots: right

Career statistics:

GP	G	A	TP	PIM
475	120	195	315	762

1989-90 statistics:

GP	G	A	TP	+/-	PIM	PP	SH	GW	GT	S	PCT
75	22	26	48	2	104	0	2	6	0	157	14.0

LAST SEASON

Games played total (highest in four seasons) tied second highest of career (missed time with eye and groin injuries); ditto goal total. Led club in game-winners.

THE FINESSE GAME

Like each of the Sutters, Ron's total as a player is greater than the sum of his parts — particularly in the finesse game. Sutter is not a glamorous skater, but his less-than-fluid skating stride doesn't hinder him in his exceptional puck pursuit. Lacking from that stride is the agility and quickness that add up to finesse player finesse ability. Improved balance would make him a better skater. He doesn't have great speed, but he is quick to jump through holes.

So too would improved skating help his offensive game, making up for his lack of NHL elite level hand skills; Sutter can be a little tough with the puck. Neither his hands nor his feet will carry him past a defender, so Sutter's better off leaving the puckhandling to a teammate.

Because of his puck pursuit (and Sutter's play without the puck is the foundation of his finesse game), Ron will force scoring opportunities. He'll have to convert the loose pucks he forces near the net, because he lacks the ability to blow the puck past a goaltender from farther out. He must be offensively opportunistic.

Sutter is an excellent faceoff man, one of the game's best; hand speed and eye/hand coordination are the keys here, aided by his wide stance — he gets down almost to the blade on his stick when he positions himself for faceoffs.

THE PHYSICAL GAME

Though neither exceptionally big nor especially tough (he is loath to drop his gloves), Sutter is an extremely physical forward, hitting at every opportunity. He willingly takes a pounding in his checking role, and will go into the corners against anyone — regardless of size.

That willingness may very well be the root of Sutter's injury problems.

THE INTANGIBLES

He is an irritating and annoying player to play against, and many would credit his yapping and refusal to back up his generally obnoxious behavior for that annoying reputation. But he's also annoying to play against because he is successful in his role.

His balance of credible offense and checking ability make him valuable to Philadelphia. His team philosophy and intensity add to that value.

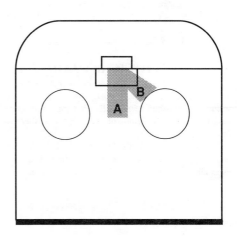

RICK TOCCHET

Yrs. of NHL service: 6
Born: Scarborough, Ontario, Canada; April 9, 1964
Position: Right wing
Height: 6-0
Weight: 205
Uniform no.: 22
Shoots: right

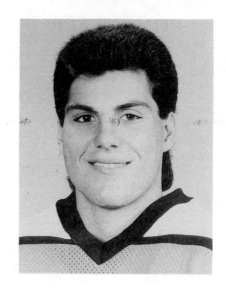

Career statistics:

GP	G	A	TP	PIM
419	162	200	362	1,431

1989-90 statistics:

GP	G	A	TP	+/-	PIM	PP	SH	GW	GT	S	PCT
75	37	59	96	4	196	15	1	0	0	269	13.8

LAST SEASON

Assist and point totals were career highs, games played total tied career high and goal total was second best of career. Led club in goals, assists, points, power play goals and shots on goal. Third on club in PIM total. Missed four games with back spasms.

THE FINESSE GAME

Substance over style is the best way to describe Tocchet's finesse game. He's not a great skater at the NHL level (his choppy stride is the reason for that), but we certainly don't mean he's a poor skater. Rather, his skating gets the job done — taking him to the net and in and out of corners (frequently with passengers). His skating strength combines with his power so that Rick runs over pretty much anybody.

Most noticeable of his finesse skills is Tocchet's wrist shot — accurate, hard and fast, and made better by Tocchet's improved ability to shoot off the pass and while in motion. As his SOG total attests, he shoots quickly and often.

While not necessarily a gifted playmaker or smart player (in terms of reading situations before they develop), Tocchet uses his teammates fairly well and is unafraid to be patient when holding the puck.

THE PHYSICAL GAME

The physical game is the key to Tocchet's success, and he plays that game robustly — and at a level virtually unmatched in the NHL. He controls the corners and the boards because of his strength, and there is no one he will not hit.

Tocchet is a ferocious hitter — he hurts people when he hits them — and his strength makes him especially effective in traffic; it also is the contributing factor to his shot, which he can deliver even while being checked.

He is also one of the NHL's true heavyweights in terms of fighting, but he can forced into poor penalties.

THE INTANGIBLES

Tocchet is among the NHL's elite players, certainly to be graded with an "A" if grades were being awarded. He would be a front-line player on any club, and a certain 50-goal and 100-point scorer on a more successful team.

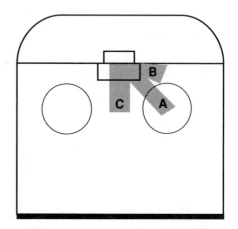

KEN WREGGET

Yrs. of NHL service: 6
Born: Brandon, Man., Canada; March 25, 1964
Position: Goaltender
Height: 6-1
Weight: 195
Uniform no.: 35
Catches: left

Career statistics:

GP	MINS	G	SO	AVG	A	PIM
254	14,014	975	2	4.17	15	118

1989-90 statistics:

GP	MINS	AVG	W	L	T	SO	GA	SA	SAPCT	PIM
51	2,961	3.42	22	24	3	0	169	1,560	.892	12

LAST SEASON

Goals-against average was career low. Finished fourth in NHL in shots faced. Missed time with a pulled hamstring.

THE PHYSICAL GAME

A goaltending catch-phrase is "squaring himself to the puck". What that indicates is a goalie who plays a standup, angle-cutting style, a goalie whose style of play is such that he challenges the shooter and, with economy of movement, just lets the puck hit him. Wregget is just such a goalie.

Wregget has good size and he maximizes it by coming out of the net and staying on his feet. He uses his size to advantage on screen shots and other play around the net by moving to the shooter.

That's important, because he's not a great skater. He doesn't regain his stance particularly well when getting off the ice, and he's in trouble when flopping around the crease which results in trouble with his short game. He does, however, move well in and out of the net — as well as across the crease. When he stays on his feet, he regains his stance well for the second save.

Wregget is not exceptionally skilled with his hands, but he does have a good glove. He does have trouble, however, containing shots to his glove and will often be forced to make second saves off those uncontrolled rebounds. He doesn't handle the puck well, but he does have the strength to ice it.

THE MENTAL GAME

Wregget sees the puck well (one reason why he's so successful coming across the crease or getting his glove in front of shots), and he combines that vision with good anticipation to make the most of his positional play. He's also canny enough to knock the net off its moorings once a twice a game as the situation warrants.

He's demonstrated through various playoffs that he can carry a club, but his tendency to pressure himself often leads to breakdowns on his part. He goes beyond concentration to worry, and that takes a lot out of him — so much so that he can be completely out of gas within the game's opening minutes and has to get pulled because he has nothing left.

THE INTANGIBLES

Wregget's a hard worker, a player who would be a number one goalie on any team without Ron Hextall. Trade rumors continue to abound regarding the Flyers' goaltending situation, so Wregget may get the chance to be that No. 1 goalie — in Philadelphia or elsewhere — within the foreseeable future.

PITTSBURGH PENGUINS

TOM BARRASSO

Yrs. of NHL service: 7
Born: Boston, Mass., USA; March 31, 1965
Position: Goaltender
Height: 6-3
Weight: 206
Uniform no.: 35
Catches: right

Career statistics:

GP	MINS	G	SO	AVG	A	PIM
334	19,163	1,108	13	3.47	22	239

1989-90 statistics:

GP	MINS	AVG	W	L	T	SO	GA	SA	SAPCT	PIM
24	1,294	4.68	7	12	3	0	101	748	.865	8

LAST SEASON

Games played was career low (missed 24 games with hand injury, plus time off for personal leave).

THE PHYSICAL GAME

Great size and foot work are the keys to Barrasso's goaltending success. He uses his bulk to fill the net when challenging shooters, and he uses his quick feet to cover the bottom of the goal. That's important, because Barrasso is a butterfly goalie, going to the ice often.

He recovers quickly when down, regaining his stance and/or readying himself for the second shot. He does have a tendency to be vulnerable when the play moves across the net (because he's already on the ice), leaving the net's corners unguarded. His size works for him here too, though, because even when on his knees he takes up a lot of net. His glove hand is one of the better in the NHL, though he has occasionally demonstrated a tendency to allow long shots high to that side.

Puckhandling is the second strong aspect of his game; he's the second best puckhandler in the League behind Ron Hextall. Barrasso is capable of making long breakaway passes to his forwards, but he doesn't demonstrate the same puck control with his rebounds; he can be careless with rebounds off his upper body, his stick and his pads.

He can also be careless in his angle play, losing his position in the net and giving up the short post.

THE MENTAL GAME

Barrasso is a smart player; he anticipates the play well and generally puts himself in position to see the puck. He fights for every goal and will bounce back from bad games, but he also has a streaky tendency.

He can also be goaded into bad penalties.

THE INTANGIBLES

The biggest question is a difficult one to ask. Barrasso took personal leave from the team last year to accompany his wife and sick daughter as the youngster took cancer treatments. We're certainly not saying that Barrasso should try to ignore his family, but the Pens must be wondering what mental and emotional state Barrasso will be in this season.

He's gone a long way to beating his selfish rap (though critics might confuse his confidence with cockiness), and has gone to great pains to be a better team man.

PHIL BOURQUE

Yrs. of NHL service: 3
Born: Chelmsford, Mass., USA: June 8, 1962
Position: Left wing/defense
Height: 6-1
Weight: 206
Uniform no.: 29
Shoots: left

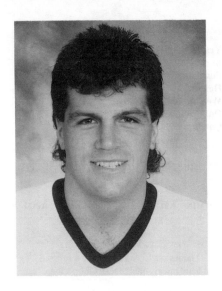

Career statistics:

GP	G	A	TP	PIM
208	45	59	104	271

1989-90 statistics:

GP	G	A	TP	+/-	PIM	PP	SH	GW	GT	S	PCT
76	22	17	39	-7	108	2	1	3	1	110	20.0

LAST SEASON

Goal and PIM totals were career highs. Missed three games with back spasms.

THE FINESSE GAME

Primary among Bourque's finesse skills is his skating. He has good skating strength and a fair dose of speed, so he can be a good forechecker in terms of puck pursuit (and also in penalty killing situations). Not tremendously agile, Bourque is more of a straight-ahead dynamo than he is an artist on skates.

His puckhandling is his other strong suit, and Bourque likes to carry the puck. He'll rush it up-ice, but he can be predictable in his rushes — he'll cut outside and swoop around a defender instead of stutter-stepping or skipping past him (that's where the lack of agility comes in). Compounding that, Bourque doesn't get a great read of the ice when carrying the puck. He's okay with teammates ahead of him, but his playmaking doesn't extend to a complete command of the ice.

He looks to use his teammates, but because he can be forced to bad ice his playmaking skills can be minimized. His speed carries him to the net and the loose pucks that gather there, and it is from that area that he will be most successful as a scorer.

THE PHYSICAL GAME

Bourque is unafraid of contact, and he initiates a lot of physical play in the offensive zone. His skating strength helps him drive through checks when hitting, and it also carries him through checks when being hit. Add his good size and strength, and you have an effective corner and boards player.

THE INTANGIBLES

No one was more adversely affected by Gene Ubriaco's firing than was Bourque. Ubriaco gave Bourque a lot of responsibility, and Bourque responded. His makeup — attitude, work ethic and versatility (he also plays defense) — should be enough to guarantee him a regular spot in the Pens lineup, regardless of who's coaching.

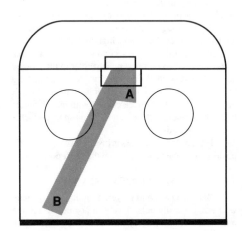

ROB BROWN

Yrs. of NHL service: 3
Born: Kingston, Ontario, Canada; April 10, 1968
Position: Right wing
Height: 5-11
Weight: 185
Uniform no.: 44
Shoots: left

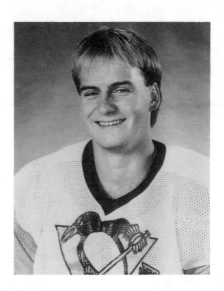

Career statistics:

GP	G	A	TP	PIM
199	106	133	239	276

1989-90 statistics:

GP	G	A	TP	+/-	PIM	PP	SH	GW	GT	S	PCT
80	33	47	80	-10	102	12	0	3	0	157	21.0

LAST SEASON

Finished second on club in goals, fourth in points. One of two (Paul Coffey) Pens to play all 80 games. Tied for first (Mark Recchi) in shooting percentage.

THE FINESSE GAME

Luckily for Brown, he doesn't have to make the NHL on his skating — if he did, he wouldn't make the American League. So what makes Brown an NHLer? His superb hand skill and his ability to get into scoring position.

Brown is always around the net, looking for whatever garbage can be converted into goals. His scorer's sense always puts him where the openings and the puck are, and his soft hands send the puck toward the back of the net in a flash (he's got an excellent release on his shot). Brown needs just the slightest opening to get his shot off and — as his shooting percentage indicates — Brown is exceptionally accurate when he fires.

Unlike most scorers, Brown isn't averse to passing the puck, something he does well. Again, his hands and hockey sense are the keys here. He is a good puckhandler (he certainly doesn't have to worry about his feet out-speeding his hands), making plays in traffic and under pressure — he's not afraid to hold onto the puck.

Except for his balance (which is the second major physical finesse skill that allows him to operate in traffic), his skating is the weakest of his finesse skills. Otherwise, Brown lacks rink-length speed, outstanding quickness or agility.

Though he thinks offense first, Brown does work at his defense. Here is an area where his skating deficiencies show.

THE PHYSICAL GAME

Though lacking good size, Brown willingly plays a physical game. He hits when he can (though he won't overpower anyone with his strength) and — as he demonstrates by working in the crease — he'll certainly take hits to make his plays. Balance is the key to his success, and Brown can score regardless of body position.

He also excels at tipping and deflecting the puck because of his eye/hand coordination, one reason why he'll occasionally take faceoffs.

THE INTANGIBLES

Brown's reputation precedes him. The opposition can't stand him because he's cocky, arrogant and a loudmouth on the ice. His agitation serves to get the opposition off their game, and there's nothing he likes more than to score after someone's taken a shot at him.

Essentially an excellent kid, his work ethic is far from good (especially in practice) but Brown puts out in games. Increased upper body strength would be a benefit because of his work in the trenches.

Some think he's the NHL's most overrated player; we don't agree. We said last year that he's capable of scoring 50 goals a year and, in the near future, Brown should hit that milestone.

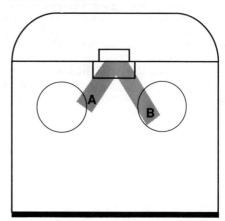

ROD BUSKAS

Yrs. of NHL service: 8
Born: Wetaskiwin, Alberta, Canada; January 7, 1961
Position: Defenseman
Height: 6-1
Weight: 206
Uniform no.: 7
Shoots: right

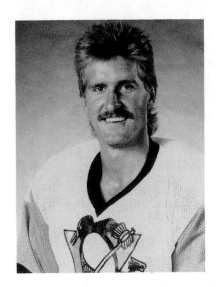

Career statistics:

GP	G	A	TP	PIM
448	16	51	67	995

1989-90 statistics:

GP	G	A	TP	+/-	PIM	PP	SH	GW	GT	S	PCT
23	0	3	3	-3	49	0	0	0	0	12	0.0

LAST SEASON

Games played was career low (34 games with ankle injury). Was traded to Vancouver and then traded back to Pittsburgh.

THE FINESSE GAME

Buskas is a limited finesse player: no better than average as a skater (lacking exceptional agility, quickness or strength); weak — but improved — in passing and puckhandling. To his credit, Buskas makes the most of his modest skills by not making too much of them; he plays within his limits.

Though essentially a one-play player, Buskas has worked to read the play coming at him and has thus improved his sense of the game. Because of that, he'll force the play wide of the net and closes what openings his skating will get him to near the goal.

His offense will come almost completely from the point, but it is practically non-existent. Once in a very great while he'll sneak into the faceoff circle for a shot.

THE PHYSICAL GAME

Here is where Buskas can make his best contributions. His takeouts are strong and he can clear the front of the net, but he will have trouble with the League's bigger forwards in those traffic areas. In essence, he is more of a pusher and shover than he is a punishing hitter.

THE INTANGIBLES

Because of his injury and trades, Buskas' report has remained essentially unchanged. He is a very popular team man, and his initial departure to Vancouver may have been the final straw in the players-versus-management squabbles that cost Tony Esposito and Gene Ubriaco their jobs last season.

Rod, through sheer dint of hard work, has made himself into a fairly dependable fifth or sixth defenseman, but he will always have to work in order to keep his hold on an NHL roster spot.

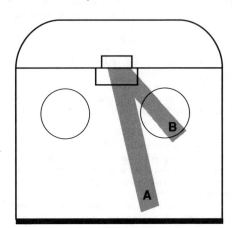

JAY CAUFIELD

Yrs. of NHL service: 2
Born: Lansdale, PA., USA; July 17, 1965
Position: Right wing
Height: 6-4
Weight: 240
Uniform no.: 16
Shoots: right

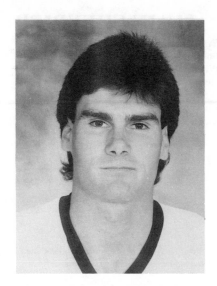

Career statistics:

GP	G	A	TP	PIM
99	4	7	11	453

1989-90 statistics:

GP	G	A	TP	+/-	PIM	PP	SH	GW	GT	S	PCT
37	1	2	3	0	123	0	0	0	0	6	16.7

LAST SEASON

Missed 18 games with a finger injury.

THE FINESSE GAME

There isn't one. By default, Caufield's best skill is his skating — and that's not saying a lot. He doesn't have the balance, the quickness or the agility to skate at the NHL level. About all Jay can do is get up and down the ice — and at 25 years old, that's not going to get much better.

He can't handle the puck while skating, and he has almost no passing skill or sense of the ice. If he scores, it's going to be from in front of the net on a loose puck with the goalie out of position.

THE PHYSICAL GAME

This is why Jay is in the NHL. He doesn't check particularly well (because he has neither the mobility nor the smarts to do), but if he happens to catch someone that check will hurt. He's tremendously strong and in excellent muscular condition — not surprising considering that he was a linebacker in college.

Caufield is Pittsburgh's designated tough guy, but while he's willing to assume that role he's less than the NHL's worst nightmare. For one thing, he doesn't have the balance to be a good fighter (disagreeable though it may be, there's a skill in throwing a punch while on skates). Because of that, Jay can't get all of his strength behind his punches, and his fights become wrestling matches.

THE INTANGIBLES

Quiet and personable off the ice, Caufield knows what his job is on the ice. He accepts that role willingly, and it is that acceptance that keeps him in the NHL; he also works exceptionally hard at improving his skills before, during and after every practice. Of course, he also spars when practice is over. But his lack of skill means he can't be used in skating games — or in close ones — and Caufield will always be vulnerable to replacement because of that.

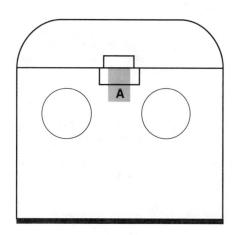

ALAIN CHEVRIER

Yrs. of NHL service: 4
Born: Cornwall, Ontario, Canada; April 23, 1961
Position: Goaltender
Height: 5-8
Weight: 170
Uniform no.: 30
Catches: left

Career statistics:

GP	MINS	G	SO	AVG	A	PIM
231	12,094	834	2	4.14	11	35

1989-90 statistics:

GP	MINS	AVG	W	L	T	SO	GA	SA	SAPCT	PIM
42	2,060	4.25	17	16	3	0	146	987	.850	8

LAST SEASON

Acquired from Chicago at trading deadline. Games played total was second lowest of career.

THE PHYSICAL GAME

Chevrier is an angle goaltender, though he doesn't challenge shooters as well as he could. One reason for that is because of his skating. Since he is only an average skater, Alain can't be overly aggressive when challenging because he won't get back into the net in time for rebounds or the second save. He does have good balance on his feet and can regain his stance quickly after sprawling.

His reflexes are good and his glove hand is fairly solid, but he'll have trouble with low shots just inside the posts and high to the stick side (again, because these spaces are open due to his not cutting the angle well enough).

He's not afraid to go behind the net and cut the puck off as it rips around the boards and he can handle the puck fairly well in getting it to his defensemen.

He stays in the net too deep and too long on screen shots, hoping for an extra second of time for the reflex save and to get a better view. He would do better to square himself to the puck.

THE MENTAL GAME

Chevrier suffers concentration lapses that result in successive goals, or goals from bad angles. He can give a good 15-20 minutes and then his concentration starts to slip and his confidence begins to go. Additionally, he's not mentally strong enough to play for long stretches — say, four or more games consecutively. He does not do well when he comes into a game cold.

He anticipates the play well and is especially sharp that way in action around his net. By and large, Alain will come back strongly from a poor outing, but his inability to hold his concentration is bound to affect him again.

THE INTANGIBLES

He may not be pleased about it, but Chevrier should expect to serve as caddie to Tom Barrasso. That position hasn't thrilled Chevrier in the past, and there's no reason to imagine it will please him now either.

PAUL COFFEY

Yrs. of NHL service: 10
Born: Weston, Ontario, Canada; June 1, 1961
Position: Defenseman
Height: 6-0
Weight: 200
Uniform no.: 77
Shoots: left

Career statistics:

GP	G	A	TP	PIM
733	283	669	952	1,074

1989-90 statistics:

GP	G	A	TP	+/-	PIM	PP	SH	GW	GT	S	PCT
80	29	74	103	-25	95	10	0	3	1	324	9.0

LAST SEASON

Led NHL defensemen in goals, assists and points (finished ninth overall in League scoring, fourth overall in assists and third overall in shots on goal). Finished second on club in scoring, first in SOG total. One of two Pens (Rob Brown) to play all 80 games; games played total was five-season high. Plus/minus was club's worst.

THE FINESSE GAME

Skating is unquestionably the best of Coffey's skills, just as Coffey is unquestionably among the NHL's top skaters — he could be no worse than second or third in terms of pure skating. He has explosive acceleration and foot speed, and Coffey combines that speed with incredible balance. The result is phenomenal agility and lateral movement ability. He has the tightest turning radius of any NHL player. He is predictable, in that he likes to break down his right wing.

His offensive ability is based on his skating, and upon his ability to handle the puck while at top speed — which is a skill almost as impressive as his skating. He carries the puck better than any defenseman in the NHL, is an excellent one-touch passer and always looks for a breaking winger or open teammate at the blue line when distributing the puck.

He can score any way from anywhere, and he must shoot the puck to be effective. He'll go to the net with the puck and use his hard, accurate wrist shot, but his laser-precise slap shot is just as effective.

Coffey plays his defense through his skating — taking chances and challenging where no other player could succeed — but he is also prone to getting caught in the offensive zone. He also plays his own game in the defensive zone — looking to break — and the combination of getting caught and rushing early make him unreliable defensively.

THE PHYSICAL GAME

He'll push and shove in the corners, but Coffey is not a physical player. He'll give up the puck to avoid a hit, and can be out-muscled in front of his own net — when he remembers to go to the front of his net to cover the opposing forward camped there.

THE INTANGIBLES

Coffey is a leader for the Pens because of his Stanley Cup and international experience, and he could exercise a little more leadership by shoring up his defensive play during the regular season. He knows how to win in the playoffs (and ups his game appropriately), but that knowledge is rendered useless when the Pens don't make the post-season.

And really — he'd have had to score 25 even-strength points (a total of 128 points total) just to be an even player.

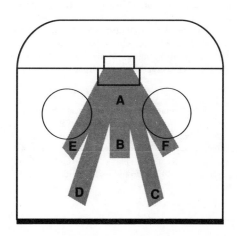

JOHN CULLEN

Yrs. of NHL service: 1
Born: Puslinch, Ontario, Canada; August 2, 1964
Position: Center
Height: 5-10
Weight: 187
Uniform no.: 11
Shoots: right

Career statistics:

GP	G	A	TP	PIM
151	44	97	141	250

1989-90 statistics:

GP	G	A	TP	+/-	PIM	PP	SH	GW	GT	S	PCT
72	32	60	92	-13	138	9	0	4	0	197	16.2

LAST SEASON

Finished third on club in goals, assists, points and shots on goal (21st overall in NHL). Missed seven games with hepatitis.

THE FINESSE GAME

Puck skills are the best of Cullen's finesse abilities, and he demonstrates those abilites well in both even-strength and man-advantage situations. He can carry and work with the puck at full speed, and he has the touch to ease or snap a pass to a teammate with just the smallest opening — hence his power play success. He is a playmaker, and looks for his teammates.

He combines his exceptional puckhandling with better than average (though not as good as his puck work) skating. Though lacking in rink-length speed, Cullen has a high level of agility and quickness. He is a shifty, darting skater, and a difficult one to contain. His balance further complements his hand skills, making him very effective in traffic.

His ice reading and hockey sense combine with his one-step quickness and lateral movement to get to him loose pucks — an area in which he clearly improved last season.

His hand skills extend to his shot, which he releases with good quickness. His touch and balance make him dangerous from the traffic areas near the front of the net, and his quickness gets him open from further out.

THE PHYSICAL GAME

Feisty, aggressive, agitating — these words accurately describe Cullen's physical play, despite his relative lack of size. Cullen is unafraid of contact and will initiate hitting all over the ice against any member of the opposition. His physical play is made doubly valuable because of his ability to follow hits with constructive plays.

His size does work against him in defensive zone checking, no small reason for his poor plus/minus rating. Because of his eye/hand coordination, Cullen will more than hold his own on faceoffs.

THE INTANGIBLES

We told you that Cullen had developable skills, and he demonstrated that last season. With a full season of Mario Lemieux in the lineup (and where would the Pens have been if they didn't have Cullen while Lemieux was out?), and drawing the requisite number of checkers, Cullen should have the freedom to duplicate those numbers this year.

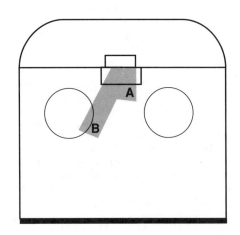

CHRIS DAHLQUIST

Yrs. of NHL service: 4
Born: Fridley, Minn., USA; Dec. 14, 1962
Position: Defenseman
Height: 6-1
Weight: 196
Uniform no.: 4
Shoots: left

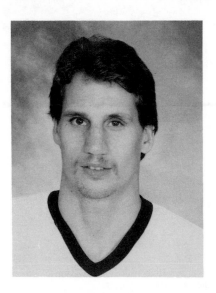

Career statistics:

GP	G	A	TP	PIM
173	9	24	33	189

1989-90 statistics:

GP	G	A	TP	+/-	PIM	PP	SH	GW	GT	S	PCT
62	4	10	14	-2	56	0	0	0	0	57	7.0

LAST SEASON

Games played total was career high. Joined Penguins from International Hockey League end of October, 1989.

THE FINESSE GAME

Finesse-wise, the best skill Dahlquist brings to the rink is his skating. Though he is a little weak in his turns, he is a fairly mobile player up and down the ice. While he cannot be counted on to contain the point offensively, Dahlquist is a strong defensive player; his skating is one reason for that (as he steps up at his own blue line) and his sense is another.

Chris reads the defensive play well, and he uses the skating ability he does have to force the play as far away from his net as he can. He plays well positionally, moves the puck when he can (although he can be forced into turnovers) and generally plays within his limits.

His offfensive contributions will be limited to goals from the blue line — probably no more than five-seven per year.

THE PHYSICAL GAME

Here is where Dahlquist makes his best contributions. He hits and takes the man out every time, and is very effective at keeping the man out of the play. He covers the front of the net fairly well, althoughshiftier skaters will give him fits as they dart in and out of the crease. He plays a fairly smart physical game, and makes that game more valuable by keeping himself on the ice and out of the penalty box.

THE INTANGIBLES

Dahlquist is a very coachable player, one who has improved his game tremendously. He has become too good for the International League, but there may be several factors mitigating against full-time NHL employment: He lacks strong confidence in his play and ability; he has a tendency to make big errors; and he is 28 years old — old to be learning the NHL game.

That said, his is a style of play the Pens need on the blue line.

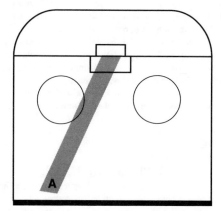

GORD DINEEN

Yrs. of NHL service: 7
Born: Toronto, Ontario, Canada; September 21, 1962
Position: Defenseman
Height: 6-0
Weight: 195
Uniform no.: 5
Shoots: right

Career statistics:

GP	G	A	TP	PIM
400	14	65	79	568

1989-90 statistics:

GP	G	A	TP	+/-	PIM	PP	SH	GW	GT	S	PCT
69	1	8	9	6	125	0	0	0	0	38	2.6

LAST SEASON

PIM total was career high. Plus/minus was club's second best (tied with Mark Recchi). Missed three games with a broken finger.

THE FINESSE GAME

Dineen's modicum of finesse skills lie in the puckhandling and shooting areas, although he's not skilled enough to survive in the NHL solely as an offensive defenseman. He can carry the puck from his end if the forechecking isn't too heavy, and he can take advantage of his teammates if given sufficient time and space, but heavy traffic is going to give him problems.

His shot from the blue line is low and hard, but his long release makes it easily blocked. Vision and ice reading deficiencies are one reason for those blocked shots, and his inability to read and react at NHL speed is why Dineen has trouble in traffic situations.

His defensive reads have the same problem, and that's why he has gets deked and has trouble with defensive zone coverages. Not helping is his no-better-than-average skating ability. Dineen has trouble turning, though he moves up and back as well as could be expected. Lack of mobility haunts him in one-on-one situations, and he's going to give up the blue line because he won't be able to close the gap on the puck carrier.

THE PHYSICAL GAME

Dineen is a fairly tough and aggressive player (he carries a mean streak, which helps), hitting whenever possible and making the opposition pay the price for scoring goals. He completes his checks along the boards to eliminate the opposition from the play.

THE INTANGIBLES

Fanatical work ethic is what keys Dineen's NHL success; he simply refuses to be cowed by his inadequacies or mistakes. He plays with desire and intensity, and is at his best when he stays within his abilities. He plays in pain, and his character traits make him a leader.

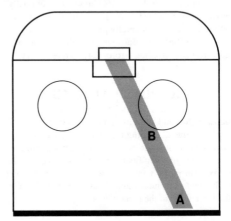

BOB ERREY

Yrs. of NHL service: 7
Born: Montreal, Quebec, Canada; September 21, 1964
Position: Left wing
Height: 5-10
Weight: 177
Uniform no.: 12
Shoots: left

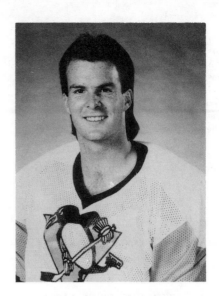

Career statistics:

GP	G	A	TP	PIM
361	85	96	181	341

1989-90 statistics:

GP	G	A	TP	+/-	PIM	PP	SH	GW	GT	S	PCT
78	20	19	39	3	109	0	1	1	0	127	15.7

LAST SEASON

Games played total was career high, point and PIM totals second highest. Plus/minus was second best among regular forwards.

THE FINESSE GAME

Skating is the best of the finesse skills Errey has to offer — in particular, his speed. Errey is very fast on his skates, and he combines that speed with the assets (balance, lateral movement and quickness) that make him an exceptional skater; he'll draw penalties because of his speed. Those skills also meld with his play-reading ability to make him a good forechecker (although he's better in pursuit of the puck than he is at closing holes) and penalty killer.

Though he demonstrates patience (and, therefore, confidence) with the puck, Errey needs the extra time he takes to make plays because neither his hands nor his brain are at the level of his feet. The same time/space idea also serves for his scoring. His shot isn't great, but his quickness will get him to a lot of loose pucks near the net. He'll have to cash those in for goals.

Errey is not an intrinsically talented defensive player. Rather, he uses his speed to make up for his mistakes. Regardless, his plus/minus rating (and the fact that last season he finished second on the club in that category) is an accurate encapsulatiuon of his defensive play — especially given the fact that the Pens were *minus*-41 as a team.

THE PHYSICAL GAME

Bob isn't gifted in the size category, but someone forgot to tell him that. He likes to hit and play and play a physical game, and Errey knowns that he needs to hit and run — because he can and will be out-muscled when trapped along the boards.

He is afraid of no one but, though his stickwork and elbowing often incite the opposition (it's also well within character for him to run the goalie), Errey will not fight.

THE INTANGIBLES

Errey is essentially a self-made player, a determined player who works through his weaknesses. Like a Sutter, he does the dirty work that so often keys a team's success.

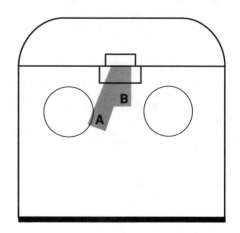

RANDY GILHEN

Yrs. of NHL service: 3
Born: Zweibrucken, West Germany; June 13, 1963
Position: Center
Height: 5-10
Weight: 190
Uniform no.: 19
Shoots: left

Career statistics:

GP	G	A	TP	PIM
142	13	17	30	107

1989-90 statistics:

GP	G	A	TP	+/-	PIM	PP	SH	GW	GT	S	PCT
61	5	11	16	-8	54	0	0	1	0	67	7.5

LAST SEASON

Assist and point totals were career highs, despite missing 11 games with a knee injury.

THE FINESSE GAME

Though he might be a step slow for the NHL, Gilhen makes up for the flaw with other finesse skills. His strong skating stride makes him relentless in pursuit of the puck, and he can deliver some speed if given enough room to take off — all of which makes him a good forechecker and fairly good penalty killer. In short, his skating will keep him confined to checking duty.

Keeping him in that defensive pigeon-hole is the fact that Gilhen is not creative offensively. He gets a fairly good read of the ice when the play is ahead of him, but otherwise his vision is unexceptional.

The best of his finesse skills is his shot, which is definitely of NHL calibre — once he gets it off. His slap shot is very heavy, but Gilhen takes too long in releasing it. The rest of his hand skills are, like the majority of his finesse skills, unexceptional.

THE PHYSICAL GAME

Gilhen is a willing physical player, if not a dominating one. He'll take the body whenever he can, although when playing center he isn't often called on to work the wood. He'll fight if forced to.

There is a question about his durability, and ability to withstand 80 games of NHL pounding.

THE INTANGIBLES

A role player of limited skills, Gilhen is nevertheless valuable because of his attitude and work ethic. He's a good team man, and adds versatility to the lineup because of his ability to play all three forward positions.

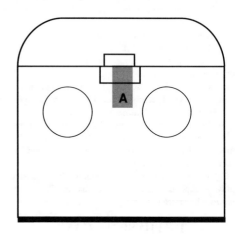

RANDY HILLIER

Yrs. of NHL service: 9
Born: Toronto, Ontario, Canada; March 30, 1960
Position: Defenseman
Height: 6-1
Weight: 186
Uniform no.: 23
Shoots: right

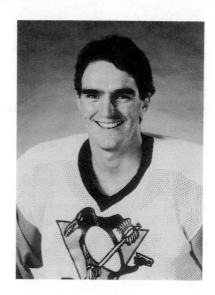

Career statistics:

GP	G	A	TP	PIM
476	14	107	121	815

1989-90 statistics:

GP	G	A	TP	+/-	PIM	PP	SH	GW	GT	S	PCT
61	3	12	15	11	71	0	0	1	0	45	6.7

LAST SEASON

Missed one game with bruised buttocks, 10 games with a broken thumb, and five games with a charley horse. Plus/minus rating was the club's best.

THE FINESSE GAME

Hillier is a limited player in the finesse areas of the game, lacking exceptional ability in the skating and puckhandling departments. Neither would be labelled any better than average, and as the talent in the League improves both categories will be downgraded further.

He lacks speed or agility in his skating, touch and hockey sense in his puckhandling. Hillier must be content to force the opposition wide of the net, for he doesn't have the ability to step up and force a play. On the offensive end, his contributions will be minimal.

Hillier does have ability in getting the puck from his end quickly, and he must move the puck rapidly in order to be effective. Intelligently, that is just what Hillier does. Once the puck has gone, Hillier does not move up to support the attack.

THE PHYSICAL GAME

In order to be valuable, it is in the physical game that Hillier must make his contributions. He is a tough hockey player, mean in front of his net, and he makes the opposition pay the price for scoring.

Hillier is also good on his takeouts, effectively eliminating his man in the corners (when he can catch him).

THE INTANGIBLES

He's got a good attitude, he's coachable and he works hard, but what you see with Hillier is what you get. He's no better than a sixth defenseman, and that status — along with his propensity toward injury — make him dispensable.

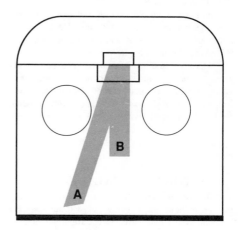

JIM JOHNSON

Yrs. of NHL service: 5
Born: New Hope, Minn., USA; August 9, 1962
Position: Defenseman
Height: 6-1
Weight: 190
Uniform no.: 6
Shoots: left

Career statistics:

GP	G	A	TP	PIM
366	14	90	104	635

1989-90 statistics:

GP	G	A	TP	+/-	PIM	PP	SH	GW	GT	S	PCT
75	3	13	16	-20	154	1	0	0	0	72	4.2

LAST SEASON

PIM total was second highest of career, third highest on team and first among defensemen. Missed three games with a back injury and two with a hip injury.

THE FINESSE GAME

Johnson is very smart defensively, and he takes advantage of his above average skating skill to play a challenging defensive style. He meets the play well at the blue line, stepping up well on the puck carrier in order to force the opposition's play as far from the Pens' net as possible.

Though his skating makes him a good checker, he amplifies his defensive play by not getting caught challenging at the opposing blue line. He acts as the safety valve, forechecking and shooting infrequently. He uses his defensive angles very well.

His puckhandling is an underrated part of his game. Not that he would ever be confused with teammate Paul Coffey (and not that Johnson wants to be, which is an indication of his smarts — staying within himself), but Jim can work well with the puck in moving it from his zone. He is a good first-passer, and he has the poise and patience to make not just the right play but a good play.

THE PHYSICAL GAME

Johnson is a physical player — hitting, clearing the front of the net and blocking shots with authority. He has both good strength and balance, and that combination allows him to hit in the corners to take the opposition off the puck and to then remain vertical and in position to make a play to his forwards. In other words, his physical play makes his finesse play more valuable.

He is also smart about his physical play, keeping himself on the ice and out of the penalty box.

THE INTANGIBLES

For what it's worth (and some would say it's like shovelling against the tide), Johnson is Pittsburgh's best defensive defenseman — and we don't mean to impugn his talents by saying so in this way. His attitude and work ethic (in both practice and games) are impressive, and he's a very dedicated and coachable athlete.

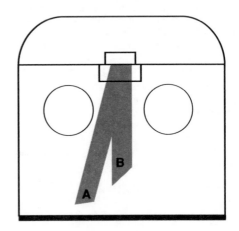

JIM KYTE

Yrs. of NHL service: 7
Born: Ottawa, Ontario, Canada; March 21, 1964
Position: Defenseman
Height: 6-5
Weight: 210
Uniform no.: 3
Shoots: left

Career statistics:

GP	G	A	TP	PIM
455	14	26	40	897

1989-90 statistics:

GP	G	A	TP	+/-	PIM	PP	SH	GW	GT	S	PCT
56	3	1	4	-10	125	0	0	0	0	23	13.0

LAST SEASON

Games played total was second-lowest full season mark of career.

THE FINESSE GAME

There really isn't one — and that's not meant in disrespect to the work Kyte's put in to improve his abilities. He has improved his skating speed and balance to become more mobile, but Jim can do little else but keep up with his teammates or the opposition. He can still be beaten one-on-one because of his trouble turning and his poor defensive reads.

He doesn't handle the puck all that well, so his play is going to have to be the simple one off the boards and out of the zone — as quickly as possible. He is little of a factor offensively, rarely becoming an attacker and rarely even following the play in an offensive mode, though he does have a good slap shot from the point. He'll be the first defenseman to fall back.

THE PHYSICAL GAME

Kyte must play a physical game to be effective, and we'll go one step further — he must fight in order to stay in the NHL, because he isn't skilled enough to survive just on banging bodies along the boards (if he can catch them to begin with).

He makes good use of his size and strength in front of his own net. He's mean defending the crease, especially while penalty killing. As a fighter, he can be one of the League's better pugilists.

BUT ...

THE INTANGIBLES

... Kyte doesn't want to fight any more. And without discussing the moral or ethical value of that stance *outside* the NHL, *inside* the NHL he doesn't have enough talent to play — and not for lack of trying.

He's worked very hard to improve his skills but, at age 26, they're not going to get any better. What got him to the NHL is his toughness and that's what will keep him here, but Jim has lost the mental edge necessary to succeed as a fighter.

MARIO LEMIEUX

Yrs. of NHL service: 6
Born: Montreal, Quebec, Canada; October 5, 1965
Position: Center
Height: 6-4
Weight: 210
Uniform no.: 66
Shoots: right

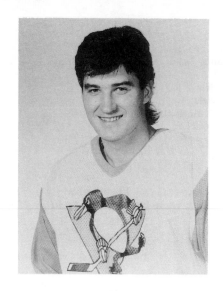

Career statistics:

GP	G	A	TP	PIM
427	345	493	838	424

1989-90 statistics:

GP	G	A	TP	+/-	PIM	PP	SH	GW	GT	S	PCT
59	45	78	123	-18	78	14	3	4	1	226	19.9

LAST SEASON

Games played total was career low (recurring back injury). Finished fourth in the NHL in assists and points. Led Pens in all point categories, was second in shots on goal. Plus/minus was club's third worst, poorest among forwards.

THE FINESSE GAME

Where to start with Mario Lemieux, maybe the most talented player to ever play in the NHL?

His physical assets — reach, strength, balance — key his finesse assets and cannot be divorced from them. His puckhandling is extraordinary, and he is the NHL's best one-on-one player; he can stickhandle through an entire team and deke the goalie, and is a threat to do so every time he has the puck. Credit his size and reach here (he does anything he wants with the puck in any situation — in traffic or wide open — and at any speed), but the softness of his hands is the key to that skill.

That touch combines with his sense (itself a combination of sight, anticipation and general hockey intelligence) to make Mario no worse than the second-best passer in the game — and if he decided to forego his own scoring opportunities and had teammates like Jari Kurri, Lemieux might just surpass Wayne Gretzky in this category.

His goal-scoring may be the most articulate in NHL history, and Lemieux just may be the League's best-ever goal scorer. There is no way in which he cannot — and will not — score. He can blow the puck past any goaltender, and needs just the slightest opening — whether from a distance or in close — to do so.

Few (if any) players can match his balance, and he is unstoppable (and many times unstoppable even when fouled) because of his skating strength.

THE PHYSICAL GAME

In plain muscular strength, Lemieux is unspectacular. But combine his balance, reach, build and sense and suddenly he is quite spectacular indeed. You can't move him from where he plants himself, you can't separate him from the puck, and you can't intimidate him. He takes people off the puck — so what if he won't win any most muscular body contests? He also likes to use his strength and size to jump through on faceoffs.

In a negative vein, Lemieux can be very cavalier with his stick — downright dirty, at times. He can be goaded into retaliation when closely checked.

THE INTANGIBLES

What can't he do? Well, he's weak in faceoffs, he's never played a full season, and his attitude remains questionable. Those weaknesses can be remedied by A) practice B) proper incorporation of conditioning aspects into his training repertoire, and C) tough question.

Lemieux is an enigma, but one thing is certain: as he goes, so go the Pens. How Lemieux approaches this season (when the Pens, for the fourth time in seven seasons introduce a new coach) is one question that can only be answered at season's end.

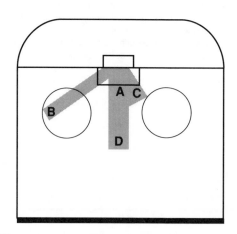

TROY LONEY

Yrs. of NHL service: 5
Born: Bow Island, Alberta, Canada;
September 21, 1963
Position: Left wing
Height: 6-3
Weight: 205
Uniform no.: 24
Shoots: left

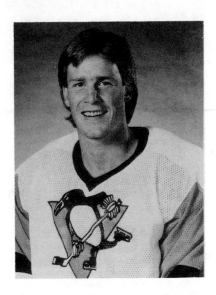

Career statistics:

GP	G	A	TP	PIM
330	47	59	106	671

1989-90 statistics:

GP	G	A	TP	+/-	PIM	PP	SH	GW	GT	S	PCT
67	11	16	27	-9	168	0	0	1	0	78	14.1

LAST SEASON

Point totals were career bests, games played total second best. Second on club in PIM total. Missed 12 games with a hand injury.

THE FINESSE GAME

Finesse is not where Loney's game shines, despite last season's career-best numbers. His skating is not good, especially in terms of agility or mobility — he has difficulty turning and he also lacks any real speed or quickness. His checking is done simply by following the puck as best he can.

His hand skills and playmaking ability (combining hands and smarts) are negligible. Loney needs lots of time and space to make an offensive play, and will never be better than fair (and isn't that now) in using his teammates.

Loney doesn't handle the puck well in traffic, which means that he will not be weaving through crowds en route to the net and he will not be finessing shots through small openings in the net. In short, 10-15 goals is about right for a season's production, and those goals will have to come from near the net with the goalie out of position.

His defensive play could best be described as decent — made so through his work.

THE PHYSICAL GAME

Loney has size and he uses it — that's what keeps him in the NHL. He can be effective along the boards and in the corners because of his size, reach and strength, even though he is of dubious value in the secondary (move the puck after gaining it) phase.

He willingly sacrifices his body, and that's best articulated when he kills penalties — where Troy blocks shots with abandon. Despite what the PIM total might indicate, Loney is not primarily a fighter.

THE INTANGIBLES

Loney is a big, honest checker — the kind of guy who maximizes his talent through work. He's a top team man with an excellent attitude. Health remains a question, as Loney has played fewer than 70 games in each of his three full NHL seasons.

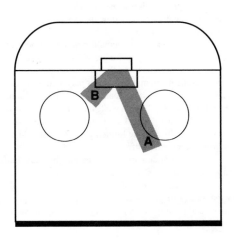

JOE MULLEN

Yrs. of NHL service: 9
Born: New York City, N.Y., USA; February 26, 1957
Position: Right wing
Height: 5-9
Uniform no.:
Shoots: right

Career statistics:

GP	G	A	TP	PIM
646	341	382	723	140

1989-90 statistics:

GP	G	A	TP	+/-	PIM	PP	SH	GW	GT	S	PCT
78	36	33	69	6	24	8	3	5	0	236	15.3

LAST SEASON

Acquired by Penguins for draft choice in June 1990. Finished third on Calgary in goals, tied for first in shorthanded goals (Theo Fleury and Paul Ranheim), tied for second in game winners (Gary Roberts) and second in shots on goal total. Point total was seven-season low.

THE FINESSE GAME

There are two keys to Mullen's finesse game, one physical — his balance — and one mental — his anticipation.

First, Mullen's superior balance powers his total finesse game by allowing him to maintain body position and retain the puck despite checking. Thats important, because Mullen plays in the game's high-density areas. Joe also possesses outstanding acceleration ability (which he uses to break into the clear), and he has tremendous one-step quickness (which he uses to dart into openings after loose pucks). He moderates his speed excellently, never allowing the opposition to predict what he will do.

His goal scorer's anticipation and great hockey sense show him those openings, and then he uses his vision and hand skills to get the puck to his teammates. Joe is unselfish and makes the best play at all times. If that means a good pass to a teammate in better position, then that's the play Mullen makes. His hand skills also allow him to carry the puck well, and they combine with his skating skills to make Mullen very shifty should he gain an opening himself.

He is very dangerous when he has the puck, but more so around the slot or just inside the faceoff circle. His shot selection is excellent: forehand or back hand, wrist, slap or snap. Mullen's shot is keyed by his quick wrists and release. He is good at one-timing his shots and can score from anywhere in the zone.

THE PHYSICAL GAME

Because of — and not in spite of — his size, Mullen is one of the toughest players in the NHL. He's completely unafraid of traffic, and Mullen will do his own mucking in the corners by consistently initiating contact.

As such, he takes more abuse per pound than almost any other NHLer (which is not to say he won't help the referee by diving). His balance is, once again, the key, and his skating strength makes difficult to dislodge from the puck.

THE INTANGIBLES

Mullen is a character player and top team man, as well as being a top player. Those first two areas are areas where the Pens could improve, and Mullen can become an on-ice leader for Pittsburgh.

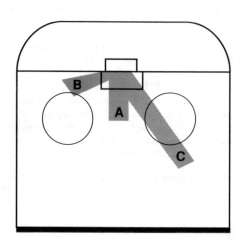

BARRY PEDERSON

Yrs. of NHL service: 10
Born: Big River, Sask., Canada; March 13, 1961
Position: Center
Height: 5-11
Weight: 185
Uniform no.: 10
Shoots: right

Career statistics:

GP	G	A	TP	PIM
618	227	400	627	443

1989-90 statistics:

GP	G	A	TP	+/-	PIM	PP	SH	GW	GT	S	PCT
54	6	25	31	-13	39	1	0	1	0	80	7.5

LAST SEASON

Acquired (along with Tony Tanti and Rod Buskas) from Vancouver in exchange for Dave Capuano, Andy McBain and Dan Quinn. Games played total was second lowest of career (missed 15 games with a broken thumb).

THE FINESSE GAME

Hockey sense has always been the strength of Pederson's game. He has excellent anticipation and vision, and those assets reveal the whole ice surface to him both offensively and defensively.

Barry puts his mental prowess to work in league with his physical finesse skills. He's a very good skater with strength, balance and quickness. Though not exceptionally fast, Barry's combination of quickness and balance makes him a very agile player — one who is difficult to trap defensively.

His skating is complemented by his puckhandling, and the opposition is forced to respect his ability to take the puck into the openings himself or to lead his teammates into those openings with excellent passes. He doesn't make the most of his ability, however, because he doesn't challenge the defensemen; Pederson's tendency is to go wide with the puck.

For a guy with his shot, Pederson doesn't shoot anywhere near enough. He's dangerous from the slot with a hard wrist shot, and Pederson also has long-range scoring capability.

His skills make him valuable in all situations, and Barry is also a complete player, very strong in the positional and defensive aspects of the game.

THE PHYSICAL GAME

Pederson plays a fairly physical game, despite his less-than-exceptional size. His balance and sturdiness afoot help him greatly in this, keeping him vertical and ready to make plays after collisions. His hitting is also made more effective by his ability to make plays off the boards. He'll always initiate contact to knock an opponent off the puck and will take a hit to make his own plays.

Strong forearms and wrists power his shots, just as they power his hands for faceoffs, an area where he does well.

THE INTANGIBLES

Pederson is a good team man, the kind of player Pittsburgh needs. He has never really regained his intensity after his arm surgery (to remove a growth), and that is why his 100-point seasons are behind him.

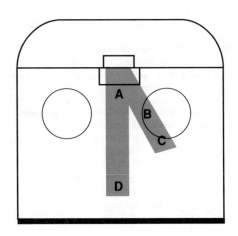

MARK RECCHI

Yrs. of NHL service: 1
Born: Kamloops, B.C., Canada; February 1, 1968
Position: Center
Height: 5-9
Weight: 185
Uniform no.: 8
Shoots: left

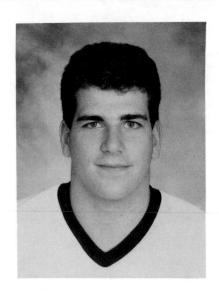

Career statistics:

GP	G	A	TP	PIM
89	31	38	69	44

1989-90 statistics:

GP	G	A	TP	+/-	PIM	PP	SH	GW	GT	S	PCT
74	30	37	67	6	44	6	2	4	1	143	21.0

LAST SEASON

First full NHL season. Finished third overall in rookie scoring (second in goals, fourth in assists, third in shorthanded goals, sixth in shots on goal, first in both power play goals and shooting percentage). Joined the Penguins from the International Hockey League on October 18, 1989. His plus/minus was best among the club's forwards.

THE FINESSE GAME

Recchi is a very talented player who brings a high level of skating, puckhandling, shooting and hockey sense to his game. He is a very dynamic skater with great mobility, the root of which is his quickness and balance. Those quantities combine to give him excellent agility and lateral ability, allowing him to change speed and direction within a step, and his skating makes him very dangerous from the blue line in.

Complementing his foot skills are his hand skills. Mark can operate with the puck at his top speed, whether that means carrying it himself or passing it to an open teammate. He uses his teammates well, and one reason he does so is because of his hockey sense — he sees the holes and leads his wingers to them (he is just as able to exploit those holes himself because of his quickness).

His hand skills extend to his shot, which is very quickly released and will beat NHL goaltending. Recchi is an accurate shooter (as his shooting percentage implies) and he forces goalies to make saves; his shot creates opportunities. He is a scorer, and has a scorer's sense of positioning and timing.

He is a consistent defensive player, attentive to his assignments.

THE PHYSICAL GAME

Considering his size, Recchi is a pretty tough player. He'll take the poundings necessary to make his plays, and he's unafraid of contact. That's good, because that physical willingness will open space for his finesse game.

THE INTANGIBLES

In all, an auspicious debut for Recchi. He's already demonstrated an ability to contribute in all situations (his skills make him a specialty teams regular), and he scored at a fairly regular pace last season (consistency is always good).

Of course, repeating is always a tough thing to do — especially now that he's no longer an unknown. He's got the talent to post at least the same numbers, but Recchi will be facing tighter checking this season. Let's see how he fares.

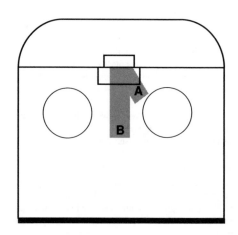

KEVIN STEVENS

Yrs. of NHL service: 2
Born: Brockton, Mass., USA; April 15, 1965
Position: Left wing
Height: 6-3
Weight: 220
Uniform no.: 25
Shoots: left

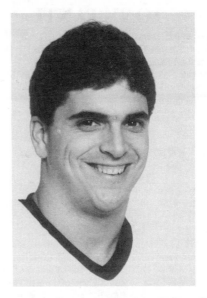

Career statistics:

GP	G	A	TP	PIM
116	46	46	92	198

1989-90 statistics:

GP	G	A	TP	+/-	PIM	PP	SH	GW	GT	S	PCT
76	29	41	70	-13	171	12	0	1	0	179	16.2

LAST SEASON

First full NHL season; all point totals were career highs. Led team in PIM total, tied for second on club (Rob Brown, Tony Tanti) in power play goals. He missed four games with a hip pointer.

THE FINESSE GAME

Like Cam Neely and Rick Tocchet, Stevens has the ingredients to become one of the NHL's best power forwards. He is a very strong skater, if not a graceful one, and once he gets his feet moving is very difficult to stop. That inertia (an object in motion tends to stay in motion) helps Stevens in his puckhandling.

Because his agility doesn't create space for his puckhandling (his agility doesn't measure up to his skating strength), Stevens must gain operating space with the puck another way; his strength gains him that space.

Kevin is also intelligent enough to know that his best play is to give up the puck, take the defenseman with him and camp by the net. Once there, he puts his good hands (strong, quick release with touch for the small openings) to work by making the goalie make saves.

Because he is still not completely acclimated to the NHL's speed and his defensive responsibilities, his defensive play will lag behind his offense.

THE PHYSICAL GAME

While he has the tools for physical dominance, Stevens doesn't necessarily have the mentality. He has to be reminded to play his size and take advantage of his God-given ability. Which is not to say he's afraid of contact. Rather, concentration and intensity on the NHL scale are the things Stevens has to develop, and he showed signs last year of discovering that consistency.

He's big and strong and controls the corners and traffic areas when he's on his game; he's more likely than not to come out of a confrontation with the puck. He uses his good strength and balance to best effect by plugging the front of the net, especially on the power play. He can get shots off while being checked, and that's a credit to his arm, wrist and shoulder strength.

He also showed last season that he's more than willing to fight.

THE INTANGIBLES

While we say that Stevens has the Neely blueprint all over him, it is worth noting that Neely — just two months younger than Stevens — has four more NHL seasons under his belt. The point is, Stevens will need additional time to grow into the player Cam Neely took six seasons to become.

Much of Pittsburgh's future success is riding on Stevens' broad shoulders. He has a good attitude, though he does need to be pushed occasionally. He played much of last season in pain — his hands were killing him from fighting, and he still picked up 29 goals.

That speaks well of his character, dedication and future.

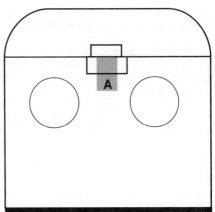

TONY TANTI

Yrs. of NHL service: 8
Born: Toronto, Ontario, Canada; September 7, 1963
Position: Right wing
Height: 5-9
Weight: 185
Uniform no.: 9
Shoots: left

Career statistics:

GP	G	A	TP	PIM
571	265	238	503	511

1989-90 statistics:

GP	G	A	TP	+/-	PIM	PP	SH	GW	GT	S	PCT
78	28	36	64	-10	72	12	0	0		1	192	14.6

LAST SEASON

Traded, along with Barry Pederson and Rod Buskas, from Vancouver to Pittsburgh in exchange for Andy McBain, Dan Quinn and Dave Capuano. Games played total was second highest of career. Tied for second on club (Rob Brown, Kevin Stevens) in power play goals.

THE FINESSE GAME

Primary among Tanti's fairly considerable finesse skills is his shot, which is very underrated. Tony's release is exceptionally quick, maybe the best in the NHL; that's why he can score goals. The puck is gone as soon as it touches his stick and he always forces the goalie to make a save. He shoots off the pass very well, and he needs only the slightest opening; Tanti loves to go upstairs on goalies. He is also very good on tip-ins because of his eye/hand coordination, and he augments that skill by using a big blade on his stick.

Tony uses his excellent skating ability to get into scoring position and to create openings. His great balance and agility make him extremely difficult to contain, and his one-step quickness and ability to change direction within a stride will snare him most any loose puck.

His anticipation keys his ability to get into scoring position, but he can also use that ability to make plays. But make no mistake: Tanti is a finisher, not a playmaker.

THE PHYSICAL GAME

Tanti isn't a physical player, but he's fairly willing to get involved by taking hits to make his plays — as he must when crashing the crease for loose pucks.

He's pretty sturdy on his feet, so Tony can be effective in hit-and-run missions for the puck against the boards but will be overwhelmed if trapped in the traffic areas.

THE INTANGIBLES

Tanti's job is to spread out the Penguins firepower, and make opposing teams pay some checking attention to another line beside Lemieux's. Though he has a way to go to regain his 40-goal form (he's lost some of his jump), Tanti must still be considered an offensive threat and treated as such.

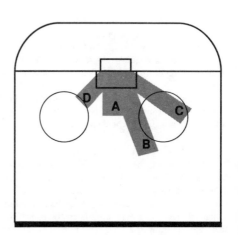

WENDELL YOUNG

Yrs. of NHL service: 3
Born: Halifax, N.S., Canada; August 1, 1963
Position: Goaltender
Height: 5-8
Weight: 185
Uniform no.: 1
Catches: left

Career statistics:

GP	MINS	G	SO	AVG	A	PIM
101	5,231	369	14	4.23	7	16

1989-90 statistics:

GP	MINS	AVG	W	L	T	SO	GA	SA	SAPCT	PIM
43	2,318	4.17	16	20	3	1	161	1,267	.8738	

LAST SEASON

Games and minutes played totals were career highs.

THE PHYSICAL GAME

Young is a standup goaltender. He plays his angles well, but he has difficulty with clearing rebounds.

He is also weak when he is off his feet and flopping around. He does not move particularly well yet, but Wendell does have quick feet and a deceptive glove hand.

He handles the puck well when he is out of the net and can move it to his defensemen, but his lack of skating skill and balance shows up when he is unable to regain his stance quickly for a second save.

THE MENTAL GAME

Young has got a mental toughness that allows him to bounce back from bad goals or games. He holds his concentration well and has demonstrated good anticipation, making him difficult to beat in the bang-bang plays around the net.

Young has the ability to respond to pressure and make the big save and nothing gets him down. If he keeps that attitude, he'll flourish.

THE INTANGIBLES

Just when it seemed safe for Young to take a permanent place in the Pittsburgh lineup — albeit behind Tom Barrasso — along comes Alain Chevrier. Young played respectably during Barrasso's absence, but the presence of Chevrier likely means a ticket to the minors for Young.

ZARLEY ZALAPSKI

Yrs. of NHL service: 3
Born: Edmonton, Alberta, Canada; April 22, 1968
Position: Defenseman
Height: 6-1
Weight: 204
Uniform no.: 33
Shoots: left

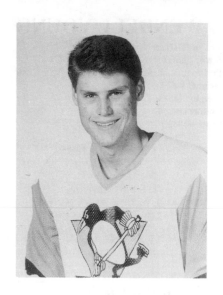

Career statistics:

GP	G	A	TP	PIM
124	21	66	87	101

1989-90 statistics:

GP	G	A	TP	+/-	PIM	PP	SH	GW	GT	S	PCT
51	6	25	31	-14	37	5	0	2	0	85	7.1

LAST SEASON

Point totals fell in second full NHL season. Missed 16 games with broken collarbone, 13 games with knee injury.

THE FINESSE GAME

Right now, Zalapski is a player whose parts are greater than his whole. He is an excellent skater with exceptional skating strength and balance. His strength gives him speed and acceleration, and his balance gives him great agility — Zalapski is an extremely mobile defenseman who can hit the holes in all directions (forward, backward and laterally), as well as challenge at both blue lines.

His puckhandling would be his second best skill, and Zalapski likes rushing the puck — sometimes too much so. He must show better judgement in his rushes (something greater NHL experience will give him). He moves well with the puck at all speeds, controlling it well in traffic, but his breakout passes must be delivered harder so they are not intercepted.

His hockey sense allows him to join the play as a fourth attacker, to find open teammates (he passes extremely well to both sides) and to pick off opposition passes in the Pittsburgh zone.

Zalapski can score from the point with a good slap shot, but he must shoot more (last season's average was a paltry 1.67 shots per game).

THE PHYSICAL GAME

He's got good size, and one look at him tells you that Zalapski is in good physical condition, but Zarley can be overpowered by the opposition. While he can succeed against some opponents because of his superior hand and foot skills, players of equal ability will gain position on him. Improved strength would help here.

He is not otherwise a punishing hitter, and he is not likely to fight.

THE INTANGIBLES

Zalapski entered the NHL after the 1988 Winter Olympics with the reputation of being the second most talented player (outside of Brian Leetch) not in the NHL. He has not come closer to that promise.

Because of his superb skills, Zalapski has a tendency to coast and needs to be reminded to work. For that reason, some say he is not easily coached. We say he has the talent to be one of the NHL's top defensemen, and a stable year both personally (he's been badly injured in both of his NHL seasons — and what does that mean?) and team-wise (in terms of team coaching and success) will give us a better read of his true ability.

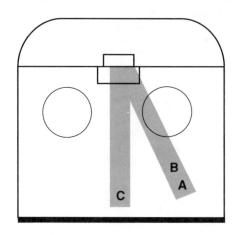

QUEBEC NORDIQUES

JOE CIRELLA

Yrs. of NHL service: 8
Born: Hamilton, Ontario, Canada; May 9, 1963
Position: Defenseman
Height: 6-2
Weight: 205
Uniform no.: 2
Shoots: right

Career statistics:

GP	G	A	TP	PIM
559	54	173	227	1,007

1989-90 statistics:

GP	G	A	TP	+/-	PIM	PP	SH	GW	GT	S	PCT
56	4	14	18	-27	67	1	0	0	0	76	5.3

LAST SEASON

Games played and point marks were full-season career lows (13 games missed with broken foot, 11 games out with injured back). Plus/minus mark was second best among defensemen.

THE FINESSE GAME

Cirella is a limited finesse player, and he makes what few skills he has less effective because of his questionable applications. He is not a good skater, possessing neither exceptional speed nor balance. His back-skating and lateral movement (especially to his right) lag behind his forward skating, but instead of playing within his limitations Cirella is apt to challenge the puck and the opposition in all three zones — thus getting caught out of position.

He can carry the puck from the defensive zone if necessary, but his puckhandling is one-dimensional because he lacks the ability to read the play as it develops. He's okay if the play is in front of him (as in breakout passes), but even then he can be forced into hurrying his passes — along with the resulting errors — if strongly forechecked.

He's talented enough to take passes well in the offensive zone, and Cirella shoots the puck well while in motion. That makes his shot more effective, with his wrist shot more of a threat than his slap shot.

THE PHYSICAL GAME

Cirella will hit and uses his decent strength to some degree of success in the defensive zone, but he is not especially aggressive and is less successful in his application against the League's bigger players — he's just not strong enough to consistently win the battles in the crease or the corners against the Neely-Tocchet-Messier types.

One thing that sabotages his efforts is his balance. Cirella is extremely top heavy, and when he gets hit in the shoulders he'll be knocked off his feet — certainly out of his skating stance — more often than not. He'll fight for himself or a teammate when necessary.

THE INTANGIBLES

At this point of his career, Cirella (and his team) must be satisfied with him being no better than a fourth defenseman (and lower than that on a stronger team). In fact, as Quebec's youngsters develop (Fogarty, Leschyshyn, Finn, Guerard), Cirella may be moved even further down the list.

He lacks a strong work ethic, and can sometimes be downright lazy. Don't be surprised to see him in another uniform before his career is over — and maybe sooner than that.

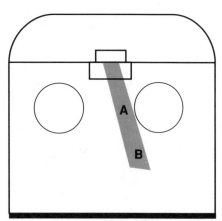

LUCIEN DEBLOIS

Yrs. of NHL service: 13
Born: Joliette, Quebec, Canada; June 21, 1957
Position: Center
Height: 5-11
Weight: 204
Uniform no.: 32
Shoots: right

Career statistics:

GP	G	A	TP	PIM
876	228	249	477	730

1989-90 statistics:

GP	G	A	TP	+/-	PIM	PP	SH	GW	GT	S	PCT
70	9	8	17	-29	45	1	0	1	1	83	10.8

LAST SEASON

Signed as a free agent by the Nordiques during the summer of 1989. Games played total was three-season low (missed five games with groin injury). Point total was full-season career low.

THE FINESSE GAME

Skating strength and balance are the keys to Deblois finesse game — physical skills though those are. Though lacking exceptional speed or quickness (and therefore a degree of the agility that would result), Deblois succeeds in his checking center role because of his strong stride and pace, and his ability to pursue the puck. His ability to recognize plays, along with his desire to close the offensive gaps, add further value to his checking role.

While he has a pretty strong wrist shot (once he gets it off), Deblois is of almost no value offensively. He lacks a scorer's release or sense of the net, and his puckhandling ability is not much better. He will almost never beat a defender one-on-one and, because he's neither exceedingly intelligent nor creative in the offensive zone, he'll make the first play he can see.

He needs to be in close proximity of the goal to score, and he'll get most of his goals on second efforts and rebounds.

THE PHYSICAL GAME

His physical willingness can betray him with injury, but Deblois is a fairly strong physical player. His takeouts are good, and he has enough strength and balance to knock the wind from the opposition's sails when he hits them.

THE INTANGIBLES

Health. Age. New management and coaching. Deblois gained a new lease on his NHL life as a checking center but, at age 33 and on a weak team, there's no telling when that lease expires.

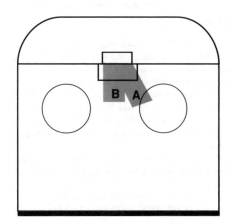

STEVEN FINN

Yrs. of NHL service: 4
Born: Laval, Quebec, Canada; August 20, 1966
Position: Defenseman
Height: 6-0
Weight: 198
Uniform no.: 29
Shoots: left

Career statistics:

GP	G	A	TP	PIM
269	10	28	38	709

1989-90 statistics:

GP	G	A	TP	+/-	PIM	PP	SH	GW	GT	S	PCT
64	3	9	12	-33	208	1	0	0	0	74	4.1

LAST SEASON

Goal total tied career best, assist and point marks set career marks. PIM total was club's third highest, second among defensemen. Missed four games with a shoulder injury.

THE FINESSE GAME

The finesse aspects of the game are not the high points of Finn's contributions to the Nordiques. His skating remains no better than average at the NHL level (an improving NHL level, we might add) and his mobility and speed must improve if his game is to improve. Currently, he must play his position conservatively — that is, he must angle the opposition to the boards and wide of the play, instead of stepping up and closing the gap, because his mobility leaves him vulnerable at his blue line.

He can skate the puck from the zone when necessary, but Finn is a better player when he moves the puck to the breaking forwards.

His hand skills are no better than average (and may be lower) in most every category. He has difficulty taking the puck off the boards, doesn't carry the puck exceptionally well, and doesn't shoot the puck well (his release is way too long, and his shot strength is debatable).

Smartly, he stays within his limits and doesn't force offensive plays at the opposing blue line or through neutral ice.

THE PHYSICAL GAME

Finn makes a very strong contribution (yes, pun intended) to the Nordiques in the physical aspects of the game. He is a very aggressive player, frequently crossing into the mean category, and he'll make the opposition pay for coming to the Quebec net (cross-checks, heads into goal posts and the like). At the least, he takes the body in all sections of the defensive zone, and he is strong enough to thwart the NHL's bigger players. He needs to remember to complete his takeouts so the opposition doesn't sneak back into the play.

He is a willing fighter, but not among the League's heavyweights, and sacrifices his body to block shots.

THE INTANGIBLES

He's an honest player, the kind who will make mistakes but is putting out a strong effort. Don't get the wrong idea from our finesse critique — Finn is a fairly stable defensive defenseman. We just think he can be better.

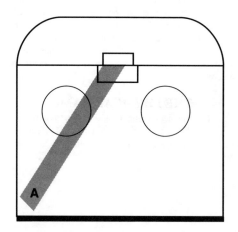

BRYAN FOGARTY

Yrs. of NHL service: 1
Born: Brantford, Ont., Canada; June 11, 1969
Position: Defenseman
Height: 6-2
Weight: 198
Uniform no.: 43
Shoots: left

Career statistics:

GP	G	A	TP	+/-	PIM	PP	SH	GW	GT	S	PCT
45	4	10	14	-47	31	2	0	0	0	93	4.3

LAST SEASON

NHL debut. Plus/minus rating was NHL's worst. Spent time in Halifax of the American Hockey League.

THE FINESSE GAME

Fogarty is a supremely skilled player, one who can grow into one of the NHL's truly elite performers. His skating is exceptional in each area (speed, quickness, balance and strength), giving him agility and fine lateral movement; Fogarty moves as well east/west as he does north/south. He acceleration ability lets him put his skating to great use by rushing the puck, and Fogarty's hand skills back him up here — they are the equal of his foot skills.

He controls the puck excellently, whether rushing it or skimming a pass to a breaking forward. His hockey sense is at the same level as his physical finesse skills, and his anticipation and vision reveal the openings into which he sends his teammates. Fogarty has very soft hands, and he can deliver the pass of the moment — snapped hard, or feathered lightly; he easily finds the open man and his patience gains openings for those men.

He will not just join the rush but will lead it, gaining the offensive blue line and dishing off when he can. Fogarty will charge the net for passes and shots, and he shoots quickly, frequently and accurately. He can afford to take those chances because his skating will overcome bad decisions.

Fogarty certainly has the ability to step up and force the play at the blue line, and will make that play better taking the puck away and sending it up ice. All of his skills make him a power play regular.

THE PHYSICAL GAME

Fogarty has good size, but he is essentially a finesse player. He'll work in the trenches in the corners and in front of the net, and he's not likely to be intimidated by the opposition, but his job is to be the breakout and not takeout defenseman.

He'll take men out and tie them up, but he is not a thunderous (or even heavy) hitter.

THE INTANGIBLES

All of this is written in "perfect world" prose, as in this is what Fogarty is capable of in his perfect world. He has shown all the signs of great potential, but he is clearly not yet ready to assume the Bobby Orr-Paul Coffey mantle carved for him (not all the blame for that minus-47 rating should be laid at the Nordiques' feet).

Which is not to say Fogarty won't reach that potential — don't mistake us, we're not coming down on him. Rather, what we say here is that Fogarty needs much more NHL experience in order to maximize his skills, more time to learn to make correct decisions, more time to grow into the player he can be. A stable playing and management environment in Quebec (to say nothing of a coach who can teach him NHL defense) will go a long way in bringing Fogarty closer to his stardom.

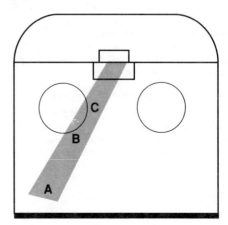

MARC FORTIER

Yrs. of NHL service: 3
Born: Sherbrooke, Quebec, Canada; February 26, 1966
Position: Center
Height: 6-0
Weight: 192
Uniform no.: 9
Shoots: right

Career statistics:

GP	G	A	TP	PIM
143	37	46	83	85

1989-90 statistics:

GP	G	A	TP	+/-	PIM	PP	SH	GW	GT	S	PCT
59	13	17	30	-16	28	3	1	1	0	89	14.6

LAST SEASON

Games played total was career high, despite stint at Halifax of the American Hockey League.

THE FINESSE GAME

Intelligence and anticipation — the elements of hockey sense — are the best aspects of Fortier's game. He's not a great skater, lacking the dynamic speed necessary for that tag, but his sense will put him the right place at the right time. His balance is also suspect, meaning that his agility and lateral movement will be questionable.

He makes up for that skating deficiency with outstanding hand skills and, once again, smarts. He sees the ice well and maximizes his chances by keeping his head up. He also does the simple things that guarantee success, like keeping the rink on his forehand. He has soft hands and uses his teammates well, and he can operate from the traffic areas because of his hand skills; his hands make him a 50-50 bet to hold onto the puck after being checked — improved balance would improve the equation.

Fortier's soft hands allow him to work well close to the net, where he can capitalize on sudden openings, and those hands also scare the opposition enough that he can draw penalties. His speed isn't good enough to put him on the penalty killing unit, but he'll see power play time because of his hands and eyes.

THE PHYSICAL GAME

Fortier has expanded his physical game in a positive way. Where previously he was unafraid of contact, greater NHL experience has shown him to be unafraid of initiating contact. He has become an aggressive —

but smart — player, hitting and taking the body well in all three zones.

THE INTANGIBLES

Fortier is a good kid, willing to work on his deficiencies in order to improve. He plays well at home and on the road, and that speaks well for his work ethic and character. He has the opportunity to become the club's second scoring center (though he's been played at wing in order to compensate for his slowness afoot), but with the pending arrival of Kip Miller and Mats Sundin, Fortier may not have long to cement that spot.

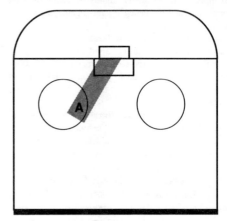

PAUL GILLIS

Yrs. of NHL service: 7
Born: Toronto, Ontario, Canada; December 31, 1963
Position: Center
Height: 6-0
Weight: 195
Uniform no.: 23
Shoots: left

Career statistics:

GP	G	A	TP	PIM
527	84	138	222	1,260

1989-90 statistics:

GP	G	A	TP	+/-	PIM	PP	SH	GW	GT	S	PCT
71	8	14	22	-24	234	0	1	0	0	68	11.8

LAST SEASON

Games played total was full-season career low (eight games, Guillain Barre syndrome). PIM total was second highest of career, tops on the team.

THE FINESSE GAME

The finesse game is not where Gillis best demonstrates his NHL aptitude. The weapon he best brings to bear is his skating, where strength and balance serve to make Gillis one of the NHL's better checkers. His leg strength makes him an almost tireless skater, and that strength also serves him as he drives through his checks or fights for the puck along the boards.

He has a degree of foot speed and that helps in his puck pursuit, making him a good forechecker and penalty killer. His anticipation is relatively good, but he is confined more to following the puck than he is to beating it to its destination.

His hand skills aren't good — maybe not even average — in terms of offensive ability. He doesn't handle or carry the puck particularly well, and so is largely unable to take advantage of any loose pucks his checking creates. He'll have to be an opportunistic scorer because of that.

His hand skills do extend to faceoffs, where his good eye/hand coordination and hand speed make him one of the NHL's better men on the draw. He'll take those late-game, defensive zone faceoffs.

THE PHYSICAL GAME

Gillis is a very aggressive player, frequently crossing the border into mean because of the liberties he takes with his stick. He plays bigger than his size, hitting anything he can reach; he's rarely out-fought for a puck.

Though an agitator and a hitter, Gillis is not likely to fight to back up his tough play.

THE INTANGIBLES

The worst thing that can be said about Gillis is that he may be trying to do too much to fill the void left by the departure of Dale Hunter; there are times when he is too aggressive, too anxious to stir the pot. Any coach, however, will live with those errors of commission. Gillis is a worker and an excellent team man — the type of character a weaker team needs as a leader.

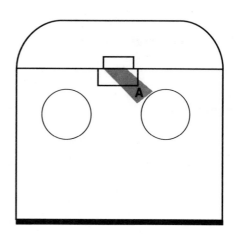

SCOTT GORDON

Yrs. of NHL service: 1
Born: South Easton, Mass., USA; February 6, 1963
Position: Goaltender
Height: 5-10
Weight: 175
Uniform no.: 30
Catches: left

Career statistics:

GP	MINS	AVG	W	L	T	SO	GA	SA	SAPCT	PIM
10	597	5.33	2	8	0	0	53	368	.856	0

LAST SEASON

NHL debut. Joined Quebec from Halifax of the American Hockey League on January 29, 1990, returning to Halifax March 5.

THE PHYSICAL GAME

Gordon is a standup, challenging goaltender who succeeds by playing his angles, squaring himself to the shooter and letting the puck just hit him. He is a good skater with good balance, and so he moves from post to post and in and out of the net efficiently; that means that when he moves, he doesn't open up holes in his stance.

He has quick hands and feet and will combine those assets with his good balance to equal strong success in scrambles around his net. His balance and foot speed quickly take him to the ice and return him to his stance ready for the next save.

Gordon handles his rebounds well, directing them away from the front of the net, and he also helps himself around the net by moving the puck to his defense. He communicates well with his defense, directing traffic near his net.

In short, he is a triumph of substance over style.

THE MENTAL GAME

Gordon is very tough mentally — he'd have to be, or he wouldn't have survived his tenure in the East Coast Hockey League. He has excellent concentration and vision, and he is always prepared to play. He also has big save capability.

THE INTANGIBLES

Gordon showed very well during his stint with Quebec (and signed a new contract because of his performance), and any number of observers have been impressed with his play at all levels. He is an extremely hard worker, taking ice early and staying late to work on his game, and he is well liked by his teammates. He will have competition in the Quebec net this season (notably from Stephane Fiset and incumbent Ron Tugnutt), and his age (27) may work against him.

But his positives outweigh his negatives, and he can be a positive player for the Nordiques.

MIKE HOUGH

Yrs. of NHL service: 3
Born: Montreal, Quebec, Canada; February 6,1963
Position: Left wing
Height: 6-1
Weight: 192
Uniform no.: 18
Shoots: left

Career statistics:

GP	G	A	TP	PIM
162	31	33	64	204

1989-90 statistics:

GP	G	A	TP	+/-	PIM	PP	SH	GW	GT	S	PCT
43	13	13	26	-24	84	3	1	0	0	93	14.0

LAST SEASON

Fourth stint with Quebec. Missed six games with a groin injury, 14 games with a shoulder injury, two games with a broken nose, 12 games with a broken thumb.

THE FINESSE GAME

The finesse game is not yet Hough's game, not at the NHL level. Hough lacks exceptional speed or agility in his skating, so he finds himself consigned to the checking role on his line. He does have good skating strength and smarts, so he can be an effective forechecker and relatively effective penalty killer (though he does suffer some in that role because of his skating).

Because he concentrates so heavily on his checking (despite what the plus/minus rating says), Hough will not score significantly at the NHL level. He does get opportunities near the net because of his checking (and because he tends to play with an offensive center), and most of his scoring will be done within 20 feet of the goal.

He doesn't handle the puck particularly well, and he'll need some time to move it to his teammates.

THE PHYSICAL GAME

Hough is tough enough for the NHL, and his skating strength helps him greatly. He'll track down the opposing puck carrier and take him off the puck, and as long as there's sufficient time and space Hough will make the pass to his linemates. He's not an overwhelming hitter, but he'll go into the corner against anyone and make the most of size.

THE INTANGIBLES

He may only make the NHL as a checker (if he can stay healthy — which is a question in and of itself), but Hough will stay in the League because he's smart, he knows his role, and he plays it. He's a worker in all situations, and that sits in his favor. Otherwise, as with other role players, he's eminently replaceable.

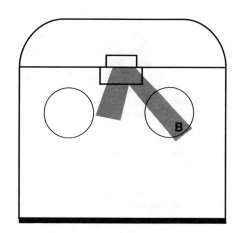

TONY HRKAC

Yrs. of NHL service: 3
Born: Thunder Bay, Ontario, Canada; July 7, 1966
Position: Center
Height: 5-11
Weight: 165
Uniform no.: 28
Shoots: left

Career statistics:

GP	G	A	TP	PIM
187	37	85	122	40

1989-90 statistics:

GP	G	A	TP	+/-	PIM	PP	SH	GW	GT	S	PCT
50	9	20	29	-4	10	3	0	0	1	70	12.9

LAST SEASON

Acquired from St. Louis along with Greg Millen in exchange for Jeff Brown. Games played and all point totals were career lows. Plus/minus total was club's best. He missed two games with a bruised shoulder, and also spent time in Halifax of the American Hockey League.

THE FINESSE GAME

The strengths of Hrkac's game lie in the offensive and finesse areas of the game. He's a good skater, shifty and quick enough so that he looks faster than he actually is. His skating is complemented by his anticipation/hockey sense and his stick skills. He uses these two skills to both exploit and create openings.

He reads the ice very well and can excel at setting up his wingers, and he's shown that he can read and execute plays at the NHL level. He's a creative passer who knows how to use all of the offensive zone. He has the hand skills to be an above average NHL playmaker, but he should also learn to balance his selflessness with selfishness and take greater advantage of his speed by going to the net when he can.

Tony generally puts himself at a shooting disadvantage by setting up teammates closer to the net. Then, when they kick the puck back to him, he has to shoot through traffic. He does, however, dart around the goal, so he'll pick up some points on loose pucks.

Those smarts don't always show themselves defensively, where Hrkac has sometimes been less than dependable.

THE PHYSICAL GAME

Hrkac's size is always going to be a concern. While he has shown, on occasion, the willingness to get involved along the boards, Hrkac doesn't have the strength to succeed in this style of play. What's more, without discussing muscling for the puck, bigger forwards are just going to reach around or over him.

THE INTANGIBLES

When he wants to apply himself, Hrkac can be a dynamic offensive player. He must toughen his work ethic so that he is prepared to play each night, or else his stints in the minors — to say nothing of the possibility of his moving to another team — are likely to grow.

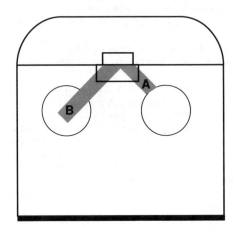

JEFF JACKSON

Yrs. of NHL service: 4
Born: Chatham, Ontario, Canada; April 24, 1965
Position: Left wing
Height: 6-1
Weight: 195
Uniform no.: 25
Shoots: left

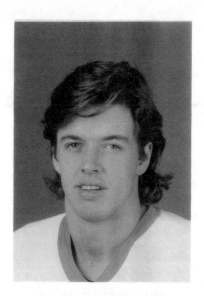

Career statistics:

GP	G	A	TP	PIM
252	35	47	82	307

1989-90 statistics:

GP	G	A	TP	+/-	PIM	PP	SH	GW	GT	S	PCT
65	8	12	20	-21	71	0	1	0	0	73	11.0

LAST SEASON

Games played total was second highest of career (despite missing five games with a charley horse, one game with an arm injury, and five more games with a knee injury). Point total was also second highest of career.

THE FINESSE GAME

Strength and a degree of mobility are the hallmarks of Jackson's skating skill. Though not exceptionally agile (he lacks the greater degree of quickness for that asset), Jackson does have the balance necessary to both work along the boards and to maintain a turning radius smaller than that of a battleship. He's not overwhelmingly fast, but his strength gets him where he has to be. That makes him good in his puck pursuit and a decent checker.

Jackson has not shown anything above average in his hand skills so, despite his ability to motor past defensemen, his offensive contributions in both scoring and playmaking will be minimal. He is smart enough to look for options when he has the puck (and not just do everything himself), but his hands are not fast enough for consistent NHL success. He will generally make the first play he sees.

Jackson has a good slap shot from the left circle, but needs to shoot it more instead of driving past the defenseman and into the corner with the puck.

THE PHYSICAL GAME

Jackson makes the most of his physical gifts by using his skating strength against the opposition when along the boards. He's consistently physical in bodying the opposition, and his strength and balance allow him to work fairly well in traffic areas.

His skating strength will help him drive the net, where the opposition is forced to take penalties to stop him. Jackson has also shown that he can be mean, in that he'll hit opponents from behind with his stick, and he will fight to back up his plays. He is not, however, a feared fighter in the NHL.

THE INTANGIBLES

As always, health remains the big question regarding Jackson. He is otherwise a role player, where what you see is what you get. As such, he is vulnerable to replacement.

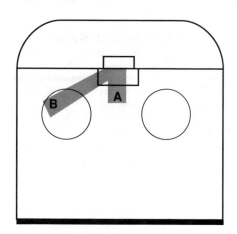

IIRO JARVI

Yrs. of NHL service: 2
Born: Helsinki, Finland; March 23, 1965
Position: Left wing/right wing
Height: 6-1
Weight: 198
Uniform no.: 11
Shoots: left

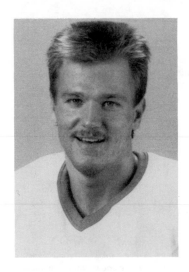

Career statistics:

GP	G	A	TP	PIM
116	18	43	61	58

1989-90 statistics:

GP	G	A	TP	+/-	PIM	PP	SH	GW	GT	S	PCT
41	7	13	20	-11	18	1	0	1	0	52	13.5

LAST SEASON

Bounced up and down between Quebec and Halifax of the AmericanHockey League.

THE FINESSE GAME

Jarvi has the typical European skills of skating and puckhandling. He has good speed and quickness, and a nice touch of balance, making him an agile forward with good lateral movement.

He handles the puck well when he carries it and has the ability to make use of his teammates, but Jarvi is not quite acclimated to the speed of the NHL game; greater experience should help alleviate that problem.

Jarvi can handle the puck in tighter circumstances because of his good hands and his balance, and his hockey sense puts him in scoring position near the net.

He uses that anticipation well in specialty team situations, where he has been used with some degree of success.

THE PHYSICAL GAME

Jarvi isn't much of a physical forward, in terms of imposing himself on the oppositon, but he has no fear of the congested areas. He willingly goes to the traffic area near the front of the net to convert loose pucks, and he'll take his knocks to make his plays.

Just don't expect him to smack anyone into the cheap seats.

THE INTANGIBLES

He's a very talented offensive player, but still relatively unproven at the NHL level. Jarvi has the skills and determination to improve, but what role he will fill is up to the new Nordiques management.

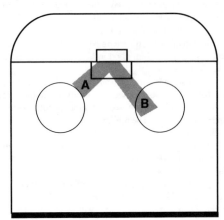

GUY LAFLEUR

Yrs. of NHL service: 16
Born: Thurso, Quebec, Canada; September 20, 1951
Position: Right wing
Height: 6-0
Weight: 185
Uniform no.: 10
Shoots: right

Career statistics:

GP	G	A	TP	PIM
1,067	548	777	1,325	397

1989-90 statistics:

GP	G	A	TP	+/-	PIM	PP	SH	GW	GT	S	PCT
39	12	22	34	-15	4	6	0	2	0	100	12.0

LAST SEASON

Signed as a free agent by the Nordiques during the summer of 1989. Finished third in team scoring, second in power play goals. Missed 16 games with an ankle injury, 25 games with a fractured cheekbone.

THE FINESSE GAME

He doesn't have the speed he once had, but Lafleur is still a very good skater. Though retaining a portion of his agility and lateral movement, he no longer eludes the opposition as he once did. Still, his skating retains a creativity, a freshness, a lack of mechanical rehearsal that no one in the NHL can match.

Lafleur controls the puck well when he carries it, and he can lug it at his top speed. His hands are good, and he can fake his way through a string of defenders. Once through, his tremendous hockey sense and vision (he's lost nothing in that regard) combine with his hand skills to deliver good passes to his teammates, passes that lead his mates into the clear.

His sense also puts him in good scoring position; without looking, he knows the puck is going to the point — so he heads to the net for a pass or a rebound.

The one thing that would make his skating and puckhandling better would be if he shot more. Guy can create the openings, but he hesitates in his shooting. It's not that he can't get the message from his brain to his hands fast enough (he can still get his shot off) — perhaps he just wants to be a team player and find a teammate.

THE PHYSICAL GAME

Never known as a physical player, Lafleur demonstrated that he can take the rough going despite his age. He still operates best in open ice, more so now that he's lost a degree of the foot speed that used to let him get to the boards for the puck and get away.

Nevertheless, he has been significantly injured in both of his comeback years. His health will continue to be a concern.

THE INTANGIBLES

Over an 80 game slate, Lafleur's numbers would have been 24 goals and 68 points — not bad for an "old man". Of course, the odds of his playing a full season are long ones. Still, Guy can play the game without hurting his team. Apparently the Quebec management realizes that contributions can be made not only in points but in attitude — which means Guy should be fine here.

He remains a team's hardest and most enthusiastic worker, and the attitude and spirit he can convey to younger players is beyond measure.

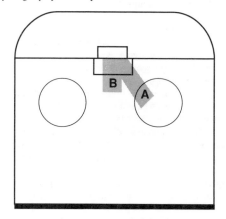

CURTIS LESCHYSHYN

Yrs. of NHL service: 2
Born: Thompson, Man., Canada; September 21, 1969
Position: Defenseman
Height: 6-1
Weight: 205
Uniform no.: 7
Shoots: left

Career statistics:

GP	G	A	TP	PIM
139	6	15	21	115

1989-90 statistics:

GP	G	A	TP	+/-	PIM	PP	SH	GW	GT	S	PCT
68	2	6	8	-41	44	1	0	0	0	42	4.8

LAST SEASON

Plus/minus was club's third worst. Games played, point and PIM totals fell from rookie year levels.

THE FINESSE GAME

For a player with his size and bulk, Leschyshyn is a surprisingly mobile skater. Though not a speed demon like, say, Paul Coffey, Leschyshyn has good speed because of his stride, and good foot speed for quickness. Those components combine with his balance to make him a strong skater in all directions — forward, backward and laterally.

His finesse ability continues through his hand and stick skills. He can move the puck very well, as his hands are soft enough for good passes to both sides and his sense is strong enough to show him the openings and his teammates. What Leschyshyn must continue to work on is his ability to react at the NHL level. He finds the open man in the offensive zone well enough, but could improve in doing the same while being checked in his own end.

He's unafraid to charge the net from his point position, and he'll carry the puck deep when he gains the opposing blue line. Again, as with his breakout passes, greater NHL experience will help him better choose the correct times for these rushes.

He has a good shot from the point, low and hard to the net for rebounds, and Leschyshyn should learn to shoot more — as his shots on goal total indicates.

He continues to play his defense reactively rather than actively, but he must learn to step up and close the gap on the puck carrier if he wants to maximize his skating ability. Here too, better familiarity with the speed of NHL play will help his play reading. Currently, he concentrates more on the puck than the man.

THE PHYSICAL GAME

Leschyshyn will sacrifice his body to block shots, and that indicates his intensity and physical willingness.

He has good size and strength, but not necessarily the requisite meanness to truly punish the opposition in front of his net. He plays efficiently physically, therefore, taking out the man fairly well in both the corners and the crease, but no one is afraid of mixing it up with him.

He makes his degree of physical play more effective by virtue of his ability to make plays coming out of the corner.

THE INTANGIBLES

Don't get the wrong idea here — we know that Leschyshyn is only in his second NHL year, and that he plays with a weaker team. Instead, we are saying that he has barely scratched the surface of his fairly considerable potential. This isn't his fault — he just needs time (and a more stable environment) in which to do so.

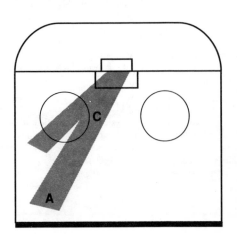

CLAUDE LOISELLE

Yrs. of NHL service: 8
Born: Ottawa, Ont., Canada; May 29, 1963
Position: Center
Height: 5-11
Weight: 190
Uniform no.: 20
Shoots: left

Career statistics:

GP	G	A	TP	PIM
417	73	92	165	804

1989-90 statistics:

GP	G	A	TP	+/-	PIM	PP	SH	GW	GT	S	PCT
72	11	14	25	-27	104	0	3	0	0	128	8.6

LAST SEASON

PIM total was career low. Led club in shorthanded goals. Missed three games with a separated shoulder.

THE FINESSE GAME

The finesse part of the game is not the best apsect of Loiselle's contributions to Quebec; his skills top out at average — at best. His skating is marked not by speed or agility but by strength and balance. He has a wide stance and generates a lot of power because of it (allowing him to drive through checks) as well as providing Loiselle with a strong base — he's hard to knock off his feet. However, because his feet are planted so far apart, his agility tends to go right out the window.

He succeeds as a checker and as a penalty killer because of his puck pursuit, but Loiselle also has a fair degree of anticipation and ice vision he can bring to bear. Loiselle is unable, however, to convert that modicum of hockey sense into offensive success. He is not creative offensively (he demonstrates his lack of offensive understanding by consistently taking himself to his backhand), needing time and space to find his teammates, and his hand skills don't do anything to help his offense either. What goals he does collect will have to come on miscues in the opponent's zone — he does have a quick shot.

THE PHYSICAL GAME

Loiselle generally plays bigger than his size, taking the body forcefully in all three zones. His balance keeps him upright (one instance where that wide stance helps) after hitting, and his checks can wear down the opposition.

He is also liberal in the use of his stick, but he will not fight to back up the ruckuses he creates. Because of his good hand and arm strength, as well as eye/hand coordination, Loiselle excels at faceoffs.

THE INTANGIBLES

Loiselle succeeds by staying within his limitations and by working extremely hard. He is, however, a role player at best — and role players are always liable to replacement.

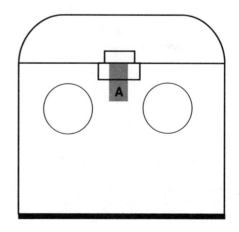

MARIO MAROIS

Yrs. of NHL service: 11
Born: Ancienne Lorette, Quebec, Canada;
December 15, 1957
Position: Defenseman
Height: 5-11
Weight: 190
Uniform no.: 44
Shoots: right

Career statistics:

GP	G	A	TP	PIM
840	73	339	412	1,593

1989-90 statistics:

GP	G	A	TP	+/-	PIM	PP	SH	GW	GT	S	PCT
67	3	15	18	-45	104	2	0	0		0	108	2.8

LAST SEASON

Point total was second lowest of career (lowest for a full season). Plus/minus mark was team's second worst, third worst in NHL. He missed 12 games with a shoulder injury.

THE FINESSE GAME

The offensive part of the game has long been Marois' NHL strength, and a decade in the big league has done nothing to change that. He is a good skater from north to south, in that his forward and backward mobility is good; he even has a reserve burst of speed that can catch the opposition napping, although Marois is less able to bring that to bear as his career progresses. He is not a dynamic lateral skater, and remains vulnerable one-on-one because of his slow turns.

His offensive rushes are now few and far between, with Marois more likely to move the puck than he is to skate it. That's not to say, given the opportunity, that Marois won't take off for the offensive zone. Rather, he's playing patiently not forcing situations. He handles and moves the puck well while skating (always has), will follow the play up-ice, and can certainly find the open man; that's why he'll see power play time.

Those same levels of vision and puck movement are present in the defensive zone. Marois also plays the man fairly well, staying in position and sticking with his check. These are recent improvements.

THE PHYSICAL GAME

Marois will hit whenever he can and has a mean streak that makes him difficult for opposing forwards to ignore. He will slash or elbow in front of the net and will do the same while fighting for the puck in the corners or along the boards.

He hits the opposition, rather than just pushing and shoving in the corners, and the hitting jars the puck free. Marois has the ability to take advantage of those loose pucks, making his hits more effective.

THE INTANGIBLES

He carried a reputation for being self-centered, but Marois' maturity and stability (as indicated by the poise he has developed over the last several seasons) have made him a leader for Quebec. He remains dedicated and committed to the game.

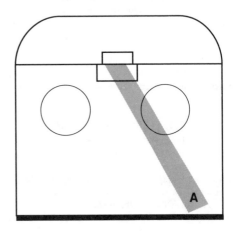

TONY MCKEGNEY

Yrs. of NHL service: 12
Born: Montreal, Quebec, Canada; February 15, 1958
Position: Left wing
Height: 6-1
Weight: 215
Uniform no.: 14
Shoots: left

Career statistics:

GP	G	A	TP	PIM
853	303	302	605	468

1989-90 statistics:

GP	G	A	TP	+/-	PIM	PP	SH	GW	GT	S	PCT
62	18	12	30	-29	53	5	0	0	0	107	16.8

LAST SEASON

Acquired from Detroit in exchange for Robert Picard. Games played total was second lowest full-season total of career; ditto goal total. He missed time with a groin injury.

THE FINESSE GAME

McKegney's a good skater, whose strength gives him speed and acceleration down the wing. Tony does have a degree of agility (and some lateral movement), but his is mostly a straight ahead speed. It is that speed that puts him in the clear and allows him to use his tremendous shot. He can also be a good checker because of his speed, making quick transitions up and down the ice.

His shot is excellent, laser-like and quickly released, and McKegney must use it to be successful. It is hard and accurate, and McKegney uses it whenever possible; he wants the puck when he's in shooting position.

His offensive diligence makes him a solid bet for an annual 25 goals, and that diligence can extend to the defensive zone where he has the capability to play well positionally. His anticipation and vision — his hockey sense — help him at both ends of the ice, but a dose more of defensive patience wouldn't hurt.

THE PHYSICAL GAME

Tony has good physical abilities — and excellent strength — but he doesn't always use those abilities the best he can. He can be very effective along the boards and especially in front of the net, because — once he plants himself — Tony's balance makes him very difficult to move. But there are times when he could be using those assets to muscle the puck in the corners or along the boards, but he's found instead outside the scrum and waiting for the loose puck to come to him.

He'll take the rough going and return it, but he is not a dirty player.

THE INTANGIBLES

Streakiness as a scorer has always been McKegney's blessing/curse. He can make strong contributions to any club in terms of scoring, but his play is essentially limited to that one dimension.

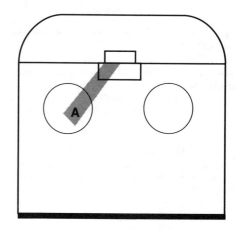

KEN MCRAE

Yrs. of NHL service: 1
Born: Winchester, Ont., Canada; April 23, 1968
Position: Center
Height: 6-1
Weight: 195
Uniform no.: 12
Shoots: left

Career statistics:

GP	G	A	TP	PIM
104	13	19	32	259

1989-90 statistics:

GP	G	A	TP	+/-	PIM	PP	SH	GW	GT	S	PCT
66	7	8	15	-38	191	0	0	1	0	83	8.4

LAST SEASON

Third stint with Nordiques. PIM total second highest among forwards. Missed seven games with elbow injury, six games with bruised shoulder.

THE FINESSE GAME

McRae's skating is questionable — but improving — at the NHL level. He still would be ranked as a no better than average skater, but he gets by because of his strength and determination, rather than on any exceptional skating skill (speed, quickness, agility). That skating strength does power his physical game, driving him to the net on offense, and through his checks when hitting. His balance also helps here, keeping him vertical after his many collisions.

His ability to make offensive plays at the NHL level is restricted to going into the corner and digging the puck out, but his hand skills aren't such that he'll wheel and deal his way into open space; given sufficient time and space he'll get the puck to his teammates, but right now he's a "hit the guy and what do I do next with the puck," type player.

He can shoot the puck, but again, needs to improve his ability at the NHL level. He is a very good stick checker, taking the puck from the opposition quickly and easily, but that hand speed hasn't yet manifested itself into NHL goal scoring ability. He'll have to be opportunistic near the net to score.

THE PHYSICAL GAME

Here is where McRae shines, as his PIM total might indicate. He is a tough, tough kid, absolutely fearless. He uses his body very well and is helped in that by his balance (making him a very effective traffic player) and skating strength. He makes the opposition pay for the puck.

He can also use his strength to hold off the opposition, and he can cross the line from rough to mean.

THE INTANGIBLES

McRae is a banger, and he could become a very dangerous player if and when his hands and feet catch up to his physical willingness. He has an excellent attitude and great desire, and he has the work ethic to improve — which must be encouraging to Quebec because McRae is only 22 years old.

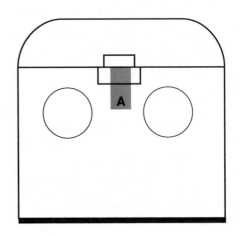

MICHEL PETIT

Yrs. of NHL service: 7
Born: St. Malo, Quebec, Canada; February 12, 1964
Position: Defenseman
Height: 6-1
Weight: 205
Uniform no.: 24
Shoots: right

Career statistics:

GP	G	A	TP	PIM
422	53	130	183	965

1989-90 statistics:

GP	G	A	TP	+/-	PIM	PP	SH	GW	GT	S	PCT
63	12	24	36	-38	215	5	0	0	0	137	8.8

LAST SEASON

Acquired from New York in exchange for Randy Moller. Finished second on the club in scoring, assists and PIM total (first among defensemen in the last category) despite four-season low in games-played total (he missed time with a back injury, as well as two games with a concussion). Point total equalled career best.

THE FINESSE GAME

Petit is an excellent skater, equipped with good balance and speed, but what makes him exceptional in this department is his agility. He has good lateral movement and change-of-direction skills for a man with his size and bulk, which could make him an above-average player in all three zones.

But doesn't, because Petit's hockey sense and playmaking abilities are not at the level of his skating. While he's smart enough to keep the play ahead of him, on the whole his play-reading and vision abilities are of the first-play variety. He doesn't get a great look at the ice before making a breakout pass, so Michel will make the first play he sees.

His skating should allow him to step up on the opposition, and Petit will do so to make hits part of the time, but he doesn't make a play after that check. And more likely, Petit will just react to the opposing winger and fall back. In all, his total play without the puck, though already improved, can be better.

He can be a dangerous offensive force, for Petit will rush if given the chance. He handles the puck and shoots it well, but he doesn't shoot anywhere near enough for a guy that gets so many opportunities.

THE PHYSICAL GAME

The physical game is the best plus Petit brings to Quebec. He's big and has very good strength, which he is not afraid to use against anyone. He can hurt people when he hits them, and Petit hits often — sometimes *too* often.

On penalty killing, for example, where he's needed to clear the front of the net, Petit is often concerned with ramming a puck-carrying opponent into the boards — taking himself out of the play and turning a 5-on-4 into a 4-on-3.

He'll drop the gloves when necessary, and he has also become very liberal in his use of his stick on the opposition. Michel is also talented enough to make a play after taking an opponent off the puck.

THE INTANGIBLES

As long as he stays within his limits, Petit can be a valuable player. But he must concentrate on unextravagant things: take the body, move the puck, follow the play. The more chances he takes, the more chance he has of making a mistake.

Interesting, too, to note that the contract squabbles that led to his trade from New York continued in Quebec.

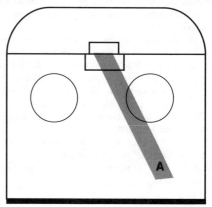

JOE SAKIC

Yrs. of NHL service: 2
Born: Burnaby, B.C., Canada; July 7, 1969
Position: Center
Height: 5-11
Weight: 185
Uniform no.: 19
Shoots: left

Career statistics:

GP	G	A	TP	PIM
150	62	102	164	51

1989-90 statistics:

GP	G	A	TP	+/-	PIM	PP	SH	GW	GT	S	PCT
80	39	63	102	-40	27	8	1	2	1	234	16.7

LAST SEASON

Led club in all point categories, and shots on goal. Finished tenth in NHL scoring. His plus/minus rating was worst among club's forwards.

THE FINESSE GAME

Sakic is an excellent skater in all facets of that skill, possessing speed, quickness, strength, agility and balance. He is a shifty player and he uses his agility and lateral movement to great effect. Between his quickness and his agility, Sakic will either get to most every loose puck or evade most any defender.

His balance (which obviously powers his agility) enables him to succeed in traffic, driving the net and maintaining body position despite the defenders he drags along. His skating strength also allows him to body his man off the puck, something he does efficiently and in all three zones.

Sakic's hand skills complement his skating. He easily makes plays after checks and can come out of the corner with the puck, and he melds his soft hands (he passes excellently to both sides) with his outstanding hockey sense to become an excellent playmaker. He always has his head up, looks for give-and-goes, and has the patience to draw defenders to him in order to open space. He handles the puck at top speed and in tight quarters.

He is a scorer as well as a playmaker; he is very creative without the puck and knows how to get into scoring position. Sakic's exceptional sense and patience are the keys here. He has an excellent selection of shots, all of which are outstanding. He delivers his shots quickly to the net, and his accurate touch forces the goalie to make saves. Joe also has a great backhand, which he uses freqeuntly.

Sakic has great understanding of his defensive responsibilties and he fulfills them conscientiously, plus/minus mark (a testimony to his ice time) to the contrary.

THE PHYSICAL GAME

He's not the biggest guy, but Sakic plays a complete game — and that includes the physical aspect. He takes the body and works willingly in traffic, and he sacrifices his body to make plays.

THE INTANGIBLES

Sakic is now clearly the main man in Quebec, and the Nordiques couldn't have found a better cornerstone. He is a dedicated, responsible, character individual who will be the foundation of any future Nordiques success. Any team could use a player with his spark and leadership ability.

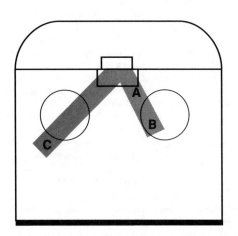

RON TUGNUTT

Yrs. of NHL service: 2
Born: Scarborough, Ont., Canada; October 22, 1967
Position: Goaltender
Height: 5-11
Weight: 150
Uniform no.: 30
Catches: left

Career statistics:

GP	MINS	G	SO	AVG	A	PIM
67	3,629	250	0	4.13	4	4

1989-90 statistics:

GP	MINS	AVG	W	L	T	SO	GA	SA	SAPCT	PIM
35	1,978	4.61	5	24	3	0	152	1,080	.859	2

LAST SEASON

Led Quebec goalies in games played with career best appearance and minutes played totals. He missed time with a knee injury, and rehabilitated in Halifax of the American Hockey League.

THE PHYSICAL GAME

Tugnutt's game is based in his angle play. He will challenge the shooters whenever possible, and he can rely on his quick reflexes whenever necessary (which in Quebec is frequently, considering the club allowed the most goals and second most shots in the NHL last season).

He has good balance and quickness, and his strong skating makeshim solid laterally; he moves as well across the crease as he does in and out of the net. His balance gets him back into his stance quickly after he extends himself or leaves his feet, and he needs that balance because he goes down early when he's struggling.

Ron has excellent reflexes. His quick feet block the shots toward the corner, and his glove matches his feet for speed. Because of his speed, he'll get a piece of many of the pucks that beat him for goals.

He handles the puck behind the net, but right now Tugnutt concentrates on first things first and doesn't dally out of the net.

THE MENTAL GAME

He prepares to play well, and Tugnutt has the ability to maintain his concentration within games and from contest to contest. He has had a tough time recovering from early goals, but Tugnutt is generally a confident player not easily shaken by goals or games.

THE INTANGIBLES

Tugnutt is an enthusiastic player, one who works hard always. He went a long way last season toward cementing a roster spot in Quebec, though the solid late-season play of Scott Gordon and the expected debut of Stephane Fiset may chip away at Tugnutt's base.

CRAIG WOLANIN

Yrs. of NHL service: 5
Born: Grosse Pointe, Mich., USA; July 27, 1967
Position: Defenseman
Height: 6-3
Weight: 205
Uniform no.: 6
Shoots: left

Career statistics:

GP	G	A	TP	PIM
296	16	65	81	479

1989-90 statistics:

GP	G	A	TP	+/-	PIM	PP	SH	GW	GT	S	PCT
50	1	10	11	-11	57	0	0	0	0	60	1.7

LAST SEASON

Acquired from New Jersey in exchange for Peter Stastny. Games played total was second lowest of career; ditto point total. Goal total was career low. He shuttled in and out of the New Jersey lineup, and spent time in Utica of the American Hockey League.

THE FINESSE GAME

Wolanin is at a number of career plateaus, not the least of which come in the finesse skills department. After showing continued improvement in his skating abilities (more quickness and power, better balance and agility) for each of his NHL seasons, he topped (bottomed?) out last season. Being benched and traded can take some of the blame for that, but the argument is of the chicken/egg variety. If his play was good enough he'd get ice time, but he can't maintain his level of play without ice time.

Craig plays a basic positional style of defense, forcing play wide of the net as often as not. He's helped by the fact that he pivots well and is able to keep pace with the opposition, but must constantly remind himself to rein in his wandering tendencies. He reads the rush toward him fairly well and is not often beaten one-on-one.

As with his skating, his offensive play-reading and playmaking skills have stilled. His puckhandling and movement is below average, and he wavers in making his decisions. Still, he often enough shows the ability to make the right choices. Overall, though, he is less than a sure-thing.

He can shoot the puck fairly well from the blue line, and his shot is a heavy one, but he doesn't shoot anywhere near often enough.

THE PHYSICAL GAME

When he hits, Wolanin hits well for a big guy. By that we mean his balance is very good, keeping him upright after hitting and ready to get back into the play. Essentially however, Wolanin remains a prisoner of his size. Though he can be extremely mean in front of the net he isn't mean enough often enough.

He is tremendously strong, but Wolanin does not consistently apply his size in front of the net or along the boards. He consistently fails to complete his checks, pushing and shoving instead of taking the body.

He is willing to sacrifice his body by blocking shots but, in short, Wolanin plays smaller than he is. He is not a fighter.

THE INTANGIBLES

There is an argument to be made that Wolanin is the classic case of the wasted 18-year-old — draft pick forced to play in the NHL long before he was ready. There is also an argument to be made that Wolanin never got the coaching and direction he needed to get in New Jersey. Both of these would be true.

However, there is also the argument to be made that Wolanin hasn't applied himself as strongly as he could (perhaps understandable under his circumstances) and after five years he has shown nothing that points to his being a top defenseman. There is potential — and at age 23 Wolanin is certainly still young enough to reach it — but how hard will it be to teach this young old dog some new tricks?

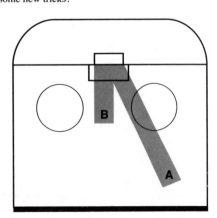

ST. LOUIS BLUES

ROD BRIND'AMOUR

Yrs. of NHL service: 1
Born: Ottawa, Ont., Canada; August 9, 1970
Position: Left wing/center
Height: 6-1
Weight: 200
Uniform no.: 19
Shoots: left

Career statistics:

GP	G	A	TP	+/-	PIM	PP	SH	GW	GT	S	PCT
79	26	35	61	23	46	10	0	1	1	160	16.3

LAST SEASON

Brind'amour's first NHL season; he played five playoff games during 1989. Finished sixth among rookies in scoring, fifth in goals and assists, third in plus/minus, power play and first goals, and fifth in shots. He was third on St. Louis in goals and power play goals, and he led the club in plus/minus.

THE FINESSE GAME

Brind'amour's finesse potential is outstanding. He's already an excellent skater at the NHL level, combining speed and strength into a dynamic package. His balance is outstanding and provides him with a high degree of agility, but it combines with his strength to make him an irresistible force along the wood, in the corners and in front of the net. Brind'amour goes to the net and is very strong on the puck.

He has the confidence in his ability to stickhandle and carry the puck, and he's already demonstrated that will make plays at the NHL level. He certainly has the intelligence and hockey sense to get good reads and, though he falters in puck movement occasionally (he'll make the read but his hands won't move fast enough), Brind'amour is already good and will get better.

He uses his physical and mental finesse skills to great result in all three zones, getting into position to score offensively (he works very well in the traffic area in front of the net because of his balance and hand and arm strength) or to cover his position defensively.

He has a good shot and likes to go high with it, and Brind'amour should shoot more. His skills have already made him a regular on both penalty killing units.

THE PHYSICAL GAME

Brind'amour's physical potential matches that of his finesse game. He is already big and strong, so much so that he can dominate a corner situation. His balance has already been discussed, but he uses it in conjunction with his strength to drive opponents off the puck. His upper body strength is just as good, and will gain him the puck after a corner scrum.

He hits hard, often and willingly, and Brind'amour initiates contact all over the ice. There are occasions when he will not use his size and strength consistently, but greater experience in the pace of both NHL's games and the season itself should solve that problem.

THE INTANGIBLES

Brind'amour has already been compared to a young Bryan Trottier, and those are big skates to fill. Since he's been moved to wing comparisons to Cam Neely or Rick Tocchet (at least in terms of physical play and scoring) may be more apt. Whatever, Brind'amour's debut was a terrific one. He'll have a tougher time achieving that performance this season (he's not a surprise any more and will see better checking) but this is a player whose attitude and work ethic insure a very bright future.

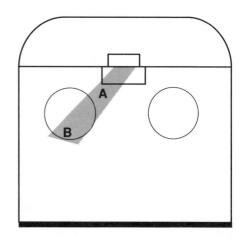

JEFF BROWN

Yrs. of NHL service: 4
Born: Ottawa, Ontario, Canada; April 30, 1966
Position: Defenseman
Height: 6-1
Weight: 202
Uniform no.: 21
Shoots: right

Career statistics:

GP	G	A	TP	PIM
285	63	146	209	203

1989-90 statistics:

GP	G	A	TP	+/-	PIM	PP	SH	GW	GT	S	PCT
77	16	38	54	-26	55	8	1	3	0	284	5.6

LAST SEASON

Acquired from Quebec in exchange for Greg Millen and Tony Hrkac. Point total was second highest of career; he led Blues defensemen in scoring. Plus/minus was the club's worst.

THE FINESSE GAME

Jeff's combination of power, quickness and strength give him speed, acceleration and outstanding lateral ability — all combine to make him an excellent skater. He can jump into an opening or change direction within a stride, and his lateral movement is especially pronounced when he's skating backward and controlling the puck at the offensive blue line.

He's an excellent puckhandler, and Brown loves to carry the puck from the defensive zone to lead an attack, charging to — and then blasting a shot from — the offensive right faceoff circle.

Brown sees the play well when it is ahead of him, so he can get the puck to an open teammate in any zone. He uses his outstanding skating ability to control play in the offensive zone (though he could improve his judgement on pinching in), and combines his containment ability with his vision and anticipation to lead a teammate into an as-yet-unopen opening.

Brown has a good shot from the blue line, low and hard, and he also likes to charge the net on give-and-gos.

Jeff's defense is still questionable, in that he succeeds more on talent than he does on sense — forcing plays by charging at puckcarriers to create turnovers — instead of making the safe defensive play. Jeff also has a concentration flaw, becoming hypnotized by the puck rather than covering his side of the net. He'll also get trapped in the offensive zone when he is crowded to the corner and forced to his backhand, from which he makes blind, weak passes that lead to turnovers.

THE PHYSICAL GAME

Brown doesn't really have a physical game. His skills would allow him to take the body well, but Jeff sometimes-just-kinda gets in the way. Of course, any degree of physical play is amplified by his terrific ability to make a play out of a confrontation. Otherwise, his play in the corners and the front of the net is no better (and could be worse) than average.

He is able to use his body to protect the puck from the opposition, particularly at the offensive blue line where Brown is very good at keeping the puck away from defenders.

THE INTANGIBLES

Brown has always been at odds with Nordiques management (and former coach Michel Bergeron) so it was no surprise to see him bounced from Quebec. The bone management always picked with him concerned his intensity during games and practices, and Brown must show that a new working environment will lead to a new attitude.

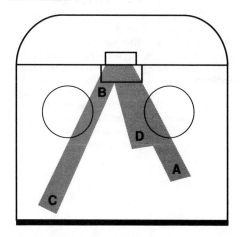

GINO CAVALLINI

Yrs. of NHL service: 6
Born: Toronto, Ontario, Canada; November 24, 1962
Position: Left wing
Height: 6-1
Weight: 215
Uniform no.: 17
Shoots: left

Career statistics:

GP	G	A	TP	PIM
382	87	103	190	348

1989-90 statistics:

GP	G	A	TP	+/-	PIM	PP	SH	GW	GT	S	PCT
80	15	15	30	-8	77	1	0	4	0	134	11.2

LAST SEASON

Played 80 games for the second time in career. Point total was four-season low. Plus/minus total was third worst among forwards.

THE FINESSE GAME

Skating would be the best of Cavallini's finesse skills, and it is certainly the asset that best allows him to play his strong physical game. He has excellent strength and balance, though is less gifted in the agility/shiftiness areas. His stride will take him to the puck, and isgood enough to put him in position to hit the opposition; he'll be the first forechecker.

Cavallini can create loose pucks and scoring opportunities with his checking, but he is not a gifted passer or playmaker. As he checks by pursuing the puck (and not through anticipation), so too does he make plays — look up, and move the puck, rather than hold the puck and create opportunities. He also lacks hands soft enough for effective playmaking, but the 15-20 goals he'll score a year are pretty good numbers for a checker.

THE PHYSICAL GAME

Cavallini makes excellent use of his size and strength, both of which are above average — he may be St. Louis' best hitter. His stride drives him through his checks, and Cavallini has the strength to hurt people when he hits them — certainly, he'll at least wear down his targets.

His good upper body strength combines with his skating to make him hard to pin against the boards on takeouts — in other words, he'll always be in your face. He'll also use his strength to go to the net.

He makes his physical play even more effective by playing smartly; as his PIM total indicates, Cavallini stays on the ice and out of the box.

THE INTANGIBLES

He must play physically to be successful — that's Cavallini's key. He's a hard worker, and we think one of the NHL's more underrated players.

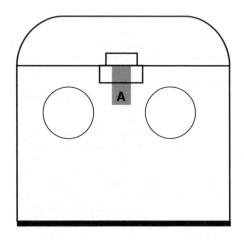

PAUL CAVALLINI

Yrs. of NHL service: 3
Born: Toronto, Ontario, Canada; October 13, 1965
Position: Defenseman
Height: 6-2
Weight: 200
Uniform no.: 14
Shoots: left

Career statistics:

GP	G	A	TP	PIM
223	18	71	89	394

1989-90 statistics:

GP	G	A	TP	+/-	PIM	PP	SH	GW	GT	S	PCT
80	8	39	47	38	106	2	1	0	0	135	5.9

LAST SEASON

Games played and all point totals were career highs; he led the Blues' defense in assists and his plus/minus rating was the NHL's best.

THE FINESSE GAME

Cavallini is a strong finesse player, one who has developed and will continue to improve at the NHL level. He is a fine all-around skater, strong in speed, agility and balance, and he uses those assets in all situations: challenging and closing the gap at his blue line, rushing the puck, forechecking and containing the point. In all, he uses his skating to play a strong active (versus re-active) style.

He complements his skating with intelligence. Where previously he had been weak in his play-reading ability, Cavallini now plays cautiously so as not to hurt his team. He has learned to hold his defensive position and to not chase the puck, and he will only challenge at the point when he can do so safely.

He finds the open man well at both ends of the ice and works well at turning the play around quickly in his own zone. His offensive strength comes from his passing, but Cavallini also has a degree of goal-scoring skill. He has a good — not great — shot and will get most of his goals from the blue line, but he'll charge the net when given the chance.

His skills make him a specialty teams regular.

THE PHYSICAL GAME

Cavallini has good size and strength and he uses both skills without hesitation. He's a tough, willing kid who hits frequently and intelligently, and he's also unintimidated — he'll go after the Dave Mansons and the like. He's very involved in the traffic areas.

His balance helps greatly here by keeping him vertical and ready to make plays after collisions, and

Cavallini certainly has the ability to make those plays. He is not a fighter.

THE INTANGIBLES

Right now, Cavallini is the Blues' best all-around defenseman. He gained a degree of well-deserved attention by being selected to the All-Star Game last season, and it is a measure of how unknown he is that fans raised their eyebrows and asked, "Paul *who*?" after his selection. Rest assured, the rest of the NHL knows exactly who he is.

He is a worker, enthusiastic, determined to improve, coachable, and a top team man well-liked by his teammates. What else could you want?

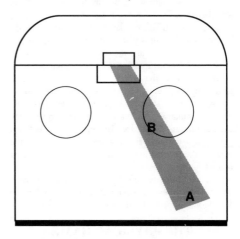

BRETT HULL

Yrs. of NHL service: 3
Born: Belleville, Ontario, Canada; August 9, 1964
Position: Right wing
Height: 5-11
Weight: 190
Uniform no.: 16
Shoots: right

Career statistics:

GP	G	A	TP	PIM
228	146	116	262	73

1989-90 statistics:

GP	G	A	TP	+/-	PIM	PP	SH	GW	GT	S	PCT
80	72	41	113	-1	24	27	0	12	0	385	18.7

LAST SEASON

Played 80 games for first time. Finished fifth in NHL with career bests in goals and points. Led NHL in goals, power play goals and shots on goal, finished second in game winning goals. Led club in all above categories.

THE FINESSE GAME

All right, let's get this out of the way: Brett Hull has the best shot in the NHL. Mike Bossy used to have it, other players can score in more ways, but Hull has the best shot in the NHL. Period.

His boomer off the wing was legendary before he even made the NHL, and Hull has made himself a more dangerous player by adding to his repertoire. The same wrist and hand strength and speed that power his slap shot also key his wrist and snap shots, which he now uses more than the big blast. He shoots excellently off the pass, and the exaggeration — if it is exaggeration at all — is only slight when we say he can score from anywhere.

He shows great anticipation offensively and jumps into the holes beautifully. In short, he has a goal scorer's sense. He'll always take the offensive option (as his plus/minus demonstrates), and he is very dangerous in open ice — note the power play numbers. Hull also looks to use his teammates but make no mistakes — he's going to shoot first and ask questions later. His SOG total shows that: 385 last season, versus 305 in 1988-89.

His improved foot speed means he's even better at getting into scoring position, so even though his skating is not at the level of his shooting, it no longer lags far behind.

The one downside is his defense, which remains questionable at best. Improved attention in his defensive zone would improve his deserved plus/minus rating.

THE PHYSICAL GAME

Not previously known as a physical player, and certainly not to be mistaken for Cam Neely or even teammate Gino Cavallini, Hull nevertheless has begun to assert himself more physically. He charges the net and goes to the traffic areas, and his improved strength has helped him win these confrontations. He still prefers open ice, but the physical dimension he's added to his game has helped him improve — and will continue to do so.

THE INTANGIBLES

We like Brett Hull a lot; we'd like him more if he could fold a better defensive attitude into his game. But we would be remiss if we didn't discuss his improved work ethic as demonstrated by his working out in the off-season, by his weight loss so as to be quicker and stronger, by his clearer focus during games.

He recognizes his need to push himself and and has shown the maturity to do so. He'll need every ounce of that character this season as he attempts to live up to the standards — and big contract — he has earned for himself.

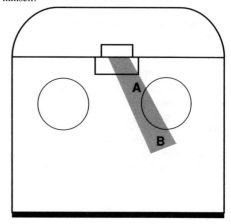

CURTIS JOSEPH

Yrs. of NHL service: 1
Born: Keswick, Ontario, Canada; April 29, 1965
Position: Goaltender
Height: 5-10
Weight: 170
Uniform no.: 31
Catches: left

Career statistics:

GP	MINS	AVG	W	L	T	SO	GA	SA	SAPCT	PIM
15	852	3.38	9	5	1	0	48	435	.890	0

LAST SEASON

Signed as a free agent by the Blues in summer of 1989. Joined St. Louis from Peoria of the International Hockey League on January 1.

THE PHYSICAL GAME

Joseph is a fundamentally sound goaltender, one who plays his angles well and relies on his challenging style to stop the puck (an intelligent style to play, given his size) but isn't afraid to use his strong reflexes.

He moves well in and around the net, and his balance and quickness take him to the ice and back to his feet quickly for his second save. He generally controls the puck well in terms of rebounds (clearing them to the corners and away from the front of the net) and his skating will allow him to help his teammates by flagging down loose pucks.

Joseph's quickness works for him in his short game — bang-bang plays around the net like passouts or criss-crosses, as well as in scrambles.

THE MENTAL GAME

As he demonstrated down the stretch and in the playoffs, Joseph has big save capability. He handles pressure well and still maintains his focus and concentration, retaining his intensity from period to period and game to game.

He understands and anticipates well, and his concentration is helped by his vision; few are the shots he won't see on their way in.

THE INTANGIBLES

Joseph's late-season heroics showed he's worth the kind of money the Blues plunked down for his services two summers ago. Like many rookie goalies during their first NHL playoff action he's shown well, but only time will tell if Joseph's rookie season more closely parallels that of — say — Ken Dryden or that of one-hit wonder Steve Penney. And, already 25 years old, time is not something Joseph has a lot of.

MIKE LALOR

Yrs. of NHL service: 5
Born: Buffalo, N.Y., USA; March 8, 1963
Position: Defenseman
Height: 6-0
Weight: 193
Uniform no.: 26
Shoots: left

Career statistics:

GP	G	A	TP	PIM
311	6	59	65	366

1989-90 statistics:

GP	G	A	TP	+/-	PIM	PP	SH	GW	GT	S	PCT
78	0	16	16	-6	81	0	0	0	0	79	0.0

LAST SEASON

Games played total was career high. Missed time with a groin injury.

THE FINESSE GAME

Lalor's is an understated (and thus underrated) style, but don't let understated fool you — he's a very efficient and successful defensive defenseman.

No one of his finesse skills stands out more than any other, which is not to say that his skills are unremarkable. On the contrary, because he skates and moves the puck so well and so smoothly — because all his gears mesh — nothing he does seems exceptional. His skating in both the vertical and horizontal dimensions is strong and sound, and he complements his skating skill with good play-reading ability and hockey smarts: Lalor challenges very well at his blue line because of his mobility and brains.

He doesn't use his skating to rush the puck (and will be paired with a partner who does), instead choosing to make not only the right pass but a good one to a breaking forward (his one flaw, and he has improved in each of his seasons, is reading and reacting to NHL-speed forechecking). Otherwise Lalor does not frequently handle the puck.

Clearly he is not a goal scorer. He will not venture from his blue line position while in the offensive zone, so any point he gets will come from there.

These skills make him a penalty killing regular.

THE PHYSICAL GAME

More and more, Lalor is using all his tools and that includes his size and strength. He controls the front of the net against most every opponent, using his size, reach and strength to neutralize the forward or move him from the crease. Lalor has also improved his take-outs along the boards.

He does all this smartly, keeping himself out of the box and on the ice. He has a good reach and can poke check effectively or deflect the puck.

THE INTANGIBLES

Lalor is a smart, coachable and willing player, the kind of player who commands attention from his teammates when he speaks. Though a late bloomer by NHL standards (remember the maxim that says a defenseman needs five seasons to hit his potential? Last season was Lalor's fifth, and he is already 27 years old.), he can still improve his already strong game. As it is he is an integral part of any Blues success.

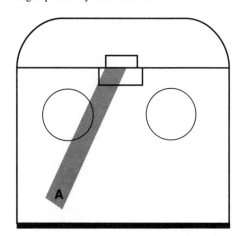

DAVE LOWRY

Yrs. of NHL service: 4
Born: Sudbury, Ontario, Canada; January 14, 1965
Position: Left wing
Height: 6-2
Weight: 175
Uniform no.: 10
Shoots: left

Career statistics:

GP	G	A	TP	PIM
264	41	30	71	443

1989-90 statistics:

GP	G	A	TP	+/-	PIM	PP	SH	GW	GT	S	PCT
78	19	6	25	1	75	0	2	1	1	98	19.4

LAST SEASON

Games played, goal and point totals were career bests. Tied for team lead in shorthanded goals (Adam Oates).

THE FINESSE GAME

Lowry is strong skater, equipped with good balance and that helps him in his physical game. Because of his skating, and because Lowry has a degree of vision and anticipation, he is a good and enthusiastic checking forward. He is also smarter defensively than most young players.

Offensively, Lowry hasn't shown that he is especially gifted at the NHL level. He doesn't handle or carry the puck with particular skill, nor has he demonstrated an ability to use his teammates. Lowry can bang in the corners, but has no clue what to do after he gets the puck.

He doesn't have especially good hands, so Lowry will have to score from close to the net with junk goals. His shot is — at best —average, but he'll take advantage of some of the loose pucks his checking creates.

He is a regular on the penalty killing unit.

THE PHYSICAL GAME

Lowry is a physical player, bringing size and toughness to the rink. He does yeoman work in the corners by hitting when he can, and he enjoys that style. He is effective that way, jarring the puck loose from the opposition and he plays that way at both ends of the ice. His insistent physical play will wear down the opposition.

He is strong on his skates and uses his size and strength to best advantage in front of the opposition net, where he is very difficult to dislodge.

THE INTANGIBLES

Lowry is another of those players where the plus/minus gets tossed out the window. Because of his defensive proficiency, he's always on against the opposition's best. Hence, a relatively poor plus/minus rating.

He's a hard worker who has toiled off-ice to strengthen himself on-ice.

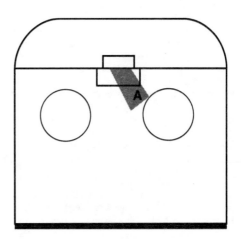

PAUL MACLEAN

Yrs. of NHL service: 9
Born: Grostenquin, France; March 9, 1958
Position: Right wing
Height: 6-2
Weight: 205
Uniform no.: 15
Shoots: right

Career statistics:

GP	G	A	TP	PIM
682	318	338	656	944

1989-90 statistics:

GP	G	A	TP	+/-	PIM	PP	SH	GW	GT	S	PCT
78	34	33	67	2	100	12	0	6	1	141	24.1

LAST SEASON

Goal total was a three-season low, assist and point totals four-season lows. Finished second on the club in goals, power play goals, and game-winners, first in shooting percentage (fourth in NHL).

THE FINESSE GAME

MacLean's primary finesse weapon is his shot. While he has other assets that contribute to that shot's effectiveness (and we won't ignore them), the bottom line is that he is the scorer he is because he shoots the puck the way he does. MacLean's shot is very heavy and he matches that strength with quickness of release. Together, those skills allow him to score from the distances, from the traffic areas, and while being checked. Not surprisingly, he is a power play standout.

The rest of MacLean's hand skills trail his shooting skill only slightly. He takes the puck off the boards very well, and he has the ability to skim a pass to a teammate or to step away from the boards with the puck and make a play himself. He handles the puck well in traffic and gets rid of it when necessary; MacLean rarely overhandles the puck.

As with every other scorer, hockey sense is also key and MacLean has it. He sees the play very well and has excellent anticipation, so MacLean easily moves into scoring position

His skating is less dynamic than his hand skills, but that doesn't mean his skating is inferior. On the contrary, MacLean succeeds because of his skating. His balance serves him well in his battles for the puck along the wood, and really comes to the fore when he plants himself in front of the net. He doesn't have a whole lot of speed, but his degree of quickness combines with his balance to give him a fair amount of agility for close quarters work.

His defense, on the other hand, is less inspired than his offense.

THE PHYSICAL GAME

MacLean's balance and hand skills key his physical game, letting him dig the puck from the corner and carrying him to the front of the net. Those assets combine with his size and strength to make him difficult to contain in the crease.

THE INTANGIBLES

He can be lazy and inconsistent in the use of his skills (as his defensive numbers illustrate), and sometimes even paradoxical (he might be second into the corner, but he'll take the abuse in front of the net). Whatever, after nine seasons what you see with MacLean is what you get — and what you get is 35-40 goals a year.

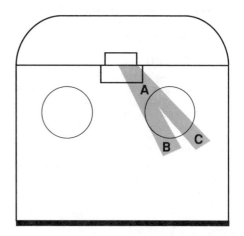

RICK MEAGHER

Yrs. of NHL service: 10
Born: Belleville, Ontario, Canada; November 4, 1953
Position: Center
Height: 5-8
Weight: 175
Uniform no.: 22
Shoots: left

Career statistics:

GP	G	A	TP	PIM
667	141	164	305	377

1989-90 statistics:

GP	G	A	TP	+/-	PIM	PP	SH	GW	GT	S	PCT
76	8	17	25	4	47	0	2	1	0	99	8.1

LAST SEASON

Goal and point totals were full-season lows; he missed time with a rib injury. His plus/minus rating was third best among full-time forwards. Tied for team lead in shorthanded goals.

THE FINESSE GAME

Skating and smarts are — finesse-wise — what make Meagher so valuable, and what keep him in the NHL despite his eligibility for SocialSecurity. He is an excellent skater with outstanding agility, lateral movement and quickness, and he complements that skill with surprising (for his size) strength afoot. His hockey sense and anticipation skills show him how to best thwart the plans of the centers he's checking, and his one-step quickness lets him close openings and beat those centers to the puck.

His smarts make him an excellent positional player at both ends of the ice, and he is a very aggressive penalty killer.

Meagher has some touch around the net from the slot area, but (despite the fact that his speed will get him around some defensemen) he lacks the power to blow the puck past a goaltender from farther out — he is a minimal offensive threat.

THE PHYSICAL GAME

One reason — a very major reason — why Meagher performs as well as he does is because of his conditioning. He is in excellent shape physically, and works hard throughout the year to remain in top shape.

He checks not just with his mind but with his body, using his great balance and strong upper body to bump bigger players off the puck. There are times in the defensive zone, however, when his size will betray him against stronger players. Still, he grinds it out as well as he skates, and he's not above stirring the pot by putting his stick into the opposition after the whistle.

His good hand/wrist strength and eye/hand coordination make him an above average faceoff man.

THE INTANGIBLES

Meagher is everything you'd want in a veteran player, a man of great character and desire, intelligence, a tremendous work ethic. In short, a leader on and off the ice. To accomplish what he has as a defensive center, to be plus-4 after playing against Lemieux, Gretzky, Yzerman, Savard and the like — well, that just shows how fine a player he is. Which, by the way, we told you last season.

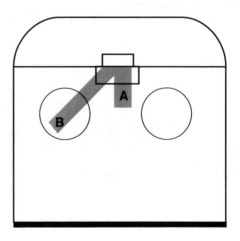

SERGIO MOMESSO

Yrs. of NHL service: 4
Born: Montreal, Quebec, Canada; September 4, 1965
Position: Left wing
Height: 6-3
Weight: 200
Uniform no.: 27
Shoots: left

Career statistics:

GP	G	A	TP	PIM
269	62	87	149	571

1989-90 statistics:

GP	G	A	TP	+/-	PIM	PP	SH	GW	GT	S	PCT
79	24	32	56	-15	199	4	0	4	1	182	13.2

LAST SEASON

Games played, PIM and all point totals were career highs. Plus/minus mark was club's second worst, poorest among forwards.

THE FINESSE GAME

Momesso's skating would best be described as marginally better than average. He has some speed and agility in his stride, but the thing that holds him back is his balance — or lack thereof. He's a big guy and his balance is correspondingly high, which means he can be pushed off the puck and knocked to the ice when hit, or when hitting. He likes to work from the outside in, as in taking the defense wide and then muscling inside.

His general hand skills are of a higher caliber. He handles the puck well and has a nice touch around the net. He's opportunistic in getting to loose pucks (one reason why he'll jam the net on the power play), but he can also score from the distances with his wrist and slap shots (he needs to deliver his powerful slap shot faster). His hand skills combine with his sense to allow him to use his teammates, especially as he makes plays from the corner.

Sergio is not much defensively, mostly through lack of effort. He doesn't pay close attention to his check and he has a tendency to wander out of position in the defensive zone.

THE PHYSICAL GAME

He's a corner and boards type of guy, and Momesso good use of his size and strength as he rumbles along the wood. His efforts can be undone by the aforementioned balance problem (which obviously is not a good thing for a physical player), but he generally succeeds.

Momesso is not a real tough guy (despite his PIM total), nor is he a feared fight.

THE INTANGIBLES

A popular team player, Momesso needs to be reminded to work; he can lose his intensity (his defensive play is one indication of that). When he has his head in the game, he can be a positive contributor for the Blues, and we maintain that he has the talent to score 30 goals a season — if he wants to.

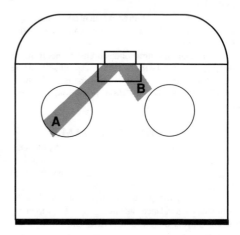

ADAM OATES

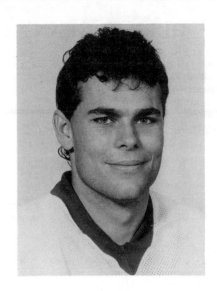

Yrs. of NHL service: 5
Born: Weston, Ontario, Canada; August 27, 1962
Position: Center
Height: 5-11
Weight: 185
Uniform no.: 12
Shoots: right

Career statistics:

GP	G	A	TP	PIM
326	77	224	301	95

1989-90 statistics:

GP	G	A	TP	+/-	PIM	PP	SH	GW	GT	S	PCT
80	23	79	102	9	30	6	2	3	1	168	13.7

LAST SEASON

Games played, PIM and all point totals were career highs. Led club in assists (third best in NHL) and was second in scoring. Plus/minus was third best among regulars, second among forwards.

THE FINESSE GAME

Courtesy of his hands and his head, Oates is a great passer. He is an excellent puckhandler at any speed and in most any situation, and he has the hand skills to match the pass to the situation: feathered over sticks or snapped through traffic. He takes the puck off the boards very well, and he passes equally well to both his forehand and backhand sides.

Those stick skills are complemented by excellent hockey sense and intelligence. Oates reads the ice very well, seeing openings before they develop and creating openings with his anticipation and patience. He'll lead his teammates to the openings, and he is particularly successful with the entire play ahead of him — that's why he plays the point on the power play (Brett Hull in the slot is his favorite target). His puck control and reading skills also make him a valuable penalty killer.

He gains scoring position for himself through his hands and his hockey sense, but he lacks the touch of a true goal scorer (quickness and heaviness of release). His hands make him very effective in traffic situations, and he'll score his 25 goals a season from near the net.

His foot skills are not of the same caliber as his hand skills. Oates lacks breakaway speed or acceleration ability, but he does have good balance and a degree of foot speed; the last two ingredients make him a fairly agile skater, and serve to further amplify his puck-handling.

He is a smart defensive player, attentive to his responsibilities in all three zones.

THE PHYSICAL GAME

He'll use what size and strength he has, but Oates is not a physical player — his size and strength mitigate against him. He can be out-matched and out-muscled in tough games (which limits his effectiveness) through no fault of his own, so he'll need brawnier linemates. By the same token, the opposition must play physically against Oates in order to neutralize him.

His hand speed also makes him good on faceoffs.

THE INTANGIBLES

Oates is very intelligent on and off the ice, and his performance last year (though colored partly by Brett Hull's success) is no fluke. His attitude and work ethic see to his success, and will continue to do so.

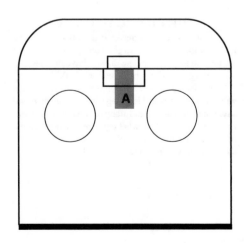

HERB RAGLAN

Yrs. of NHL service: 4
Born: Peterborough, Ontario, Canada; August 5, 1967
Position: Right wing
Height: 6-0
Weight: 200
Uniform no.: 25
Shoots: right

Career statistics:

GP	G	A	TP	PIM
203	23	36	59	519

1989-90 statistics:

GP	G	A	TP	+/-	PIM	PP	SH	GW	GT	S	PCT
11	0	1	1	-5	21	0	0	0		0	13	0.0

LAST SEASON

Games played was full-season career low; broken hand suffered in November 1989 sidelined him for the season.

THE FINESSE GAME

Raglan is a strong skater and he gets up and down the ice well because of that strength, but there isn't a lot of finesse in his play. He lacks real NHL speed or agility (and he's got the turning radius of a battleship), but his strength makes him a relentless skater. He's very difficult to get away from (he has an underrated degree of smarts), which in turn makes him a good checker, fairly strong defensively, and a tremendous player without the puck.

His hand skills approximate the level of his foot skills finesse-wise. He neither carries nor passes the puck especially well, and doesn't shoot exceptionally either. He'll shoot from the faceoff circle, and from the left wing circle too (remember his bad turns) because he rotates around the net and stays deep on the left wing side, but he'll have to do his scoring from in close.

THE PHYSICAL GAME

Raglan's strength makes it difficult to dislodge him from the puck, so he's a good player for the front of the net and in traffic (but he doesn't have the hands to score in tight; he'll just cause commotion).

Raglan hits hard, really punishing the opposition with his checks, and Herb eagerly uses his size and strength in the corners and along the boards. His physical effectivness is somewhat tempered by the fact that he won't make the play out of the corner, but his points are all going to come via his physical style.

He is a tough player, and he'll fight too.

THE INTANGIBLES

We told you last season that injury will keep Raglan from the lineup ("His physical style betrays him with injury, so that's the biggest question mark: How often will he be in the lineup to contribute?"), and we say the same thing now. We've left his report essentially unchanged because of his absence.

Aside from that, he is a fine character player with a great team attitude and an outstanding work ethic.

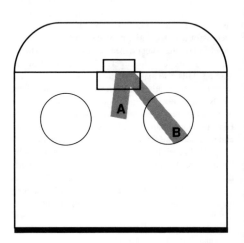

VINCENT RIENDEAU

Yrs. of NHL service: 2
Born: St. Hyacinthe, Quebec, Canada; April 20, 1966
Position: Goaltender
Height: 5-10
Weight: 185
Uniform no.: 30
Catches: left

Career statistics:

GP	MINS	G	SO	AVG	A	PIM
76	4,429	262	1	3.55	1	10

1989-90 statistics:

GP	MINS	AVG	W	L	T	SO	GA	SA	SAPCT	PIM
43	2,551	3.50	17	19	5	1	149	1,271	.883	6

LAST SEASON

Games and minutes played totals were career highs. He missed 10 games with a finger injury.

THE PHYSICAL GAME

At his best, Riendeau is a challenging, angle-cutting goalkeeper. He comes out over the crease on long shots, making his not-great-size work to his best advantage. He doesn't have great confidence in this style onscreens, or during scrambles in front or shots from nearer the net — he'll hang back in the net instead of coming to the top of the screen. NHL shooters will beat him to the corners with shots in those instances.

He has fairly good reflexes and a good catching glove and will get away with that reflex style in some instances, but quick passes and plays from behind and around the crease will overcome his defenses.

His skating and balance are part of the equation here. He is not an exceptional skater, particularly in lateral (post-to-post) situations, and criss-cross exploit that weakness; his lack of mobility also makes him vulnerable to dekes. He also doesn't track the puck around the net as well as he could.

He does stand up well on stick-side shots, perhaps because Riendeau knows he has a weakness there; he has a tendency to allow goals to sneak between his body and his stick arm. He leaves stick rebounds in front.

THE MENTAL GAME

In terms of game-to-game concentration, intensity and preparation, Riendeau isn't bad. He keeps himself in games and within a personal groove fairly well, making him a relatively dependable and consistent performer.

His anticipation and vision, however, could be improved. If they were, they would better counter ther flaws in Riendeau's game.

THE INTANGIBLES

He's just 24 years old, and an NHL sophomore, so Riendeau has plenty of time to mature. He will be pushed, however, by the emergence of Curtis Joseph, the free agent signed by St. Louis during the summer of 1989.

GORDIE ROBERTS

Yrs. of NHL service: 11
Born: Detroit, Mich., USA: October 2, 1957
Position: Defenseman
Height: 6-1
Weight: 195
Uniform no.: 4
Shoots: left

Career statistics:

GP	G	A	TP	PIM
836	50	306	356	1,272

1989-90 statistics:

GP	G	A	TP	+/-	PIM	PP	SH	GW	GT	S	PCT
75	3	14	17	-12	140	0	0	0	0	56	5.4

LAST SEASON

Point total was career low.

THE FINESSE GAME

Time and 15 seasons of professional hockey have taken their toll on Roberts. He needs to play the game smartly now (not that he should ever not have), as opposed to playing through skills alone. He has slowed down in his skating (no surprise), but he still retains enough mobility to make the occasional challenge at the blue line, but he's got to play a positional and angle-forcing game to contribute to the Blues.

He can turn the play up-ice fairly quickly if unchecked, but Roberts has also become susceptible to turnovers; when hurried, he'll throw the puck up the middle — and he is hurried more and more as time goes by. Generally, though, he finds the open man ahead of him.

He's not much of a goal scorer, but he does have a good slap shot from the point that he gets away quickly and on target, and that makes it good for rebounds or deflections. Roberts will also charge the net for a return pass on a give-and-go.

THE PHYSICAL GAME

For a guy without the greatest size Roberts plays an extremely effective physical game, willingly bringing the best of his less-than-exceptional size and strength to play at all times. Roberts can also hit hard and he does, but his game is best when he takes the body and moves the puck. He has the strength to keep the front of his net clean and he can also steer the opposition wide of the net and hold them out of the play for as long as necessary.

THE INTANGIBLES

Steady play and strong work ethic are the pluses Roberts brings to the Blues, important attributes in light of the number of younger defensemen rotating in and out of the lineup. That said, the emergence of some of those younger players may force Roberts to the sidelines.

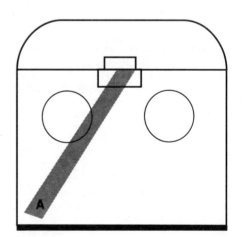

CLIFF RONNING

Yrs. of NHL service: 2
Born: Vancouver, B.C., Canada; October 1, 1965
Position: Center
Height: 5-8
Weight: 175
Uniform no.: 7
Shoots: left

Career statistics:

GP	G	A	TP	PIM
132	40	53	93	36

1988-89 statistics:

GP	G	A	TP	+/-	PIM	PP	SH	GW	GT	S	PCT
64	24	31	55	3	18	16	0	1	0	150	16.0

LAST SEASON

Played in Europe for 1989-90 season; re-signed with St. Louis in May of 1990.

THE FINESSE GAME

Ronning is a neat little package of finesse skills. He's an excellent skater with superior quickness and agility; those are his best assets and are particularly valuable on the power play — where Ronning excels.

He also has outstanding playmaking smarts. His hockey sense, his understanding of the game's flow and his ability to not just see but to find openings is excellent. Cliff can make the most of those openings himself (with his skating) or by using his teammates. He passes well because of his soft hands.

Ronning has a good shot, not extremely powerful but very quickly released (thus making his ability to jump into an opening even better). He's also accurate with his shot, forcing goaltenders to make saves. He'll score best from near the net, where he can use his good hands in tight.

His defense is conscientious, and Cliff plays a fairly good positional game in all three zones.

THE PHYSICAL GAME

There really isn't one. Not that he isn't willing, but Cliff doesn't have a lot of strength to bring to bear, certainly not a lot of size. He's not afraid (Ronning will cover the Jim Korns of this world when they go to the Blues net), but so what? Once caught, Ronning is going to be out-muscled and out-reached by bigger and stronger opponents.

He must stay away from crowds to succeed.

THE INTANGIBLES

We've included Ronning this season because of his new contract with the Blues, but that new deal doesn't guarantee him anything in the way of NHL ice-time. He'll be behind Peter Zezel and Adam Oates *at least*, followed by Rick Meagher as the club's checker.

As we said last year, the thing with Ronning is you have to decide how many small players to have on the ice at one time — he must be joined by big linemates.

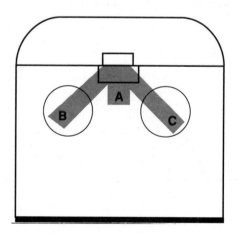

HAROLD SNEPSTS

Yrs. of NHL service: 15
Born: Edmonton, Alta., Canada; October 24, 1954
Position: Defenseman
Height: 6-3
Weight: 210
Uniform no.: 5
Shoots: left

Career statistics:

GP	G	A	TP	PIM
979	37	191	228	1,959

1989-90 statistics:

GP	G	A	TP	+/-	PIM	PP	SH	GW	GT	S	PCT
46	1	4	5	-1	36	1	0	1	0	15	6.7

LAST SEASON

Acquired by St. Louis along with Rich Sutter in exchange for Adrien Plavsic. He missed some time with a wrist injury.

THE FINESSE GAME

The finesse game has never been Harold's game, and it is less so today than ever before. He was never a great skater and has almost no speed to speak of. In fact, he can not keep up with the play as it moves around him, either by skating forward or backward, and he is apt to be beaten one-on-one by opposition forwards who go around him as if he didn't exist.

He is very weak at handling the puck in his own end and frequently has his back to the play, meaning that he'll make bad, blind passes around the boards or up the middle.

But Snepsts makes his play effective by staying away from his weaknesses; he doesn't, regularly, for example, handle the puck.

He has almost no mobility — and absolutely no interest — in playing within the offensive zone. He will not pinch in to the play and has an impotent shot from the point.

THE PHYSICAL GAME

Harold puts fear into the opposition and makes them pay for camping in front of his net. Snepsts loves to hit and can do so with authority, and he has learned to temper that desire with common sense.

Snepsts doesn't run around the defensive zone in search of prey, but waits for the opposition to come to him. And then he lets them have it. He clears men from the slot well because he is big and strong. He adds size to the defense and keeps things honest in his zone.

THE INTANGIBLES

The key to Harold is his play in front of the net. He is also a great team guy and has a good sense of humor, so he's important in the locker room too.

Harold's time with St. Louis may be limited because of several younger defensemen on the verge of full-time NHL, but Snepsts can still contribute to a degree.

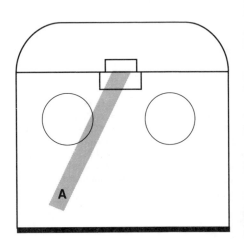

RICH SUTTER

Yrs. of NHL service: 7
Born: Viking, Alta., Canada; December 2, 1963
Position: Right wing
Height: 5-11
Weight: 185
Uniform no.: 23
Shoots: right

Career statistics:

GP	G	A	TP	PIM
516	99	108	207	936

1989-90 statistics:

GP	G	A	TP	+/-	PIM	PP	SH	GW	GT	S	PCT
74	11	9	20	-3	155	0	1	1	1	122	9.0

LAST SEASON

Was acquired from Vancouver along with Harold Snepsts inexchange for Adrien Plavsic. Point totals were full-season career lows. PIM total was club's third highest.

THE FINESSE GAME

Finesse has never been big in any of the Sutters and Rich is no exception. He is no better than average a skater at the NHL level in terms of his balance and agility, but he has power in his stride and can accelerate well. For a straight-ahead guy, that's about par for the course.

Sutter has difficulty handling the puck, especially as he skates up-ice and cutting to his right. He has a sense of the game and can read its ebbs and flows (and that's why he succeeds as a checking forward) but he can't do much offensively.

He'll never score more than 25 goals a year and many times won't even come near that mark. His shot is undistinguished and won't often fool NHL goaltending, so he'll have to be opportunistic and score off scrambles and loose pucks created by his checking.

In short, he is not an exceptionally skilled player.

THE PHYSICAL GAME

As with every Sutter, Rich is a physical player. His own style begins at chippy and moves swiftly to dirty, as he hits anyone in an enemy uniform and finishes the check with his stick. Naturally he refuses to fight after stirring up all kinds of troubles, and that just frustrates the opposition more.

Rich is good on the boards and will run at anyone, but is no good after hitting because he's unlikely — for two reasons — to make a play: First, he lacks the requisite hand skills. Second, his balance isn't good enough for him to stay vertical after all those collisions. Those flaws make his physical play one-dimensional.

THE INTANGIBLES

Sutter's work ethic is unassailable. He's an honest hockey player, but he'll never approach the heights hit by any of his five brothers.

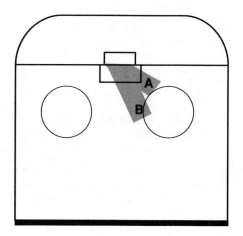

STEVE TUTTLE

Yrs. of NHL service: 2
Born: Vancouver, B.C., Canada; January 5, 1966
Position: Right wing
Height: 6-1
Weight: 180
Uniform no.: 35
Shoots: right

Career statistics:

GP	G	A	TP	PIM
124	25	22	47	10

1989-90 statistics:

GP	G	A	TP	+/-	PIM	PP	SH	GW	GT	S	PCT
71	12	10	22	-6	4	1	1	1	0	92	13.0

LAST SEASON

PIM total was league-low for a skater playing at least 70 games. Missed four games with a shoulder injury.

THE FINESSE GAME

Tuttle's physical finesse skills are average. He possesses a fair degree of balance and quickness, making for good agility (the ingredients for penalty killing duty) but is otherwise an unexceptional skater.

He handles the puck no better than averagely at NHL speed, and his ability to use his teammates is on the same level. Like his other skills, Tuttle's shot is also average — lacking the quickness of release and strength of delivery that would make it a more distinguished weapon.

What makes him effective as a finesse player is his hockey sense — his anticipation and ice-reading ability. Tuttle uses these mental skills to a good degree as a forechecker and smart defensive player. He has a degree of the same smarts offensively (he's the kind of player who knows to come down the wing with the puck and then open up to middle of the ice so as to see the action and make a play) but is hampered by his skill level.

THE PHYSICAL GAME

As with his finesse skills, Tuttle's physical skills would be described as no better than average. He'll get to the puck and muck around, but he's a 50-50 bet to succeed in taking it from the opposition. He doesn't help himself in these situations either, because he has a habit of coasting into traffic areas instead of keeping his feet moving.

Improved strength would allow him to compete better.

THE INTANGIBLES

As mentioned last year, Tuttle has to fight the Blues' depth chart; he's not going to displace Brett Hull or Paul MacLean, and when Herb Raglan is healthy Tuttle gets knocked to number four on the right side. Where he fits in with the Blues or, more accurately, how often he fits in with the Blues is a question to be answered.

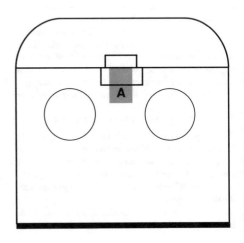

PETER ZEZEL

Yrs. of NHL service: 6
Born: Toronto, Ontario, Canada; April 22, 1965
Position: Center
Height: 5-10
Weight: 195
Uniform no.: 9
Shoots: left

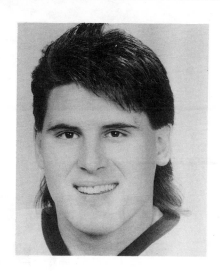

Career statistics:

GP	G	A	TP	PIM
435	133	253	386	287

1989-90 statistics:

GP	G	A	TP	+/-	PIM	PP	SH	GW	GT	S	PCT
73	25	47	72	-9	30	7	0	3	0	158	15.8

LAST SEASON

Point total tied career high. Finished third on club in scoring, second in assists. Plus/minus was club's fourth worst, second poorest among forwards. Missed four games with a bruised shoulder.

THE FINESSE GAME

Zezel is a skilled finesse player, and primary among his physical finesse skills is his footwork and skating. By now the whole world knows that he was a professional soccer player in the NASL, and Zezel uses his feet better than any player in the NHL — especially on faceoffs, where Zezel will tie up the opposition's stick before kicking the puck to one of his own wingers.

But he's an excellent skater on top of the fancy footwork, possessing speed, quickness, agility and strength. He's got excellent one-step moves, is hard to knock off the puck and has a very tight turning radius, and he complements his skating with a strong degree of hockey sense and play-reading ability. Zezel shows poise with the puck and looks to use his teammates, and he can be fairly creative in his passing.

His hand skills are strong (he carries or passes the puck equally well), and he also has a good selection of shots. His wrist shot is quickly released and generally accurate, forcing the goaltender to make a save, but he also has the power to score from a distance and is good at getting defensemen to set screens.

His finesse talents alone are enough to force the opposition into taking penalties, but Zezel augments that penalty-drawing ability with some of the League's best dives. He can also — when he puts his mind to it — be a strong defensive player because of his skills. Those skills make him a power play regular.

THE PHYSICAL GAME

Balance is the key to Zezel's physical game, for it allows him to plant himself and make plays despite checking and body position. Strength of course is a key here, and Zezel can get off shots while being checked, and he also uses these assets in his own hitting.

He is not above putting his stick into the opposition but does not back up that stickwork by fighting.

THE INTANGIBLES

Intensity is the question about Zezel — as long as he keeps his intensity level high, his play ranks accordingly. It's not that Peter isn't a hard worker or that he doesn't care, because he is and he does — he just needs to maintain his focus from night to night and shift to shift. There might also be a concern about his conditioning, as he'll take shorter and shorter shifts late in the game.

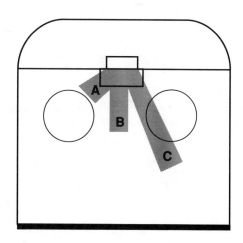

TORONTO MAPLE LEAFS

ALLAN BESTER

Yrs. of NHL service: 6
Born: Hamilton, Ontario, Canada; March 26, 1964
Position: Goaltender
Height: 5-7
Weight: 155
Uniform no.: 30
Catches: left

Career statistics:

GP	MINS	G	SO	AVG	A	PIM
199	10,716	723	7	4.05	8	30

1989-90 statistics:

GP	MINS	AVG	W	L	T	SO	G	SA	SAPCT	PIM
42	2,206	4.49	20	16	0	0	165	1,296	.873	4

LAST SEASON

Games and minutes played totals were second highest of career. Led four Leaf goalies in those totals, as well as in wins. Spent two weeks in Newmarket of the American Hockey League.

THE PHYSICAL GAME

Though his frequent flailings and floppings may seem to belie it, Bester is a standup goalie. He challenges the shooters well, which is smart considering he's only 5-foot-7; after all, if he were to hang back in the net and depend solely on reflexes to stop the puck, he'd develop a terrible case of whiplash from watching pucks sail over his shoulders.

That doesn't mean Bester squares himself to the puck as well as he could, so he'll frequently react to shots that are nowhere near the net.

He moves to the top of the screen — again, playing the percentages — and generally forces the opposition to make the first move. Bester is well balanced on his skates and that's important, because he often needs to regain his stance quickly after leaving rebounds from his pad and glove saves.

He has a quick glove hand and will block the puck, but not catch it, frequently juggling it till it falls to the ice. He'll leave rebounds in front from his pad saves too, but is otherwise good about clearing the puck.

He holds the post well and has a quick left foot, but Bester is just average in his lateral movement from post to post. He doesn't handle the puck well and that creates all kinds of defensive confusion.

THE MENTAL GAME

Bester is a worrier, always fidgeting about doing his best and sometimes that mitigates against him. He has a tendency to lose his concentration because he's worrying about how he's playing instead of stopping the puck, and then he allows goals.

One sign that his concentration is good is his vision of the puck. When his concentration is on he sees it well, following the play all through the offensive zone. That allows him to make saves based on anticipation.

THE INTANGIBLES

His position as Toronto's number one goalie isn't cast in cement, but the Leafs have shown themselves reluctant to invest that status in either Peter Ing or Jeff Reese. Add in Bester's standoff-ish and arrogant attitude (he's not real popular among his teammates), and he may not get the nod for team chemistry reasons. Still, with Mark LaForest gone, there may very well be a three-way rotation and Bester should have the inside track for the number one slot.

WENDEL CLARK

Yrs. of NHL service: 5
Born: Kelvington, Sask., Canada; October 25, 1966
Position: Left wing
Height: 5-11
Weight: 194
Uniform no.: 17
Shoots: left

Career statistics:

GP	G	A	TP	PIM
227	108	57	165	760

1989-90 statistics:

GP	G	A	TP	+/-	PIM	PP	SH	GW	GT	S	PCT
38	18	8	26	2	116	7	0	2	0	85	21.2

LAST SEASON

Games played, goal and point totals were three-season highs. Suffered early season knee injury, missed four games with a shoulder injury, then was sidelined for season with knee injury suffered in January.

THE FINESSE GAME

Whereas some players are greater than the sum of their parts, Clark is lesser than the sum of his. His skating stride is a strong one and he does have speed up the wing, so once he gets his 200 pounds rolling he can run over most anyone. Problem is, he lacks agility and balance. That means he can't work in tight spaces unless he's already got a head of steam going so he can run people over, and it also means that when he hits people he's going to fall down and be useless in the subsequent play.

As such he actually undermines the value of his wrist shot, which is one of the NHL's very best. That shot is hard, heavy and accurate and Clark could score 40 goals a season with it. But to do that he has to get into the open and to get into the open he has to get away from defenders, and he doesn't know how to do that without running them over.

Clark has demonstrated little to no ability to see and react to the play at the NHL level, which is why both his assist numbers and plus/minus rating are so poor and why his power play totals are good. He doesn't look to use his teammates and even if he did lacks the requisite anticipation skills for anything beyond the most rudimentary play. He doesn't understand the concept of space, and certainly doesn't realize that if he passed the puck he might be able to get into the open. To Clark, the game begins and ends with the space he occupies; that's why he overhandles the puck.

His understanding of positional play is poor, made worse by his determination to crash into every opposing body he can find on his way back to the defensive zone. His inability to read and react doesn't help.

THE PHYSICAL GAME

Clark is a very strong physical player, and his physical game reflects his abilities. He hits hard and often, regardless of circumstance (though he is more determined at home than on the road, but not undetermined in away games) and opponent. He has the power and strength, through his skating, to really drive the opposition and hurt them when he hits and Clark enjoys all aspects (yes, that means fighting) of a physical game.

Overall, he is a very strong, very tough, very aggressive player. But he is also very inconsistent, doing all these things some nights, some of these things other nights, none of these things still other nights.

THE INTANGIBLES

Health is the big one, and Clark's style does nothing to help him in that regard. He's an enthusiastic and spirited player, but he doesn't play smartly and hasn't demonstrated the willingness to fold his game into the Leafs' overall style. He can be the franchise player the Leafs sorely need (assuming health), but he's not yet mature enough to assume that status.

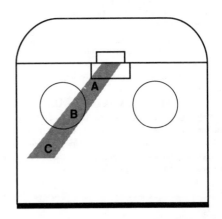

BRIAN CURRAN

Yrs. of NHL service: 6
Born: Toronto, Ontario, Canada; November 5, 1963
Position: Defenseman
Height: 6-5
Weight: 220
Uniform no.: 28
Shoots: left

Career statistics:

GP	G	A	TP	PIM
331	6	32	38	1,336

1989-90 statistics:

GP	G	A	TP	+/-	PIM	PP	SH	GW	GT	S	PCT
72	2	9	11	-2	301	0	0	0	0	21	9.5

LAST SEASON

Games played and all point totals were career bests. Was team's lowest scoring regular, but led club in PIM total.

THE FINESSE GAME

Curran is not a good skater and he knows it, so he doesn't get himself into places his poor skating can't get him out of. He has no speed to speak of and almost as little mobility, but Curran does play his defensive angles fairly well, and his size helps him force the play wide of the Toronto net.

Brian does not handle the puck particularly well — and he knows that too — so he usually leaves that task to his defense partner. When he does handle the puck in his own zone, Curran is liable to a turnover if forced.

Offensively, Curran is virtually non-existent. He almost never forces the play at the opposing blue line, smartly preferring to fall back to defense. He rarely shoots the puck and any goals he will get will come from a shot from the blue line.

THE PHYSICAL GAME

Curran has accumulated some of the most useless penalty minutes ever. He fights almost at the drop of a hat but he doesn't intimidate anyone, certainly not in the sense of a Joe Kocur or Bob Probert. He's not a real cheap shot artist either so he's not accomplishing much with all those minutes.

In terms of pure physical play, Curran takes the body fairly well, but he is not a punishing hitter despite his size. He doesn't possess strength equal to his size, and he can get muscled off the puck along the boards or in front of the net.

In all, despite his great size and large penalty minute total, Curran is no more than average as a physical player.

THE INTANGIBLES

Willing he may be, but few are the players that Brian Curran scares. As long as Curran holds up his end of the bargain defensively, the Leafs can afford his extra-curricular activities. Otherwise he's no great shakes as a defenseman, and even less as a fighter.

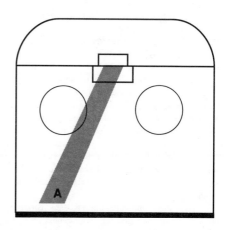

VINCENT DAMPHOUSSE

Yrs. of NHL service: 4
Born: Montreal, Quebec, Canada; December 17, 1967
Position: Center/left wing
Height: 6-1
Weight: 185
Uniform no.: 10
Shoots: left

Career statistics:

GP	G	A	TP	PIM
315	92	164	256	197

1989-90 statistics:

GP	G	A	TP	+/-	PIM	PP	SH	GW	GT	S	PCT
80	33	61	94	2	56	9	0	5	1	229	14.4

LAST SEASON

All point totals were career bests. Finished second on club in points and shots on goal total, first in assists. Played 80 games third time in four NHL seasons, finished 18th in overall League scoring.

THE FINESSE GAME

Hand skills are Damphousse's bread-and-butter, and his ability to distribute the puck is as directly related to his hand ability as it is to his hockey sense — and that's not such an obvious point.

For example, if Damphousse's sense were so great he would know where to be as a scorer and how often to shoot the puck — two aspects of the game that he had a solid understanding of but needed to strengthen nonetheless. That's why he now gets into better scoring position, and that's why he shoots more often — an increase of almost 20 percent from 1988-89 to 1989-90 (190 SOG two seasons back versus 229 last season).

Just as he adjusted as a shooter, Damphousse adjusted as a playmaker. He has exceptional innate puckhandling ability and he controls the puck well at all speeds. But while he uses that puckhandling ability to tease the defense he's also using his mind to anticipate plays and opportunities to use his teammates. And now that Damphousse can read and react at a more consistent NHL level, he'll use his teammates better. He passes the puck well and with good touch, and he can pass or shoot off the stickhandle. He likes to go one-on-one versus the defense, and the defense should be wary of his deking ability.

His skating is probably the least demonstrative of his skills. He has a degree of both quickness and speed, so he can be a fairly mobile and agile player, and he can use his skating at both ends of the ice.

THE PHYSICAL GAME

He protects the puck well with his body and he does establish good position along the boards, but Damphousse isn't a real factor physically. Willing does not always mean able (as in when he gets tired defensively while battling along the boards trying to gain the puck or impede his check), and though he can lean on guys enough to get his hands some time to work this area isn't where Damphouse will show best.

THE INTANGIBLES

Despite his less than dynamic skating skills, Damphousse might be better as a center — the open ice is where he can best exploit his hand skills while minimizing his lack of physical effect. He is a quiet but earnest young man, one who is already en route to becoming a top NHLer and can have better seasons yet.

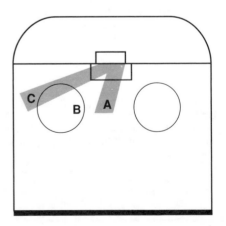

TOM FERGUS

Yrs. of NHL service: 9
Born: Chicago, Ill., USA; June 16, 1962
Position: Center
Height: 6-3
Weight: 210
Uniform no.: 19
Shoots: left

Career statistics:

GP	G	A	TP	PIM
621	210	310	520	450

1989-90 statistics:

GP	G	A	TP	+/-	PIM	PP	SH	GW	GT	S	PCT
54	19	26	45	-18	62	4	0	2	0	120	15.8

LAST SEASON

Games played total was career low, goal, assist and point totals were second lowest of career. Missed 26 games with groin injuries. Plus/minus rating was club's worst.

THE FINESSE GAME

Fergus's NHL skills are concentrated in his hand skills. He handles the puck very well, smooth with it at all of his speeds and good in traffic. He passes well to both sides, demonstrating the touch that allows him to either fire or feather his passes as the situation requires, but he undercuts his puck work by generally ovehandling the puck in the offensive zone.

That may be because he has great confidence in his shot — and he should. He is an exceptional shooter and has one of the NHL's very best wrist shots, so good he can beat goalies with it (and does) from the blue line.

That said, Fergus doesn't often do the things that would give him success. Together with the already mentioned overhandling of the puck, Fergus also avoids the traffic areas where his soft hands would do the most damage; you won't often find him in front of the net. He also doesn't shoot the puck enough when he does have it, and that too is a failing attributable to his one-extra-play mentality.

His foot skills lag behind his hand skills, though not by much. He's a fairly agile player for a guy with his size and bulk, and he's got a bit of acceleration in his stride as well. In short, he can get around a defender for a play but his overhandling of the puck short-circuits his work.

His defensive play verges on the apathetic.

THE PHYSICAL GAME

Fergus is a finesse player with size. If he used his body to gain position near the net he could easily prey on rebounds and loose pucks because of his soft hands. He doesn't work in the traffic areas along the boards either, which is just as well because he's going to get out-muscled anyway.

In short, he avoids contact when he can.

THE INTANGIBLES

Fergus is a smart player, but he is undone by his lack of concentration and intensity. He plays a comfortable unmotivated game, and to expect anything else from him is to court disappointment.

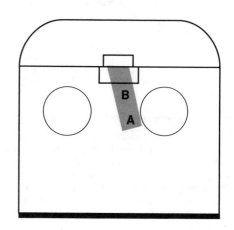

LOU FRANCESCHETTI

Yrs. of NHL service: 6
Born: Toronto, Ontario, Canada; March 28, 1958
Position: Left wing
Height: 6-0
Weight: 190
Uniform no.: 25
Shoots: left

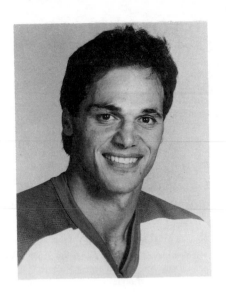

Career statistics:

GP	G	A	TP	PIM
407	57	73	130	689

1989-90 statistics:

GP	G	A	TP	+/-	PIM	PP	SH	GW	GT	S	PCT
80	21	15	36	-12	127	0	2	4	0	76	27.6

LAST SEASON

Acquired by Toronto from Washington in June 1989 in exchange for a 1990 draft pick. Games played and all point totals were career highs. Plus/minus rating tied for team's second worst (John McIntyre, Dave Hannan), but finished second in shorthanded goals and PIM total among forwards, and led club in shooting percentage.

THE FINESSE GAME

About the best thing that can be said of Franceschetti's finesse skill is that he skates with some power and strength in his stride, and this ability helps him in his checking game — he's a very good bodychecker, when he can contain the opposition and hit them.

He's otherwise unremarkable in his finesse ability, succeeding more through effort than skill. He doesn't handle or pass the puck especially well, and he'll need time to make his plays because he lacks hockey sense or anticipation skills.

His board work is limited by the fact that he hasn't the hands to make plays coming off the wood, and his shot won't be effective from the distances; in order to score he'll have to be near the net with plenty of time and space.

THE PHYSICAL GAME

Franceschetti makes the most of his physical game by playing a consistently strong, tough style. His bodychecking is good (as mentioned) and he has the strength to wear down the opposition. He plays with almost no regard for his body, kamikaze-like in his charges into the opposition. He doesn't have great balance, so his own hitting can sometimes take him out of the play.

He uses his body all over the ice and does so with a degree of intelligence, meaning he's not always on search and destroy missions but takes the hits as they come. He's a good fighter and generally finds himself unchallenged.

THE INTANGIBLES

Franceschetti is a worker and a grinder. He wears his style on his sleeve, demonstrating heart and desire every night. We would not, however, say that he is a 20-goal scorer; that's an aberration. But that's okay, because he's not on the team for goals, he's there to provide some grit.

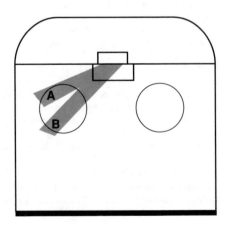

TODD GILL

Yrs. of NHL service: 4
Born: Brockville, Ontario, Canada; November 9, 1965
Position: Defenseman/left wing
Height: 6-0
Weight: 180
Uniform no.: 23
Shoots: left

Career statistics:

GP	G	A	TP	PIM
258	26	74	100	428

1989-90 statistics:

GP	G	A	TP	+/-	PIM	PP	SH	GW	GT	S	PCT
48	1	14	15	-8	92	0	0	0		0	44	2.3

LAST SEASON

Games played and point totals were full-season career lows. Missed one game with a sore back.

THE FINESSE GAME

Gill is a contradiction as a player in a number of ways. For example, he is a primarily offensively oriented player and plays that way yet he has never been able to marshal even average numbers in any particular season — despite his skating and puckhandling ability. But then again, maybe his skills aren't as strong as previously described.

He's got some good speed in his forward skating and he can handle the puck at that speed, but he lacks the agility — especially laterally — that would improve his essentially straight ahead style. And that lack of agility really hurts when he plays defense, as Gill has problems pivoting to follow the puckcarrier.

He overhandles the puck when skating up front, and that's because his vision isn't good enough to show him another play. As a defenseman he's less prone to that error because he can see the open men in front of him.

He likes to join the attack from either position and he has the hand skills to score from in tight after crashing the net, but he's more likely to just stickhandle himself into the corner because of his poor reads of the ice.

THE PHYSICAL GAME

Gill likes to play a physical game, likes to hit in open ice and be a force along the boards and likes to fight, but he's a contradiction here too. He doesn't have all the tools to regularly win those battles (balance and strength) despite his willingness, and he's done nothing in his four-plus NHL seasons to improve either of those skills so he can succeed more frequently.

THE INTANGIBLES

Gill's a popular player among his teammates and a gutsy kid — we're not faulting his intentions. There's just a shortfall here between the perception of his talents and the reality of the numbers posted thus far. And we wonder how many more chances he'll get to prove himself to the Maple Leafs.

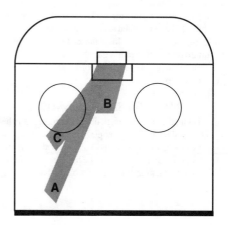

DAVE HANNAN

Yrs. of NHL service: 6
Born: Sudbury, Ontario, Canada; November 26, 1961
Position: Center
Height: 5-10
Weight: 185
Uniform no.: 9
Shoots: left

Career statistics:

GP	G	A	TP	PIM
445	75	108	183	628

1989-90 statistics:

GP	G	A	TP	+/-	PIM	PP	SH	GW	GT	S	PCT
39	6	9	15	-12	55	0	1	0	0	39	15.4

LAST SEASON

Games played total was five-season low; missed at least 23 games with knee injuries and subsequent surgery. Plus/minus rating was club's second poorest (tied with Lou Franceschetti and John McIntyre).

THE FINESSE GAME

Hannan is an average skater, meaning that he possesses neither outstandingly good or outstandingly poor speed, agility or quickness. He succeeds more by effort than by skill, but he can fill a role as a fourth-line forward or checker.

He's not very skilled in playmaking, lacking both the hand skills and the hockey sense to make this part of the game work. He is reading the play a little better, but Hannan's foot skills aren't developed enough for him to take real advantage of what his modest ice vision shows him.

He doesn't handle the puck real well, so Hannan will have to have time and space to make his plays. His checking can create some loose pucks, but his shot lacks the quick release that might gain him some goals.

Because of his eye/hand coordination, Hannan is good on faceoffs.

THE PHYSICAL GAME

Hannan can dig the puck out of the corners and he has no fear about bumping people, which is the strongest aspect of his game. Hannan will use his body to make the play and is unafraid to hit or be hit. He plays bigger than his size, making the most of what he has.

THE INTANGIBLES

Dave doesn't have the natural ability to score, but because of his attitude and work ethic, the players have a lot of respect for him. More of a leader than a follower, he's an extremely hard worker. His attitude has kept him in the NHL, but his modest skills may very well have him finishing the season — perhaps even starting it — in some place other than Toronto.

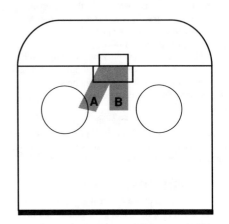

AL IAFRATE

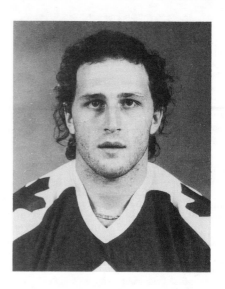

Yrs. of NHL service: 6
Born: Dearborn, Mich., USA; March 21, 1966
Position: Defenseman
Height: 6-3
Weight: 217
Uniform no.: 33
Shoots: left

Career statistics:

GP	G	A	TP	PIM
430	78	154	232	433

1989-90 statistics:

GP	G	A	TP	+/-	PIM	PP	SH	GW	GT	S	PCT
75	21	42	63	-4	135	6	1	0	0	153	13.7

LAST SEASON

Assist and point totals were career highs; finished eighth in scoring among NHL defensemen, first among Leaf defenders. Suffered a late season knee injury.

THE FINESSE GAME

Iafrate is a very gifted finesse player, and the best of his finesse abilities is unquestionably his skating. He has great speed and agility, and those qualities are made more intimidating by his size. He motors up and down the right wing like nobody's business, and he loves to cut to the enemy net off his rush. He can do that because of his lateral ability, which is very high. Iafrate has one-step quickness that he uses to change speed and direction within a step, and if the opposition has any hope of stopping him they've got to stop him in the neutral zone.

He uses his skating to challenge the puck all over the ice and many of those challenges are foolish one, but his mobility gets him out of those jams. He doesn't really get good reads of the ice, so if he doesn't orchestrate the offensive play by rushing the puck he's going to have to make the first play he sees. His reads are especially weak defensively, where Iafrate succeeds only because of his skating ability.

He complements his skating with very good puck skills. Iafrate will sooner rush the puck from his zone than pass it, but he also undercuts his ability by overhandling the puck in contained situations; of course, he has difficulty taking advantage of his teammates once he's contained because he doesn't see the ice well.

He shoots the puck very well, as his win in the shooting segment of the All-Star skills contest demonstrated, but he could use his shot as more of an offensive weapon by shooting to score instead of just getting the puck to the net. Ironically, in this one skill he is not selfish enough. He'll move off the point for shots, and he shoots well off the pass.

THE PHYSICAL GAME

Iafrate plays an inconsistent physical game in that he doesn't mind hitting and will initiate some contact, but he doesn't really enjoy a physical game and he's more likely to push and shove than he is to hit. He doesn't get the most he can from his size, so he'd have to be said to play smaller than he is.

THE INTANGIBLES

Every year writers (and we are not excluded) claim that players have a certain potential — and after five or six years we say that a player either has or has not reached his potential, based on his numbers. But we forget that reality dictates a player's ability, not potential. So what if Al Iafrate has the potential to score 30 goals and 100 points? The point is — and the point to finally be recognized — is that he will not hit those numbers. He is a 20-goal, maybe 50-point scorer. That is what he has done in the past, that is what he will do in the future.

And the reason why he will not bridge the gap between potential and reality is because of his attitude. He's not a bad kid, but he lacks confidence in his abilities, and lacks the concentration and intensity necessary to counter that lack of confidence.

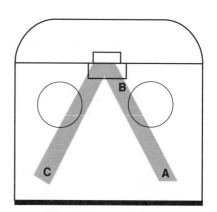

JOHN KORDIC

Yrs. of NHL service: 4
Born: Edmonton, Alta., Canada; March 22, 1965
Position: Left wing
Height: 6-2
Weight: 210
Uniform no.: 27
Shoots: left

Career statistics:

GP	G	A	TP	PIM
216	17	16	33	772

1989-90 statistics:

GP	G	A	TP	+/-	PIM	PP	SH	GW	GT	S	PCT
55	9	4	13	-8	252	3	0	0	0	48	18.8

LAST SEASON

Goal, point and PIM totals were career highs. Finished second on the club in PIM, first among forwards. Missed two games with groin injury, as well as time with team-mandated suspension.

THE FINESSE GAME

Kordic is an extremely limited finesse player at the NHL level. His skating is below average in terms of speed and agility, meaning Kordic will have great difficulty keeping up with the pace of NHL play.

He could compensate for that with a high degree of hockey sense, but Kordic lacks that skill as well. He gets no read of the ice beyond the most elementary, and he understands little of the implications of a particular play.

He has little skill with the puck, whether it be carrying it passing it or shooting it. The best that can be said of his finesse game is that he attempts to play positionally, but since he doesn't understand anything beyond straight line play a creative winger can do a lot of damage if matched against him.

THE PHYSICAL GAME

Kordic likes to be a physical presence, but he lacks the skill to play a physical game that goes beyond fighting. For one thing he can't catch anyone to hit them. Should he happen to corner somneone Kordic can hit pretty hard — kind of like being hit by lightning, and just as rare.

He is, of course, a more than willing fighter. That's why he's in the NHL.

THE INTANGIBLES

Kordic had a host of off-ice problems last year that manifested themselves in his team-oriented discipline and lack thereof. So the main question is one of mindset: is Kordic ready to devote himself to playing hockey? Of secondary consideration is the fact that, like any other limited player, Kordic is subject to replacement by the first player who comes along and is tougher and/or a degree more talented. And for what it's worth, he's not real popular with his teammates.

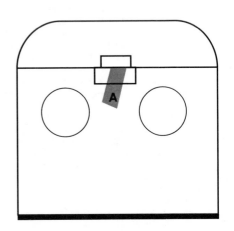

TOM KURVERS

Yrs. of NHL service: 6
Born: Minneapolis, Minn., USA; October 14, 1962
Position: Defenseman
Height: 6-0
Weight: 205
Uniform no.: 5
Shoots: left

Career statistics:

GP	G	A	TP	PIM
394	59	191	250	201

1989-90 statistics:

GP	G	A	TP	+/-	PIM	PP	SH	GW	GT	S	PCT
71	15	37	52	-9	29	9	1	1	0	156	9.6

LAST SEASON

Acquired from New Jersey in exchange for Toronto's first draft choice in 1991. Second among Leaf defensemen in scoring, first in power play goals. Plus/minus rating was worst among defensemen.

THE FINESSE GAME

Skating and puckhandling make Kurvers an effective offensive defenseman. He complements good skating speed and quickness with balance for agility and lateral movement. Kurvers then makes his skating better by combining it with his good-to-very-good puck carrying ability; he handles the puck well at all speeds.

Because of these skills, Kurvers is apt to skate the puck over center ice and join the attack. However, that doesn't mean Tom will lead the rush to the net. Rather, because he likes to run the offense from the offensive blue line, he'll carry it to center and then get it to a breaking winger before setting up camp at the left point.

Kurvers contains the point well with his quickness and anticipation, and he makes good passes to his teammates from there because of his vision. As such, he's a power play natural. He has a fine shot from the blue line, low and almost always on net, and Kurvers will almost always move to the center of the line to improve his shooting angle; he'll also move to the slot.

His defensive zone work is less outstanding, but Kurvers is nevertheless competent. He generally makes good decisions regarding outlet passes, but he can be rushed into mistakes.

THE PHYSICAL GAME

Kurvers is not much of a physical player, despite good size. He's probably going to be out-muscled should he get trapped along the boards (and that's an area of

the ice best left to Kurvers' partner), but he does have the skills to make plays from the boards.

THE INTANGIBLES

With Al Iafrate on the club, Kurvers' role is no longer that of generating all the offense the defense can muster (as it was in New Jersey). Rather, he'll be looked on to provide consistent offense to support Iafrate, and Kurvers' presence also serves to insure that the opposition can no longer key on one set of defensemen.

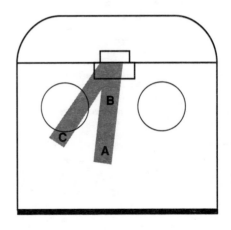

GARY LEEMAN

Yrs. of NHL service: 7
Born: Toronto, Ontario, Canada; February 19, 1964
Position: Right wing
Height: 5-11
Weight: 175
Uniform no.: 11
Shoots: right

Career statistics:

GP	G	A	TP	PIM
459	152	206	358	380

1989-90 statistics:

GP	G	A	TP	+/-	PIM	PP	SH	GW	GT	S	PCT
80	51	44	95	4	63	14	1	5	0	256	19.9

LAST SEASON

Led team in goals and points with career bests in all point categories. Plus/minus was second best among fulltime players, best among forwards. Finished second on club in game winners, tied for first (Daniel Marois) in power play goals and first in shots on goal total. Finished 16th in overall NHL scoring, eighth in goal scoring. Played 80 games for third time in last four seasons.

THE FINESSE GAME

Leeman is an explosive offensive player, and his skating and stickhandling abilities are the keys to his tremendous offensive potential. He is a very mobile skater with abilities in all aspects of skating: speed, acceleration, balance, quickness and agility. He can even combine these elements to augment his otherwise average strength, using these skills to move bigger and stronger players off the puck. In particular, it is his quickness and ability to change directions and speed within a step that make him so dangerous when carrying the puck.

His hands are as talented as his feet, so he can rush with the puck at full speed or dip, cut and sway around defenders once inside the offensive zone. To have any hope of stopping him the defense must play his body, but even then Leeman has the ability — courtesy of his soft hands and his balance — to either absorb the hit and still make a play (because he's kept good body position) or simply lean away from the check. He passes off the stickhandle as well as he carries the puck, and he hits open men anywhere.

His eyes will light up when he sees the net, and that's because he knows how good a scorer he is. Leeman's shot is accurate and quickly released and he really can score from anywhere. He one-times the puck exceptionally well and makes his excellent shot better by practicing patience and forcing the opposition (both defense and goaltender) to commit itself.

THE PHYSICAL GAME

Leeman is an aggressive player, one who plays bigger than his size and strength would dictate. He'll go to the traffic areas in front of the net or in the corners, but he's not a bruiser in the classic sense. In other words, he'll go where he has to to score, but don't expect him to be in the corners doing the yeoman work of digging the puck out for someone else. He's also a good fighter, suprisingly so for a guy his size.

THE INTANGIBLES

Though he's a fairly well-rounded player Leeman is capable of taking some poor gambles; the attitude that allows that has not always served to make Leeman popular among his teammates. He's a very talented player and it is easy for him to play comfortably, so he needs to be reminded about working hard and working for the team.

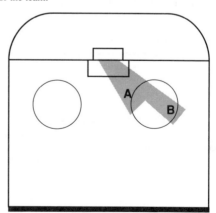

KEVIN MAGUIRE

Yrs. of NHL service: 3
Born: Toronto, Ontario, Canada; January 5, 1963
Position: Right wing
Height: 6-2
Weight: 200
Uniform no.: 20
Shoots: right

Career statistics:

GP	G	A	TP	PIM
189	19	25	44	598

1989-90 statistics:

GP	G	A	TP	+/-	PIM	PP	SH	GW	GT	S	PCT
66	7	9	16	-4	121	0	0	1	0	69	10.1

LAST SEASON

Acquired from Buffalo in exchange for Jay Wells. Games played total was career high. Missed time with late season knee injury.

THE FINESSE GAME

Not much of one. Maguire is a strong skater, but not a particularly graceful one. He has neither rink-length speed nor one-step quickness, and his lack of agility is attributable to that missing foot speed.

He doesn't handle the puck particularly well, and he has no real vision or sense of the ice and the offensive game. He succeeds as a checking forward because of his desire (his strong stride helps him close gaps and stay with his man) and physical play.

Any goals he scores will have to come on loose pucks near the net, as Maguire doesn't have a shot that will fool NHL goaltending.

THE PHYSICAL GAME

This is why Maguire is here. He'll bang whatever bodies he can catch, and his skating stride helps him drive through his checks. He can punish the opposing defensemen — if he can catch them — and that serves to make him a decent forechecker.

He also fights. A lot.

THE INTANGIBLES

We told you last season that, because of his limited ability, Maguire wouldn't last long in Buffalo. Maguire may just find himself on the short end again in Philadelphia as the Flyers attempt to rebuild.

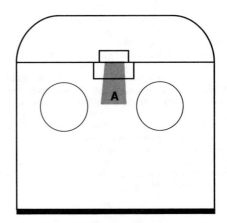

DAN MAROIS

Yrs. of NHL service: 2
Born: Montreal, Quebec, Canada; October 3, 1968
Position: Right wing
Height: 6-0
Weight: 190
Uniform no.: 32
Shoots: right

Career statistics:

GP	G	A	TP	PIM
144	70	60	130	158

1989-90 statistics:

GP	G	A	TP	+/-	PIM	PP	SH	GW	GT	S	PCT
68	39	37	76	1	82	14	0	3	1	183	21.3

LAST SEASON

Games played total fell, but all point totals rose, in second NHL season. Finished second on club in goals, tied for first (Ed Olczyk) in power play goals. Shooting percentage was second best among regulars. Missed 11 games with shoulder injury.

THE FINESSE GAME

Marois is a very gifted player in most every finesse category. Like all goal scorers, his sense of the ice and the partnership his sense forms with his hand and foot skills so he can create the ability to get open is very high. Marois is a creative and dangerous offensive player, very good without the puck and excellent at getting into scoring position. His sense tells him where the openings will be and he gets there to put his skills to work.

The primary skills obviously rest in his hands, and Marois's hand skills are as sophisticated as his hockey sense. His puck control is excellent in all situations, whether it be in motion or in traffic. He controls the puck very well in the confined space near the net from which he's going to do his damage, and he needs just the slightest opening to finesse the puck home. He takes passes well while in motion, just as he carries the puck well at his top speed, and he can also shoot off the pass or stickhandle. His quick shot release is a key to his scoring.

The third skill in the scoring triumvirate is skating and Marois is gifted in this area as well. He has the speed to pull away from many NHL defenders, and he also has the quickness and agility to dart into an opening or sacrifice premium body position but still get the job done (as well as using those assets to stay away from the opposition while carrying the puck).

He plays a fairly conscientious defensive game (to be plus-1 on a team that is minus-21 is a good indication) and he feasts on power play time because of the additional open ice.

THE PHYSICAL GAME

Marois's got size, but not a lot of bulk or strength. He's perfectly willing to take and give checks to make plays, but he's going to be at a disadvantage in those close quarter situations. His finesse skills amplify his physical willingness and Marois won't be intimidated; he certainly should keep the physical element in his game, but could better help himself succeed if he added some sorely needed muscle — if only to protect himself from the knocks he's taking.

THE INTANGIBLES

He's a pretty skilled player, and the fact that Marois did better in his sophomore season than he did in his freshman year speaks well for his talent and potential. It's not unusual for a player's second-year numbers to fall, as he no longer sneaks up on the opposition; they know all about him, and he has to learn to work through increased checking. Which is not to say that scenario won't happen this year, but the Leafs have to be greatly encouraged by Marois's development.

And we think there's more on the way.

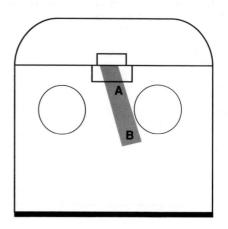

BRAD MARSH

Yrs. of NHL service: 12
Born: London, Ontario, Canada; March 31, 1958
Position: Defenseman
Height: 6-3
Weight: 220
Uniform no.: 8
Shoots: left

Career statistics:

GP	G	A	TP	PIM
930	19	165	184	1,127

1989-90 statistics:

GP	G	A	TP	+/-	PIM	PP	SH	GW	GT	S	PCT
79	1	13	14	14	95	0	0	0	0	50	2.0

LAST SEASON

Plus/minus was club's best.

THE FINESSE GAME

Marsh is like a grammar lesson: slow, slower, slowest.

Marsh is like Old Man River: He must know something to just keep rolling along.

But what Marsh is most like is death and taxes: He's always there. Not through any great feat of skill either, unless you call desire skill. Rather, he is the ultimate triumph of function over form. By now, after almost 1,000 NHL games, Marsh should be as mobile as a dinosaur trapped in the La Brea tar pits — and sometimes he looks the role. But damned if he isn't in your face, forcing you to the boards and holding you there so long you think you might be married to the guy.

And damned if the puck doesn't always skitter off his stick to an open Leaf teammate; funny how that happens. Of course, you can't rightly remember how he got it on his stick in the first place — must be that thing about being in the right place at the right time.

Just like all those times he falls down and the puck happens to hit him before it gets to the net. We all know Marsh doesn't have the quickness to sprawl in front of 80-MPH shots; those pucks just hit him by mistake.

THE PHYSICAL GAME

As with his finesse skills, Marsh uses his physical skills to their best degree because of his intelligence; he puts himself in positions to succeed. He remains a strong player and he uses that strength to neutralize the opposition along the boards or in front of the net, no doubt helped in that last aspect by the fact that he's also one of the League's best holders.

THE INTANGIBLES

We hope no one misinterprets our poking fun at Marsh in the finesse section as serious commentary. Marsh deserves all the credit in the world for showing that even if you are slower than water running uphill you can still play at a high level in the NHL. Because of his work ethic and character, Marsh remains a leader and an example for the younger Leafs.

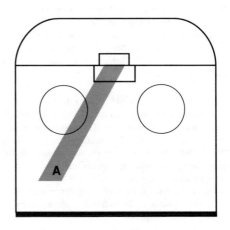

JOHN MCINTYRE

Yrs. of NHL service: 1
Born: Ravenswood, Ontario, Canada; April 29, 1969
Position: Center
Height: 6-1
Weight: 175
Uniform no.: 44
Shoots: left

Career statistics:

GP	G	A	TP	+/-	PIM	PP	SH	GW	GT	S	PCT
59	5	12	17	-12	117	0	1	1	0	44	11.4

LAST SEASON

First NHL season. Missed four games with thumb injury. Plus/minus was tied (Dave Hannan, Lou Franceschetti) for club's second worst.

THE FINESSE GAME

McIntyre is a fairly skilled player built more along the lines of ramrod play than dipsy-doodling around. He is a strong skater and he uses his good speed and strong stride as a checking center. He's going to succeed by staying in the opposition's face and holding, hooking and so on; McIntyre's not the kind of checker to dart around, swoop in and out closing passing lanes — he doesn't have that agility or sense of the ice.

McIntyre's hand skills are at the fair level and developable now, with greater NHL experience the key. He has fairly good hands and sense, so he knows what to do on the ice; now he just needs to better acclimate himself to the speed of the NHL game.

He can use his sense in a positive way in his checking, but again he needs a better understanding of the feel of the game's speed before he operates on his brain and not his skating. His scoring will be done the same way — directly related to his physical skills, and not his mental ones. He needs to be near the net to score now, opportunistically cashing in on loose pucks his checking creates.

THE PHYSICAL GAME

McIntyre is a wiry player, but he has good strength and he is aggressive in how he uses his strength. Feisty, pesky and tough are also good words — the point being he is unintimidated by either his surroundings or the players he is checking. He uses his body effectively to work his man off the puck, and he has the ability to be a dominating force in the traffic and corner areas.

He is also a well-conditioned player, and that skating stamina helps him keep pace in his work against the League's top centers.

THE INTANGIBLES

McIntyre is a sparky, spirited player, one who puts his heart and soul into every gamne. He works hard and is enthusiastic and coachable, and he certainly has talents to be more than just a checking center. Greater NHL experience will better reveal the extent of his possible contributions, but he is already a valuable member of the Leafs because of his attitude.

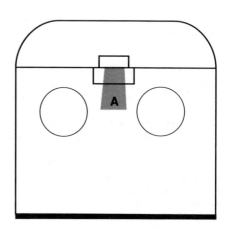

ED OLCZYK

Yrs. of NHL service: 6
Born: Chicago, Illinois, USA; August 16, 1966
Position: Center/right wing
Height: 6-1
Weight: 200
Uniform no.: 16
Shoots: left

Career statistics:

GP	G	A	TP	PIM
467	177	256	433	441

1989-90 statistics:

GP	G	A	TP	+/-	PIM	PP	SH	GW	GT	S	PCT
79	32	56	88	0	78	6	0	4	0	208	15.4

LAST SEASON

Assist total was career high, point total second highest of career, goal total three-season low. Finished third on the club in points and shots on goal, second in assists.

THE FINESSE GAME

Since so much of his game and success are puck-oriented, it is only appropriate that Olczyk's best skills have to do with direct work with the puck. He is a fine passer to both sides of the ice and his great touch is enhanced not only by his anticipation and hockey sense but by his poise and patience. Olczyk is uanffected by pressure from the opposition and, in fact, pressures the opposition with his long panic zone — he simply waits for the defense to cave in and then makes his moves, so that he not only makes a correct play (and he does that most always) but often a good play.

Good as his passing ability is, his shooting skill is better. He is an excellent shooter, one who can hit any area of the net from most any place on the ice. His touch makes him especially dangerous in the traffic area near the net (he also gets into scoring position excellently), where he shoots so quickly and with such placement that he'll put the puck in the net before anyone has even realized he's shot it. Of course, he's just tailor-made for the power play.

Obviously he has to be able to back up his puckhandling ability with mobility, and Olczyk is a good skater. He's got good strength on his feet (useful in traffic), as well as a degree of speed and agility uncommon in bigger men.

He's a fairly conscientious defensive player, regardless of the plus/minus rating.

THE PHYSICAL GAME

Tough, he ain't. Olczyk's got the size to be an intimidating player, but he plays a very passive physical game. He's content to go to the traffic areas to get loose pucks but won't necessarily mix it up with the defense to *cause* those loose pucks. He is, in short, a finesse player with size — and he plays smaller than he is.

He also could improve his conditioning, as he takes short shifts and comes off the ice after 30 seconds as if he were half-dead.

THE INTANGIBLES

Olczyk is a pretty straightforward player, in that he knows what he can do and that's what he does. He does almost nothing to improve himself and is content to take what his talent alone will give him, which is not to say that he doesn't care or doesn't put out when he's playing — we're just saying that he likes to be comfortable. An attitude, by the way, which has not endeared him to his teammates.

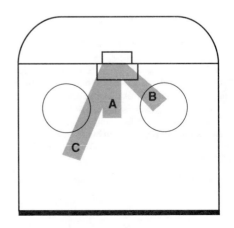

MARK OSBORNE

Yrs. of NHL service: 9
Born: Toronto, Ontario, Canada; August 13, 1961
Position: Left wing
Height: 6-2
Weight: 205
Uniform no.: 12
Shoots: left

Career statistics:

GP	G	A	TP	PIM
624	172	263	435	763

1989-90 statistics:

GP	G	A	TP	+/-	PIM	PP	SH	GW	GT	S	PCT
78	23	50	73	2	91	3	1	6	0	137	16.8

LAST SEASON

Assist and point totals were career bests. Finished third on the club in assists, first in game winners.

THE FINESSE GAME

Osborne is a better than middle-of-the-road player, made so more because of his work ethic than any superlative finesse skills. He is a strong skater in terms of sturdiness and power (his stride gives him some rink-length speed), but he's a not a really gifted player in terms of mobility or one-step quickness.

He shoots the puck very well, using his strength to drive his shot. He lacks a truly quick release and his accuracy also leaves something to be desired, but Osborne's shot is so heavy that if a goalie doesn't get all of it it's going into the net.

His hand skills and hockey sense are on a level below that of his skating and shooting, but Osborne's perseverance makes his modest talent better. He's not gifted with particularly sensitive hands, and because Osborne must go full throttle in order to make his skating a weapon his puckhandling falls behind his footwork. And too, he doesn't have an exceptional sense of the ice so his plays are going to be one-dimensional. When he's got his head up he can get the puck to his teammates.

THE PHYSICAL GAME

Osborne is gifted in the physical areas of the game, courtesy of his size and strength. He plays an active physical game all over the ice and he can be an effective physical player, but his skating can betray him because his balance is high. Consequently he won't always be ready to make plays after collisions, as he'll have to take a second or two to regain his footing.

He is a finely conditioned player and can play a physical style all night long for 80 games a season because of his physical shape.

THE INTANGIBLES

Though he has a tendency to be moody, Osborne is a hard worker and a fine team player. He gives the best of everything he has at all times, and it is that dedication that makes him successful.

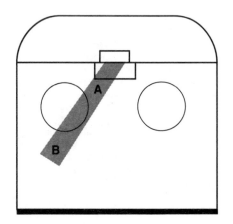

ROB RAMAGE

Yrs. of NHL service: 11
Born: Byron, Ontario, Canada; January 11, 1959
Position: Defenseman
Height: 6-2
Weight: 200
Uniform no.: 8
Shoots: right

Career statistics:

GP	G	A	TP	PIM
835	120	380	500	1,822

1989-90 statistics:

GP	G	A	TP	+/-	PIM	PP	SH	GW	GT	S	PCT
80	8	41	49	-1	202	3	0	1	0	196	4.1

LAST SEASON

Games played total was five-season high, point total four-season best. Plus/minus rating was second best among defensemen, shots on goal total highest among defenders.

THE FINESSE GAME

Mobility has always been the key to Ramage's NHL success, and it remains so even after a decade's service. He is a good skater in all directions, but it is his lateral ability that has allowed him to be the active rather than reactive defenseman he's been. His skating combines with his vision to allow him to challenge the puck at both blue lines.

Ramage is a good combination of offensive and defensive abilities. He sees the ice well and that allows him to join the Leafs rush as a fourth attacker or to even carry the puck himself, but that vision also teams with his hand skills to help him get the puck to an open teammate — something Ramage does well at both ends of the ice.

He passes the puck and otherwise controls it well, and he uses his slap shot from the point for his goals (he likes to shoot high).

THE PHYSICAL GAME

Ramage is a gifted physical player, blessed with size and strength. He is very tough in front of his own net, and he also does an excellent job of taking out men along the boards; only the NHL's strongest forwards will out-wrestle him. He plays a consistent and sometimes downright mean physical game regardless of the score, the period, or the venue.

He fights but he's not a great fighter, and Ramage can also be guilty of being over-aggressive; he can be goaded into poor penalties.

THE INTANGIBLES

Ramage is a very positive team personality, a player who sacrifices personal gain for team gain. His maturity, dedication and work ethic make him a natural leader, and he's a good choice as captain of the Maple Leafs.

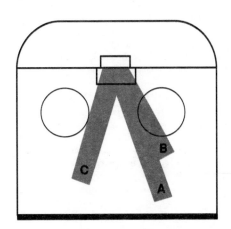

DAVE REID

Yrs. of NHL service: 4
Born: Toronto, Ontario, Canada; May 15, 1964
Position: Left wing
Height: 6-1
Weight: 205
Uniform no.: 14
Shoots: left

Career statistics:

GP	G	A	TP	PIM
242	46	66	112	70

1989-90 statistics:

GP	G	A	TP	+/-	PIM	PP	SH	GW	GT	S	PCT
70	9	19	28	-8	9	0	4	1	0	97	9.3

LAST SEASON

Games played, assist and point totals were second highest of career. Led club in shorthanded goals.

THE FINESSE GAME

Very little about Reid's game attracts attention. He is no better than average as a skater, possessing neither great speed nor exceptional agility.

His puckhandling skill is at the same level. Reid doesn't carry the puck with any exceptional flair but that's okay because he doesn't think with any particular creativity, so neither asset is hampered by the inability of the other.

He neither passes nor shoots the puck with any great skill, so he's going to need lots of time and space to make any kind of play — including scoring.

Even in his role as a defensive player he's nothing out of the ordinary. He's willing to play defense (which is a pretty smart decision on his part since he won't make the NHL on his offense) and plays fairly well positionally, but he contributes little else beyond that positional play — and even that is marginal.

THE PHYSICAL GAME

As with his finesse game, Reid brings little of above average value to his physical game. He uses his body to get in the opposition's way, but he doesn't really impose himself on the opposition via hitting (and probably can't do so consistently because of his modest skating skill).

THE INTANGIBLES

Reid is a fourth-line player who has found some NHL life as a checker. He can continue in the NHL in that role but, as with any other one-note player, is always on the bubble because of his limited contributions.

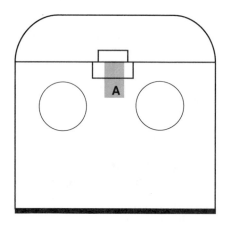

410

LUKE RICHARDSON

Yrs. of NHL service: 3
Born: Ottawa, Ontario, Canada; March 26, 1969
Position: Defenseman
Height: 6-3
Weight: 215
Uniform no.: 2
Shoots: left

Career statistics:

GP	G	A	TP	PIM
200	10	27	37	318

1989-1990 statistics:

GP	G	A	TP	+/-	PIM	PP	SH	GW	GT	S	PCT
67	4	14	18	-1	122	0	0	0	0	80	5.0

LAST SEASON

Assist and point totals were career highs; ditto PIM total. Plus/minus rating tied for second best among defense (Rob Ramage).

THE FINESSE GAME

"Be not too tame neither, but let your own discretion be your tutor." Shakespeare wrote that in *Hamlet*, and we thought we'd offer it as a parallel while discussing Richardson's skills. He can be a thunderous hitter (and why are we discussing this in the finesse area?) but his judgement in deciding when to hit and when not to needs work (now you know why we're discussing it here).

For a guy with his size and bulk, Richardson is a very good skater. He has speed and quickness, and most of all he has the agility to challenge the puckcarrier — something Richardson loves to do. The problem is he does this without regard to consequence: When he slams someone Richardson looks like a genius. When he goes to hit and the play goes around him, he looks a little less smart. The key to his success will be to develop his judgement and to sharpen his read and react skills. Outside of his challenging mistakes, Richardson plays a fairly disciplined and successful defensive game.

He has good skills in terms of puckhandling, passing and shooting. Richardson moves up-ice well with the puck, dishing it to open teammates at both ends of the ice. In these cases, his discretion is the better part of valor. He shoots fairly well from the blue line, and he'll generally be successful in his pinchs and forechecks.

THE PHYSICAL GAME

In this case, talent and the application thereof mesh at a fairly high level. Richardson has excellent size and strength and he brings them to bear as the team's best 1-on-1 defensive bodychecker. He's very strong in front of the net and his strength and balance allow him to out-wrestle most other players along the boards or in the corners.

Strong as he is, Richardson is not generally a fighter.

THE INTANGIBLES

He's a very coachable kid and Richardson needs that attention; he needs positive feedback to raise his confidence. He has solid skills and can grow into an above average NHL player, something his excellent attitude, desire and work ethic almost guarantee.

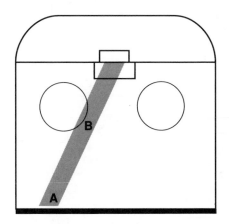

VANCOUVER CANUCKS

GREG ADAMS

Yrs. of NHL service: 5
Born: Nelson, B.C., Canada; August 1, 1963
Position: Center
Height: 6-3
Weight: 185
Uniform no.: 8
Shoots: left

Career statistics:

GP	G	A	TP	PIM
392	152	152	304	135

1989-90 statistics:

GP	G	A	TP	+/-	PIM	PP	SH	GW	GT	S	PCT
65	30	20	50	-8	18	13	0	1	1	181	16.6

LAST SEASON

Games played total was full-season career low. Led team in goals, power play goals and shots on goal (tied with Dan Quinn). Missed two games with groin injury, 12 games with a broken cheekbone. PIM total was lowest among regulars.

THE FINESSE GAME

Adams is a goal scorer (sometimes) and he plays like a goal scorer. He shoots the puck with good strength and quickness, and he gets himself into good shooting position near the net. He can also bring the puck from a distance. He gets into position by knowing to be around the net, and then his quick shot takes over.

He is an otherwise unremarkable finesse player, an unexceptional skater despite his very good balance — a skill he uses in tandem with his reach to lean away from checking and still get his shot off. He has no real speed or agility, and his lack of foot speed for quickness means he can't translate his balance into lateral movement.

Adams can carry the puck up ice fairly well (credit size and leaning ability again), but his limited skating combines with his limited sense and view of the ice to make him a limited playmaker. Almost any work he does with his teammates is incidental.

His defense suffers by virtue of his slow skating and poor reads of the ice.

THE PHYSICAL GAME

Adams has exceptional reach, as we've already discussed, but his great size is contradicted by his lack of strength. He has no real bulk, so he can be taken off the puck by smaller and/or stronger forwards. He does use his body to protect the puck extremely well; his wingspan is almost unmatched (only Mario Lemieux and Joel Otto comes to mind) in the League.

THE INTANGIBLES

It's hard to consider a guy as likely to score 20 goals as he is to score 30 a goal scorer — even harder to consider when his poor defense minimizes nearly half (17 even-strength goals last season, with Adams a minus-8) of his goal contribution. He's an inconsistent player who has shown no sign of making his game a dependable one.

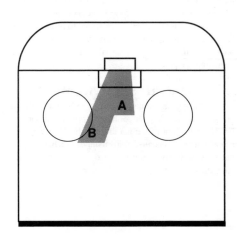

JIM BENNING

Yrs. of NHL service: 9
Born: Edmonton, Alta., Canada; April 29, 1963
Position: Defenseman
Height: 6-0
Weight: 185
Uniform no.: 4
Shoots: left

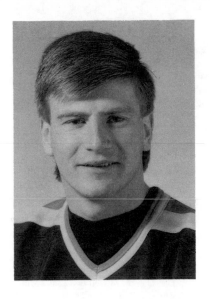

Career statistics:

GP	G	A	TP	PIM
605	52	191	243	461

1989-90 statistics:

GP	G	A	TP	+/-	PIM	PP	SH	GW	GT	S	PCT
45	3	9	12	4	26	0	1	0	0	49	6.1

LAST SEASON

Games played, all point and PIM totals were career lows. Plus/minus rating was club's third best. Missed four games due to injury and did not dress for final 11 games (according to the Canucks).

THE FINESSE GAME

Skating and puck abilities are the skills Benning brings to his NHL game. He is a very mobile player and — when his confidence is high — has no hesitation in using his skating skill at both blue lines. He has very strong acceleration and lateral movement abilities, using them defensively to control the gap and step up on the puck carrier (and then turn the play around) and to contain the point and continue the Canucks offense at the opposing blue line.

Benning gets pretty good reads of the ice and is fairly smart with the puck, but he will make the occasional high-risk play and get burned when a simpler off-the-boards play would have succeeded. He can also be forced into runovers by strong forechecking.

His offense is generally confined to following the rush and posting up at the blue line, where he'll dish the puck to open teammates. His goals will come on a good shot from the point.

THE PHYSICAL GAME

Benning has some size, but he's not really a physical player. He gets good body position along the boards or in front of the net and can have success because of that and because of his balance and hand skills, but he's probably going to get out-muscled in strict strength situations.

THE INTANGIBLES

Benning had become a fairly dependable player during the last season or two, and can be that again if the Canucks want him to play; he was benched late in the season as the Canucks went with younger defensemen, but Benning is only 27 and has plenty of NHL time left. He just might have that time with another team.

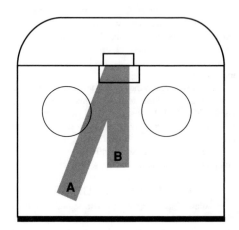

STEVE BOZEK

Yrs. of NHL service: 8
Born: Kelowna, B.C., Canada; November 26, 1960
Position: Left wing
Height: 5-11
Weight: 180
Uniform no.: 14
Shoots: left

Career statistics:

GP	G	A	TP	PIM
521	141	142	283	260

1989-90 statistics:

GP	G	A	TP	+/-	PIM	PP	SH	GW	GT	S	PCT
58	14	9	23	-3	32	0	1	2	0	105	13.3

LAST SEASON

Assist and point totals were full-season career lows. Plus/minus rating was second best among forwards.

THE FINESSE GAME

Skating in general and speed in particular are the weapons Bozek brings to bear in his finesse game. He has tremendous acceleration and rink length speed but he is also extremely quick, able to change direction and to stop and start within a stride. His balance and foot speed are the keys to that skill, and that quickness makes him a good checker and penalty killer.

The rest of his finesse game is based on his speed, and sometimes suffers because of it. Bozek's sense of the game is no better than average, so that he checks reactively rather than actively (and as a forechecker he is better at puck pursuit than he is at containing). Offensively he has the same flaw — the rink goes by so quickly Bozek can't get a good look at it.

His ability to get to loose pucks powers his scoring ability, which is also not very high. He plays the game at 100 miles per hour, gets 100 scoring chances and can't score because his hands are terrible. Bozek lacks smarts around the goal, so he will have to feast off of rebounds and other opportunistic-type scoring chances.

THE PHYSICAL GAME

Bozek is in great condition, and his ability to just skate and skate reflects that. He is not a big player and he lacks the bulk to absorb punishment, thus resulting in injuries. He is not a player to initiate a lot of contact or to work successfully in the traffic areas, but he does have the strength to hold his own in a one-on-one battle for the puck.

THE INTANGIBLES

Bozek is a role player with a very positive attitude, working as hard as possible at all times despite his infrequent playing status.

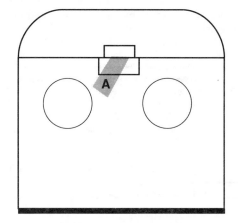

BRIAN BRADLEY

Yrs. of NHL service: 3
Born: Kitchener, Ontario, Canada; January 21, 1965
Position: Center
Height: 5-10
Weight: 170
Uniform no.: 10
Shoots: right

Career statistics:

GP	G	A	TP	PIM
194	50	80	130	129

1989-90 statistics:

GP	G	A	TP	+/-	PIM	PP	SH	GW	GT	S	PCT
67	19	29	48	5	65	2	0	0		1	121	15.7

LAST SEASON

All point and PIM totals were career bests. Missed 10 games with thumb injuries. Led forwards in plus/minus rating.

THE FINESSE GAME

Bradley is a very highly skilled finesse player. He is an excellent skater in the nifty-shifty class with great agility and quickness to power his darting style. His balance and lateral ability are very high, and he'll get to loose pucks — or even force them — with his combination of quick feet and fast hands.

He has excellent stick skills that are marked by the same quickness that mark his skating. He handles the puck very well and he likes to exploit his quickness by going one-on-one with defensemen down the left wing; he'll almost always carry the puck over the blue line.

His sense and quick stick would argue for his ability as a playmaker (and he does keep his head up to use his teammates; Bradley gets the puck to them well), but his tendency to overhandle the puck in hopes of just one more fancy move sometimes works against his playmaking ability.

He uses his skating ability to get into the opening for shooting and he shoots the puck a lot, using his excellently released shot to force goalies into making saves. He'll also succeed in front of the net because of his ability to get to loose pucks and to quickly send them goal-ward.

He is a defensively responsible player.

THE PHYSICAL GAME

Bradley doesn't bring much to the table in the physical game, mostly because he lacks both the size and the strength to do so (not that those deficiencies have to stay deficiencies — see Steve Yzerman and Pat LaFontaine for proof). He'll get into trouble in any muscular situation, and that especially hurts him in his defensive battles for the puck.

His strength will remain a concern as players in the NHL grow bigger and stronger.

THE INTANGIBLES

Bradley has shown that he can contribute in the NHL, but he is the kind of player who will have to be bracketed by big wingers who will clear space for him. He could and should add whatever degree of strength he can to his game — it can only help.

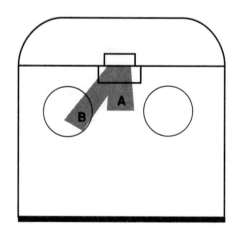

GARTH BUTCHER

Yrs. of NHL service: 8
Born: Regina, Sask., Canada; January 8, 1963
Position: Defenseman
Height: 6-0
Weight: 200
Uniform no.: 5
Shoots: right

Career statistics:

GP	G	A	TP	PIM
541	27	95	122	1,412

1989-90 statistics:

GP	G	A	TP	+/-	PIM	PP	SH	GW	GT	S	PCT
80	6	14	20	-10	205	1	0	1	0	87	6.9

LAST SEASON

Games played and goal totals tie career highs. Second on club in PIM total (first among defensemen).

THE FINESSE GAME

Butcher is a limited finesse player who maximizes his skills through fairly intelligent application of his modest abilities. He's not a great skater but he does have enough mobility to play an active defensive game at his blue line, stepping up and challenging the puck carrier when possible. The League's fastest skaters will get Butcher turned to take advantage of his limited mobility. He insures success at the offensive end by rarely pinching in or forechecking.

An offensive defenseman in junior, Butcher has the ability to rush the puck from the defensive zone when necessary. Again, he tempers this skill intelligently and tends to leave that action to his partner; Butcher serves more as the takeout and not breakout defenseman. He sees the forward breaking and generally makes smart plays, but he can be forced into giveaways via determined forechecking.

His offense is going to come from the point on a strong slap shot, and Butcher knows to keep that shot low to the ice for tip and deflection possibilities.

THE PHYSICAL GAME

He's not the biggest or strongest guy, but Butcher plays a very physical and aggressive defensive zone game. He punishes the opposition in front of the Canucks' net and takes the body well in the corners and along the boards.

He's not a great fighter (certainly the rest of the League's fighters aren't afraid of him), but Butcher will go with anyone in protection of a teammate.

THE INTANGIBLES

One thing Butcher also does well is instigate incidents that create power plays for the Canucks via his constant yapping at the opposition. Butcher is smart that way, the same way his smartness about staying within his game has molded him into a fairly dependable defensive defenseman. He's a good team man and an honest, dedicated player.

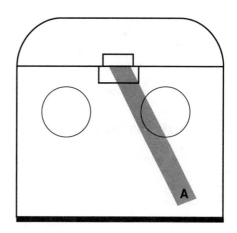

VLADIMIR KRUTOV

Yrs. of NHL service: 1
Born: Moscow, Soviet Union; June 1, 1960
Position: Left wing
Height: 5-9
Weight: 195
Uniform no.: 17
Shoots: right

Career statistics:

GP	G	A	TP	+/-	PIM	PP	SH	GW	GT	S	PCT
61	11	23	34	-5	20	2	0	1	0	81	13.6

LAST SEASON

First in the NHL. Missed four games while returning to USSR for family matter.

THE FINESSE GAME

Krutov is a goal scorer — at least that's what his history says. He uses his skating style (one based more in strength than speed) to bull his way into shooting position and then he unloads a dynamic and (at its best) bullet-like shot at the net.

He also gets into scoring position well without the puck, and his innate hockey sense and anticipation get the credit there. Krutov is a good stickhandler and can use his hand skills to get into the clear. While not the speediest skater he does have a high degree of agility, and these factors contribute to his getting into the clear and ready to accept passes.

He shoots well off the pass and is more of an in-tight scorer than he is a long-range bomber.

His defense is perfunctory, and Krutov frequently looks uninterested in his own end of the ice.

THE PHYSICAL GAME

Krutov has the cannonball-build to be effective in traffic. He aborbs hits with his fire-hydrant body and continues to the net uninterrupted — you might even call him a Soviet power forward. He'll take the knock necessary to score, and will succeed in his drives to the net because of his strength.

THE INTANGIBLES

To many people Krutov is the ultimate Soviet carpetbagger — and his poor physical condition worked in tandem with his poor performance (versus expectations) to confirm the suspicion that all Krutov (and, by extension, all Soviet players) wanted was North American currency. The Canucks counted quite heavily on both his performance and that of his center Igor Larionov to help them improve in the NHL standings, and they were sorely disappointed. What will this year bring? Well, Krutov has promised to be in shape and to put forward a better effort. We shall see.

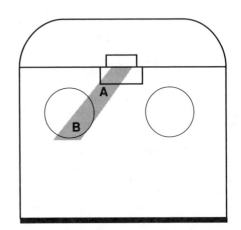

IGOR LARIONOV

Yrs. of NHL service: 1
Born: Voskresenk, Soviet Union; December 3, 1960
Position: Center
Height: 5-9
Weight: 165
Uniform no.: 18
Shoots: right

Career statistics:

GP	G	A	TP	+/-	PIM	PP	SH	GW	GT	S	PCT
74	17	27	44	-5	20	8	0	2	1	118	14.4

LAST SEASON

First NHL season. Missed two games with a groin pull, three with a wrist injury and one with the flu.

THE FINESSE GAME

Larionov is a very creative player, and his finesse skills allow him to play that creative game. He sees the ice exceptionally well and looks to use his teammates at all times, but he has not yet gotten completely acclimated to the pace and crowding of the NHL game; he will have to make his plays faster if he is to make as much use of his vision as he can.

Larionov's hand skills back up his mind. He has glove-soft hands, hands with the touch to put the puck anywhere in any situation. He handles the puck well himself, and his skating is a further complement to his creativity. Larionov is a small, nifty, darting kind of player — not unlike Denis Savard, though nowhere near as dynamic. Still, his hand and foot skills make him a dangerous player in contained circumstances while his brains make him a dangerous player in open ice.

His skills have not yet extended to strong defense, and even Larionov's goal-scoring ability is less pronounced than his playmaking. He will take great advantage of time and space around the net (his balance and lateral ability combine with his soft hands here) in order to score his goals.

THE PHYSICAL GAME

Larionov doesn't really have one. His strength and thus his ability to perform in traffic (and therefore the NHL) are suspect. He can be worked off the puck when trapped in one-on-one situations, and that particularly hurts defensively.

THE INTANGIBLES

For return based on anticipation, Larionov was a disappointment last season. Not that he wasn't motivated or didn't care — rather, the new experiences of the NHL and North American life took their tolls on him (there were nights when you forgot he was even in uniform). Now the question is, can he marshal the resources for the Canucks that once made him a world-class center? Because, based on last year, he was an ordinary player.

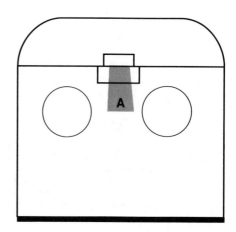

DOUG LIDSTER

Yrs. of NHL service: 6
Born: Kamloops, B.C., Canada; October 18, 1960
Position: Defenseman
Height: 6-1
Weight: 200
Uniform no.: 3
Shoots: right

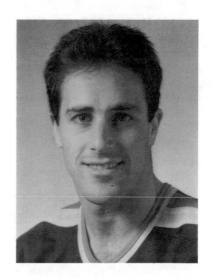

Career statistics:

GP	G	A	TP	PIM
451	47	168	215	374

1989-90 statistics:

GP	G	A	TP	+/-	PIM	PP	SH	GW	GT	S	PCT
80	8	28	36	-16	36	1	0	0	1	143	5.6

LAST SEASON

Played 80 games for second time in career. PIM total was full-season career low. Finished second in scoring for defensemen and first in shots on goal for defenders, and plus/minus rating was second poorest among Canuck defenders.

THE FINESSE GAME

Lidster is a talented finesse player with above average ability in all finesse skills. He is an excellent skater with fine mobility up and back and superior ability laterally. He doesn't have rocket-like acceleration or exceptional rink-length speed, but Lidster's foot speed and balance combine to make him a very strong one-step player. He can get loose pucks because of that skill, as well as change direction and start and stop within a stride.

His skating makes him an active versus reactive player at both blue lines. He controls the gap well on the incoming forward (stepping up to challenge and thwart offensive drives), and he also uses his skating to contain the offensive point and quarterback the Canucks' play for the opposing blue line. Lidster will use his skating to come off the point for shots and to become an attacker on rushes from the Vancouver zone.

He has fine hockey sense and anticipation skills (especially offensively), but he has a tendency to make mistakes by trying to do too much — home run plays from his own end, when shorter and more efficient passes would work better. Still, he uses his good hand skills (Lidster rushes and passes the puck very well and with touch) in tandem with his brains to be a potent transitional and offensive force.

The one thing he lacks finesse-wise is an exceptional point shot, and he doesn't use the one he has enough anyway, but his wrist shot from the faceoff circle is a good weapon.

He plays regularly in all specialty team situations.

THE PHYSICAL GAME

Essentially a finesse player with a degree of size, Lidster uses his body to gain good position along the boards or in front of the net. That positional play, rather than outstanding strength or earthshaking hitting, keys Lidster's physical game. He can be out-muscled when wrestling for the puck, but he does complement his body position game with his ability to make plays coming away from the boards.

He is always in good physical condition and has a good recovery rate (the ability to be back at full-strength quickly after a shift), and that's important because he's going to play 30 minutes a game.

THE INTANGIBLES

An intelligent and reliable player (Vancouver's most dependable player), Lidster's one downside is that he plays at the same intensity level at all times. He plays a generally unemotional game and that's one reason why he's so reliable, but it's also a reason why he hasn't taken greater advantage of his skills.

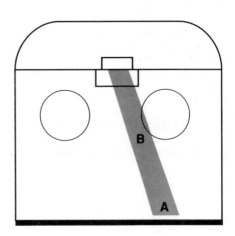

TREVOR LINDEN

Yrs. of NHL service: 1
Born: Medicine Hat, Alta., Canada; April 11, 1970
Position: Center/right wing
Height: 6-4
Weight: 200
Uniform no.: 16
Shoots: right

Career statistics:

GP	G	A	TP	PIM
153	51	59	110	84

1989-90 statistics:

GP	G	A	TP	+/-	PIM	PP	SH	GW	GT	S	PCT
73	21	30	51	-17	43	6	2	3	0	171	12.3

LAST SEASON

Finished third on the club in scoring, first in shorthanded goals. Plus/minus rating was second poorest among forwards. Was second in game-winners, fourth in shots on goal. Assist total grew, goal total fell in second season. Missed one game with a hyperextended elbow, six games with separated shoulder.

THE FINESSE GAME

Just as Linden's hallmarks as a player are in the physical aspects of the game, so too are his best finesse aspects ones based on strength and power. He is a very strong player on his feet and his balance is to be credited here. His strength allows him to remain upright after hitting (which is something Linden does a lot of) and also allows him to drive through his checks, and his balance combines with his deceptive foot speed to give him a better-than-anticipated ability to move laterally.

His ability with the puck is good and very likely to get better, despite his tendency last season to overhandle the puck in many situations. Linden can handle the puck smoothly as he moves up ice and he can give or take passes to both sides in stride. He has good touch and can feather or fire a pass as the situation dictates, and his high degree of hockey sense maximizes his puck work. Linden knows how to get into scoring position, but he also knows how manipulate his teammates into that position as well.

That strong degree of anticipation and vision is also present in Linden's defensive game, regardless of the plus/minus rating. He is a very strong positional player, very reliable in all three zones. That mental sense also serves him as a forechecker, and he is a very strong reader of the offensive zone.

THE PHYSICAL GAME

Linden has excellent size and strength and he not only knows how to use them, he uses them. His skating strength allows him to drive the net, just as it allows him to drive through his checks in the corners to take the opposition off the puck.

He can get his shots away while being checked, and Linden also plays a smart physical game by avoiding wandering and foolish penalties.

THE INTANGIBLES

Last season was probably about as bad a season as Linden could have had as an NHL sophomore. He over-did everything in attempts to do every positive thing himself, and then when he was just beginning to straighten himself out mentally, when he was beginning to regain his poise, he got hurt.

But though this was a short-term disaster for Linden and the Canucks it will have long-term benefits. For one thing, Linden realized what he was doing and took steps to return to his freshman form. And, it showed him how to deal with adversity. No way should anyone be down on this kid, who — though just 20 years old — possesses the poise, intensity, work ethic and maturity that will make Linden one of the NHL's very best players.

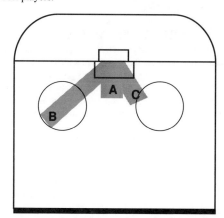

JYRKI LUMME

Yrs. of NHL service: 1
Born: Tampere, Finland; July 16, 1966
Position: Defenseman
Height: 6-1
Weight: 190
Uniform no.: 21
Shoots: left

Career statistics:

GP	G	A	TP	PIM
86	5	29	34	59

1989-90 statistics:

GP	G	A	TP	+/-	PIM	PP	SH	GW	GT	S	PCT
65	4	26	30	17	49	0	0	1	0	109	3.7

LAST SEASON

Acquired from Montreal in March 1990 in exchange for a draft choice. Led all rookie defensemen in plus/minus rating, was third in overall rookie defensemen scoring.

THE FINESSE GAME

Lumme is a highly skilled offensive player, the kind of player who can generate offense from defense but can also make the kind of mistakes that result in big goals-against. He is an excellent skater and puck carrier and clearly likes to be a playmaker — he has a very creative sense of the ice and likes to make the high-risk play that can sometimes backfire. He needs to develop a better sense of risk.

He is a fine skater and he uses his skating to great effect at both ends of the ice, though he has a tendency to gamble a bit too frequently at his own blue line when challenging the puck; still, his skating can bail him out of those holes.

Lumme finds the open man very well at both ends of the ice, and he also rushes the puck and joins the attack prudently. He uses his skating to contain and conrol the point, and it is from the blue line that he will get most of his goals.

THE PHYSICAL GAME

Lumme is a fairly tough player, not one who will necessarily devastate the opposition with his hitting but a player who will take his lumps and get his nose dirty. He is helped greatly in his physical play by virtue of his finesse skills of balance and hand speed, so he can certainly make plays in traffic and coming off the boards. He uses his body to gain good position in one-on-one battles for the puck.

THE INTANGIBLES

Lumme was one of those players whose presence drove veterans Jim Benning and Robert Nordmark to the bench late in the season, and he is one of those players on whom the Canucks will be counting heavily in the future. As for immediately, he can expect to see heavier checking pressure from the opposition, as he is no longer a secret to the NHL. Let's see how he responds under both the internal pressure to succeed from the Canucks and the external pressure from the rest of the NHL.

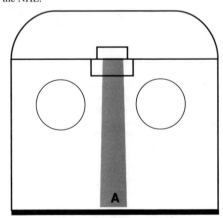

ANDREW MCBAIN

Yrs. of NHL service: 7
Born: Scarborough, Ontario, Canada; January 18, 1965
Position: Right wing
Height: 6-1
Weight: 205
Uniform no.: 9
Shoots: right

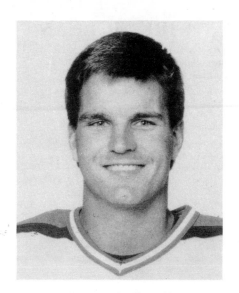

Career statistics:

GP	G	A	TP	PIM
475	110	143	253	494

1989-90 statistics:

GP	G	A	TP	+/-	PIM	PP	SH	GW	GT	S	PCT
67	9	14	23	-11	73	4	0	0	0	106	8.5

LAST SEASON

Acquired from Pittsburgh in January 1990 along with Dan Quinn and Dave Capuano in exchange for Barry Pederson, Tony Tanti and Rod Buskas. Games played and all point totals were four-season lows. Missed six games with bruised ribs and five games with the flu.

THE FINESSE GAME

The greatest portion of McBain's NHL success has come on the power play. There are two reasons for that: his skating and his shot.

Andy's skating is no better than good, marked more by strength on his skates than it is by quickness or agility. His strength has given him some degree of speed off the wing, and his ability to move with the puck at that speed does force the defense to back up. But, for the most part, McBain's skating doesn't strike fear into the opposition — and it certainly doesn't get him into the clear in 5-on-5 situations.

But when the ice opens up on the power play Andy uses his strength afoot to plant himself near the net, where he exploits loose pucks with his quick shot.

Because he's not a creative player, McBain isn't much of a playmaker. He's improved his ability to see and react at the NHL level, but the bulk of his assists are going to come on the power play.

His defense is atrocious. His skating and playreading are part of that, but McBain doesn't try awfully hard either.

THE PHYSICAL GAME

In order to succeed, McBain must uses his good size and strength consistently. He has to play aggressively, but he's reluctant to do so. For a straight-ahead player with size, that's a grievous flaw. He is a one-play player, making a hit if he can but having very little idea what to do afterward.

THE INTANGIBLES

McBain is a streaky player, but his attitude has come a long way in the last five years. A better work ethic would make him a better player, but after seven NHL seasons what you see with Andy McBain is what you get.

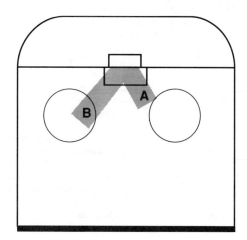

KIRK MCLEAN

Yrs. of NHL service: 3
Born: Willowdale, Ontario, Canada; June 26, 1966
Position: Goaltender
Height: 6-0
Weight: 195
Uniform no.: 1
Catches: left

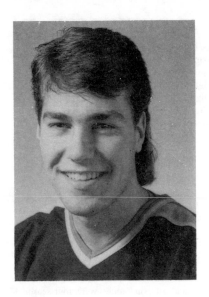

Career statistics:

GP	MINS	G	SO	AVG	A	PIM
152	8,867	511	5	3.46	6	20

1989-90 statistics:

GP	MINS	AVG	W	L	T	SO	GA	SA	SAPCT	PIM
63	3,739	3.47	21	30	10	0	216	1,804	.880	6

LAST SEASON

Led NHL in games and minutes played with career highs in both categories. Posted career-best win total.

THE PHYSICAL GAME

McLean is an excellent standup goaltender, one who makes best use of his his good size by playing an active challenging game. He squares himself to the puck very well and allows the efficiency of his angle-cutting style to do the work for him. Because of this ability, he's going to have to be attacked with re-directed shots — tips and deflections will take advantage of his style.

He is a very good skater with good balance, so he moves in and out of the net, as well as from post to post, very well (he does have some difficulty remaining compact in his stance when moving laterally, so there'll be five-hole opportunities). His balance serves to get him to the ice and back into his stance very quickly, and his overall skating ability allows him to leave the net to flag down loose pucks.

He handles the puck conservatively but well, and he helps himself greatly when passing it to his defensemen. He is also a very good pokechecker and will use his stick around the net to break up plays and deflect pucks. He has a fine catching hand and is generally very strong in protecting the upper half of the net.

He is much quicker with his feet than would be expected for a tall goalie, so he actually benefits from the stereotype as shooters try to beat him low to the corners (of course, his style aids him greatly in eliminating those options). However, his standup style can be a weakness on scrambles around the net as bang-bang plays find the openings he allows by staying on his feet.

THE MENTAL GAME

McLean has become a very strong competitor mentally, maintaining his concentration through games and over long stretches of time. He has also developed the facility of retaining his calm and composure after giving up quick goals; McLean just sticks with basics, standing up and letting the puck do the work. In fact, the sign that Mclean is struggling is when he flops to the ice an inordinant amount of times. He sees the puck very well and has good anticipation ability, and prepares well to play each game.

THE INTANGIBLES

McLean won the goalie segment of the All-Star skills competition, and while we wouldn't say that makes him the NHL's best goaltender we would say that his performance in Pittsburgh is quite representative of his overall ability. He seems to thrive on work and responsibility and — as one of the NHL's top 10 goalies — (though generally unknown in the east) is the cornerstone of future Canuck success.

LARRY MELNYK

Yrs. of NHL service: 8
Born: Saskatoon, Sask., Canada; February 21, 1960
Position: Defenseman
Height: 6-0
Weight: 195
Uniform no.: 24
Shoots: left

Career statistics:

GP	G	A	TP	PIM
432	11	63	74	686

1989-90 statistics:

GP	G	A	TP	+/-	PIM	PP	SH	GW	GT	S	PCT
67	0	2	2	-27	91	0	0	0	0	45	0.0

LAST SEASON

Plus/minus rating was club's worst. Missed at least four games with a recurring back injury.

THE FINESSE GAME

Because he has limited finesse skills, Melnyk has to operate on smarts. And his smarts tell him to stay within his limited finesse skills.

He's not exceptionally mobile, and that's because of his skating stance — all his weight is on his heels, cutting down the speed and lateral movement he can generate.

Melnyk counters that seeming flaw by playing a solid defensive angle game. He forces the opposition into a narrower and narrower lane wide of the net, and he screens off the opposition effectively once they're forced to the corner.

He is not at all offensive minded and will pinch into the offensive zone only on the rarest of occasions. He does not have an exceptional shot and he hardly shoots at all for that matter.

THE PHYSICAL GAME

Melnyk has good size and strength, and he marshals them both to succeed in the corners and the front of the net. He can be out-maneuvered in front of the net because of his less-than-exceptional balance, but he uses his strength to counter that. He's a pretty tough player.

He willingly sacrifices his body to block shots and is aggressive in a non-fighting way.

THE INTANGIBLES

Melnyk would be called an honest hockey player, a guy who brings everything he has to offer to each of his performances. He makes his modest skills better by playing within his limitations but, with the Canucks using the last month of last season to audition youngsters, Melnyk may not be long for Vancouver.

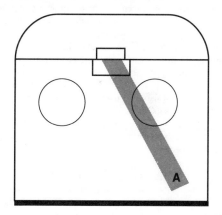

ROBERT NORDMARK

Yrs. of NHL service: 3
Born: Kalix, Sweden; August 20, 1962
Position: Defenseman
Height: 6-1
Weight: 200
Uniform no.: 6
Shoots: right

Career statistics:

GP	G	A	TP	PIM
191	11	64	75	191

1989-90 statistics:

GP	G	A	TP	+/-	PIM	PP	SH	GW	GT	S	PCT
44	2	11	13	-16	34	1	0	0	0	86	2.3

LAST SEASON

Missed seven and then nine games with back spasms. Games played and all point totals were career lows.

THE FINESSE GAME

The finesse aspects of the game are Nordmark's strengths, particularly in the playmaking department. As always, skating is the foundation of hockey ability and Nordmark is an excellent skater (speed and quickness combined with balance for agility and very strong lateral ability), but his passing skills and hockey sense account for the bulk of his success.

He sees the ice very well at both blue lines, getting good reads of open men and the direction a play can take. He plays a fairly active game defensively by stepping up to challenge the puck carrier, and Nordmark thus forces turnovers. Then he takes the second step of turning the play around by making good decisions for the transition game. He gets the puck to his wingers very well because of his vision and good touch. Nordmark will also carry the puck when necessary, not forcing rushes that don't exist.

He reads the offensive blue line well and can get the puck to the open man. His shot is good, but he'll pass to a better-positioned teammate.

THE PHYSICAL GAME

He has the size and bulk (and he certainly has the mobility and intelligence) to play a physical game, but Nordmark is a largely unphysical player. He does use his body to establish good position in one-on-one confrontations along the boards or in front of the net, but he doesn't initiate a lot of actual hitting. Conversely, hitting will wear him down both during games and over the course of the season.

He will sacrifice his body by blocking shots.

THE INTANGIBLES

Nordmark can be an above average player in the NHL, but he needs to maintain his intensity — he needs to be reminded to pick up the level of his game. Considering the number of younger and more eager players the Canucks iced late last season, Nordmark may find himself sitting more or playing somewhere else.

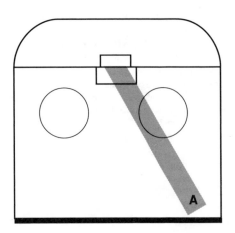

DAN QUINN

Yrs. of NHL service: 7
Born: Ottawa, Ontario, Canada; June 1, 1965
Position: Center
Height: 5-11
Weight: 180
Uniform no.: 7
Shoots: left

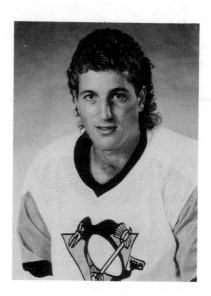

Career statistics:

GP	G	A	TP	PIM
513	199	299	498	314

1989-90 statistics:

GP	G	A	TP	+/-	PIM	PP	SH	GW	GT	S	PCT
78	25	38	63	-17	49	11	0	5	0	181	13.8

LAST SEASON

Acquired from Pittsburgh along with Andrew McBain and Dave Capuano in exchange for Barry Pederson, Tony Tanti and Rod Buskas in January 1990. All point totals were five season lows, but he led the club in scoring (second in both goals and assists) and shots on goal. Was second in power play goals and led in game-winners.

THE FINESSE GAME

Dan is a very good finesse player, with his skating and hockey sense tops among his finesse skills. His skating is excellent in all areas, especially those that comprise mobility: balance and quickness. He's got great foot speed and can make moves in any direction — and at any speed — within a stride. That gives him great lateral movement and, while he also has the strength needed for breakaway speed, Dan is more a darter than a rocket.

His hockey sense makes his skating more effective, as his anticipation and vision allow him to lead his teammates into openings or to exploit those openings (courtesy of his quickness) himself.

Of course, his hand skills are largely responsible for his ability to make plays. Quinn has great hands with a real soft touch and he's able to make his plays — whether feathering passes or carrying the puck himself — at full speed.

Because his skills get him into the open quickly, Quinn is an opportunist at goal scoring. He'll get those loose pucks because of his quickness, and that skill combines with his sense to put him in the clear on the power play. He gets his shot away quickly, and shoots frequently.

THE PHYSICAL GAME

Quinn has incorporated a willingness to accept contact into his game, and that has helped him succeed (his finesse skills let him work favorably in traffic — especially his balance). He does not, however, initiate a great deal of contact, so Quinn will most likely be found on the edges of traffic, hoping to be in the clear when the puck squirts free. If he is caught in traffic, the opposition will most likely take the puck from him, because he is not overwhelmingly strong.

THE INTANGIBLES

He'll be counted on to be Vancouver's primary scoring center, and he'll face — for the first time in his career — the opposition's primary checkers. He's a consistent player, which will help the Canucks, but not the greatest team guy (which will not help the Canucks).

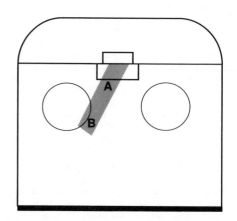

PAUL REINHART

Yrs. of NHL service: 11
Born: Kitchener, Ontario, Canada; January 6, 1960
Position: Defenseman
Height: 5-11
Weight: 205
Uniform no.: 23
Shoots: left

Career statistics:

GP	G	A	TP	PIM
648	133	426	559	277

1989-90 statistics:

GP	G	A	TP	+/-	PIM	PP	SH	GW	GT	S	PCT
67	17	40	57	2	30	9	1	1	2	139	12.2

LAST SEASON

Games played total was three-season high, goal total five-season high. Finished second on team in scoring, first in assists. Plus/minus rating was club's second best. Missed six games with an ankle injury and seven games with a back injury.

THE FINESSE GAME

Reinhart is an outstanding playmaker, maybe the best unknown offensive defenseman of his generation. He has excellent hockey sense, vision and anticipation, so he'll find open men or create open men by his manipulation of the puck and the ice in front of him. His ability to read and react is very high at both the offensive and defensive ends of the ice — in fact, react is a weak word to use because Reinhart always plays an active game.

His skating is the skill that most directly allows him to physicalize his mental abilities. Reinhart is an excellent skater in all directions, with exceptional balance and agility; his lateral movement is outstanding. So good is his skating that, although he plays without contact, the opposition cannot get the puck past him. His low center of gravity combines with his leg strength to give him exceptional sturdiness afoot, and he is very difficult to knock off the puck.

He rushes the puck and joins the attack excellently, and his puckhandling ability is just as strong as his other skills. His passing to both sides and in all situations is superb — once he gets the puck in the Vancouver zone it's as good as gone because Reinhart finds and delivers the puck to the open man excellently. He has a strong, low slap shot from the point, but he will move to the deep slot if he can.

All his skills make him a natural for specialty teams duty, and he is especially dangerous in power play situations because of his abilities in open ice.

THE PHYSICAL GAME

The physical game is not really Reinhart's game. He'll bang and bump along the boards, but he wants to skate with a guy, flick out his stick to poke the puck away and then turn the play up ice. His balance serves him very well in traffic situations, but Reinhart won't put himself into traffic all that frequently (and how much does his fragile back have to do with that?).

He gains body position very well in front of the net, but he won't pound anyone into oblivion — he'll play the opponent's stick, or the pass to the slot.

THE INTANGIBLES

We're not kidding when we talk about Reinhart being unknown; you never hear his name mentioned when people talk about skilled defensemen. It's almost as if, between his back problems and his trade to Vancouver, he's been forgotten. Well, don't tell the Canucks that. How important is Reinhart to Vancouver? To start, he makes all the Canucks better players — and the 25 minutes on-ice he logs are 25 minutes Vancouver doesn't have to worry about getting the puck from its zone.

His health will always be a concern, but Reinhart — who is an exceptional athlete and very positive person — gives all of whatever he has every day.

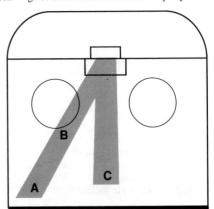

JIM SANDLAK

Yrs. of NHL service: 5
Born: Kitchener, Ontario, Canada; December 12, 1966
Position: Right wing
Height: 6-4
Weight: 219
Uniform no.: 19
Shoots: right

Career statistics:

GP	G	A	TP	PIM
292	67	67	134	360

1989-90 statistics:

GP	G	A	TP	+/-	PIM	PP	SH	GW	GT	S	PCT
70	15	8	23	-15	104	1	0	1	1	135	11.1

LAST SEASON

PIM total was career high and third highest on club, assist and point total full-season career low. Missed five games with separated shoulder.

THE FINESSE GAME

The best finesse asset Sandlak has is his shot, and it is an excellent asset. Sandlak shoots with great power in both his slap shots and wrist shots, and those shots are good enough to consistently beat NHL goaltending. They are both heavy and fast to the net, and a quicker release would only improve Sandlak's goal-scoring numbers.

Two things may mitigate against his development into a true goal scorer: skating and anticipation. Sandlak has very good strength in his skating and is very sturdy on his feet (solid attributes in his burgeoning physical game) and that sturdiness is important when he plugs the net on the power play, but it is not a substitute for agility or speed — two assets Sandlak lacks at the NHL level. Sandlak would especially benefit from better quickness, as that would allow him to better exploit loose pucks when he's around the net.

His anticipation and hockey sense are not much better. Sandlak doesn't exhibit the true goal scorer's ability to get into scoring position, and he is also handicapped in the use of his teammates because of that absence of anticipation — not that he has great passing skills either.

Both his slowness afoot and his poor sense of the ice make him an iffy propostion defensively.

THE PHYSICAL GAME

The potential is scary, and so is Sandlak's use of his talent. He has excellent size and strength, the type only a handful of NHL players could claim, yet Sandlak is exceptionally inconsistent in his application of his talents.

Sandlak *must* hit to be effective, but he does so on infrequent occasions and backs away from the confrontations that follow his banging around. Sandlak has trouble even doing simple things, like fighting through checks, consistently.

He is, therefore, essentially a finesse player with size, and he generally plays smaller than he is.

THE INTANGIBLES

Both the Canucks and Sandlak are haunted by Cam Neely, and the Canucks are afraid that that is exactly what Sandlak will develop into should they dispatch him from Vancouver. But Neely's first five NHL seasons looked like this goal-wise: 16-21-14-36-42. Sandlak's look like this: 1-15-16-20-15.

The Canucks' restraint in their dealing with Sandlak is admirable, remarkable even considering what they've gotten in return. But Sandlak ain't no Cam Neely. He has shown nothing to demonstrate that he will ever rise above third or fourth line status.

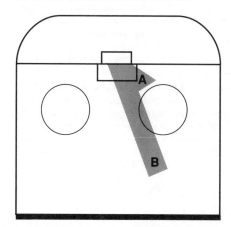

PETRI SKRIKO

Yrs. of NHL service: 6
Born: Laapeenranta, Finland; March 12, 1962
Position: Right wing
Height: 5-10
Weight: 175
Uniform no.: 26
Shoots: right

Career statistics:

GP	G	A	TP	PIM
452	167	198	365	213

1989-90 statistics:

GP	G	A	TP	+/-	PIM	PP	SH	GW	GT	S	PCT
77	15	33	48	-21	36	3	1	2	0	172	8.7

LAST SEASON

Goal total was career low, assist and point totals second lowest of career. Plus/minus rating was club's second worst, poorest among forwards. Missed three games with the flu.

THE FINESSE GAME

Skriko is an excellent skater, with outstanding speed his best finesse weapon. He has great acceleration ability and he drives the defense backward with that skill, but he complements his speed with strong lateral ability. Skriko is also a very agile skater with great quickness, so he changes directions and stops and starts dynamically and within a stride.

His skating allows him to do a lot of one-on-one work versus the defense, sometimes too much so. Skriko handles the puck well at his top speeds, but he mitigates his playmaking because he doesn't see the ice well at his best speed. He works to use his teammates and has good passing skills, but his overhandling of the puck is a negative balance against his playmaking ability. Still, he commands a good degree of hockey sense.

He shoots the puck with outstanding quickness and accuracy, which allows him to take advantage of his quickness by converting loose pucks around the net into scoring chances. Skriko will circle to his forehand for most of his scoring opportunities.

His sense and anticipation combine with his one-step quickness to make him a power play natural.

THE PHYSICAL GAME

Skriko is a pretty tough guy for his size, and he'll cross the line into the chippy category. But for all his willingness he doesn't have a lot of strength to back up his attempts. He'll play the body and work the corners and boards, but he's going to be far more effective in open ice. His defense also suffers because of his lack of strength as he is unable to control the bigger forwards he's matched against.

That lack of strength also serves to undercut his conditioning, leaving him fatigued during the season. He has played a full season only once.

THE INTANGIBLES

Skriko is a worker, very determined and focussed on the ice, and he's among Vancouver's five most talented players. But at 28 years old his NHL road seems shorter than longer, and it wouldn't be surprising to see him playing for another team.

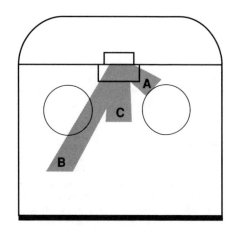

STAN SMYL

Yrs. of NHL service: 12
Born: Glendon, Alta., Canada; January 28, 1958
Position: Right wing
Height: 5-8
Weight: 190
Uniform no.: 12
Shoots: right

Career statistics:

GP	G	A	TP	PIM
851	260	399	659	1,469

1989-90 statistics:

GP	G	A	TP	+/-	PIM	PP	SH	GW	GT	S	PCT
47	1	15	16	-14	71	0	0	0	0	58	1.7

LAST SEASON

Games played and all point totals were career lows. Missed three games with an elbow injury, 24 games with a knee injury, six games with a bruised back.

THE FINESSE GAME

Not much left here finesse-wise. Stan's skating strength and balance power him in his physical play, but he lacks exceptional quickness or agility.

His hockey sense is still high, and Smyl uses his ability to check and play well defensively. The anticipation, good vision and understanding he used when he was an offensive threat continue to serve him in his defensive game.

Stan can still dig the puck out of the corner and make a play with it, but the chances of his getting to the net in time to complete the give-and-go are now remote. He will need to be opportunistic for his goals from now on.

THE PHYSICAL GAME

Smyl plays a robust physical game — always has, always will. He's a very aggressive player, and his balance and strength allow him to keep playing that style. He barrels around in the corners and along the boards, and he remains very strong and very difficult to knock down. But now that style results in injuries.

He'll fight when he has to.

THE INTANGIBLES

As we mentioned last year, his age and his health will get in Smyl's way more and more from now on

(because of his injuries last season we've left this report essentially unchanged). He is still a team leader supreme, a hard worker who brings everything he can muster physically and mentally to the rink everyday.

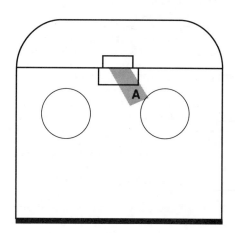

STEVE WEEKS

Yrs. of NHL service: 9
Born: Scarborough, Ontario, Canada; June 30, 1958
Position: Goaltender
Height: 5-11
Weight: 165
Uniform no.: 31
Catches: left

Career statistics:

GP	MINS	G	SO	AVG	A	PIM
253	14,347	876	5	3.66	2	14

1989-90 statistics:

GP	MINS	AVG	W	L	T	SO	GA	SA	SAPCT	PIM
21	1,142	4.15	4	11	4	0	79	623	.873	4

LAST SEASON

Games played total was second lowest of career, goals-against-average career high.

THE PHYSICAL GAME

Weeks is a good skater and has learned to rein in his forays around the ice and that has made him a better goaltender. In previous seasons he roamed all over the ice to pick up loose pucks and, because his puckhandling isn't good, would turn the puck over and have to scamble back to the net.

Steve is a good angle goaltender and he is particularly good at shots at his feet because he keeps his entire skate blade on the ice as he kicks his foot out, rather than raising the toe as he moves, so he'll get that shot headed for the far post.

He is good on screen shots because he moves to the top of the screen. Weeks has a good glove hand above his waist, but it is suspect below his waist. He directs pucks to the corners well but fails to control rebounds from high off his chest protector.

Steve is also weak on the short side and that indicates a failure to cut the angle completely and a failure to be completely squared to the puck. He is not very quick to regain his feet after going down and that's because he usually winds up on his butt rather than his knees, and there's no way to be mobile in that position.

THE MENTAL GAME

Weeks runs the gamut in the mental aspect of his game. He prepares to play well and enters the game with a high level of concentration. He can maintain that concentration over the course of the game, and can in fact turn in a some big games, but if he allows a bad goal he's done for the night. Bad goals devastate him and he lacks the mental toughness to put that goal from his mind and re-focus his concentration.

He can marshal himself for big saves.

THE INTANGIBLES

Weeks' style demamds a team that cleans up the front of the net, something the Canucks didn't do last season. He is a hard worker and a strong team man, a competitor who has the temperament and ability to play 25-30 relatively consistent games a season.

WASHINGTON CAPITALS

DON BEAUPRE

Yrs. of NHL service: 9
Born: Kitchener, Ontario, Canada; September 19, 1961
Position: Goaltender
Height: 5-8
Weight: 155
Uniform no.: 33
Catches: left

Career statistics:

GP	MINS	G	SO	AVG	A	PIM
375	21,204	1,289	6	3.65	4	158

1989-90 statistics:

GP	MINS	AVG	W	L	T	SO	GA	SA	SAPCT	PIM
48	2,793	3.22	23	18	5	2	150	1,362	.890	24

LAST SEASON

Games played total was second highest of career; ditto win total. Missed five games with a groin injury, nine games with a thumb injury.

THE PHYSICAL GAME

Beaupre is essentially a butterfly goaltender, one who lives or dies because of his reflexes. He has outstanding hand and foot speed, and he complements those assets with a high degree of balance. Combined, his foot speed and balance get him to the ice and back into his stance quickly, and those skills also make him a good skater — he moves in and out of his net well. Still, Beaupre doesn't primarily challenge shooters and will sit back in his net. He also moves well from post to post.

His hand speed matches his foot speed, and all his reflexes are aided by his vision; Beaupre picks up the puck very well. Nevertheless, he handicaps himself in play around the net by playing that butterfly style and leaving open net — especially to the corners.

He is less than a sure thing when he leaves the net to track down loose pucks, and he is aggressive in protecting his territory, whether that means pushing or slashing an opposing player.

THE MENTAL GAME

Beaupre is among the more jittery in his profession, in that he needs to be constantly reassured regarding his performances. His confidence and concentration abilities are fragile things, and he's a streak goalie because of that.

He has a tendency to let his concentration waver during games and that results in bad goals — goals from which he does not recover. He is unnerved by criticism and needs a pat on the back and not a kick in the ass in order to succeed.

THE INTANGIBLES

We told you last year that Beaupre would be Washington's number one goalie, and he certainly demonstrated that throughout the regular season and the playoffs until he was hurt. Consistency will always be a problem with Beaupre, and he needs time and encouragement to work himself out of the slumps he works himself into.

But Beaupre may not get sufficient amounts of either, now that the Caps have Mike Liut to fall back on.

DINO CICCARELLI

Yrs. of NHL service: 10
Born: Sarnia, Ontario, Canada; February 8, 1960
Position: Right wing
Height: 5-10
Weight: 180
Uniform no.: 22
Shoots: right

Career statistics:

GP	G	A	TP	PIM
693	385	360	745	776

1989-90 statistics:

GP	G	A	TP	+/-	PIM	PP	SH	GW	GT	S	PCT
80	41	38	79	-5	122	10	0	6	0	267	15.4

LAST SEASON

Played 80 games for just the second time in his career, hit the 40-goal plateau for fifth consecutive season. Led club in goals and points, tied for team lead in power play goals (Michal Pivonka) and game winners (Dale Hunter). Finished second in shots on goal. Plus/minus rating was third worst among regulars.

THE FINESSE GAME

Whatever it takes to be a goal scorer, Ciccarelli has it. He's an excellent skater with breakaway speed, balance and quickness — he's a very mobile and agile player. He retains body position because of his balance and can get his shot away while being checked. His one-step quickness will get him to loose pucks, and his speed and lateral movement will get him around defenders and into prime scoring position.

His hockey sense is that of a scorer, showing him where to lurk or dart in order to get the puck and shoot. Ciccarelli seems to come from the shadows for loose pucks and interceptions, and that is his sense and skating working in tandem. His outstanding hand skills make the most of the opportunities his brains create; he accepts passes in stride or not (credit balance again), and he has a wide array of shooting weapons that allow him to put the puck anywhere he wants. His wrist shot is quickly released (the key to goal scoring), hard and accurate for best results from the traffic areas, and his slap shot off the wing is just as dangerous. He can pass as well as he shoots, but Ciccarelli will shoot before looking to dish off.

One of his favorite moves is to post up behind the net and slide to the slot for a pass or loose puck. He excels on the power play, where his one-step quickness gets him to that crossing puck to one-time it home. He works especially well from the left side.

THE PHYSICAL GAME

He doesn't have great size, but Ciccarelli is a tough, feisty player. He shows up to play in every game and cannot be intimidated, as evidenced by the work he does in front of the net; he'll take his punishment to score his goals. This is where his balance serves him best.

Dino definitely initiates contact and likes to dish out the bodywork that creates more space for him in which to work. He has good strength and can apply it along the boards to muscle the opposition off the puck, but he is most effective in the open ice.

THE INTANGIBLES

Ciccarelli has a short fuse and can be goaded into stupid penalties. On the other side, he isn't above diving for penalties. He maintains his intensity and desire (sometimes too much so as the poor penalties attest) throughout a game and a season, and he remains Washington's one truly consistent offensive threat.

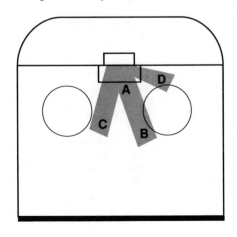

GEOFF COURTNALL

Yrs. of NHL service: 6
Born: Victoria, B.C., Canada; August 18, 1962
Position: Left wing
Height: 6-1
Weight: 195
Uniform no.: 14
Shoots: left

Career statistics:

GP	G	A	TP	PIM
430	159	162	360	599

1989-90 statistics:

GP	G	A	TP	+/-	PIM	PP	SH	GW	GT	S	PCT
80	35	39	74	27	104	9	0	2	1	307	11.4

LAST SEASON

Games played and assist totals were career high marks, goal and point totals second highest of career. Finished second on club in all point categories and power play goals, but led club in shots on goal and plus/minus ranking.

THE FINESSE GAME

Skating and shooting are Courtnall's claims to fame, and they are the assets that power his NHL game. He has blazing speed to the outside and he's most likely to use his speed to break up the wing and blast the puck home, but Courtnall can also claim a fair degree of agility and change of pace. So while he can drive the defense off the blue line he can also make better use of the immediate ice vacated in front of him.

His shot is the second ingredient that makes him a good scorer, and the fact that he shoots often and from anywhere demonstrates his skill. He has good touch and gets to the net's tougher areas, and he also has the strength to drive the puck past the goalie from a distance. Courtnall is very dangerous on the power play.

He is primarily a shooter, but Courtnall has amplified his game so as to at least make an attempt to use his teammates. His puckhandling lags behind his skating when he's at full speed, but at a slower clip he demonstrates a fair degree of skill.

Because of his shot and ability to get open, Courtnall has become a power play mainstay. His defensive play has also improved, with Courtnall showing better understanding of the opposition attack and then using his great speed to break it up.

THE PHYSICAL GAME

Courtnall has good size and strength and is willing to use them when checking. In fact, he can stun some people because of the strength generated by his legs.

He will initiate contact going into a corner and will take hits to make plays, but he is a better open-ice player than he is a mucker.

THE INTANGIBLES

Courtnall's an enthusiastic player, the kind of guy well-liked by his teammates and coaches. He's shown he can succeed as a scorer if given the opportunity and confidence from the coaching staff, and he's become an important part of the Capitals.

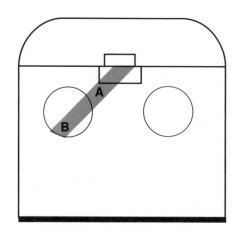

JOHN DRUCE

Yrs. of NHL service: 1
Born: Peterborough, Ont., Canada; February 23, 1966
Position: Right Wing
Height: 6-2
Weight: 200
Uniform no.: 19
Shoots: left

Career statistics:

GP	G	A	TP	PIM
93	16	10	26	114

1989-90 statistics:

GP	G	A	TP	+/-	PIM	PP	SH	GW	GT	S	PCT
45	8	3	11	-3	52	1	0	1	0	66	12.1

LAST SEASON

Shuttled back and forth between Washington and Baltimore of the American Hockey League.

THE FINESSE GAME

All aspects of Druce's game are based on strength, so his finesse game is no exception. His skating is powered by his strength. He has a fair degree of speed and acceleration ability, and the force generated by his speed combines with his balance to make him a successful traffic player. Druce can drive the net while being checked because of that strength, and he can also drive through his checks for the same reason.

He has fairly good hand skills and, again, they are powered more by his strength than by his sensitivity. His goals aren't usually going to be pretty ones but will instead be triumphs of substance over style. In other words, he'll score from near the net.

He has good sense of the ice defensively and plays with a concentration on his defensive responsibilities (plus/minus aside). Druce lacks great reads of the ice, so his current ability to use his teammates is limited.

THE PHYSICAL GAME

Here is where Druce has his best opportunity to shine. He has good — better than good — NHL strength and size, and he uses his assets enthusiastically (though he could do better consistency-wise). He plays well in all types of games and is unafraid of confrontations in the corners or front of the net.

He will certainly accept hits to make his plays, and Druce will hand out more than his share as well. His aforementioned driving skating skill keys his hitting, and his own total body strength makes him the fine traffic player that he is.

THE INTANGIBLES

The NHL's Central Scouting Bureau said of Druce in 1985, "He can come up with the big goal because of his toughness around the net." Druce's 1990 playoff was just one testament after another to that five-year old prediction. He is a coachable player, one who will sacrifice for his team, and if he can keep his intensity level at the plateau he reached during the playoffs he will be a player to be reckoned with.

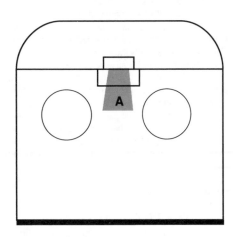

KEVIN HATCHER

Yrs. of NHL service: 5
Born: Detroit, Mich., USA; September 9, 1966
Position: Defenseman
Height: 6-4
Weight: 215
Uniform no.: 4
Shoots: right

Career statistics:

GP	G	A	TP	PIM
372	58	121	179	603

1989-90 statistics:

GP	G	A	TP	+/-	PIM	PP	SH	GW	GT	S	PCT
80	13	41	54	4	102	4	0	2	0	240	5.4

LAST SEASON

Games played, assist and point totals were career highs. Finished second on club in assists and led Caps defensemen in scoring. Finished third on club in shots on goal.

THE FINESSE GAME

We mention "surprising mobility for a big man" a lot in this book. For Hatcher, the phrase should be altered to "astonishing" — his skating is clearly the best of his finesse skills. He's improved his first-step explosiveness so that he now has real dynamic acceleration ability, and Hatcher uses that skill in tandem with his agility to join the play immediately as a third attacker, to jump off the point and head to the net, or to step up to lead a rush. He also uses his skating just as well defensively for gap control, and he makes his skating more effective by playing an alert defensive game.

His hand skills mesh well with his foot skills, and Hatcher is a solid bet to carry the puck from his zone. He handles the puck well at top speed, and certainly is a force when he controls the point. He passes well (as his numbers indicate) because he gets a good view of the ice, but he is less likely to use his teammates when he leads a rush; his typical play there is to gain the blue line and bomb the goalie.

Hatcher looks for the pass as he heads to the net offensively, and he has the hands to score from in close — he can roof the puck in tight. His shot from the point is very good — low and hard for tips, deflections and screens.

All of his skills make him a specialty teams regular.

THE PHYSICAL GAME

Just as he makes the most of his finesse abilities, so too does Hatcher use all of his physical tools. He's huge, obviously, but unlike many big guys who play or played a more passive physical game (Willie Huber, Uwe Krupp, Kjell Samuelsson) Hatcher hits — hard and often. He punishes the opposition in front of the net and in the corners and does so without drawing penalties; it's hard to imagine him being out-muscled in a one-on-one confrontation.

His physical ability amplifies his finesse skill by allowing him to make plays after hits, and Hatcher is not afraid of fighting; he's a pretty tough fighter, as a matter of fact.

THE INTANGIBLES

This guy makes us look like geniuses. We said last year that defensemen fit into the five-year theory and that this was Hatcher's fifth year — and that big things were expected from him. We also said a guy this big and strong should play 80 games.

Presto. Hatcher produces his best season ever, game 1 through 80. And believe us — he's got plenty of room for an encore.

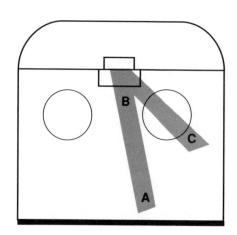

BILL HOULDER

Yrs. of NHL service: 1
Born: Thunder Bay, Ont., Canada; March 11, 1967
Position: Defenseman
Height: 6-3
Weight: 210
Uniform no.: 2
Shoots: left

Career statistics:

GP	G	A	TP	PIM
79	2	16	18	42

1989-90 statistics:

GP	G	A	TP	+/-	PIM	PP	SH	GW	GT	S	PCT
41	1	11	12	8	28	0	0	0	1	49	2.0

LAST SEASON

Games played and point totals were career bests. Was spotted in and out of lineup.

THE FINESSE GAME

Houlder's skills, though still in the development stages, are the kind that will never leap out at you. Rather, his skills are of the quiet and efficient variety. He's an average skater at the NHL level, and he needs to improve his ability and turns in order to improve his skating overall. Still, he's a strong enough skater to challenge extensively at the offensive blue line and Houlder shows good poise in that decision making.

He also shows poise and confidence when working with the puck in his own end. Houlder will look over his options in order to make a smart play, and that patience bodes well for his future NHL development. He handles the puck fairly well when he carries it, but Houlder will be more of the steady, stay-at-home defensive type. He plays fairly well positionally, but needs to step up more in his own zone and to angle the opposition toward the boards instead of allowing a lane nearer the middle of the ice.

He will not make great point contributions offensively. Look for him to tally a handful of goals per year off shots from the point.

THE PHYSICAL GAME

As with his finesse game, Houlder's physical game will be more marked by its efficiency than it will spectacular hitting. He takes the body well along the boards, pinning his man and keeping him out of the play as necessary. Houlder controls the front of the net fairly well, getting inside position and maintaining it through leverage and strength.

THE INTANGIBLES

Houlder must still be referred to as a prospect, but he will certainly play full-time in the NHL. Look for the Caps to up his icetime this season.

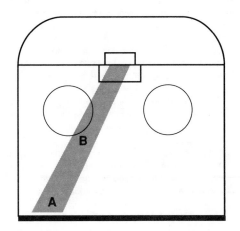

DALE HUNTER

Yrs. of NHL service: 10
Born: Petrolia, Ontario, Canada; July 31, 1960
Position: Center
Height: 5-10
Weight: 190
Uniform no.: 32
Shoots: left

Career statistics:

GP	G	A	TP	PIM
762	205	432	637	2,235

1989-90 statistics:

GP	G	A	TP	+/-	PIM	PP	SH	GW	GT	S	PCT
80	23	39	62	17	233	9	1	6	0	123	18.7

LAST SEASON

Hunter played 80 games for the seventh time in his career. He was third on club in PIM total, second in plus/minus rating. Goal, assist and point totals were four-season highs.

THE FINESSE GAME

Hidden beneath his gruff game style, Hunter demonstrates a fine mind for playreading and a good dollop of hockey sense. That sense is what make him one of the NHL's most underrated — if not the most — forechecker (of course, his chippy style does tend to divert attention from his skills).

Hunter uses his good skating ability (good speed, very good balance and strength) in conjunction with that hockey sense to see the openings the opposition would like to exploit, and to then close them. He uses his balance and strength when hitting to drive through his checks and to remain upright after collisions, and he also uses his balance to plug the front of the net.

Hunter can also make some plays because of his vision and anticipation, and it is those "invisible" abilities rather than his physical finesse skill (he doesn't have the greatest hands) that allow him to get the puck to his teammates. That sense also serves to put him in scoring position, though his physical play is just as likely to carve out space for him.

He's not a great puckhandler or scorer so Hunter will have to be in fairly close proximity of the net to score, and in order to get there he's going to have to go in a straight line. He is not a dipsy-doodle player.

THE PHYSICAL GAME

Tough and sometimes dirty play — and the willingness to play that way at all times — is what characterizes Hunter's NHL strength. Though lacking great size, Hunter will get in a corner and dig the puck out against anyone regardless of size or reputation. He succeeds in the confrontation situations because of his upper body and arm strength (we've already mentioned his lower body strength).

He hits a lot, sacrifices his body by frequently blocking shots and just may be the NHL's top pest. His penalty minutes are not of the gentle (trip, hold) variety, he uses his stick and elbows with impunity, runs goalies, and rarely backs up his actions with his fists.

He is also an outstanding faceoff man.

THE INTANGIBLES

If you play against him, you hate him. If you play with him you love him. Hunter is a fierce competitor and an excellent team man, always playing with heart and guts. Like Bobby Clarke, Hunter does whatever is necessary to win — making him a very important ingredient in any Capitals success.

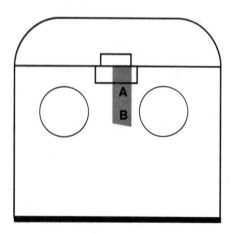

CALLE JOHANSSON

Yrs. of NHL service: 3
Born: Goteborg, Sweden; February 14, 1967
Position: Defenseman
Height: 5-11
Weight: 200
Uniform no.: 6

Career statistics:

GP	G	A	TP	PIM
200	15	87	102	99

1989-90 statistics:

GP	G	A	TP	+/-	PIM	PP	SH	GW	GT	S	PCT
70	8	31	39	7	25	4	0	2	0	103	7.8

LAST SEASON

Missed 10 games with a back injury. Tied for second best plus/minus among defensemen.

THE FINESSE GAME

Passing, poise and patience are the things that make Johansson a valuable commodity to the Capitals — one of their two quarterbacking defensemen. Johansson has the European skill of skating (good speed and quickness to get to the puck, along with agility to move from the zone), where he closes the gap turns the play up-ice alertly, as well as containing the offensive blue line.

But it his his vision and hand skills that come to the fore. He sees the play in his end very well when finding the open man, using his vision and patience to make not just the right play but a good play — he makes good, strong decisions. The same applies for Johansson's work at the offensive line, where he moves the puck with alacrity. He also uses his vision and skating abilities to jump up into the rush as it heads up-ice.

He'll charge the net for shots if he can, and Johansson is also smart enough to just lay the puck on net when he's rushed. He is otherwise not a big goal scorer, largely because he doesn't shoot the puck often enough.

THE PHYSICAL GAME

Strength and balance are the keys to Johansson's physical game. He is certainly not a thumper, not by any means, but he can take the body and gain the puck because of his ability to remain upright and to make a play coming out of the corner.

He'll need to play smartly in front of his net, playing the sticks of bigger opponents, because Johansson cannot match the Neelys and Kerrs of the NHL for strength. He's not afraid to get his nose dirty but really, that's not his job.

Johansson will sacrfice his body to block shots.

THE INTANGIBLES

Johansson is a fine complement to Kevin Hatcher, forcing the opposition to divide its attention between the two defenders instead of concentrating on one player. He has the potential to improve on his point totals and overall play, especially as he is just 23 years old.

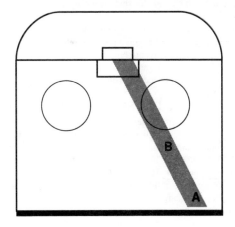

BOB JOYCE

Yrs. of NHL service: 3
Born: St. John, N.B., Canada; July 11, 1966
Position: Left wing
Height: 6-1
Weight: 190
Uniform no.: 27
Shoots: left

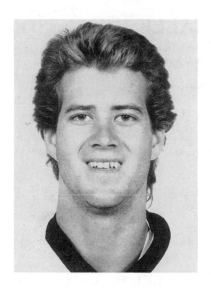

Career statistics:

GP	G	A	TP	PIM
139	31	46	77	82

1989-90 statistics:

GP	G	A	TP	+/-	PIM	PP	SH	GW	GT	S	PCT
47	6	10	16	-6	26	1	0	1	0	62	9.7

LAST SEASON

Acquired from Boston in exchange for Dave Christian in December 1989. Games played and point totals were career lows. Missed 17 games while with Washington because of knee injury.

THE FINESSE GAME

The strengths of Joyce's game rest more in the physical categories than the finesse ones, but he does have some very good finesse skills.

He shoots the puck fairly well (with some quickness and accuracy), so he's a threat from near the net — say, 15-20 feet away. His hand skills go beyond just shooting the puck, as Joyce operates well with the puck in traffic; that's good, because he does his best work from the slot and along the boards — just don't mistake him for Denis Savard. He also has good hand strength, so he'll get his shot off when being checked, hooked or leaned on.

Joyce is a strong skater equipped with powerful strides, good balance (giving him a degree of agility unexpected in a player of his size) and — once he gets going — speed. His acceleration skill should improve as his NHL experience deepens.

THE PHYSICAL GAME

Joyce's size, balance and strength key his game — particularly as he likes to hang around in the slot for his opportunities. He's not a big thumper, but Joyce has good strength and uses it well in his contests in the corners for the puck. His size and strength are made more valuable by his ability to make a play coming out of the corner, especially because his balance keeps him vertical after hits.

He's very strong on the puck along the boards, and Joyce also makes sure to finish his checks. He generally plays a tough game.

THE INTANGIBLES

Essentially, Joyce is heading into another rookie season. His term in Boston was clearly a wash, so much so that the Bruins got rid of him in favor of a player seven years older.

Joyce needs to energize his game and must show the determination to perform at the high NHL level he is capable of.

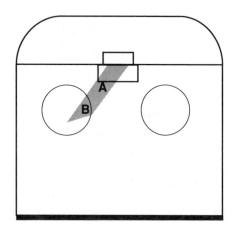

ROD LANGWAY

Yrs. of NHL service: 12
Born: Formosa, Taiwan; May 3, 1957
Position: Defenseman
Height: 6-3
Weight: 215
Uniform no.: 5
Shoots: left

Career statistics:

GP	G	A	TP	PIM
853	50	258	308	785

1989-90 statistics:

GP	G	A	TP	+/-	PIM	PP	SH	GW	GT	S	PCT
58	0	8	8	7	39	0	0	0	0	46	0.0

LAST SEASON

Langway failed to play 80 games for the sixth consecutive season; games played was full-season career low (six games knee injury, 10 games arthroscopic surgery). Point total was full-season career low, and he failed to score a goal for first time in career. Plus/minus rating was second best among defensemen.

THE FINESSE GAME

A dozen-plus professional seasons have taken their toll on Langway's finesse ability, but he retains a good degree of his abilities; we won't go so far as to say he's getting better with age, but let's say Rod has found a way to stall the aging process.

He's still a mobile skater, though more and more he relies on his smarts and positional ability to get the job done — that's the sign of experience. He'll still make an occasional foray to the slot for a shot, but those journeys are few and far between. He stays with the play well, and can still control the gap between himself and the puck carrier.

He moves the puck from the zone alertly, and Langway loves to use the reverse (change the direction of the puck) when he's doing so. He handles the puck fairly well, and he makes his puckhandling better by not forcing plays or doing things he cannot do.

He's never been a scorer and will take even fewer forechecking and pinching chances now.

THE PHYSICAL GAME

Langway has always been a hitter, and he remains a strong physical player. His willingness is mitigated now, however, by his decreasing mobility — you can't hit what you can't catch. Still, in a limited space confrontation, Langway is going to punish the opposition.

He's always been smart with his physicality, playing efficiently when taking the body and avoiding penalties, but as the League gets younger and stronger Langway will be forced to do more holding and interfering.

THE INTANGIBLES

Langway still has his lion-hearted determination but, without putting too fine a point on it, the spirit may be willing but the flesh rebels. That's natural, considering his time of service and style of play. He remains a character player with a strong work ethic and is a leader (though he used to be *the* leader) for the Caps.

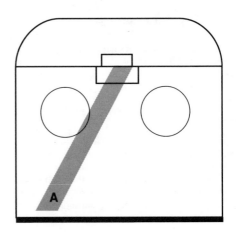

STEPHEN LEACH

Yrs. of NHL service: 3
Born: Cambridge, Mass., USA: January 16, 1966
Position: Right wing
Height: 5-11
Weight: 180
Uniform no.: 21
Shoots: right

Career statistics:

GP	G	A	TP	PIM
178	32	35	67	223

1989-90 statistics:

GP	G	A	TP	+/-	PIM	PP	SH	GW	GT	S	PCT
70	18	14	32	10	104	0	0	2	0	122	14.8

LAST SEASON

Goal, point and PIM totals were career bests. Plus/minus rating was third best on club. Missed five games with a hand injury.

THE FINESSE GAME

Everything Leach accomplishes on-ice is created by his skating. He's got great speed up and down the rink, and he can be a good checker because of that. He still needs to develop a change of pace, to think in terms of saving his ice so as to maximize his speed, but that should come with greater NHL experience.

In the meantime he uses his skating for relentless puck pursuit all over the ice, though he is not so undisciplined as to chase the puck in his own end (he has improved his defensive understanding significantly). His skating will also carry him to the front of the net and it is from there that he will have to do most of his scoring, because his hands have not yet caught up to his feet.

He needs better ice reading abilities so as to get into scoring position better and to better use his teammates. Right now, he's kind of one-dimensional in his offense. Leach does have a fairly good set of hands, in that he can go upstairs with the puck when he's in tight to the net. Currently, he must be opportunistic for his goals.

THE PHYSICAL GAME

Leach has demonstrated the willingness to be opportunistic to score. He'll go to the front of the net and take his beatings, and he'll go into the corners with anyone — unafraid is a good word to use.

His strong skating keeps him strong on the puck, and his low center of gravity (read, *balance*) aids him in his physical game by keeping him upright after collisions. Nevertheless, his size is always going to be a concern in both the continued success and overall health areas. Greater strength would greatly aid his cause.

THE INTANGIBLES

There have been some nights when Leach has taken some pretty bad beatings, but he just comes right back the next shift and the next game. He's a great competitor with heart and courage, attributes that will serve him well in the NHL. That said, he still has some major improvements to make in order to round out his game.

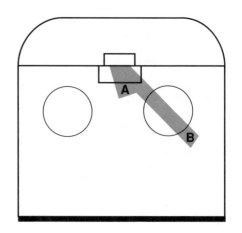

MIKE LIUT

Yrs. of NHL service: 11
Born: Weston, Ontario, Canada; January 7, 1956
Position: Goaltender
Height: 6-2
Weight: 195
Uniform no.: 1
Catches: left

Career statistics:

GP	MINS	G	SO	AVG	A	PIM
607	35,198	2,035	24	3.47	12	20

1989-90 statistics:

GP	MINS	AVG	W	L	T	SO	GA	SA	SAPCT	PIM
37	2,161	2.53	16	16	1	4	91	962	.910	0

LAST SEASON

Acquired from Hartford in exchange for Yvon Corriveau in March 1990. He missed 15 games due to knee surgery while with Hartford, and games played total was second lowest of career. He led the League in shutouts, and finished second overall in goals-against-average and save percentage.

THE PHYSICAL GAME

Liut is a good skater, moving in and out of his net very well. His good balance allows him to rapidly regain his stance when he leaves his feet, so as to be in position to make a second save if a rebound is given. He uses his skating to track down loose pucks and control them for his defensemen, and Liut will pass it to a defenseman or forward quickly for a breakout. He excels at poke checking the puck away from incoming forwards.

Liut generally handles his rebounds, sticking them to a corner or covering them if necessary to keep them from the opposition. He has a good glove hand and will catch anything he can (he cheats to that side), but is less sure on his stick side, where pucks bounce high in the air off his blocker. He also leaves the puck at his feet after left pad saves on shots from the right point. Liut is weak on the short stick side and can fall prey to shots low to the ice, most noticeably on the stick side again and also between the legs, as he is a little slow snapping his pads closed.

He takes advantage of his size when he does go to the ice, occupying large areas of net. However, because he goes down early on screen shots, he leaves himself vulnerable on subsequent shots.

THE MENTAL GAME

Anticipation and preparation are big parts of Liut's game. He's ready to play in each of his starts, but he can give up goals in bunches if scored on early. Then he regains his composure and buckles back down to business.

He's a very smart player — hockey sense would be the term used if he skated out. Liut understands the game and its flow very well, and he uses that sense to his advantage on cross-ice passes or re-directions.

THE INTANGIBLES

We've taken shots at Liut in previous years for folding his tent in big games but he showed some real toughness last spring when, after being blown out of the water by the Rangers in game one of their series, he came off the bench in game two and played masterfully throughout the remainder of the series.

Certainly he is the best goaltender the Capitals have ever had, and he's got one or two more kicks at the can left in him. By the way, we told you he'd be moved from Hartford last season.

445

ALAN MAY

Yrs. of NHL service: 1
Born: Barrhead, Alberta, Canada; January 14, 1965
Position: Right wing
Height: 6-1
Weight: 200
Uniform no.: 16
Shoots: right

Career statistics:

GP	G	A	TP	PIM
83	8	10	18	361

1989-90 statistics:

GP	G	A	TP	+/-	PIM	PP	SH	GW	GT	S	PCT
77	7	10	17	-1	339	1	0	2	0	67	10.4

LAST SEASON

Acquired by Washington from Los Angeles in June 1989. Games played, all point totals and PIM mark were career highs. Finished second in NHL in PIM total, leading club in that category.

THE FINESSE GAME

Shall we use the word "limited" in discussing May's finesse ability? He is no better than average in his ability to play the game at the NHL level, and that may be a generous assessment. He has no real skating talent and is very limited in his mobility, though his balance is good.

May neither handles nor shoots the puck with distinction; whole games can pass without his getting near the puck, let alone controlling or shooting it. He is, however, a fairly conscientious defensive player and — for a player whose finesse skills are as modest as they are — his plus/minus rating really isn't bad.

THE PHYSICAL GAME

May beats people up. He is an instigator, something unbecoming for a guy with his size and fistic prowess, but he also knows his role and fills it willingly. He sticks up for his teammates and is a very tough — fearless — player.

THE INTANGIBLES

May is a hard worker, focussing on improving his game so as not to be a liability. But so does every tough guy. He'll be here until someone tougher comes along.

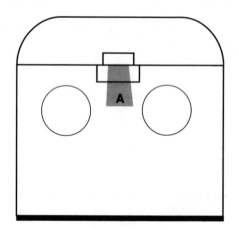

KELLY MILLER

Yrs. of NHL service: 5
Born: Lansing, Mich., USA; March 3, 1963
Position: Left wing
Height: 5-11
Weight: 185
Uniform no.: 10
Shoots: left

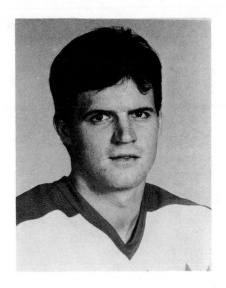

Career statistics:

GP	G	A	TP	PIM
394	75	114	189	231

1989-90 statistics:

GP	G	A	TP	+/-	PIM	PP	SH	GW	GT	S	PCT
80	18	22	40	-2	49	3	2	2	0	107	16.8

LAST SEASON

Played 80 games for second time in career.

THE FINESSE GAME

Speed and more speed is what Miller brings to his NHL game, and it is that asset that allows him to succeed as a forechecker and penalty killer. Miller uses that speed to chase the puck, and he is one of the few players in the NHL who can pressure the puck and cause turnovers through that skill alone. He also has great balance and strength on his skates, so when he does close on the puck carrier he can drive through the opposition to force the puck loose.

In an offensive sense, Miller can blow by defensemen because of his tremendous speed and he's also learned to moderate his pace (to save ice, in the vernacular) so as to increase his unpredictability and free space for his teammates.

Still, though his hand skill has improved, his hands are nowhere near as sensitive as his feet — he's essentially an outside route and in player. His anticipation is good, but is not at a goal-scoring level. In short, he is going to have to cash in on the loose pucks his checking creates. He'll score no more than 20 goals a season and he'll score those goals from 25 feet and in, because Miller lacks the hands to score from further away.

THE PHYSICAL GAME

Miller is small, but he uses every ounce and inch of his size. He hits relentlessly and because he has good strength to drive through his checks he can wear down the opposition. He is also fearless, and will go into the corner against any opposing player.

He also knows enough to go to the front of the net when he has to, and Miller is strong enough to drag a checker with him.

THE INTANGIBLES

Miller is a supremely dedicated player, one with an exemplary work ethic on and off the ice. His excellent character and attitude make him a leader for the Capitals.

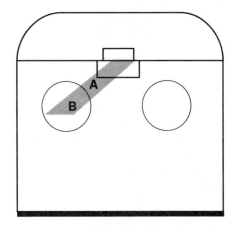

MICHAL PIVONKA

Yrs. of NHL service: 4
Born: Kladno, Czechoslovakia; January 28, 1966
Position: Center/left wing
Height: 6-2
Weight: 200
Uniform no.: 20
Shoots: left

Career statistics:

GP	G	A	TP	PIM
273	62	106	168	153

1989-90 statistics:

GP	G	A	TP	+/-	PIM	PP	SH	GW	GT	S	PCT
77	25	39	64	-7	54	10	3	0	0	149	16.8

LAST SEASON

Games played and all point totals were career highs. Led club (tied with Mike Ridley) in shorthanded goals and (tied with Dino Ciccarelli) in power play goals. Plus/minus was second worst on club, worst among players with 40 or more games played.

THE FINESSE GAME

Skating and hockey sense are the hallmarks of Pivonka's finesse ability. He reads the ice and finds openings well for himself and his teammates, and that ability has developed over the course of his NHL career. Pivonka knows how to get into scoring position, and he knows how to manipulate the ice so as to get his teammates there as well.

He is an excellent open-ice skater with a powerful stride for speed, as well as balance and quickness for agility and lateral movement. He combines these skills with his sense to create strong puckhandling ability; Pivonka wants the puck and he wants to challenge the opposition with it, and his increased skill at reading and acting at NHL speed has made him a more potent offensive player. All these skills make him a valuable specialty teams player.

His shot lags behind his otherwise high-quality hand skills, so he'll have to be fairly opportunistic to score. He almost never uses a slap shot, so Pivonka will have to rely more on his positioning and quick release in order to score than he can count on his strength. His goal total demonstrates how he needs open-ice — Pivonka scored just 12 times while at even-strength.

He remains a questionable defensive player.

THE PHYSICAL GAME

Pivonka is not a physical player, plain and simple. He initiates little contact, and accepts even less — despite his high degree of success in the traffic area near the net. His balance and hand skill indicate that he should have a high degree of success in bumping the opposition off the puck and making a play from the wood, but Pivonka doesn't apply himself in this way.

We repeat: He must learn that an element of physical play opens up a finesse game.

THE INTANGIBLES

Now this is more like it. The numbers he put up last season are far more representative of Pivonka's skill than anything else he's done to date in the NHL. Now he must maintain his intensity (a difficult thing for Pivonka to do, as he is not an emotional player) and put *at least* like numbers on the boards this season.

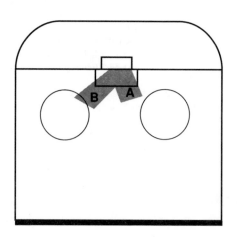

MIKE RIDLEY

Yrs. of NHL service: 5
Born: Winnipeg, Man., Canada; July 8, 1963
Position: Center
Height: 6-1
Weight: 190
Uniform no.: 17
Shoots: right

Career statistics:

GP	G	A	TP	PIM
382	152	204	356	207

1989-90 statistics:

GP	G	A	TP	+/-	PIM	PP	SH	GW	GT	S	PCT
74	30	43	73	0	27	8	3	3	0	124	24.2

LAST SEASON

Games played total was second lowest of career, point total second best. Missed six games with a lung injury. Led team in assists, shorthanded goals (tied with Michal Pivonka) and shooting percentage (third overall in NHL in last category).

THE FINESSE GAME

The heart of Ridley's game lies in his skating, though not in the classical senses of speed and dynamic motion. Rather, he has almost extraordinary balance and it is that skill that powers his skating. Ridley is essentially a straight-line player — which is not to say he can't turn or think creatively. Instead, Ridley's strength on his skates lets him drive the opposition back and literally skate through them. He works exceptionally well in the traffic areas in the corners and the front of the net, despite his relative lack of quickness or speed. His balance does make him very agile, and helps him make plays or shoot while being checked.

His hockey sense, anticipation and vision are very strong and give him good reads of both his own position and those of his teammates all over the ice. He complements that sense with good passing skills to make strong use of his teammates (he'll not just spot the open man but will lead teammates to openings), and his hand skill extends to puckhandling and shooting; he forces the goaltender to make saves.

His skills make him a specialty teams regular, and they also serve to make Ridley a strong defensive player and solid two-way performer.

THE PHYSICAL GAME

Ridley is a quietly aggressive player, in that he consistently and successfully takes the body and wins one-on-one battles all over the ice — without bouncing anyone into next week. His balance is the key here, as already mentioned, and Ridley makes the most of it as he drives through checks along the boards and gains the puck; he'll come out of collisions vertical and ready to go. He amplifies his physical ability with his playmaking ability out of the corner.

He not only initiates contact but willingly accepts it to make his plays, regardless of abuse. He also sacrifices his body by blocking shots.

THE INTANGIBLES

Ridley is a very dedicated player and a hard worker, but he needs to have more confidence in his abilities — he can fall into funks because he worries about his performances. Nevertheless, he's a character player and a quality person.

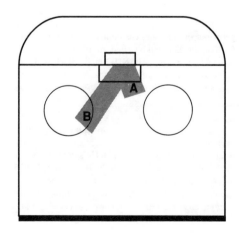

BOB ROUSE

Yrs. of NHL service: 6
Born: Surrey, B.C., Canada; June 18, 1964
Position: Defenseman
Height: 6-1
Weight: 210
Uniform no.: 8
Shoots: right

Career statistics:

GP	G	A	TP	PIM
434	13	76	89	894

1989-90 statistics:

GP	G	A	TP	+/-	PIM	PP	SH	GW	GT	S	PCT
70	4	16	20	-2	123	0	0	2	0	72	5.6

LAST SEASON

Games played total was five season low (knee injury, eight games), while assist and point totals were career highs.

THE FINESSE GAME

Average would be the best way to describe Rouse's modest degree of finesse skill. He's not an outstanding skater in any of the skill's areas (speed, balance, quickness or lateral movement), and so will have to rely on positional play in order to be successful; Rouse is not the kind of defenseman who will be forcing the play and controlling the gap at the defensive blue line.

His lack of foot speed leaves him susceptible to forechecking and turnovers. If he can turn back up-ice with the puck he'll usually move the puck efficiently. He reads the play defensively, as he sees and understands the rush coming at him well and he steers the opposition to the boards smartly. He must, if he is to be successful.

Rouse rarely carries the puck, leaving that task to his partner. His play is to move it up to the forwards to get it out of the zone. His contributions from the offensive blue line will be a handful of goals a year on a shot that is just average by NHL standards. He will cheat to the top of the faceoff circles for shots, but that is the extent of his offensive fireworks.

THE PHYSICAL GAME

He has the size and the strength to be an above average NHL defender, but Rouse must be reminded to use his abilities night after night. He's got the requisite mean streak to really punish the opposition, but his inconsistent use of his size undercuts his efforts. Rouse can clear the front of the net very well because of his strength and meanness. He hits well and hard — rather than just pushing and shoving along the boards — and can muscle the opposition off the puck.

When he wants to.

THE INTANGIBLES

When he plays outside his limitations (as in trying to be too cute while moving the puck) or when he plays below his capabilities, Rouse is not a positive contributor to the Capitals. That is a very small window of allowable error, but it is a window inside of which Rouse must fit if he is to be a meaningful performer for Washington. To reach that level of stability he must increase his intensity. He is a worker and can improve, but he must want to make the commitment.

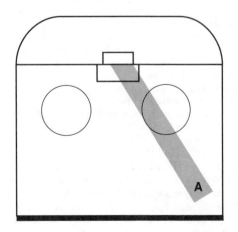

NEIL SHEEHY

Yrs. of NHL service: 6
Born: International Falls, Minn., USA; February 9, 1960
Position: Defenseman
Height: 6-2
Weight: 215
Uniform no.: 15
Shoots: right

Career statistics:

GP	G	A	TP	PIM
344	17	45	62	1,192

1989-90 statistics:

GP	G	A	TP	+/-	PIM	PP	SH	GW	GT	S	PCT
59	1	5	6	8	291	0	0	0	0	32	3.1

LAST SEASON

Missed five games with a groin injury, four games with a knee injury. Plus/minus rating tied (Bill Houlder) for defense's best, and he led defense in PIM total (second on club). He was Washington's lowest scoring regular.

THE FINESSE GAME

Though neither outstandingly fast nor exceptionally agile, Sheehy is a good skater — strong on his feet and improving in the areas of balance and foot speed. He moves fairly well forward and backward and maintains his position well when checking in his own zone, but is not likely to step up and challenge the puck carrier.

His puckhandling is more than adequate. He sees the open man and makes the smart plays, and Neil can also handle the puck and rush it when necessary, though he prefers to move the puck rather than skate it.

Sheehy can move in to contain the point and keep play in the offensive zone, but he rarely pinches in. As well, he will not frequently become a fourth attacker in the offensive zone. In short, he recognizes his limitations and doesn't force his offensive game beyond its boundaries.

THE PHYSICAL GAME

Sheehy is a pretty tough and pretty mean character, and he enjoys playing that way. He can really punish the opposition in front of the net, though his consistency in this area is questionable. He uses his size and strength well in hits and takeouts along the boards, and can be a good fighter — but it takes a lot to get him to drop the gloves.

THE INTANGIBLES

Here's a guy who knows what has gotten him into the NHL and what will keep him here, and we're not just talking about toughness — although that's a big part of it. Rather, Sheehy is a very intelligent player who knows how to stay within the limits of his game and how to maximize his modest skills.

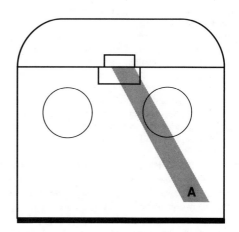

SCOTT STEVENS

Yrs. Of NHL service: 8
Born: Kitchener, Ontario, Canada; April 1, 1964
Position: Defenseman
Height: 6-1
Weight: 215
Uniform no.: 3
Shoots: left

Career statistics:

GP	G	A	TP	PIM
601	98	331	429	1,630

1989-90 statistics:

GP	G	A	TP	+/-	PIM	PP	SH	GW	GT	S	PCT
56	11	29	40	1	154	7	0	0	0	143	7.7

LAST SEASON

Games played total was career low (17 games with broken foot, plus late-season shoulder injury), assist and point totals second lowest of career.

THE FINESSE GAME

Though primarily thought of as a physical player, Stevens possesses a high degree of finesse skill. He's an excellent skater in all aspects of that skill, with speed, lateral ability and strength, and his balance keys both his agility and physical game — it powers that lateral skill, and allows him to remain vertical after hitting.

He combines his skating with his strong hockey sense and puckhandling ability to make not just correct passes but good passes to breaking forwards and open teammates. His sense and skill combine defensively to give him good reads of the play coming at him and to allow him to close the gap on the incoming forward; here his hand skills allow him to turn the puck quickly up ice. He finds the open man excellently at both ends, and his passing is more effective by virtue of his patience; he genrrally can't be forced to make mistakes.

His hand skill extends to his puckhandling, and Stevens is unafraid of rushing the puck or charging the net. His strength and balance help him make plays while checked, and Stevens can one-time the puck. He has a hard and accurate slap shot but his release lags behind his other shooting skills, so his shot can be blocked.

THE PHYSICAL GAME

Stevens may be the League's strongest physical player, and maybe its best too. His superior upper *and* lower body strength put him at the elite level, allowing him to control any area of ice easily. His upper body power allows him to out-muscle anyone, and his leg strength allows him to drive through his checks and make them truly punishing.

That leg strength and balance power his great skating and make his physical game that much more effective, because he is always on the vertical side of his collisions. He's also an excellent fighter, though largely unchallenged nowadays.

THE INTANGIBLES

We like Stevens a lot, but somehow we're struck by the idea that he's treading water in Washington, unable to play the admittedly wild physical game that first characterized his play (but terrorized the opposition), unable to move into *the* position of leadership because of the continued presence of Rod Langway, unable to fully use the offensive skills he can bring to bear because of the presence of Kevin Hatcher and Calle Johnasson — in short, neither fish nor fowl and no closer to that Norris Trophy he has always been supposed to win.

Are we alone in this thought?

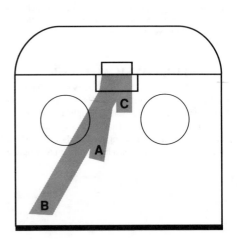

JOHN TUCKER

Yrs. of NHL service: 7
Born: Windsor, Ontario, Canada; September 29, 1964
Position: Center
Height: 6-0
Weight: 197
Uniform no.: 12
Shoots: right

Career statistics:

GP	G	A	TP	PIM
365	124	170	294	148

1989-90 statistics:

GP	G	A	TP	+/-	PIM	PP	SH	GW	GT	S	PCT
46	10	21	31	8	12	2	0	1	0	69	14.5

LAST SEASON

Acquired from Buffalo in January 1990. Games played total was second lowest of career, goal total lowest of career.

THE FINESSE GAME

Tucker's greatest finesse skill, the one that really powers the rest of his game, is his outstanding anticipation. He sees the openings excellently and he combines his anticipation and excellent vision with his superior hand skills to exploit those openings in a number of ways.

John is an exceptional passer; his sense is one reason and his hand skill is another. He passes well to both sides and has great touch, so his passes are always easy to handle. He uses his passing to either hit a breaking teammate, or to lead a teammate into an opening.

His hand skills extend to his puckhandling ability, and they dovetail well with his skating. Not seemingly spectacular, Tucker nevertheless has excellent agility and lateral movement. His balance and foot speed are the keys here — especially his excellent one-step quickness. His skating and hand skills allow him to make plays while moving, and he's able to slip away from his man quickly to get clear.

John combines his hand, foot and sense skills to great success in the tight quarters around the enemy net. He needs just the slightest opening to get free and then finesse the puck home, but he also has the strength to score from farther out.

THE PHYSICAL GAME

He's got better size than he seems to have; John's a solid six-feet, 190 pounds, but his style has him playing smaller. Tucker doesn't impose himself on the opposition, but he's not intimidated by the opposition. He willingly goes to the traffic areas and takes whatever abuse is necessary for him to make his plays.

And considering his propensity toward injury, it might not be a bad idea for him to stay away from contact.

THE INTANGIBLES

Perhaps his new surroundings will be the key that unlocks the door to Tucker's considerable potential, a potential Tucker has never fully brought to bear in the NHL. He can come through in big games but, paradoxically, Tucker's been unable to harness his talent consistently night to night.

Of concern too should be his attendance record. He's never played a full season and has played more than 65 games just once.

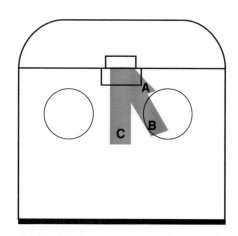

WINNIPEG JETS

SCOTT ARNIEL

Yrs. of NHL service: 9
Born: Kingston, Ontario, Canada; September 17, 1962
Position: Left wing
Height: 6-1
Weight: 188
Uniform no.: 9
Shoots: left

Career statistics:

GP	G	A	TP	PIM
626	139	169	308	492

1989-90 statistics:

GP	G	A	TP	+/-	PIM	PP	SH	GW	GT	S	PCT
79	18	14	32	4	77	1	1	4	0	123	14.6

LAST SEASON

Acquired from Buffalo in June 1990 along with Phil Housley and Jeff Parker in exchange for Dale Hawerchuk. Point total was third lowest of career.

THE FINESSE GAME

Attitude has made Arniel what he is, which is a top NHL checker. None of his skills are particularly outstanding. As a skater he has some speed and pretty good balance (he's sturdy on his feet), but Arniel lacks the quickness that would create true agility.

His hand skills are of the same ilk as his foot skills. The degrees of vision and anticipation that he does possess don't translate into great offensive numbers. He doesn't get into scoring position and he doesn't move the puck so teammates do either. Rather, the goals he will score come from being opportunistic — his checking will free pucks and Arniel will cash in on those opportunities; he won't blow the puck past anyone.

His skating pace makes him a good forechecker and a better penalty killer. He is a strong defensive player, and it is there that he makes his contributions.

THE PHYSICAL GAME

Arniel's got good size and strength and can be tough in the corners, but he is generally inconsistent in the use of his size. Some nights he'll hit, others he'll push and shove. Some nights he won't go into the high density areas, others he does nothing except get trapped along the boards.

His balance and skating strength (along with his durability) make him an ideal candidate for physical success. He gets better results when he uses all his assets — and that includes the physical one — than when he does not.

He is one of the few forwards who sacrifices his body to block shots.

THE INTANGIBLES

Arniel is a very hard worker and a very coachable player — that is how he has gotten to his position as a top checker. Arniel must be out-worked for the opposition to have a chance of beating the Jets.

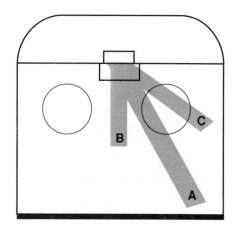

BRENT ASHTON

Yrs. of NHL service: 11
Born: Saskatoon, Sask., Canada; May 18, 1960
Position: Left wing
Height: 6-1
Weight: 210
Uniform no.: 7
Shoots: left

Career statistics:

GP	G	A	TP	PIM
793	244	286	530	474

1989-90 statistics:

GP	G	A	TP	+/-	PIM	PP	SH	GW	GT	S	PCT
79	22	34	56	4	37	3	0	5	0	167	13.2

LAST SEASON

Games played total was three-season high, goal total six-season low. Finished fourth in team scoring.

THE FINESSE GAME

Ashton's finesse strengths lie in his strength. His skating is marked by his balance, power and sturdiness and he uses those assets to generate speed and acceleration ability. He also uses that balance and strength to drive the net and plow through traffic, and his balance gives him a strong degree of agility — perhaps a surprising amount of mobility for a man with his bulk.

He's a shooter and a scorer and he plays that way, taking the puck and just going when he's got it. He'll selfishly overhandle the puck in search of his opportunity to shoot, so he can't be said to have a good sense of the ice or to use his teammates well; he's not a smart player.

That shot, however, is a dynamic weapon; Ashton can beat any goaltender because of his accuracy and quick release. His hand skills extend to his puckhandling (excepted as noted above re: overhandling), especially since he moderates his speed so his hands can keep up with his feet; his hands will work in tandem with his agility to get him around the defense.

He is a fairly responsible defensive player.

THE PHYSICAL GAME

Ashton is a strong player in a sort-of demonstrative way. He uses his body to knock the opposition off the puck and to work through traffic and his balance keeps him vertical after collisions, but he's not a driving or spectacular hitter. His checking will cause loose pucks and he certainly has the hand skills to make a play coming away from the boards.

His excellent balance helps him get goals in tight, and his willingness to play in the traffic area in front of the net keys much of his scoring success.

THE INTANGIBLES

You know how you sometimes find yourself saying of someone: "He means well,"? Well, that's Ashton — he means well and wants to contribute and he needs to feel that he is contributing in order to continue doing so. He'll score his goals, and he can contribute to any club in that way.

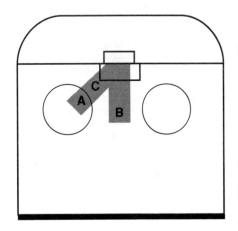

STEPHANE BEAUREGARD

Yrs. of NHL service: 1
Born: Cowansville, Quebec, Canada; January 10, 1968
Position: Goaltender
Height: 5-11
Weight: 185
Uniform no.: 30
Catches: right

Career statistics:

GP	MINS	AVG	W	L	T	SO	GA	SA	SAPCT	PIM
19	1,079	3.28	7	8	3	0	59	570	.896	4

LAST SEASON

First NHL season. Joined team in January 1990 from Moncton of the American Hockey League.

THE PHYSICAL GAME

Beauregard is a very mobile goaltender, one with strong skating ability. As might be expected, then, he uses his skating and balance to move in and out of his net in a challenging, angle-cutting style. He squares himself to the puck very well and uses his balance and mobility to move well around his crease and to follow the play.

His lateral movement keys his ability to go smoothly from post-to-post, and Beauregard uses his skating ability to get out of the net and flag down loose pucks. He handles the puck well, and will help himself by using his stick around the goal.

His reflex ability is high, and both his hands and feet are quick. He likes to catch the puck when he can so as to control rebounds, but also handles rebounds well off other parts of his body.

THE MENTAL GAME

Beauregard has very strong concentration skills and he maintains that concentration very well. That concentration manifest itself in his ability to see and get to the puck, and few are the shots that will beat Beaurgard that he hasn't at least touched as they go by. Beauregard is also a confident player, the kind of goaltender who knows he can make the saves when called upon.

THE INTANGIBLES

Like crease-mate Bob Essensa, Beauregard made a strong NHL debut. Of course, he is just 22 years old to Essensa's 25, so Beauregard has some more time on his side. But his past shows he may not need that time cushion; he led the International League in goals-against-average during their playoffs in 1988-89, and playoff success is always a good indicator.

He has a bright future ahead of him.

457

LAURIE BOSCHMAN

Yrs. of NHL service: 11
Born: Major, Sask., Canada; June 4, 1960
Position: Center
Height: 6-0
Weight: 185
Uniform no.: 16
Shoots: left

Career statistics:

GP	G	A	TP	PIM
786	201	312	513	1,964

1989-90 statistics:

GP	G	A	TP	+/-	PIM	PP	SH	GW	GT	S	PCT
66	10	17	27	-11	103	3	1	1	0	87	11.5

LAST SEASON

Games played and point totals were six season lows, goal total was career low. Missed three games with a finger injury, eight games with a League-mandated suspension. PIM total was second highest among forwards, plus/minus rating lowest among forwards.

THE FINESSE GAME

The physical game has always been Boschman's strength, more so now as his skills show the erosion caused by a decade of NHL wear. His quickness has decreased noticeably (as has the agility that comes from quickness), but Boschman remains a strong skater with balance and sturdiness afoot.

He uses that skating skill as a checker and defensive-type player, more a a puck pursuer than as a defensive genius; his is a game of work and effort tempered by smarts, instead of the other way around. He does have a degree of vision and anticipation but his play in both directions would have to be categorized more as opportunistic (as in taking advantage of a situation) than they could be called creative.

He doesn't finish well around the net and will have to be in fairly close proximity of the goal to score. His passing skills are not much more sophisticated than his scoring skills.

THE PHYSICAL GAME

He is still a feisty, physical, chippy player — and his determination suggests that that quality will remain undiminished. He's been an aggressive player throughout his career, less so in the last season or two; he may be finding he has a more difficult time getting near anyone to hit. Though more inclined to instigate and provoke, Boschman will drop the gloves.

He is a very good faceoff man.

THE INTANGIBLES

Boschman's a worker — that part of his game returned to a degree last season (after a season's absence). But he is still a limited player, one who can now function only in specific situations — and any player who can contribute only in particular situations will always find himself replaceable.

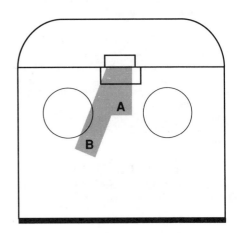

RANDY CARLYLE

Yrs. of NHL service: 14
Born: Sudbury, Ontario, Canada; April 19, 1956
Position: Defenseman
Height: 5-10
Weight: 200
Uniform no.: 8
Shoots: left

Career statistics:

GP	G	A	TP	PIM
915	137	470	607	1,288

1989-90 statistics:

GP	G	A	TP	+/-	PIM	PP	SH	GW	GT	S	PCT
53	3	15	18	8	50	2	0	0	0	92	3.3

LAST SEASON

Games played, assist and point totals were career lows; goal total tied career low. Plus/minus rating was second highest among defensemen. Missed eight games with leg injury, then further time with late-season knee injury.

THE FINESSE GAME

In Carlyle's case, skills and smarts sit in a direct balance. What his skills may no longer accomplish on their own, his smarts allow him to pull off. Carlyle has unquestionably lost a step in his skating so loose pucks may elude him or opposing players may get behind him, but he generally uses his excellent sense and vision to counter those physical flaws. He still sees the ice extremely well and is a very strong read and react player, and Carlyle retains enough confidence in his skating to challenge the puck intelligently at both blue lines.

His strong positional play is half the battle, because from there he can put his hand skills to work in either carrying or passing the puck from the Winnipeg end. He still finds open men very well at both blue lines and that skill comes to the fore in man-advantage situations. Exception: strong forechecking which takes advantage of his diminished skating can force Carlyle to make blind, panicky passes around the boards.

Not primarily a goal scorer, Randy's points will come on a low and accurate point slap shot; he'll cheat to the faceoff circle if he can.

THE PHYSICAL GAME

Carlyle will play as tough a game as he can manage, which means he shows up against everyone and gets shown up by forwards with better strength and driving power; Carlyle's penalties will be of the obstruction/interference kind, and he'll be forced into them by forwards he cannot contain.

THE INTANGIBLES

Even when he's not playing Carlyle is an important element of the Jets — a wholehearted and positive team man. He doesn't have the capability to play well for 80 games, but he has enough heart for 180 games. That makes him a leader for the Jets.

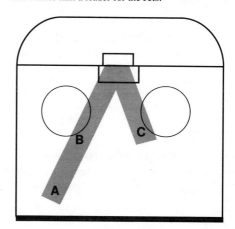

SHAWN CRONIN

Yrs. of NHL service: 1
Born: Flushing, MI, USA; August 20, 1963
Position: Defenseman
Height: 6-2
Weight: 210
Uniform no.: 44
Shoots: right

Career statistics:

GP	G	A	TP	PIM
62	0	4	4	243

1989-90 statistics:

GP	G	A	TP	+/-	PIM	PP	SH	GW	GT	S	PCT
61	0	4	4	-16	243	0	0	0	0	30	0.0

LAST SEASON

Cronin's first in the NHL. Led club in PIM total. Plus/minus total was club's worst. Missed two games with shoulder injury.

THE FINESSE GAME

Not much of one. Cronin's finesse skills are below what would be the NHL average. He is a ponderous skater without great mobility in any direction, and so he must play a strictly reactive game at both ends of the ice. He cannot afford to challenge for the puck at any time because he will not be able to recover should he fail; the best he can hope for is to stay with the puck carrier defensively so as to force him wide of the net, and even that is doubtful.

He can neither handle nor pass the puck with any notable ability, and his shooting ability is also below average.

THE PHYSICAL GAME

Cronin is in the NHL to fight, and he is a tough fighter. He doesn't use his size or strength to any other great degree, though he will do what he can to clear the front of the net. He can be goaded into penalties because he takes every hit as a personal affront and cannot let it go unchallenged. In other words, his physical play isn't very smart.

THE INTANGIBLES

As with any player whose talents are limited in one category or another, Cronin is eminently replace-able by the first player who comes along and is a little tougher, or smarter or more talented but still tough. And at age 27, he doesn't have a lot of time left to carve out an NHL career for himself.

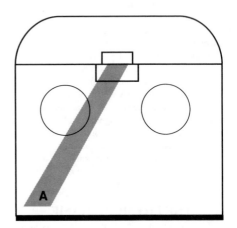

GORD DONNELLY

Yrs. of NHL service: 5
Born: Montreal, Quebec, Canada; April 5, 1962
Position: Right wing
Height: 6-1
Weight: 202
Uniform no.: 34
Shoots: right

Career statistics:

GP	G	A	TP	PIM
325	19	25	44	1,118

1989-90 statistics:

GP	G	A	TP	+/-	PIM	PP	SH	GW	GT	S	PCT
55	3	3	6	3	222	0	0	0	0	43	7.0

LAST SEASON

Games played, all point and PIM totals were three-season lows. Finished second on club in PIM total.

THE FINESSE GAME

As a finesse player, Donnelly has just enough to get by at the NHL level. He's certainly no better than average as a skater, and that's only in the vertical plane of skating — up and down the ice. Laterally, Donnelly is below average.

His ability to work with the puck at the NHL level is also limited. Donnelly doesn't handle the puck well and he does the smart thing of not handling it frequently. He won't rush the puck up-ice but he will get into the action often enough for a shot or two a game. He'll get his goals from the front of the net.

He has a linear understanding of the game, meaning he can see the play in front of him and counter that (or make an attempt to counter it) but he doesn't anticipate secondary options.

He is a fairly conscientious player defensively, so he can play in situations other than those demanding toughness.

THE PHYSICAL GAME

Donnelly is one of the NHL's heavyweights, a top fighter. He maintains himself physically and is always in top shape. He otherwise lacks the skills to play a more-rounded physical game (can't hit what you can't catch) so his excellent strength is wasted in that regard.

THE INTANGIBLES

Donnelly knows his role and embraces it. He adds toughness to the club and the emotion that a good fight can add, and he is also a strong character and team player. However, he will never be more than a fourth line winger — so like every limited player he is always subject to replacement.

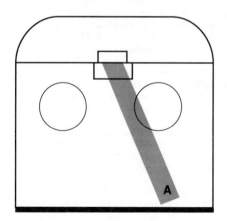

DAVE ELLETT

Yrs. of NHL service: 6
Born: Cleveland, Ohio, USA; March 30, 1964
Position: Defenseman
Height: 6-1
Weight: 200
Uniform no.: 2
Shoots: left

Career statistics:

GP	G	A	TP	PIM
458	91	197	288	498

1989-90 statistics:

GP	G	A	TP	+/-	PIM	PP	SH	GW	GT	S	PCT
77	17	29	46	-15	96	8	0	1	0	205	8.3

LAST SEASON

Games played total was three season high, assist total second lowest of career. Plus/minus rating was club's second worst, shots on goal total second best. Missed three games with back spasms.

THE FINESSE GAME

Ellett is a very skilled finesse player in almost every aspect of thr finesse game. Skating is the primary skill needed for finesse success, and Ellett is an excellent skater. He has very good speed and quickness, and fine agility as well(*maybe* a shade under his other skating skills). All together they make him a very mobile player, one with the ability to dictate play at both blue lines. His transition game is excellent, with Ellett using all of his skills to turn the play around at the defensive blue line, although he does have a tendency to be too puck conscious and can get deked because of that.

His skating and puck ability show best on the power play, where he is one of the NHL's best players. He controls the offensive blue line with ease, containing the point, pinching in and moving the puck smoothly and efficiently in all of the Jets' power play schemes. He is a better player on the power play than he is at even strength.

That puck skill extends to Ellett's puck carrying ability; he excellently rushes the puck from his zone and joins the play as an attacker after dishing off. He combines his exceptional hand skills with good hockey sense to see both openings and teammates, and Ellett will exploit both. He can find the open man, but he can also lead the man to the hole with a good pass. Or, he'll jump into that opening himself courtesy of his foot speed — and then let his puckhandling bedevil the opposition.

His shot is also exceptional, low and hard to the net; it creates all kinds of opportunities for rebounds and deflections.

THE PHYSICAL GAME

Ellett has good size and strength and he uses these skills in an efficient, rather than spectacular, way. He establishes body position excellently in one-on-one

situations (and his finesse skills take over from there), but that also means he will be out-wrestled by as strong — and sometimes not as strong — players who play a more vociferous hitting game.

He could be more physical in his play in front of the net, and he could be more physical in his takeouts in the corners. He is not a fighter per se, but will fight if sufficiently provoked.

THE INTANGIBLES

He has all the skills in the world, but that plus/minus rating is a big sticking point when trying to sell Ellett as one of the League's best overall defensemen — it takes a lot of work to be minus-15 when you're team is an overall plus-8. We're not questioning his character; Ellett's got good work habits and is a good team guy, but we wish he'd show as much enthusiasm for his defense as he does his offense.

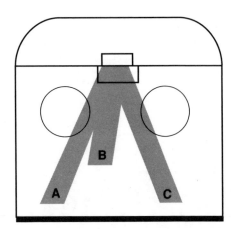

PAT ELYNUIK

Yrs. of NHL service: 2
Born: Foam Lake, Sask., Canada; October 30, 1967
Position: Right wing
Height: 6-0
Weight: 185
Uniform no.: 15
Shoots: right

Career statistics:

GP	G	A	TP	PIM
149	59	70	129	124

1989-90 statistics:

GP	G	A	TP	+/-	PIM	PP	SH	GW	GT	S	PCT
80	32	42	74	2	83	14	0	3	1	132	24.2

LAST SEASON

Games played, all point and PIM totals were career high. Finished tied for team lead in goals (Paul Fenton), second in points, first in power play goals and shooting percentage (second overall in NHL in last category).

THE FINESSE GAME

Hand skills and sense, rather than the customary skating base, are the keys to Elynuik's NHL success. He handles the puck well when carrying it, though he is not likely to stickhandle around an entire team. He has good passing skills and looks to use his teammates, but his best hand skill by far is shot: hard, accurate and quick. Those are the marks of a scorer. He also has the ability to score from further away; he's dangerous anywhere from the top of the circles in. His soft hands serve him very well in the traffic areas in front of the net, and he'll cash in often because of the quickness of his shot.

Elynuik uses his outstanding hockey sense to empower his hand skills. He sees the ice very well for himself, using his sense to get into scoring position, but he also sees and anticipates well for his teammates. Though he is a very creative player without the puck, Elynuik also opens up ice for his teammates via his passing.

His speed and quickness make him a good skater, and added strength on his skates would make him that much better since he works in the crowded areas of the ice.

Elynuik uses his skills defensively, certainly well enough that he can't be considered (as are many goal scorers) a one-way player.

THE PHYSICAL GAME

Elynuik is not a physically inclined player, which is not good for a player who can do well in a physical game. Added strength in both his upper and lower body would help, as would the knowledge that a physical game can open up a finesse game.

THE INTANGIBLES

Elynuik is right on schedule as far as development is concerned. He's a big part of their future as the Jets move into the Nineties as a club in transition. Elynuik is a hard working, honest kid who wants to be coached and wants to improve. His next step, that of moving to the 40-goal plateau, will be a difficult one, but he has the potential to reach that goal.

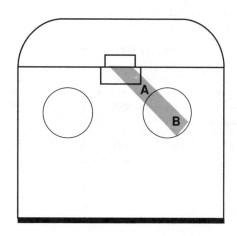

BOB ESSENSA

Yrs. of NHL service: 2
Born: Toronto, Ontario, Canada; January 14, 1965
Position: Goaltender
Height: 6-0
Weight: 160
Uniform no.: 35
Catches: left

Career statistics:

GP	MINS	G	SO	AVG	A	PIM
56	3,137	175	2	3.35	2	2

1989-90 statistics:

GP	MINS	AVG	W	L	T	SO	GA	SA	SAPCT	PIM
36	2,035	3.15	18	9	5	1	107	988	.892	0

LAST SEASON

First full NHL season; played 20 games during 1988-89. Led four Winnipeg goalies in games and minutes played, as well as goals-against-average.

THE PHYSICAL GAME

Essensa plays a game based on his quickness and reflexes, and is fairly successful that way because of his innate hand and foot speed. He will challenge shooters but his style is at least a hybrid one, with the reflex game the dominant one; clearly the style works, for he has had six winning seasons (overall) out of the last seven campaigns.

He does have a tendency to leave his feet early, so re-directed goals and longer shots to the extremities of the net are more likely to be successful against Essensa than are direct-attack drives. In his favor, his quickness will get him to a lot of those re-directed pucks around the net, and he'll be strong in scrambles around his crease.

He has good balance (one reason why he can pop up and down) and his skating is fairly strong, so he can move in and out of his net.

THE MENTAL GAME

Essensa has a strong mental outlook and corresponding concentration skills; he prepares well for games and maintains his concentration within contests and over a period of time, and he has the ability to forget bad goals. That indicates the strong confidence and positive outlook needed for NHL success. His preparedness and intensity give him some big save abilities.

THE INTANGIBLES

A pretty strong rookie year for Essensa, even though he did get a taste of the NHL last season (and the Jets got enough of a taste for him that they knew they could dispatch both Pokey Reddick and Daniel Berthiaume). Twenty five years old is a little old for an NHL debut, especially for a goalie, but Essensa has more than a handful of seasons at his — and the Jets' disposal. He can be an above average NHL goalie.

PAUL FENTON

Yrs. of NHL service: 4
Born: Springfield, Mass., USA; December 22, 1959
Position: Left wing
Height: 5-11
Weight: 180
Uniform no.: 11
Shoots: left

Career statistics:

GP	G	A	TP	PIM
273	75	58	133	137

1989-90 statistics:

GP	G	A	TP	+/-	PIM	PP	SH	GW	GT	S	PCT
80	32	18	50	2	40	4	1	1	1	152	21.1

LAST SEASON

Goal and point totals were career highs. Played 80 games for second consecutive season. Tied for team lead (Pat Elynuik) in goals.

THE FINESSE GAME

Paul succeeds more on brains and determination than anything else. He does have some foot speed, but his rink-length speed and his balance are not exceptional at the NHL level.

His quickness combines with his vision and anticipation to make him a good forechecker, and he can exploit some openings near the net because of that. He'll force some loose pucks around the net through his angle play and quickness, and his hands are good enough to score from in close — which he'll have to do, because he otherwise does not shoot the puck well.

He's not a gifted puckhandler, but he does pursue the puck well. He's very aggressive at getting to the puck but is not as strong when he is on it as you'd like.

THE PHYSICAL GAME

He's neither exceptionally big nor exceptionally strong, but Fenton is exceptionally willing — and that's how he performs. He goes to the net and takes his beatings, but he hangs in and succeeds because of that. He won't often out-muscle the opposition, so he'll have to out-think and out-work them.

THE INTANGIBLES

Fenton is an over-achiever — or at least an excess achiever. He is a tremendous worker with strong character, and he must maximize his pluses (like scoring and working hard) in order to minimize his minuses (like inability to physically handle the opposition). As long as he does that — and he always has — he can continue to enjoy a degree of success at the NHL level, but we're not prepared to say that he is a 30-goal scorer.

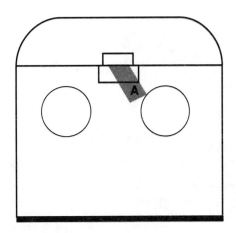

PHIL HOUSLEY

Yrs. of NHL service: 8
Born: St. Paul, Minn., USA; March 9, 1964
Position: Defenseman
Height: 5-10
Weight: 179
Uniform no.: 6
Shoots: left

Career statistics:

GP	G	A	TP	PIM
608	178	380	558	386

1989-90 statistics:

GP	G	A	TP	+/-	PIM	PP	SH	GW	GT	S	PCT
80	21	60	81	11	32	8	1	4	0	201	10.4

LAST SEASON

Acquired from Buffalo in June 1990 along with Scott Arniel and Jeff Parker in exchange for Dale Hawerchuk. Games played, assist and point totals were career highs. Finished third on Buffalo in scoring, second in assists (fourth in points among NHL defenders). Plus/minus was that club's fourth best, third among defensemen.

THE FINESSE GAME

Beginning with his skating and running the gamut of his finesse skills, Housley's abilities are of the world-class variety. He is an excellent skater, superior in his agility and mobility. His stride is fluid, with tremendous acceleration, superb balance and quickness. He uses his skating exceptionally well in all circumstances, both offensively and defensively.

Housley's skating skill allows him to step up and close the gap at the defensive blue line; he closes the gap excellently on the puck carrier, and he turns the play around very quickly. His skating and mobility also allow him to challenge and pinch in at the offensive line, and he drives the opposition off the blue line with his skating. The opposition must play his body in order to stop him.

He handles the puck extremely well and has rounded into a superb playmaker from all angles of the play — in front, along-side and behind. He'll join every rush as an attacker, and will go as far as the net if he sees an offensive chance.

He uses his teammates very well (and is a power play natural), but Housley has remained a goal-scoring threat despite his improved playmaking. He has a good wrist shot that he likes to deliver from the high slot and he can slap the puck well (quick, not heavy) from the point.

THE PHYSICAL GAME

He'll never knock somebody into the middle of next week, but Housley has added a physical element to his game that complements his finesse skills. He can rub an opponent off the puck along the boards, and his quick stick and feet allow Housley to take the puck and turn it around.

His front of the net coverage is average, made better by his smarts; instead of bulling around, Housley just lifts the opposition's stick or intercepts the pass. In fairness, the play in the trenches isn't Housley's to make — that's his partner's job.

THE INTANGIBLES

Last season was Housley's finest point-wise, and maybe every other way-wise too. He's become much more reliable defensively than he's given credit for, but he'll now have to make the transition to a new team. The Jets are a skating club, however, and Housley should show well because of that.

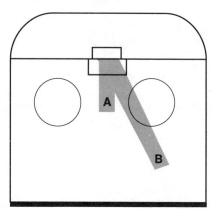

PAUL MACDERMID

Yrs. of NHL service: 6
Born: Chesley, Ontario, Canada; April 14, 1963
Position: Right wing
Height: 6-1
Weight: 205
Uniform no.: 23
Shoots: right

Career statistics:

GP	G	A	TP	PIM
417	75	93	168	844

1989-90 statistics:

GP	G	A	TP	+/-	PIM	PP	SH	GW	GT	S	PCT
73	13	22	35	5	169	4	0	3	0	85	15.3

LAST SEASON

Acquired from Hartford in December 1989 in exchange for Randy Cunneyworth. Plus/minus rating was second best among full-time forwards. Games played and all point totals were three-season lows. PIM total was third highest on club.

THE FINESSE GAME

MacDermid's serviceable finesse game is predicated on his skating — especially his balance. MacDermid's balance keeps him vertical after hits and ready to continue the play. That's important, since Paul is in the lineup because of his physical play. He has fairly good speed and agility (good enough so that the opposition can't just get out of his way when MacDermid lines them up) and he uses those assets as a good forechecker.

Paul has average hockey sense or anticipation ability, hence he's an average goal scorer and play maker. He'll collect most of his goals on muscle work around the crease (he's handy there on the power play). His hands are also good enough for him to finesse the occasional goal into an opening.

THE PHYSICAL GAME

Paul hits hard and often, and those hits will cough up the puck and hand it to the Jets. He can level most players if he hits them squarely and he has a pretty good penchant for doing that. Paul goes in the corners and bangs around and he is very successful there, often forcing the puck free.

THE INTANGIBLES

MacDermid is a very hard worker and his scoring success last season made his already valuable physical play even more important to the Jets, because guys who can hit *and* score are tough to find.

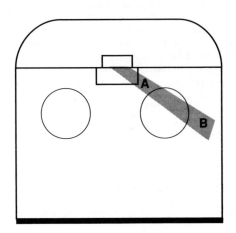

MOE MANTHA

Yrs. of NHL service: 8
Born: Lakewood, Ohio, USA; January 21, 1961
Position: Defenseman
Height: 6-2
Weight: 210
Uniform no.: 22
Shoots: right

Career statistics:

GP	G	A	TP	PIM
582	72	270	342	460

1989-90 statistics:

GP	G	A	TP	+/-	PIM	PP	SH	GW	GT	S	PCT
73	2	26	28	8	28	0	1	0	0	114	1.8

LAST SEASON

Plus/minus rating was second best among defensemen. Missed two games with an eye injury.

THE FINESSE GAME

Mantha's skills are in the offensive arena. He clears the zone and creates the attack because he's a skater with good speed, and his puckhandling is above average. If he cannot skate with the puck Mantha can move it up ice well because he is a good passer.

Mantha is a scorer and his particular area of importance is on the power play, where he reads the play extremely well and finds the open man or takes off on his own through an opening to score.

Moe likes to shoot from the slot and he has a good shot from there, and he also drifts along the boards to the outer edge of the faceoff circle. He shoots often.

His defense is nothing to write home about. He tries his butt off defensively but can still make bad decisions: blind passes, hurried passes, delayed passes.

THE PHYSICAL GAME

Moe is not as physical a player as he should be and that's one reason for his defensive mistakes: if he was more involved and accepted hits he wouldn't make those hurried passes.

He's not strong in front of the net, and he'll allow the opposition to camp in front of the net.

THE INTANGIBLES

Mantha's intensity and willingness to apply himself night after night have always been questionable. Another question has to do with the group of young defensemen the Jets have accumulated, making Mantha's tenure with Winnipeg a precarious one.

DAVE MCLLWAIN

Yrs. of NHL service: 2
Born: Seaforth, Ontario, Canada; January 9, 1967
Position: Center
Height: 6-0
Weight: 190
Uniform no.: 20
Shoots: right

Career statistics:

GP	G	A	TP	PIM
170	37	36	73	104

1989-90 statistics:

GP	G	A	TP	+/-	PIM	PP	SH	GW	GT	S	PCT
80	25	26	51	-1	60	1	7	2	0	180	13.9

LAST SEASON

Acquired by Winnipeg from Pittsburgh in June 1989 along with Randy Cunneyworth and Ric Tabaracci in exchange for Jim Kyte, Andrew McBain and Randy Gilhen. Led club in shorthanded goals with second best NHL total. Games played and all point totals were career highs.

THE FINESSE GAME

McLlwain is a good skater, strong and balanced on his feet but with above average NHL speed, quickness and agility.

His history shows him to be a scorer, and though McLlwain spent last season on a checking line (where he was able to put his scorer's anticipation and vision to good use) he still created many offensive opportunities. He also killed penalties well, combining his skating and hockey sense to an obvious good result. As such, his plus/minus number is deceiving.

He has good hands and can handle the puck at the opposition's blue line; carrying the puck would open up more room and force the opposition to back up. He can make good passes and works fairly well in traffic, and increased NHL experience should better demonstrate that.

Dave shoots the puck well, but needs a quicker release to consistently beat NHL goaltending. He's opportunistic (which is good, because his forechecking will create loose pucks) and will do most of his scoring from near the crease. He'll succeed there because of his sensitive hands that can operate in traffic.

THE PHYSICAL GAME

McLlwain has good size and balance, but he could benefit from some added weight and muscular strength in his upper body. That would add another dimension to his checking. He is not generally a physical player, and a physical dimension would greatly help his finesse game.

He uses his body now not so much for hitting as he does for getting in the way. He doesn't out-muscle the opposition along the boards, rather he tries to put his balance and hand skills to work in gaining the puck.

THE INTANGIBLES

McLlwain is a very talented youngster, one who needs just a little more seasoning to reach his NHL potential. He is an intelligent, enthusiastic and coachable player.

TEPPO NUMMINEN

Yrs. of NHL service: 1
Born: Tampere, Finland; July 3, 1968
Position: Defenseman
Height: 6-1
Weight: 190
Uniform no.: 27
Shoots: right

Career statistics:

GP	G	A	TP	PIM
148	12	46	58	56

1989-90 statistics:

GP	G	A	TP	+/-	PIM	PP	SH	GW	GT	S	PCT
79	11	32	43	-4	20	1	0	1	0	105	10.5

LAST SEASON

Finished second in assists among defensemen; games played and point totals were all career highs.

THE FINESSE GAME

Numminen is a talented finesse player, and greater NHL experience will continue to bring those talents forward. He's a very mobile skater, using speed, quickness and agility to cover a lot of ice; Numminen has the ability to shift gears and to change direction within a stride or two. He can challenge the puck at both the offensive and defensive blue lines and his plays there can be good ones in and of themselves, but he does need to develop a better sense of opportunity he has a fine complement of finesse skills.

He gets good reads of the ice and he uses his vision and anticipation in conjunction with his puckhandling ability to orchestrate rushes from the Jets' zone. He'll also use his skating skill to support an offensive rush as a late attacker.

His vision and hand skills combine to make him a good playmaker, and he has little trouble finding open men at both ends of the ice. Numminen's good hand skills extend to his shot; he shoots in stride and off the pass very well, but he doesn't consistently come off the point for closer opportunities.

THE PHYSICAL GAME

He is not primarily a physical player, and Numminen must incorporate a degree of strength and ability into his game. He can be worked off the puck in contact situations despite his balance, and he can be out-wrestled in front of his net. At this point, he *must* be paired with a tough, physical partner who can compensate for the absence of Numminen's physical game.

THE INTANGIBLES

A strong sophomore season for Numminen, but he still must show the willingness and ability to correct the flaws in his NHL game re physical play.

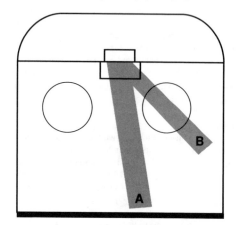

470

FREDRICK OLAUSSON

Yrs. of NHL service: 4
Born: Vaxsjo, Sweden; October 5, 1966
Position: Defenseman
Height: 6-2
Weight: 200
Uniform no.: 4
Shoots: right

Career statistics:

GP	G	A	T	PIM
262	36	132	168	106

1989-90 statistics:

GP	G	A	TP	+/-	PIM	PP	SH	GW	GT	S	PCT
77	9	46	55	-1	32	3	0	0	0	147	6.1

LAST SEASON

Games played was career high, all point totals second highest of career. Led all Jet defenders in points (fifth on the club) and was third on team in assists. Missed one game with a virus.

THE FINESSE GAME

Olausson is an outstanding — *outstanding* — player in terms of skills, one of the highest skilled players in the NHL and therefore in the world. Simply, there is nothing he cannot do. His skating is exceptional — superior — in every aspect, so good that he can singlehandedly pick up a game's tempo by switching from defense to wing. He has speed, power, quickness and balance, and he uses these skills to dominate play at both blue lines: he dictates the way play will go because of his ability to close the gap and turn the play around defensively, and to contain and control the point, to pinch and forecheck, offensively.

His hockey sense is as strong as his skating. He sees the entire ice and his teammates' relationships to each other, to the opposition and to the goals with exceptional clarity, and he sees this in *all* situations better than any Winnipeg defenseman. He can rush the puck and lead an attack from the Jets' zone with ease (he handles the puck smoothly at any speed), or just as easily spring a teammate for a breakout. He joins the rush in any case as a full-fledged attacker.

He has an exceptional shot — Al MacInnis-exceptional — that makes him a dangerous offensive weapon, but Olausson does not shoot enough. One reason his point total fell last season is because he knocked some 30 shots (almost 20 percent) of his shot total from two seasons back.

All of his skills make him a clear choice for specialty play duty.

THE PHYSICAL GAME

His physical game is as complete as is his finesse game. Olausson is big and strong, and he is also tough and unintimidated. He hits, he bumps, he takes the body, he establishes good positions, he out-wrestles, he pins men to the boards, he clears the net — all these skills have improved as he's grown more accustomed to the NHL's game, and could improve still more as he learns to impose himself on the opposition to a greater degree.

THE INTANGIBLES

Fredrik, we're begging you — shoot the puck more. See, 'cause if you do you'll score goals. And if you score goals NHL observers (read, *media in non-Winnipeg cities*) will pay attention when you play. And when they pay attention they will see that you are an All-Star and Norris Trophy winner in the making.

Do you get where we're coming from? With the departure of Dale Hawerchuk, Olausson may be the Jets' most talented player. However, with the arrival of Phil Housley, Olausson may be slotted for trading — especially if the Jets believe that he will return to Sweden before too long. But Housley is not the player Olausson is and can be — which is one of the NHL's very best performers.

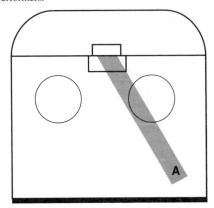

JEFF PARKER

Yrs. of NHL service: 2
Born: St. Paul, Minn., USA; September 7, 1964
Position: Center
Height: 6-3
Weight: 194
Uniform no.: 29
Shoots: right

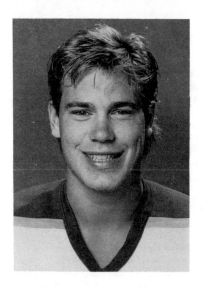

Career statistics:

GP	G	A	TP	PIM
137	16	19	35	161

1989-90 statistics:

GP	G	A	TP	+/-	PIM	PP	SH	GW	GT	S	PCT
61	4	5	9	-9	70	0	0	0	0	61	6.6

LAST SEASON

Acquired from Buffalo in June 1990 along with Phil Housley and Scott Arniel in exchange for Dale Hawerchuk. Point totals fell in second full NHL season. Missed four games with the flu and suffered a late-season back injury.

THE FINESSE GAME

Parker is primarily a grinder, and that's because his skating isn't particularly exceptional and his offensive mindset is not especially creative.

He has a big stride that takes him where he's going, and there's some speed and quickness to be brought to bear, but Jeff succeeds more on desire than skating talent.

While he reads the play in front of him fairly well, and combines that read with his modicum of skating talent to be a good forechecker and defensive player, Parker doesn't translate that read into offense; the game is still a little too fast for him. And since he thinks in straight lines, his offense is going to be straight forward: opportunistic and direct — he'll have to score on loose pucks that his checking has created, despite his big shot.

His defensive game is very sound, and Parker covers his man way back into the Buffalo zone. He understands and executes his defensive responsibilities, and he'll see penalty killing time because of that.

THE PHYSICAL GAME

Jeff has great size, but he doesn't really do anything with it. He's not timid, but neither does he impose himself on the opposition. He's very strong and can control the corners, but he must play tough in order to be effective. His physical play is somewhat mitigated by the fact that he can't do anything after he wins the puck.

His reach helps him snare loose pucks and tie up the opposition, and his eye/hand coordination and arm strength make him a good faceoff man.

THE INTANGIBLES

Parker needs to be reminded where his strengths are. He is not a fancy player and cannot play in the NHL as a fancy player. He must use his physical gifts in order to contribute, and even then he will get above the role of checking center. He has the silhouette of Joel Otto, but has yet to show that he can play as consistently and as physically (and as meanly) as Otto.

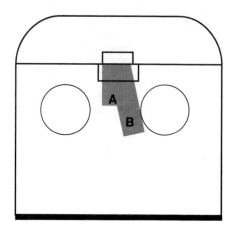

GREG PASLAWSKI

Yrs. of NHL service: 6
Born: Kindersley, Sask., Canada; August 25, 1961
Position: Right wing
Height: 5-11
Weight: 190
Uniform no.: 28
Shoots: right

Career statistics:

GP	G	A	TP	PIM
427	128	133	261	123

1989-90 statistics:

GP	G	A	TP	+/-	PIM	PP	SH	GW	GT	S	PCT
71	18	30	48	-4	14	7	0	6	2	122	14.8

LAST SEASON

Acquired by Winnipeg from St. Louis in June 1989. Tied for team lead (Doug Smail) in game winners, but goal total was full season career low. Missed five games with a shoulder injury.

THE FINESSE GAME

Paslawski is a kind of "good news/bad news" player, in that he has NHL skills but doesn't always bring them to bear. He's a good skater and he has good movement and speed in his skating, but he doesn't always use his skating to his best ability by forcing the defense to retreat or by jumping into holes.

He's shown that he has good vision and anticipation, that he can see the openings, but — again — he doesn't always exploit them. When he does he's successful, but Paslawski also shows a tendency to delay moving to openings.

Greg can be a sniper and definitely has talent that could be further developed. The problem is, Paslawski waits for the holes to open, rather than forcing them open with his speed and better-than-average puck sense. That shows in his power play goal total, where the open ice is created for him; almost half of his goals came on this specialty team — making him a less than dynamic even strength player.

He's fairly good with the puck and does look for his teammates, but don't look for him to thread any needles with his passes.

THE PHYSICAL GAME

One area that Paslawski has shored up is his physical game. He's become more involved along the boards, taking the body alertly and putting his hand skills to work from the traffic areas. He's still not a corners and boards player — and isn't built for success in that style — but his game is more well-rounded. Still, he prefers the outside to the inside.

THE INTANGIBLES

Overall, Paslawski is a well-balanced player. He's effective in all three zones and has begun to push himself, but he is still a player who plays comfortably. He needs to be pushed.

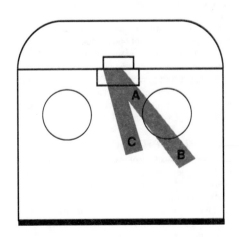

DOUG SMAIL

Yrs. of NHL service: 10
Born: Moose Jaw, Sask., Canada; September 2, 1957
Position: Left wing
Height: 5-9
Weight: 175
Uniform no.: 9
Shoots: left

Career statistics:

GP	G	A	TP	PIM
676	188	206	394	456

1989-90 statistics:

GP	G	A	TP	+/-	PIM	PP	SH	GW	GT	S	PCT
79	25	24	49	15	63	1	1	6	0	165	15.2

LAST SEASON

Games played total was five year high; ditto assist and point totals (the latter second highest of his career). Plus/minus was club's second highest, tops among forwards. Tied for team lead (Greg Paslawski) in game winners.

THE FINESSE GAME

Smail is a phenomenally quick skater, maybe the quickest in the NHL. He makes that skill more important by also having rink-length speed and good hockey sense, (and he makes his speed and quickness more effective by always showing speeds other than "Full" — that makes him unpredictable, a particular advantage when killing penalties) so that he can be a checker, an excellent penalty killer, and an offensive contributor.

His anticipation and quickness will get him the loose pucks that his checking helps create, and he can convert those loose pucks to the tune of 20 goals a season.

His hand skills are otherwise not at the level of his skating skill. He's not a great puckhandler, but Smail controls the puck while in motion and can get the puck to his teammates if given ample opportunity — but he won't thread needles with his passes. He likes to stutter-step just over the blue line to get the defense committed, and then jump in another direction, when he carries the puck.

THE PHYSICAL GAME

Smail is unaware of his size, which is another way of saying he plays bigger than he is. He uses his quickness and surprising strength to ambush opponents along the boards, and then he uses his quickness to escape their clutches. Don't mistake his abstention from a grinding game as fear; he simply knows he'll get outmuscled if trapped. That's why the hit and run missions don't become extended stay vacations.

He also uses his stick fairly liberally — which serves to irritate the opposition enough that they retaliate and the Jets get power plays.

THE INTANGIBLES

Smail is a dedicated athlete, approaching each game as if it were his first NHL contest. He may not have the greatest hockey sense or the best hands, but Smail makes up for any deficiency he has by working hard each night.

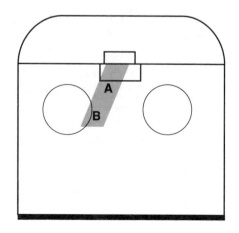

THOMAS STEEN

Yrs. of NHL service: 9
Born: Tocksmark, Sweden; June 8, 1960
Position: Center
Height: 5-10
Weight: 195
Uniform no.: 25
Shoots: left

Career statistics:

GP	G	A	TP	PIM
667	186	388	574	554

1989-90 statistics:

GP	G	A	TP	+/-	PIM	PP	SH	GW	GT	S	PCT
53	18	48	66	2	35	5	0	3	1	129	14.0

LAST SEASON

Led club in assists, finished third in points. Games played total was career low. Missed two games with the flu, 21 games with back pains.

THE FINESSE GAME

Steen's skills are highly developed ones used quietly, and they are quiet for one reason: he doesn't shoot the puck enough.

If Steen shot the puck more we'd know all about his great skating ability — the speed, quickness and lateral ability he uses to force loose pucks, to pounce on said pucks, to drive defensemen off the blue line, to get into scoring position, to change speed and direction within a stride.

If Steen shot the puck more we'd know all about his outstanding hockey sense, vision and anticipation — his ability to read the ice both offensively and defensively, to find open teammates and even to create open space himself, to read and react to the play as it develops.

If Steen shot the puck more we'd know all about his fine puckhandling skills, his ability to make plays in traffic and to get the puck to his teammates in most any situation. If he shot the puck more we'd know all about his quick and accurate shot, and how he gets into position to use it.

Why would we know these things if Steen shot the puck more? Because goal scorers get ink — conscientious, dependable, reliable two-way players do not. Until now.

THE PHYSICAL GAME

Just as his finesse game is a complete one, so too is Steen's physical game. He doesn't have great size or outstanding strength, but Steen's brains and balance allow him to gain good body position in many one-on-one confrontations — and from there his finesse skills take over. He is unafraid of any area of the ice or any member of the opposition, and will willingly impose himself on opposing players. Though breaking down one European stereotype through his willing physicality, Steen reinforces another by being very mean with his stick.

THE INTANGIBLES

He is a leader through attitude and effort, and he is Winnipeg's best all-around player, bar none.

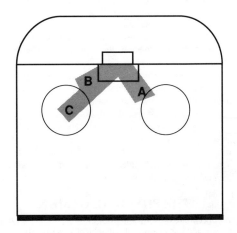

PETER TAGLIANETTI

Yrs. of NHL service: 4
Born: Framingham, Mass., USA; August 15, 1963
Position: Defenseman
Height: 6-2
Weight: 200
Uniform no.: 32
Shoots: left

Career statistics:

GP	G	A	TP	PIM
207	10	37	47	604

1989-90 statistics:

GP	G	A	TP	+/-	PIM	PP	SH	GW	GT	S	PCT
49	3	6	9	20	136	0	0	1	0	57	5.3

LAST SEASON

Games played, assist and point totals fell for third straight season. Missed several weeks with knee injury, one game with sore throat, five games with League-mandated suspension. His plus/minus rating was the club's best.

THE FINESSE GAME

As the numbers might indicate Taglianetti is not a strong offensive or finesse player. He isn't the most mobile of defenders in the NHL and that means two things: First, he must make intelligent decisions about challenging the puck at either blue line, and second, he can be beaten to the outside because of his less than great pivots. He must always keep his feet moving so as to force the opposition as wide as possible as often as possible.

His offense will be played the same way, with Taglianetti contributing from the blue line only. He will skate up with the attack but will not join the rush as a fourth attacker. He can carry the puck when he skates but he needs to make quick passes and decisions, or else he renders his puckhandling ineffective by overhandling; he's much better off with simple, up-to-the-breaking-winger plays.

He is not an offensive force, but will join the play at the offensive blue line and score some goals from the point with a good low slap shot (he'll see occasional power play time because of that shot).

As a lefthanded player he's better off on the left side — that way, the entire ice surface would be on his forehand and he could take the puck off the boards better. When playing the right side, he has a little trouble taking the puck on his backhand.

THE PHYSICAL GAME

Taglianetti is a big, strong and tough physical player, and it is in this realm that he proves his value to the Jets. He succeeds in and enjoys a physical game, and is very willing and very aggressive in his hitting. He has good size and strength and hits hard along the boards, although he can be knocked off the puck on occasion because of his high center of gravity. He'll fight if he has to.

THE INTANGIBLES

Work ethic and determination are the keys to Taglianetti's game, a game marked more by over-achieving and desire than by anything else. He's a great team man and his behavior is leadership by example.

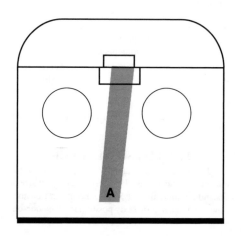

INDEX OF
PLAYERS